CAMBRAI 1917

The Myth of the First Great Tank Battle

BRYN HAMMOND

Weidenfeld & Nicolson

LONDON

First published in Great Britain in 2008
by Weidenfeld & Nicolson

1 3 5 7 9 10 8 6 4 2

© Bryn Hammond 2008

A CIP catalogue record for this book
is available from the British Library.

ISBN 978 0 297 84553 9

Typeset at The Spartan Press Ltd,
Lymington, Hants

Printed and bound at CPI Mackays,
Chatham ME5 8TD

Weidenfeld & Nicolson

The Orion Publishing Group Ltd
Orion House
5 Upper Saint Martin's Lane
London WC2H 9EA

An Hachette Livre UK company

The Orion Publishing Group's policy is to use papers that
are natural, renewable and recyclable products and made
from wood grown in sustainable forests. The logging and
manufacturing processes are expected to conform to the
environmental regulations of the country of origin.

www.orionbooks.co.uk

Contents

List of Maps and Diagrams

Preface

HINDSIGHT IS FREQUENTLY the enemy of objectivity. Our perhaps understandable national obsession with the casualties suffered by the British Army in France and Flanders during the large offensive battles of the First World War (and especially on the first day of the Battle of the Somme – 1 July 1916) means that we often forget the nature of Britain's original commitment as an alliance partner with France and Russia. Our attention is drawn again and again away from some of the conflict's fundamental truths. Moreover, even today the war's events continue to be distorted and shaped to fit moulds produced by those looking at events that occurred many years after the original conflict. Nowhere is this more clearly evident than in the fighting associated with the last large-scale British offensive of 1917, known as 'The Battle of Cambrai'.

The events that took place around the French town of Cambrai between 20 November and 8 December 1917 are now buried beneath the accumulated legends and misrepresentations built up over ninety years. Here, as with the battle of the Somme, the focus has been, and continues to be, on the events of the battle's first day. Interpretation of the events of that day has depended on the personal experience accounts of a few highly biased individuals. During the First World War, the view of the battlefield available to many British tank commanders was via a small fixed letter-box-sized aperture and each tank man's knowledge of battlefield events was, therefore, extremely limited. In the same way, the accounts of those who have described the battle's events with their focus chiefly, and firmly, fixed on the events of the first day are inevitably both partial and narrow. To achieve a wider understanding of the battle's events and significance, it is essential to appreciate how Britain's army developed during the war.

Britain went to war in 1914 as the world's greatest naval power. Its initial contribution in land forces had little significance – except as a symbol of British determination to support its allies and to deliver on its treaty promise to protect Belgium. Although the manner in which the first British Expeditionary Force (BEF) – the small land force committed because of the demands of coalition warfare to fight alongside the French – grew from six infantry and one cavalry division has often been described, the massive effort required by Britain and its Empire to place 67 divisions in the field *on the Western Front alone* is rarely acknowledged and massively underappreciated. To equip those divisions with appropriate weapons and paraphernalia, and instil appropriate tactics for the nature of the fighting they encountered, was even more demanding. To build a supply and communication infrastructure capable of supporting and sustaining this army on foreign soil was a monumental task. Nevertheless, these goals were achieved. Furthermore, that same force had become, by the second half of 1918, the best equipped and most tactically skilful military force in the world. Unmistakably, and contrary to the views promoted by many (particularly the Nazis) that the German Army in the First World War was undefeated in the field and was 'stabbed in the back' by politicians at home, the British Army broke the German field army in 1918. It did so by skill at arms, superior tactics and greater material strength. That it nevertheless incurred heavy casualties was as much due to the nature of the weapons deployed on all sides as the decisions made by the senior commanders and politicians. Whilst new technology might reduce casualties, it was more likely to inflict them in greater numbers than in any previous conflict. The British Army's attack at Cambrai clearly demonstrated this.

The 1917 Battle of Cambrai was one of the most significant milestones in the BEF's progress. Yet, obscured by subsequent events, its true significance has been misunderstood and descriptions of its events distorted. It might, indeed, be seen as a milestone on a different road from that for which it is remembered. In order to understand its importance, we must look, not forwards to the inter-war years and the Second World War, but back to the outbreak of the Great War and the events of the first three years of that conflict. Only then can the real successes and failures of the men who fought and the commanders who led them be seen for what they were. This book seeks to do precisely that: to cut through the myth and the (sometimes deliberate) misinformation associated with this frequently misrepresented battle and to present an account focusing not on hindsight but on the evidence of those who participated.

Bryn Hammond, November 2007

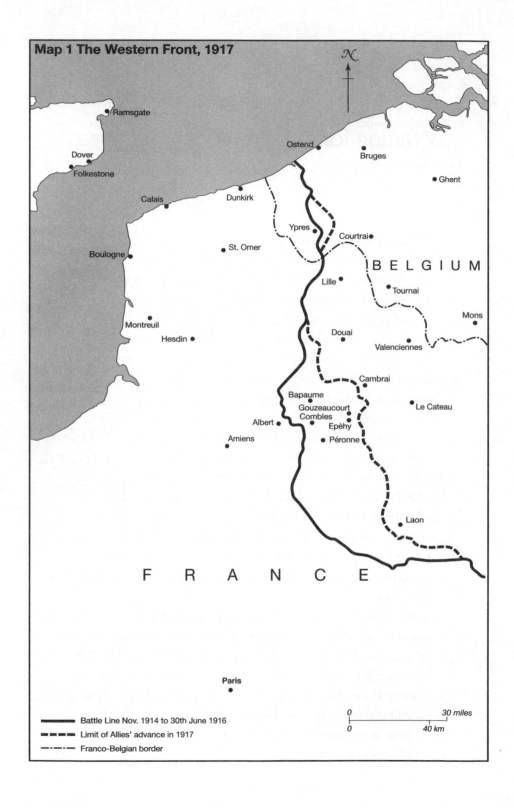

Map 1 The Western Front, 1917

N

Ramsgate

Dover

Folkestone

Calais

Dunkirk

Ostend

Bruges

Ghent

St. Omer

Ypres

Courtrai

BELGIUM

Boulogne

Lille

Tournai

Mons

Montreuil

Douai

Hesdin

Valenciennes

Cambrai

Bapaume

Gouzeaucourt
Combles

Le Cateau

Albert

Epèhy

Amiens

Péronne

Laon

FRANCE

Paris

——— Battle Line Nov. 1914 to 30th June 1916

━ ━ ━ Limit of Allies' advance in 1917

—·—·— Franco-Belgian border

0   30 miles
0   40 km

CHAPTER ONE

Waiting for the great leap forwards

WHEN BRITAIN WENT to war in support of its allies France, Russia, Serbia and Belgium against Germany and Austria–Hungary in August 1914, its small professional army, though highly skilled, was poorly prepared and ill-equipped for the type of warfare it was to encounter. Britain's army was for policing its Empire. It comprised only 247,798 'Regulars'. These were supported by about 270,000 part-time 'Saturday Night Soldiers' of the Territorial Force, originally intended for service at home to cover the Regulars called overseas. As a small professional force, its infantry were trained to develop the kind of rapid, aimed rifle fire that could defeat massed attacks by poorly armed indigenous peoples. Its artillery principally used light, manoeuvrable guns firing shrapnel ammunition at targets usually directly visible to the gun crews.

As the British Expeditionary Force (BEF) manoeuvred into position on the left flank of the French Army along the Franco-Belgian border, few among its number realized the extent of its shortcomings in both training and equipment for the European war it was about to fight. This was especially true of the artillery – and this above all proved to be an artillery war.

In purely numerical terms, the artillery of the BEF was undoubtedly outgunned by its allies and opponents. But more importantly, in the types of guns the BEF possessed and their capabilities, the British soon found their artillery, ammunition and training inadequate for their task.

Germany alone, because of her strategic plan to burst through the forts guarding the frontiers of Belgium and France, had supplied her artillery with a significant number of heavy howitzers.[1] These guns were capable of firing a large shell on a high trajectory at a low velocity,

1

and were therefore suitable for bombarding fortified or entrenched positions. Thus the German Army had a considerable head start on its opponents in possessing types, if not numbers, of artillery appropriate to the character of warfare that was to develop soon after the initial clash of arms.

Moreover, although the war initially seemed to conform to the expected models as one of manoeuvre, this proved an illusion. The German Army, striving to complete the vision of victory first defined by its principal strategist of the late nineteenth century, Alfred von Schlieffen, had launched itself first against the armies of Belgium and France. The plan was to storm through the Low Countries – Luxembourg, Holland and especially Belgium – into north-east France in an endeavour to defeat the French Army within six weeks. It was assumed that a rapid victory would allow Germany then to turn eastward in support of its Austro-Hungarian ally and complete the defeat of Russia.

The BEF which landed in France consisted of two army corps (each of two infantry divisions) an additional infantry brigade and one cavalry division, and had been expected to play little part in any land operations. The anticipation was that the massively superior French Army would shoulder the main burden of the fighting. However, the British soon found themselves directly in the line of advance of one of the chief thrusts of the German forces. First at Mons and then Le Cateau they learned the painful lesson that skill at arms, and particularly the ability for rifle-armed infantry to aim and shoot rapidly, counted for little against an enemy vastly superior in numbers that was supported by a good supply of powerful artillery.

French and British forces retreated for many miles under the force of the inexorable German onslaught until a combination of Allied determination, good fortune and errors of judgement by the German commander-in-chief, Helmuth von Moltke, presented an opportunity to counter-attack. This counter-attack in September 1914, subsequently known as the First Battle of the Marne, resulted in Von Moltke's replacement by Erich von Falkenhayn and a serious reverse for Germany, whose forces were in turn required to retreat. However, they did so to a defensive line on the Aisne river and here began to construct the first defensive positions combining earthwork entrenchments and larger subterranean shelters or 'dugouts' with barbed wire that in increasingly sophisticated form became characteristic of trench warfare on the Western Front. Since the defenders were supported by artillery and machine-guns that could be used to assail any attacker foolish enough not to construct protective defences for their troops to occupy, the French and British armies also began to 'dig in'. At first, attempts were made by both sides to outflank their opponents' positions northwards in what was subsequently dubbed 'The Race to the Sea'. Nevertheless, the final result was a series of trench lines that ran from the North Sea to the Swiss border. Stalemate and stagnation ensued.

Such positions gave an enormous advantage to the defender in this new style of warfare and, since the German positions were almost entirely constructed on French and Belgian soil, the onus to attack and overcome these defences lay with the armies of these two nations and their ally, Britain. German endeavours to break the trench stalemate largely ended with the close of the year 1914, although in early 1915 some attempts were made to penetrate the allied defences by the use of innovative technologies such as poison gas. It was not until 1918, however, that Germany was to return to the strategic offensive. Britain and France could not afford the luxury of sitting back to wait upon their opponent's next move. France's enemies must be driven from French soil and British support was not only expected, but demanded.

Thus, four fundamental elements gave the fighting on the Western Front in the First World War its unique character: artillery; trenches; barbed wire and machine-guns. Each presented both a problem and a solution in the particular circumstances encountered in France and Belgium between 1914 and 1918. Trenches and barbed wire entanglements of increasing depth and sophistication offered the defender a measure of security against attacks by enemy infantry, but by their very nature made it many times more difficult for the infantryman behind them to screw his courage to the sticking point and advance to the attack under the maelstrom of fire and steel. Breech-loading artillery of enormous destructive power, becoming available in unprecedented numbers, seemed capable of sweeping aside any obstacles standing in its path, allowing the infantry to advance almost unopposed to capture ground previously held by the enemy. Yet, the same destructive power when wielded by the defenders could obliterate such an infantry advance in minutes. Machine-guns too were a double-edged weapon: on the one hand, a means to support an infantry advance with rapidly developed firepower of great volume; on the other, an instrument for the deadly destruction of massed infantry attacks by a small number of defenders in concealed and well-protected positions.

Meanwhile, the necessity for the artillerymen to locate targets that they could not observe directly fuelled the requirement for more detailed and accurate maps from which the enemy positions could be plotted. These maps in turn depended on survey work by engineers and photographic reconnaissance by the newest addition to each combatant's armed forces: aircraft. The need to protect the aircraft and their crews engaged in these tasks vital to the work of the artillery, or prevent the enemy from conducting the same work, was the prime reason for the development of 'scout' or fighter aircraft and led, inevitably, to aerial combat. Not only on the ground, but also in the skies above, the war's character was being formed.

This was the first modern industrial war and the means to kill the enemy were increasingly sophisticated and ever more effective. Such warfare required the recruitment and training of armed forces on a previously unimagined scale. When war was declared, Britain had appointed Field Marshal Earl Kitchener, its most distinguished imperial soldier still capable of shouldering the enormous burden of responsibility, as its Secretary of State for War. Kitchener understood that the commitment of Britain's land forces to support her allies would probably be a long-term one: three years or more of war. Therefore, Britain must rapidly expand its army in support of the mighty endeavour upon which it had embarked. To do so, he decided it would be necessary to recruit, equip and train a mass volunteer army of hundreds of thousands, perhaps millions.

Nevertheless, whilst doing so, Britain still had to demonstrate to its coalition partners that it was prepared to commit men and *matériel* to the cause. In the last months of 1914, however, the battered BEF's chief objective was to cling on for survival. In defensive positions around the Flemish town of Ieper (Ypres), the dogged defence of the remaining Regulars, bolstered in small measure by the arrival of the first Territorial units from Britain (the strictures on their home service had been raised and many had agreed to serve abroad because of the enormity of the military crisis) and units from the Indian Army, frustrated German attempts to seize the Channel ports. The experience of this First Battle of Ypres (October–November 1914) was to have a significant influence on several of the BEF's senior commanders and especially the man destined later to become its commander-in-chief, Sir Douglas Haig. The ancient fortress town was at the heart of the region familiarly termed 'the cockpit of Europe' and firmly embedded in the psyche of Britain's army through the battle honours carried on each regiment's colours. Now the psychological bond to this, the last sizeable Belgian town unoccupied by the Germans, was to have increased emotional resonance for Britain. Britain had gone to war ostensibly to protect Belgium and was determined to defend the unconquered remnants of that land.

With the expansion of the BEF in early 1915 and the arrival of the first trickle of appropriate equipment and ammunition, the British felt in a position to oblige their French allies and take a more active role in assisting their military operations. At the battle of Neuve Chapelle (10–13 March) the British learned how difficult the deadly conundrum of trench warfare was going to be to crack. In part because of the paucity of resources for making an attack, the British planned a short intensive artillery bombardment lasting only 35 minutes, followed by an infantry attack to capture the village of Neuve Chapelle and break through the German trench lines. This attack was initially successful, and an advance of up to 1,200 yards accomplished, but it soon lost momentum. The Germans brought up their reserves and reformed their defensive lines. Without adequate supplies of artillery ammunition and fresh infantry, the attack could not be pushed forward again and offensive operations were stopped. This was to be a problem repeatedly encountered by all sides in the fighting. Each combatant nation possessed the means to break *into* the enemy's defensive positions, but not *through* them.

The battle of Neuve Chapelle had significant consequences for both sides. The Germans were moved to strengthen their defensive positions by adding more barbed wire and greater depth to their trench systems – an approach they continued to follow in the west until early 1918. For the British, the belief was that a longer and heavier preliminary bombardment to destroy the German defences before the infantry advanced on a wide front would have made the latter's task altogether easier. In common with their French allies, the British commanders were of the view that artillery was to conquer, infantry only to occupy. This was to prove an erroneous conclusion, but was to shape the conduct of the BEF's military operations until at least mid-1917.

Throughout 1915, for each successive battle longer and heavier artillery bombardments were planned as the prelude to each infantry attack. Of course, the greater the weight of shells fired on the attack front, the more shell-torn the terrain over which the infantry must advance became. But although the BEF continued to expand in numbers of men and guns, in 1915 it never had adequate resources of artillery or ammunition to accomplish the ambitious plans made for each battle. Furthermore, as each attack was made on a wider front than the last, the concentration of shells per yard of German position attacked was also diminished, decreasing the artillery's effectiveness.

Various attempts were made to compensate for these shortcomings and difficulties. At the battle of Loos in September 1915, plans were made for the release of clouds of poison gas (first used by the Germans on 22 April 1915 at the Second Battle of Ypres) before the infantry attack, in an attempt to supplement the artillery. The secret weapon's contribution was not a great success, but the initial infantry assault went well. Once again, however, the arrival and counter-attack of German reserves prevented a breakthrough of the defences and the fighting developed into a long, drawn-out slogging match to little purpose and with heavy casualties to both sides.

The failure of the Loos attack ultimately resulted in the dismissal of the BEF's commander, Sir John French, and his replacement as commander-in-chief by his subordinate, Sir Douglas Haig. Haig was to retain this position for the rest of the war. To it he brought extraordinary self-belief and a conviction that he, and he alone, was the right man to lead the largest British Army ever in existence to victory and to ensure the British Empire not only survived, but survived renewed in vigour, the greatest crisis it had ever faced.

Douglas Haig was an austere and rigorously self-disciplined Scot. The dry facts of his life are well documented. Born in 1861 he enjoyed all the benefits of privilege that a scion of a moneyed Victorian family would expect: an Oxford education followed by a commission in a fashionable cavalry regiment – in which capacity he might complacently have settled to enjoy society's advantages, whilst exercising authority for his country's good and, thereby, securing easy political and financial rewards. However, at this point, Haig's life path veered from the norm. In 1896 he attended the newly established Staff College at Camberley, ensuring his future military career would be largely more cerebral than physical. Yet he experienced both action and personal danger during his active service in the Sudan and during the Boer War, where as a staff officer to Sir John French he impressed as a more than capable officer. In the Edwardian army, where staff officers of ability could be sure of some advancement, he enjoyed a series of regular promotions through hard work and application in administrative appointments in Britain and India. He worked with both military and civil administrators in military reforms such as the creation of the Territorial Force in 1908. By August 1914, he held the rank of Major General and commanded the two divisions based at Aldershot that formed I Corps of the BEF when it was mobilized on the outbreak of war. It is useful, therefore, to remind ourselves that in these dry facts there was little to suggest that Douglas Haig was ultimately to demonstrate the intellectual, political and military abilities to lead his command (the largest force Britain had ever before, or since, put in the field) to triumph in November 1918. Although born into the Victorian era, Haig would adapt to the enormous demands of twentieth century warfare in quite remarkable fashion.

All this was in the future. In 1916 Haig's command grew from 42 to 62 Divisions. The BEF was divided into four (and, later in the same year, five) Armies. Kitchener's decision to build a large army capable of fighting a long war was finally bearing fruit: whole divisions of volunteers had been arriving in France throughout 1915 and early 1916. These had joined the tens of thousands of men of the Territorial Force who had agreed to serve outside Britain and who also went to France in complete divisions. Haig now had nearly a million men under his command. In addition, greater numbers of guns, shells, machine-guns, aircraft and other material resources were available than ever before. Given the appalling casualties suffered by the French Army in 1914 and

1915, Britain was about to deploy a military force in the field that would give her a significant say in the conduct of military operations.

Nevertheless, the first major offensive conducted by Haig was neither at the time of his choosing, nor for the strategic objectives that he felt were key. Haig had wanted to attack at Ypres, wishing to drive the Germans further away from the Channel ports. He was prevented from doing so by the massive attritional offensive launched by the Germans against the French Army at Verdun in February 1916. The Verdun attack had been designed not to break through the French defences, but to erode French morale and military strength. The Germans hoped to force France to commit excessive numbers of men in defence of the fortress town of Verdun, which like Ypres had great symbolic, as well as a lesser strategic, significance. Britain's commitment to coalition warfare as a junior partner meant Haig was obliged to launch an attack astride the Somme River in July 1916, at least in part to relieve pressure on the forces of her beleaguered ally. Haig's preferences took second place to the strategic necessity of taking some of the terrible burden of the 'mincing machine' of Verdun from French shoulders.

Haig's plans for the 1916 Somme Offensive were based on experience gained in the offensive operations conducted by the BEF in 1915. Haig had been the army commander responsible for almost all of these attacks and had reached some flawed conclusions as a result. As with earlier battles, a prolonged artillery bombardment (this time of unprecedented length and ferocity) would precede the infantry assault with the intention of smashing the German front line defenders into submission and obliterating their positions. On this occasion, perhaps more than on any previous one, the view from the BEF's high command was that the infantry (many of whom were volunteers with little, if any, experience of front-line combat) would only be required to occupy, and hold, the shattered remnants of the German positions.

Yet again, however, the mistakes of previous attacks were repeated. Because of the wide attack frontage, the concentration of guns per yard of trench to be captured was reduced and no attempt was made to take into account the increased depth of the German trench systems. The strength of the defences on a front where there had been relatively little fighting for some time and where, consequently, the Germans had been able to prepare deep and strong dugouts for the protection of their front-line troops, was spectacularly underestimated. There were still too few guns firing the high-explosive shells capable of smashing trenches and dugouts. The long preliminary bombardment of the German defences had two other crucial failings: it provided a clear indication to the Germans of an impending attack in this sector, thereby removing any possibility of surprising the defenders and, furthermore, it drew valuable resources away from the very necessary task of overcoming the German artillery through what was termed 'counter-battery fire'.

It was also true that, despite a massive expansion in numbers in all branches of the BEF, the officers and men of most of this force had not received adequate training in, or had sufficient experience of, modern industrial warfare. All these factors in combination produced a day of catastrophe unparalleled in the history of the British Army. The first day of the Battle of the Somme, 1 July 1916, ended with 57,470 British casualties. Those killed on that fateful Saturday numbered 19,240 and many more would subsequently die of their wounds.

Yet the losses at the outset of the battle did not so impair the BEF's fighting capabilities that it could no longer conduct offensive operations. Although the first day of the Somme Offensive was a serious reverse, there were 141 other days of the campaign during which the men of the British Army (and especially the ever-optimistic Haig) maintained their belief that they were defeating the Germans. However, although suffering heavy casualties and many reverses at the hands of their skilful and determined enemy, the British learned the tough lessons of the nature of trench warfare; gradually developed new and more sophisticated tactics, and acquired hard-won experience.

And, whilst they did so, the flow of guns, ammunition and equipment continued and grew stronger. Ever-more powerful guns capable of firing high explosive shells with increasingly sophisticated fuzes were provided for the artillery. Better aircraft were provided for the Royal Flying Corps (RFC), whose important aerial reconnaissance work in support of the artillery was increasingly acknowledged. New weapons (especially the tank, which made its first appearance in warfare during the Somme battles on 15 September 1916) were also tried in the hope that they would provide the key to unlock the trench warfare conundrum. Infantry too received increasing numbers of machine-guns,

Lewis guns (portable automatic rifles), trench mortars, grenades and other equipment. Tactics and techniques were adopted that were considerable advances on what had gone before. The vital necessity for artillery not only to help infantry to capture and occupy German positions but also to prevent their opposite numbers from getting into action was increasingly recognized as a priority and techniques to locate accurately the position of German artillery batteries, such as flash-spotting and sound-ranging, combined with artillery spotting by aircraft, were all applied to this task and developed and refined. Across all branches of the army the British had to learn what would work and what would not in the unforgiving context of modern industrial warfare. Perhaps the steepest part of this jagged 'learning curve' was encountered in the months from July to November 1916.

By the end of the Somme battle, despite heavy losses to themselves, the British and French had inflicted grievous harm on their German opponent. Indeed, the wound was so deep that one German staff officer subsequently referred to the Somme as 'the muddy grave of the German field army and of the faith in the infallibility of German leadership'.[2] German casualties during the battle have been estimated at anywhere between 450,000 and 600,000. These losses prompted the German High Command to come to a momentous decision. In September 1916, whilst the Somme battle was in progress, they ordered the construction of a new and sophisticated defensive position between Arras and Laon known as the *Siegfried Stellung* and termed the 'Hindenburg Line' by the British. They would withdraw to this new position in order to shorten the defensive line held whilst still remaining on French soil and to husband Germany's most precious resource: its fighting troops.

The decision to adopt this policy was taken by Paul von Hindenburg and Erich Ludendorff, the men who assumed supreme command of the German Army after Erich von Falkenhayn's resignation as Chief of the General Staff in August 1916. They saw this strategic move as part of a wider policy whereby unrestricted submarine warfare would be used to compel Britain to conclude a separate peace leaving France isolated with German troops still occupying French territory. The withdrawal of German troops to the Hindenburg Line in March 1917 was an indication of the harm the British and French had inflicted on the Germans in

1916, but it also ensured that the task of winning the war was made even harder in the west from that point forward.

In conjunction with their revised defensive posture, the Germans developed new tactics of 'elastic defence in depth', specifically designed for use in combination with the complex defensive positions they had constructed. Although the Germans did not use this specific term, it aptly describes its intended purpose. The German defensive line should only reluctantly bend without breaking before springing back to recover lost ground. The German tactical guidance for this doctrine recognized that 'stout hearted men with iron nerves form the real backbone of defence'.[3] The initial success of any attack was an illusion. Defenders of the forward positions (the outpost line) would fall back in the face of the assault, allowing the attackers to advance on the main line of resistance which was to be, as far as possible, concealed from British artillery observation either on a reverse slope or perhaps camouflaged by woods. It was usually also at, or beyond, the extreme range of all but the heaviest guns of the British field artillery, which were typically sited some considerable distance behind their front line. Once again, this main line of resistance might be overrun but the attackers who occupied it would themselves be subjected to heavy artillery fire and infantry counter-attack to drive them back out of the position, inflicting major casualties in the process. The British were to encounter these tactics in the battles of 1917.

With the advent of 1917, Douglas Haig hoped finally to be able to launch an offensive in the salient surrounding Ypres in Flanders. Whilst an emotional attachment to this sacrificial ground cannot be discounted, Haig had what he believed were sound strategic reasons for planning and executing an offensive in Flanders. Firstly, by their proximity to the Channel ports of Calais, Dunkirk and Boulogne, the Germans threatened the BEF's supply lines. Secondly, this relatively short distance from the ports meant that a British offensive near Ypres could be more easily supplied than, say, another Somme attack. Thirdly, and of especial importance in Haig's success in gaining support for his plans, a Flanders offensive offered the opportunity for the capture of the Belgian ports of Ostend and Zeebrugge, which the Germans had established as major bases from which to attack shipping in the Channel and the Atlantic with destroyers and submarines. The prospect of removing the U-boat thorn from Britain's side ultimately provided a powerful case for Haig's cherished offensive. Other possible strategic goals, such as the opportunity to turn the German flank and capture the important rail junction at Roulers only reinforced his arguments.

Nevertheless, it was not easy to secure support for his ambitions. Britain's Prime Minister, David Lloyd George, had been appalled by the Somme casualties, for which he held Haig accountable, and was bitterly opposed to any major new offensive proposed by the British Commander-in-Chief. However, this was some way ahead. In February 1917 Lloyd George delivered a snub to Haig when he committed the BEF to support a new French offensive without Haig's consent. In a conference with the French Army's recently appointed commander-in-chief, Robert Nivelle, he agreed that the BEF would take over more miles of trenches on the Western Front from the French and launch a large-scale diversionary attack at Arras to draw away German reserves from the French attack on the Chemin des Dames.

Lloyd George's actions permanently soured relations between him and Haig. The latter dutifully ordered a British attack which commenced on Easter Monday (9 April) 1917 at Arras but after some initial success the attack ground to a halt, along with the whole Nivelle Offensive. With the failure of French plans and Nivelle's subsequent dismissal, Haig was in a strong position to push for his own attack. In effect, in the absence of any other viable plan for offensive operations on the Western Front, Haig's Flanders offensive was assured of (albeit grudging) support and his planning permitted to go ahead. Rumours (subsequently proved to be true) of mutinies amongst units of the French Army demoralized by three years of war and the Nivelle Offensive, and the March 1917 revolution in Russia which threw considerable doubt over Russian assistance on the Eastern Front, further strengthened his case.

The first blow delivered by British forces as part of the plan for the Flanders attack was the operation to capture the Messines Ridge, at the southern end of the Ypres Salient, launched on 7 June 1917. On this occasion considerable success attended the battle's first day largely because of three exceptional factors. First and foremost, the absence of a preliminary bombardment of the German positions on Messines Ridge meant the attack was a complete surprise. Crucially linked to this was the sudden explosion of 19 underground mines beneath key German strongpoints. Many of these mines had been dug and charged with explosives over the course of two or more years and had then lain dormant and undiscovered in the interim. The Royal Engineer Tunnelling Companies responsible for their construction had worked long and hard to gain the upper hand over their German counterparts in the war underground and the attack at Messines was the culmination of their efforts. Of course, this was unlikely to be repeated in subsequent British attacks. Thirdly, the attack was for strictly limited objectives. German attempts to counter-attack were therefore met on more advantageous terms than those occasions when the attackers had been overstretched in endeavours to reach over-ambitious objectives or had gone beyond the range of their supporting artillery. Indeed, British casualties in the attack were surprisingly heavy and the great majority resulted from attempts to go beyond the original objectives.

After the battle of Messines, there was an operational pause and preparations were made for what was clearly regarded by the BEF's most senior commander as Britain's war-winning offensive. It was to be almost seven weeks before the main attack was launched as Haig's decision to transfer responsibility for the attack from one army commander, the methodical Herbert Plumer, to another, Hubert Gough (perceived by Haig as more aggressive and therefore better suited to offensive operations), was worked through. During this period, the commitment of resources in preparation of the offensive was phenomenal. Enormous numbers of guns were manoeuvred into position. Infantry divisions were trained in the tactical principles that would allow them to tackle the principal element of German defences in the Ypres Salient, the *mebus* or concrete blockhouse. Large models of the ground over which the attack was to take place were constructed behind the lines and both officers and men encouraged to go and visit them in order better to inform their understanding of their tasks in the attack. The RFC flew countless photographic reconnaissance and air observation missions in support of the preparations. A total of 216 tanks of the latest type were assembled (from a force originally known as the Heavy Branch Machine Gun Corps but about to be officially renamed as the Tank Corps immediately before the battle's opening), in preparation for what has never previously been recognized as the first mass use of tanks by the BEF – an indication of the battle's importance in Haig's eyes.

Yet, despite the enormous effort, there were fundamental problems which had not been overcome and which played a significant part in shaping the battle. Particularly difficult to surmount were the difficulties arising from the fact that the pre-offensive preparations were easily observed by the Germans occupying defences on the low ridges around three sides of the town. This meant that not only was the attack being launched from a relatively narrow bulge (only approximately 8–9 miles wide at its widest point, the 'neck') in the British defensive line, but that this salient made it virtually impossible to move troops, guns, tanks, ammunition and supplies without German knowledge. Equally, it made it very difficult to attack any part of the German positions without German artillery and infantry holding other parts of the line around the salient to fire into the side, or flank, of the attackers.

Concealment was a particular problem in these circumstances, especially for the largely static heavy artillery. Manoeuvring a battery of guns or howitzers into previously prepared positions without being observed was problematic at the best of times. But in the relatively cramped space behind the front line positions in the Ypres Salient, artillery positions were especially difficult to conceal and good ones were as rare as hen's teeth. Almost as soon as an artillery battery assumed its position, the Germans were aware of the fact and could bring fire to bear on it. The resulting artillery duels were a desperate attempt by both sides to establish superiority over their opponent whilst, inevitably, suffering large numbers of casualties to gun crews and their guns in the process. This is why the Third Battle of Ypres ('Third Ypres') is frequently described as an artilleryman's battle.

Then there was the use of tanks. Theoretically, these new weapons had shown during their limited employment on the Somme, at Arras and at Messines that, although very slow-moving, large targets for artillery with a frequent tendency to suffer mechanical breakdown, if used as close support weapons they could help infantry neutralize concrete strongpoints and capture trench positions. They were particularly effective for overcoming machine-guns – sometimes simply by driving over the gun and its crew. However, since their first use on the Somme, the Germans had learnt much about the strengths and weaknesses of tanks. The intelligence, guile and inventiveness that made the German Army such a difficult and resourceful enemy for the British to defeat was again in evidence in the Germans' responses to tanks. In particular, the tank's vulnerability to artillery fire and inability to operate in woods was known to the Germans. Whilst tanks were strong enough to fell large trees and drive over them, they were vulnerable to the tree stumps and shattered remnants of tree trunks which often pierced, or at least damaged, the tank's less armoured underbelly. This, in turn, could result in damage to the tank's engine – especially the fly wheel close to this bottom plate. Such damage would, quite literally, stop a tank in its tracks. When Haig's Flanders offensive began on 31 July 1917 these factors were to define the tank operations in the same way as the German elastic defence in depth tactics were to define the infantry's battle.

Visitors to the Ypres Salient today will note immediately as they head out of the town on the Menin Road that there are significant expanses of woodland on either side of this road, the main axis of the British advance when the battle opened. Further north in the vicinity of St Julien, the flat farmland is largely free of woods. Consequently, here tanks enjoyed considerable success in support of the British 39th and 51st Divisions, each of which accomplished all their objectives. However, astride the Menin Road, where infantry of 8th, 24th and 30th Divisions initially made good progress, problems arose as the shell-shattered woods were approached. The Germans used the remnants of the latter in the manner in which they used barbed wire against infantry: as a means to channel the tanks into killing zones where they could be tackled and destroyed by direct artillery fire. Then the infantry were tackled using the elastic defence in depth principle.

However, it was not the destruction of the tanks that left the infantry isolated and vulnerable to the German counter-attack. It was the absence of artillery support and infantry reserves. Consequently, the three divisions of II Corps were soon driven back with very severe casualties. With sufficient support from their own field artillery, the infantry could, perhaps, have held onto their gains despite the tank losses. Certainly, without the ability to hurry sufficient guns forward, an advance beyond the first 3,000 yards or so left the infantry too isolated.

And then came the rain. On the afternoon of 31 July, it began to fall and did so on 12 of the next 15 days. As it fell, the shell-torn landscape of the Ypres Salient flooded. The delicate Flanders drainage system had been destroyed by repeated artillery bombardment: ditches became rivers; fields became lakes; the clayey loam became glutinous mud. Haig's Flanders offensive became waterlogged and stalled.

Yet further attempts were made to continue what had been started. On 10 August, an infantry attack by two divisions accomplished little. It was a similar story on 16 August, although this time eight divisions were involved. There was still no breakthrough and although an advance of around 1,500 yards was made in the north, there was little, if any, progress elsewhere. With the coming of the rain, conditions had become too bad for tanks to operate with any degree of success and the Tank Corps headquarters staff began to look beyond its 'swamp maps' of the salient with the intention of securing support for an attack on more favourable ground.

This decision is usually presented as a form of rebellious response to GHQ's decision to commit tanks on the 'wrong ground' in the first place. Since the source for this line was John Frederick Charles Fuller, then chief staff officer of the Tank Corps, it has carried considerable credibility. In the interwar years Fuller's writings were hugely influential and allegedly inspired German military commanders such as Heinz Guderian and Erwin Rommel to develop the tactics that made the German Army's use of armour so successful in the early years of the Second World War. As a consequence his interpretation of the events surrounding the Tank Corps' involvement in Third Ypres have been accepted largely unchallenged.

But, on closer examination, the appreciation by Fuller and the Tank Corps' senior field commander, Brigadier General Hugh Elles, that the terrain of the Ypres Salient was, and would probably remain, unsuitable for the large-scale employment of tanks in support of the offensive was only logical. It was the proper response of a good military headquarters staff searching to ensure it made as effective a contribution as possible to the war effort. With the main thrust of future attacks in the Salient likely to meet the same type of ground the first attacks had foundered on, it was time for a change of ideas. This was not rebellion, but pragmatism, and enjoyed the full support of GHQ.

Nevertheless, despite this not unnatural desire to escape the mire and slough, the tanks' service in the salient continued and on 19 August, in an action near St Julien, a notable tactical success was achieved when twelve tanks supporting nine infantry platoons managed to secure the capture of four especially troublesome strongpoints for very few casualties. They did so in remarkable fashion. Because the inundated farmland was too greatly churned and broken by shell fire and so heavy with water, the only available option was to attack along the remnants of the St Julien–Poelcappelle road. This road ran behind the line of strongpoints, allowing the tanks to fire into the entrance of each *mebus*. Importantly, a smokescreen provided by the artillery masked the attack. The commander of one of the two attacking divisions had estimated that an attack without tanks could have cost his division 600 casualties. Since casualties amongst the tank crews and infantry totalled less than 30, the obvious conclusion to be drawn was that the tanks could significantly reduce infantry losses.

The attack (which became known as the 'Cockcroft' action after one of the strongpoints captured) was important not only for the success achieved but also because many connected with the Tank Corps both at the time and subsequently had a different interpretation of its significance to their peers. Later writers have often perpetuated a view that the action was a radical departure from previous tank operations. Yet, in fact, apart from the novelty of the tanks moving in single file along the road rather than in line abreast, the success of this attack was based on the firmly established principles that defined a successful tank operation. These were prior liaison (and, if possible, training) between the tank arm and the infantry, the allotment of specific objectives to individual tanks and the cooperation of artillery, especially in the provision of smoke. All these factors were of enormous importance in the coming Cambrai battle.

Many in the Tank Corps also believed that the success on 19 August guaranteed the Tank Corps' survival; basing this on a belief that prior to the action there had been moves afoot to disband the tank arm. Although close examination of the evidence does not support this, undoubtedly the Cockcroft attack gave the men of the Tank Corps a greater belief in their own abilities. One tank commander who took part was certainly correct when he wrote:

It was by far the most complete success achieved by tanks up to that time. It proved conclusively their *potentialities* [my emphasis] as economisers of life – a point upon which their advocates had been insisting from the beginning. It was a striking example of their moral effect . . . Dozens and scores of tanks were thrown away in the Salient after the Cockcroft with no adequate return for the sacrifice, but there was no more overt talk of abolition or even reduction.[4]

Second Lieutenant Douglas Browne, 'G' Battalion, Tank Corps

The Ypres Offensive continued for the next three months during which time the Tank Corps' involvement was limited but in many ways mirrored the experience of infantry with small local success lost in a welter of casualties, huge expenditure in materials, effort and men, frustration and, especially from October onwards, rain and mud. By employing attacks for strictly limited objectives and then meeting the German counter-attacks on more favourable terms with immense artillery support from September 1917 onwards, the British forces developed an effective counter to the German defensive tactics. Meanwhile the infantry's tactical drills were so successful in dealing with the many strongpoints they encountered that the German high command ordered its infantry to abandon what had effectively become death traps and use them only for shelter from the artillery before any British attack. Instead German infantry were instructed to sight advancing troops from positions in the countless shell holes that pock-marked the face of the Ypres Salient.

Yet these were attritional successes. Given unlimited time this approach might have worked. That it did not succeed was due to many factors. Some, such as the unfavourable weather and its effects on the terrain, in combination with the massive use of heavy artillery, are well known and understood. Others are less easily discerned. In particular it should be noted that until 1918 none of the combatants had developed the means to sustain an initial success and develop it into a comprehensive strategic victory *regardless of conditions of terrain, etc*. In late 1917, they were all still very much in the dark. Cambrai provided a signpost to the way ahead, but it did not provide all the answers.

It is important to remember that the fighting in the Ypres Salient continued throughout the period in which the Cambrai attack was being prepared, and almost to the point at which the latter attack was launched. The Third Battle of Ypres officially ended on 10 November. British casualties amounted to more than 275,000 men, German casualties being over 200,000. Whilst the British Official History emphasizes the fact that 'it was impossible to start the Cambrai offensive until the fighting at Ypres had been brought to a conclusion',[5] this statement ignores the fact that, by late 1917, the BEF was capable of planning and preparing further offensive operations whilst already in the process of conducting a battle on the scale of Third Ypres. Whether it had adequate resources in men and *matériel* to accomplish another offensive was quite another matter. However, its ability even to contemplate doing so on this occasion, and to do so repeatedly on subsequent occasions, was to give it a major advantage over its opponents for the last year of the war. It was quite plainly a very different force in every way from the one that first went to war in 1914.

CHAPTER TWO

Armies and Weapons

THE BATTLE OF Cambrai represented an important landmark in the evolution of the British Expeditionary Force. To appreciate its significance, it is especially important to understand the condition and nature of the British Army in 1917. Contrasts and comparisons with their German opponents also underline the sophistication of the evolutionary process and help contextualize the decisions taken in planning and executing the Cambrai attack. There were superficial similarities between the war experiences of the British and German armies. Both expanded considerably during the course of the war, both recruited on a regional basis, both used schemes for reservists and part-timers to increase the size of their forces rapidly during the first months of war. However, these apparent similarities masked a host of differences.

In 1914 the German Empire consisted of 26 states that included free cities, principalities, duchies and kingdoms. There was, in fact, no single German Army as the five largest states retained their own armies after German unification in 1871. These were the kingdoms of Prussia, Bavaria, Saxony and Württemberg plus the Duchy of Baden, which provided its own army corps. Whilst the Prussian army formed the nucleus of the German army (the *Kaiserliches Heer*), the units drawn from the other states maintained a separate identity through their insignia and regimental titles and customs. A single overall General Staff (the *Oberste Heeresleitung*, or OHL) was the key to their coordination. In addition, the troops of all these states used the same personal weapons and wore the same basic field grey*

---

* German infantry commonly referred to themselves as 'feldgrau' as a result but, unlike the term 'Tommy' used to describe British troops, this was not a term favoured by their opponents, who preferred 'Fritz', 'Boche' (spelt variously 'Bosche', 'Bosch' and 'Boche') or 'Hun'. The term 'Jerry' (which appears in accounts here) was less common in the Great War than afterwards.

uniforms, enhancing their cohesiveness. These combined forces created an army of almost 700,000 active troops in 669 infantry battalions, 633 artillery batteries, and 550 cavalry squadrons. Reservists and others who were called back to serve on the outbreak of war expanded the numbers in arms to approximately 1.75 million and there were about the same number of men again in what were essentially second-line reservist and territorial units, termed *Landwehr* and *Landsturm*. During the course of the war, the army expanded from 50 to over 250 divisions and approximately 13.4 million men served in it.

The key difference, other than size, between this continental mass army and its British opposite number in the First World War was in their respective intended purposes. Germany's army was for fighting a continental war against any of its immediate neighbours who, especially in the case of France and Russia, could produce equally strong, or even stronger, land forces. Germany maintained a large standing army, supported by an even bigger pool of men who had trained and served in the army and who could be called back to serve again, with the expectation that this would be the agency by which it would achieve its political aims to become the leading power in Europe.

The British Army had never been intended for such a role. Its shape and form had been defined in reforms of the late nineteenth and early twentieth centuries, which had provided for the maintenance of a small standing army of professional soldiers, supported by reservists and territorials. The infantry and cavalry in particular recruited largely on a county-based system of administrative depots and regimental districts dividing up the country. This county-based structure was also maintained for the organization of the Territorial Force and the Reserve. It provided a ready means, on the outbreak of war, for Kitchener's volunteers to be integrated into the existing regimental structure and formed the basis for an *esprit de corps* in many units. Whether volunteers enlisted through regimental administrative headquarters or joined the army as part of a locally-organized initiative, they and their mates who had enlisted at the same time became members of new battalions of long-established regiments.

For over a year of industrial warfare, the British government resisted the military's calls for conscription, choosing instead to rely on volunteers and then a variety of measures to persuade the less willing to register for military service. One such measure was attestation – the so-called 'Derby Scheme' – which promised that men who voluntarily registered their name would only be called upon for service when necessary. Married men would only be called up once the supply of single men was exhausted.

One who attested under the Derby Scheme was Stan Bradbury. His two brothers had already enlisted and in November 1915, as the pressure to find manpower for the army continued to develop, Stan (despite the fact that he was involved in essential war work) was required to register. He was prepared to play his part. His employer was considerably less enthusiastic for him to do so:

> Great efforts were being made to recruit the whole of the manpower of the country and I began to feel my position rather acutely. Many times I requested my employer to release me in order to join up but he insisted on my staying with him, especially as I was engaged on work of national importance. The latter fact was of little consolation to a guilty conscience. The hint however was constantly given to me that it would not be to my future benefit to act in opposition to my employer's wishes.[1]
>
> Stan Bradbury

Bradbury's story illustrated why the Derby Scheme was not a success, even though Stan himself was prepared to cooperate:

> The Scheme enabled men to enlist and after so doing they were placed in Groups according to age and occupation; then the various Groups were called up for service as required. I was placed in Group 5. Within two weeks Group 5 was called up, but my employer appealed at the Local Tribunal and obtained my postponement to Group 10. This availed me very little as the next ten Groups were called up together. However, he made desperate attempts to secure my release and was successful in putting off the evil day until April 1st 1916. I must have been an indispensable sort of chap.[2]
>
> Stan Bradbury

With insufficient numbers of men attesting and clear signs the war was going to be a long one, the Military Service Act was passed in January 1916, which introduced conscription for single men. This was subsequently extended to cover married men as well. Conscription was undoubtedly used to ensure men were taken into military service, but this did not mean that there were no longer many willing recruits. For some, it was the opportunity they had waited and longed for. For example, Billy Kirkby had wanted to join the army ever since 1914, but had been prevented from doing so because he was too young. In February 1917 he at last travelled to Saltburn to enlist: 'I was looking forward with pleasure and anticipation to serving my King and Country in the war to end war.'[3] For others, it was simply 'the done thing':

> When I was due to leave Winchester, at the end of July 1916, com-
> pulsory military service for men over the age of 18½ had been
> introduced; but in my case it would never have occurred to me, or to
> anyone else at the school, to do anything but join the army. It was also
> regarded as natural to apply for a commission. Accordingly, in June, I
> went to Salisbury for a brief interview with a retired general (who asked
> me if I liked cricket) and applied for a commission in the field artillery.[4]
> Frank Paish

The widely held belief in the rightness of Britain's cause in the war amongst lads raised on stories of the Empire and the stirring deeds that had conquered half the world are especially difficult for the modern reader to comprehend. Nevertheless, the views of young men like Kirkby and Paish were by no means exceptional. They were driven by a genuine desire to 'do their bit'.

So, the British Army (like the German) consisted in 1917 of regulars, reservists, volunteers, part-timers, and conscripts. However, it was a truism of the British Army at least that, by late 1917, none of this mattered. It was now impossible to categorize any unit as truly Regular, Territorial or 'New Army'. Divisions, brigades, infantry battalions, artillery batteries now comprised men who had come to military service via a variety of different paths; some willingly, others less so. Further- more, following the losses on the Somme in 1916, it was no longer possible to make generalizations about any unit's regional character. Under national mobilization measures, even those who readily joined often found themselves serving in unlikely units. Many men from the English shires found themselves in a kilt before the war's end – just as many Scottish and Welsh volunteers and conscripts served in Regular battalions of English county regiments and men from London were to be found in regiments like the Northumberland Fusiliers. Men were simply sent where needed.

Like the German Army, the British Army in 1917 represented a coalition of nations in arms. The war saw the British place an increasing reliance upon troops from the Dominions and Empire to supplement those from Britain. Australian, Canadian, Indian, New Zealand and South African troops all served on the Western Front. There were also regiments from the West Indies and Newfoundland (which was a separate Dominion from Canada at this time). Many in these units volunteered their services in the belief they were fighting to protect the 'Mother Country'. Men from Canada, India and Newfoundland are of particular importance in the Cambrai story.

Both sides organized their armies in corps, divisions, brigades and infantry battalions, but for the German infantry the regiment was the significant formation, whilst the British infantryman chiefly identified with the battalion he served in. Each battalion was numbered: the Germans identified theirs by roman numeral and regimental number – *III/52* being the third battalion of *Infanterie Regiment 52* – the British system gave a further indication of whether the battalion had its origins as a Regular, Territorial or 'New Army' battalion. Thus, the Loamshire Regiment might consist of the 1st and 2nd Battalions, which would be the 'Regular' battalions (the 3rd Battalion might only exist as a depot battalion for new recruits back in Britain), the 1/4th and 1/5th or 'First-Fourth' and 'First-Fifth' (and, possibly, the 2/4th and 2/5th) would have been Territorial units, whilst the 6th, 7th, 8th, 9th and 10th Loamshires would have been raised as Kitchener, New Army or Service battalions. Of course, some regiments had more Regular, Territorial or New Army battalions than others, whilst some, such as the London Regiment, were wholly Territorial in origin.

By 1917, the principal tactical unit for the German infantry was the *Gruppe*, or squad, of 9 men under a *Gefreiter* (Corporal). In the BEF, it was the platoon. This was a larger formation but was subdivided into four sections, each of 12 men under a non-commissioned officer (NCO) such as a corporal or sergeant. The platoon was commanded by a subaltern (a Lieutenant or Second Lieutenant). Four platoons made a company and four companies a battalion. Four battalions constituted a brigade in the BEF and three brigades formed a division.

In the BEF each section was trained and equipped in 1917 to specialize in the tactical use of a particular weapon and were termed 'Bombers', 'Rifle Grenadiers', 'Lewis Gunners', and 'Riflemen'. The former were skilled in the use of the Mills Bomb, or hand grenade. Rifle grenadiers were trained and equipped to use their rifles to fire special grenades to a greater range than the Mills bomb could be thrown. The Lewis gun section was responsible for the handling of, and ammunition supply to, the automatic rifle of that name with which the platoon could enhance its firepower in support of the riflemen. These sections were trained to act in combination when meeting opposition such as pill-boxes. The Lewis gunners would provide covering fire while the rifle grenadiers shot at the loopholes through which the Germans fired; then the bombers and riflemen could close with the pillbox's occupants to kill or capture them. Similar combinations could be used against other types of resistance. The whole formed an extremely flexible tactical unit.

No amount of training, however, could prepare the infantry for the conditions of trench warfare and only when a man was in the front line could he really learn the essential skills of survival. Most did so in the company of older hands like Thomas Suthren Hope:

A new battalion, a mixture of youth and age just arrived in France, has been attached to us for training in trench warfare . . . Now that they have become efficient at soldiering in Blighty, they have come out here to find that most of the rules they have been taught don't apply when up against the real thing.[5]

Thomas Suthren Hope, 1/5th King's (Liverpool) Regiment, 165th Brigade, 55th Division

On one occasion, Hope's turn on sentry duty was with 'a fresh-faced youth of nineteen' a little excited at being actually in the front line, all eagerness and expectancy.

I explain to him the lie of the land in front, point out the supposed machine-gun emplacements in the Jerry lines, our own posts in front of our wire, and a hundred other things a soldier should know about his particular part of the line. To all this I add my own pet theories and devices for cheating death. How to take a slanting look through the sandbagged loophole. One sees just as much and doesn't provide such a good target for a watchful sniper in the opposite lines. The spare cartridge stuck in the rifle sling. It is easier and quicker to insert than a new clip when one counts life by seconds. How to distinguish the different shells by their sound, and the necessity of judging accurately the interval between the bursts. The best way to approach a Jerry trench – erect and not bent double – then, if you going to be unfortunate enough to be hit it will be on the legs and not in the stomach, and leg wounds aren't really dangerous while stomach wounds are. And above all, I impress upon him the necessity of taking advantage of every bit of cover. Ignoring it may look brave and impressive, but if you have a desire to live out here it is much easier accomplished by making use of all the natural safeguards. In that way only can you get the last laugh, as a dead man can't even grin.[6]

Thomas Suthren Hope, 1/5th King's (Liverpool) Regiment, 165th Brigade, 55th Division

Veterans who had seen and survived combat knew that it was the infantry, and the infantry alone, who must take and hold the positions occupied by their enemy counterparts. All other arms were intended to assist in this process, or (in the case of the cavalry) exploit its successful completion.

Experienced infantrymen knew that their hopes of survival in any attack depended to a great extent on the artillery doing its job. The constant background refrain to trench warfare was the thunder of the guns. Never before had so many, and so heavy, guns been employed in warfare. Their destructive powers were enormous and every combatant nation depended on them.

The artillery of each army was divided into the lighter guns of the horse and field artillery and the heavier siege guns and howitzers. German guns were limited to a relatively small number of models and new developments were often enhanced versions of existing models – indicating that from the start of the war the German artillery's equipment was largely appropriate to its tasks.

In the BEF, the guns were the responsibility of three branches of the

Royal Artillery – the Royal Horse Artillery (RHA), the Royal Field Artillery (RFA) and the Royal Garrison Artillery (RGA), who manned the heavy weapons. The horse-drawn 18-pounder (pdr) and its lighter equivalent (used by the RHA), the 13-pdr, together with the 4.5-inch howitzer formed the majority of the field artillery's strength. They had maximum ranges between 5,500 and 7,300 yards (between 3 and 4 miles). During the course of the war the heavier artillery included anything from 6-inch guns and howitzers to 12-inch and even 15-inch guns. Some of the largest guns were on railway mountings. By late 1917 the most important and numerous large artillery pieces were the 6-inch and 8-inch howitzers, the 60-pounder gun and the 9.2-inch siege howitzer. Throughout the war the introduction of new gun types meant that the effective range of the artillery increased and this, in turn, meant they had to be aimed with greater accuracy since the longer the range, the more any error was magnified.

Typically in the British Army, there was little love lost between the branches of the Royal Artillery. In one camp were the RFA and RHA who focused a great deal on horses and horsemanship, seeing the necessity for rapid and effective deployment as the crucial factors in their successful employment in battle. In the other were the officers and men of the RGA. Generally employed in defensive coastal forts, they focused on technical questions and complex calculations pertaining to the use of heavy guns against targets such as enemy warships. Such technical matters were of little interest to the gunners of the other branches. Ultimately, however, whilst the verve and energy of the horse and field gunner could do much in taking the fight to the Germans, it was to be in gunnery as a science that the key to victory lay.

Because of the opportunities offered by combat experience against the Boers in South Africa between 1899 and 1902, the advances in British artillery equipment prior to the war had been rapid. Richard Foot joined the Officer Training Corps in 1908 and witnessed the changes. The first gun he trained on betrayed its ancestry:

> Except that it was loaded at the breech, instead of at the muzzle, the
> 15-pdr BL gun . . . was little different from the field-gun of the
> Napoleonic wars. Its carriage was a simple axle with a pair of wheels,
> and its trail, equipped with a spade end, had a sprag, spring attached,

to reduce the recoil and back movement of the trail spade. Each time it was fired, the wheels would leap six inches or more from the ground, as the trail dug into the earth behind. After four or five shots, the wheels would have to be manned, often with drag ropes on the axle, and the gun hauled forward again by the sweating gunners on to firm ground.[7]

Second Lieutenant Richard Foot, London University OTC

The 15-pounder was a 'BL' or 'breech-loading' gun, so called because when this model was being developed it was still customary to load a 'cannon' at the muzzle. Each time the gun was loaded, it required the shell, propellant charge and the means to explode this charge to be loaded separately. However, thanks to new technology its successors, introduced after the South African War, could be termed 'QF' or 'quick firing'. The introduction of a spring recoil mechanism made the field-gun more stable, allowing the gunners to relay it on its target while it was being reloaded. But what really made these guns 'quick firing' was the ammunition they fired since the gun was generally loaded with a single unit of shell and brass cartridge case in one piece. However, the new 4.5-inch QF howitzer was a contradiction since its 35-lb shell and its brass cartridge case were still loaded separately!

Nevertheless, for the early years of the war, the type of shells with which the BEF's artillery was equipped was not appropriate for the tasks it was required to perform. Up to 1915, British shells were nearly all shrapnel:

Shrapnel shells were intended to burst in the air, over the enemy's head, and to disperse a cone of round lead bullets from the point of burst. Air burst required a nice calculation of the time spent in trajectory to the point over the target, and the fuze of the shell was set to explode at the end of that time. This was the theory, but the practice was very different. All sorts of variables had to be taken into account; the barometric pressure which varied the flight of the shell; the temperature which varied the rate of burning of the powder train of the fuze; the difference in height above sea level of the gun and the target; the degree of wear in the barrel of the gun, which varied the muzzle velocity. It was largely a matter of luck, or successful correction by trial and error, to get [the shell] to burst in the right place.[8]

Lieutenant Richard Foot, 2nd Hertfordshire Battery, Royal Field Artillery

The purely practical problem of setting the fuze for each shell was greater in wartime than anticipated before it. Fuze setting was done by moving a graduated ring on the fuze, but the graduations were small and difficult to see in darkness or heavy rain. These were precisely the conditions frequently encountered on the Western Front.

But what the gunners of the BEF soon realized they needed most of all were high explosive (HE) shells. When these became available, the performance differences were marked:

> It was not till 1917 that shrapnel shell began to disappear, and both 18-pdr and 4.5-inch howitzer got a plentiful supply of high explosive shell, designed to fragment on impact by a simple contact fuze. This combination made the gunners' contribution to the battle very much more effective than in the earlier years of the war in all sorts of ways. The rate of fire was much increased by this simplification of the gunner's task. The 18-pdr, well emplaced, and with a skilled detachment to serve it, could, at a pinch, fire fifteen aimed shells in a minute, and the 4.5-inch howitzer twelve. An order of '5 rounds gun fire' to a six-gun battery would produce a smother of thirty shells on a target in half-a-minute.[9]
>
> Major Richard Foot, D/310 Battery, 62nd Division

High explosive shells in themselves were very useful but in combination with one of the key British technological developments of the war, they became supremely effective. This was the No. 106 instantaneous fuze:

> The usual fuze contained a slight delay and the shell penetrated a foot or two into the ground before exploding. For wire-cutting, this entailed two disadvantages: first, a crater which impeded the progress of attacking troops; and second, the slight upward trajectory of the shell splinters, which caused most of them to miss the wire. The only technique used for wire-cutting by artillery was therefore shrapnel, bursting low at short range, which was rarely possible. But with the introduction of the instantaneous fuze, No. 106, wire-cutting with high-explosive shells became the most effective method.[10]
>
> Second Lieutenant Frank Paish, 53rd Battery, 2nd Brigade, Royal Field Artillery, 6th Division

These advances in weaponry were important, but it was in artillery techniques and associated sciences such as survey and aerial photography that the most remarkable developments took place during the war's early years.

As was the case with the armies of the other major combatants, at the end of the nineteenth century most artillery training in the British Army had been based on the assumption that the normal method of shooting would be over 'open sights' in the same way a rifle was aimed and fired. Artillerymen would look along the gun sights at a target visible from the gun position. Where the enemy possessed artillery, it was expected that they would do the same thing. Artillery training was largely concerned, therefore, with practising how to get into action quickly and how to achieve as high a rate of fire as possible. It was clearly an advantage to get in the first shot and to shoot more rapidly than your opponent.

The fighting in South Africa had hinted at the flaws in these artillery tactics. Gunners who tried to shoot over open sights necessarily exposed themselves to view and became targets for their enemy counterparts who, if they fired 'indirectly', could remain hidden. As a result, British artillery training manuals and tactical guidance stressed that indirect fire was to be the primary form of artillery fire. However, although the artillery doctrine set down in the 1906 edition of *Field Artillery Training* provided detail on how indirect fire should be used, the majority of field (as opposed to siege) artillery units still trained principally in direct fire techniques. Only the heavy guns of the RGA trained extensively in indirect fire.

The first engagements of the Great War only served to reinforce the South African experience and demonstrated that, as one writer put it, 'the game was not worth the candle'.[11] At Le Cateau in August 1914, the British artillery largely operated from forward positions and, as a consequence, thirty-eight guns were captured and many gun crews killed, wounded or captured. Direct fire was soon given up and seldom used again. Artillery instead fired from concealed positions, usually at targets invisible to the gun crew, often several miles away. This experience was the same for all combatants.

Indirect fire meant that gunners were unable to see their target and had to be told, firstly, where to aim and, secondly, the distance to the target. The first was addressed by aiming in the horizontal plane (calculating the 'line', 'direction' or 'azimuth'), whilst the second depended on aiming in the vertical plane where the 'elevation' of the guns helped set the expected 'range' or fall of the shells. When positioning a gun battery, it was first essential to ensure all the guns of the battery were firing in the same direction. This was usually accomplished by firing at a visible object or prominent feature:

> Gun-layers pointed their guns by aiming so many degrees and minutes right or left of some conspicuous object, as determined by the director (a sort of primitive theodolite), which measured the angle between the line to the object and the calculated line to the target. In actual operations, the guns were invariably laid with the help of two aiming posts, laid out by map, and where possible corrected by firing on some identifiable point in the German lines, the zero line, from which all orders were given as so many degrees or minutes right or left of zero. The use of aiming posts had the additional advantage that it was possible to fix small lamps to them for firing at night.[12]
>
> Second Lieutenant Frank Paish, 53rd Battery, 2nd Brigade, Royal Field Artillery, 6th Division

These aiming posts, or 'Bearing Pickets', were iron pins or pegs carrying labels giving coordinates and lists of bearings to suitable points. They were originally introduced on the Somme by Captain Bertram Keeling of 4th Field Survey Company to help a 12-inch railway gun fire along the straight Albert–Bapaume road, which was extensively used by the Germans as a supply route. The problem was how to ensure this gun was correctly aimed so as to hit the road which was 13 miles away (especially in the dark). The solution was to provide an accurately surveyed marker close by and then calculate the bearing to the target from this. This technique was soon in wide use but it was to be another year before its real possibilities were finally realized.

A concomitant problem arising from these artillery techniques was the loss of surprise resulting from preliminary ranging. Until accurate maps were available and equally accurate means to locate targets so that a battery of guns could reasonably expect to land its shells on, or near, its target, it was necessary to employ a technique known as registration. For a battery to 'register' on a target, one gun would have to fire ranging shots at the target. This shooting would be observed from the front line trenches or from an aircraft and corrections to the range and direction of the gun's fire would be communicated back to the battery by the observers until the gun was 'on' the target, at which point the other guns of the battery could take their line of fire and range from this gun. This process, frequently long and laborious, was adequate to some degree for static targets such as strongpoints and trench lines but alerted any enemy artillery officer with even a modicum of knowledge of the gunner's trade that his battery was being registered and of the possibility of an infantry attack. It also offered him the opportunity to relocate his guns to a new, and therefore unregistered, position.

Then there was the need to cut gaps in the German barbed wire:

Before Cambrai, we had always had before any major attack these enormous bombardments – the Somme, I think, was over a week; at Arras it was 7 days plus one because it wasn't considered long enough . . . One difficulty was how to get the wire cut so the infantry could advance and the only way of cutting the wire was to cut lanes with 18-pounder fire, which had to be done very slowly, largely by individual guns, very careful ranging and observed fire. 18-pounder fire was the only thing that really cut the wire satisfactorily for the infantry to go through. There was a need for a long bombardment; the German positions in 1916–1917 had been occupied for two or more years and they were 'strongpoints' – very strong. There were very well dug-in gun positions and so on and so forth. All these things need to be dealt with with accurate and observed fire. If you are going to need accurate, observed fire, you had to allot several days for it. Of course, you lost strategic surprise at once, you even lost tactical surprise because it was comparatively easy for the Germans to sit there watching where their wire was being destroyed and saying 'Well, presumably if they are cutting the wire at point A over there, that's where they are going to attack'.[13]

Lieutenant Kenneth Page, 40th Brigade RFA, 2nd Division

The introduction of aircraft in the war opened many possibilities to the combatant nations – not least of which was the ability aircraft offered to observe what was on 'the other side of the hill' and, if possible, photograph it. Photographic aerial reconnaissance meant that artillery had to deploy various methods of deception to conceal the position of the guns.

> With the introduction of aerial photography the technique of camouflage grew in importance. The airman's eye might not be able to detect the presence of guns even when flying over them at 1,500 feet, but a photograph taken from 4,000 to 6,000 feet would reveal their location unless the whole area was carefully camouflaged. The interpretation of aeroplane photographs became a highly skilled work, on which specially trained men were employed.[14]
>
> Second Lieutenant Frank Lushington, 244 Siege Battery, Royal Garrison Artillery

Such photographs did not normally show the guns themselves. The process of interpretation was intended to glean information from various clues such as the shadows cast by the guns, the tracks leading to possible gun emplacements, the 'blast' marks immediately in front of the guns where grass scorched through firing showed as lighter than unburnt grass, and freshly dug earth. From early 1917 camouflage officers were increasingly employed to devise and provide means to disguise these effects of light, shade and tone and they issued large quantities of rolls of wire and fish netting on to which small strips of coloured canvas had been knotted, and bundles of material of a canvas texture called 'scrim'.

> The wire netting was erected on poles and supported over the gun and its emplacement, the object being to create a perfectly flat overhead cover which in plan should symmetrize with the surroundings, and conceal the black shadows cast by the gun and other objects in or near the pit. This cover aimed at the production of another surface which should have the effect of absorbing and reflecting about the same amount of light as the surrounding grass, and consequently appear of the same tone in the photograph.[15]
>
> Second Lieutenant Frank Lushington, 244 Siege Battery, Royal Garrison Artillery

Since the artillery of all combatants worked hard to conceal themselves by going to ground and hiding behind buildings and in woods it became increasingly difficult to locate hostile artillery batteries. Virtually the only indication of their position was the flash of a gun when it was fired, which was difficult to see except at night. Aeroplanes spotting these 'flashes' could only fix their position roughly. The valuable work of aerial reconnaissance could locate gun pits, but could not show whether the pits were occupied or empty. Other means had to be found for locating the position of enemy batteries.

When a battery was shooting and the enemy territory could not be seen and errors corrected visually from the actual shots falling on the ground, the artillery used a technique known as 'shooting off the map' or 'predicted shooting' instead. Map shooting obviously required accurate maps. Herein lay a major problem. Whilst Belgian maps were reasonably accurate and up to date, the French maps the BEF possessed were those of Napoleon's time. It was necessary, therefore, for special units of the Royal Engineers to accurately survey the land the BEF was fighting on. These surveyors eventually became known as 'Field Survey Companies' and, using a combination of aerial photographs and a completely new surveying technique, they completed the first survey of the British front by the spring of 1916 – but not without some cost:

> In 1915 our main object was to complete new trench maps of the whole of our front by the end of the year. Drawing-office hours were from 8.00 am to 10.00 pm, 7 days a week; three of the draughtsmen had to be sent home with impaired eyesight. The topographers surveyed as close up to the line as possible, often in weather which before the war would have been considered impossible to work in, and beyond their area the detail was revised and trenches added by compilation from cadastral plans and air photographs.[16]
>
> Lieutenant Frederick John Salmon, 3rd Field Survey Company, Royal Engineers

Having done so, they could fix the position of each British artillery battery and supply the battery commander with an accurate map showing his own position and the position of all his targets. This specially prepared map was known as a 'plotting table' or Artillery Board, owing to the fact that the map was mounted on a zinc-covered board to prevent shrinkage. By reading the targets on this board it was only a matter of simple calculation to work out the angle and elevation of the gun.

The ability to attack targets without the help of an observer became more and more essential. Harassing fire against German supply columns and troop movements was a vital and continuous part of the artillery's role. So too was the support of infantry against attacks, or SOS fire. Night firing became increasingly common and had to be from the map or against a target located in daylight under probably different meteorological conditions. Corrections for wind, barometric pressure and temperature would therefore have to be calculated and applied. Further calculations based on variations in quality of ammunition were also introduced.

Of vital importance were the process of calibration and the calculation of each gun's muzzle-velocity. Each artillery piece had its own characteristics based on how it had been made, how much it had been used, and so on. The gunner's object was to find out the gun's power so adjustments could be made to make the guns of a battery shoot alike. These factors varied with time:

> All guns tend to lose muzzle-velocity gradually, as the corrosion of the bore, just in front of the firing-chamber, allows an increasing amount of the gas created by the explosion of the firing-charge to escape past the shell. For a time this can be corrected by increasing the elevation of the gun to allow for the 'calibration error'. When, however, the corrosion gets beyond a certain point, the gun not only loses range but becomes increasingly erratic, and has to be sent in for a new inner barrel.[17]
>
> Second Lieutenant Frank Paish, 53rd Battery, 2nd Brigade, Royal Field Artillery, 6th Division

In 1917, therefore, although some gunners might still speak of their art, there was no avoiding the science.

Field survey enabled the position of British artillery to be located but for the Artillery Board to be of use it also had to indicate the position of German artillery. Two techniques were developed to complement the work of observers on the ground and in aircraft. These were termed 'flash-spotting' and 'sound-ranging'. It is undoubtedly true that although the units who engaged in these tasks and in the work of field survey were tiny and they may seem to have taken a very small part in the battles of the Great War, their work had an importance that was disproportionate to their numbers.

The basic idea of flash-spotting was simple. Trained observers using special instruments looked for the muzzle flash of German guns firing. At best this appeared as a bright red spot, but more usually it was a reddish glow with a red heart in the middle or sometimes only a glow. By day only a flash or a smoke puff might be seen. The important element was systematic observation. There were over a hundred survey posts stretched along the Western Front and spaced at convenient distances from one another. Two or three miles was about normal, but the most important thing was that every part of the front as far as was practicable should be covered by at least three posts. This was more difficult in rolling country like the Cambrai sector but, conversely, height helped and made various aspects of observation easier.

Each post's essential equipment consisted of an instrument with which to take bearings, a telephone, a chronometer, a log book, a stop watch, and a press key. Other items included binoculars, maps, electric torches, notebooks, and similar odds and ends. Survey posts usually had 8–10 men, generally with an NCO in charge. A post had a map of its own front mounted on a board. On this map was marked all the known information about hostile batteries. By means of a thread fixed at the post's position, the observer could plot bearings on this map quickly. If two or more posts got bearings to a gun that was firing, they could fix its location and pass it on to the artillery. As the survey posts became better organized into groups (with an officer commanding each group), a system was developed for properly coordinating and synchronizing bearings from different posts. When bearings had been taken from two or more posts to a gun flash, some means had to be devised for determining whether they had been observing the same gun flash. This was initially done by recording the time of every observation, but a later development was the Flash and Buzzer (F&B) Board, which was generally in use by November 1916.

The Flash and Buzzer Board was a special type of telephone switchboard by which Group headquarters could communicate with posts. The special feature of this switchboard was the addition of a small light and a buzzer on each line. By depressing the key in the post the observer lit up the light on the board and at the same time sounded the buzzer. At Group headquarters a skilled coordinator could decide whether two or more posts were observing the same flash. The board prevented any chance of one post's observations being influenced by another.

In sound-ranging a simple principle was used for a complex application.

> When a gun is fired three separate noises are made. The first is the 'onde-de-choc'; next is the sound of the charge exploding in the gun's breech; and last is the noise of the shell exploding. Six petrol tins in a semi-circle were equipped with a simple microphone – just a wire – and placed in a curved line about 500 yards from the front. Each was wired to a film at a station a mile or so away which carried six separate lines, and which could be activated by pressing a switch. When a gun was fired each line would give a kick, the first being from the petrol tin nearest to the gun, and followed by two further kicks from the subsequent noises. From this information and a knowledge of the speed and direction of the wind the precise situation of a German gun could be computed. Even more, its bore, i.e. the size of its shell (the two best-known were the 9.2s and the 5.9s), could be identified, and, by reference to the book of statistics, the maker's name – usually Krupps as far as I can remember. The system could also work in reverse i.e. it could be used for ranging our guns on the target.[18]
>
> Private Harold Edwards, 15th (Civil Service Rifles) London Regiment, 140th Brigade, 47th Division

Accurate location of German batteries depended upon the coordination of recordings from three or more stations and the time interval between its arrival at each station.

All sorts of external interference needed to be filtered out by trained observers or by seemingly Heath Robinson devices. The most important of these was the 'Tucker microphone'.[19] Because the 'shell-wave' caused by a high velocity shell travelling faster than sound made a loud, high-pitched crack, it often completely drowned out the low boom of the gun firing it. This report was not easy to hear, but had a bigger pressure behind it, causing windows to rattle and so on. By electrically heating a thin wire stretched over a hole in an ammunition box, it was possible to distinguish between the boom and crack. The change in pressure caused by a gun report produced a jet of air which cooled this wire, lessening its electrical resistance, and a galvanometer recorded the effect. Shell-waves and equally unwanted high-pitched sounds such as rifle fire hardly registered but a gun report produced a large kick. Insects drawn to the heated wire were deterred by wire mesh.

A sound-ranging section could only operate if these sounds reached its recording stations. The great enemy, therefore, was an adverse wind. This would render the sound of the gun report as received by a ground-station faint or inaudible. Conditions were ideal when the wind was blowing from the gun towards the observer. The effect of wind was far more important than the effect of hills or other obstacles and so the recording microphones of a sound-ranging section could be placed almost anywhere. Unfortunately, the wind on the Western Front generally blew from the British towards the German lines. However, it was a very useful technique in most other weather conditions, particularly mist and fog.

Sound-ranging sections also depended on complex wiring systems with double wires running from HQ to the six microphone stations and two forward Observation Posts. This was reckoned to total about forty miles of wire, and it had to be good wire with a low resistance and freedom from earths and other faults, a much higher standard than that demanded of telephone cable.

Whilst the Germans also employed sound-ranging units, the British were much more successful in their implementation. The need to locate and neutralize enemy artillery batteries became recognized as increasingly important and all these measures were coordinated under counter-battery staff officers, colloquially termed 'counter-blasters'.

The counter-battery organisation was extremely well run and very complex. You had a counter-battery officer at Corps who kept very complete records and maps, which were circulated regularly. Every gun position seen firing was entered on the map and it was given a number so that an aeroplane seeing it fire could send down the signal 'GNF' – which meant 'Gun Now Firing' – GNF number so-and-so and the counter-battery staff would know at once that that battery there was in action and they could get somebody onto it. Counter-battery work improved as time went on as we got more and more heavy artillery.[20]
Lieutenant Kenneth Page, 40th Brigade RFA, 2nd Division

The counter-blasters could only coordinate the artillery effectively because they had good maps, the position of the British guns was precisely located, the position of enemy guns was also accurately identified, and they had the means of laying their guns correctly on these targets without previous registration. These were all critical features that defined the artillery's role in the Cambrai battle.

Cambrai is forever associated with the tank. But, to appreciate its role in, and contribution to, the battle, it is absolutely essential to forego the myth of the all-conquering, invincible, unstoppable armoured behemoth and instead to look at the reality of the tank as it was in its state of development in 1917.

The tank in the Great War was crudely simple in design and construction when compared with subsequent models. However, when British industrial techniques and might were applied to solving the problems arising from the developing stalemate on the Western Front, the technological response was essentially pragmatic, adequately effective in combat but ergonomically appalling. A true 'first' in the history of warfare, its designers and creators had little to guide them in their decisions regarding necessary construction materials, motive power and armament for actual combat.

In October 1914, as operations began to stagnate, an energetic and intelligent officer, Colonel Ernest Swinton, applied his mind to the problems being encountered in France and Belgium. Swinton was Assistant Secretary to the Committee of Imperial Defence and advised the war cabinet on military matters. His first thoughts were that 'some form of armoured vehicle immune against bullets, which should be capable of destroying machine guns and of ploughing a way through wire'[21] was required and imagined that these machines would have tracks, referring to them as 'caterpillars'. Swinton was to be a key figure in the invention of the tank. His drive did much to help the idea of tanks become a reality. His superior, Maurice Hankey, took up the cause and circulated a paper to the War Cabinet (now known as the 'Boxing Day Memorandum') in which he wrote of a machine-gun armed, caterpillar track-driven, armoured vehicle capable of crushing barbed wire and of providing cover for advancing infantry.

This in turn fired the imagination of Winston Churchill, who although First Lord of the Admiralty lost no opportunity to involve himself in a variety of matters outside his position's purview. Churchill too proposed armoured and machine-gun armed vehicles with cater-pillar tracks. It is remarkable, therefore, that from its inception, many of the key people who made the design a reality (and Churchill was probably the most important of all), imagined many of the tank's key features and had a clear idea of its role that, ultimately, matched its use in reality. For, above all, the tank was to prove most effective as an infantry close-support weapon and as a means to overcome barbed-wire defences.

Churchill's establishment of an Admiralty Landships Committee in February 1915 provided a forum from which, eventually, a coordinated programme for developing the tank grew and its decision to build eighteen prototype models led to the involvement of the agricultural machinery manufacturers, Messrs. William Foster, Ltd. of Lincoln. Foster's participation in turn saw the introduction of two key engineer-ing figures into the tank story: William Tritton and Lieutenant Walter Wilson. Tritton was the managing director of Foster's and the very image of an Edwardian businessman in bowler hat and three-piece, whilst Wilson was a Royal Naval reserve officer who had built a reputa-tion as a designer of motor cars and lorries. Together they produced the solution to one of the biggest difficulties in the manufacture of the first tanks: how to make the tracks sufficiently durable and yet light and flexible enough for use in battle.

Whilst designers were striving to create a viable armoured vehicle, significant political developments were taking place in Britain. The formation of the Asquith Coalition in May 1915 and the related resignation of Churchill from his post as First Lord of the Admiralty could have put paid to the Landships Committee and the Admiralty's experiments. That it did not was largely thanks to Churchill's successor, Arthur Balfour, who allowed work to continue and encouraged key Admiralty personnel to remain involved. The political reorganization after the coalition was formed also saw the creation of the Ministry of Munitions under David Lloyd George on 9 June 1915. This was to have important consequences for tank production as, in February 1916, the Ministry took over control of production of the new weapon. Large-scale tank manufacture depended on their inclusion in the industrial mobilization programme the Ministry was responsible for. It seems unlikely that, without the Ministry's active involvement, the tank would have been anything other than an experimental novelty. So much industrial capacity was already taken up with production of other munitions, that there was little spare available when the tanks were ready to go into full production.

Although representatives of the War Office, Ministry of Munitions and the Landships Committee saw a demonstration of a wooden mock-up of the tank in September 1915, it was not until January 1916 that the first working prototype, called 'Mother', appeared. Later, because of production and supply problems, only 50 were available for use on the Somme in September 1916. Douglas Haig, who had been led to believe by Swinton (amongst others) that he could expect to have considerably more ready and considerably earlier, decided to employ them in what he hoped would be the critical phase of the Somme battle. This attack, subsequently termed the Battle of Flers-Courcelette, opened on 15 September 1916.

In the attack, a sizeable proportion of the allotted tanks broke down and only a small number proved of any use. However, the achievements of a few in this attack and in what has dismissively been termed 'penny packet' attacks subsequently on the Somme, demonstrated to Haig and his senior commanders that there was enough in the new invention to merit requests for larger numbers to be manufactured and, when these were not available, to use whatever tanks were to hand (including poorly armoured training tanks) for the Arras battle in April 1917. Haig also appointed one of the most capable members of his headquarters staff, Lieutenant Colonel Hugh Elles, to replace Ernest Swinton as commander of the tank forces in France and, it seems, Elles was permitted a free rein by Haig in appointing his staff.

Hugh Elles was a highly regarded member of Haig's own staff when appointed to command the tank units in France in October 1916. He was 36 years of age, 'admirably good looking', urbane and intelligent. 'Immensely popular' with 'a good deal of personal charm and power of leadership', Elles was the ideal man to lead the new tank arm with the appropriate mixture of élan and common sense. Importantly, to Haig and his staff he was 'one of us'. Elles also seems to have well understood the tank arm's status as part of a much larger force: the BEF. 'Universally liked and admired', his personal qualities nicely balanced those of the acerbic Major John Fuller, who acted as his chief staff officer.[22]

Officers and men who joined the tank arm were generally volunteers. After the first occasion tanks were used on the Somme, the tank force went through a period of reorganization and expansion. During this time, many men were drawn by invitations to volunteer and, to some extent, the prospect of serving with the tanks offered similar attractions to the Royal Flying Corps (RFC). However, for some the reasons for joining were altogether more prosaic. Horace Birks had served as a lance corporal on the Western Front until he was wounded on 1 July 1916. After hospitalization he was sent to an Officer Cadet Battalion at Cambridge. Whilst there he heard about the new tank arm:

> Our company commander put a notice on the board saying that volunteers were required for a new branch of the Army and only those who were picked men would be selected. We gave our names in to the company orderly room. They took very few of us. We were told nothing about it except that it was a new service. Of course, rumour being what it is, one guessed it must be them because they'd just come out then. It was just getting common news that they'd got tanks. As far as I can remember about a third of us were selected. Personally, I volunteered for it because I was sick of walking about in France. I thought the infantry work was no good to me at all. I knew nothing about tanks.[23]
>
> Second Lieutenant Horace Birks, No. 11 Company, 'D' Battalion, Heavy Branch, Machine Gun Corps

In France, the newly appointed chief staff officer of the newest corps in the Army described the curious amalgam of men that the expansion of the Heavy Branch, Machine Gun Corps had drawn as volunteers:

> Frankly, I had never seen such a band of brigands in my life. The reason became apparent directly I was told that recruitment had been opened to the whole Army in France, for this naturally meant that every disgruntled man or 'impossible' soldier had sought an escape from his surroundings by applying to join the Heavy Branch. There were cavalrymen, infantrymen and gunners; ASC* men, sappers and

* Army Service Corps

42

actually a sailor, though how he had found his way to Bermicourt I cannot say. There were men in trousers, men in puttees, men in trench boots and men in kilts. There was every type of cap badge and deficiency in cap badges: the men looked exactly what they were – the down-and-outs of bawling sergeants and unfriendly corporals.[24]

Major John Fuller, Headquarters, Heavy Branch, Machine Gun Corps

Yet it was one of the achievements of Hugh Elles, Fuller and their staff in France and of the organizers and trainers in England that these men were moulded into a genuinely homogenous unit with a true esprit de corps during the early months of 1917 – a fact recognized in the granting by Royal Charter of the title 'Tank Corps' in July 1917.

Whilst these organizational changes were taking place, a number of technological changes were made to the Mark I tank used on the Somme in the light of the combat experiences of the tanks' first few months of service. However, essentially, the Mark IV tank that saw service at Messines, Third Ypres and Cambrai was very similar to its predecessors. Its strengths, weaknesses and peculiarities were a direct product of the circumstances in which the tank was designed and produced, the conditions in which they were called upon to fight and the lessons of those battles. When detailed, the tank's characteristics make the achievements of their crews all the more remarkable and admirable.

The Mark IV tank came in two varieties: the 'male' was armed with two 6-pdr. Hotchkiss QF 57 mm naval guns and four Lewis guns, its 'female' consort had six Lewis guns.[25] These weapons were mounted in housings called 'sponsons' on the sides of the tank, except for one Lewis gun in the front of the tank. The 'male' version weighed 32 tons, whilst the 'female' weighed 28 tons. Crews soon realized there were other important differences in the two types:

Everybody wanted a male tank. I was a junior officer. I got a female. The male tank was the thing because it had a gun and it was a more formidable weapon altogether. You could get out of it easier because it had quite a biggish door on the back of the sponson. But the female tank had doors [close to] the ground. And it was very difficult to get out of. If there was a fire or anything like that it was odds on that some of you would get hurt.[26]

Second Lieutenant Horace Birks, No. 11 Company, 'D' Battalion, Tank Corps

Both types had a crew of eight who fought together in a single compartment. As one former tank man remarked, 'It doesn't seem possible that you can squeeze eight men in there, but you could.'[27] Space was cramped still further because it was shared with a six-cylinder Daimler-Knight sleeve-valve 105 hp engine. This engine though large 'didn't have enough power really for the weight of the tank'.[28] This was the chief reason for the first tanks' lack of speed. On good going, such as metalled roads, a Mark IV tank might achieve 3.7 mph, but over the shell-torn terrain of the Western Front a rate of 25 yards per minute (i.e. less than 1 mph) was more usual.

Considerable heat and carbon monoxide fumes came from the engine. Although a fan drew air from the stuffy interior to cool the radiator and sucked in fresh air in an attempt to provide ventilation, the temperature inside the tank frequently reached over 50° Celsius (125° Fahrenheit). Despite the petrol and cordite fumes the crew dared not open a flap or loophole to get fresh air for fear of the enemy machine-gun bullets, and the excessive heat could cause vomiting and exhaustion. Most crews could perhaps endure about eight hours' continuous action but then required 48 hours' rest.

The engine generated noise as well and this proved a major handicap to steering the tank:

As you can imagine the noise was terrific in the tanks and the stench and the heat and if I had to signal that I wanted to turn, I would have to turn round and bang on the engine cowling on this side or that side to one of the gearsmen at the back.[29]

Second Lieutenant Edward Leigh-Jones, B9 'Black Bess', No. 4 Company, 'B' Battalion, Tank Corps

Leigh-Jones' reference to the gearsmen highlights the tank's complicated steering system:

In those days the tank was a very primitive machine. It had a driver who worked the pedals and accelerator and so on, [and] an officer who sat beside him and worked the brakes. Then there were two men at the back – one on each side of the centre portion of the tank because on each side there was a gearing which was called a secondary gearing, so you could drive if you liked with one side of the tank in top gear and the other side in second gear – the result would be, of course, that the tracks would move unevenly and the tank would swing in its movement and that was the chief method of turning. You had to put the clutch out and get the man at the back to put the appropriate gear in. It was a very tricky business. There were two other men on each side. A man with a six-pounder gun and the other with a machine-gun. So there were eight men in that tank altogether. There wasn't that much room for dancing![30]

Captain Mark Dillon, 'B' Battalion, Tank Corps

Most importantly, in order to turn, it was usually necessary for the tank to stop. This meant that it presented a large stationary target to the German artillery. The necessity for secondary gears (and men to operate them) was a result of the design process, as it was discovered that the tank's weight would overstrain the transmission system. Other aspects of the design caused further problems. One was visibility for the crew:

The front visors could only be lifted a matter of 45° which gave the driver and the officer a view of the front horns of the tank and very little else. You had to get your direction from these periscopes, which were not very effective. The driver and the officer had two small round periscopes which you pushed through the top which gave you an additional quite clear view, but a very restricted field of vision.[31]

Second Lieutenant Horace Birks, No. 11 Company, 'D' Battalion, Tank Corps

This meant tank commanders were dependent on their crews for information concerning events on the battlefield to either flank and, consequently, the problems of internal communication were again an issue. The gunners themselves were not in a significantly better position than the driver and commander:

You could see nothing except just that little bit where the gun goes out. You could see nothing else when you were inside the tank. We had a limited view just along the sights of the gun. All we saw was their trench more or less. You couldn't tell whether you were shooting at anybody or not when you first went in. You fired generally along their trenches on each side.[32]

Private Eric Potten, F23 'Foggie II', No. 17 Company, 'F' Battalion, Tank Corps

In order to make *effective* use of the 6-pounder guns with which the male tanks were equipped, it was again necessary to stop the tank. However, to avoid German artillery fire, tanks fired on the move as far as possible. Even firing the gun was complicated by the noise in the tank and tank gunners often had to rest their hands on their gun to feel if it fired or not.

Combat experience led to the development of certain items of equipment intended to assist the tanks to play their part in the attack. One such item was the 'unditching gear' used after a tank fell into a shell-hole and 'ditched'. This was a solid hardwood beam, which ran the whole width of the track and had chains fitted to it with bolts. These chains were attached to the track before the tank was driven forward on to the beam, which gave the tracks purchase on which to climb out of difficulty. Of course, the crew normally had to get out of the tank whilst under fire to fit the chains to the tracks.

A problem for the crew that was less easy to solve was 'splash':

> When the outside of the tank's armour is struck by machine-gun bullets, it causes the hardened steel on the inside to flake off. In the process of the flaking off a spark is created. So, when the succession of machine-gun bullets strikes the tank you get a display of sparks just like a Catherine wheel.[33]
>
> Private Reginald Beall, 'A' Battalion, Tank Corps

These flakes were known as 'splash'. However, their effects were potentially more harmful than simple pyrotechnics.

> One experienced a lot of injury from splash from the inside of the plates. You had a machine-gun playing on the outside of the plates, the inside where the bullets hit it would flake away in little red-hot splinters and we were issued with masks – visors – to protect our faces. The trouble was you couldn't see a damn thing through them so we rarely wore them. You'd see tank crews coming out of action very often looking as if they had come from a piratical expedition because their faces would be running with blood and their arms and hands too. Of course, it is only superficial but it was quite nasty all the same.[34]
>
> Captain Mark Dillon, 'B' Battalion, Tank Corps

In fact, eye injuries to crew members were often more than superficial, but the issuing of leather and chainmail face masks, whilst designed to help prevent these injuries, served to exacerbate the problems of visibility for gunners and drivers.

Tank crews were well aware of the advantages and disadvantages of their machines by comparison with the lot of the infantry and that an infantryman might regard the tank man's work of a few hours' action in an armoured box as 'cushy'. However, as Horace Birks recognized: 'The infantry who had any knowledge of tanks wouldn't come within a mile of them because they attracted all the enemy fire. The mugs got close . . . because they thought they'd get shelter.'[35] Furthermore, the unique conditions in which the crews fought, when known to the infantry, often earned their respect and admiration, tinged perhaps with the belief that anyone prepared to contemplate volunteering for such work must surely be slightly unhinged.

The combination of barbed wire, machine-guns and artillery had done much to ensure that opportunities for cavalry to operate in their traditional role on the Western Front at least were almost non-existent – although during the Somme battles, in the fighting connected with the German retreat to the Hindenburg Line and the Battle of Arras, brief opportunities for cavalry employment did manifest themselves.

Whilst the Germans retained significant quantities of cavalry principally for use in the wider open spaces of the Eastern Front, many have questioned why the British Army in France maintained a Cavalry Corps of five divisions throughout 1917 and into 1918 when there was so little prospect of it being used. The answer was quite simple: cavalry remained the only viable option to exploit any opportunity created by the infantry, artillery and tanks for breaking through and beyond the German defensive positions. Since the British cavalry were trained principally to act as mounted infantry (although still capable of charging with sabres drawn when necessary) and carried exactly the same rifle as the infantry for that especial purpose, horses remained the fastest way to get significant numbers of men to where they were needed. Without the equivalent of armoured personnel carriers or other robust motor transport for infantry, and with the tanks clearly too slow to be an arm of exploitation, it was still hoped the Cavalry Corps could deliver victory if employed correctly.

But, whilst the cavalry saw no action, or served dismounted as trench garrisons, those of its leaders who by their character might have pursued their task with drive if the occasion arose, instead grew impatient for excitement. Many transferred to other arms, such as the RFC and, indeed, the tanks. Although many who remained still demonstrated the fighting spirit expected of them when the time came, on the Western Front at least the cavalry remained an under-utilized and expensive resource to maintain. However, until appropriate circumstances for their employment could be created, they drilled their men and groomed their horses and waited for their time.

The foregoing account of the artillery and the associated methods of survey, aerial photography and reconnaissance indicates that, from the earliest days of the war, air operations were constantly linked to the ground fighting. There were tremendous developments in technology in the air during the war relating not just to the flying and aerial combat abilities of the aircraft, but also in their associated equipment. Whilst the 'scout' or fighter aircraft were fitted with new and more deadly means to increase their effectiveness as killing machines, the photo reconnaissance aircraft acquired more accurate cameras and the bombers more efficient means for delivering their relatively small, but sometimes effective, burdens onto targets.

During the Somme battles of 1916, the Royal Flying Corps expanded dramatically, and the German Air Force concentrated its best aircraft and pilots against it. Although the RFC enjoyed some success in the air battle, by early 1917 its German opponents had considerably more technically advanced aircraft. The Arras offensive became known as 'Bloody April' for the RFC as its pilots and observers suffered severe casualties in their efforts to continue operations in support of the ground forces. For, despite all losses and setbacks, the RFC never shirked from its responsibilities towards the artillery and infantry on the ground and continued a desperate and ferociously aggressive policy against its German opponents. Its scouts sought out combat rather than avoiding it, and its reconnaissance aircraft continued to fly mission after mission to secure vital information or give necessary support to the troops below.

One consequence of the losses of 'Bloody April' was that the RFC's equipment, training, aircraft production and organization were all reviewed and improved and the force began to take a formidable shape as a weapon of war. In particular, the first use of aircraft to bomb and machine-gun (or 'strafe') ground forces created a remarkable change in the conduct of military operations and soon became an essential part of any attack. The use of bombers to attack targets such as lines of communication, airfields, ammunition dumps and reserve troops many miles behind the front line was an important step towards the realization of the modern concept of 'deep battle'. Third Ypres saw this ground attack work (especially in cooperation with infantry), develop and become an important aspect of the RFC's overall role in offensive operations. But it was at Cambrai where this work was first successfully incorporated into the overall battle plan for the 'all-arms battle'. By this time, new and improved aircraft had been brought into service – although in some cases they arrived just days before the battle was set to begin. Many British pilots felt that with the Sopwith Camel, SE5a, Bristol Fighter F2b, Airco DH4 and the rugged Armstrong-Whitworth FK8, they were finally getting the machines with which to match their German opponents' Pfalz DIII, Fokker DR1 and Albatros DV fighters. However, these were still formidable opponents and, in the right hands, could still prove more than a match for the majority of RFC pilots.

In 1917, the German Air Force had more than doubled its numbers of fighters and, thereby, reinforced the cult of the 'ace' – the efficient and deadly aerial killer. In Manfred von Richthofen, their 25-year-old leading ace, they had a man whose reputation was such that as the 'Red Baron' he had acquired something of the bogeyman status of a children's fairy tale for many British and French fliers. This he only sought to enhance by painting his aircraft's fuselage bright red so that his enemy were immediately aware of his presence in combat. By encouraging the pilots of his unit (*Jagdgeschwader I*) to decorate their planes in similarly bright colours and patterns, he created an instantly recognizable 'Circus' with an immediate moral advantage when it met its opponents in combat. Richthofen maintained the elite character of his command through a careful selection process:

> Richthofen was very firm on one point: he kept in the *Staffel* only such pilots who really accomplished something. He observed each beginner for a time [and] then if he became convinced that the person concerned

was not up to the requirements that Richthofen placed on a fighter pilot – whether due to his moral character or due to his technical ability – that person would surely be sent away.[36]

Leutnant Friedrich-Wilhelm Lübbert, *Jasta 11, Jagdgeschwader I*

Nevertheless, there was nothing of the myth about Richthofen's reputation as an efficient killer, as his total of 61 'kills' by the beginning of November 1917 proved. Although the Allies had greater strength in the air in late 1917, the German Air Force stood undoubtedly stronger than at any previous point in its history. This would prove an important factor in determining the Cambrai battle's ultimate outcome.

CHAPTER THREE

The Clockwork Battle

AT THE BEGINNING of August 1917, the Tank Corps faced a difficult dilemma. It was clear to its chief staff officer, Lieutenant Colonel John Fuller, that the Ypres Offensive was 'stillborn' as far as the tanks were concerned. The inundated terrain and continuing downpours would prevent large-scale tank operations in the salient – and such operations were what Fuller craved. Short of stature and bald, he was a man of remarkable intellect – by common consent the brightest and most gifted of the undoubtedly talented and relatively young Tank Corps staff. Fuller, at 39, was somewhat older than most of his peers. He aspired to be a great military commander, in pursuit of which he read widely, studying closely the lessons of every military campaign from those of classical history to Napoleon, Lee and Grant. He was also under-employed. His considerable abilities ensured he did not find his staff duties especially onerous and this meant he enjoyed opportunities to write theoretical papers on tank employment – opportunities that must have been envied by many others on the staff of divisions, corps or armies. Fuller's study and reading of military history convinced him that only operations on the grand scale achieved more than a footnote in the history books. He was determined that the tanks would not be consigned to the marginalia in this manner.

What Fuller had to acknowledge, however, as a serving officer in the British Army, was that tank involvement or otherwise in the current offensive was not a matter of personal choice. The Ypres Salient was where the main fight against the Germans was being conducted on the Western Front in late 1917. For the moment, at least, the Tank Corps must continue to make whatever contribution it could to the British offensive. Fuller undoubtedly believed that the war must be won by the

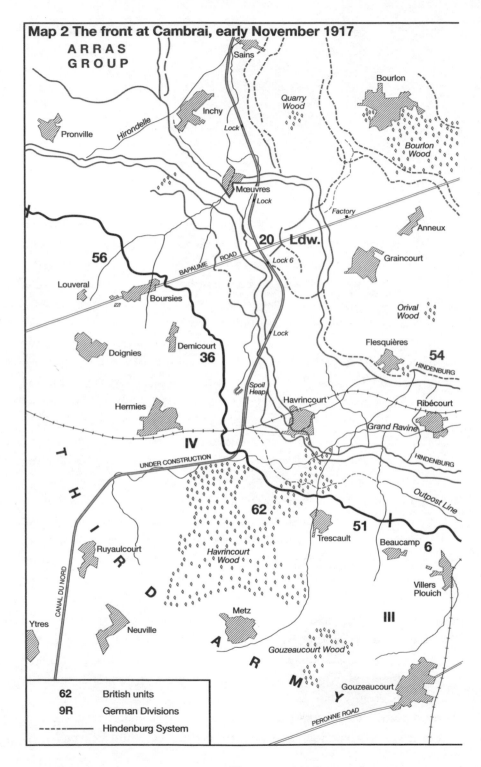

Map 2 The front at Cambrai, early November 1917

ARRAS
GROUP

Sains

Bourlon

Inchy

Quarry
Wood

Pronville

Hirondelle

Lock

Bourlon
Wood

Mœuvres

Lock

Factory

Anneux

20 Ldw.

Graincourt

56

Lock 6

Louveral

Boursies

BAPAUME ROAD

Orival
Wood

Doignies

Demicourt

36

Lock

Flesquières

54

HINDENBURG

Hermies

Spoil
Heap

Havrincourt

Ribécourt

Grand Ravine

IV

HINDENBURG

UNDER CONSTRUCTION

62

Outpost Line

51

Ruyaulcourt

Havrincourt
Wood

Trescault

Beaucamp

6

CANAL DU NORD

Villers
Plouich

Ytres

Metz

Neuville

III

Gouzeaucourt Wood

Gouzeaucourt

PERONNE ROAD

THIRD ARMY

62	British units
9R	German Divisions
--------	Hindenburg System

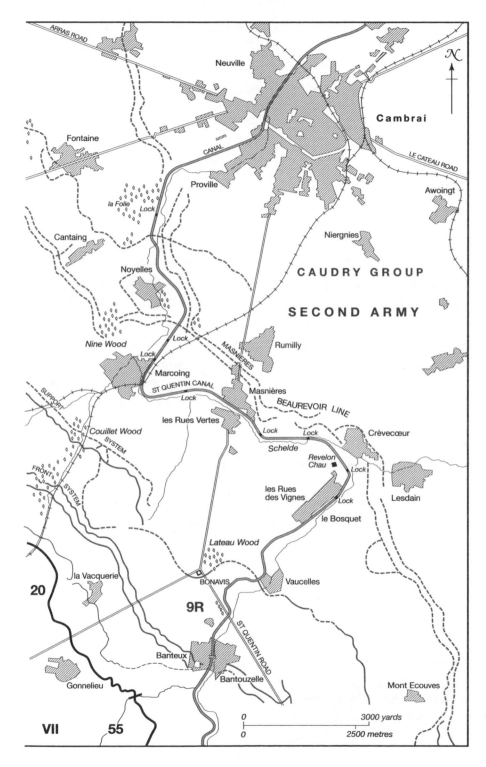

defeat of the German Army. So he turned his attentions to considering whether other parts of the Western Front offered possibilities for tank use.

Whilst two British armies were engaged in the main attack at Ypres, three other such armies had responsibility for continuing the war in one form or another on other parts of the line. Each did their job diligently: improving defensive positions, launching raids, looking for opportunities to carry out offensive operations. The RFC squadrons under their command continued to fly photographic reconnaissance missions to help with the intelligence picture, RE Field Survey Companies worked to provide increasingly accurate maps that were as up-to-date as possible and the flash-spotters and sound-rangers dutifully logged all possible positions occupied by German artillery batteries.

One such sector was the Cambrai area held by Third Army under its still relatively new commander, General the Honourable Sir Julian Byng, who had assumed command after the departure of General Sir Edmund Allenby for the Middle East theatre in June 1917. Byng had previously commanded the Canadian Corps when it had captured the hugely important Vimy Ridge on the opening day of the Battle of Arras on 9 April 1917. He was 57, a talented sportsman, a lover of the theatre and the arts, admired for his integrity and humanity and an intelligent, determined and resourceful military commander. His star was definitely in the ascendancy with Douglas Haig.

It was no mere coincidence that Byng commanded Third Army with responsibility for the Cambrai sector. Clearly, it was intended as an opportunity for him to get some army command experience under his belt in an area where the Germans maintained a less than aggressive posture and where he could benefit from the support of three experienced corps commanders: Lieutenant Generals Sir Charles Woollcombe (IV Corps), Sir William Pulteney (III Corps) and Sir Thomas Snow (VII Corps) – all older men and safe pairs of hands.

The German High Command, OHL, recognized that somewhere, somehow, they had to be able to bring divisions shattered by the fighting around Ypres to rest and recuperate and refresh themselves with new drafts of reserves. Since June 1917, the Cambrai sector had served this purpose well. The deep trenches and thick barbed wire of the *Siegfried Stellung* allowed OHL to exercise a degree of confidence that here its sore-tried troops could get some respite. According to Ober-leutnant Zindler of the German *54th Division*, 'The sector was excellently fortified, with very broad, exceptionally strong wire entanglements, and good deep dugouts; it was therefore called 'the Sanatorium of the West'.[1] At the same time, in many ways, it served a similar purpose for the BEF. An artillery officer recounted how

> We spent a very quiet summer down opposite the Hindenburg Line near Havrincourt. A most delightful summer for about three months from June to early September. It was really a thoroughly peaceful war and we enjoyed it immensely. It was rather like the French fronts: the Germans didn't shoot at us and we didn't shoot at them.[2]
>
> Lieutenant Kenneth Page, 40th Brigade RFA, 2nd Division

The relative peacefulness of the sector had provided the opportunity for the British to construct more substantial trench positions than they might normally, as the attacking force, be expected to build. Lieutenant Charles Austin and 12th King's Royal Rifle Corps (KRRC) were in the same trench sector at Gouzeaucourt Wood from the beginning of October to early November:

> [The dugouts] were very good, deep with good stairways down. I imagine they were built by miners because they were so well-supported by timber. The cooks used to prepare the food in a portion of the room and we used to live quite well. I would imagine the floor of the dugout was probably at least 12 feet underground; you had six feet to move around in and six feet of solid earth above you . . . From my recollec-tion, I should think it was probably an area about ten or twelve feet square. This would be a company dugout, which would mean there were about four, five or six officers sharing. We had a good table and the mess down there. There was another dugout for the signallers and perhaps the Lewis gunners. The ancillary troops to the headquarters were in a dugout which must have been quite near. This was a particularly good 'training for warfare' area and it was all set out and really very comfort-able. [The Germans] could have been as much as 1,200 yards away.[3]
>
> Lieutenant Charles Austin, 12th KRRC, 60th Brigade, 20th Division

For Captain Geoffrey Dugdale of 61st Brigade's staff, the sector 'was so quiet that it was difficult to restrain the men from walking about on the top. Also an order had to be sent to battalions forbidding the men to shoot at game, owing to the likelihood of casualties from spent bullets behind our line.'[4] Nevertheless, the bird and animal life of the region continued to suffer severely in those summer months.

However, the BEF's ethos was never to lapse into total passivity. The important thing was to dominate the Germans. If this persuaded them into quietude, so much the better.

> We were astonished to observe German soldiers walking about within rifle range behind their line. Our men appeared to take no notice. I privately made up my mind to do away with that sort of thing when we took over; such things could not be allowed. These people evidently did not know there was a war on. Both sides apparently believed in the policy 'live and let live'.[5]
>
> Captain Geoffrey Dugdale, Headquarters, 60th Brigade, 20th Division

The difficulty was that attempts to dominate produced entirely predictable results:

> Time passed very peacefully, as the Germans were very quiet. My battalion snipers had the time of their lives; never before had they been given such targets. We literally kept a game book of hits for the first three days; after that the Germans did not show themselves so much; also they started to retaliate.[6]
>
> Captain Geoffrey Dugdale, Headquarters, 60th Brigade, 20th Division

The tranquillity of the 'sanatorium' was about to be seriously disturbed.

The rolling chalk downland of the region was dotted with villages, copses and woods of various sizes, of which the two largest were Bourlon Wood – a dense and largely undamaged forest approximately one mile square occupying a prominent ridge behind the German lines – and Havrincourt Wood immediately behind the British front line, almost twice the size but reduced somewhat by the Germans' clearance of trees to give their artillery and infantry improved fields of fire. For between these two woods and south-west of the town of Cambrai ran the sophisticated wire and trench systems of the *Siegfried Stellung* – Germany's iron resolve to retain her grip on her French opponent's throat here in all its stark reality.

Despite these formidable defences, the BEF had been aware of the possibilities the Cambrai sector offered for offensive operations for some time, and had contemplated various plans for breaking the German defences between Banteux and Havrincourt. This sector was, in fact, almost exactly the one over which the eventual attack took place. However, it was in August 1917 when Brigadier General Hugh Tudor, who commanded 9th Division's artillery, conceived the idea of a surprise attack in the IV Corps sector that his unit occupied, and the crucial elements of the final plan for the attack were born.

The 46-year-old 'Owen' Tudor was handsome, tall and intelligent. In his plans for the use of artillery in action a weapon that was a bludgeon in the hands of many other commanders became a rapier and, as the war progressed, his ideas became increasingly sophisticated and detailed. It was Tudor who first saw the possibilities offered by combining recent developments in artillery techniques, and especially the 'silent registration' of guns, and the use of tanks for a particular task on the battlefield.

Tudor recognized that if the usual 'noisy' process of registering guns on their targets could be avoided, surprise on the First World War battlefield became a real possibility. If the guns could be positioned to bring reasonably accurate fire on their opposite numbers and on the German trenches without their knowledge, there remained only the problem of how to deal with the barbed wire, which previously could only be slowly destroyed by long preliminary bombardments. This process had been greatly improved by the introduction of the No. 106 instantaneous fuze in early 1917 – an important technological innovation which finally enabled the instantaneous detonation of high explosive shells on contact with barbed wire or the ground before the shell could bury itself in the earth. However, the BEF's assiduous process of post-battle analysis in an endeavour to 'learn and disseminate the lessons of the fighting' had already pointed to the fact that tanks could overcome barbed wire by simply crushing it flat – a fact of which Tudor was well aware. Thus it was that the Royal Artillery, and *not* the Tank Corps, arrived at the formula that formed the basis of what ultimately became the plan for an attack at Cambrai.

Tudor discussed his ideas with Brigadier General Hugo De Pree, the chief staff officer of Woollcombe's IV Corps, and De Pree developed them into a full-blown plan for a surprise operation with limited objectives, which was then presented to Woollcombe. The latter forwarded it on to Byng's Third Army headquarters with his support and a recommendation that a Tank Corps officer be invited to look at the proposed battle ground which was, essentially, the front between two canals – the St Quentin Canal on the right and the unfinished and as yet still-dry Canal du Nord on the left.

Meanwhile, at Tank Corps headquarters in early August, Fuller's search for an alternative area for tank employment had produced a flawed idea for what he termed a 'tank raid' to capture the German-occupied town of St Quentin. Fuller soon revised this project in the light of criticism from his chief, Brigadier General Hugh Elles. First the front was changed, and then the plan's objectives. Now it became an operation in the vicinity of Cambrai planned to last no longer than 48 hours. Over 200 tanks would perform a 'hit-and-run' attack to destroy as many German guns as possible on a front between Banteux and Ribécourt. Fuller also proposed using low-flying aircraft to compensate for any inadequacies in the number of guns to support his attack. His concept of a 'raid' recognized the problems the St Quentin Canal might present to tanks attempting to go further east. It also assumed that the Germans had sufficiently large numbers of guns deployed in this sector to merit the use of such large tank numbers and, to some degree, ignored the very obvious limitations of the slow-moving tanks. Since the Cambrai sector was the responsibility of Third Army, the Tank Corps plan also found its way to Byng's headquarters.

The almost-simultaneous arrival at Third Army of two plans with very different origins but which were, in many ways, complimentary was serendipitous. However, between late August and mid September, it was Byng and his Third Army staff who constructed a plan based on elements of both Tudor and Fuller's ideas and which proposed the use of cavalry to exploit any successful breakthrough of the Hindenburg Line. This was subsequently acknowledged by Hugh Elles of the Tank Corps: 'The plan was Byng's, the choice of place was his too. He also propounded the scheme of attack without bombardment.'[7] On 16 September, Byng presented this detailed plan to Haig, who later wrote in his diary: 'I discussed some operations which Byng proposed after lunch, and I told him I would give him all the help I could.'[8] Securing

Haig's support for the plan was a necessity but was made considerably easier by the fact that, whilst the Ypres Offensive was in progress and Haig retained hopes of its success, he did not have to deliver on any promise made for attacks elsewhere. By early October, however, as hope of all-out success for the Ypres Offensive bled away in the morass of mud that the Salient had become, Haig gave his approval for Third Army to proceed with preparations for the attack.

When Byng outlined his army's plan to his corps commanders and their staffs on 26 October he stressed that the essential elements of the plan were absolute secrecy in the preparations of the offensive and complete surprise. The Germans must know *nothing* of what was being prepared. Six infantry and five cavalry divisions, together with three tank brigades (a total of nine tank battalions) would be used for the attack. The process of assembling over a thousand guns of all calibres was set in motion. Because there would be no prior registration of the guns, there were doubts about their ability to fire an accurate creeping barrage. Consequently, it was decided to employ a 'lifting' barrage instead. This would start on the German first line and lift to each successive defence line without traversing the ground in between. It would, therefore, be easier to track the barrage's course. In addition, there was less effect on the intervening ground, a fact that would assist the tanks.

Of the forces available to Third Army, the quality of the artillery units is all too frequently ignored. By late 1917 the Royal Artillery had come through the 'Gunner's Battle' at Ypres where it had engaged in a deadly duel with its German counterparts. Its casualties had been heavy but, undoubtedly, its morale and skill at arms were undiminished. Here perhaps more than anywhere else in the BEF was the quality of units consistent and high. On the other hand, the quality of the cavalry forces available was absolutely unknown. Few units had participated in mounted action since the autumn of 1914. Furthermore, many senior cavalry commanders were chary of the combination of wire and machine-guns to be found on the industrial battlefield and their consequent caution was likely to work in direct opposition to the thrust needed for exploitation of any success.

Regarding the infantry, on the right was Snow's VII Corps whose experienced 55th Division would only make a diversionary attack. Next to it, Pulteney's III Corps would use 12th, 20th and 6th Divisions to make the initial assault. These were all reliable divisions and their respective commanders – Major Generals Arthur Scott, William Douglas-Smith and Thomas Marden – could all be entrusted to perform their work steadily. Ostensibly, 6th Division was a 'Regular' division whilst the other two were 'New Army' or 'Kitchener' divisions raised on the outbreak of war. However, in reality, such labels now meant little since the huge casualty lists of the war had broken down such differentiations. Similarly, Major General Beauvoir de Lisle's 29th Division – which was to pass through the assault divisions before securing the further objective of the Masnières–Beaurevoir Line – was also notionally a 'Regular' division with a record of service at Gallipoli, the Somme, Arras and Ypres.

Next in the line was IV Corps, which was made up of 36th Division (a 'New Army' division, which only had a flank role), 62nd Division and 51st Division. The last of these had acquired something of a reputation (which it did nothing to suppress and, indeed, rather shamelessly sought to perpetuate) as one of the top assault units of the BEF. In part, this was merited, although any attack or raid in which 'Scottish' infantry were used was usually seen as the work of this Highland formation, despite the presence of two other 'Scottish' Divisions on the Western Front and other 'Scottish' units scattered widely throughout the BEF. The division had seen extensive service in fighting from November 1916 to September 1917, firstly on the Somme, and then on several occasions at Arras and during the Ypres Offensive. Whilst it could not claim a reputation as 'ever-victorious', its fighting qualities were obvious to its friends and enemies.

These qualities, and the formation's reputation, owed themselves to some extent to the division's remarkable commander. Major General Montague Harper was 52 at the time of the battle. He began his military service as a Royal Engineer and completed his training at the Staff College, Camberley, in 1901 before taking an appointment at the War Office. He later returned to the Staff College as an instructor. In 1911, as assistant to the Director of Military Operations (DMO), Brigadier General Henry Wilson at the War Office, he completed most of the detailed planning for the mobilization of the BEF on the left flank of the French Army in the event of a European war. In August 1914, he had the opportunity to see how well his and Wilson's meticulous plans worked when he travelled to France as part of GHQ. Having briefly succeeded Wilson as DMO, he subsequently commanded an infantry brigade before taking over 51st Division in September 1915.

Harper was a distinctive figure amongst the BEF's high command. He was described by Edward Spiers* as:

> Fine looking, with an aquiline nose and snow-white hair though his moustache was black, he was known as 'Uncle', and also as 'Old Arper' after an incident which had occurred at Abbeville in 1914. Some visiting politicians, passing the Operations 'A' Office, asked Wully Robertson the meaning of the letters 'O.A.' stuck prominently on the door. 'Old 'Arper,' said Wully, laconic as usual.[9]
>
> Lieutenant Colonel Edward Spiers, British Military Mission, Paris

Tall and with his distinctive shock of white hair, Harper was generally popular with his peers and the men he commanded as indicated by the almost universal soubriquet 'Uncle' (or, occasionally, 'Daddy'). He could, however, be stubborn and occasionally demonstrated a lack of acceptance of the authority of his seniors, which on at least one occasion bordered on insubordination. He was not a Scot: this might have been a problem when commanding a division with an intense Caledonian character, but he had served with territorial soldiers and had developed a good understanding of their particular character, and especially how to tap in to the streak of individualism that such men had. This proved more than a counter-balance to his 'Englishness' and, according to one of his staff, Harper was 'decidedly the right man for this somewhat feudal gathering of the clans'.[10] Indeed, he sought to strengthen, not destroy, the division's clannish nature. This same officer, Lieutenant Colonel Walter Nicholson, also described him as 'having the makings of a great general'.[11] His subordinate officers at least were undoubtedly fiercely loyal and Nicholson observed the division's 'magnificent *esprit de corps*' which he attributed largely to Harper's personality, for 'There was no happier selection than in the choice of General Harper for the 51st Highland Division. They exactly suited one another.'[12]

---

* Edward Louis Spiers changed his name to the Anglicized 'Spears' in 1918.

Harper has been portrayed as the epitome of the 'donkey' general. Yet, having passed Staff College he was, like Douglas Haig, entitled to be termed 'an educated soldier'. But, more than this, he was dedicated to his work – as Edward Spiers indicates after a meeting with Harper before the 1917 Arras battles:

> The new mental attitude of the Command was conveyed to me vividly by General Harper, whose Division, the 51st (Highland), was to take part in the attack. After asking me how the French were getting on and what formations they had employed when following the Germans to the Hindenburg Line, he explained his methods of training. The time had come, he said, when soldiers should use their brains again, and this principle he certainly applied. The advance in tactical instruction in his and other divisions since the Somme was extraordinary.[13]
>
> Lieutenant Colonel Edward Spiers, British Military Mission, Paris

Harper's great strength was training – about which he was passionate and thorough. He was particularly keen to develop the individual soldier's initiative. According to one staff officer, 'He had a touch of showmanship which troops like when it is combined with efficiency.'[14] The high regard in which he was held was emphasized in a report by his corps commander during the 1917 Ypres Offensive:

> During the past three months of strenuous work in Flanders I have formed a high opinion of this officer. He has an intimate up-to-date knowledge of infantry tactics and is thorough in his training methods. His division is organised from top to bottom in all departments, and he handles it in a masterly manner in active operations. I knew the 51st Division before General Harper commanded it and then considered it ill-organised and unsoldier-like. It is now one of the two or three best divisions in France and its fighting record is well known. I attribute its success mainly to its present commander and recommend him for promotion to a Corps.[15]
>
> Lieutenant General Sir Ivor Maxse, Headquarters, XVIII Corps

In summary, Byng and Woollcombe must have considered themselves blessed with the presence of a crack division commanded by such a highly regarded general officer.

They might also have felt heartened by the quality of the man at the head of IV Corps' other assault division at Cambrai, 62nd Division's Walter Braithwaite. As one of his subordinates later described him:

> This was a true 'beau sabreur', tall and lean, handsome with a hawk eye, immaculate in dress, courteous and concise in speech, with a ready wit that was never unkind. He came to the division under the cloud of having been on Ian Hamilton's staff at the Dardanelles failure; and he cannot have been very happy to find himself committed to the making of an untried Territorial Army second line formation.[16]
>
> Major Richard Foot, D/310 Battery, Royal Field Artillery, 62nd Division

In October–November 1917, therefore, Braithwaite was deep in the task of forging his command into an efficient fighting unit. His division had last seen terrible loss and little success in operations at Bullecourt in April and May 1917. Since then Braithwaite's work had proceeded apace, despite a very real personal tragedy that undoubtedly gnawed at his emotions almost constantly:

> His only son had been reported 'missing, believed killed' in the Somme battle, and early in 1917, as we advanced over the area, Braithwaite spent hours walking alone over the shell cratered area where his son had last been seen, hoping to find some trace of him. But as a General, he never allowed this personal tragedy to appear; it did, I am sure, make him tender to our youth, and we admired him almost with affection. He was a splendid soldier.[17]
>
> Major Richard Foot, D/310 Battery, Royal Field Artillery, 62nd Division

That Braithwaite's work in 'making the division' was still incomplete is indicated by his appointment of a new brigade commander in the immediate period prior to the battle. This was Brigadier General Roland Bradford who, upon appointment to command 186th Brigade, became the youngest to attain that rank in the British Army. He was just 25.

Bradford was born at Etherley, County Durham, in 1892, the youngest son of a mining engineer for the Stobart Collieries in that area. On leaving school he took a commission in a territorial battalion of the Durham Light Infantry (DLI) before successfully completing competitive exams to join the Regular Army in 1912. In service with three battalions of the DLI, he favourably impressed those ranked above him and, in October 1916, during fighting on the Somme, he was awarded the Victoria Cross for his gallantry and leadership.

It was not just his personal bravery that secured his 'fast track' promotion to brigade command. Bradford also possessed great strength of character, charm and single-mindedness and exhibited great consideration for the welfare of his men. He had a fine tactical mind and sparkling intellect. In describing operations, he was concise and lucidly explained any situation before distilling the fundamentals of each action into lessons for the future. What made Bradford's views particularly palatable to those senior to him was that he expressed them in terms they understood. In particular, he, like them, recognized that there was much in the pre-war army training that he had received that was still applicable to the warfare now encountered. His views on tanks, expressed in late April 1917, demonstrated this and, incidentally, showed how advanced his own thoughts on their use already were:

> Tanks should go with the infantry. This gives confidence to our men and helps demoralise the enemy. If they came on later the enemy is more prepared and will be able to devote more attention of his artillery to dealing with them. I consider that tanks might be used extensively for carrying of artillery ammunition and also stores for infantry. Cannot smoke barrages be established to hamper observation?[18]
>
> Lieutenant Colonel Roland Bradford, 9th Durham Light Infantry, 151st Brigade, 50th Division

Thus, although 186th Brigade was eventually given a difficult and important task on the first day of the attack, it had an energetic and tactically astute commander at its head.

Behind the assault divisions, Third Army's chief reserves were three markedly different divisions. The very inexperienced 40th Division at least had the merit of some familiarity with the Cambrai sector, having taken part in the follow-up advance of British forces when the Germans had withdrawn to the Hindenburg Line in March 1917. Although, as a consequence, it was up to full strength, its fighting qualities were unknown. By contrast, the presence of the veteran Guards Division, albeit still recovering from its last wounding engagement at Passchendaele on 12 October, offered Byng some reassurance. Finally, 59th

Division, although notionally a 'second-line territorial' division, had performed well during fighting in the Ypres Salient in September 1917.

As Third Army's logistical preparations proceeded, Lieutenant Robert Ross described the hive of activity:

> There was no peace from Arras down to Gouzeaucourt but feverish haste as of bees that had wasted the summer months in lazy nothing-ness and were anxiously afraid the winter might catch them honeyless. And there was work to be done . . . We were some of the bees. This hutment camp, so it was whispered among officers' servants – always the most authentic news vendors – was to be honoured not very long ahead by elevation to the peerage – to the dignity of Corps HQ. And when Corps comes within ten miles of the front somebody is about to be hurt. Our part was to lay the nerves of such a body.[19]
> Lieutenant Robert Ross, RE Signal Service, III Corps

Whilst he did so, he witnessed the remarkable transformation taking place in Gouzeaucourt, a village behind the front line in III Corps' sector:

> Gouzeaucourt was an empty rambling collection of decaying farm-houses and barns, smashed in a haphazard sort of fashion, a kind of 'out to hurt you, but only a little at a time' just as a kindly dentist relieves you of your molars. But as October appeared, the village became the home of a silent population. Every wall had as neighbour an 8-inch howitzer, a 6-inch naval gun or some other piece of destruc-tion not used in agriculture, all fantastically disguised as 'Queens of the May' or 'Jacks in the Green', clothed as they were in shapeless garments of netting festooned with green rag or canvas painted in grotesque splashes of colour by a mad artist, and arranged cunningly to break line and shadow. Every barn held its dragon – its strange occupant – here a shell dump – here a Trench Mortar store – there a dressing station all prepared and ready for its grim work of patching. But what was of most interest – the massive form of tanks, decked and painted as the guns. These were the greatest mystery of all the 'mysteries' of Gouzeaucourt.[20]
> Lieutenant Robert Ross, RE Signal Service, III Corps

In Ross' evocative phrase, 'By the end of October, Gouzeaucourt was more iron than brick.'[21]

With a major offensive in the offing, 3rd Field Survey Company had to work flat out in surveying the proposed attack area and preparing accurate maps and 'Artillery Boards', whilst also locating and marking appropriate sites for the multitude of batteries to be used:

> For these operations we had two survey parties living in dugouts up the line. Captain Calder Wood . . . took the northern area round Havrincourt Wood (IV Corps) and I the southern round Gouzeaucourt (III Corps). Despatch-riders took our observations back to headquarters every evening. The computers worked all right, and the draughtsmen, who made the 'artillery boards', started at 1.00 a.m. and carried on through the day. Boards for battery positions which had been surveyed on one day were usually delivered to the artillery the following evening. There was only about a fortnight to do the work in, and the weather was usually wet or foggy. Unconventional methods had to be adopted. The Lucas lamp was found to be excellent for penetrating fog, and much triangulation and traverse work was done with it. For the first time such an 'unsoldierly trinket' as an umbrella appeared at the front, as we had to carry on with theodolite work in the rain.[22]
>
> Lieutenant Frederick John Salmon, 3rd Field Survey Company, Royal Engineers

In this manner, Salmon, Calder Wood and their teams worked right up until the morning of the battle.

It is easy to underestimate what was needed for the BEF to mount a further major offensive whilst the last embers of the Ypres Offensive faded and died. An incredible flow of men, supplies and guns headed steadily southwards from the Salient from late October onwards. More than 150 new battery positions had to be fixed by survey and prepared. Many guns of all sizes only moved to the Cambrai front in the first two weeks of November. The necessity for surprise was part of the reason for this late move, but the fighting in Flanders was also still in progress during much of the planning period for the Cambrai attack. In total, 1,003 guns would be concentrated by Third Army for the attack (see Table A).

Table A: Guns by Type	III Corps	IV Corps	Total
13-pounder	36	18	54
18-pounder	264	234	498
4.5-inch howitzer	66	66	132
60-pounder	54	42	96
6-inch gun	8	4	12
6-inch howitzer	72	68	140
8-inch howitzer	14	16	30
9.2-inch gun	1	1	2
9.2-inch howitzer	16	12	28
12-inch howitzer	4	4	8
15-inch howitzer	2	1	3
	537	466	1,003

Source: *Official History, 1917*, Vol. 3, p. 28.

The numbers in themselves were impressive, but what was even more so was the fact that, during this move, most batteries went through the essential process of recalibrating their guns and calculating each gun's muzzle velocity – factors critical to their ability to deliver accurate predicted fire when the attack opened. In some cases, the process went even further:

> Our march, which lasted several days and took us through St. Pol and Doullens, finished at a large farm a few miles south-west of Albert. Our main work during our short stay there was to test our guns on an artillery range that had been constructed in the old Somme battle-field . . . The main object of the tests was by repeated firing of each gun, to work out the average calibration error . . . One of our guns tested to be too bad to keep, and was exchanged for a new one. It must be remembered that the number of shells fired per gun was enormously larger than had been expected when the gun was designed.[23]
> Second Lieutenant Frank Paish, 53rd Battery, 2nd Brigade, Royal Field Artillery, 6th Division

Experienced artillerymen understood what this process might mean:

> The 18-pounders were sent two at a time, to a range in rear and
> carefully calibrated. From this it was clear that no preliminary registra-
> tion of targets would be necessary, and, to avoid alerting the enemy
> that a big scale attack was starting, there would be no lengthy
> bombardment of their trenches.[24]
>
> Corporal Frank Webster, 255th Brigade, RFA, 51st Division.

The new method of calibration by ascertaining the muzzle velocity of
each gun was undoubtedly seen as a step forward, although some
mistrusted its efficacy. Nevertheless, many saw the possibilities offered
if surprise really could be achieved.

Although large numbers of tanks were on hand, Third Army's expectation was unquestionably that massive artillery strength would be the key
to the battle's success. Nevertheless, the available tanks – 378 fighting
tanks and a further 98 supply and 'special purpose' tanks (see Table B) –
clearly had a very specific and important task in the battle plan in
making passages for the infantry and cavalry through the German wire.
It was this anticipated role that provoked conflict between the Tank
Corps and Third Army when, on 29 October, Fuller and Major
General Louis Vaughan, Byng's chief staff officer, clashed over the
latter's view that 'in the initial attack tanks could not be too numerous'
and that, therefore, no tanks would be held in Army or Corps reserve.
Vaughan and Third Army clearly understood the tanks' primary role as
wire-crushing. Employing the maximum number of tanks in the battle's
early stages for this task might well lessen the likelihood of infantry
being held up by the wire, thereby reducing their vulnerability to fire
from surviving German machine-guns. On the other hand, holding
back a reserve of tanks for use on the second and subsequent days of
operations offered a more cautious but sensible approach. Unfortunately for Fuller, and possibly for the plan's overall chances of success,
Vaughan won the day. He was supported by Byng who, according to
Fuller, stated that 'I cannot go against the wishes of my Corps and
Divisional commanders'[25] over this matter.

Table B: Number of tanks available for Cambrai attack, 20 November 1917

378	Fighting Tanks (nine battalions at 42 tanks each)
54	Supply Tanks and Gun Carriers (7)
32	Wire Pulling
2	Bridging Tanks
9	Wireless Tanks (one per battalion)
1	Transport Tank (to carry telephone cable for Army HQ).
476	Total

Source: *Official History, 1917*, Vol. 3, p. 28.

The first task for the two infantry corps was to organize the training of assault divisions with the Tank Corps – an important element of the battle planning and recognized by both Third Army and the Tank Corps as critical to successful cooperation on the battlefield. Third Army then circulated two papers entitled *Tank and Infantry Operations without Methodical Artillery Preparation* and *Notes on Infantry and Tank Operations* on 30 October giving more detailed instructions on how tanks and infantry would work together and providing important additional information about tanks for those – and there were still many – who had never seen them or been in action with them before.

Tank and Infantry Operations without Methodical Artillery Preparation was quite definitely Fuller's creation: a blueprint for successful tank co-operation with infantry against the Hindenburg Line. He expounded his underpinning philosophy:

> I decided that, as the governing principle was surprise, the easiest way to coordinate action was to reduce tactics to a drill. In fact, the idea I had in my head was to elaborate a tank and infantry ceremonial parade – leaving nothing to the imagination of the performers. In short, Cambrai was to be a clockwork battle.[26]
>
> Lieutenant Colonel John Fuller, Headquarters, Tank Corps

Success, therefore, would come via Fuller's prescription. He laid down a simple drill by which tanks were to lead the infantry through the German wire and protect them during their attack. Simplicity was especially important given that a maximum of ten days was available for training in infantry and tank cooperation.

In Fuller's tactical guidance tanks operating against each objective were to constitute one 'Tank Echelon' divided into two waves – the 'Advanced Tanks' and the 'Main Body Tanks'. The Advanced Tanks would normally comprise 'one-third of the total tanks employed against any one objective'. Since tank sections were reduced from four tanks to three for the attack in most (but not all) tank battalions, this essentially meant the tanks operated in a pyramid formation. Each Advanced Tank was to work slightly ahead of its Main Body partners, suppressing German fire. Meanwhile the infantry would follow the Main Body Tanks through the wire and trenches. Subsequently, Advanced Tanks would become a reserve to the Main Body. The Main Body was to give direct assistance and protection to the advancing infantry. Fuller considered it inadvisable to allot more than a platoon to follow each tank. This recommendation was based on the width of the path tanks could create through wire. Other platoons could follow behind. Infantry were to advance in section single files (or 'worms'), the easiest formation for passing through wire gaps. Since units would have to assemble in darkness, the note included a diagram illustrating how a tank company and infantry battalion might form up. (The formations recommended by Fuller are illustrated in Diagrams 1 and 2.)

There is something in the word 'clockwork' that prompts unease when applied to the maelstrom of warfare. Fuller's plans for a 'clockwork battle' were no exception. Unquestionably, he had excelled in creating such detailed plans in a very short period of time and under immense pressure. However, with the experience of three years' war, he must surely have been aware that such prescriptive instructions with their diagrams in which men became dots, tanks boxes and the terrain a snow-white featureless plain could not stand the test of battle. For, although the tank's progress across the battlefield might resemble a clockwork toy, men are men, the battlefield is a random environment in which events change their course in moments and, most importantly, the Germans could not be relied upon simply to watch the 'ceremonial parade'.

Nevertheless, what Fuller had defined was a framework in which the divisions of III and IV Corps could train with tanks. His ideas also meshed well with the suggested means for getting a 32-ton tracked vehicle across the Hindenburg Line. This was the fascine. Based on a medieval siege device, the fascine was an enormous bundle of brushwood 'about 5 feet in diameter, like an enormous toilet roll',[27] carried on the top of each tank and secured there by chains. Each weighed over 1 ½ tons.

The construction of these enormous bundles was a colossal task undertaken by men of the Chinese Labour Corps working in combination with the tanks. By the autumn of 1916 the demand for workers to carry out vital logistical work behind the front lines on the Western Front had become critical and the British had approached the neutral Chinese government to provide men who would be non-combatants, but part of the BEF. This lead to the formation of the Chinese Labour Corps. These men would do all kinds of manual labour, freeing up others for active service. The men were volunteers, peasants drawn by the rewards of daily pay, food, care and clothing far beyond those they could get in China. They laboured long and hard to produce over 300 fascines for monstrous machines the like of which many had never before seen. They gathered smaller bundles of brushwood, or faggots, together which were then bound together to make one large bundle.

Of course, the fascine mounted on each tank's roof made it an even larger target for the German artillery, but this was considered a small cost for the intrinsic value of providing each tank with a means to get over the Hindenburg Line trenches. The manner in which they were to be used was simple:

> They had one sole object. The Hindenburg Line had been dug deep down to make it tank-proof, the theory being that when a tank goes over a big trench, its nose dips and then it goes through and starts to rise, the engine is insufficient to pull the tail up and the tail drops. Now, you dropped the fascine in from the nose. And when the tail started to drop it hit the fascine and it rode up. It reduced the angle of ascent. And you pulled yourself out.[28]
>
> Second Lieutenant Horace Birks, No. 11 Company, 'D' Battalion, Tank Corps

Equally simple was the way in which they were released from on top of the tank. According to Private Fred Collins of 'B' Battalion, 'You used to have to touch a lever – the driver did this – just touch a lever and it'd drop in the trench. Then the tank'd go over it and you'd be on the other side.'[29]

Diagram 1: Tank Company and Infantry Battalion forming up for the attack

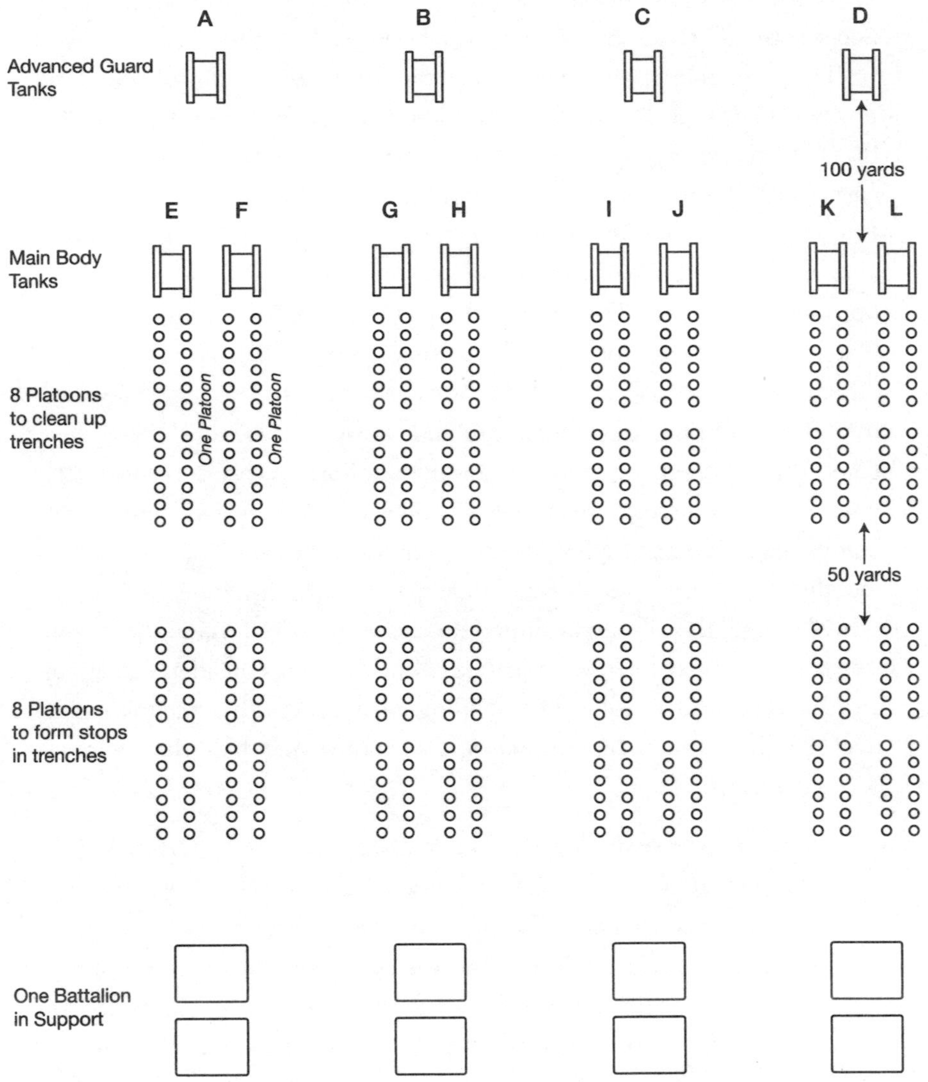

A, B, C and D are the Advanced Tanks, EF, GH, IJ and KL are the Main Body Tanks. According to 'TANK AND INFANTRY OPERATIONS WITHOUT METHODICAL ARTILLERY PREPARATION', "Immediately behind these are placed 8 platoons each on a file frontage, that is two sections in single file side by side, and two in similar formation behind them, these 8 platoons form the Trench Cleaners. At 50 yards distance behind the Trench Cleaners come 8 more platoons in similar formation, these are the Trench Stops. Behind these, at whatever distance considered necessary, are drawn up the supports in two lines, consisting of 8 platoons each as shown ..."

Diagram 2: Tactical Formation adopted by 6th, 20th and 12th Divisions for operations with tanks, 20 November 1917

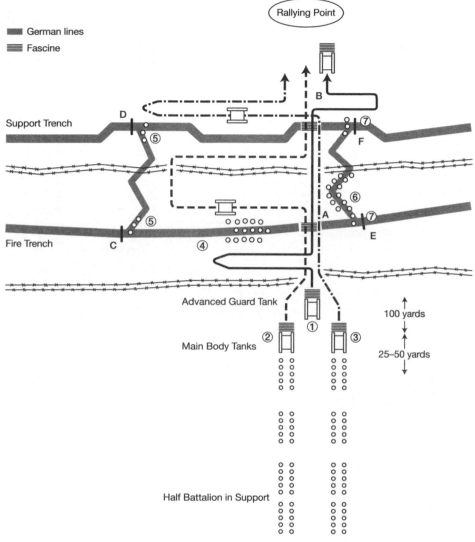

1. Advanced Guard Tank crushes wire, creates gap and moves to left along front of fire trench, before returning to cross fire trench at **A** and support trench at **B** and advancing to Rallying Point.
2. Left Main Body Tank drops fascine at **A** and crosses fire trench, before turning left along rear of fire trench. Then turns right to crush gap in second wire entanglements and crosses support trench at **B**.
3. Right Main Body Tank crosses fascine at **A**, crushes a gap in second wire belt and drops fascine and crosses support trench at **B**. Turns left along rear of support trench to rake it with fire before returning to advance on Rallying Point.
4. Infantry 'trench cleaners' follow Advanced Guard Tank.
5,6,7. Infantry 'trench stop' parties follow Left Main Body Tank and block trenches at **C** & **D** and follow Right Main Body Tank to block trenches at **E** & **F**.

73

Of course, once dropped a fascine could not be recovered, so tank tactics had to ensure sections could cross successive trench lines. Fuller's drill took account of this. Advanced Tanks would cross the German wire and turn left, moving close to the trench parapet without crossing the trench until the Main Body tanks and infantry were over. The Main Body tanks would cross the trench at the same spot, thereby economising on the use of fascines. One tank would move down the trench line, whilst the other went on to the support trench where, if necessary, it would drop its fascine and cross, before turning left and working down the trench. After clearing these areas, Advanced and Main Body tanks would reinforce the echelon attacking the next objective. Fresh infantry would accompany this tank echelon.

Ingenuity was also applied to the question of how to get cavalry through the Hindenburg Line wire. Whilst infantry could simply walk over wire crushed into the ground, some more effective means was required to ensure no wire damaged the horses' hooves. Tanks were detailed to cooperate with 1st Cavalry Division to clear the Trescault–Ribécourt road for the cavalry's advance, whilst others were to clear the Villers Plouich–Marcoing road and the road through La Vacquerie.

> The first wave of battle tanks would pass over the wire. Behind was a collection of tanks specially fitted for dealing with this wire, with the intention of clearing the wire off the ground to enable cavalry to pass through. This was effected by fitting each tank with a grapnel and a steel cable. The tank passed into the belt of wire, dropping the grapnel as it proceeded. [It] passed through the wire, turned to the right and proceeded parallel to the belt of wire. The effect was to roll the grapnel and roll up the wire, pulling up stakes and everything, until we had a mound of wire as high as a cottage – at which point the tank would go no further on account of the tremendous weight of this wire, and the cable was cut. The tank left to join the other fighting tanks in the battle, leaving behind it a gap from which every strand of wire and every post had been torn and rolled up.[30]
>
> Captain Stuart Hastie, Tank Corps

In the midst of all the planning and preparations, Haig and his command were struck by a bombshell. On 24 October, in what became known as the Battle of Caporetto, an attack by nine Austrian and six

German divisions on the Isonzo river had reversed the trend of slogging Italian advances that had pushed the Austro-Hungarians towards contemplation of their own defeat. Instead the Italian Second Army was routed. By the end of the first day, an advance in places of almost 16 miles had been achieved and, over the course of the next eighteen days, an overall advance of more than 62 miles was made. Italian morale was shattered and Italy was left on the brink of political and military collapse. This was something Britain and France could not allow and on 26 October Haig was asked by the War Cabinet to send two divisions to the Italian Front at once. Two more soon followed.

This had an important influence on the Cambrai plan. Effectively, it reduced Haig's already greatly diminished pool of units for the operation still further. It also meant that he had fewer reserves with which to exploit any success or to commit to the attack if matters were not progressing as they should. It placed greater demands on those units that he did retain, and subsequently enforced a subtle change in the nature of the Cavalry Corps' involvement. Finally, it reinforced Haig's desire to secure some form of achievement on the Western Front that would take the pressure off the Italians and stop the War Cabinet (and, in particular, the Prime Minister, Lloyd George) from taking away more of his divisions for employment on other fronts.

With the opportunity offered by the winding down of operations in the Ypres Salient, in early November Haig could give closer attention to Byng's plans. As a consequence, Third Army were obliged to make a number of amendments before issuing the final plan for what became known as 'Operation GY' on 13 November. In the past (for example on the Somme), Haig's interventions had been to broaden the objectives set for the attack and, often, to have over-ambitious expectations. However, on this occasion, he added definition to aspects of the operational plan.

The initial object was to clear a quadrilateral area defined by the St Quentin Canal, the Sensée river, Canal du Nord and forward defences of the Hindenburg Line, aiming to cut off and destroy the German divisions holding the area. For Haig it was vitally important that the ridge occupied by Bourlon village and wood be captured by IV Corps on the opening day. This was much more important than the capture of Cambrai itself by the Cavalry Corps, since it offered observation into

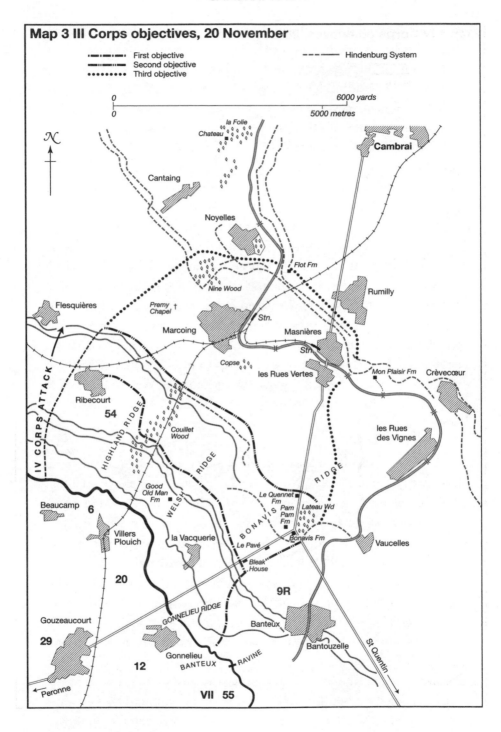

Map 3 III Corps objectives, 20 November

First objective
Second objective
Third objective
Hindenburg System

0   6000 yards
0   5000 metres

𝒩

la Folie
Chateau
Cambrai
Cantaing
Noyelles
Flot Fm
Rumilly
Nine Wood
Flesquières
Premy †
Chapel
Stn.
Marcoing
Masnières
les Rues Vertes
Stn.
Mon Plaisir Fm
Crèvecœur
Copse
Ribecourt
54
HIGHLAND RIDGE
Couillet
Wood
les Rues
des Vignes
WELSH RIDGE
BONAVIS RIDGE
Good
Old Man
Fm
Le Quennet
Fm
Lateau Wd
Pam
Pam
Fm
Beaucamp 6
Villers
Plouich
la Vacquerie
Le Pavé
Bonavis Fm
Vaucelles
20
Bleak
House
9R
IV CORPS ATTACK
Gouzeaucourt
Banteux
29
GONNELIEU RIDGE
Bantouzelle
St Quentin
Gonnelieu
Peronne
12
BANTEUX
RAVINE
VII 55

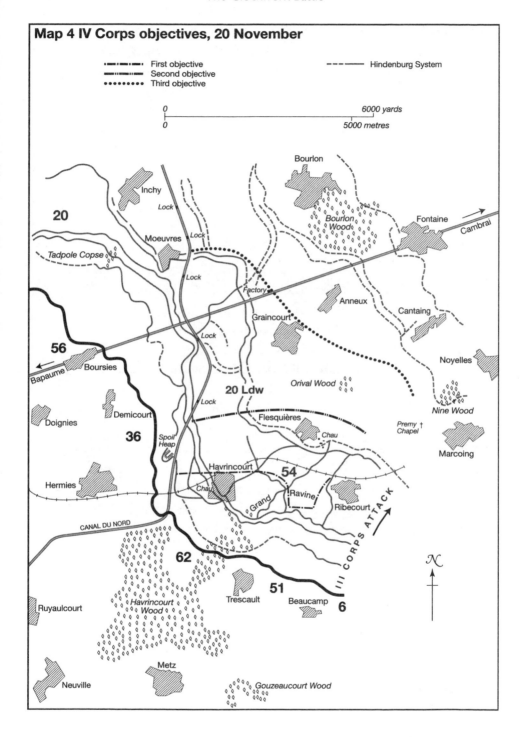

Map 4 IV Corps objectives, 20 November

First objective
Second objective
Third objective
Hindenburg System

0   6000 yards
0   5000 metres

Bourlon

Inchy

20

Lock

Bourlon
Wood

Fontaine

Moeuvres   Lock

Cambrai

Tadpole Copse

Lock

Factory

Anneux

Cantaing

Graincourt

Lock

56

Noyelles

Bapaume   Boursies

Orival Wood

Nine Wood

Doignies   Demicourt

20 Ldw

Flesquières

Premy †
Chapel

Marcoing

Spoil
Heap

Chau

36

Havrincourt

54

Hermies

Chau

Grand   Ravine

Ribecourt

CANAL DU NORD

III CORPS ATTACK

N

62

Ruyaulcourt

Havrincourt
Wood

Trescault

Beaucamp

51

6

Metz

Neuville

Gouzeaucourt Wood

the rear of German positions to the north and west as well as over the attack front. Nevertheless, he urged III Corps' thrust to seize the crossings of the St. Quentin Canal at Masnières and Marcoing to be undertaken boldly on as wide a front as possible. The infantry were not to wait for the cavalry.

Byng's final plan therefore defined three stages for the attack:

(1)   The breakthrough of the Hindenburg Position; the seizing of the canal crossings at Masnières and Marcoing, and the capture of the Masnières–Beaurevoir line (the German Second Position) beyond;

(2)   the advance of the cavalry, through the gap made, to isolate Cambrai and seize the crossings of the Sensée river; and the capture of Bourlon Wood;

(3)   the capture of Cambrai and the quadrilateral defined by Haig and the defeat of the German forces cut off.

Haig rightly emphasized the need for bold and daring action by all arms, but especially the cavalry who needed to get across the St Quentin Canal without delay. However, neither Haig, Byng nor indeed anyone at Tank Corps Headquarters, seems to have applied much thought to the matter of getting *tanks* across the canal or what to do in that regard if the canal crossings had been destroyed. Fuller's awareness of the potential for the canal to limit tank operations on the right flank did not mean he provided any solution to the problem. The BEF at this time did not possess portable bridges capable of bearing a tank's weight. If the bridges were destroyed, the infantry and cavalry would be on their own.

Haig laid particular stress on one aspect of the plan – that he would stop the offensive after 48 hours, or even earlier, if the results gained did not justify continuation. The time period was not arbitrary but based on the expected time it would take for the Germans to get reserves to the battle front. The war had taught the generals of both sides this important time-critical fact:

The order for a unit to entrain is by no means the same thing as its arrival. It has to march to the entraining station, where trains have to be got ready for it. On the various lines the trains can only follow each other at certain definite intervals of time, and the normal duration of the journey has to be added to all this. So it generally took two or three days for a division, using some thirty trains, to reach its destination. It could seldom be done in less.[31]

General Erich Ludendorff, *OHL, Kaiserliches Heer*

Haig's status as commander-in-chief of the BEF meant, of course, that the detail of military operations was not his sole concern. Another crucial aspect of his job was liaison with the French. In this he had, since the beginning of November, experienced the frustration of an enthusiastic ally, but one who did not conform to Haig's hoped-for model of cooperation. He had informed the French commander-in-chief, General Philippe Pétain, of the plan in outline on 1 November. Pétain was looking for further opportunities for offensive action after the recent successful application of his strategy of the limited offensive at Malmaison on the Chemin des Dames. He hoped to participate in the attack and made plans for two cavalry divisions and three infantry divisions to exploit a British success by striking southward through any gap on the second or subsequent day of the battle. Haig had hoped the French might simply take over some of the British defensive front. Instead the issues relating to French involvement were to dog preparations for Haig until the eve of the battle.

CHAPTER FOUR

'Simple tactical exercises . . . colossal binges'

JOINT TRAINING OF tanks and infantry started at the beginning of November at various locations including the Tank Training School at Wailly, at Humières and at Bray-sur-Somme. Each division supposedly had ten days allotted to it, allowing infantry battalions a maximum of two days each. However, there were substantial differences in timings and practical arrangements and the majority of infantry units did other forms of battle training first. Consequently, training time with real tanks was limited.

Second Lieutenant Wilfrid Bion of 'E' Battalion, Tank Corps recalled his battalion's first encounter with the infantry of the division his unit was to work with. There was mild amusement at their commanding officer's garb as they waited:

> The section and tank commanders of the battalion were taken by car to some country of chalk downland. We waited at a cross-roads at the bottom of a declivity; on higher ground was a small group of officers including the Colonel 'wearing a French letter', as someone said about his transparent raincoat.[1]
>
> Second Lieutenant Wilfrid Bion, No. 14 Company, 'E' Battalion, Tank Corps

Soon the group heard a faint but distinctive sound – the skirl of bagpipes:

> Over the crest there presently appeared the first files of marching men, battalion after battalion of kilted troops. We watched the rhythmical sway of the kilts as the battalions went by. Nothing was said, for we all knew who they were. In that war the 51st Division, Highland Territorials, had won a reputation second only to the Guards. In their

own opinion, and many could be found to share it – even amongst the enemy – they ranked even higher. For steadiness and reliability the Guards could not be matched. But the virtue that was their strength also led to the defect of rigidity in some situations where the flexibility of the 51st would have been more valuable. We had already learned in our very slight and brief experience that our lives depended on the stout hearts of the infantry who were in action with us . . . We watched in silent relief the troops who would be in action with us. The 51st Division? Someone meant business – at last![2]

Second Lieutenant Wilfrid Bion, No. 14 Company, 'E' Battalion, Tank Corps

Training of 51st Division with its cooperating tanks was especially thorough according to several tank men. Major William Watson, a company commander of 'D' Battalion, indicates it was exemplary:

We trained with the splendid 51st Division for ten days, working out the plans of our attack so closely that each platoon of Highlanders knew personally the crew of the tank which would lead it across No Man's Land. Tank officers and infantry officers attended each other's lectures and dined with each other. Our camp rang at night with strange Highland cries. As far as was humanly possible within the limits of time, we discussed and solved each other's difficulties, until it appeared that at least on one occasion a tank and infantry attack would in reality be a 'combined operation'.[3]

Major William Watson, No. 11 Company, 'D' Battalion, Tank Corps

Horace Birks of the same tank company recalled his training as consisting of:

simple tactical exercises by day and the most colossal binges at night. Looking back on the exercises one realises how very simple and ineffective they were. In the circumstances, it was difficult to do more than practice very simple evolutions with the infantry. Liaison, at any rate, with our battalion of the Black Watch was very close, very intimate, very cordial and both sides understood precisely what was required and expected.[4]

Second Lieutenant Horace Birks, No. 11 Company, 'D' Battalion, Tank Corps

However, some felt that the tank training with the division had not been thorough and that 51st Division's staff had very definite ideas on

Diagram 3: Tactical Formation adopted by 51st and 62nd Divisions for operations with tanks, 20 November 1917

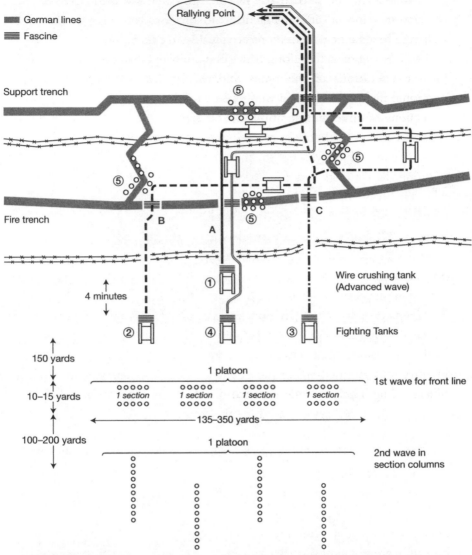

1. Wire Crushing Tank breaks wire at **A**, drops fascine and crosses fire trench. Then breaches next wire entanglements and turns either right or left along support trench, before following other tanks across support trench at **D**.

2,3. Left and Right Flank Tanks break wire and cross fire trench at separate points (**B & C**) and turn right or left along rear of fire trench.

4. Remaining Fighting Tank crosses fire trench at **A** and drops fascine at **D** before advancing to Rallying Point.

5. Infantry parties for each objective clear trenches and create 'stops' before remaining to garrison that position when it has been secured.

what they could do and essentially said 'We will do our stuff. Hope you can do yours.' Whatever the truth of this, what rankled with some in the Tank Corps and particularly its chief staff officer was the division's decision to adopt a different tactical formation to that expounded by Fuller. (These tactical formations are illustrated in Diagram 3.)

On 7 November, therefore, 51st Division issued its tactical guidance for the operations of the tanks and infantry in cooperation. The divisional instructions stated that tanks would operate in three waves, in sections of three, in line abreast. The first wave of 'Wire Crushing' (W.C.) Tanks would consist of one section per infantry battalion. To deal with all objectives up to and including the first objective, 36 Fighting Tanks (eighteen per Brigade front) formed a second wave. The third wave of 24 Fighting Tanks (twelve per Brigade front) would tackle positions beyond the first, and up to and including, the final objective. Infantry 'following immediately behind' tanks were to be extended in two ranks, and not move in file, whilst 'Infantry detailed for further objectives should move in Section Columns until necessary to extend on account of hostile fire'.[5]

Meanwhile, in 62nd Division an organic process was in progress where the original ideas as to formation were considerably modified as the possibilities and limitations of the tanks became known to the infantry and the methods of the infantry attack were seen by the tank officers. The Tank Brigade commander, Colonel Christopher Baker-Carr, whose units participated in this training and the subsequent attack with the two divisions, made no criticism of these tactics at the time. Indeed, he was full of praise for the training and liaison work done prior to the battle.

The changes made to the attack formation cannot be denied yet their significance has been greatly exaggerated. In the first place, in deciding to adopt a different method of attack to Fuller's, Harper and his staff were not alone, for Braithwaite and 62nd Division also adopted an altered modus operandi. Secondly, both divisional commanders did nothing that others of equivalent rank had not done in other operations as indeed they were encouraged to do if necessary by their training and by Field Service Regulations. Thirdly, it seems likely that Harper (and, presumably, Braithwaite) were concerned that infantry in columns (or 'worms') would suffer heavier casualties and be less able to return fire than troops in 'wave' formation. Fourthly, 51st Division's considerable experience based on five previous occasions of working with tanks had clearly demonstrated that these large lumbering objects drew German machine-gun and artillery fire and that infantry should, as a consequence, keep a safe distance from them. Finally, a change in tactics was not simply imposed; tactics were tested in training and adjusted based on the evaluation of this training.

On 10 November Fuller produced an appendix to his original training note. It gave definite guidance to tank commanders about matters such as the distance to be maintained between tanks and clearly stated that infantry advancing behind tanks should keep about 100 yards behind them. There is no suggestion that Fuller produced this guidance to counter instructions issued by 51st and 62nd Divisions, but neither did it influence them. By now, both divisions had trained with tanks in their own tactical methods for some time. Harper, certainly a stubborn commander, disregarded the guidance – presumably considering it irrelevant. His own arrangements put a greater distance between infantry and tanks. It seems likely that Harper was now concerned over the tanks' ability to crush barbed wire and the plan's dependence on this, thus accounting for his 'extreme scepticism'[6] of the whole plan as subsequently recalled by Brigadier General George Craufurd of the neighbouring 18th Brigade.

Harper was not the only one to be sceptical of these new methods of attack. Some senior artillery commanders (especially Major General Robert Lecky, the chief artillery officer of Third Army) were equally unconvinced about the effectiveness of 'silent' registration. Nevertheless, despite his doubts, Lecky had thrown himself behind the plan when his objections were over-ruled. Harper, meanwhile, presumably felt sufficiently confident of the regard in which he was held by Haig and Byng to feel he could do much more for his infantry in the attack.

The opportunity for infantry to see tanks close up and to witness their capabilities provided a tremendous boost to the morale of the men of the BEF such as Private Billy Kirkby of 2/6th West Yorkshires:

A day came when we moved from our camp to a battle front in miniature – a series of trenches defended by rows of barbed wire. Several tanks were already there in attacking position. We lined up behind them and followed them to see, to our astonishment, these massive new and mysterious machines stride over the wire, crushing it into the ground as if it was so much waste paper. Then as we continued to follow, our amazement increasing, as they surmounted the huge trenches, without effort, turning to bring their deadly quick-firing guns and their Lewis guns to bear upon the defenders. Of course, there were no defenders, but the lesson was clear. No defences, however strong, no machine-gun fire or small arms fire, etc, would stop these thickly armoured monsters, driven forward by their powerful engines whose deep throbbing was music to our ears. Only a direct hit by shell fire would stop them as it would stop anything.[7]

Private Billy Kirkby, 2/6th West Yorkshires, 185th Brigade, 62nd Division

It took an experienced veteran like Kirkby's friend, Jim Turnbull, to cool the enthusiastic ardour of the men after such an impressive display:

We returned to camp, full of enthusiasm, continuing to marvel at the extraordinary powers of these wonder weapons. That night our hut buzzed with our excited comments though none of us had the slightest idea we would follow them into battle . . . At this point up came Jim Turnbull. 'You boys are becoming too excited. Remember those tanks still move very slowly. As I see it, the danger is if they are caught by a heavy, concentrated, artillery barrage. Their attack must be a surprise one without any warning of any kind and in mass, just before dawn. You know, lads, catching the Germans on the hop so that the tanks are on them before they have time to wonder what has hit them.'[8]

Private Billy Kirkby, 2/6th West Yorkshires, 185th Brigade, 62nd Division

Nevertheless, Kirkby and many of his mates were still optimistic after seeing the tanks' power. Only the test of battle would prove whether this optimism was misplaced.

Another who witnessed the tanks' capabilities was Second Lieutenant George McMurtrie of the Somerset Light Infantry:

We were marched to a small valley where many tanks were moving about. All that morning and afternoon we were hard at it practising the platoon in attack with tanks going in front. Obviously the 'stunt' we were going into was going to be a pretty big one and tanks were to take a big part. Sir Douglas Haig was expected that day but did not turn up

85

in the end. The second day we were at the tank school at Bray, we carried out a Battalion attack with the tanks and we all had a ride back after the attack was over. Some of us were lucky enough to get inside, but most climbed up on the outside of the tank and had a ride for about a mile. They were extraordinary machines. They went at a slow walking pace and as they weighed about 35 tons, anything that got in the way was simply crushed. When going through a belt of barbed wire, the posts were either driven into the ground or broken. We saw one tank going up a hill and it went straight through a belt of wire with six rows of stakes about 5 foot high and 9 inches in diameter. All the stakes were either driven right into the ground or broken.[9]

Second Lieutenant George McMurtrie, 7th Somerset Light Infantry, 61st Brigade, 20th Division

Meanwhile, for men of 29th and 40th Divisions, it was clear that they would shortly be called upon to play their part in offensive operations. But there was an air of artificiality about their training:

We have had a field-day today. 'Uncle Har'* was one of the umpires, and looked very fine on his big horse and with his bright red tabs and brassard. We all got rather wet in the morning, but got dry again by the afternoon.

It is great fun when we move from one position to another. I blow my whistle and wave my arms round and round, and immediately all the men jump up and carry off the guns and the tripods, and the ammunition, and all the things they have, and pack them like lightning into the limbers, which are like boxes on wheels. Then crack go the whips, the men scramble up somehow on to the limbers; and the good little mules go galloping off as fast as they can till I stop them, and everybody and everything tumbles out again, and a new position is taken from which to fire. We don't really fire on field-days, which makes things a little bit silly, but all the same it is great fun. I like the real firing best, especially when you see the horrible Germans fall or scuttle for shelter, as we often could see them when we were in the line.[10]

Lieutenant Algernon Hyde Villiers, 121st Company, Machine Gun Corps (MGC), 40th Division

* i.e. Major General Montague Harper.

Second Lieutenant Eric Marchant, writing to his father, knew from the battle training his unit was receiving that a 'stunt' was soon to take place. However, he remained unconvinced of its potentialities for shortening the war:

> We are continuing our usual training, but have now got on to attack formations and tactics again, so there is certain to be some entertainment in the near future. I feel certain that the war will be over by about July 1925![11]
>
> Second Lieutenant Eric Marchant, 1st Essex Regiment, 88th Brigade, 29th Division

In the attack, 29th Division was to advance from reserve and secure crossings over the St Quentin Canal. To do so, the division was allotted a company of 'A' Battalion tanks. Consequently, 88th Brigade repeatedly practised crossing a canal in cooperation with tanks. There was some concern at GHQ regarding the tasks set for 29th Division. In mid November, the divisional commander, de Lisle, received a visit from a member of Haig's staff:

> For three consecutive nights the men would be marching; on the morning of the 20th, they would have to march ten miles to the place of assembly, and then fight their way forward for three or four miles. He wanted to know if I could rely on their endurance to consolidate the ground won, as we could not expect to be relieved until the night of the 21st. I had full confidence in the endurance of my men.[12]
>
> Major General Beauvoir de Lisle, 29th Division

De Lisle's confidence was admirable but as yet he had no clear idea as to the scale of the work his division would actually be called upon to perform.

Because of their mechanical frailties and in particular the lack of durability of their tracks, the tanks could not be concentrated behind the British front line under their own power. Instead, they were brought up closer to the front line on rail flat cars. Normally one such train would move a company of twelve tanks. The sheer logistical effort involved in moving the tanks to the railhead before they were deployed to their various starting points was immense, and the responsibility of Captain Charles Weaver Price:

As Staff Captain (Q) of HQ Tank Corps the instructions given me about fourteen days before the battle were to supervise the concentration of over 300 tanks at the Plateau siding (near Albert and close to The Loop siding where we assembled in September 1916). The tanks, with personnel arriving on trains, were quickly placed under cover of woods, necessary repairs and adjustments made, and, finally, loaded on trains for dispatch to their several kicking-off points for battle. On account of fear of observation by the enemy, the whole of the detraining and entraining had to be done during darkness, even torches and Helleson lamps being used very sparingly. The whole scheme was successfully carried out. But not without some terribly anxious times. The very first train to arrive was delayed several hours through rear coaches running off the line and causing several deaths and injuries to personnel.[13]

Captain Charles Weaver Price, 'Q' Branch, Headquarters, Tank Corps

One serious problem that developed was the gradual collapse of the special trucks for carrying tanks. They had already suffered much hard wear and had a switchback appearance. Several had to be scrapped, but, fortunately, enough held together to move the last tank. The process of loading and unloading each train of twelve tanks was one in which the tank drivers had now developed considerable dexterity after the practice offered by the Ypres Offensive. Each tank had to be driven up a ramp and along the length of the rail flat cars. When unloading, the tanks were driven off forwards onto another ramp. The clearance on each side of the tank was only 3–6 inches whilst on the trucks. Yet twelve tanks could be loaded or unloaded in 20 to 30 minutes.

From the railhead, tanks were driven to concealed positions behind the British front. In order to shield them from the eyes of German aerial observers, each tank carried camouflage netting. Secrecy dictated that no work could be done on the tanks during day time, only at night.

It was not only on the ground where preparations were in full flow. In the air, the RFC had been photographing the German defences for some time. To enable the reconnaissance aeroplanes to do so, the scout pilots had to fly mission after mission to protect them from German predators. After an especially difficult period in early 1917 when the better, faster aircraft of the Germans had wrought havoc on the brave pilots and out-classed machines of the RFC, the British squadrons were finally receiving aircraft with which they would compete on almost equal terms with their opponents until the end of the war. In early November, 46 Squadron RFC had re-equipped with the Sopwith Camel Scout and the pilots were getting to know their new aeroplanes.

> I've done five flights today, including two short ones on the Camel. First impressions – more room in the cockpit, so you can take a deep breath without feeling you're going to burst the fuselage at the seams . . . Second, the exciting pull of the 130 hp Clerget, and the surge of power at full throttle. Third, her amazing lightness on the controls, lighter even than a Pup, which is gentle-sensitive, while the Camel is fierce, razor-sharp. She turns with lightning quickness to the right. You have to be careful taking off, as the engine torque veers her to the left, and you have to apply full right rudder, but it's easy enough once you get the knack. I've not fired the guns yet, that's a pleasure to come. Our one Camel has been taking off and landing all day as a succession of pilots tried their hand. Marvellously, nobody has broken it.[14]
>
> Lieutenant Arthur Gould Lee, 46 Squadron, RFC

Pilots like Lee experienced a genuine thrill at their opportunity to try, and test to the limits, the new technology with which they were being supplied and it was with genuine, almost boyish delight, that Lee described his new aircraft's 'handsome silver-finish cowling, with dark brown struts and woodwork' and his 'longing to test the guns properly before the dirty work starts'.[15] Meanwhile, the squadron practised a new skill: low-level bombing of ground targets. Lee was pleased, but somewhat disconcerted, to discover he was fairly adept at this task – in practice sessions at least:

> Dropping dummies at the aerodrome target, with no bullets to bother me, I found it surprisingly easy to get close results, in fact mine were much the best in the squadron. My proudest four, dropped one at a time, were all within a yard or two of the target, compared with other people's 100 yards, and one man's 170 yards. I hope this unexpected skill doesn't land me into any awkward jobs![16]
>
> Lieutenant Arthur Gould Lee, 46 Squadron, RFC

Also equipped with Camels, 3 Squadron conducted similar practice 'bombing' sessions:

[We were] kept very fully occupied in between the usual patrols in getting used to the new form of armament which was to be tried out when the proper time came. This, in brief, amounted to the Sopwith Camel Scouts being adapted to carry light bombs by means of a rack attached to the underside of the fuselage, carrying four 20lb Hales bombs, the releases being controlled by a Bowden cable arrangement in the pilot's cockpit. The pilots practised a great deal and with dummies aimed into a nearby shell crater and found accuracy more difficult to attain than had been anticipated, as allowance had to be made for speed and height while using their machines as launching platforms. It was found that about 500 feet was the lowest they could safely fly when diving to launch a bomb as they would be following the bomb down and would have to allow themselves time to pull up and away from the violent explosion directly underneath.[17]

Captain Howard Brokensha, 3 Squadron, RFC

After almost two weeks of steady practice, the pilots felt sufficiently confident of being able to hit their objective under ordinary conditions, but had no idea as to how things would turn out in actual combat. Then they were informed of their mission:

At length the squadron was briefed on the coming attack on Cambrai and the three flights assigned their various objectives and told the date and time when this was to take place, each of the flights being given different targets . . . The objective of 'B' Flight was an enemy aerodrome about twelve miles behind the lines which they were to try and put out of action and, at the same time, destroy as many aircraft as possible.[18]

Captain Howard Brokensha, 3 Squadron, RFC

These attacks on German airfields were an important element of Third Army's 'deep battle' plan, which aimed not only to tackle the front-line defences but the rear areas, reserves, supplies and communications of the Germans. This was an early vision of a very 'modern' battle.

The delights of his new Sopwith could not blind Arthur Lee to the developments taking place around him for long. Pausing to reflect in his diary, he could draw only one conclusion:

> Something unpleasant is certainly brewing. We all feel it. First 3 and 46 both getting Camels in such a hurry. Then this intensive practice in low level bombing, and low cross-country flying, which our neighbours 64 were doing even in England. Another squadron, 84, with SE5a's under Major Douglas, has arrived at the other end of the aerodrome, and other squadrons have come to this area. Every village in the forward zone is crowded with troops . . . including artillery, and masses of cavalry with horse-lines everywhere. And there are hundreds of tanks around, too, from the air you see their tracks sprawling across the countryside. They move at night, but you can see them in daytime, hiding under camouflage in the woods beyond Bapaume. Obviously, a big push is coming any time now.[19]
>
> Lieutenant Arthur Gould Lee, 46 Squadron, RFC

Finally, Lee learned that his task in the battle would be to tackle German gun positions that might hinder or stop the advance of the tanks. Understandably, he was too concerned about how this affected his own chances of surviving the coming days to appreciate that this was an important tactical advance. Specifically, the ground attack squadrons engaged for the same work as 46 Squadron were intended to provide additional surety to the tanks in case German guns escaped the attention of the British artillery. But for Arthur Lee, an air fighter, it was difficult not to be disappointed:

> Imagine after waiting all those months for Camels, striving not to be shot down on Pups, and looking forward to toppling Huns two at a time with my two Vickers, to find myself switched to ground strafing![20]
>
> Lieutenant Arthur Gould Lee, 46 Squadron, RFC

Douglas Haig spent the period 13–15 November inspecting troops and watching the tanks and infantry in training. Eric Marchant, who saw him on 15 November, described the impressive sight that evening in a letter to his father:

> This morning we started off soon after 9.00 a.m. with a pack horse carrying the [wireless] equipment and took up a position in a valley.

Whilst we were waiting having got into communication with headquarters we watched the troops getting into their positions. It was a
wonderful sight. The whole division was out, and the country seemed
alive with men in 'battle order'. Sir Douglas Haig, who had come over
to see the fun, passed us, with our own General and some of the staff.
He looked very fit and full of beans, and was riding a perfectly
magnificent charger.[21]

Second Lieutenant Eric Marchant, 1st Essex Regiment, 88th Brigade, 29th Division

This letter provided an opportunity to give a hint of possible imminent
action, anticipating possible concern on his parents' part: 'We shall be
having some thrilling entertainment in the course of a few days,' he
wrote, 'and writing may be difficult or impossible. So don't get the wind
up if there is a period of drought in the flow of news.'[22]

During his visits, Haig availed himself of the opportunity to
emphasize that the presence of tanks did not remove responsibility
from the infantry in the attack. Covering fire from Lewis guns and rifles
was needed during all stages of the advance and it was essential that
infantry commanders acted with boldness and determination.[23] He also
reminded both Byng and his superior, General Sir William Robertson,
Chief of the Imperial General Staff, that the operation would be
stopped at once if it appeared likely to entail greater losses than he
could afford or the general situation did not justify continuation. The
criteria for this decision were, however, not clearly defined.

The question of the nature and timing of French involvement in the
attack had not yet been resolved and the days immediately prior to the
attack were spent by Haig and his staff in navigating the difficulties of
coalition warfare. Haig hoped that if the French were involved they
would take over command of Sir Thomas Snow's VII Corps on the
right of the attack and operate through that sector and emphasized to
Byng the importance of capturing and holding the canal crossing at
Crèvecoeur to facilitate any possible French action. The suggestion
that two cavalry divisions and three infantry divisions might be available to participate in the attack was obviously welcome, but Haig could
not control their use. Instead, his staff found themselves with the
burden of adjusting supply arrangements because of the likely presence
of a large body of French troops in Third Army's rear areas at Peronne

on the morning of the battle. Haig and Byng therefore felt all of the inconvenience and none of the benefits of their ally's ardour for involvement.

With the days of training ending, the infantry realized the attack was imminent. Confirmation came soon enough for Benjamin Parkin and 186th Brigade parading before their new brigadier, Roland Bradford. Parkin, like many, was well aware of this young man's remarkable reputation. Bradford entirely lived up to his 'billing':

> After the inspection he mounted his white horse and addressed us somewhat as follows: 'Officers and men of 186th Brigade. You are shortly going into battle when we expect great things from you. Your record is good and that of the Division is good. We are given a position of honour in the Order of Battle and our doings will be followed by the authorities here and at home. The Commander-in-Chief – Sir Douglas Haig – and the Army Commander – Sir Julian Byng – and the Divisional Commander – General Braithwaite – all send their wishes for your success. The experiment of surprise is being tried – and we are confident of success. I want you to pray for the success of these operations. "More things are wrought by prayer than this world dreams of." You will have an opportunity tomorrow of attending a service of the Holy Communion. Go there and pray. And may God bless you all.' There was not a man present who was not moved by his eloquence and sincerity. I still have in my mind the picture, his moving forwards and backwards on his horse as he delivered the address.[24]
>
> Second Lieutenant Benjamin Parkin, 2/4th Duke of Wellington's Regiment, 186th Brigade, 62nd Division

For Parkin, at least, these words were inspirational. Those of a fellow officer, Lieutenant Zohrab, that night reminded him of the great undertaking they were now a part of:

> Zohrab, in his theatrical way, began: 'You know, Parkin, old man, you want to visualise this movement as a whole. Here in the dead of night are thousands and thousands of troops marching silently on parallel roads. There is a great machine operating this wonderful night march. You and I are small units in this great Army – but isn't it grand to take

part in it – the grand unseen assembly march to battle. Little does the Boche suspect this! I wonder whether he has an inkling. I wonder!'[25]

Second Lieutenant Benjamin Parkin, 2/4th Duke of Wellington's Regiment, 186th Brigade, 62nd Division

It was, therefore, with some disappointment that Parkin learned he and another officer would not go into action with the battalion:

We were told that we hadn't been sufficiently long with the men during their training – but our names were sent as spare officers to the battalion, and thence to brigade and division. We were told that all spare officers were given jobs somewhere for division and brigade were asking for officers to do this and that job connected with the operations.[26]

Second Lieutenant Benjamin Parkin, 2/4th Duke of Wellington's Regiment, 186th Brigade, 62nd Division

Parkin was detailed to an Aeroplane Dropping Station, receiving messages regarding the battle's progress from contact patrols of 15 Squadron RFC. It was an important, but disappointing, assignment.

There were disappointments for others too. The bitter experience of the Somme battles had taught a powerful lesson. In every big operation a proportion of the men had to be withdrawn to create a nucleus for reforming each unit, should it meet with a disaster.

Unfortunately I was chosen personally, partly because I was daily expecting a transference to the MGC and partly because I was the only subaltern in 'A' Company who had been 'over the top' before.[27]

Second Lieutenant Wilfrid Taylor, 6th Buffs, 37th Brigade, 12th Division

In the Tank Corps, Private Fred Apthorpe of 'E' Battalion could barely conceal his excitement when he wrote a brief note in his diary: 'I am going in the tank with the Capt[ain]. Great preparation and great excitement among the boys. We have got notice to prepare,' only to add shortly afterwards, 'I am not to go with the Capt after all as the Major is going and there is no room for me. Very disappointed.' Finally, 'They have gone and who knows whether they will return.'[28]

It was different for those who had seen battle before. When such men knew they were going into action again, their past experiences fed their dread of what was to come:

> We were to be in it again. Battle, sudden death, and maiming. Gone was my buoyant anticipations of July last year. Gone was that exhilarating ambition to be 'in' at these 'glorious' affairs. Gone was my youthful idea of doing my damnedest for my 'king and country'. I was war-weary, mentally bruised, and fed up . . . The 'push' was looming nearer, like a huge, hypnotising, menacing ogre, and I was 'feart' as never before. I was 'feart' of showing I was 'feart'.[29]
>
> Private Frank Brooke, 1/4th Seaforth Highlanders, 154th Brigade, 51st Division

This was what many of those who had survived the Somme, Arras, Third Ypres (or perhaps all three) had been brought to by late 1917. This was the lot of the poor bloody infantry – and knowing it made it all the worse.

During the final days before the battle, the pace of preparations increased. Although the Field Survey Companies continued their work in locating battery positions for the artillery, the guns to occupy them arrived almost immediately afterwards. Major Ambrose Dudley's battery of 13-pounders had been camped for three days waiting their turn. Around them the nocturnal activity hinted at the scale of the forthcoming attack, but the night cloaked its imminence from the Germans:

> . . . I shall never forget the contrast of those hours of light and darkness. By day the perfect stillness of the countryside was amazing . . . By night the scene was one of feverish, but carefully regulated activity.
>
> The roads were packed with guns, ammunition, wagons and vehicles; a constant, steady stream. Traffic control posts were stationed at all the crossroads and turnings, pointing out the routes to be taken. Along the tracks by the side of the roads tanks slowly crawled their way eastwards. At all the advanced camouflaged ammunition dumps column upon column of wagons were filling up and taking their loads ever eastwards.[30]
>
> Major Ambrose Dudley, RHA, Royal Artillery

When Colonel Henry Rochfort-Boyd took him into the front zone, the work of the surveyors meant all was ready:

> On reaching the neighbourhood of the front system the colonel led us off the main road, down a side lane, which led across a small valley, to a village on a rise ahead of us. When we reached the lowest part of the valley we turned off the lane on to the rough grass.
>
> 'Here,' he said, 'is your position. Your guns will be brought into action in broken line, and the position of your directing gun is marked by this peg. To it are attached your telephone lines, leading back to my headquarters.' He explained to us the rough lie of the front line and the direction of his HQ, and instructed me, before I returned to the wood, to go forward and reconnoitre our own lines and those of the Germans, and on return to camp to come to him for further orders. He then left us.[31]
>
> Major Ambrose Dudley, RHA, Royal Artillery

After examining the surrounding country and marking out with pegs the site for each gun, Dudley and his accompanying officer hoped to get a distant view of the German positions:

> As we walked through the village we were amazed to find it packed with camouflaged artillery of all calibres: 18-pounders, heavy howitzers, and even super-heavy howitzers. Every ruined house, every hedge and hollow concealed them, perfectly hidden from view by most careful and elaborate camouflage.[32]
>
> Major Ambrose Dudley, RHA, Royal Artillery

On 18 November specifics of the attack were revealed to him and, on the following day, explained to the battery's officers and men. That evening, after dark, the battery established its wagon-lines at a suitable distance behind the gun position, and from there the detachments marched straight up to the guns. Dudley had already been provided with the last essentials for his work on the morrow:

> A barrage map was given me, showing our allotted zone and giving the details of the 'lifts' to be carried out, and our guns, being established in position, were accurately laid by compass and director by my captain and myself.[33]
>
> Major Ambrose Dudley, RHA, Royal Artillery

For Frank Paish and his battery, the final details of their part in the opening of the offensive were remarkable:

> The colonel called a meeting of battery commanders in our mess, and afterwards the major gave junior officers instructions for the attack, including maps of a creeping barrage, to be fired without preliminary bombardment, or even registering, lasting over three hours. Our battery had an opening range of 1,300 yards (the shortest I had ever fired at), and a closing range of over 4,700 yards. The rate of fire was to be two rounds a gun a minute, with each round of shrapnel followed by one of high explosive and one of smoke. We were also told about the use of tanks, of which there had been many rumours, and the intended use of cavalry to exploit the initial success, if one could be obtained.[34]
>
> Second Lieutenant Frank Paish, 53rd Battery, 2nd Brigade, Royal Field Artillery, 6th Division

Paish was quick to see the advantages the well-drained chalky ground offered his guns by comparison with the Salient as 'there was no need to make gun-platforms, only the usual semi-circle little trench behind each gun, in which to swing the spade at the end of its trail'.[35]

Still the survey work continued and into the night of 19–20 November. Once more the surveyors had cause to acknowledge the benefits given by the Lucas lamps in their night-time work:

> The lamps enabled us to work after dark, and on the last day I gave line to the latest arrival, a 9.2 railway gun belonging to 442 Siege Battery at 2.00 a.m.[36]
>
> Lieutenant Frederick John Salmon, 3rd Field Survey Company, Royal Engineers

Moving several hundred large, noisy tracked vehicles into close proximity to the front line prior to the attack was a major challenge and a remarkable achievement. It owed much to the work of the Tank Corps' chief intelligence officer, the 30-year-old Captain Elliot Hotblack. Described by Fuller, who admired him greatly, as 'conscientiously' brave and a 'mixture of Abelard and Marshal Ney'[37] he was a natural soldier, whose 'sense of duty, his standard of discipline, his extreme efficiency, and his astonishing courage were an invaluable asset'.[38] His reconnaissance work, conducted at enormous personal risk prior to each major battle in which the Tank Corps was to fight, resulted ultimately in the award of the DSO and Bar and MC and Bar. It also meant he was wounded on five occasions. Hotblack's devoted subordinates were the battalion and company reconnaissance officers who performed the detailed work. One such was Captain Mark Dillon of 'B' Battalion.

> I had the job of reconnoitring the route up to the front. We reconnais-
> sance officers were told where the attack was going to be before our
> commanding officers knew it. The choice [of the Cambrai front] was a
> splendid one. It hadn't been fought over much and the going was very
> good. One really couldn't ask for better conditions.[39]
>
> Captain Mark Dillon, 'B' Battalion, Tank Corps

To get the tanks forward to their assembly positions before the attack, it was impossible to use the roads, because the tanks chewed the surface up and the roads were needed for other traffic. Instead,

> you had to find a route that would enable you to waddle along and get
> into your position without ditching and disturbing the roads and
> without upsetting other people who were also fighting the war – such as
> gunners, signallers and other people. So the tanks would be able to find
> their way, one laid down white tape with a black mark in the middle.
> There might be half a mile of this, and you'd dodge in and out of
> various obstacles. As a rule, having found my route up to the front
> trenches, I used to start my tape at the front trench and lay it back. Of
> course, you couldn't lay it in daytime because it would be seen from the
> air.[40]
>
> Captain Mark Dillon, 'B' Battalion, Tank Corps

A major problem to be overcome were the signal wires that were laid everywhere and were so essential to the communication infrastructure of the BEF:

> You could spot them alright, because we used to trip over the damn
> things! They were all over the countryside. They cut across like a
> spider's web, wherever you went. Sometimes they were up on poles if
> they had to cross a road or something like that, but you tried to avoid

disrupting signal wires, because they were part of the essential framework of the battle.[41]

Captain Mark Dillon, 'B' Battalion, Tank Corps

Having laid out a route suitable for the tank company one evening, the reconnaissance officers' task was to lead the tanks forward the following night. This was a difficult and risky enterprise requiring a cool nerve under pressure, as Dillon discovered:

I had a very nasty experience, which was apt to happen when guiding tanks at night. We had shrouded torches. I got caught up in some barbed wire. The leading tank was bearing down on me and I couldn't stop it. I couldn't get free of the wire. However, I flashed my torch and held it up as high as I could so as to shine into the driver's visor. He stopped with a volley of oaths. You should never flash your light at the driver like that because it blinds them – but that was my purpose. He stopped the tanks and I got free. I explained what had happened and we went on from there.[42]

Captain Mark Dillon, 'B' Battalion, Tank Corps

But there were more scares to come:

The next thing that happened was, I think, the most agonising moment of my life. We got along on our tape very nicely and we were getting among the gun emplacements when we ran out of tape. What on earth had happened?! Somebody, probably some gunners, had come in in the dark, seen this tape, cut it and taken it out of the way because they didn't want anyone interfering with their liberty. It was a frightful moment. I was lost in the middle of nowhere! If those tanks had not reached their starting point, the lives of hundreds of men would have been lost. It was up to me to find it. Luckily I had my compass with me and a rough idea of the direction to go. I set my luminous compass and tramped off rather hopefully with the tanks. With the grace of God we crossed a road or track, and I realised then more or less where I was. By casting about right and left we came on the other end of the tape and were able to follow it to our conclusion. But I was never more thankful than when I found the end of that tape and guided those tanks up to their starting point behind the trenches.[43]

Captain Mark Dillon, 'B' Battalion, Tank Corps

Once in position and camouflaged, the tanks were given a final mechanical overhaul by their crews:

> It was really staggering the amount of essentials that each tank took on board. That is, if they all got issued with a like amount to ours. We had trebled up for this Cambrai attack. It struck us as being too much by a long chalk. The extra .303 ammunition was left in their original boxes. The extra 6-pounder ammunition was loose. Petrol in 2-gallon cans was stacked anywhere it could be stacked. There was precious little room for the gunners to operate their guns when it was finally arranged in some kind of makeshift order. We weren't at all a happy band. Somebody was expecting too much.[44]
>
> Private Reginald Beall, 'A' Battalion, Tank Corps

Like many other tank crews, Beall and his fellows had grave doubts regarding the magnitude of the task before them and their ability to accomplish it. It was, however, too late for most to do anything other than, in the popular phrase of the day, 'soldier on'. Yet, in one case at least, someone was desperate enough to attempt drastic measures, as Captain 'Jake' Wilson discovered:

> When filling up with petrol before the start, one driver came to me in trouble, one petrol tin containing water (the petrol having been flogged) had been poured into the tank. In reply to my question, 'How do you know?' he answered that he 'was suspicious of the sound' and, tasting the last few drops, was sure it was water. The whole tank was hurriedly emptied and even at that late hour we had taken the precaution of siphoning out the low lying drains before refilling.[45]
>
> Captain 'Jake' Wilson, No. 26 Company, 'I' Battalion, Tank Corps

Experienced tank officers like Wilson knew that, in all likelihood, this was no accident but, rather, an attempt to prevent the tank's (and therefore its crew's) participation in the battle. Yet, of course, he could not be sure. It remained to be seen if tank and crew would withstand the rigours of action.

Five divisions of cavalry were also moving forward ready to be launched when the breakthrough was effected. Their presence engendered a thrill of excitement for some, contempt and irritation in others.

Certainly there was a pernicious view of the cavalry as something of a waste of space amongst some in the BEF in late 1917. This was epitomized in the remark of Major Adrian Hodgkin, a chemical weapons adviser on Third Army's staff who saw 'much nasty messy cavalry about in the area, all over the road as usual and blocking traffic in all directions'.[46]

Even in the cavalry there were those, like Captain Geoffrey Dent, whose diaries and letters did not suggest a particular desire to 'ride for the G in Gap'.* Writing to his mother on 19 November he dwelt long on his recent sporting endeavours:

> We have been here two or three days. A most sporting place, as it is all deserted and out of cultivation, miles of grass. I killed a dozen of the best rats yesterday in the stream. The day before we had a most amusing fox hunt with Humphrey Barclay's old bull mastiff and a mixed pack of terriers, etc . . . There is some very good duck shooting here by the river and swarms of partridges . . . I shall certainly get a gun if we stop here.[47]
>
> Captain Geoffrey Dent, 2nd Machine Gun Squadron, 2nd Cavalry Brigade, 1st Cavalry Division

He ended with a hope that 'we spend the winter here, as it is a very sporting place and no French civilians'.[48] However, Dent's commanding officer would undoubtedly have been happier to read of these exploits than the detail of the forthcoming attack and Dent did, in fact, preface his comments by remarking that: 'I expect to have some news for you soon and will write as soon as possible, but may be busy for a day or two.'[49]

There were undeniably those amongst the cavalry who did all they could to prepare for the attack and knew the importance of their task. Lieutenant Samuel Williams of Lord Strathcona's Horse wrote how, immediately prior to the attack's launch: 'everybody was in a fever of expectancy and excitement so that there was little or no sleep for

---

* This phrase originated with the British Army's 'Bingo' system for giving map references – a system which had existed since the 18th Century and which was still being used in 1914. It vaguely identified objectives, locations or targets on maps as 'south of the O in Bleak House' or 'near the B in Broad Wood'. Cavalry were expected to ride their gee-gees for the G.

anyone',[50] whilst his brigade commander, Brigadier General 'Jack' Seely, even conducted a personal aerial reconnaissance of the putative battleground:

> It was fortunate that I did so, because I spotted a sunken road, with no obstructions in it, leading through the German support lines to Masnières . . . I saw the Canal at Masnières, and wondered what chance there was of our crossing it by the bridge. Clearly it was impossible to get over it at any other place in the neighbourhood.[51]
>
> Brigadier General 'Jack' Seely, Canadian Cavalry Brigade, 5th Cavalry Division

The value of such aerial reconnaissance depended on the abilities of the observer. Seely's endeavours were at least an attempt to learn more in anticipation of the attack.

The seemingly unending flow of men, guns, tanks and supplies continued under cover of darkness for several nights. Much use was made of horse-drawn transport, but the logistics required to carry out the attack could not have been put in place without a great deal of help from one under-appreciated asset the BEF possessed: mules. Indeed, one artillery officer, Second Lieutenant Edmund Fisher of 36th Divisional Ammunition Column, was so impressed by their contribution that he was moved, in a letter to his young son, to write: 'The more I see of mules, the more I think they will win the war – I shall never wish for a horse except for hunting.'[52]

Infantry of 6th, 12th, 29th, 51st and 62nd Divisions moved up to their concentration areas behind the front by road and rail between 13 and 17 November.* On the last two nights before the battle, a series of reliefs allowed those infantry who were not already occupying the front line to take up positions ready for the assault. Stan Bradbury's battalion, 1/5th Seaforth Highlanders, moved forward from the ruins of Metz-en-Couture:

> The night was terribly dark; we paraded in the street about midnight and after much palaver set off for the trenches. After leaving the village we marched for about two miles over open country passing along the side of Havrincourt Wood. On the way we encountered many tanks

---

* 20th and 36th Divisions were already in the line.

slowly making their way towards the line ready for the attack next morning. It seemed to us impossible that the Germans would not hear them as they made such a noise in the stillness of the night. There was very little gunfire taking place.[53]

Private Stan Bradbury, 1/5th Seaforth Highlanders, 152nd Brigade, 51st Division

It was Robert Ross who perhaps best captured the atmosphere of the eerie night scenes of the final preparations:

And so those preparations went on in a crescendo of effort ending in a very fortissimo on the last two nights – the troops themselves – thousands of them – hours and hours passing – without a song – without a glow of cigarette – a ghost-like army – soulless.[54]

Lieutenant Robert Ross, RE Signal Service, III Corps

George McMurtrie's 7th Somerset Light Infantry in full fighting order left Sorel at 2.30 p.m. on 18 November. Every man wore his webbing equipment with water-bottle filled. He had his 170 rounds of ammunition and a haversack instead of a pack. Wire-cutters, wire-snippers, wire-breakers, and SOS rockets were also taken. There was by no means complete confidence that the tanks would clear the wire adequately:

We passed through Heudicourt. About 5.30 p.m. the battalion fell out under the cover of a wood, and the cookers which had come with us had tea for the men. After a short wait, we went forward once more, it was beginning to get dark, and we were also getting tired. We met guides at Cemetery Road and from here onward we had a rotten journey, the path was slippery and was just on the edge of a steep cutting. One man fell over and broke his thigh, a commotion ensued and as our company was in the rear it was disastrous. It was a pitch-dark night, there was a good sprinkling of oldish men, who couldn't see or march well in the dark. Everyone began to spread out, some began to curse and we stood a good chance of losing touch with the company in front. Luckily we just managed to keep in touch and at last arrived at the trench we were to occupy.[55]

Second Lieutenant George McMurtrie, 7th Somerset Light Infantry, 61st Brigade, 20th Division

The following morning offered a chance to see the terrain over which they would attack, including La Vacquerie – a small ruined village on the far slope of the valley. In the evening, the final measures were undertaken prior to Zero Hour:

We issued two bombs per man and a shovel or pick. In the evening after 'stand down', one party was sent out to cut the wire in front of our line, to make a clear path for the infantry the next morning. I was detailed to take a work party and fill in the trench where the tanks for our companies were to pass over. We filled in the portion of the trench with only one interval whilst the enemy sent over a few trench mortars, which came pretty near us but luckily did not actually hit anyone. After having filled in the trench, we started back, dim shapes were moving about all over the place, lights here and there, shouts in the distance, officers and men going to and fro; everybody was busy.[56]

Second Lieutenant George McMurtrie, 7th Somerset Light Infantry, 61st Brigade, 20th Division

With Zero Hour now so close, there was desperate concern that the secret, so closely kept, might be given away at the last. It was with a mix of horror and outrage, therefore, that McMurtrie's returning work party observed the British lines:

All along a line about 200 yards behind the front line lights were flickering at times. This was the gunners training their guns. They had been unable to fire any sighting shots so you can imagine the difficulty they had, to make certain that they did not hit the advancing infantry when the attack began. We were all very annoyed at the time at their poor light discipline. When in the front line I am afraid one often thinks of one's own safety before other people's comforts or necessities and that night all our nerves were very much on edge.[57]

Second Lieutenant George McMurtrie, 7th Somerset Light Infantry, 61st Brigade, 20th Division

Perhaps fear of discovery of the attack preparations made McMurtrie and his men more susceptible to such dark imaginings, but there is nothing to suggest that the Germans observed any such preparations. Of much greater concern were the prisoners taken in three raids the Germans launched on the nights of 18 and 19 November. Two were against the flank divisions (36th and 55th), whilst the last was against 20th Division. Of the raid on 36th Division, the BEF from Haig downwards was set to wondering, like Benjamin Parkin: 'How much did those two men know of the Stunt? How much or how little have they told? Has the Boche got any inkling or suspicion from their replies?'[58] The answer was that interrogation of these prisoners suggested to the Germans that an attack near Havrincourt was being prepared, although the date was not known. The Cambrai sector was the responsibility of General Georg von der Marwitz's *Second Army*, on the left of Crown Prince Rupprecht of Bavaria's Army Group. Consequently, Rupprecht contacted *Oberste Heeresleitung* (OHL) with a warning that 'The British having failed in Flanders, partial attacks may be expected on other parts of the front.'[59] Later, on the night of 19–20 November, General Theodor Freiherr von Watter's *Caudry Group* (part of *Second Army*) issued a further order warning its men that tanks might be used in any anticipated attack. Of course these were only hints at the really huge undertaking the British were about to launch. There is no suggestion, for example, that the Germans expected a surprise attack by British artillery. They could not imagine the power of the guns gathered to assault them.

Three divisions of *Caudry Group*: *20th Landwehr*, *54th* and *9th Reserve* defended the proposed attack front. Some regiments of the *20th Landwehr* contained a high proportion of very young recruits or middle-aged men, whilst *54th Division* had been through the mill at Ypres in August and was recuperating. However, although the defenders were weak in artillery and short of ammunition for what guns they had, the defensive positions they occupied were well sited and constructed. Nevertheless, it was to prove extremely fortuitous for the Germans that *Generalmajor* Otto Havenstein's *107th Division* began arriving at Cambrai from the Russian Front on 19 November.

In the last hours before Zero, the tanks made their final move to their start positions:

> In the silence – the rumbling silence – those quaint occupants of
> Gouzeaucourt had come to life once again – chuffed and spluttered,
> then slid like reptilian monsters of other ages up the street, by ravine

and sunken road until dozens of them actually straddled across our support and front line trenches.[60]

Lieutenant Robert Ross, RE Signal Service, III Corps

For the infantry in the front line, the noise of the approaching tanks seemed impossibly loud. Surely the Germans must hear:

At midnight a continuous roar in the distance informed us that the tanks were moving up to their positions. Everybody was in a dither of excitement. The noise of their approach got louder and louder; minute by minute our anxiety increased, as we could not think it possible that the enemy could help hearing the outrageous noise they were making. As they approached their positions in the dark the guides in front were shouting directions at the top of their voices. We were expecting every minute the German batteries to open up along the whole front line with all the guns they could bring to bear. The tank close to me made the most shattering noise. It seemed to have an open exhaust and the captain, or whoever was in charge, seemed to have no realisation of his close proximity to the enemy. However, he got the great hulk into its allotted position, and at last stopped his engine, and still nothing happened.[61]

Captain Geoffrey Dugdale, Headquarters, 60th Brigade, 20th Division

Other infantry units still had a final move to occupy their starting positions. The previous year's fighting on the Somme had taught the benefits of providing the men with food before the attack. Harry Adams recalled how:

We marched up towards the line with fighting order, shovels, flares, 3 bandoliers of ammunition and a tin of 'bully beef'. After marching all night we arrived at the assembly point at 4.00 a.m. where we found everything very quiet. The cooks came up with us and made porridge and tea before we went over.[62]

Private Harry Adams, 6th The Queen's (Royal West Surrey Regiment), 37th Brigade, 12th Division

Lieutenant Charles Austin's men were less well served. Although given hot tea at midnight, their 'breakfast' was less appetising. As Austin recalled, 'We were given rice, cold rice – it wasn't my idea of going into battle on a diet of cold rice laced with rum'.[63]

The final arrangements indicate the huge risk of detection the last hours presented, and what the cost might be if the assembled troops were discovered by the Germans:

> About 1.00 a.m. on the night Nov 19th–20th we heard the tanks being moved up into position. Soon after that the Kings' relieved us in our support line. At 3.00 a.m. we all went round and issued rum to the men; most of them were pretty cheery but all of us felt very cold and I shall never forget that tot of rum. It warmed me up and improved my morale. The battalion that was relieving us were in the same trench and the result was absolute chaos; men everywhere. At 4.00 a.m. we got the men out of their shelters and we went forward by platoons to our assembly positions. Our Company was in support to 'B' Company and when we advanced we had to follow 'B' Company about 150 yards behind. 'B' Company were just behind the front line. There was a large flat expanse of grass on which we assembled with a good many shell-holes scattered over it. The tanks were already there and soon 'B' Company also turned up. We got the men into shell-holes so that they would have some protection if the enemy suddenly commenced shelling. It was a cold misty morning and here we were waiting for 6.20 a.m. which was Zero hour to advance. In front of us were the tanks and 'C' Company. The tanks were moving about a little and making what we thought was an awful noise. One hundred yards behind us were two or three rows of guns, light 13-pounders, 18-pounders, trench mortars, machine-guns nearly wheel to wheel and everyone had his nerves at concert pitch.[64]
>
> Second Lieutenant George McMurtrie, 7th Somerset Light Infantry, 61st Brigade, 20th Division

Discovery now would mean disaster and with this constant worry, the last hours seemed to drag by. Faith, in God and their cause, sustained men like Private Billy Kirkby at this time. Kirkby, like many others, spent some of the time before Zero Hour in silent prayer. Then:

> I raised my head greatly strengthened and immensely comforted by my prayer. Though young – still a teenager without any experience of war – I had great faith in our cause, convinced it was our duty both as

individuals and as a nation to fight to the death to defeat all predatory powers so that we retained our freedom from persecution and all forms of international intimidation.[65]

Private Billy Kirkby, 2/6th West Yorkshires, 185th Brigade, 62nd Division

This patriotic fervour was genuinely felt by numerous young men of the day, despite three years of war and the horrendous losses inflicted in the fighting. In many it was too deeply ingrained for them to reflect on. There were no doubts in Kirkby's mind about the rightness of Britain's cause and he was by no means exceptional.

Zero Hour for the ground forces was 6.20 a.m. but for the RFC squadrons intended for the attack on the German aerodromes, their start time was considerably earlier, at 5.00 a.m. All those detailed for the attack had turned in early to get as much rest as possible. When they were woken at about 4.30 a.m. on 20 November with hot tea and biscuits it was still dark with a good deal of mist and low cloud about. Whilst these conditions persisted it was impossible to take off. Howard Brokensha, commanding a flight from 3 Squadron, described the wait in unusually detached fashion, writing in the third person:

> There was no wind to speak of, only the mist slowly lifting and the dawn breaking through. Five o'clock came and still they waited tensely, chafing at being late as they listened to the terrific roar of the barrage which had started only a few miles away . . . They waited with something more than the usual quaking feeling in their stomachs that was always felt by pilots just before taking off on a mission or patrol, not knowing what would happen or which of them would be posted as missing at the end of the day, and this, too, in spite of their having had a tot of spirits to warm them up while waiting.[66]
>
> Captain Howard Brokensha, 3 Squadron, RFC

Finally, at 5.30 a.m., the wait was over. They took off and assumed formation, although not without difficulty because of the low clouds and mist. Then, at about 150 feet, they flew towards their targets:

> Each pilot had a strip map of the route pasted to the right-hand wooden strut of his machine, and this gave him a guide as to landmarks to be crossed and the approximate times, while maintaining a set

compass course and a speed of 100 miles per hour, about their
maximum at ground level.[67]

Captain Howard Brokensha, 3 Squadron, RFC

Their low altitude at least gave them a chance of finding their targets.
Good fortune would, however, be necessary if they were to do so.
Elsewhere, DH4s of 18 Squadron scheduled to make reconnaissances on
the morning of the attack were also faced with difficult weather conditions
but their squadron commander was under tremendous pressure to get
into action:

Cloud and mist were down to ground-level, making flying almost
impossible, but the new Wing Commander pressed me to send up our
pre-arranged reconnaissances. By a strange coincidence, as I expostu-
lated on the telephone, two Martinsydes collided in the mist just above
my office and crashed. Delay was then granted, for an hour or so.[68]

Major Ranald MacFarlane Reid, 18 Squadron, RFC

The needs of the ground forces in the attack finally overcame the
caution of the airmen. Most, if not all, recognized that it was, quite
simply, a question of getting on with the job.

For the infantry and tanks, the wait was nearly over. Despite the mist
which helped cover their presence, for many the tension was almost
unbearable.

No one who has ever been in an attack can forget the night before. We
all looked forward to it with excitement, we were all highly strung and
all of us thought – What will become of me? – I hope I do my job well –
Have the enemy knowledge of our attack?[69]

Second Lieutenant George McMurtrie, 7th Somerset Light Infantry, 61st Brigade, 20th
Division

For Major Douglas Wimberley, waiting with his machine-gun crews
in the support trenches, the moments prior to Zero were a strange mix
of false joviality and inner turmoil:

I shall never forget the last half hour before Zero – it was perfectly quiet
and the November dawn had a sharp nip of cold to herald its coming.
The men lay about the parapet of the trench through which the last of

the assaulting troops had passed, sipping their warming tea, cracking quiet jokes which the soldier indulges in at all times except when very tired. We officers sat in a bunch, and one thought was uppermost in all our minds – would it be a walk-over as intelligence had promised, or had this ghastly stillness a more significant meaning and would Zero be ushered in by the usual heavy counter barrage and the crack, crack of the German maxims.[70]

Major Douglas Wimberley, 232nd Company, MGC, 51st Division

Amongst the divisional, corps and army staffs, there was only helpless anxiety as the last minutes ticked away. They had done all they could by way of preparation:

We stood in a little group outside the hut which served for our headquarters and fixed our eyes on the long grey line of the road along the edge of which the guns lay waiting. At 6.18 a.m. there was not a sound.[71]

Brigadier General Austin Anderson, Royal Artillery, Headquarters, 62nd Division

The artillery and tanks were ready. If they did their tasks well, they believed the plan had a good chance of success. However, both were only auxiliaries to the infantry. Once more, it was time for the 'poor, bloody infantryman' to find the sticking point for his courage and step into the terror of battle:

Calmly, deliberately, as though on parade, we climbed out of the trench among the shell holes, fixed bayonets, stood for a few moments with our grand Lee Enfield rifles fully loaded, a Mills Bomb in each pocket, cloth bandoliers round our shoulders full of extra rounds of ammunition and carrying a pick or shovel for digging emergencies if they arose between trenches. Our Hour had come . . . This was it.[72]

Private Billy Kirkby, 2/6th West Yorkshires, 185th Brigade, 62nd Division

CHAPTER FIVE

Shock and awe

A T 6.20 A.M. on 20 November, the dull grey morning was violated by the tremendous roar of over one thousand artillery pieces giving vent to their fury. It is all but impossible to imagine what such a bombardment was like. Those who witnessed it were astounded.

> Suddenly the silence of the coming dawn was shattered by such an earthquake and fire as surely was never heard before by men. Though the ground shook with the thunder of our massed guns, it was the breathtaking circle of multi-coloured flames rising like millions of gigantic fireworks which produced a sight so breathtaking, so altogether awe-inspiring, as to root us to the ground, unable to take our eyes away from the beauty of man's explosive power appearing like some ethereal glory rather than the concentrated hellish force which would tear men apart leaving them little more than shapeless, shattered flesh and blood.[1]
> Private Billy Kirkby, 2/6th West Yorkshires, 185th Brigade, 62nd Division

The sheer power of the barrage inspired growing confidence in some of those waiting to attack. For Second Lieutenant Horace Birks of 'D' Battalion, Tank Corps, 'It was the most sustaining thing that happened in the war – to see the Germans were getting it and not us,'[2] whilst a Royal Engineer officer, Robert Ross, on hearing the drum fire, felt 'Nothing could survive; every living thing must perish down to the parasites of the trenches. The very earth must have been riven and obliterated.'[3] Lieutenant Basil Henriques of 'G' Battalion, Tank Corps, experienced mixed feelings of humanity and humility: 'All one could ejaculate was "Poor old Fritz!" and then beneath one's breath "God make thy presence felt to me and make me strong and brave." '[4]

Nevertheless, experience had taught some to wait for signs of how the Germans responded before drawing conclusions about the prospects for success:

> We could hear the rumble of the tanks as they disappeared into the dawn most closely followed by the first wave of the assaulting Highlanders. One, two, three minutes passed. We held our breath. Not one single hostile gun had fired. It was almost five minutes before a few little pip-squeaks began to burst, followed by the crack here and there of a sleepy machine-gun. At this our morale went up with a bound. The Boche had been caught napping. If he could not do better than this, we could hardly help walking through him.[5]
>
> Major Douglas Wimberley, 232nd Company, MGC, 51st Division

For others whose first battle this was, the terrible destructive power of the artillery, and man's helplessness in trying to resist it, was suddenly and shockingly revealed.

> Punctually to the tick, Hell was let loose. All my theoretical Battle collapsed in a moment. All my indifference and curiosity or newness or inexperience or whatever you may call it disappeared in a flash. The reality came as a thunderbolt – something for which I had never been prepared. From that moment I was no longer an 'Officer just out', I was a poor specimen of humanity possessed with something indescribable. I wanted to find a hole in the earth to go down and down and down and hide myself from it all. I couldn't hold my water. I simply grovelled full length at the bottom of the trench trying to dig my fingernails into the earth. Oh God! Give me courage. I thought of my wife and boy. My parents. Oh, smash that picture from my mind! Stop those guns or let me get out of it! No! It's impossible – I'm in it and I shall never get out! I don't know how long I lay there but I felt and knew that the others were lying flat too at the bottom of the trench. Once I caught the face of Graham. He had his teeth and lips snarling like a terrible vicious dog.[6]
>
> Second Lieutenant Benjamin Parkin, 2/4th Duke of Wellington's Regiment, 186th Brigade, 62nd Division

Some German artillery did get into action. Although the counter-barrage near Havrincourt was relatively weak, those enduring it could not estimate its power.

Shells were bursting all round us. This time they were not over there –
somewhere else – they were not theoretical. Here they were – just here.
God! That was pretty near. The trench is blown in. A tree on the
roadside by the trench had a direct hit and crashed with that noise only
associated with crashing trees. And then the debris of earth and stones
fell over us and mingled with the smell of explosives – that never to be
forgotten smell. Something dropped on my leg a little bit sharper than a
stone. I picked it up and immediately dropped it. It was hot! . . . 'You
may be caught in the enemy's counter-barrage.' At the time this had
meant nothing but a theoretical barrage. Afterwards I learnt that this
particular barrage was a weak one. But then I didn't think so.[7]

Second Lieutenant Benjamin Parkin, 2/4th Duke of Wellington's Regiment, 186th
Brigade, 62nd Division

Fear and the desire for self-preservation in such conditions drove all
other thoughts from men's minds.

I am ashamed to relate that from Zero until the enemy's barrage
weakened or until perhaps I got more accustomed to it, I never once
gave a thought to the boys who were going to attack. I cannot remember when my senses returned and when that unholy fear departed. But
they did go and I pulled myself together.[8]

Second Lieutenant Benjamin Parkin, 2/4th Duke of Wellington's Regiment, 186th
Brigade, 62nd Division

Without prior registration, artillery batteries had no concerns about
the flash from their guns giving away their positions. Work by the RE
Field Survey Companies also allowed batteries to be placed far forward
in 'silent' positions close to the front line from which they could fire
deep into the German defences. However, as they did so, an unexpected problem arose.

As the nearest tank passed me I was alarmed to see that it was heading
slightly across my line of fire. At our very short opening range the guns
had very little trajectory, and although care had been taken to see that
our shells would clear the low crest three or four hundred yards in front
of us, I was by no means sure they would clear the crest with a tank on
it, especially if it was carrying a fascine. When, therefore, the tank

approached my line of fire, I ordered my section to stop firing until it was over the crest.[9]

Second Lieutenant Frank Paish, 53rd Battery, 2nd Brigade, Royal Field Artillery, 6th Division

But the guns continued their calculated death-dealing programme of 'barrage lifts' for over three hours after the tanks had passed, pausing for intervals on each of the German defence lines before lifting again. For this was a 'jumping', not a creeping barrage. So, for example, in IV Corps' sector there were nine major 'jumps' between the first German defences and the reverse slope of the Flesquières Ridge. The ground between each jump might, therefore, remain relatively unscathed by shellfire. The consequent advantages in terms of smoother going for infantry and tanks had been expected. But disadvantages now manifested themselves in the potential to leave defensive positions and units unharmed. The artillery fired steadily and relentlessly. 'Two rounds a minute does not sound a high rate of fire,' wrote Frank Paish, 'but it was one which could be maintained for a long period only with difficulty.'[10] This was because the guns, being industrial machines, required careful maintenance by their crews. Guns that overheated would soon break down.

As soon, therefore, as the paint began to burn, the guns were taken out of action, one at a time, while buckets of water were poured down their elevated muzzles, and poured out again, black and boiling, from their depressed ones. With one gun out of action most of the time, the battery was effectively reduced to five guns firing at any one time; even so, we must have fired about two thousand rounds during the barrage.[11]

Second Lieutenant Frank Paish, 53rd Battery, 2nd Brigade, Royal Field Artillery, 6th Division

On the flanks of the main attack, diversionary attacks without tanks were launched by 56th (London) Division to the north and 55th (West Lancashire) Division to the south. The latter was the more substantial. Although it enjoyed initial success, ultimately the attackers suffered over 600 casualties. The northern attack involved the use of various *ruses de guerre*:

At 6.30 a.m. the whole of our artillery on the Army front opened fire on the enemy lines whilst men in the line hurled smoke bombs ahead of them to cover our movements from the line of our trenches. Then the dummy tanks were run out from cover; the dummy men were waved by others to and fro. And so, as the smoke cleared, the enemy got a fine view of our attack.[12]

Lieutenant Kenneth Palmer, 513th Field Company, RE, 56th Division

Fear that this was part of a major attack in this sector prompted the Germans to blow up the Bapaume–Cambrai road bridge over the Canal du Nord. Since IV Corps had expected to use this road as its principal route for supplies and reinforcements during the advance, the bridge's destruction had far-reaching consequences.

In the main attack, the sight of over four hundred tanks in action against them might reasonably have been expected to demoralize the German defenders. Nevertheless, one tank battalion introduced an additional element of surprise in their appearance on the battlefield.

Prior to the advance we lay up in a roofless factory. To go up to the start all the tanks put their noses to the factory wall and pushed! The wall went over with a thud and we climbed out over the debris.[13]

Major Edward Carter, No. 8 Company, 'C' Battalion, Tank Corps

Tank crew members without previous combat experience now discovered what a uniquely appalling experience going into battle in a tank of the Great War was:

We moved forward over fairly even ground at about 4 miles per hour. The noise inside was absolutely deafening; the eight-cylinder engine was going at full speed, both six-pounder guns were firing as rapidly as possible and I was emptying drum after drum from the machine-gun. Any order I gave to Fagg – the driver – who was close beside me, had to be shouted in his ear and any order given to the NCO – Sergeant Harkness – was given in a similar manner. Everything else had to be done by signs.[14]

Lieutenant Kenneth Wootton, Tank A29, 'Apollyon II', No. 2 Company, 'A' Battalion, Tank Corps

For the raw Private George Brown it was uncomfortable, but fascinating:

> When we moved off . . . it seemed a long time before we were given the order to open fire. At first we were just firing in the general direction of the enemy lines. Even at this early stage, the atmosphere inside the tank was beginning to get unpleasant: the fumes from the engine, the cordite fumes, the heat from the exhaust pipe, which was now red-hot. The noise was terrific: the rattle of the Lewis guns, the empty cartridge cases landing on the floor of the tank, and the driver banging onto the engine cover signalling to the secondary gearsmen. Sometimes the two gunners on one side of the tank were not in a position to see any targets on which to fire; this enabled them to relax and perhaps have a drink from their water bottles.[15]
>
> Private George Brown, H50 'Hurricane', No. 24 Company, 'H' Battalion, Tank Corps

The rolling downland proved ideal tank country. One tank crewman described driving on the green grass as 'like running over plush carpet'.[16] Others recalled the mud of the Ypres Salient:

> After driving over such impossible ground as we had been doing in Belgium, where even a few yards might cause endless difficulties and delays and often completely hold you up, this ground on Welsh Ridge seemed almost like an ordinary field and was, in fact, actually so in most places, except for trenches, gun-pits and so on with shell holes fairly widely distributed and almost entirely absent over quite long stretches.[17]
>
> Lieutenant Kenneth Wootton, A29 'Apollyon II', No. 2 Company, 'A' Battalion, Tank Corps

Because of the fascine each tank carried, tank commanders like Wootton were forced to expose themselves to greater danger in order to navigate the tank:

> The periscope usually used was one that you pushed through a hole in the roof of the cab over your head. Owing to the fascine on top, this was not possible. I now and again lifted the flap on my side and very cautiously peered out to see if anything was in front of us. As the light was by now improving, things gradually became more or less distinct

through the morning haze. So I crossed No Man's Land, dividing the time between firing off the Lewis gun, peering out the flap, and shouting to Fagg.[18]

Lieutenant Kenneth Wootton, A29 'Apollyon II', No. 2 Company, 'A' Battalion, Tank Corps

The German barbed wire, which was the chief reason for the employment of tanks en masse in the battle, had been expected to present major problems. However, the reality proved different:

We had to depend upon what we had learned from maps and photographs and we knew pretty well the hazards of the Hindenburg Line with its masses of wire. It had been said that it was 50–100 yards deep, the wire, and we anticipated that might be a serious obstacle.

I crossed the first line. The wire didn't prove to be any obstacle at all. The artillery had done their job very well and the element of surprise – the heavy gas shelling, no preliminary bombardment at all – had made it almost a cakewalk, one might say.[19]

Second Lieutenant Edward Leigh-Jones, B9 'Black Bess', No. 4 Company, 'B' Battalion, Tank Corps

Captain Mark Dillon too marvelled at the manner in which the barbed wire was overcome:

I had never seen myself such a depth of barbed wire. I suppose it was 10 yards deep and about 4 feet high, so dense that you could barely poke a broom handle through it. It was quite impassable to any man or beast and of course would never be destroyed by artillery fire in a month of Sundays. But the tanks went through it, and I personally followed their tracks and walked straight through on the track without any trouble at all as if it had been a carpet.[20]

Captain Mark Dillon, 'B' Battalion, Tank Corps

Dillon also witnessed the work of the wire-pulling tanks, specially assigned to clear paths for cavalry and artillery to advance through:

There were tanks with anchors on the end of a steel rope. These cleared the wire by driving into the wire, two abreast, dropping their anchors, turning away from each other and going down the length of the wire dragging the anchor after them. The result was to drag those enormous barbed wire defences into balls about 20 feet high. It cleared the ground as clean as a whistle. There wasn't even a scrap of anything left – not even weeds! I don't know how they got the anchors out of the ball of wire, but that was somebody else's business![21]

Captain Mark Dillon, 'B' Battalion, Tank Corps

In III Corps, the tactical drills and the manoeuvres in which the tank crews and infantry had trained were almost slavishly applied, but to good effect:

We went forward as fast as we could – which wasn't very fast. The tank was under fire, but not so much. A lot of Germans got down into the dugouts. We sort of picked them off as we went along. When we got through the line, one tank went forwards, and dropped its fascine in the German trench. When it had dropped its fascine it went along the front of the trench – the British side – and the next tank came over, dropped another fascine and went along the side and then the next one having something to go on went through. It might have dropped its fascine if it was needed or it may have kept it in case it got held up by a small trench. The tanks were shooting along the German trenches. Then the infantry coming on behind mopped them up.[22]

Private Eric Potten, F23 'Foggie II', No. 17 Company, 'F' Battalion, Tank Corps

The infantry's advance was almost mechanical, just as Fuller's 'ceremonial' drill had demanded:

We had formed up in artillery formation. When we came to the gap in the wire, each section and each platoon ran through the gap and took up the same formation on the other side. This manoeuvre we had practiced over and over again at Sorrel – men going in front with flags to represent the tanks . . . Everything seemed to be going very well. We were all smoking hard and all of us officers had our whistles ready and were giving directions just like a field day.[23]

Second Lieutenant George McMurtrie, 7th Somerset Light Infantry, 61st Brigade, 20th Division

The tactical manoeuvres allowed little room for human emotion. The advance was the cold, dispassionate translation of the blueprint for the ruthless destruction of all opposition. Indeed, the brutal efficiency of some tank crews had to be tempered by the commonsense requirement to conserve ammunition and use the appropriate tool for the job:

> German gunners, dug into the sides of the slopes, came out and tried to drag their machine-guns, which were mounted on a sort of sled, up the slopes and thus were easy shots for the tanks. I had to interfere because the 6-pounder gunners would use their guns when the tank machine-guns were more effective.[24]
>
> Major Edward Carter, No. 8 Company, 'C' Battalion, Tank Corps

For many, there was something unreal about the initial advance:

> It was extraordinary the luck we had that day. All the German shells landed on spots which our men had just left, [but] a few came unpleasantly near and the German machine-gun fire was pretty hot so that we were not at all sorry to get down into the valley, into dead ground.[25]
>
> Second Lieutenant George McMurtrie, 7th Somerset Light Infantry, 61st Brigade, 20th Division

Despite the previous indications that an attack could be expected, the Germans were completely surprised. The British artillery's destructive power was overwhelming as Artur Pries, an officer of *Reserve Infanterie Regiment 90*, describes:

> Suddenly all of the enemy's artillery began to fire madly right along our division's sector. The incendiary shells illuminated the whole front, left and right, as far as the eye could see, as if the entire area was on fire. We barely had time to instruct this battalion to follow our orders, when our own position and likewise the other commands in our rear were covered in a veritable hailstorm of shells of every imaginable calibre. Our telephone lines were shot to pieces straight away and could not be restored despite the utter fearlessness of our radio operators and engineers.[26]
>
> Artur Pries, *Reserve Infanterie Regiment 90, 54th Division*

German accounts of their defence in this sector highlight the dogged resistance of the trench garrisons:

> No. 7 Company with two platoons, that of Vizefeldwebel Noffeck and mine, was in the second trench. The platoon of Offizierstellvertreter

Wolf kept watch in the first line. The combat strength of the whole Company I'd estimate at about 100 rifles. About six in the morning*, a barrage was put down on the right of the neighbouring unit's sector, and after an hour this also started on our sector. During the bombardment I myself took over observation duties. After about an hour the fire went beating towards the rear. In the same moment, enemy tanks appeared in our first line. At once I raised the alarm. The tanks unnerved one private, lately arrived from Russia, yet he was carried along by the example of the others, whose bearing was blameless. Nobody was coming back from the front line.[27]

Leutnant R. Heinrich, *Reserve Infanterie Regiment 19, 9th Reserve Division*

Without adequate artillery support, Heinrich and his men attempted to tackle the tanks with rifle and machine-gun fire.

A tank appeared at the end of the communications trench in which we were standing. It was unable to advance over the first line. Leutnant Raberg, the company commander, tackled it with frontal fire from one machine-gun, whilst my platoon and I launched ourselves over the open ground from the right flank. Our artillery was not firing. Unfortunately, I didn't succeed in getting closer than 50 metres to the tank, and there I was halted by fire from the right flank. Many of my people had been hit in our dash forward. I had only two men with me, and with these I opened an effective fire at short range against the occupying tanks and the Tommies with them. The enemy hid behind the tank. Then one of my men called to me: 'Herr Leutnant! We've got company!' I went to him and observed two tanks behind us. I turned around and, at that moment, I stopped a bullet through the right shoulder.[28]

Leutnant R. Heinrich, *Reserve Infanterie Regiment 19, 9th Reserve Division*

Heinrich, though wounded, remained on his feet.

Together with my lads, I only got as far as the second line, where I received an emergency dressing from a medical officer. Leutnant Raberg gave the order to retire. He was killed the same day. The

* German clocks were one hour ahead of those used by the British.

Tommies then came to the area where I was and took me and my lads prisoner, as well as the medical officer.[29]

Leutnant R. Heinrich, *Reserve Infanterie Regiment 19, 9th Reserve Division*

Meanwhile, despite the weather conditions, the pilots and observers of the RFC did all they could to support the assault. On this opening day of the battle it was not the romantic work of the scout (or fighter) that was crucial to the battle's chances of success. It was the altogether more journeyman toil of the bomber and of the artillery spotter. The aircraft tasked with attacking the German airfields were the main instrument of what modern military theorists would term the 'deep battle' concept designed to tackle every element of the German defences. Soon after Zero, these RFC squadrons appeared low over the advance. Howard Brokensha of 3 Squadron described their experiences:

> They were flying near enough to the trenches to be able to see the tanks going into action and crawling over the crater-pitted ground, many of them already out of action and lying crippled on their sides. Seconds later they were crossing the trenches so low that they could see the frantically firing gunners below them giving a wave of the hand as the planes passed through their flaming barrage which from above looked just like a long carpet of tongues of flame.[30]

Captain Howard Brokensha, 3 Squadron, RFC

Incredibly none of his flight was hit. Visibility had improved slightly and the flight flew on, still in formation, at about 500 feet, allowing them to clear any hazards such as hills and pick out landmarks as a check on their position.

> There was just time to test their guns and make sure the bomb releases were ready to hand when almost before they realised it they flew slap into the enemy aerodrome, taking the occupants completely by surprise.[31]

Captain Howard Brokensha, 3 Squadron, RFC

Splitting up as arranged, the pilots made individual dives at the hangars and some planes on the ground, bombing and machine-gunning as they went. Brokensha felt certain some good hits were achieved and at least two machines damaged, but the attempts at bombing suffered because the pilots had to drop in and out of the low clouds, frequently losing sight of their targets.

Thinking it was time to return as most of their ammunition and fuel had been expended, Brokensha joined up with the only two machines of his flight he could locate and signalled them to follow him homewards. But they were then all surprised to see and hear tracers crackling past their machines as a number of German aircraft got into the air. Brokensha was quickly separated from the others and had his hands full with two German aircraft closely following him, trying to get into a favourable position for a decisive burst.

> In the mist and bad visibility all these machines were soon lost to each other, however, and he soon decided that it would be wiser to try and reach his home base before it was too late, with the likelihood of being taken prisoner into the bargain. So, turning his machine due west he started hedge-hopping towards the lines after firing several green signal lights but without having been able to get in touch with any of his flight who by now were probably widely scattered.[32]
>
> Captain Howard Brokensha, 3 Squadron, RFC

Despite an erratic compass and a growing concern over whether his fuel would last, Brokensha got safely back to a British airfield. However, 3 Squadron had lost three pilots killed and two taken prisoner in their mission.

The important contribution of these RFC squadrons and their success in suppressing German aircraft operating against the offensive was clear to one renowned British ace:

> About 8.30 we left the ground, and flew along the Bapaume–Cambrai road at 300 feet, as the heavy clouds were down at this height. We arrived at Havrincourt Wood and saw smoke and gun flashes everywhere. From 200 feet we could see our tanks well past the famous Hindenburg Line, and they looked very peculiar nosing their way around different clumps of trees, houses, etc. We flew up and down the line for an hour, but no sign of any Hun machines about, although the air was crowded with our own.[33]
>
> Captain James McCudden, 56 Squadron, RFC

The efficacy of the 'jumping' barrage in dealing with opposition in some key areas had been considerably doubted by the British high command, so several RFC squadrons were tasked with operating in a ground-attack role. Since German artillery was known to be in Lateau Wood, Sopwith Camels from 'C' Flight, 46 Squadron, were to bomb these batteries of 150 mm (5.9-inch) guns. Arthur Lee was one of the pilots:

> It was a ghastly morning – low cloud, mist, occasional rain. It was 6.30 before we could see to take off in formation, when we were immediately in the clouds. How [our CO] found the way, I don't know. Nearly forty miles across country in mist and rain, and never more than 100 feet from the ground. We followed blindly, our attention fully taken in keeping formation.[34]
>
> Lieutenant Arthur Gould Lee, 46 Squadron, RFC

Soon reduced to three aircraft, 'C' Flight pressed on. They passed over the wide trenches of the Hindenburg Line, and the vast belts of barbed wire, through which the tanks had crushed many lanes.

> From then on the mist was made denser by the smoke-screens laid in front of the advancing tanks which still hung around. We quickly catch up the first wave. Everything flashes by like a dream, and as we rush forward at ninety miles an hour, twenty feet up, I get split-second glimpses that remain vividly in the memory.
>
> The ragged line of diamond-shaped monsters, thirty to fifty yards apart, stretching into the mist on either flank, rolling unevenly forwards, their tracks churning round, their exhausts throwing out blue-grey smoke. Behind each tank, a trudging group of infantry, casually smoking, looking up at us. Other knots of infantry stroll along a little in rear, between the tanks. I see a disabled tank, flames leaping up, the troops standing helplessly around. A chance shell bursts between two tanks, knocks down a small bunch of soldiery like ninepins.[35]
>
> Lieutenant Arthur Gould Lee, 46 Squadron, RFC

The Camels reached the Hindenburg support line where, having previously kept loose formation, they now broke up and climbed, ready to dive and bomb:

At once, we're in the clouds, and have to drop. So there we are, the three of us, whirling blindly around at 50–100 feet, all but colliding, being shot at from below, and trying to bomb places accurately. Even at this frantic moment, my mind switches to my beautifully dead-on practice bombing on our bullet-free smoke-free aerodrome, but I don't have the time to laugh.[36]

Lieutenant Arthur Gould Lee, 46 Squadron, RFC

In a real battle, choosing specific targets was impossible:

The main thing was to get rid of the darned bombs before a bullet hit them. I saw a bunch of guns right in line for attack, so dived at 45 degrees and released all four bombs. As I swung aside I saw them burst, a group of white-grey puffs centred with red flames. One fell between two guns, the rest a few yards away.[37]

Lieutenant Arthur Gould Lee, 46 Squadron, RFC

His aircraft then suffered damage from ground fire:

This makes me go hot. I dive at another group of guns, giving them 100 rounds, see a machine-gun blazing at me, swing on to that, one short burst and he stops firing.

As I climb up, a Camel whizzes past me out of the mist, missing me by a yard. It makes me sweat with fright. This is too dangerous, and I lift into the cloud to 300 feet, stay there half a minute, come down. Lateau Wood is behind me. There isn't much room below, I nearly hit a high tree, swerve violently, skim through tree-tops with the mist clinging to the branches, then suddenly no trees, an open road. I fly along it, trying to get my breath. My heart is racing, and it isn't through being at 20,000![38]

Lieutenant Arthur Gould Lee, 46 Squadron, RFC

Elsewhere, four DH5s from 64 Squadron attacked batteries on the reverse of Flesquières Ridge, at the limits of the artillery barrage's range. At 7.00 a.m. they found the German batteries fully active, firing from gun-pits. The pilots bombed the positions, claiming at least one direct hit, and machine-gunned the detachments. A pilot flying over the same position at 7.45 a.m. could find no activity of guns or personnel. Several dead men and horses were lying around the pits. Whilst this might indicate artillery opposition had been overcome, another possibility was that the guns had been withdrawn from their pits (positions known to the British), and were moving to fire from elsewhere.

Near Havrincourt, six more DH5s from 68 Squadron (an Australian unit), operating in pairs dropped bombs on the best obtainable targets; the fog was so thick that low-flying in flight-formation was impossible. This was risky work (their leader was mortally wounded by ground-fire), but offered some rewards. Artillery batteries were attacked and the gunners driven off.

The derring-do of these antipodean airmen was typified by Lieutenants Gordon 'Skipper' Wilson and Harry Taylor. Taylor, like many Australians of the Great War, had been born in England.[39] During his military service he had already been awarded the Military Medal. His courage was further demonstrated on 20 November:

> Taylor and I found the enemy being massed to repel the attack –
> confused and dazed by surprise. Close together we dived down and
> opened our machine-guns on the Germans, pulling up to the level of the
> fog again (about thirty feet off the ground), and letting a bomb drop as
> we rose. For a few moments we continued this, scattering and
> demoralising troops, and preventing them from concentrating their fire
> on our own men. Then, as I zoomed up after a burst of machine-gun fire
> and turned to dive again, I missed Taylor. For a moment I thought he
> must have pulled up into the fog to clear a machine-gun stoppage. The
> next second the red light of a pilot-rocket showed up beside me. I
> guessed that it was fired by Taylor, and meant he was in distress.
> Another red light followed rapidly. Then I saw him down on the ground
> wrecked and among the enemy. That he was sufficiently alive to fire his
> rockets was amazing. His machine was just a heap of wreckage. One
> wing lay twenty yards away from the rest of the heap, from which Taylor
> had scrambled and was now firing his rockets to attract my attention.[40]
> Lieutenant Gordon Wilson, 68 (2 Australian) Squadron, RFC

Whilst in the air, Taylor had been the hunter. On the ground he was the vulnerable prey, as his fellow pilot realized.

> Fifty yards or so away from him were scattered groups of the enemy,
> who had stood off as his machine came down . . . I saw them turn as

they realised that Taylor had crashed, and lift their rifles to fire. I dived at them immediately and scattered them again. It showed Taylor that I had seen his signals.[41]

Lieutenant Gordon Wilson, 68 (2 Australian) Squadron, RFC

Taylor's desperate fight for self-preservation was keenly watched by Wilson:

Crouching behind a slight mound, he pulled out his automatic and fired at some Germans who rushed towards him as I pulled up ready for another dive. Then, as I dived and scattered the Germans again, he dashed back a few yards, dropped to the ground, and fired again. He repeated this until he had got back maybe sixty yards from his machine and nearer to our own men, and then I saw him surrounded by a small band of British soldiers. He picked up the gun of a fallen man, and he and his little party lay firing at the enemy, who were gradually creeping up and spreading out fan-shape to surround them.[42]

Lieutenant Gordon Wilson, 68 (2 Australian) Squadron, RFC

Wilson, however, in his desire to help his stranded friend, had neglected his own safety:

For a while I saw snapshots of the unequal contest as I dived down and zoomed up repeatedly to try and scatter these groups of Germans. Then there was a crashing sound against my head and I was blinded. Two bullets had pierced the windscreen and dust from the triplex glass had been flung into my eyes. Pulling back the 'joy-stick' and giving the engine full throttle, I climbed up into the fog away from hostile fire, to wait until my eyes cleared. For a while I flew about anywhere . . . climbing up clear of enemy fire. Gradually the glass-dust got washed from my eyes, and I was able to see again.[43]

Lieutenant Gordon Wilson, 68 (2 Australian) Squadron, RFC

Now he returned to where he had left Taylor, but neither he nor his party were there:

Here and there a German jumped up from behind cover and dashed forward between the mud-splashes of falling shells. Little rips in the canvas of my aeroplane wings told me that others unseen were firing at me. It seemed certain that Taylor and his party had been captured or killed and that the ground was in possession of the Germans.[44]

Lieutenant Gordon Wilson, 68 (2 Australian) Squadron, RFC

Reluctantly, therefore, Wilson flew to a forward landing ground to report the loss of Taylor and receive further orders.

For all their undoubted bravery, these pilots and their aircraft could only supplement the artillery's work. They could never wholly compensate for the absence of effective artillery counter-battery fire – as subsequent events demonstrated. Nevertheless, their work drew considerable admiration from Captain James McCudden, who had an opportunity to observe the pilots and machines of the ground attack squadrons at another advanced landing ground near Bapaume:

The machines were mostly DH5s which were employed in low bombing and ground strafing. It was really wonderful to see these fellows come back from a show all shot about, load up with some more bombs and ammunition, and then go off again to strafe the Hun. There was quite a fair percentage coming in wounded too, which was to be expected under the circumstances.[45]

Captain James McCudden, 56 Squadron, RFC

On the ground, the chief problems encountered by Pulteney's III Corps in the advance on the first objective came from the villages and fortified farms incorporated into the Hindenburg Line. On the extreme right, 12th (Eastern) Division attacking with two brigades led by 'C' and 'F' Tank Battalions faced its first tough challenge at Bleak House on the Péronne–Cambrai road. This strongpoint had not been shelled by the heavy artillery but eventually fell to tanks and infantry working in a model of close cooperation.

The efficiency with which Bleak House was captured contrasted with the problems encountered elsewhere when cooperation between tanks and infantry was less satisfactory:

I had to take Lone Farm,* we were to use tanks and my troops weren't very, very keen. I told them that we were going to take the farm and we were going to have a tank go ahead, make sure the wire was gone and

---

* Davies is mistaken here. In fact, the farm was Sonnet Farm.

everything . . . We'd never had that before. So we followed the tank. Every time it stopped, we dropped down. Then we went forward again.

I remember the tank stopped and started to veer round. So I crawled forward. I got up and I didn't know where to look in a tank! I was trying to find somewhere I could talk to somebody inside, when a little aperture opened and an officer said, 'This is as far as we go.'

So I said, 'Come outside and talk to me,' but he wouldn't come out. I thought: 'But the tank's supposed to go and take the farm with me!' So I crawled back and said 'Right, we take the bloody farm on our own!' So we did![46]

Second Lieutenant Jim Davies, 8th Royal Fusiliers, 36th Brigade, 12th Division

This was typical of the problems of implementing tactical theory in the grim reality of battle. Instructions concerning tactics could only be useful as a framework in which real men and tanks tried to work together. No amount of tactical prescription and training could wholly anticipate or overcome battlefield conditions. Yet, despite these difficulties, by 8.00 a.m. 12th Division had taken its first objective.

On 12th Division's left, 20th (Light) Division's initial advance on the slopes of the Gonnelieu spur and Welsh Ridge and into the valley beyond by 60th and 61st Brigades encountered slight opposition, although there was some artillery retaliation. As 61st Brigade advanced on La Vacquerie, the key position in the German first line of defence in this sector, it encountered growing resistance:

There was a sunken road in the side of the hill leading to La Vacquerie. So far, we had been very lucky and had had very few casualties. By now the enemy had more or less got over the surprise and their machine-guns were beginning to be effective; bullets were whistling just over our heads. We had to keep pretty low to avoid being hit. Several men were hit here by machine-gun bullets. I shall never forget a Lance Corporal who had come out and joined the battalion the same time as I did – he was crying like a frightened baby and asking to go home . . . He got home but not in the way he wanted, for at that moment he was shot through the stomach.[47]

Second Lieutenant George McMurtrie, 7th Somerset Light Infantry, 61st Brigade, 20th Division

With 61st Brigade were tanks from 'I' Battalion. One section was that commanded by Captain 'Jake' Wilson. After the unfortunate incident the previous night when water had been poured in the fuel tank, Wilson doubted his tank's reliability. Predictably, when the advance began, it did not get far:

Having got to the enemy front line the engine conked out with water in the jets. This was the pivot tank in which I was travelling. I had to make a quick decision and ran the gauntlet to the left rear tank commanded by [Second] Lieutenant Parsons, which became the pivot.[48]

Captain 'Jake' Wilson, No. 26 Company, 'I' Battalion, Tank Corps

Surely confirming that Wilson was generous in his interpretation of the circumstances of this mishap, Parsons' tank had suffered a similar 'accident' prior to the attack and also experienced difficulties.

I started off almost midway between Villers Plouich and La Vacquerie, after my driver accidentally put a can of water in the gas tank. We only got into No Man's Land when we stopped and had to disconnect the gas lines and suck out as much of the water as we could, before we were able to go again. We spent nearly 40 minutes in the middle of the German barrage, and instead of leading the attack we became part of the second wave.[49]

Second Lieutenant George Parsons, Tank I35, No. 26 Company, 'I' Battalion, Tank Corps

But tank I35 played a significant part in the attack:

We successfully silenced any enemy machine-guns that were plastering our lookout slits, paving the way for the infantry following in our wake to mop up and take La Vacquerie on our right flank almost without cost.[50]

Captain 'Jake' Wilson, No. 26 Company, 'I' Battalion, Tank Corps

La Vacquerie's fall saw the first flood of prisoners for 20th Division. McMurtrie's initial response was that of the victor towards the vanquished:

They all had their hands up in the air and were running as fast as they could. It was one of the funniest things I have ever seen, these poor devils running along, their heads bobbing up and down and their eyes starting out of their heads, running for dear life and not knowing where to go or what to do. We sent out two men with fixed bayonets who brought them to the CO. When I saw them closer, I felt very sorry for them, but they seemed pleased that we had not shot them as they expected.[51]

Second Lieutenant George McMurtrie, 7th Somerset Light Infantry, 61st Brigade, 20th Division

The attack of 60th Brigade was led by eighteen tanks of 'A' Battalion. On the right was Lieutenant Kenneth Wootton's section. Its orders were to tackle a strongpoint in the German front line and on no account to leave until the position's capture was confirmed by an infantry officer. At the front trench, Wootton's tank drove along the parapet firing into the trench in the prescribed fashion. Having accomplished this, Wootton decided to get outside to find out more about the situation.

Telling the Sergeant to keep the tank there till I returned I cautiously opened the door of the left sponson . . . and peered out. Then, drawing my revolver, I jumped down from the doorway, ran round the back of the tank and leaped down into the trench. There was no one to be seen in the trench, so I turned to the right and quickly but cautiously made my way down the trench and after passing one or two traverses came upon a few of the Infantry that had made the attack with us; they were extremely cheerful and said they had got into the trenches very easily and did not think they had had any men either killed or wounded.[52]

Lieutenant Kenneth Wootton, A29 'Apollyon II', No. 2 Company, 'A' Battalion, Tank Corps

Hurrying along the maze of trenches, passing other groups of infantry, Wootton now sought out their officer.

On rounding a bend, I found myself facing a large man about to lunge at me with his bayonet and I, pointing my revolver at him; we stood like this for a second and then realised we were friends instead of enemies, we both exclaimed something like 'all right – British', in a very relieved tone. He said he had heard me coming and thought I was a Jerry. I was wearing no hat which made matters worse, quite against the regulations, but I couldn't stand shrapnel helmets. We wore no hat inside a tank and I had omitted to put one on.[53]

Lieutenant Kenneth Wootton, A29 'Apollyon II', No. 2 Company, 'A' Battalion, Tank Corps

With this lucky escape and having found the officer, Wootton's section could now press on for the second objective.

Amongst the infantry of 60th Brigade, 12th King's Royal Rifle Corps (KRRC) encountered the most resistance. Whilst attacking the first objective, one company lost all its officers and many NCOs. Here 20-year-old Rifleman Albert Shepherd, who had already rushed a machine-gun single-handed, took command of the remnants of his platoon. Luckily securing a tank's assistance, he and the platoon's survivors then took their objective. Shepherd was subsequently awarded the Victoria Cross.

The difficulties Shepherd faced and the vagaries of battlefield co-operation between tanks and infantry are underlined by the experience of Charles Austin, of the same battalion, at Good Old Man Farm – a fortified strongpoint just short of the Hindenburg Support Line:

> I commanded a company and was given four tanks. We had some machine-gun fire that was very troublesome and killed and wounded a lot of men. In the battle, when I tried to communicate, I couldn't do so because of the noise all around us. I hammered on the tank door with the butt of my revolver and got no response at all – they weren't interested! I wanted to alert the tank to the machine-gun that was shooting us up but the tank [saw] the machine-gun itself, tackled it, and cleared the way.[54]
>
> Lieutenant Charles Austin, 12th KRRC, 60th Brigade, 20th Division

With Good Old Man Farm taken, Austin's company advanced towards the Hindenburg Support Line.

> A tank was moving ahead of us and into the German wire [which] was not very high but coiled – and very deep. I would think it was thirty or forty feet at least. Dreadful stuff to get caught up in, because you couldn't get any cover at all. I mean you were a sitting target if you got into the wire . . . We didn't get into it – we approached it and the

German machine-gun fire was so devastating that we really had to lay down or be killed.[55]

Lieutenant Charles Austin, 12th KRRC, 60th Brigade, 20th Division

Although a tank was with his unit, Austin once more experienced problems in securing its assistance. Without wireless communication or an intercom system to speak to the tank's crew, all such requests had to be by mouth and face-to-face:

I tried to draw its attention to this machine-gun but I couldn't make contact. The noise of battle was so much. The tank did eventually silence the machine-gun but before it did so, we were pinned down in our approach to the wire and the machine-gunner was very efficient – he shot up the ridge which was immediately in front of the wire and he killed my entire section.[56]

Lieutenant Charles Austin, 12th KRRC, 60th Brigade, 20th Division

Austin's anguish was intensified because these men had died needlessly.

They didn't do what I told them. When I realised the machine-gun was skimming the ridge, I crawled forward – into the German wire. I reckoned they wouldn't shoot actually into the wire because they wouldn't expect a target there. I signalled the section into the wire and they didn't follow me. While I was in that wire, pinned down by this machine-gun before the tank destroyed it, I was shot – couple of bullets through the left leg. Now if I'd been where I was prior to moving forwards, I'd have had those machine-gun bullets through my head or body. I reckon that I saved my life that morning by moving forward.[57]

Lieutenant Charles Austin, 12th KRRC, 60th Brigade, 20th Division

Despite his wounds, Austin wasn't totally incapacitated and remained in action:

When you're shot, all that seems to happen is that you just get like a nasty punch, that's all. I didn't realise quite what had happened. I certainly hadn't got time to take my puttees off and look at my leg and fuss about it then, and it wasn't bleeding badly. There were just a couple of holes. I got up, so did the two or three survivors, and we moved forwards with the rest of the company. We were the leading section at that time.[58]

Lieutenant Charles Austin, 12th KRRC, 60th Brigade, 20th Division

Once the machine-gun had been dealt with, Austin and his platoon survivors could negotiate the wire. There was no resistance in the Hindenburg Line. Some German dead lay about the trench, but the survivors had fled down the support trenches. By now, Austin's wounds were becoming too much to bear:

I was stiffening up, I could only hobble. I found a stick and met up with a young German officer who had given up and who was disarmed. We walked back together to a dressing station. I don't know quite how far but it was an Advanced Dressing Station – I expect a mile or so.[59]

Lieutenant Charles Austin, 12th KRRC, 60th Brigade, 20th Division

Austin later discovered he had bullets through both calves, but no bones broken. He knew he was lucky. His medical treatment provides an excellent example of the standards of post-battle care:

Because I wasn't a stretcher case I sat on the steps of the ambulance that took me back to a forward casualty hospital. There the wounded were queuing up for an anti-tetanus injection and I had mine. Just a jab in the arm. They used the same needle, I noticed, for everybody. By the time they got to me it was hellishly blunt and they had to have about three punches at my [left arm] to get the needle in. Then I went into the hospital which was a big tented forward dressing station. All the beds were occupied by severely wounded people, so I was given a floor to lay on. The nurses were ever so busy doing their job. They'd been up all night cutting sandwiches and I got the most beautiful plate of sardine sandwiches – which I was very pleased to have.[60]

Lieutenant Charles Austin, 12th KRRC, 60th Brigade, 20th Division

He was subsequently evacuated to Rouen. As Austin acknowledged, 'I was very fortunate.'[61]

In the centre of the attack, 'B' and 'H' Tank Battalions made steady progress leading the two assault brigades of 6th Division. Their attack was covered by a good artillery barrage that included a substantial proportion of smoke shells. It was hoped this would not only screen the tanks but also deceive the Germans into thinking that large quantities of gas were being used:

> Our observation post was placed behind the front line, in a position which would give us a very fine view of the country behind the enemy lines. For quite an appreciable time we could see very little of what was going on, owing to the smokescreen; but we could hear the machine-guns and small artillery which the tanks carried firing from our front. The troops following the tanks disappeared into the smoke, so for the moment we had little or nothing to do.[62]
>
> Captain Geoffrey Dugdale, Headquarters, 60th Brigade, 20th Division

Mark Dillon, as a reconnaissance officer for 'B' Battalion, was expected to follow the attack on foot:

> I went forward with my Company Commander and followed the tanks keeping them fairly well in sight – probably a couple of hundred yards behind. You can't see very much. There's always a certain amount of smoke and dust about a battlefield . . . miserable-looking people trudging forward carrying their rifles slung over their backs and tanks going ahead of them. There was no resistance from the Germans. One chap had a rifle bullet through his thigh, making rather a to-do about it. So I bandaged him up with a field dressing and left him on the side of the track where the ambulance people would pick him up. But there were very few casualties.[63]
>
> Captain Mark Dillon, 'B' Battalion, Tank Corps

Generally the advance to the first objective by Dillon's 'B' Battalion operating with 16th Brigade and 'H' Battalion with 71st Brigade went well. However, Major Gerald Huntbach, commanding No. 22 Company in 'H' Battalion, witnessed an alarming incident early on when one of the advanced tanks (H4 'Harvester') suddenly veered violently to the left, crossed the Beaucamp–Ribécourt road, across the advance of the Main Body tanks and came to rest on the edge of a dump of trench mortar bombs. Huntbach ran to help the tank's occupants.

> Inside were a remnant crew, alighting and gasping. The tank had been on fire under the engine bonnet, from a flooding carburettor, and four of the crew, including the first driver, had been sick from Pyrene fumes

and had dropped out. While they recovered, I boarded 'Harvester' and Parsons, my runner, and I started the engine.[64]

Major Gerald Huntbach, No. 22 Company, 'H' Battalion, Tank Corps

Extricating the tank, Huntbach was soon joined by the recovering tank men and their commander, Second Lieutenant Robert Davis. Huntbach, Davis and his remaining men took 'Harvester' towards the now-visible Ribécourt. From the tank's top hatch, Huntbach surveyed the battlefield.

I had a grandstand view of all 'B' Battalion tanks, with some of 'C' and 'F' almost racing down Welsh Ridge. It was magnificent, and it was war all right. They were doing what always paid with [Great War] tanks, maintaining fire against all local targets . . . The whole fleet took the wire in their stride, and the cunning little manoeuvre of each section of three tanks at the two main trenches was perfectly executed.[65]

Major Gerald Huntbach, No. 22 Company, 'H' Battalion, Tank Corps

Meanwhile, 'Hilda', with Brigadier General Hugh Elles aboard, ditched somewhat ignominiously before reaching Ribécourt. The Tank Corps commander was seen walking briskly back towards Beaucamp, carrying the Corps' slightly tattered 'standard' with him. 'Harvester' and the other tanks of 'H' Battalion pushed on.

I saw one male tank using its 6-pounders with good effect on enemy positions. Two of our tanks were out of action, the crews had baled out, they waved to us; eventually we lost sight of them. We were now firing onto the German lines, and we saw many prisoners being escorted by our troops away from the trenches, many of them wounded.[66]

Private George Brown, H50 'Hurricane', No. 24 Company, 'H' Battalion, Tank Corps

The first objective of 71st Brigade included Ribécourt village. Its capture was the task of 9th Norfolks, whose commander observed

the leading line of tanks, followed by the [1st] Leicesters, crossing our trenches and starting across No Man's Land – a wonderful spectacle in the half light of the early morning. Ponderous, grunting, groaning, wobbling, these engines of war crawled and lurched their way toward the enemy lines, followed by groups of men in file. Overhead our shells were pouring over. The barrage lifted from the enemy's outpost trench to the other side of the hill, where we knew that Unseen Trench was getting it hot; but the slowness of those tanks! It is at these moments that one itches for quickness and rapidity, and the slow, deliberate action of these monsters was exasperating. Neither tanks nor Leicesters were clear of our lines when we reached 'A' Company. I have never seen men in better fighting spirit. They all stood up and cheered when I reached them.[67]

Lieutenant Colonel Bernard Prior, 9th Norfolks, 71st Brigade, 6th Division

Prior had decided to go over with his battalion, the better to observe its progress after it had crossed the ridge in front of the British line.

I was anxious to get on and over the hill, so as to be able to get a view of the Promised Land, and then be able to control the fight. In the advance we came across [Captain Samuel] Blackwell with 'D' Company. He told me that both Cuthbert and Cubitt had been wounded, and that he himself was hit but could carry on. That was the last I saw of him, for he was killed later on. When the doctor examined his body he found that the first wound was a terrible one; despite which he continued to lead his company, crossed the Hindenburg Line, and initiated the attack against the final objective before being shot.[68]

Lieutenant Colonel Bernard Prior, 9th Norfolks, 71st Brigade, 6th Division

Prior, realizing the need to do whatever possible to control the battalion attack, pressed on to Unseen Trench.

Here I found a number of 'C' Company who were evidently not quite sure what their next action was, for I heard one man say, 'Well, what do we do now?' I shouted out, 'Now, my lads, you'll take the ruddy village,' at which they laughed and clambered out of the trench with me.[69]

Lieutenant Colonel Bernard Prior, 9th Norfolks, 71st Brigade, 6th Division

Prior and 'C' Company had outstripped both the tanks and the other three companies. Instead of being in support, they now found themselves leading.

Ribécourt was immediately in front of us. I could see parties of the enemy running through the streets. Our artillery was putting down a smoke barrage on the farther side of the village, and several houses were on fire and blazing merrily. I had to decide whether to hang on in our present position and wait for the arrival of the tanks and the three other companies, or push 'C' Company in. The enemy already showed signs of recovering from the initial surprise. We were now being shelled pretty persistently and accurately, as well as machine-gunned. I determined to take immediate action, and directed [Captain Gerald] Failes to push forward at once, take the part of the village lying on this side of the ravine, and hold the bridge crossing it. 'C' Company swept on and effected this in brilliant fashion, securing a large bag of prisoners.[70]

Lieutenant Colonel Bernard Prior, 9th Norfolks, 71st Brigade, 6th Division

Having secured the bridges, the clearing of Ribécourt beyond the Grand Ravine fell to the other companies. Prior observed their action with undisguised pride:

'B' Company had gone through and were in the village. I saw 'A' Company make a beautiful attack on the line of houses on the left of the village, supported by a male tank whose gun was in action. 'A' Company was attacking by sectional rushes, covering the advance by rifle fire, and I could not help feeling that my efforts at open warfare training whilst at Tinques had not been wasted.[71]

Lieutenant Colonel Bernard Prior, 9th Norfolks, 71st Brigade, 6th Division

There was an anxious wait for news of 'D' Company.

Cheering messages from 'A', 'B', and 'C' Companies, reporting complete success, began to come in, the runners arriving with broad grins and puffing German cigars . . . At last a message from 'D' Company reporting complete success.[72]

Lieutenant Colonel Bernard Prior, 9th Norfolks, 71st Brigade, 6th Division

By 9.00 a.m. Ribécourt had fallen and almost 500 prisoners were taken, although 'mopping-up' of sporadic resistance from some houses was still necessary. This resistance continued for some time and had important consequences.

Operation orders now dictated a pause of 48 minutes, before fresh units took up the advance once more. Initial success gave rise to wild rumour:

First to pass us were the walking wounded – a surprising few – but each and all radiant of the first fruits of victory. They set no bounds upon their powers of exaggeration. Quite a number had seen our fellows crossing the Canal. A few swore the cavalry were in Cambrai. How I wished I had not known that the Canal line was six miles from the old front line; then I might have believed it, and felt happy too.[73]

Lieutenant Robert Ross, RE Signal Service, III Corps

Although in IV Corps, 51st (Highland) and 62nd (West Riding) Divisions had adopted tactical formations that deviated from Fuller's 'ceremonial drill'; this made little difference in the attack on the Hindenburg front trench. For 62nd Division's attack against the village and chateau of Havrincourt, of the 60 tanks* emerging at Zero from concealed laying-up places within Havrincourt Wood to advance along its edges, only 50 actually got into action, and all were late since the distance they had to travel to get into action had been underestimated.

On the division's left, 187th Brigade experienced problems early on because of the absence of their tank support. However, the brigade commander, Brigadier General Reginald Taylor, had sensibly emphasized the principle now established that the infantry were on no account to wait for tanks. That they obeyed was fortunate since 'their' tanks soon caught them up, but not before the infantry had dealt with a number of strongpoints in the German outpost line prior to pushing on to the first objective. The defenders of Chateau Wood offered the chief resistance with heavy rifle and machine-gun fire. Nevertheless, the leading infantry companies reached the German front line, whilst those following advanced on the west half of Havrincourt village.

The division's other brigade, 185th, experienced an equally unsatisfactory start: its tanks were also delayed, despite the urgency with which they had gone forward:

6.20 a.m. and away we went. Engines running in top gear – no need for quiet now – down the slope into the lane of Trescault village, up a side track, across our front line trench, hell for leather we pelted, into No

---

* All of 'G' Battalion plus 16 from each of 'D' and 'E' Battalions: No. 19 Company with tanks from 'D' and 'E' on the west side preceded 187th Brigade; Nos. 20 and 21 on the east side with 185th Brigade.

Man's Land, just as dawn was breaking, straight for the German trenches. The tank was ordered to keep on the extreme right of Havrincourt Wood (the remainder spreading out right and left, fan-wise, as soon as our front line was crossed) and we hugged the edge of the wood pretty closely, the artillery barrage which had opened at zero falling just in front of us.[74]

Lance Corporal Ernest Thwaites, No. 21 Company, 'G' Battalion, Tank Corps

Both sides' trenches were close together here on the eastern edge of Havrincourt Wood and British artillery had not been able to shell the German positions. But the area was also covered in smashed tree stumps and fallen trees – obstacles that any sensible tank commander was at pains to avoid since they could easily ditch a tank or cause it severe mechanical damage by pushing the bottom plates up against the engine. Consequently, lacking artillery and tank support, Billy Kirkby's battalion, 2/6th West Yorkshires, almost immediately encountered problems when they advanced.

We were suddenly in the midst of violent enemy machine-gun fire. Suddenly the soldier next to me was badly hit, giving a look of anguish as the blood from his wound spread over and from his mouth. The last I saw of him was his desperate turn, using all his remaining strength as he staggered back towards the stretcher bearers who would be follow-ing our advance. Man after man was hit as we experienced the power of the enemy machine-guns.[75]

Private Billy Kirkby, 2/6th West Yorkshires, 185th Brigade, 62nd Division

Despite this, the advance continued, although for Kirkby the 'fog of war' proved a singularly appropriate phrase:

The grey mist of the morning was obscuring my vision so that I seemed to be advancing alone towards the enemy trenches in front. A solitary young soldier without any previous experience of battle, almost over-come by the terrible thought that all my gallant comrades had fallen. I pushed forward, ready for whatever might come. Then several Ger-mans emerged, charging towards us. I gripped my rifle firmly, about to open fire on them, when I was utterly astonished to see their hands rise above their heads; their faces, their whole attitude one of fright and shock. I waved them on to captivity as once again the mist dispersed.

The early morning mist had horrified me by creating the illusion of a lone warrior advancing within the great battle, but now as it cleared I was more than comforted by the appearance around me of West Yorkshiremen.[76]

Private Billy Kirkby, 2/6th West Yorkshires, 185th Brigade, 62nd Division

Kirkby's company, under Captain Walter Moorhouse, successfully reached and occupied the Hindenburg Line without yet enjoying tank assistance. Here, however, they had to wait for another company of the battalion to come up on their left. When they did the advance could continue. The scent of a major success was clearly in the men's nostrils, leading to acts of irrational bravado:

The enemy had retreated from their first line of trenches. We searched them thoroughly. Satisfied no single German remained, we continued our attack. A sergeant wounded, though not seriously, stood irresolute, wanting to continue the attack but finding the increasing effects of his wound making progress difficult. Three of us stood round him arguing against his efforts to continue while the enemy's murderous fire continued to inflict casualties all around us. Nature seemed immune in the midst of our hotly-disputed argument and I noticed a solitary flower at my feet, a sign of the beauty of the earth and its indifference to the madness of man.

'Get out of it, Sarge, before you drop down helpless, overcome by that ____ wound of yours. Don't be such a damned fool.' He had given a look of despair. 'I wanted to be with you boys until we had captured Havrincourt.' Blood was now appearing through his puttees from his wounded leg. He gave a groan as we gently turned that massive frame of his around, walked with him a few paces seeing he could manage. The last I saw of him was his massive figure stumbling back to our rear.[77]

Private Billy Kirkby, 2/6th West Yorkshires, 185th Brigade, 62nd Division

The tanks had now joined the attackers, although Ernest Thwaites' tank suffered a further delay.

From my 'bus' we saw hardly any enemy to fire at, as we crept up the outskirts of Havrincourt Wood, until we came into a sunken road, opposite the village, where we became badly ditched. We were held up here for a while, until we could get the fascine* lowered, a sniper in the wood meantime taking pot shots at Sykes, as he released the chains. Once down, however, the tank rose easily over and gained firm ground again, and we were soon on our way.[78]

Lance Corporal Ernest Thwaites, No. 21 Company, 'G' Battalion, Tank Corps

On IV Corps' right-hand was 51st (Highland) Division. Its attacking brigades, 153rd and 152nd, were to work with 'D' and 'E' Tank Battalions respectively. In front of both brigades worked the wire-crushing 'Rovers' well in advance of the 'fighting' tanks. Following these came the infantry. Paths through the wire were cleared easily enough but, next to 62nd Division, tanks with 153rd Brigade encountered an exceptional problem. Here the front trench was wider and deeper than elsewhere. Four tanks became stuck and several others ditched or broke down. Three somewhat puzzlingly withdrew because of a shortage of supplies. The infantry, however, falling back on their own resources and tactical training, took the trench and overcame various points of resistance in the support line, capturing in the process over 600 prisoners. The two battalions themselves sustained less than 120 casualties.

During the early advance, the Flesquières Ridge was subjected to the attentions of both the RFC and the Royal Artillery, as William Watson witnessed:

Beyond the enemy trenches the slopes, from which the German gunners might have observed the advancing tanks, were already enveloped in thick white smoke. The smoke-shells burst with a sheet of vivid red flame, pouring out blinding, suffocating clouds. It was as if flaring bonfires were burning behind a bank of white fog. Over all, innumerable aeroplanes were flying steadily to and fro.[79]

Major William Watson, No. 11 Company, 'D' Battalion, Tank Corps

Watson, following his tank company forward, witnessed the infantrymen's delight at their success in a captured regimental headquarters; scene of some hard fighting:

The trench-boards were slippery with blood, and fifteen to twenty corpses, all Germans and all bayoneted, lay strewn about the road like

* Actually the tank's unditching beam.

141

drunken men. A Highland sergeant who, with a handful of men, was now in charge of the place, came out to greet us puffing at a long cigar. It was indeed difficult that morning to find a Highlander without a cigar. He invited us into a large chamber cut out of the rock, from which a wide staircase descended into an enormous dugout. The chamber was panelled deliciously with coloured woods and decorated with choice prints. Our host produced a bottle of good claret, and we drank to the health of the 51st Division.[80]

Major William Watson, No. 11 Company, 'D' Battalion, Tank Corps

Meanwhile, champing at the bit to get on was Douglas Wimberley with his Vickers machine-guns:

We impatiently waited for a word that the Support Line had been taken. It was getting lighter every minute and we could see the third wave of 'kilts' leaving the front line. I knew that they would not go forward so soon unless all was well, and so, without waiting, we moved forward with all sixteen guns.[81]

Major Douglas Wimberley, 232nd Company, MGC, 51st Division

Indeed, the contrast to the Flanders offensive was remarkable:

When we got to the front line, we were met by Webb with a broad smile, which told us at once that all was well, we pushed over for a little tiny copse of stunted trees which marked the line over the crest which was to lead us to our predetermined barrage position by a trench called, on British maps, 'Unseen Support'. We moved slowly across the eight hundred yards of No Man's Land with the heavily burdened men, but everyone was all smiles. We could see on our right a Company Headquarters, of the 5th Seaforths, moving forward and, but for a few little tired, inoffensive, pip-squeaks from some German guns a long way off, and an isolated MG, all was quiet. What a difference from our experience two months before at Ypres! In fact, for about half an hour, it was almost like a field day at home.[82]

Major Douglas Wimberley, 232nd Company, MGC, 51st Division

Waiting as part of the 1/5th Seaforth's reserve company was the very un-Scottish 'Jock', Stan Bradbury:

In the semi-darkness the country in front which dipped down into a valley known as 'The Ravine' and then rose up towards a high ridge known as Flesquières Ridge, was lit by the bursting shells and the flares of the enemy's guns, the tanks and the men being silhouetted against the fiery light. A more beautiful, yet terrible and impressive, sight could not be portrayed by the greatest artist living. It was the sight of a lifetime and never to be forgotten.[83]

Private Stan Bradbury, 1/5th Seaforth Highlanders, 152nd Brigade, 51st Division

As dawn came, the attack's success became clear.

It was really a marvellous sight. We could see the tanks going down the slope towards the Grand Ravine in front of us, and we could see the lines of Jocks going down with them. We could see a certain number of Germans running about, who had obviously decided to trust to their legs rather than remain in the deep dugouts where they would have probably met the Mills Bombs of the Jocks coming along.[84]

Major Douglas Wimberley, 232nd Company, MGC, 51st Division

Although 152nd Brigade's other assault battalion, 1/8th Argyll and Sutherland Highlanders, had a fight overcoming some strongpoints, Stan Bradbury's battalion encountered little opposition:

I assisted the signallers in their work and took and received messages from those who had gone along with the first wave of troops until our turn came to leave the trench and go forward, which we did immediately the enemy's front line had been consolidated. On the way we passed scores of prisoners making their way towards our lines. Practically the whole of the enemy's troops occupying the line had been taken by surprise and captured in their dugouts without having any chance of showing resistance.[85]

Private Stan Bradbury, 1/5th Seaforth Highlanders, 152nd Brigade, 51st Division

Those captured included the headquarters staff of a German battalion. This was the remarkable achievement of Lance Corporal Robert McBeath, assisted by a tank. McBeath, who had already tackled a machine-gun single handedly, was subsequently awarded the Victoria Cross. Clearly, cooperation between the Highland battalions and the tanks was good at this stage:

As the light grew we could see our first line forging ahead. To us it looked as if the enemy's surprise was complete. We could even see the

Highlanders signalling the tanks on at crossing points of trenches and other obstacles.[86]

Second Lieutenant Wilfrid Bion, E40 'Edward II', No. 14 Company, 'E' Battalion, Tank Corps

Bion, too, noted the unreality of the day's events so far:

The battlefield was set out like a diagram; the functions of infantry, gunners and tanks slotted together with such perfection that it seemed as if we were more pieces of a Staff Officer's dream than soldiers at war. Small pockets of German prisoners were being marched back, filled more with curiosity than fear as the spectacle unrolled before them. It was as if the British Army had decided to have a mock field day on territory already in use by enemy troops. They seemed awfully decent about it and indeed quite keen to watch what we were doing.[87]

Second Lieutenant Wilfrid Bion, E40 'Edward II', No. 14 Company, 'E' Battalion, Tank Corps

Tank crews and infantry both had a great surprise at the Grand Ravine:

Everybody thought it was going to be an obstacle. We had to have a halt there for forty minutes in order not to run into our own barrage. It turned out to be a trickle of water, not a complete stop. And the Germans all packed up. There was breakfast in some of the dugouts, and the rest of the Germans were sent running back.[88]

Second Lieutenant Horace Birks, D27 'Double Dee III', No. 11 Company, 'D' Battalion, Tank Corps

This pause was to have important consequences but for those who had reached the Grand Ravine it was merely a temporary pause before the final assault on the Flesquières Ridge.

As III Corps' advance on the second objective commenced, it was time for Robert Ross to lead his command forward. Supplied with 16 miles of cable, 4 miles to be carried by each of 4 mules, his task was to establish a forward report station in a captured German post. Messages could then be sent back up the command chain. But 20 November 1917 was not a day Ross would recall fondly:

I never passed through so much scrap iron in all my life. Yards and yards, thick, ugly, terribly rusted, long, barbed. Tanks had rolled it flat into the soft soil, completely hidden in places by the matted growth of weeds. Easily negotiable by men. But I had men and mules, four-legged raving lunatics. As soon as we reached this wire, these mules seemed to sprout dozens of pairs of legs to which were attached the most ticklish tender feet that ever animal had. Tread ever so lightly and before a yard had been traversed they would each be in the most terrible tangle. The flattened wire seemed to writhe in devilish glee round their limbs – the more they kicked, the more hopelessly they became entwined – like a swimmer caught in reeds.[89]

Lieutenant Robert Ross, RE Signal Service, III Corps

Worse was to follow:

The ingenious carriers for the wire, devised by a Staff Officer, (doubt-lessly awarded the MC for the idea), functioned so capitally that No. 1 mule soon unburdened himself of his 4 miles, carrier and all, and thus enlightened dashed straight for England, home and beauty – back to Gouzeaucourt. No. 2's cable drum shifted – one became perched on top of his back while the other swung affectionately under his belly. A mule's solution to all troubles is kick – and kick again. The result: a pioneer wending his way, happily perhaps, to a dressing station with a fractured forearm. He was well out of the mess.[90]

Lieutenant Robert Ross, RE Signal Service, III Corps

Pluckily persevering, at the Hindenburg Line Ross somewhat am-bitiously attempted to get his recalcitrant carriers across the trench using a fascine as a bridge:

With a feeling of an Alexander, I lightly sprang across this famous defence line and hoped that all would follow. I had not reckoned with my mulish companions. Cajoling, swearing, beating, tugging – nothing would move these fiends incarnate. One we bodily pushed onto the fascine. Even so he beat us; gently rolled over sideways – feet up, fixed firmly in the Hindenburg Line. No. 4, after repeated refusals, backed through the wire which this time allowed him a free passage – so I ordered the muleteer 'Take the damned beast back'. The other – in the trench – we had to shoot. So forward once again with the whole day wasted – carrying as much of the wire as humanly possible to our destination – the old German signal station, which . . . we never found.[91]

Lieutenant Robert Ross, RE Signal Service, III Corps

Once again, in III Corps' advance, it was the fortified farms that had escaped severe punishment by the artillery that offered the most determined resistance. On Bonavis Ridge, Pam-Pam Farm proved tough. The strongpoint required the attention of ten tanks and the defenders only surrendered when the buildings caught fire. By contrast, Bonavis Farm, specifically targeted by a 15-inch howitzer during the first hour of the attack, was easily captured – a good indication of how important the artillery's contribution was to the day's success.

That the Germans were not completely cowed by the British attack was demonstrated at Le Quennet farm where men from 6th Royal West Kents attempting to occupy the position were either killed or captured. The defenders subsequently made a skilful withdrawal, taking their prisoners with them. The West Kents then became involved in the fight for Lateau Wood, where they succeeded in capturing a battery of 150 mm (5.9-inch) guns, (probably those previously bombed by Arthur Gould Lee and 46 Squadron), but in doing so they suffered several casualties and lost their commanding officer, Major William Alderman, who was mortally wounded.[92]

On 20th Division's front, the tanks pushed on through the German defences. Despite the attack's success so far, Jake Wilson was still able to spare a thought for the defenders:

Having flattened out the wire of the two front line trenches, which enabled the infantry to amble peacefully along, some of them enjoying a 'gasper', we made for what was considered by the enemy the impregnable Hindenburg Line.

The isolated machine-gun nests that were left behind to impede our progress were easily disposed of by our six-pounders. I remember thinking to myself that these men were much too brave to die like that.[93]

Captain 'Jake' Wilson, No. 26 Company, 'I' Battalion, Tank Corps

However, events took a sudden and dramatic turn. As the tanks advanced down the north-eastern slope of Welsh Ridge, they were totally exposed to German observation:

With hindsight, it is fairly obvious that the tanks having penetrated so far should have halted this side of the ridge, but our sights were on Cambrai. Without putting out feelers in the way of scouts and a 'recce', we went blithely and rather blindly on with the unhappy result that quite a number of tanks sustained direct hits from a battery, direct laying in the valley below. We were unlucky in getting two in as many minutes; the first smashed the left track causing us to swing to the right to receive a broadside from the second.[94]

Captain 'Jake' Wilson, No. 26 Company, 'I' Battalion, Tank Corps

George Parsons also recalled the sudden and unexpected shock as the tank was hit by artillery fire:

I remember seeing some 30 people in a sunken road or cutting (it may have been their support line) at some 400 yards range. We swung the tank 90° left and opened machine-gun fire on them until they disappeared. I saw two Germans ahead of us with a tripod machine-gun but they vanished before we could open fire. Then we were hit. The first shell hit the fascine and left track and I remember the acrid cordite smell. I tried to move the tank, but we were without traction. Then the second shell hit us on the left side and that was it. I got out and tried to hide in a very shallow shell hole, but abandoned that for a nearby trench, and in that got back some 200 yards to our advancing infantry.[95]

Second Lieutenant George Parsons, Tank 135, No. 26 Company, 'I' Battalion, Tank Corps

Wilson also managed to get clear of the tank:

Badly wounded in the face, I succeeded in crawling into a shell hole and plastering my field dressing on the wound, fortifying myself with a swig of rum from my water bottle. I remember nothing more until finding myself in a field dressing station well behind the line. Some years after, my friend showed me a letter he had received from a tank commander who had seen me on a stretcher on the way back, in which he said 'I have just seen your old friend JK being carried down on a stretcher. I am afraid you will not see him again.' Which only goes to show that things are not always what they appear to be. Even a small wound can look pretty ghastly until the mud and the blood have been cleaned away . . . [96]

Captain 'Jake' Wilson, No. 26 Company, 'I' Battalion, Tank Corps

Parsons was luckier:

I met Sergeant Marsh, who had a broken arm. From him I first heard [Wilson] had been badly wounded. All I got was a painful scratch in the flesh above my knee – really nothing. I returned with the slowly advancing infantry to my tank and stayed with it . . . The tank was smouldering – the camouflage net was on fire – I'm a bit vague after this, but I remember meeting the MO who took me to his dugout near Villers Plouich, gave me a drink, cleaned my scratch and let me sleep.[97]

Second Lieutenant George Parsons, Tank 135, No. 26 Company, 'I' Battalion, Tank Corps

There was a similar experience for the tanks of 'A' Battalion. The advance to the crest of Welsh Ridge had been largely concealed from German observation. It was quite a different matter when the tanks began to move down the north-east slopes where some German batteries had escaped the British barrage. Kenneth Wootton having resumed his place at the front of 'Apollyon II' led his section across more trenches:

We had to cross one very deep and wide trench and made ready to lower the fascine into it but the driver had spotted a small flag stuck into the top of this trench and had driven for it. We found it was marking the spot where a tank had already dropped its fascine and so we rode out over that one and kept ours in its position. We resumed our position in line with the others and after assuring myself that we were now well up, by looking through the portholes on the left and right, I once more pushed a Lewis gun through the ball-mounting in front of me.[98]

Lieutenant Kenneth Wootton, A29 'Apollyon II', No. 2 Company, 'A' Battalion, Tank Corps

Much to the discomfort of Private George Fagg at his side, Wootton fired blindly:

I fired at anything I could see that looked like a target, any rise in the ground, trench, bush, anything that might shelter someone and I dropped most of the empty drums out of the flap in front. By now the inside of the tank was terribly hot, caused by the engine chiefly and the air was heavy and close and caught your throat when you breathed; this, owing to the back-blast of the two guns and the ejector of the machine-gun and the noise was appalling. The driver had the worst of it, as the Lewis gun ejected its empty cartridge cases a few inches from his left ear. Poor Fagg was worried by this a great deal as I could see by his expression every time I put on a fresh drum.[99]

Lieutenant Kenneth Wootton, A29 'Apollyon II', No. 2 Company, 'A' Battalion, Tank Corps

As they approached what was clearly a German battery position, Wootton saw the guns had been pulled out of their emplacements in an attempt to get them away before the tanks came upon them. No doubt a few had been saved, but the advance had been too swift and surprising for most, and these were captured.

I saw one gun, with a few men by it, not far away from us and turned the machine-gun on them. My six-pounder gunner on the right side had also seen it. I remember seeing the burst of his shell a short distance behind them . . . Evidently my machine-gun and the six-pounder were too much for them, as they bolted off almost at once without apparently any of them being hit . . . I should say the six-pounder was the thing that terrified them most, as it was firing at a point-blank range, just suitable for it. Johns was the gunner on that side. He was a deadly shot – having put a shell into the opening of a pill box at Ypres – and was probably dead on target. So that gun was captured. It was annoying not to be able to actually get it ourselves, but we couldn't stop, so had to leave it for others.[100]

Lieutenant Kenneth Wootton, A29 'Apollyon II', No. 2 Company, 'A' Battalion, Tank Corps

However, the German artillery, the chief tank-killer of the Great War, was about to have its revenge.

Soon after we came almost face to face with at least four more guns, also in the open. All pointing in our direction. I remember noticing that some of the guns were unmanned, but one, at any rate, was still working. Whether I had time to fire at it I do not remember but they fired at me, just point blank and the shell struck us in front just where I was sitting and, bursting as it hit, blew a hole in the armour-plating by my left knee.[101]

Lieutenant Kenneth Wootton, A29 'Apollyon II', No. 2 Company, 'A' Battalion, Tank Corps

Wootton's was one of three tanks knocked out here.

The first thing that made me realise we had been hit was 'coming to' finding myself lying back over my seat with my head nearly on the floor and my left foot caught in something so that I couldn't move it. With the help of Fagg, I got into a sitting position and freed my foot, which was caught under the brake lever. I felt no pain of any sort, being dazed and numb all over, with a tremendous sort of singing noise in both ears and some blood running into my left eye, which I wiped with my hand now and then. I slid back off the seat and sank to the floor having no use in my legs or arms, but still feeling nothing.[102]

Lieutenant Kenneth Wootton, A29 'Apollyon II', No. 2 Company, 'A' Battalion, Tank Corps

The tank had been very badly damaged: the right six-pounder was knocked off its mounting, the engine smashed and the front was almost blown in. Incredibly, the rest of the crew were able to evacuate the tank, but Wootton realized there was one other casualty: 'The pigeon that was in a box by my feet must have been blown to pieces by the first shell.'[103]

Wootton was dragged from the tank by two of his crew and all three lay behind the tank's rear. But, knowing that if the German gun continued firing, a shell would probably come through and burst amongst them, Wootton ordered the crew to scatter and find shelter elsewhere. Together with Fagg, he finally found a British tank and Wootton was pushed inside.

It was about full up. This tank was returning from the attack, having had its driver blinded, most of its crew wounded and was picking up any other wounded tank people it could find. [Captain JP] Thompson, an officer of our company, was lying the other side with a bad head wound and quite a number of other cases were packed away wherever they could find room.[104]

Lieutenant Kenneth Wootton, A29 'Apollyon II', No. 2 Company, 'A' Battalion, Tank Corps

From this 'ambulance', Wootton travelled by stretcher to a dressing station and then in a motor ambulance to a casualty clearing station.

Field guns were not the only means by which the Germans tackled the tanks. The German 76 mm mortar had a flat-trajectory mounting specifically designed for use against tanks. One such weapon accounted for A2 'Abou-ben-Adam', commanded by Lieutenant Christopher Duncan, which was hit at a range of less than 60 yards whilst attempting to assist a company from 12th Rifle Brigade held up by a German machine-gun post. Duncan was killed. Captain Richard Wain, the section commander, had been travelling in A2. Despite being wounded, he tackled the strongpoint on foot, initially with a Lewis gun from the tank.

> Captain Wain and Stower made a dash for the trench which was nearer their door. Roberts and I left by the opposite door and were fired on by a German rifleman at point blank range. Fortunately he was a poor shot and we made the trench. Our only weapons were revolvers carried by Captain Wain, Roberts and myself. Captain Wain got on the parados and threw German 'tater-masher' bombs into the long grass.[105]
>
> Private Joseph Mossman, A2 'Abou-ben-Adam', No. I Company, 'A' Battalion, Tank Corps

Rifleman Walter Wilkinson saw some of what followed from a nearby trench.

> I was in line with the tank, a few yards to its left, and personally saw it hit. Captain Wain did not immediately leave the tank, but did so some little time later. In the meantime, there were only two other riflemen on my left. The three of us made for the trench.
>
> Almost immediately German stick bombs came falling on the trench, so we got out on the top. We had a few rifle grenades. We luckily dropped one dead in the trench. As soon as we heard the explosion we rushed into the trench. On seeing us, the enemy held up their hands and surrendered. There must have been about 20 or so of

them. Other riflemen began to come into the trench, and it was to these men we handed over the prisoners.[106]

Rifleman Walter Wilkinson, 12th Rifle Brigade, 60th Brigade, 20th Division

Mossman and Wilkinson disagree over what happened next:

It was roughly 5 minutes after the prisoners had gone that I chanced to look back at the disabled tank. As I did so, Captain Wain, with his tunic torn away at the front, his chest covered in blood, and in a pretty bad way, jumped into the trench by my side and shouted, 'Give me a bloody rifle!' That's all he said. I saw him snatch a rifle, put it to his shoulder, fire 2 rounds, and was himself shot dead in the head. He dropped, a lifeless corpse, by my side.[107]

Rifleman Walter Wilkinson, 12th Rifle Brigade, 60th Brigade, 20th Division

Mossman, on the other hand, records:

After a few minutes Wain was killed by an explosive bullet in the head and fell into the trench. Roberts and I turned round a German machine-gun and fired it into the long grass until the belt ran out. We had no further trouble.[108]

Private Joseph Mossman, A2 'Abou-ben-Adam', No. 1 Company, 'A' Battalion, Tank Corps

Whatever the precise circumstances of his death, Wain's actions earned him the posthumous award of the Tank Corps' second Victoria Cross.

Other tank battalions also encountered problems at the Hindenburg Support Line, as Edward Leigh-Jones found:

My section commander had engine trouble and stopped. As he was to go over first and I was to follow him, drop my fascine on the second [trench] and then Dickens [in B6 'Boadicea'] was supposed to go to the third one, we were in rather a jam. So I went over to Haseler's tank [B12 'Bantam'], and shouted through the bottom [of the door] under-neath the Lewis gun sponson that I'd go on, and they said 'Alright'. I hadn't been a minute away before that tank was blown up. Haseler was killed and Corporal Bamford and two or three others.[109]

Second Lieutenant Edward Leigh-Jones, B9 'Black Bess', No. 4 Company, 'B' Battalion, Tank Corps

Captain William Haseler was 25 and a relatively inexperienced tank commander. Corporal Harold Bamford, despite being only 22, was a former Coldstream Guards veteran of Mons who had won the Military Medal: two men with very different war experiences, united in death.

Despite these losses, III Corps secured its first two objectives with comparatively few casualties and with mechanical breakdown being the chief cause of tank 'casualties'. Artillery batteries were being hitched up and rushed forward to new positions in support of the attack, and tanks and infantry were pressing on towards the St Quentin Canal and the two key crossings at Masnières and Marcoing. The first tanks (from 'A' Battalion) reached the canal at Marcoing by 10.50 a.m. Meanwhile, on the extreme right, 12th Division pushed infantry patrols through Banteux, across the canal, and into Bantouzelle without encountering Germans.

To explain IV Corps' fortunes in the second stage of the battle, we should look from north to south towards the attack's centre. West of the dry Canal du Nord, the 36th (Ulster) Division's attack commenced at 8.35 a.m. with the intention of capturing the German trenches as far as the Bapaume–Cambrai Road. The 109th Brigade, operating with-out tank assistance, had waited until 62nd Division on the canal's opposite bank had advanced to a position level with its right. Now, employing an attack formation of several specially selected strong men of large physique – each armed with a Lewis gun slung from a strap over their left shoulder which they were to fire from the right hip as they moved up each trench – the assaulting infantry went forward. The defenders from *20th Landwehr Division*, having already been sub-jected to a barrage of trench mortar fire (that included an especially 'frightful' addition to the British armoury, 'thermit' incendiary bombs), showed little inclination to fight but fled northwards. The captured trenches were cleared systematically, and as each dugout encountered was dealt with by moppers-up, the entrance was marked with a notice inscribed 'Mopped'. By 9.30 a.m. the lead battalion was north of the Demicourt–Flesquières road – the second objective of the attack – and ready to push on.

For 62nd Division, Havrincourt chateau and village still offered considerable opposition. From the roofs and top windows of the houses, snipers fired down on the advancing troops, who dashed into the buildings to end this opposition. One brave but reckless German machine-gunner who had set up his gun in the centre of the village was quickly dealt with but Billy Kirkby and his mates, pressing on, continued to suffer casualties:

> One of my comrades, who had been arguing with the courageous Sergeant to turn back, was hit but much more seriously, a thick pencil-like mark of blood appearing across his face followed by the terrible spurt of blood coming from his wound. Involuntarily, he turned, caught his arm in my rifle sling, gave me a frantic look as though I held him prisoner while his wound destroyed him. I quickly freed him from my deadly hold to see him disappearing rearwards towards the help our stretcher bearers would give him as they followed our advance.[110]
>
> Private Billy Kirkby, 2/6th West Yorkshires, 185th Brigade, 62nd Division

In the midst of the battle, Kirkby then chanced upon his friend, Harry Griss, in a sunken road close to Havrincourt:

> We met face to face, exchanging enquiring and anxious looks quickly expressed in equally anxious tones . . . 'Are you alright, Harry?' He replied, 'Yes, Bill. Are you?' I just had time to answer and he had gone on. We had no sooner come within range of the German's deadly fire than he stumbled forward, his arms flung wide, his rifle flying to the ground, falling there to lie still and silent in death amid my outburst of, 'No, No, not that!' I stood motionless, too horrified by the terribly sudden death of a very great friend, so great was the blow his sudden passing inflicted upon me.[111]
>
> Private Billy Kirkby, 2/6th West Yorkshires, 185th Brigade, 62nd Division

His friend's death provoked a furious response from Kirkby:

> At long last, I snapped into action, my whole being bent upon avenging his death and the deaths and wounds inflicted on my gallant pals. Standing upright I fired round after round through the windowless openings of the houses facing us, my one aim and purpose to destroy the killers within those houses, wanting them to come out and fight in the open, not fire unseen by us.[112]
>
> Private Billy Kirkby, 2/6th West Yorkshires, 185th Brigade, 62nd Division

Resistance in Havrincourt village was finally overcome at about 10.30 a.m.

> We were still losing too many men and were ordered to circle our final goal, Havrincourt, while our tanks made a frontal attack. While we entered the village from the rear, almost without opposition, [the tanks] crushed the enemy into complete surrender as they made their successful attack. But for these wonderful new weapons of war, our losses as we sought to capture Havrincourt could have been staggering. As it was, we found the German defenders lined up in the centre of the village – a tank standing by – the prisoners ready to move off into captivity.[113]
>
> Private Billy Kirkby, 2/6th West Yorkshires, 185th Brigade, 62nd Division

For Kirkby, all his hopes and expectations of tanks had been fulfilled. Havrincourt had fallen and German resistance had crumbled. Casualties in 187th Brigade in particular were remarkably low. In Havrincourt Wood an American engineer officer witnessed some of 62nd Division's prisoners – men from the *384th Landwehr Regiment* – being brought back to the 'cages'.

> There came down the road, marching westward, a little procession of perhaps fifty figures in field-grey uniforms, the first prisoners, mute but satisfactory evidence that the enemy lines had been reached. Their faces made a curious study. There was a mixture of all sorts, from quite young boys to men of thirty-five. Some sullen, some just stupid looking, others rather interested in their new surroundings, while some were unmistakably nervous as to what might be in store, in striking contra-diction to those who were evidently not displeased to realize that the war, at least in active fighting, was for them at an end.[114]
>
> Major William Barclay Parsons, 11th Engineer Regiment (Railway), American Expeditionary Force (AEF)

In 51st Division's attack, both tanks and infantry had paused as planned at the Grand Ravine to allow the attackers to reorganize, for reserves to come forward and for tanks to be replenished and refuelled before the advance on Flesquières Ridge and village. Horace Birks recalled that 'crews dismounted, engines were switched off and tanks aired'.[115] Meanwhile, the machine-guns of companies like Douglas

Wimberley's got into position. Facing similar problems to Robert Ross in getting laden mules through the wire and trenches, Wimberley had a more pragmatic response, inveigling German prisoners into the work of clearing gaps in the barbed wire.

By means of a few signs they set to work with a will. In their eagerness at pulling away the knife-rests they cut their hands to ribbons – they needed no encouragement, if one's hand strayed anywhere near a revolver holster you could see them perform prodigies of labour – I fancy that they had seen a few of their comrades bayoneted or shot minutes previously.

In a few minutes a clear path was cut. They were a miserable lot of men, unshaven of course, but so were we, but dirty, consumptive and small, or grossly fat, some of them very young, but most middle-aged men with the cartoonist spectacles. They were a Landsturm* division of 'duds', poor devils; had never seen fighting on the Western front and they had been on the Eastern front in a very quiet sector. What a shock they must have had to see lines of great armoured tanks followed by the bayonets of the Jocks.[116]

Major Douglas Wimberley, 232nd Company, MGC, 51st Division

When the advance recommenced, the railway line part-way up the slope of the Flesquières Ridge was reached by the division's right flank at 9.30 a.m. and by the left at 9.45 a.m. Stan Bradbury witnessed the final stages of his battalion's progress:

Our troops had practically reached their objective which was the railway line running west of Flesquières. On the way a German field kitchen was captured, the cook killed, and the soup in the dixies soon devoured.[117]

Private Stan Bradbury, 1/5th Seaforth Highlanders, 152nd Brigade, 51st Division

Soon afterwards, 152nd Brigade's support battalions were crossing the railway line, just as 153rd Brigade began to arrive there. The supporting tanks of 'E' Battalion, now resupplied, were able to lead on. The battalion's losses in the advance to this point had been so few that

* Actually, Landwehr.

the remaining tanks moved closely together; six from No. 15 Company actually advanced in single file up a sunken lane.

Although slow-moving, the tanks steadily climbed the slope to Flesquières and actually began to pull away from the following infantry who had already advanced, in full combat order, over 2 miles. As the tanks began to reach the crest, they were perhaps 150 yards in front of the infantry. At this point, they were engaged by the artillery of the defending *54th Division*, including *Feld Artillerie Regiment 108*, which had previously faced French tanks on the Chemin des Dames in May 1917 and had subsequently received anti-tank training.

Some guns had survived the attacks by aircraft and the artillery barrage, which 'jumped' on at 9.25 a.m. Although a smokescreen had shielded the initial advance from German observers on the ridge, this had now dispersed. The tanks' advance was clearly visible. An anonymous German artillery officer described the action:

> When the attack began, we suffered heavy artillery fire. The enemy
> knew our position well. Soon after 9.00 we got to know that the English
> were advancing on Flesquières with many tanks. The only usable gun
> was the one on the left. We drew it into the open, and had to support a
> defective wheel with some beams. A little later the tank monsters came
> creeping to the ridge south of the village . . . We shot directly and
> disabled the leading tank with a few shells at a distance of about 950
> metres. Every time, when a tank crept over the crest, the Unteroffizier
> shouted: 'Leutnant, there's one coming . . . Let's give him it!' and he
> pointed the gun. Together with *2.Batterie Feld Artillerie Regiment 108* we
> put six tanks out of action, and we accounted for no less than three of
> them. At 11 o'clock the shooting-match was finished. We were still
> waiting, but we had only a few shells left.[118]

Anonymous Leutnant, *Feld Artillerie Regiment 108, 54th Division*

Amongst those hit were some of the six tanks from No. 15 Company. These, seeing a line of trees to their front, had veered half-right to avoid them. (Once again the knowledge of the damage that trees could do to tanks was clearly uppermost in the crews' minds.) As a consequence, they presented excellent targets for the gunners and were quickly destroyed. Seven tanks of the battalion's first wave were destroyed in this way. Meanwhile, the second wave, including Wilfrid

Bion's 'Edward II', moved into contact with the German defenders. As machine-gun bullets hammered on the tank's armour, Bion determined to tackle their source:

> Feeling my face pouring with a greasy sweat I put up my hand to wipe it away. Allen looked white-faced and scared as I saw him looking at me. I noticed that my hands were covered with blood. Another wipe with my hands showed me why; my face was streaming with blood. 'His gory visage down the stream sent.' The words repeated themselves in my mind monotonously, rhythmically, like 'Around the rugged rocks the ragged rascal ran.'[119]
>
> Second Lieutenant Wilfrid Bion, E40 'Edward II', No. 14 Company, 'E' Battalion, Tank Corps

Yet the tank went on, until suddenly, an explosion rocked the rear and Bion and his crew were forced to evacuate. The tank had a hole where the right rear driving mechanism had been; it was out of action, but fortunately the ninety gallons of petrol in the tank had not exploded. Outside the tank,

> we were under fire, but I had not the slightest idea where the bullets were coming from. They were in fact converging on us from all directions. I told O'Toole to take charge in the trench while I tried to deal with our tormentors.
>
> Taking four drums of Lewis gun ammunition attached to my waist and a Lewis gun, I clambered clumsily onto the top of the tank and set up my gun under cover, as I thought, of the fascine . . . I was not aware of any danger and therefore experienced none of the fear which might have served as a substitute for my common sense which was wholly lacking. I commanded a good view of the little copse behind the wall, this I proceeded methodically to spray. I soon exhausted almost the whole of my four drums of ammunition.
>
> By this time my escapade had stirred up a veritable hornets' nest in the copse . . . I was surprised to find German troops, led by an officer, pouring out of a gap in the left distant corner of the wall. An officer pointed his swagger stick to direct his troops to me. I swung round and opened fire on them as they were coming through the gap. At the same moment my gun jammed.

I saw it was a simple stoppage, could not clear it, and realizing that my drum had no more ammunition left fell rather than scrambled back into the shelter of the trench.[120]

Second Lieutenant Wilfrid Bion, E40 'Edward II', No. 14 Company, 'E' Battalion, Tank Corps

What followed was a series of short, mad rushes by Bion and his two remaining unwounded crew members to a trench occupied by infantry from the 1/6th Seaforths, who had now caught up with the tanks.

I reported to the Seaforth captain, Edwards, who appeared to be the only officer left in his company. While I was talking to him in the trench there was the loud crack of a near bullet. He fell forward and I saw blood and brains bulge out at the back of his skull. I was too stunned to know where or how the bullet was fired; it might have been chance but the infantry had no doubt it was aimed fire.[121]

Second Lieutenant Wilfrid Bion, E40 'Edward II', No. 14 Company, 'E' Battalion, Tank Corps

Concluding that this shot must have come from the copse, the infantry and tank men turned their fire on the suspected target.

Under the intense fire, a body detached itself, caught in some branches, hung for an instant and crashed onto lower branches, was again halted and finally dashed to the ground. The Lewis guns continued their chattering search of all tree-tops in the radius of our segment, but there was no further result. The Highlander senior NCO reported to me that there were no officers left. Would I therefore take command of the infantry? As I knew nothing of infantry fighting I asked him to stay near and advise me on my new duties.[122]

Second Lieutenant Wilfrid Bion, E40 'Edward II', No. 14 Company, 'E' Battalion, Tank Corps

'Edward II' was one of a further nine tanks from 'E' Battalion put out of action east of Flesquières. In total, 28 of the battalion's tanks had been disabled, ditched or had broken down.

To the west of the village, 'D' Battalion fared little better. As already mentioned, 'D' Battalion had paused at the Grand Ravine for forty minutes. Horace Birks was clear that this was where their problems had started:

> That halt had a most profound effect, at any rate on my company, [it] just gave them [the Germans] forty minutes to pull themselves together. We went on after that – having collected my crew who had all got out for a smoke – up to Flesquières.[123]
>
> Second Lieutenant Horace Birks, D27 'Double Dee III', No. 11 Company, 'D' Battalion, Tank Corps

Birks was sure the blame for what followed lay with 51st Division's infantry:

> It was all right up to the Grand Ravine. But after that they didn't seem to come on at all. I don't think they thought they'd get beyond the Grand Ravine. They wouldn't admit that, of course.[124]
>
> Second Lieutenant Horace Birks, D27 'Double Dee III', No. 11 Company, 'D' Battalion, Tank Corps

At the Hindenburg Support Line, the tanks were attacked by a combination of artillery and infantry, the latter using hand-grenades and armour-piercing ammunition. Ten tanks in total were lost. Birks' 'Double Dee III' was, fortunately, not one of them but still received a great deal of punishment.

> The machine-gun fire, the armour-piercing stuff from the Germans, was so intense that my front visor was cut in half. It was hanging like that, all machine-gun sprayed and completely out of action.[125]
>
> Second Lieutenant Horace Birks, D27 'Double Dee III', No. 11 Company, 'D' Battalion, Tank Corps

Nevertheless, Birks continued his efforts to deal with the German resistance around the wood outside Flesquières, but felt that without infantry support, the task was futile:

> We prowled up and down, up and down the wood, the infantry being left behind. They hadn't come on. I think they were as astonished as everybody.
>
> By that time I was getting short of petrol. And I'd been hit by 'splash' in the back. I had six crew hit altogether. And so I started to go

back. I ran into – the commanding officer – Colonel Kyngdon. He told me to go back to Trescault. And that was the end of [my] Cambrai.[126]

Second Lieutenant Horace Birks, D27 'Double Dee III', No. 11 Company, 'D' Battalion, Tank Corps.

Captain William Watson learned of the hold-up when he encountered two section commanders, Captain W.A. Wyatt and the wounded Lieutenant David Morris (Horace Birks' commander), as he trailed in his company's wake:

They told me that we were held up outside Flesquières, which was being cleverly defended by field-guns. Several tanks had already been knocked out and others had nearly finished their petrol.

We took to a narrow half-completed communication trench and pushed on up the hill towards the village, meeting the survivors of two crews of another battalion, whose tanks had been knocked out in endeavouring to enter Flesquières from the east along the crest of the ridge. The trench was being shelled. From the sound of the guns it appeared that they were only a few hundred yards away. We walked steadily up the trench until we came to the railway embankment, five or six hundred yards from the outskirts of the village, and we could go no farther, for on the other side of the embankment were the enemy and some of my tanks.[127]

Major William Watson, No. 11 Company, 'D' Battalion, Tank Corps

Recognizing the need to report the hold-up, Watson began to make his way back on foot two miles to the nearest infantry battalion headquarters.

In fact, the problem was not lack of infantry support for the tanks. Indeed, some of 153rd Brigade had managed to push into Flesquières itself, before being forced to withdraw. One tank, D51 'Deborah', commanded by Second Lieutenant Frank Heap, passed right through the village, but the infantry could not follow because of heavy fire and D51 was knocked out by five direct hits from a battery of field guns. Four of its crew were killed.[128] The problem was the lack of coordination between attacks by the tanks and infantry. However, with Watson's two fellow tank company commanders killed or captured, battlefield control had clearly broken down.

Almost as soon as the fighting on Flesquières Ridge had ended, a rumour circulated that a particularly resolute German major (or NCO – the rank varied) had continued to serve his gun right up until the moment he was killed, and was thereby principally responsible for the heavy losses suffered by 'E' and 'D' Tank Battalions there. Clearly, this was not the case. It was not solely the determined action of a single German artilleryman, but could conceivably be regarded as the inevitable consequence of the unusual combination of circumstances the tanks and 51st Division encountered on Flesquières Ridge. Certainly, too many German guns had survived the attentions of the jumping barrage or were sited beyond effective field artillery range, but many other factors played their part.

As word of the delay at Flesquières filtered back up the command chain, it was apparent that what had been potentially the most difficult position in the Hindenburg Support Line to capture was proving exactly that. The extent of the set-back was not yet known, but critical to the success of the attack now was the speed with which a response to the check at Flesquières could be organized. Since news of the (unexpectedly good) progress made elsewhere was being received, however, British commanders already had some justification for assuming that German resistance might begin to crumble here as the increasingly isolated defenders' will to continue the fight diminished accordingly.

Nevertheless, at 11.00 a.m., despite a hugely successful beginning, the outcome of the battle already hung in the balance. As tanks approached Marcoing and Masnières and the canal crossings on the right, and pressed on towards Graincourt and Bourlon Wood on the left, and as the cavalry and horse artillery were being hurried forward, the time was ripe for bold and determined action. It remained to be seen whether Third Army could capitalize to the full on its initial success.

CHAPTER SIX

'Unravelling'

AT 11.00 A.M. on that dank November morning, three years of technological and tactical innovation had brought the BEF to the brink of its most significant success in the war so far. The return of tactical surprise to the battlefield in the form of the devastating predicted barrage had been achieved through developments in artillery techniques, the RFC's diligent photographic reconnaissance and the work of the RE Field Survey Companies. The surveyors, flash-spotters and sound rangers of 3rd Field Survey Company were surely amazed by the magnitude of what they had accomplished.

In order to maintain the momentum of the attack, units of all types were now hurrying forwards in the wake of the tank and infantry advance. Most obvious to the infantry was the movement of the field and horse artillery:

> We saw several gun and ammunition columns come galloping around the hill across the other side of the valley and get under the shelter of the hill where they unlimbered and immediately opened fire again. Meanwhile the ammunition columns dumped their loads and went back for more. It was a fine sight seeing the horses racing along with the guns and it was extraordinary to watch shell after shell from the enemy just not [sic] bursting in the middle of one of the columns.[1]
> Second Lieutenant George McMurtrie, 7th Somerset Light Infantry, 61st Brigade, 20th Division

There was considerable activity further back as well. Since 8.25 a.m. 1st Cavalry Division had been on the move from Fins towards Trescault, led by 2nd Cavalry Brigade. At 10.15 a.m., bugles sounding in the British assembly trenches between Gonnelieu and Beaucamp had signalled the advance of all three brigades of 29th Division from reserve. It was a stirring scene.

> They marched, three brigades in line, each battalion in fours. I cannot describe what a wonderful sight it was. The only thing missing was a band in front of each battalion. We cheered.[2]
>
> Captain Geoffrey Dugdale, Headquarters, 60th Brigade, 20th Division

Their objectives were the canal crossings at Masnières and Marcoing.

At 11.35 a.m., 2nd Cavalry Brigade received a message from IV Corps (under whose orders 1st Cavalry Division – the brigade's parent unit – now operated) stating that Flesquières had fallen, that the road from Trescault to Flesquières was open and that the main road via Ribécourt might also be available. However, although Lieutenant Colonel Prior's 9th Norfolks had reported Ribécourt captured at 9.00 a.m., there had still been sporadic resistance from German snipers. Consequently, when the leading cavalry regiment, 4th Dragoon Guards, came under some of this fire, they halted under cover and sent back for further orders to their brigade commander, Brigadier General Desmond Beale-Browne. This did not suggest the degree of drive and urgency expected of the BEF's exploitation arm. As Beale-Browne received these reports at about 11.55 a.m., he also learned that Flesquières' capture was in doubt and was obliged to send a squadron to ascertain whether this was true. In the meantime, his brigade stopped and waited.

Cavalry in III Corps' area had also started forward. At 11.40 a.m. the Canadian Cavalry Brigade, 5th Cavalry Division's vanguard, which had been waiting since 9.00 a.m., was ordered to begin its advance from behind Gouzeaucourt towards Masnières, keeping in touch with the infantry in front.

> Off we went as fast as we could over the fifteen miles between Fins and Masnières, where we halted in a sunken road, about a mile from Masnières, while a patrol under Lieutenant Harvey VC, went forward to ascertain the conditions of the canal crossings.[3]
>
> Lieutenant Sam Williams, Lord Strathcona's Horse, Canadian Cavalry Brigade, 5th Cavalry Division

By now the advance of the tanks and infantry towards the canal had developed its own momentum. Opposition from German riflemen and machine-gunners was sporadic, poorly organized and generally swiftly overcome. The surviving German artillery was also hampered in its efforts by the terrain:

> Owing to the undulating nature of the country I could not fire with my batteries on the tanks which attacked Marcoing from Villers Plouich. From my group lookout I saw them clearly rolling down the slope into the valley as if they were in a hurry. As my telephone connections were cut I ran with my adjutant to my next battery in order to bring at least one gun into action; but we had our hands full against other objectives, so they reached the village almost unhindered.[4]
>
> Major Lorenzen, Landwehr Artillery, *20th Landwehr Division* (attached *54th Division*)

First to reach the St Quentin Canal were eight tanks from 'A' Battalion in an attempt to take the canal crossings. Second Lieutenant John Bailey, a reconnaissance officer from the battalion, acted swiftly to cut the detonator leads to the mined railway bridge in Marcoing, thereby preventing the Germans from blowing it up. The tank company commander, Major Justice Tilly, subsequently saw Bailey 'crossing the bridge with a French woman hanging round his neck. He had one arm round her which held his revolver and in the other he was waving the leads; they were both laughing and shouting.'[5]

However, the absence of supporting infantry meant Marcoing could not be satisfactorily cleared. Resistance to the tanks continued, whilst German troops still held the eastern end of the railway bridge. Indeed, although 14 more tanks (this time from 'B' Battalion) had reached Marcoing by 11.30 a.m., it seems likely that a further German attempt to blow the bridge at about this time was made. It was foiled by Lieutenant Arthur Dalby and his tank, B23 'Bandit II'. On reaching the village Dalby took his tank along the railway embankment to the bridge where he found a party of Germans running out a wire to the explosive charges. The tank's gunners opened fire, dispersing the party and killing several. Dalby and his crew subsequently used their machine-guns to scatter a group of German infantry preparing to counter-attack the bridge. A section of Royal Engineers, led by Major Basil Wilson, then arrived and the charges were finally removed. Meanwhile, several other bridges and locks, suitable for infantry from 87th Brigade of 29th Division to cross the canal, were also seized and at 12.30 p.m. a total of three infantry companies were formed up at Marcoing station on the canal's far side ready to advance on their final objective. The tanks were ready too:

> We were on our objectives at 12 o'clock, fuelled up, with ammunition, oil and grease, which had been brought along by tanks on sledges. Then we sat down to await further orders and above all to wait for the promised huge reinforcements of infantry and cavalry.[6]
>
> Second Lieutenant Edward Leigh-Jones, B9 'Black Bess', No. 4 Company, 'B' Battalion, Tank Corps

Mark Dillon noted anticipation and a little unease as he arrived at 'B' Battalion's rallying point in Marcoing:

> I found the tanks, having finished, all sitting down having mugs of tea! People were walking all about the countryside, which was open . . . The infantry were just sculling about wondering at having got through so easily. The crews were saying 'it was a piece of cake' and 'where are the cavalry which are supposed to be exploiting our advance?' That was the main theme: where are the cavalry that are supposed to burst through? We were expecting to see them coming through in hordes.[7]
>
> Captain Mark Dillon, 'B' Battalion, Tank Corps

To the tank men at least, the way to the final German defensive line and Cambrai appeared open.

As the infantry from 29th Division crossed the canal at Marcoing station, the first of 12 tanks from 'F' Battalion approached Masnières. They were led on foot by Major Philip Hamond, commander of No. 18 Company, who, upon reaching the Hindenburg Support Line, had gone 'bald-headed over the open for the bridge at Masnières'[8] with little, if any, infantry support.

> I took a man of mine, Roberts, a real rough Musselburgh ship's fireman, and each with a large Boche cigar in our mouths, we walked off to capture the town by ourselves. When we came in the civilians rushed out to welcome us and we were kissed by all and sundry.[9]
>
> Major Philip Hamond, No. 18 Company, 'F' Battalion, Tank Corps

Three tanks, accompanied by about 30 infantry scouts, arrived just after Hamond in Les Rues Vertes on the south side of the canal, immediately opposite Masnières. The first of these was F7 'Feu de Ciel II', closely followed by F27 'Fighting Mac II', and F26 'Fearless II'. Their appearance drew considerable interest from the German infantry across the canal:

> We heard the characteristic noise of tanks on the other bank. Finally, four of them emerged out of the mist, after having passed through Masnières. This was the first time our men, coming from Russia, had seen a tank. The impression was astonishing and almost comic. All stood up and looked at those monsters with the greatest interest, although they were only about 500 yards [450 metres] away and were actually firing.[10]
> Oberstleutnant D. Feuerheerd, III Battalion, *Reserve Infanterie Regiment 227, 107th Division*

The bridge was in two parts; one span across the Escaut river, then a stretch of road over the neck of land, and after that a span of reinforced concrete across the canal itself. Hamond's approach through Les Rues Vertes was quick, but not quick enough.

> It was a most laughable picnic up to then. Unfortunately, just as we came into the village the Boche managed to blow a hole in the bridge. When I got to the bridge there was no one to give a lead at all, so I tried to get some infantry to follow over and seize the houses on the other side. But there was a little sniping which was steadily increasing and I could not get anyone to help me in time. It was a rather bad place as there was only a bit of girder left when I went to see. Only one man could get over at a time and the snipers were within eighty yards of us.[11]
> Major Philip Hamond, No. 18 Company, 'F' Battalion, Tank Corps

Although an attempt had been made to blow the main span, it had not been completely successful. Hamond pondered this setback, whilst more tanks (including F22 'Flying Fox II' and F23 'Foggie II') arrived.

> We had been driving our tank all night up to the line, and fighting all day, when we eventually arrived at Masnières, five or six miles behind the Bosche lines . . . There were one or two 'busses' before us in the village, but we managed to come in for a bit of the mopping up of the

western half thereof. As soon as we had cleared that portion, the villagers came out of their cellars, and fell on our necks (quite a courageous performance considering our greasy state), bringing with them their small stores of liquid refreshment.[12]

Private Alfred Ballard, F22 'Flying Fox II', No. 17 Company, 'F' Battalion, Tank Corps

Despite the setback, Hamond was not prepared to concede the canal crossings yet. First, however, he had to deal with the snipers.

I took a tank up to the gap in the bridge and proceeded to blow the snipers out with 6-pounder shells. We did this with some success and I again tried to get some men to follow me over, but they were all dog-beat and I could not get any of the officers to make a determined effort. By this time they had found two more bridges and were crossing there, but I could not get tanks over either of them.[13]

Major Philip Hamond, No. 18 Company, 'F' Battalion, Tank Corps

Meanwhile, the tanks fired each in turn on targets directed by Hamond until they ran out of ammunition. Hamond, realizing the importance of getting across the canal, determined that F26 'Fearless II' should attempt to cross the bridge. But his plans soon went awry.

The damned tank elected to break down in the full fire of the snipers and machine-gun which by now had come up. Then it ran out of 6-pounder shells so I could not continue firing onto the houses opposite without clearing it out of the way. So I went and got Roberts and we went up to it, got the wire hawser off it, had another tank come up and shackled the two together and pulled it out of the way – but the sniping from [sic] both tanks and in front was fierce. The *pavé* road and the tanks we were working on were in a sheet of sparks. I got one tiny bit in my right leg and had a bullet burst to bits on the tank just as I was stooping to put in the shackle pin. The bits flew all over my face and eyes but I was not hurt.[14]

Major Philip Hamond, No. 18 Company, 'F' Battalion, Tank Corps

So, instead, it was F22 'Flying Fox II', commanded by Second Lieutenant Walter Farrer, that went for the bridge:

We started across, our guns delivering the goods as fast as we could slap the shells into the breaches. I was laying the right gun, and it was great

– houses full of the swine, at about 50 yards range – one couldn't miss. We placed a shell slap into each window of the houses within the traverse of the guns, and knocked the sheds on the canal banks all to blazes. We got safely across the first span and swung to the right, and crawled down the bit of road. The noise inside was terrific, the barking of the 6-pounders and the rattle of the machine-gun, added to the usual roar of the engine and road vibration, which was greatly increased by the fact that we were using 'spuds'* on a cobbled road.[15]

Private Alfred Ballard, F22 'Flying Fox II', No. 17 Company, 'F' Battalion, Tank Corps

Now 'Flying Fox II' approached the main span. Clinging to its sides were a number of bombers from the 11th Rifle Brigade:

Swinging to the right again, we started across – going strong and no one hurt except odd splinters. We had almost got across, when Grruff Crash! – the Bosche blew the far end of the span in, and we dropped smack into the canal. We thought the end of the world had come at least, but had the presence of mind to fling open all exits, and the water started to pour in from all directions, squirting in through the ports etc., like a shower bath, and through the doors in a cataract. The air inside was thick with ammunition boxes and shells which had broken loose from their holders with the shock of landing, and flew about in all directions. Something outside hit the muzzle of my gun, and as the traversing arm was under my armpit, it lifted me up, bringing my head into violent contact with the steel plating of the roof. I was thankful that I was wearing a steel helmet at the time. Luckily, our tail had lodged on some masonry, and so held the rear end of the tank out of the water. I was delayed a few seconds by the tap I had received on the head, and in the meantime the others had 'shot' out of every exit, and jumped and scrambled until they gained the road, down which they 'beat it' in great style, taking care not to bunch. I was not long in following their example and although I never shone at school as a sprinter, I imagine it would have taken a good man to catch me on that occasion, as one Bosche machine-gun in particular was knocking chunks off the road all

* 'Spuds' were metal extensions that could be fitted at intervals along the tank track's length to broaden the track and thereby spread the tank's weight when operating on softer ground.

around, but the bullets were noticeably fewer than when we started to cross.[16]

Private Alfred Ballard, F22 'Flying Fox II', No. 17 Company, 'F' Battalion, Tank Corps

'Flying Fox II' was jammed between the two broken ends of the bridge. The bridge's collapse ended any further prospect of advance with tanks in this sector. At no point in the planning of the operation does any thought appear to have been given to the possibility of such an eventuality occurring. Since no previous occasion on which tanks were used had required the rapid construction of temporary bridges capable of bearing 32 tons, the BEF in general and the Royal Engineers in particular, were not equipped or prepared for such a task. Of course, if cavalry, infantry and guns could still be got across the canal, this might not matter.

There was, therefore, little the tanks could now do – except patrol the canal's southern bank and offer supporting fire whilst others attempted to tackle German opposition in Masnières itself.

We patrolled up and down for an hour or two because the Germans were in houses on the other side of the canal and they were firing and we were trying to keep them down. It was very hot, very stuffy, of course. The smell of oil and the machine-guns . . . we were very glad to get out and get a breath of fresh air . . . Soon after we got there, we got a chance to get out on one side. We were firing across the canal, so if you got on [the other] side of the tank, you were shielded. They'd only got machine-guns there at that time so we were pretty safe, so you could get out for a breather and then get back in again.[17]

Private Eric Potten, F23 'Foggie II', No. 17 Company, 'F' Battalion, Tank Corps

It was now about 12.40 p.m. and the first units of 29th Division had also arrived in Les Rues Vertes. Amongst these was Second Lieutenant Eric Marchant's battalion, 1st Essex, in the village itself and 4th Worcesters. The latter seized a lock to the south of Les Rues Vertes and successfully got two companies of men across. These promptly came under heavy fire and were effectively pinned down, losing their commanding officer.

In Les Rues Vertes, meanwhile, an impromptu conference took place between Brigadier General Herbert Nelson, the commander of

88th Brigade, and Brigadier General J.E.B. 'Jack' Seely, commanding the Canadian Cavalry Brigade, in an attempt to establish the situation. Nelson believed that both tanks and infantry were across the canal and advancing on their final objective. Seely, however, had seen the tank's failed attempt to cross, but still sent a message back to his leading regiment, the Fort Garry Horse, to come on and continue the advance if possible, using the sunken road his aerial reconnaissance had spotted. At last it looked like the cavalry might be going for the 'G' in 'gap'.

The fight on Flesquières Ridge continued to show why this was such a key position in the attack. The gentle rise, with the village itself just behind the crest and with good observation over the approaches to the south and southeast, had suggested obvious natural advantages to the Germans when they were planning the *Siegfried Stellung*, or Hindenburg Line. It was no accident, therefore, that the principal Hindenburg Support Line was built to use the ridge position's strengths to best effect. The village and its chateau were fortified and dense barbed wire thickets constructed in front of deep, wide trenches. Battery positions for the guns of *Feld Artillerie Regiment 108* were sited on the reverse slope and two infantry battalions of *54th Division* were based in Flesquières itself. The ridge was always going to prove a tough nut to crack. The defenders, having survived the attentions of both artillery and the ground-attack aircraft of the RFC, had already stopped 'D' and 'E' Tank Battalions in their tracks and dealt a bloody check to 51st Division. They now provided further demonstration of their resourcefulness and resilience as their determined resistance continued to influence the British attack's chances of success.

On 6th Division's front, 'H' Battalion's advance on the third objective at 11.00 a.m. initially suggested that the Germans would offer little opposition:

We stopped for a little while, had some tea and biscuits from our iron rations. Later we moved on towards . . . Flesquières Ridge. The German artillery was firing from positions that must have been well out of range of our machine-guns; as yet we had not received any instructions to open fire. There was nothing to aim at, so we continued forward, hoping we would be lucky enough to survive the barrage until we reached our objective. Like the rest of the crew, I was feeling very tired and hoping that there would be a chance to have some sleep very soon.[18]

Private George Brown, H50 'Hurricane', No. 24 Company, H Battalion, Tank Corps

However, the tank battalion encountered its first significant losses when several tanks* were destroyed by direct hits from a battery of German artillery firing at short range on the ridge north of the Ribécourt–Marcoing road (the eastern shoulder of Flesquières Ridge). This was typical of what happened all over the battlefield. Beyond the trench systems and the range of the British artillery, the terrain was less shell damaged. Consequently, the tanks outpaced the already tired footsloggers and became more vulnerable to German field artillery. The ill-fated H4 'Harvester' was struck by three shells and both Second Lieutenant Robert Davis and Major Gerald Huntbach were wounded.

One of the NCOs described exactly what it was like to be inside a tank when it was hit by artillery fire:

A tank close to our right received a direct hit and burst into flames. I only saw one man roll out of the side door. The tank on our left also had a direct hit. I did not see anyone get out of that tank. All this time my officer and the side gunners were effectively using their Lewis guns.

I saw the German field gunners well in the fore loading their gun and I knew this lot was for us. There was a terrific roar and 'Hotspur' shuddered from stem to stern. I saw our left caterpillar track fly in the air. Our left nose was blown off. The tank was filled with smoke and I thought we were on fire. But not so. If that last shell had landed two feet closer to where the officer and I sat we would most certainly have both been killed and the tank completely smashed up.

The order was given, 'Abandon tank'. The crew got out. I took the front Lewis gun with me. As per our tank drill, we all ran to the front of the tank and spread out in a semi-circle. While we lay there waiting for whatever might come, a plane flew low and fired right along the semi-circle made by the crew. The bullets fell only a foot or so in front of us. Not one man was hit. At this point our officer crawled forward to the

---

* Most sources say three but it is clear that five or more tanks were hit here.

right with a Lewis gun and I understand wiped out the gun crew which had put out of action our tank 'Hotspur'.[19]

Lance Corporal Alfred Brisco, H24 'Hotspur', No. 23 Company, 'H' Battalion, Tank Corps

Another tank hit here was H9 'Huntsman'. Its commander, Lieutenant Eldred Fraser, formerly a Harley Street dentist, was also killed. George Brown's battle in 'Hurricane' was about to come to an abrupt end too:

As we were approaching Flesquières Ridge we met a great deal of resistance both from the artillery and machine gun fire. We could now see in the distance the German positions still out of range except from our own artillery.

Suddenly there was a terrible noise; without any warning a shell had ripped off our right track. The officer left the tank to have a look at the damage; he soon returned and ordered us to evacuate the tank. A few minutes later I was struck by a piece of shrapnel which cut through my left boot, injuring my foot. I took off my boot and one of our crew bandaged my foot with my field dressing. The officer and crew wished me luck, and taking some Lewis guns and magazines went on their way. The RAMC picked me up and later drove me to Peronne where I stayed in hospital for three weeks.[20]

Private George Brown, H50 'Hurricane', No. 24 Company, H Battalion, Tank Corps

The loss of two more tanks was described by Second Lieutenant Joseph Gordon Hassell:

I was in the second wave, commanding tank H7 'Harrier' and received three direct hits – tank completely put out of action. This was after we had reached all our final objectives. I had 8 men inside with a large black German dog, which had refused to run away with retreating Bosch soldiers. Apart from scratches we had no casualties.

This was due to the extremely good team work which existed between my driver, Sergeant Callaghan, and myself.

We 'sensed' trouble in the leading tank (Lieutenant [sic] the Honourable Cecil Edwardes, killed) and had just managed to swing the tank through 90° and start off downhill to our right, when the first shot took off my right track – it sailed away through the air. The second shot – a glancing blow – pushed in the roof – and the third got us right in the rear. Had we been broadside on, we should all have been done for.[21]

Second Lieutenant Joseph Gordon Hassell, H7 'Harrier', No. 22 Company, 'H' Battalion, Tank Corps

The commander of another tank section provided more detail concerning Captain Edwardes' death:

The Honourable Cecil Edwardes had reached his objective in his tank. A shell penetrated the tank from the front. It did not explode, but, passing between Edwardes and the tank driver without touching either of them, pushed back the engine of the tank. Edwardes died instantaneously of shock through heart-failure. Gerrard found him dead, sitting upright in the officer's seat with his pockets already rifled.[22]

Captain Daniel Hickey, No. 23 Company, 'H' Battalion, Tank Corps

Edwardes was the third son of the fourth Baron Kensington and, at 41, had been considerably older than many of his fellow tank officers. According to Gordon Hassell,

Edwardes had a premonition of his death. He told us the day before the action of this – settled up all his affairs. He was immensely popular and eight officers went up the day after his death, got his body out of the tank and carried him back for burial. In the absence of a Padre, I conducted such a burial service as was practicable.[23]

Second Lieutenant Joseph Gordon Hassell, H7 'Harrier', No. 22 Company, 'H' Battalion, Tank Corps

Despite these losses, 'H' Battalion tanks reached their final objective at about 1.00 p.m. Some German infantry around Premy Chapel and a few machine-guns on the outskirts of Marcoing were dealt with, but otherwise the advance was hardly contested at all. Indeed, there was something of the surreal about the day, as Major Stephen Foot, a Tank Corps staff officer discovered:

My own job was to follow up the tanks and find out from the infantry what they really thought about the way the tanks did their job. It was considered important to get these impressions from the infantry, red-hot, during the attack itself, as we should be more likely to get useful information than if we waited for the official reports after the battle. Cazalet was with me, and we talked to privates, NCOs, platoon commanders, captains, majors and colonels. Their replies were overwhelming. I have never been so proud of the Tank Corps as I was on that day, for they all said the same thing: 'The tanks were splendid – gaps in the wire top-hole – we'd follow the tanks anywhere.'[24]

Major Stephen Foot, Headquarters, 2nd Tank Brigade, Tank Corps

This in itself represented a considerable contrast to the Tank Corps' experience of infantry attitudes to their labours at Third Ypres. However, the exceptional nature of the day's events was perhaps most clearly highlighted as Foot and Cazalet approached Marcoing where, 'On the hillside above the road leading to Marcoing we came upon a large yellow flag, and sitting under its protection we found Colonel Bryce and some officers of No. 2 [i.e. 'B'] Battalion having lunch.'[25] Despite news that nearly all the battalion's tanks had reached their objectives, there was growing anxiety amongst this coterie of tank officers:

The only fly in the ointment was that there were no signs of the cavalry, who were expected to arrive and exploit the success . . . We sent off pigeon messages to everybody we could think of, asking them to hurry up. Meanwhile we sat on the hillside in the sunshine, three miles inside the former German lines, and wished that all attacks could be like this one.[26]

Major Stephen Foot, Headquarters, 2nd Tank Brigade, Tank Corps

The tanks were by this time a considerable distance ahead of the infantry, and it was not until 1.15 p.m. that units of 29th Division arrived and took over the position. All tanks, their task completed, then withdrew to their various Company Rallying Points, and the battalion's work for the day was over. This withdrawal was unfortunate given the situation in and around Flesquières itself.

The continuing hold-up on the ridge was obvious to 6th Division, as the commander of 2nd Durham Light Infantry indicates:

My objective was the farthest one, on the Premy Ridge, so we did not follow immediately behind the tanks, but went over the heads of those people who took the 1st and 2nd [sic] objectives, and then forward to our own objectives. The show went like clockwork except that

Flesquières village was not taken, and as I had been informed that this village had to be taken by the Brigade on my left before I could advance to the Premy Ridge, I naturally thought that it was so when it hove in sight. I was speedily undeceived by a hail of machine-gun bullets from it, but the shooting was high and they did not hit anybody, and we got our objective in spite of it, capturing 11 Hun guns and killing or capturing all the gunmen.[27]

Major Hugh Boxer, 2nd Durham Light Infantry, 18th Brigade, 6th Division

An attack against the German positions at Flesquières by 18th Brigade, 6th Division's left flank brigade, thrusting in behind them from the east might well have broken the deadlock there. However, the brigade commander, Brigadier General George Craufurd, had understood that his task was to ensure that III Corps' left flank was protected and, consequently, he did not act.

News of events at Flesquières continued to filter back. Throughout the morning Second Lieutenant Benjamin Parkin had waited in vain at his aeroplane dropping station for any RFC pilot or observer to drop a message concerning the progress of the attack.

And then about 1.30 p.m. low down – just over the trenches – a small aeroplane circled from Flesquières way. He signalled to us; we could see him clearly and then he let drop a cylinder with a bit of tassel attached, on to our calico. I was out in a moment, and both Graham and I took copies. The original went to 51st Division as it affected them but I despatched one of my runners to 185th Brigade Headquarters and a request to repeat to Division.

Here is the Report: -

'1.05 pm about 150 cavalry appear taking shelter behind railway embankment at K.24.c.8.1. Grand Ravine full of cavalry from K30a to K29c. Some appear to be retiring southwards. I was fired on by machine-guns from Flesquières at 12.55 p.m. 15 Squadron RFC JB Solomon, Captain.'[28]

Second Lieutenant Benjamin Parkin, 2/4th Duke of Wellington's Regiment, 186th Brigade, 62nd Division

Parkin realized that this meant that the Germans were still in Flesquières and that cavalry in the Grand Ravine couldn't get further because of fire from the village. This message was soon followed by another:

> Before we had really folded up our maps the aeroplane returned. He had been to Flesquières again – it was only 2 miles away. This was the message he then dropped: '1.25 p.m. Two tanks firing on Flesquières from K.24.d.2.7. Red Flare from K.24.c.5.2. 1.30 p.m. JB Solomon, Captain.'
>
> This message again affected the 51st Division. It showed the Highland Division was still held up at Flesquières at 1.25 p.m. and that 2 tanks were 500 yards this side of the village and that the infantry had got no further than the railway – just 3,000 yards from our position – representing 2,250 yards advance.[29]

Second Lieutenant Benjamin Parkin, 2/4th Duke of Wellington's Regiment, 186th
Brigade, 62nd Division

Parkin and his colleague, Graham, relayed these messages immediately, of course, but it was by such wholly unsatisfactory means that Great War commanders learned of the progress of the battle. The value of such information naturally depended not only on the speed of delivery but on the preparedness of the recipient to believe and act on it, as Major William Watson found when he completed his two-mile trek back to the headquarters of one of 51st Division's infantry battalions:

> The infantry colonel would not believe my report. He was assured that everything was going well, and, according to programme, we must be well beyond Flesquières. So I sent a couple of messages to my own colonel, whose headquarters were at those of the infantry brigade with which we were operating. I pointed out to the infantry colonel that, if we had taken Flesquières, it was difficult to account for the machine-gun fire which apparently was coming from the neighbourhood of the village, and half-convinced, he sent his scout officer with me to find out what was happening generally, and to endeavour in particular to approach Flesquières from the west.[30]

Major William Watson, No. 11 Company, 'D' Battalion, Tank Corps

Watson and the scout officer set out at once towards Flesquières itself.

We were tramping across the open down, happily exposed, when the battalion scout officer was convinced by a long burst of machine-gun fire that at least the western end of the village was still held by the enemy . . . We hurried on with more haste than dignity, and looking towards the village, I thought I could catch the flash of the gun in the window of a large white house. A particularly unpleasant burst, and the scout officer was crawling on his hands and knees towards a convenient trench. At that moment I knew no one wiser than the scout officer, and I followed his example. For the next five minutes the man in the window of the large white house must have enjoyed himself thoroughly. The air sang with bullets. With tremendous care we continued to crawl, until after a lifetime of suspense we came to within fifty yards of the trench. I jumped up and dashed forward, the scout officer and our two runners following me, and in a moment we were lighting our pipes and feeling acutely that somebody had made a fool of us both.[31]

Major William Watson, No. 11 Company, 'D' Battalion, Tank Corps

This was sufficient to convince Watson's companion that Flesquières was indeed still in German hands. Those in the village's immediate vicinity needed no further proof. Wilfrid Bion was still leading a detachment of infantry survivors on the fringes of the village, but his relief was on hand:

It was obvious that we had to hold our positions which we did against one powerful counter-attack on our left flank. Although the troops of the infantry battalion on our left were forced to yield some ground we held our pivotal position. We lit our marker flares when one of our reconnaissance planes came over . . . Shortly after, the Colonel of the regiment, hearing my report of the position rapidly summed it up: 'Since you have no tanks, you and your bloody Lance Corporal are no good to me. Get back to our HQ.'[32]

Second Lieutenant Wilfrid Bion, E40 'Edward II', No. 14 Company, 'E' Battalion, Tank Corps

Despite his personal bravery, which was readily acknowledged by the Highland infantry, Bion must have noticed the infantry commander's tone, which undoubtedly stemmed from a frustration with the tanks' failure to prevail over the Flesquières' defenders. During the afternoon, the infantry were to make several further attempts to over-come this opposition, but the oft-encountered problems of the Great War in coordinating attacks by the various arms without adequate means of communication once more prevented organized attacks from being made and only minor gains were made by the infantry.

In this case, however, the problems were compounded by the fact that 'Uncle' Harper had sited his divisional headquarters 8,000 yards (over 4.5 miles) behind the original British front line and, therefore, almost 7 miles from Flesquières. This obviously meant the decision-making cycle of receipt of information, response, and despatch of revised orders was greatly extended. In particular, it may have added to the problems resulting from another of Harper's decisions – in this case, a repeat of his habitual tactic of using what he deemed the minimum force necessary to take the objective. With insufficient troops to overcome German resistance in Flesquières, he had little time to decide whether or not to commit his reserves, Brigadier General Kenneth Buchanan's 154th Brigade. Harper and his staff can rightly be criticized for accepting the check at Flesquières and for the in-adequacy of their response.

Douglas Wimberley, like many in 51st Division, could see evidence of the hold-up at Flesquières and discern the likely reason:

> The attack was evidently slowing down, and a line of blazing tanks outside the village wall of Flesquières told of some good work by the German tank gunners – it was a very interesting sight for our tanks seemed to be stopped on some line on the far ridge which they could not pass.[33]
>
> Major Douglas Wimberley, 232nd Company, MGC, 51st Division

On his return journey from the front line, Wimberley's route brought him into contact with what must have been, after years of trench warfare, a remarkable sight:

> Near the craters over the Trescault–Ribécourt road, we passed a cavalry brigade, the 2nd, waiting, with their horses, to go forward. Very trim and clean they looked – Lancers, Hussars and Dragoon Guards in their steel helmets and leather jerkins and lances or sabres. I saw about ten fellows I had been at Wellington with: Palmer of the 9th Lancers

was one, Berries in a Dragoon Guards regiment, and many others. They looked very clean, I remember, in comparison to us; but then we had already been in action for twelve hours and that makes one dirtier than any job I know.[34]

Major Douglas Wimberley, 232nd Company, MGC, 51st Division

This was the cavalry brigade that had halted after encountering fire from Ribécourt. It was not until 1.30 p.m. that they moved forward again.

The lack of progress by 51st Division and the surviving tanks was an even greater setback given the good progress of infantry and tanks on 62nd Division's front. Although, as Lieutenant Basil Henriques discovered, even such a successful advance was not without its perils:

By now we were out of the zone of the gun fire, but I am not sure I did not hate the 'bitz, bitz' of the sniper and the machine guns even more. However, thank goodness, none hit me. As I advanced it seemed more like a dream than a modern battle. To compare it with July 31st was just ridiculous. We seemed to be sweeping all before us . . . At last we reached our second objective and here there was to be a halt. I caught the tanks up, although the infantry were by now behind me. We wandered about in the open as though we were at Aldershot, occasionally having to duck as a bullet went 'bitz' past overhead.[35]

Lieutenant Basil Henriques, 'G' Battalion, Tank Corps

The continued good progress of 62nd Division was due in no small measure to the drive of Brigadier General Roland Bradford, whose 186th Brigade's important and by no means easy task was to reach a line from Graincourt to the bridge on the Bapaume–Cambrai road over the Canal du Nord. (This bridge was the same one the Germans had destroyed earlier in the day because of their fears of attack in this sector.) Bradford recognized the importance of a rapid advance in increasing his brigade's chances of success:

The night before the battle, Bradford was very anxious to advance early on the 20th and take up a much more forward position. It was the ardour of youth and there was a great deal in it if things were right. I did not fully concur with Bradford, nor did I like being without some form of reserve. I felt, however, there was a great deal in what Bradford

180

said, I decided to 'chance my arm'. I gave him instructions to keep moving forward, and directly the leading Brigades had gained some initial success that 186th Brigade should push through. It was taking a bit of a risk, but if it came off it was well worth it. As a matter of fact it did come off and had a tremendous effect on the fortunes of the day. Bradford was a born leader and led his Brigade with conspicuous success.[36]

Major General Walter Braithwaite, 62nd Division

With the brigade was a company of tanks from 'G' Battalion, but all other available tanks were also to assist, acting independently. Also attached were two cavalry squadrons of the 1st King Edward's Horse. The artillery barrage was planned on a fixed timetable, hence Bradford's desire to get his men as far forward as possible before they tackled the Hindenburg Support Line. They began moving forward within Havrincourt Wood at 9.00 a.m., soon after reports confirmed the German first line had been captured.

Having leap-frogged the advance brigades, between 11.00 a.m. and 2.00 p.m. Bradford's 186th Brigade only advanced about 1,000 yards, meeting pockets of stubborn defence in their advance along, rather than across, the German defences which ran almost exactly north-south here. The attached cavalry had attempted to send patrols towards Flesquières. Although most were driven off by machine-gun fire, one patrol under Lieutenant Ian Stein reportedly reached the village's western outskirts. They found that although the front of the village and the chateau at the south-east corner were occupied strongly, this western part was only weakly held.

Benjamin Parkin's battalion, the 2/4th Duke of Wellington's, on the right of the brigade's advance was initially delayed by the check to 51st Division, but the left of the unit pressed on and reached the Graincourt area with few problems. Meanwhile, Brigadier General Bradford was well forward in his brigade's advance in order to keep control. He was therefore able to order an attack on Graincourt by two companies of the 2/4th Duke of Wellington's with tanks. The latter, however, were once again reduced by German artillery at this point. In this case, two 77mm field guns were responsible. Major Ralph Broome, an experienced tank commander, was on the spot and directed three tanks against these guns from a different direction. Lieutenant Albert 'Charles' Baker's tank, G29 'Gorgonzola II', eventually accounted for them – a feat for which he later received a bar to his MC* – enabling the infantry to capture it. The direct influence of commanders like Bradford and Broome in ensuring a successful outcome in the attack on Graincourt is worthy of note.

Although Flesquières had still not fallen, Bradford's focus was, rightly, on reinforcing success. At 3.30 p.m., with resistance in Graincourt overcome, contact established with units of 36th Division across the Canal du Nord and his own infantry established beyond Graincourt, he decided to push infantry, cavalry and tanks on towards Anneux and the factory on the Bapaume–Cambrai road. Casualties in each battalion of his brigade amounted to less than 100.

Although batteries of horse and field artillery were being pushed forward, the formal programme of artillery 'lifts' had now been completed. The gunners too took stock of their achievements so far and, in some cases, had an opportunity to examine their German counterparts' weaponry for the first time:

> That first day was a day to be remembered. We really had the sense of victory for the first time. My chief memory of the day was collecting a mixed battery of fourteen German field guns, and firing off their captured ammunition into the German back area.[37]
>
> Major Richard Foot, D/310 Battery, Royal Field Artillery, 62nd Division

Having moved forward from their observation post in 6th Division's sector, Captain Geoffrey Dugdale and his servant, Whittingham, encountered a more ambitious but misguided group of artillerymen:

> We found some of our gunners trying to turn round a battery of German guns so that they could fire them at the Germans themselves. A party of our men were watching the proceedings in silence.
>
> Looking down the barrel of one I found that I could not see through it, so I asked the man who was going to load it what was in the barrel. He said, 'There is a shell stuck in it. We will soon get it out.'

* One of these guns is now on display at the Tank Museum, Bovington, and is known as the 'Graincourt Gun'.

I mentioned that the gun was pointing to the rear towards Villers Plouich, but he seemed to think it was pointing in the right direction; also he said he was going to fire it.

Quickly and speedily all the spectators drifted away to places of safety to await results. The man fired the gun, and much to our astonishment the gun did not burst.[38]

Captain Geoffrey Dugdale, Headquarters, 60th Brigade, 20th Division

Dugdale, like many, was astounded by the German defences he encountered in the Hindenburg Line:

Here we found one of the German artillery observation posts wonderfully fitted up with an elaborate range-finding apparatus. We seized all the maps we could find in this dugout.

There appeared to be no Germans left at all. Everybody was walking about on the top and in front of our front line doing just as they liked.

Down one dugout we found a German battalion canteen, but a lot of our troops had got there first. It was obvious that our presence was very badly needed. The canteen was full of every kind of drink, from beer to brandy. Luckily the men who had discovered this canteen were men of my old battalion, so I asked two of them to collect all the brandy in sandbags, which we took to headquarters. We also took with us a large quantity of butter and cheese. We left the beer for the men to drink. They had earned it.[39]

Captain Geoffrey Dugdale, Headquarters, 60th Brigade, 20th Division

In Havrincourt, looting by Billy Kirkby and his mates was suddenly, and violently, interrupted:

I remember a sudden enveloping mighty roar . . . Instinctively we ducked low, at speed, as the two huge pillars of what had been the imposing entrance to a beautiful chateau disintegrated as a German shell burst, bricks and parts of bricks flying everywhere. We picked up the crate of apples we had been carrying, finally descending some distance into a German dugout, finding almost an underground palace with pictures on the wall and every possible comfort for the occupants, suggesting we were in what had become exclusive Officers'

183

Headquarters safe from our guns, far below ground. No wonder they had defended stubbornly as we knew to our cost.[40]

Private Billy Kirkby, 2/6th West Yorkshires, 185th Brigade, 62nd Division

Dugdale also encountered 'civilians from the villages of Marcoing and Masnières coming back through our lines, carrying what possessions they could save on their backs, driving cows and pigs in front of them'.[41]

Two tanks from 'A' Battalion, although they did not know it, were to be the ones that got closest to Cambrai on that day. Second Lieutenant Cyril Charles in A52 'Artful Alice II' and Lieutenant John Lipscomb's A55 'Aggressive II' were taken across the canal by their section commander, Captain David Raikes, and then sent forward towards 87th Brigade's final objective.

> On receipt of a message from the infantry, stating that there were machine-guns still firing from Talma Chateau, I ordered these two officers to fire into the rear of it as they went by, and also arranged for two platoons of infantry to move up on the left side of the canal to clear out the chateau. I sent both these tanks on to the right and left of Flot Farm and returned myself to bring up the other two. When I arrived with the other two tanks at Marcoing Station, I found that the infantry had not gone forward, but were prepared to go forward again if supported by tanks.[42]
>
> Captain David Raikes, No. 3 Company, 'A' Battalion, Tank Corps

Meanwhile, Lipscomb's tank received a direct hit from a shell, wounding its commander severely, shattering his right arm and inflicting terrible wounds on his right side and face. His sergeant and two of his crew assisted him towards the British lines but when within 150 yards of them he collapsed completely. The rest of the party then went on to get a stretcher to carry him, but by the time they had returned, the Germans had advanced slightly and it was impossible to get near him, one of the party being shot in the attempt. No further attempts were possible as his body was then behind German lines. Lipscomb was subsequently reported as missing, presumed dead. However, he survived – wounded and a prisoner.

Cyril Charles in 'Artful Alice II' later led a company of the Border Regiment forward in the dark and succeeded in knocking out at least one machine-gun. The infantry took 19 prisoners and captured two machine-guns. This was the limit of 'A' Battalion's advance on the day.

A German officer claimed credit for the destruction of what was perhaps Lipscomb's tank. Stressing that it was infantry with armour-piercing ammunition and not the artillery who were responsible for this deed, he described how:

> I gave the order to fire. What a joy it was, to see the shots hit the tanks, so that the sparks showered. In a moment, flames began to lick from the tank, followed by an explosion. The tank stood still and stirred no further . . . Our delight over the tanks' destruction was great. It had been an extremely unpleasant feeling, as the creature approached us and we couldn't contact the artillery . . . With the coming of darkness a patrol went out to the knocked-out tank. They found it abandoned, but discovered good loot in it. Champagne, cognac, chocolate and cake with raisins . . . This increased our delight still further.[43]
>
> Leutnant Quehl, *Reserve Infanterie Regiment 227, 107th Division*

In the meantime, the three infantry companies that had crossed the canal had been reinforced by the 1st Inniskilling Fusiliers who now led the advance on the wire of the next line of defences, known by the Germans as Siegfried II. Despite the remarkable courage of many of these men in attempting to penetrate the deep defences by cutting the wire by hand, it soon became clear that tank or artillery assistance was needed and the Inniskillings were forced to dig in for the night.

Third Army's plan had envisaged a return for the Cavalry Corps to that arm's traditional function: the rapid exploitation of success on the battlefield. The point of the operation was to create an opportunity for such action. Successful use of cavalry in this manner required opportunism, determination and élan on the part of commanders and men. Since the plan had anticipated that cavalry units might be expected to begin crossing the canal at any time after 11.00 a.m., their arrival was now eagerly anticipated by tank crews and infantry, who perhaps envisaged cheering on squadron after squadron of mounted men galloping past en route to complete the victory.

The reality was rather different. So, by the time the first cavalry from the Secunderabad Cavalry Brigade of 5th Cavalry Division reached the village and began to cross the canal, at about 2.00 p.m. (approximately an hour and a half after Mark Dillon had reached 'B' Battalion's rallying point in Marcoing), they had marched 30–35 miles in about 40 hours. Most of it had been steady, but slow, progress with none of the bravado associated with aggressive cavalry action. The machine-gun fire they now encountered made it immediately clear that there was no opportunity for mounted action here. Lieutenant George Thompson witnessed the cavalry's precipitous arrival and equally swift departure:

> As we stood outside the tank having a smoke, a detachment of cavalry came along in charge of a Major. He wanted to know why I had stopped and then enquired about the location of the enemy. I was unable to offer any information, since there was no clear forward view due to the country being well wooded. With this negative information he led his detachment across the bridge and was soon lost to sight. Almost immediately we heard machine-gun fire and back came the cavalry and they galloped back the way they had come. That was the last we saw of them.[44]

Lieutenant George Thompson, B22 'Buccaneer', No. 5 Company, 'B' Battalion, Tank Corps

The story was different farther to the left, where Nine Wood had been captured by infantry of 86th Brigade and tanks of 'H' Battalion. The tanks withdrew after their commander obtained a receipt for the wood from the infantry. Subsequently, 7th Dragoon Guards galloped to take the village of Noyelles without suffering a single casualty, and captured about 25 prisoners. This was a somewhat more spirited display than that of 4th Dragoon Guards, whose first objective was the village of Cantaing – dimly visible through the November murk and mist. Wire and machine-gun fire from the newly arrived *Infanterie Regiment 227* soon halted this advance, as a cavalry machine-gun officer later described:

> The regiment [4th Royal Irish Dragoon Guards] was leading regiment of the division and I was attached to it with my sub-section officer and my four guns. The leading squadron had quite a good show and did a

charge with one troop, killing about 15 Bosches with the sword and taking 50 prisoners. One of the guns which was with the leading troop had a good shoot, as they surprised a convoy of wagons, killed the horses and about 30 Germans and the rest surrendered. The leading troops finally got heavily counter-attacked and surrounded by a crowd of machine-guns, but got out without many casualties and rejoined the squadron, and as it was dark, dug in for the night. The other three guns we had in action covering their left all the time, and were firing on a village to keep down machine-gun fire, and stop counter-attacks. We got pretty well shelled once or twice, but very little harm done.[45]

Captain Geoffrey Dent, 2nd Machine Gun Squadron, 2nd Cavalry Brigade, 1st Cavalry Division

Consequently, the cavalry could only reinforce the infantry as they dug in around Nine Wood.

At Masnières, too, the cavalry had gone into action. The Canadian Cavalry Brigade, lead by the Fort Garry Horse, followed by the Royal Canadian Dragoons and Lord Strathcona's Horse, had waited for news of the condition of the canal crossings at Masnières. However, 'After a wait of about three quarters of an hour, a message was received from Lieutenant Harvey that the bridge had been smashed by a tank going through it.'[46]

Soon, nevertheless, they received Brigadier General Seely's orders to move forward. Part of their advance was covered by an artillery screen previously used by the Germans to hide their traffic from observation. Sam Williams captured the exhilaration of the move forward:

Crossing the open between the sunken road, where we had been halted, and this screen, we came under fire from a battery of German guns on the high ground on the other side of the canal. They were firing over open sights at us. Although we could not see the guns because of the haze, we could distinctly see the flashes of the guns, and then came the shells. I was watching the shelling pretty closely as we were coming along, and it looked very much as if the next salvo would land right amongst my troop if we did not change our path . . . Gauging the time between salvoes, I gave 'Sections Left,' which brought us into troop column to the left. We went about 150 or 200 yards to the left, then a 'Sections Right' brought us into troop frontage again. All this was at the gallop, and it worked out just fine. The shells landed just where we would have been had we not changed direction, and we missed having any casualties, which we surely would have had otherwise.[47]

Lieutenant Sam Williams, Lord Strathcona's Horse, Canadian Cavalry Brigade, 5th Cavalry Division

The Fort Garry Horse entered Les Rues Vertes around two o'clock. Unable to cross by the main town bridge, the Fort Garrys moved east to the lock which the Worcesters had discovered:

On reaching the bridge in Main Street I found that it had either been blown or broken in by the weight of a tank. I at once instructed Major Sharpe to reconnoitre a crossing on the right, stated by civilians to be suitable for horses in single file, and over which I could see the infantry crossing.

Shortly after 3.00 p.m. I received a message from Major Walker, stating that a crossing had been constructed. I forwarded this message to Brigade, advising them that I was pushing on. Major Sharpe not having returned, but a guide from the infantry reporting, I instructed Captain Campbell of 'B' Squadron to take his squadron across the canal and that I would follow with the balance of the regiment as soon as he had got over.[48]

Lieutenant Colonel Robert Paterson, Fort Garry Horse, Canadian Cavalry Brigade, 5th Cavalry Division

'B' Squadron found Major 'Tiny' Walker, the regiment's machine-gun officer, working under heavy fire to make a better crossing from massive baulks of timber – the framework of another set of lock gates which were lying to hand. Despite some casualties, he and his men persisted until the work was finished. Then 'B' Squadron took its horses in single file and crossed the bridge under fire. Several men fell into the canal and a number were drowned, but the rest reached the other side and set off at a gallop two hours later, watched by their commanding officer.

I watched 'B' Squadron crossing, which they did at 3.30 p.m., then pushed on myself to make certain that they would clear the bridge successfully. Having ascertained this, I sent a messenger to instruct 'C'

Squadron to follow. I then crossed the temporary bridge to the Lock
House, where I found Major Walker of the Machine-Gun Squadron,
and at the same time received a message from the rear that I was not to
cross the canal and was to withdraw any of my troops which had
crossed.[49]

Lieutenant Colonel Robert Paterson, Fort Garry Horse, Canadian Cavalry Brigade, 5th
Cavalry Division

This decision had been arrived at by Brigadier Generals Nelson
and Seely and Major General Walter Greenly, 2nd Cavalry Division's
commander, after the latter arrived in Les Rues Vertes soon after 3.00
p.m. All felt that it was not practicable to get a large force of cavalry
across the canal by the same route as the Fort Garry Horse squadron.
In fact, less than a mile south-east of the main bridge there was another
wooden bridge leading to Mon Plaisir Farm, which would have been
very suitable for cavalry to cross hidden from German observation and
fire. However, no one present remembered about this bridge and it
remained undiscovered. This meeting was witnessed by Sam Williams:

I happened to be in the room which was being used as the Brigade
Headquarters, when Lieutenant 'Shrimp' Cochran of the RCDs
[Royal Canadian Dragoons], who was acting as Brigade galloper, came
in to say that the Garrys were starting to cross. General Seeley [sic] and
General Greenlay [sic] conferred for a few minutes and came to the
decision that it was then too late in the day for enough light for cavalry
to operate. The decision was to stop the Garry's and bring them back
and to defer the crossing until the next morning. However, by the time
Lieutenant Cochran had galloped back with the message, the leading
squadron had crossed and were on their way.[50]

Lieutenant Sam Williams, Lord Strathcona's Horse, Canadian Cavalry Brigade, 5th
Cavalry Division

Colonel Paterson himself made an attempt to recall 'B' Squadron:

No other messenger being available, Corporal Ryan of the Machine-
Gun Squadron who had already been shot through the arm volunteered to carry a message forward to 'B' Squadron, in which I
instructed them to return at once. I then sent back a messenger to the
Brigade, advising them of the situation and pushed forward myself in

endeavour to reach 'B' Squadron, which by this time had passed through the infantry and was right out of sight over the ridge in front. The infantry gave me the direction in which they had gone, but my horse being injured by a fall into a sunken road, I was unable to catch them.[51]

Lieutenant Colonel Robert Paterson, Fort Garry Horse, Canadian Cavalry Brigade, 5th Cavalry Division

Major General Greenly issued orders curtailing further attempts to cross the canal at 3.30 p.m. However, until darkness (the sun set at 4.03 p.m.) infantry of 29th Division continued to attempt to get across the various known surviving canal bridges and drive the Germans from Masnières. It was during one such attempt that Second Lieutenant Eric Marchant of the 1st Essex – the young man who had been certain the war would last until July 1925 – was killed. His death was witnessed by several of the battalion:

He and I were with our respective platoons and we had orders to capture the bridges over a canal and a small river in the village of Masnières; the bridges were strongly defended by the enemy who had a machine-gun and several snipers concealed in houses on the other side.

Although it was a matter requiring tremendous pluck, [he] took the lead and, telling his men and mine to follow him, dashed over the first bridge. I regret to say that he and two men immediately behind him fell under a hail of bullets from the machine-gun, whilst I managed to jump under cover on the bank between the two bridges. The machine-gun was eventually destroyed by the guns of a tank on the bank and the second bridge was captured at dusk.[52]

Second Lieutenant Frank Barford, 1st Essex, 88th Brigade, 29th Division

His commanding officer was another who saw Eric Marchant die. In writing to Marchant's parents, he tried to minimize the pain of their loss by hiding the full details of the circumstances in which their son had died. However, he may have only made matters worse:

A tank had been brought up to give covering fire and when all was ready I heard him call out 'Now I'll go first, follow me closely' and then he made his dash. He was hit whilst on the bridge and at that moment the bridge collapsed, and he was precipitated into the canal, which is a deep one, in all his heavy equipment.[53]

Lieutenant Colonel Sir George Stirling, 1st Essex, 88th Brigade, 29th Division

The Canadian Cavalry still tried to seek out other points at which the canal could be crossed. Lieutenant Sam Williams was able to witness the meeting between Greenly, Seely and Nelson whilst awaiting an opportunity to report another likely crossing found north of Masnières.

Major Macdonald had learned [. . .] of another bridge to the left of Masnières and wanted permission from General Seeley [sic] to send a patrol round to report on the possibility of crossing there. As it was my turn for the next patrol, he took me with him so no time would be lost if it was agreed to send a patrol. We had just got inside the door when Lieutenant Cochran came bursting in. Realising his news was urgent we stood aside to give him precedence . . . General Seeley told him [Macdonald] to send a patrol round and further to take his squadron across and operate it if he thought it wise to do so. I thought it funny to tell him that, just after giving word to stop the Garrys from crossing. However it was not my place to question. I dashed back to my troop and called for number one patrol . . . in no time at all we were on our horses and away on our mission.[54]

Lieutenant Sam Williams, Lord Strathcona's Horse, Canadian Cavalry Brigade, 5th Cavalry Division

Williams discovered the bridge was held by a detachment of the Newfoundland Regiment.

I found the bridge to be quite passable for cavalry, its only fault being that one end was about a foot out of plumb. I sent word back to Major Macdonald, but before my messenger got there, I could see him getting the squadron mounted to come around. He brought the squadron around and then was able to size up the situation for himself. He very wisely decided that nothing worthwhile could be accomplished by trying to operate with one squadron unsupported, and especially with the light fading so rapidly. We watered the horses while the opportunity was at hand and went back again to where we had been behind the screen.[55]

Lieutenant Sam Williams, Lord Strathcona's Horse, Canadian Cavalry Brigade, 5th Cavalry Division

Thus 'B' Squadron, Fort Garry Horse was still the only cavalry unit across the canal at Masnières. The full story of their doings on the other side was remarkable.

After crossing some marshy ground under machine-gun fire they had moved north from the canal, entering the German lines by a gap cut in the wire. At this point, the squadron commander, Captain Campbell, and one or two other ranks were hit, also by machine-gun fire, and command devolved on Lieutenant Harcus Strachan:

> We moved north and encountered a camouflaged road south-east of Rumilly. This we cut under machine-gun fire and the squadron went through in sections. On crossing the road the squadron formed lines of troop columns, and immediately encountered a battery of field guns. Two guns were unmanned, the crew destroyed another, and the other fired one round point blank which missed. The squadron charged the battery, and those of the crew who were not killed, surrendered. The prisoners were left to be dealt with by our supports, and the squadron then took on the enemy's infantry, who were retreating and dis-organised. These either took refuge in shell holes or surrendered or were killed.[56]
>
> Lieutenant Harcus Strachan, 'B' Squadron, Fort Garry Horse, Canadian Cavalry Brigade, 5th Cavalry Division

Perhaps the perilous circumstances of their situation began to dawn on Strachan and his men at this point:

> The operation had been carried out at the gallop, and on nearing Rumilly, the squadron, which had about 40 casualties from machine-gun fire from flanking block-houses, were brought down to a walk, and we then seemed to be isolated. We took up a position in a sunken road about one kilometre east of Rumilly, and held out until dark, during which three telephone lines leading east were cut.[57]
>
> Lieutenant Harcus Strachan, 'B' Squadron, Fort Garry Horse, Canadian Cavalry Brigade, 5th Cavalry Division

Having despatched messengers back to Colonel Paterson, the squadron waited until dark when it was decided to fall back on Masnières.

After dark the squadron decided to abandon horses and fight its way out, all horses except five being wounded. The horses were stampeded, attracting the attention of the machine-guns, and the squadron moved off in the direction of Masnières. Four parties of the enemy were encountered on the journey, and retired leaving casualties. These were mostly working parties. On reaching the wire through which we entered, the squadron had seven prisoners, and two more were taken at the wire. At this point the party became separated and Lieutenant Cowen who had previously been hit reached home with ten other ranks and nine prisoners. The rest of the squadron, two officers and eleven other ranks, entered Masnières at the eastern entrance, and moved down Main Street, crossing the canal by the broken bridge, where a sniper was encountered and hit but not captured. There were no further casualties.[58]

Lieutenant Harcus Strachan, 'B' Squadron, Fort Garry Horse, Canadian Cavalry Brigade, 5th Cavalry Division

For his skilful and brave leadership during 'B' Squadron's ultimately futile mission, Strachan was subsequently awarded the Victoria Cross.

The first day of the battle had seen some remarkable achievements. On a front of approximately six miles, the BEF had advanced between three and four miles. Two fortified German trench systems and the outpost line that covered them, that had been designed to offer formidable resistance to any attack, had been overcome in slightly more than four hours. For approximately 4,000 casualties, over 4,000 Germans had been taken prisoner and a hundred guns had been captured or destroyed.

On the evening of 20 November, III Corps occupied positions from the front line north-east of Gonnelieu, along the Bonavis Ridge and down to about half a mile from the canal at Crèvecoeur. The 29th Division had got troops across the canal at Masnières and Marcoing, although fighting continued throughout the night at Masnières. Noyelles, north-west of Masnières, had also been taken, but the third German line of defences (*Siegfried II (S2)* or Masnières–Beaurevoir Line) remained unbroken. The left of 29th Division linked up with 6th Division at Premy Chapel and the captured positions included Nine

Wood. IV Corps' right flank, in the form of 51st Division, was, of course, still held up in the Hindenburg Support System at Flesquières. The line then ran almost due north, where 62nd Division faced eastward through Graincourt to the Bapaume–Cambrai road. Beyond the road the line ran east-west with the 62nd and 36th Divisions in touch there.

However, the success of the initial advance to some extent masked the very real inadequacies of the operational plan. III Corps had no infantry reserves to commit in support of 29th Division infantry clinging precariously to ground gained on the far side of the St Quentin Canal, and it would have been difficult to filter the surviving tanks and five cavalry divisions across without adequate bridges. In IV Corps' sector, Major General Harper still had an entire brigade, 154th, of fresh infantry to commit and there were also two brigades of 36th Division for use but, otherwise, the 40th Division, eight miles back, was the nearest possible force capable of reinforcing the success. Had the attack been made with the possibility of more reserves being available, much more might have been achieved. Perhaps this fact, more than any other, demonstrated the problems for those who viewed mechanized means of making war as satisfactory surrogates for infantry. This was simply not the case at Cambrai after day one: guns, tanks and aircraft could not provide an adequate substitute for the presence of sufficient numbers of infantry – as the second, and subsequent, days were to prove.

As 20 November drew to a close, the mist changed to rain and conditions grew steadily more dismal. Since it was late in the year, the early descent of darkness dictated several decisions to the attacking forces. In particular, it precluded the further use of cavalry, whose presence in large numbers on the roads now began to hamper the command, supply, support and reinforcement of the front-line infantry. The ebb and flow of British hopes was captured in the diary of one divisional staff officer:

> About 2.00 p.m. we heard that the cavalry, who were round here last night, had got advanced troops over the Hindenburg Line by 1.00 p.m. and all the afternoon they have been pouring through.
> If only they can get through to Cambrai tonight.

This afternoon I went up to see how things were going and visited the Prisoners' Cage. By 4.00 p.m. the Division had taken 5 officers and 329 [men], other divisions will probably get more.

The roads forward were crammed with cavalry so I got up to our Brigade HQ another way . . . When I got back about 5.00 p.m., after walking for 3 hours, I heard that the cavalry had seized the crossings over the canal at Marcoing and Masnières and that infantry had come up and were across . . . These places are only about 3½ miles from Cambrai. It is unfortunately raining now.[59]

Lieutenant Colonel Edwin Collen, Assistant Adjutant and Quartermaster General, Headquarters, 12th Division

At La Vacquerie, in 20th Division's sector, George McMurtrie observed the hubbub of activity involved in sustaining the attack – activity that was duplicated on every divisional front:

There was one incessant stream of prisoners, our own and German wounded and ambulances, ammunition columns, GS waggons with fresh supplies of SAA and bombs and RE waggons with pontoons for bridging the canal further on. All afternoon we watched the cavalry riding over the brow of the hill in hundreds and thousands; it was a very fine sight.[60]

Second Lieutenant George McMurtrie, 7th Somerset Light Infantry, 61st Brigade, 20th Division

As his unit moved forward, he noted how order was already being brought to what might appear chaotic:

Just in the middle of La Vacquerie we came across an Indian cavalry-man and there were already notices up about canteens and tea for wounded. It was remarkable how soon they had got everything in working order.[61]

Second Lieutenant George McMurtrie, 7th Somerset Light Infantry, 61st Brigade, 20th Division

The Somersets' task was seemingly straightforward – to advance towards Masnières down the La Vacquerie valley, bringing supplies with them. However, having gone into action at 6.20 a.m., the men were tired and the conditions difficult:

I shan't forget that march for a long time. I had all the webbing equipment, a sandbag of loot, which I wouldn't part with, two jerry cans of water and about 400 extra SAA. It was raining, a pitch dark night, everything was slippery, barbed wire, etc everywhere and wet through to the skin. We rolled more than marched down the slope and across the road to the right again. Here there was a conglomeration of all branches of the army; everyone tired out, everyone cursing and swearing as hard as they could go. We passed an RE officer laying telephone wire forward and soon afterwards we met the cavalry coming back, having done absolutely no good.[62]

Second Lieutenant George McMurtrie, 7th Somerset Light Infantry, 61st Brigade, 20th Division

With nightfall it was important for the weary men to find shelter:

We were all tired out by now having had a long day, no sleep the night before and a long tiring march that night; but there was nothing to do but to dig in. We started away but soon found an old German trench just in front of us so got into it. This saved us a great deal of work and we were very thankful especially as we found a dugout in the trench so managed to get some food, take off our clothes to dry and get some sleep, which was badly needed.[63]

Second Lieutenant George McMurtrie, 7th Somerset Light Infantry, 61st Brigade, 20th Division

The surviving tanks and crews rallying back after their adventures also had to find food, warmth and shelter. Edward Leigh-Jones was especially lucky:

In the escarpment of Couillet Wood, there were German dugouts with beds already made with wire covers. So we went down there and spent the night with their gramophone and the Peer Gynt Suite![64]

Second Lieutenant Edward Leigh-Jones, B9 'Black Bess', No. 4 Company, 'B' Battalion, Tank Corps

Like George McMurtrie, the tank crews also wanted to keep their souvenirs of this momentous day:

In the Hindenburg Line [trenches], there was great German sausages and all sorts of things, and wine . . . I took a pistol, one of the latest

German revolvers, off a captain and a saw-edged bayonet and I took it into the tank with me and I brought them home . . . It had got 8 bullets in it, little round brass bullets – a beautiful little thing, it was, if you could call it a beautiful thing. I brought it home on leave.[65]

Private Fred Collins, 'B' Battalion, Tank Corps

Yet despite these 'treasures', Fred Collins was soon confronted with a powerful reminder of the human suffering produced by the fighting:

There were men lay up there. Artillery men. There weren't enough stretchers to take them back . . . We'd advanced all that way and the wounded were coming back. There weren't enough stretchers . . . some were hobbling, helping others and we saw four Germans . . . they'd improvised stretchers. They'd got two long poles – where they got them from, I don't know – and their groundsheets (they were always larger than ours) and they'd fixed these groundsheets onto these poles and made a stretcher of it. They'd got a man in the centre of it. It was pitiful to see them. They came close to me and as they went by the blood was trickling out the bottom of the groundsheet. Their comrade. But they stuck with him. I never hated the Germans. I was sorry for them blokes though.[66]

Private Fred Collins, 'B' Battalion, Tank Corps

As tank units rallied, the survivors had their first opportunity to discover how their friends had fared. They could learn who the lucky ones were.

We turned about and returned to our rallying point, a little copse shaped like a 'T' close to Havrincourt Village. On arrival we found several of our company 'buses' had got back, and on comparing notes found to our satisfaction that the casualty list was very light, a few killed and a few more wounded. Certainly we were a lucky 'mob'. We parked up at 'T' Wood and endeavoured to make ourselves comfortable for the night. Sleeping inside the bus though somewhat cramped, we were too fatigued to trouble about the hardness of our beds, although in the morning I found my right hip somewhat sore from lying on the edge of an oil drum all night.[67]

Lance Corporal Ernest Thwaites, No. 21 Company, 'G' Battalion, Tank Corps

For the infantry, like Billy Kirkby, spending the night in Havrincourt cemetery, it was also time to exchange news of mates. Meeting an old friend, Dick Hardy, together they discussed Harry's death:

> Dick, like myself, felt his death a great personal loss . . . 'Bill, one thing I envy you – being the last one to speak to him, that exchange of greetings between you in the midst of death. You know, Bill, that he and I had that feeling we would both die in this battle. If it is to be my fate I would have loved to die with him, side by side, in the attack on this village.'[68]
>
> Private Billy Kirkby, 2/6th West Yorkshires, 185th Brigade, 62nd Division

Undoubtedly, such maudlin and futile thoughts were genuinely meant, though difficult for us to grasp. For these men truly were, in the midst of their lives, in death.

Elsewhere, however, there was happier news of Lieutenant Harry Taylor, the Australian pilot of 68 Squadron shot down east of Havrincourt and last seen by his fellow aviator, Gordon Wilson, with a small group of British troops about to be surrounded by German infantry.

> The party of men he had found had lost their officer. He had stayed with them till they battled their way, edging back yard by yard, to the main body of troops from whom they had advanced too far. Here he left them to try to get back to the advanced landing-ground for another machine. On the way he found the damaged aeroplane of Captain Bell, who had been shot down earlier. With the help of some troops he tried to start the engine, but it refused to work, and he continued back to the aerodrome, which he reached in time for dinner.[69]
>
> Lieutenant Gordon Wilson, 68 (2 Australian) Squadron, RFC

Eighteen machines from Wilson and Taylor's squadron had flown ground-attack missions on 20 November. Six were shot down, and another one was missing. Of the pilots, one was missing, one died of his wounds, and one was wounded. This new and untried squadron, like its fellow RFC squadrons, had taken great risks but had performed more than creditably in this unfamiliar role.

For the Canadian cavalry, the first day seemed about to offer one more cruel twist when, at 7.30 p.m. an order was received by the brigade headquarters from 5th Cavalry Division that the Canadian

Cavalry Brigade could make **Rumilly** (a mile beyond Masnières in the direction of Cambrai) their objective that night, and if the Secunderabad Cavalry Brigade could assist from the northwest of this village a bridgehead was to be seized with a view to pushing forward the following morning. Lord Strathcona's Horse was detailed for the operation. At the regiment's conference at 10.15 p.m., the palpable disquiet about a night operation pushing into the unknown was obvious:

> All officers and NCOs of the regiment attended. I think that Colonel Docherty sensed that we all felt pretty dubious about the project because he said 'Now, we will be alright, we'll all be there together and I'll be there with you and we will be all right.'[70]
>
> Lieutenant Sam Williams, Lord Strathcona's Horse, Canadian Cavalry Brigade, 5th Cavalry Division

So it must have been a considerable relief for Williams to record: 'However, just as we were filing out of the big barn in which we had held the conference, word came that the project was abandoned.'[71]

As the advanced guard units of III Corps' cavalry, the experience of the Canadian Cavalry Brigade must be noted as exceptional on the day. More typical of the general cavalry experience was that described by Frank Ash of 4th Hussars:

> We sat shivering with cold on the ground till orders came at 2.00 p.m. Then we moved up through Saulcourt and Guyencourt and arrived on the left edge of La Vacquerie at about 6.30 p.m. March up very bad owing to mud. Raining hard, no cover at all on the open hillside. Pitch dark, very cold, everyone wet through. The news was that our infantry had got the river crossing at Marcoing but not at Masnières. Off saddled and fed where we were. Howe, Norman and myself found an old Hun dugout 50 feet deep which the Huns had left hurriedly that morning. We got down to it in our saddle blankets at 8.00 p.m. after eating a tin of sausages – the first food for close on 24 hours. Lay at the bottom but full of huge mosquitoes and huge black flies. We got our nappers under our blankets and slept. 12 midnight came; sudden orders to saddle up at once. All turned out. Pouring hard and steadily. False alarm. Off saddled at 1.00 a.m. Lay down in

the rain under a waterproof sheet with Captain Scott and shivered till 6.00 a.m.[72]

Captain Frank Ash, 4th (Queen's Own) Hussars, 3rd Cavalry Brigade, 2nd Cavalry Division

It had been a frustrating day for the cavalry, typified by this story from one cavalry regimental history: 'That evening one of the officers asked the Colonel what hopes there were for the Bays of doing anything next day. He replied that he did not know what anybody else intended to do, but he had every intention of "doing something".'[73] It was now very difficult to see what that 'something' might be.

Yet for many, and perhaps for the men of the Royal Artillery and the Tank Corps in particular, there was a sense of euphoria. Snatching an opportunity to write a brief letter home, Captain George Samuel of the Royal Field Artillery summed up his elation at the tremendous success of the battle's opening:

Now you will know why I was so much in a difficulty as to how I could write to you! The results of the 'push' that we started about 6 hours ago I cannot guess (you will know before me) but I do know that it has been an absolute triumph for SECRECY. No one has dared say a word (in fact very few have known a word) about it. Since the 8th when we left our last home I have been on the move every day and have not had my boots off for several nights at a time. We have done all our marching by night and hidden ourselves by day. No fires have been allowed – in fact it has almost been a crime to show an <u>electric torch</u> at night! – <u>But</u> it's been worth it. The six hours pure joy we have had today have repaid every bit – and I am confident that we shall get further when we want to . . .

I honestly haven't had a moment to write or anything to write about also I've been pretty weary all the time. Even now I'm fairly busy as we are just in the middle of 'taking' our 'final objective' and the phone bell rings a bit. The others have gone forward to find a new 'home' – it will be on the Bosch side of the trenches!! Tonight I may sleep and dream of you where a Bosch officer last night never dreamt of the trouble awaiting him at dawn.

Think of the hundreds of tanks – think of the thousands of guns

– all got up quietly and secretly and let loose at the Hun without a thing to warn him of coming trouble. I can't get over the wonder of it.[74]

Captain George Samuel, Royal Field Artillery

CHAPTER SEVEN

Going on

DURING THE NIGHT the Royal Engineer Field Companies, the pioneer battalions and labour companies responsible for maintaining and expanding signals communications, repairing roads and bridging trench systems, had worked until exhaustion at their tasks. Yet the very nature of a success involving such a deep advance militated against them. Furthermore, the heavy overnight rain, which continued into the morning, combined with the movement of men, guns and horses had turned many roads to glutinous mud.

Captain Horace Raymond Smith, commanding 20th Divisional stretcher-bearers attached to 60th Field Ambulance, had watched the previous day's fighting from a quarry near Gouzeaucourt. Now he and his men were flung brutally into the night's chaos and an encounter with the innocent casualties of war:

> At the ghastly hour of 2.30 a.m., I received orders to take my party up to our new front line, near the canal bank. It was a grim struggle through the mud in the pitch dark, and long before reaching our forward positions my men were tired out. In the grey of the dawn we met a group of French civilians – refugees from one of the villages recaptured from the Germans. There were seven women and two men, and two of the women were carrying young children. They were plastered with mud and their white faces expressed nothing but blank despair. Exclamations of pity broke from my riflemen. Two stepped forward, carried the children over a trench and directed the women to the nearest place of safety.[1]
>
> Captain Horace Raymond Smith, 12th Rifle Brigade, 20th Division

Many civilians had remained in close proximity to the front line, basing their decision on three years' stagnation of trench warfare. Now they were in the eye of the maelstrom of battle. Unwittingly, they added to the chaotic mix already created by the poor weather and the disruption caused by blocked roads and blown bridges. The Germans had also blown mines, creating large craters in the roads near Trescault and Havrincourt. The combination had severe implications for the supply and reinforcement of the attacking forces. Supplying the tanks alone was a monumental task, in spite of the best efforts of the Tank Corps' undoubtedly talented staff:

> For the actual battle I was engaged in rushing up spare guns, ammunition, petrol, etc. Although that organizational genius, Colonel Uzielli, had arranged a most perfect system for replenishment of supplies by light railways, at times even this proved inadequate and lorries were brought into use.[2]
>
> Captain Charles Weaver Price, 'Q' Branch, Headquarters, Tank Corps

The problems Weaver Price encountered that morning, and all day, were typical of those for the whole of Third Army.

> At 5.00 a.m. . . . . I started in my car to collect more emergency supplies and convoy them to Ribécourt and Marcoing . . . Followed by six lorries packed with six-pounder shells, petrol, etc., I set out on my journey with the idea of delivering the goods and being back in Albert in time for dinner. Vain hope![3]
>
> Captain Charles Weaver Price, 'Q' Branch, Headquarters, Tank Corps

The roads forward were jammed with traffic and progress was interrupted by occasional long-range shelling. His journey provided ample evidence to support Weaver Price's respect for the men who supplied the guns, the unsung heroes of that most neglected branch of any army's vital functions: logistics.

> I always had a great admiration for the men of the Ammunition Supply Columns. It appeared to me that their work called for more control of nerves than even – say – waiting to go over the top . . . This task of mine confirmed my views and ever after I sympathised with a column waiting patiently for an enemy to cease 'plastering' the road ahead; a perfectly nerve-wracking ordeal.[4]
>
> Captain Charles Weaver Price, 'Q' Branch, Headquarters, Tank Corps

For now all Weaver Price and his lorries could do was join the endless, slow-moving procession of stores and ammunition moving east.

Amongst those who participated in the previous day's attack, the morning provided an opportunity for some to search for friends and others to share news. For Billy Kirkby and Dick Hardy the new day brought renewed pain over the loss of their friend, Harry Griss:

> I awoke to a grey morning, feeling cold and somewhat damp . . . Dick Hardy sat up, rubbed his eyes, and turning towards me said, 'Bill, where is Harry?' For a few moments he looked intently towards me as though wrestling with that confusion of mind existing between awakening from sleep and remembering all that had happened with absolute clarity. 'I remember now, Bill. He's dead. You told me how he died.' He remained silent for several minutes turning the events of the previous day over in his mind, the very personification of utter sadness . . . [5]
>
> Private Billy Kirkby, 2/6th West Yorkshires, 185th Brigade, 62nd Division

Wilfrid Bion gleaned piecemeal the fate of his fellow 'E' Battalion officers, knowing only too well the unsubtle nuance of many a tank crew's likely fate:

> Through the day I heard, bit by bit, what had happened. Quainton had escaped injury and so had two section commanders, Bagshaw and Clifford. Stokes was dead and so was Bayliss. Broome had not been in action. Cohen had been very badly wounded and it was thought was now in the hands of the military hospital. Of the rest of the company one-third that had gone into action had been killed. As usual there were few wounds as the nature of tank warfare meant that most casualties were killed outright by direct gunfire or the almost instantaneous fire caused by the burning petrol. [6]
>
> Second Lieutenant Wilfrid Bion, E40 'Edward II', No. 14 Company, 'E' Battalion, Tank Corps

Overnight, the staff at army, corps, division and brigade had worked hard to establish the exact position in their respective sectors and to make preparation for renewing the assault. In III Corps' sector, Geoffrey

Dugdale's position on a brigade staff gave him some definite knowledge of the situation:

> Our line was now in the form of a very acute salient. We had
> penetrated about four miles deep into the German lines. Therefore we
> had two flanks to defend, which were very much open to German
> counter-attack.
>
> The 12th Division on our right were facing one of these flanks; our
> front extended from Crèvecoeur along the canal bank to within a
> quarter of a mile of Masnières; from there the 29th Division held the
> line.
>
> Our left flank ended by a bridge over the canal on our side; on the
> other side of this bridge the 29th Division held the front.[7]
>
> Captain Geoffrey Dugdale, Headquarters, 60th Brigade, 20th Division

With III Corps up against the canal on the attack's right flank and with most of the canal crossings either damaged, destroyed or uncaptured, it was going to be extremely difficult to get large numbers of infantry and cavalry into a position where they could exploit the first day's success. Nevertheless, plans were laid for an attack at 11.00 a.m. by III Corps to gain the Masnières–Beaurevoir trench line east of Marcoing and Masnières and to capture Crèvecoeur. Then the cavalry could go on. Unbeknown to the British, this trench line had been absolutely undefended for several hours on the previous day. However, units of *107th Division* had now been hustled into the breach and, though they remained uncertain about the position they occupied, every minute without attack had worked to their advantage.

As a preliminary to III Corps' attack, the positions occupied by units of 29th Division and mentioned by Dugdale had been expanded during the night. Most of Masnières was cleared and patrols were sent forward towards the Masnières–Beaurevoir line. George McMurtrie with 7th Somerset Light Infantry moved up to Masnières.

> To do this we had to cross a piece of very marshy ground and the
> enemy started shelling heavily. We got across however without any
> casualties, crossed the canal by a pontoon bridge and got under cover
> of some buildings on the right edge of Masnières. Here we had to dig in
> as a Battalion in reserve to the Brigade holding the front line. The

situation at this time was as follows: In the early morning we had attacked again and captured the whole of Masnières and were then holding a line between Masnières and Les Rues Vertes. We were expecting the enemy to counter-attack at any moment and if he did we would have to go up to support our front line troops. The place we were in was as nasty as it could be.[8]

Second Lieutenant George McMurtrie, 7th Somerset Light Infantry, 61st Brigade, 20th Division

Masnières and its environs was, indeed, an unhealthy spot. Being a salient, it had many of the characteristics of the larger one around Ypres. Its smaller size did not diminish its deadly character:

We were right on the corner of the salient overlooking a lock on the canal. We were being shelled from the front, right flank and the rear and nothing is more unpleasant than being shelled from the rear. Two 'duds' dropped just by where I had placed my platoon and so I immediately put them in another place. It was only by a stroke of luck I managed to get the platoon right and thus saved a large number of casualties. All that day the enemy was heavily shelling us and the machine-gun fire was very serious too; the front line troops had been badly knocked about, so badly that they could not spare men to carry down their wounded. We helped them with their more serious cases.[9]

Second Lieutenant George McMurtrie, 7th Somerset Light Infantry, 61st Brigade, 20th Division

In addition to the expected terrors of shellfire, the occupiers of Masnières soon discovered that the German air force, largely suppressed into acquiescence by sheer weight of numbers on the first day, was very much more active on the second. George McMurtrie complained of how, throughout the day, 'German aeroplanes were flying over us at a very low altitude and occasionally machine-gunning us. There seemed to be a dearth of our machines.'[10] Captain Raymond Smith and his stretcher-bearers also encountered these aircraft:

No sooner had dawn come than a number of enemy planes flew over us. One of them suddenly dived low and started to spray us with machine-gun bullets. We were in a sunken road at the time and on my order the men scattered to either side, and no one was hit. It was, however, a most uncomfortable experience.[11]

Captain Horace Raymond Smith, 12th Rifle Brigade, 20th Division

That the German fliers were so active was all the more surprising since the rain on 21 November had kept most of the British aeroplanes grounded. Nevertheless, some contact patrols were carried out by low-flying aircraft and the movements of infantry, cavalry and tanks reported.

III Corps' 11.00 a.m. attack on the Masnières–Beaurevoir line (to be made by 88th Brigade) was pre-empted at 10.30 a.m. by a German counter-attack against Noyelles, which was one of several such efforts during the day to regain lost ground. The defence had bent. It appeared broken in places. Yet, already, the attempts to seize back territory demanded by German tactical doctrine had begun. Troop movements near Crèvecoeur associated with this attack were disrupted by artillery support from the 13-pounders of the RHA – demonstrating that shrapnel was still a potent weapon against infantry in the open. However, the Germans managed partially to retake Noyelles, and prevented 88th Brigade's attack from being attempted. During the desperate defence of Noyelles, Lieutenant Edward Horner and some men of the 18th Hussars were endeavouring to hold a corner of the village square with a Lewis gun. During one counter-attack, Horner was shot in the groin and mortally wounded. He died at a casualty clearing station at about 8.00 p.m. that evening. His death was another blow to the political and intellectual elite of British society and to the coterie of powerful families known as 'The Souls'.*

The first attack proper by III Corps did not take place for another hour. At noon 2nd South Wales Borderers, with 1st King's Own Scottish Borderers and a total of 18 tanks of 'F' and 'A' Battalions, attacked from Marcoing Station towards Flot Farm. The problem with this attack was much the same as that which affected all operations involving tanks that day. It was relatively hastily prepared, with little or no opportunity for liaison between the tank commanders and the

* Edward Horner's parents subsequently raised a memorial to their son in the parish church in Mells, Somerset. This fine equestrian statue depicting a British cavalry officer of the First World War is a beautiful tribute to a much-loved son.

infantry. This meant cooperation was always more likely to be inferior. Furthermore, time and again infantry commanders ignored the important guiding principle of this type of warfare: infantry must never wait for tanks. However, without the familiar of strong artillery and with the evidence of the previous day's work by tanks before them, it was not unnatural for them to react in this way. Cooperation was further hindered by the fact that, without fascines for their tanks, their commanders were wary of attempting to cross German trench lines, often moving laterally along them instead. This made it difficult for the infantry to follow them closely.

When 87th Brigade did attack, the tanks were met by a storm of machine-gun fire. The Germans used large quantities of armour-piercing bullets which frequently pierced the tanks' 8mm armour – to the shock and horror of the crews, who had been led to believe that this was not possible. However, it was the use of field artillery firing over open sights direct at the tanks that caused several of the tanks to be either knocked out or set on fire. As a consequence virtually no further advance was made here. Efforts to advance at Crèvecoeur saw heavy opposition and little gain. The attack of III Corps was beginning to resemble a man banging his head repeatedly against a brick wall.

In IV Corps, plans were made to complete the capture of the first day's objectives and press on hard towards Bourlon village and wood. Capturing the latter was the responsibility of 62nd Division. In 51st Division, Brigadier General Kenneth Buchanan's 154th Brigade had not been engaged in the first day's fighting. Now they were to advance as far as the Graincourt–Premy Chapel road before preparing for the capture of Fontaine-Notre-Dame and Bourlon. The veteran Frank Brooke of 1/4th Seaforth Highlanders was faced early in the morning with the prospect of an assault to clear the Flesquières Ridge (already a known centre of German resistance) and then a further advance into the unknown. Unlike the first day, the Germans would surely be expecting any such attack. Brooke suppressed all outward signs of being 'feart' at the prospect:

> The Fourth Seaforths were 'waiting' again: 'waiting' for the barrage to lift; 'waiting' for the killing and mutilating. I was in a dreadful mood of

expectancy. My nerves were screwed to the highest point. I looked around at my comrades of Fourteen Platoon. They were young, quivering with mixed elation and fear.[12]

Private Frank Brooke, 1/4th Seaforth Highlanders, 154th Brigade, 51st Division

The loss of all his pals in previous battles left Brooke feeling alone and apart from his fellow platoon members:

I felt irritable and moody. My pipe failed as a solace. I had no desire to go around the company as once. My friends were not with it. In such anxieties, thoughts and apprehensions, I 'waited'.

The maniacal barrage continued with its barbarous work. It was intended to be short, heavy, and ferocious, keeping to the 'surprise' element. Officers' whistles sounded shrilly, and 'over' we went, for the most part a yelling, tumultuous crowd. I felt no weight from the stretcher on my shoulder. From force of habit I glanced along the company's line repeatedly, seeking casualties. No one fell: it was uncanny and mystifying. There was no rattling, spitting machine-gun fire as our foremost men reached the German front line and still no casualties.[13]

Private Frank Brooke, 1/4th Seaforth Highlanders, 154th Brigade, 51st Division

The reason became clear as the Seaforths reached the Hindenburg Support Line:

Number Four Company commander reached the line and stood, as if mesmerised. I came up behind him and looked down into the broad, well-made trench. Sergeant Major Andy Ross had jumped into it and now returned below the 'Skipper'. 'There's no' a bluiddy Jerry onny-ways, sir!' he reported.

'Good Lord, Ross, that's damn funny. He's never skinned out?'

'Looks like it, sir,' said the CSM.

'Here, runner,' said the officer, hastily scribbling a message on his pad, 'cut back to Battalion HQ at the double with this. Now, Sar'-Major, we'll go to his second line.'

We went on, with a similar result. 'Jerry' had 'skinned out' alright. It was incredible, and the battalion was jubilant, its members freely prophesying the end of the war.[14]

Private Frank Brooke, 1/4th Seaforth Highlanders, 154th Brigade,
51st Division

Clearly, news that patrols from 153rd Brigade had entered Flesquières in the early hours of the morning of the 21st and found it unoccupied had not reached Brooke's unit. This news of Flesquières' fall had a remarkable effect:

During the next hour the whole character of the battle seemed to change. Our artillery had finished its bombardment except for the continuance of the heavy calibre . . . field batteries passed up the road; we got out of our trench; the road became a busy thoroughfare – getting busier. The throng and the rain made it very bad. It became thick with wet mud. And then on our right – along No Man's Land we had the pleasure of seeing lines and lines of cavalry pass forward – it seemed a never-ending stream. Then more tanks, more infantry, more working parties hurrying forward to repair the roads. Then wagons laden with shells for the forward guns. Oh, it was fine, a great relief – for a time – from the awful shelling and the noise of the guns.[15]

Second Lieutenant Benjamin Parkin, 2/4th Duke of Wellington's Regiment, 186th
Brigade, 62nd Division

As a consequence of the German withdrawal neither 153rd nor 152nd Brigade encountered much opposition in reaching the Graincourt–Premy Chapel road by 9.00 a.m. Now Buchanan's brigade was to continue the division's advance. Their attack, to commence at 10.00 a.m., would be supported by tanks of 'B' Battalion. Its objectives included the village of Cantaing. However, as the minutes ticked by and the appointed hour approached, there was no sign of the tanks. At 10.00 a.m. there was still no sign. At 10.30, Buchanan decided he could wait no longer. The infantry must attack.

In drizzling rain they went forward – the drizzle reducing visibility but, thereby, helping to screen the advance a little from German observers in Bourlon Wood. Nevertheless, the attack was soon repulsed by scything machine-gun fire. Without tanks, and with insufficient artillery support, it did not appear that progress by infantry alone was possible. However, help was at hand from a more traditional source.

At 9.45 a.m. the 2nd Dragoon Guards (Queen's Bays) of 1st Cavalry Brigade had been ordered to carry out its original task from the first day, advancing northward close to Cantaing and then on to Fontaine-Notre-Dame to exploit any possible gap in the German defences. The cavalry squadrons crossed the Hindenburg Line just beyond Ribécourt, and halted in Bois de Neuf (Nine Wood) to find out what the situation was. It was about 11.00 a.m. Clearly the infantry attack on Cantaing had been repulsed, and the village of Noyelles was partly held by the enemy.

> We had a view of . . . open country leading up the ridge along which the main Cambrai–Bapaume road runs, and which to our immediate front was commanded by Bourlon Wood and the village of Fontaine-Notre-Dame. As far as we could see, there was no German trench line between us, except some wire round Cantaing, halfway between where we were and the ridge. Whilst waiting in the wood the Colonel met a Tank Officer, who said he did not know what to do, but that he had four tanks in working order and wanted to use them. This was sufficient for the Colonel, and he decided to make good his words of the previous evening. He told the Tank Officer to advance on Cantaing, and that he himself intended to follow immediately behind with the Regiment.[16]
>
> Captain James Kingstone, 2nd Dragoon Guards (The Queen's Bays), 1st Cavalry Brigade, 1st Cavalry Division

This section of four tanks was, in fact, part of the group of 13 from 'B' Battalion who had only received attack orders at 9.00 a.m. Nevertheless, with these tanks and his own squadrons, Colonel Algernon Lawson of the Bays had found his opportunity to do 'something':

> His orders to us were that 'A' Squadron was to advance at the gallop, enter the village behind the tanks and occupy the east and north-east extremities of it; that I was to follow with 'C' Squadron and occupy the north and east edges; 'B' Squadron being kept in reserve. Soon after 11.00 a.m. the tanks advanced, and when they were about to enter the village we left the Wood and galloped forward.[17]
>
> Captain James Kingstone, 2nd Dragoon Guards (The Queen's Bays), 1st Cavalry Brigade, 1st Cavalry Division

Amongst the attackers were Privates 'Nobby' Clarke and his festively monikered mate, Christmas Knight, who captured the anticipation and tension of the wait for the order to advance:

> Enemy shells were plentiful. A lieutenant galloped along the rear, at the same time shouting, 'See that your swords are loose'. We sat tense in our saddles, waiting for the order to go forward. Everybody was 'keyed up'. Would the order ever come? I was young then, very young indeed to be a cavalryman. Barely twenty, and there were men in my troop who had campaigned in South Africa.
>
> There I sat astride a powerful bay, wondering whether he would keep his feet in the plunge that was to come, or whether he would fall in the morass: whether we should both come back triumphant or whether I should come back carrying my saddle. It never occurred to me that I should not come back. At last the orders came: 'Half-sections right, walk march! Form sections! Head, left wheel! Draw swords! Trot! Form troop! Form column of half squadron! Gallop!'[18]
>
> Private Chris Knight, 2nd Dragoon Guards (The Queen's Bays), 1st Cavalry Brigade, 1st Cavalry Division

Now the cavalry galloped to the outskirts of the village, rapidly formed sections and got on to a nearby sunken road.

> There were one or two Jerries about and we snapped them up. We got on this sunken road and lined the bank. While we were lying there a few Jocks came over, they had been fighting on the left hand side and they settled down with us. I think they were the Gordons.[19]
>
> Private William 'Nobby' Clarke, 2nd Dragoon Guards (The Queen's Bays), 1st Cavalry Brigade, 1st Cavalry Division

These were men of 1/4th Gordon Highlanders, the right-hand battalion of 154th Brigade's attack. The advance was observed by Stan Bradbury with 1/5th Seaforth Highlanders, who were busy moving forward from dugouts in Ribécourt:

> Whilst doing so we were presented with a sight which is not often seen. In front of us stretched a valley and along the road running on the right-hand side of this a squadron of cavalry were trotting, when suddenly they deployed to their left and in extended order galloped

down into the valley and swept forward onto the enemy's positions. It
was fine to watch them.[20]

Private Stan Bradbury, 1/5th Seaforth Highlanders, 152nd Brigade, 51st Division

Although Captain Kingstone recalled little opposition from the
infantry on entering the village but a considerable amount of shell-fire
coming from their immediate right flank, the village fight was harder:

> Donelly, the Irishman, went raving mad, cutting and thrusting wildly at
> retreating Germans. Germans emerged from dugouts in all directions,
> some giving themselves up, others making a fight of it with a few
> bombs. No. 1 troop received the bombs in its midst. The bomb-
> throwers were accounted for with rifle and revolver. We took many
> prisoners, but the major portion of the garrison holding the village had
> cleared out before we arrived. Very soon their machine-guns were in
> action again, and shells were dropping in and behind the village.[21]

Private Chris Knight, 2nd Dragoon Guards (The Queen's Bays), 1st Cavalry Brigade,
1st Cavalry Division

A company from 14th Durham Light Infantry of 18th Brigade also
joined in the attack on Cantaing on the initiative of their commanding
officer, Lieutenant Colonel John Rosher, and this force of combined
arms took the village and almost 400 prisoners. For the cavalrymen, the
attack demonstrated the possibilities of cavalry on the Western Front
when used in appropriate circumstances, the Bays' dash contrasting
markedly with the caution of their sister regiment in the same sector on
the previous day. But the immediate aftermath provided an equally
important illustration of what happened if cavalry were not available to
exploit success.

> We did not remain in the village but pushed forward to the northern
> and eastern outskirts, leaving only a few men to clear up the village.
> The tanks, or rather three of them, had moved on as if making for
> Bourlon Wood, and in so doing had routed a large number of enemy
> infantry, who came streaming past in disorder across our front. We did
> a lot of shooting at them. This is when another regiment of the Cavalry
> Brigade should have been sent forward. On the one occasion when
> there seemed to be a really good opportunity for Cavalry action, the

Headquarters of both Brigade and Division were miles back and out of touch with the situation.[22]

Captain James Kingstone, 2nd Dragoon Guards (The Queen's Bays), 1st Cavalry Brigade, 1st Cavalry Division

With Cantaing captured, Kingstone and Sergeant Major Arthur Tatlow rode north, past the three tanks – now knocked out by shell fire – and on into Fontaine:

There were small parties of British infantry in Fontaine and on the outskirts of Bourlon Wood, but there was no sign whatsoever of the enemy. In addition to this a large number of civilians were coming out of Cambrai, and they all said that what Germans there were – and they were only details – were in a state of great confusion. This information was immediately sent back, because it seemed that the road was wide open for advance, if only the rest of the Cavalry Brigade was brought up.[23]

Captain James Kingstone, 2nd Dragoon Guards (The Queen's Bays), 1st Cavalry Brigade, 1st Cavalry Division

Kingstone was surely mistaken concerning British *infantry* in Fontaine. The advance of 154th Brigade had halted when it had encountered enfilade fire on the left from Cantaing Mill and Bourlon Wood. Perhaps the men he saw were other dismounted cavalry patrols. The capture of Fontaine would require a separate effort.

The Bays' advance was almost catastrophic for a party of senior German regimental officers of *Reserve Infanterie Regiment 52*:

I rode in the lead with the commander of III Battalion, Major Bohtz. Just as we crossed the lock bridge west of La Malière, we received machine-gun fire from the left . . . I then met our signals officer, Leutnant Ahrens, who told me that the regimental commander was coming on the road towards us. I trotted along to report the arrival of the battalion commanders to the regimental commander. The machine-gun fire was getting stronger. I jumped down from Saul, who was getting nervous because of the bullets whistling in the crossfire. He raced off, no doubt into the arms of the English. I went on by foot, met Major Frühling with Leutnant Hansen and gave him my report. They were on foot, but he had their horses with them. I also met Leutnant Dietz, adjutant of III Battalion.[24]

Leutnant Herbert Ulrich, III Battalion, *Reserve Infanterie Regiment 52, 107th Division*

It was at this moment that British cavalry appeared from Nine Wood and the eastern exit of Cantaing, advancing on a broad front in the direction of Fontaine.

We scattered, the commander, with Leutnants Hansen and Dietz, on their horses in a northerly direction, I without Saul through a dry trench in a north-westerly direction towards Cantaing. In a flash I found myself surrounded by six riders, who charged at me with sabres drawn. The leader shot at me with a pistol from 5 metres, obviously without hitting me. Infantry fire came from Cantaing, so they took their leave of me and went to continue their hunt in the direction of Fontaine.[25]

Leutnant Herbert Ulrich, III Battalion, *Reserve Infanterie Regiment 52, 107th Division*

Evading being chased once more by cavalry, Ulrich was delighted to find on his return from Cantaing that his horse, Saul, had returned unharmed. His superior, Bohtz, was less lucky and was captured.

There was an interesting dichotomy between the conclusions to be drawn from the action at Cantaing according to a cavalry participant like Kingstone and those of the 'conscientiously' brave Tank Corps Intelligence Officer, Captain Eliot Hotblack, who despite being wounded on several prior occasions, roamed the battlefield on foot gleaning whatever information he could regarding the tanks' performance in battle. Hotblack was altogether less sanguine about the cavalry's cooperation with tanks:

In our attack, which was hastily organised, both infantry and cavalry were trying to gain ground under cover of the tank advance. The enemy's machine-gunners were very active, but their exact positions were hard to locate. As the machine-gunners opened fire, the infantry went down, and though the ground was open their casualties were slight, while they remained down. The tanks then hunted for the enemy's machine-gunners, who ceased fire whenever the tanks were near them; on each of these occasions the infantry on the left of the tanks were able to get forward. With the cavalry, however, the problem was much harder. Each time the German machine-gunners got onto them the cavalry had to go back a considerable distance to get cover. Whenever the tanks created an opportunity to advance, the cavalry were too far off to make use of it; by the time the cavalry tried to advance again, fresh machine-gun fire was brought to bear on them and back they had to go. I was very impressed by the fundamental difference between the cooperation with tanks of infantry and cavalry; the fact that mounted men cannot take cover by lying down renders their close cooperation with tanks extremely hard to achieve. If the cavalry dismount and advance on foot, the problem is a simple one; but then they simply become infantry.[26]

Captain Eliot Hotblack, Headquarters, Tank Corps

Of course, Hotblack did not impugn the work of the cavalry when operating independently of the tanks and, however it had been achieved, Cantaing had definitely fallen.

I got orders, round about noon, from Hardie at Brigade to say that the Boche were in full retreat; we had almost reached Cantaing, and that our tanks were already in it – and that I was to collect my transport, pick up my guns, on the way, on the limbers and collect in Flesquières, and be prepared for open warfare.

This was exciting news. It meant we were through the barbed wire zone at last – there were no proper trenches in front of us, and visions of a triumphant march through Cambrai opened before me. I sent off immediate orders to Hastings to rally the transport and fighting limbers, and bring them along the Trescault–Ribécourt road, and orders to my Section Commanders to make dumps of guns and ammunition by hand along the roadside where they could be picked up.[27]

Major Douglas Wimberley, 232nd Company, MGC, 51st Division

The 1/4th Seaforths were ordered forward again, ready to advance on Fontaine.

We marched off. On both sides of the road were ex-German dug-outs and gun-pits. A couple of days ago the road was full of guns pounding away at us. In one place one of our 'heavies' had dropped on a gun and its team. Dead gunners lay in queer, distorted shapes rapidly decomposing. Dumps of engineers' tools had been hurriedly left; there was every sign of a hasty evacuation.[28]

Private Frank Brooke, 1/4th Seaforth Highlanders, 154th Brigade, 51st Division

Wimberley's machine-gunners found progress slow – balked by the volume of horse-drawn and foot traffic on the roads and the efforts of the Germans to delay their progress:

The road was packed with reinforcing infantry, field guns, shells for the guns already up, lorries full of stone for mending the road and filling up the mine craters; cavalry, armoured cars [i.e. tanks], a company of cyclists – hundreds of men and guns trying to pass through the narrow break before it could be closed up. After about half a mile the stream stopped altogether, and there we stuck.

I cursed with rage, as we were losing precious minutes, and then rode forward, cross country, to find out what was causing the block. About half a mile on I found it – it was all owing to the wretched mine craters blown by the Boche across the road at the front-line system, some heavy howitzers were in front – they dared not leave the road as they would sink up to the axle in the soft ground – and were holding all up behind them.

I rode back at the gallop and took my limbers a wide detour over a cross country track – empty though they were it was hard work for the animals, and it was a path only possible to infantry or very light transport. The other side of the crater we rejoined the road and here we found our tired sections with their dumps. I am convinced that these mine craters, which in spite of the sappers' efforts took twenty-four hours or more to bridge over, had a great deal to do with our not being able to exploit our initial success.[29]

Major Douglas Wimberley, 232nd Company, MGC, 51st Division

Moving on up, Brooke's battle experience instead of calming his nerves fed his anxiety and gloom, manifesting itself in heavy sarcasm:

Still in our column of platoons we reached a main road. Away in the distance was a small wood, and word was passed along to halt at this wood for a meal. No one knew how much further we had to march. We trudged through the mud, our boot soles feeling painfully thin.

Buildings came into view, all with huge, German crosses painted upon them. I caught a glimpse of wintry-green fields, queerly refreshing. Shell-holes had all disappeared. The wistful rumours freely circulated. We reached the wood and halted gratefully. Small fires were lighted, dixies filled from water-bottles, and put on to boil. I produced a tin of bully beef and an onion, and Jock [Webster] fished out the bread and biscuits for us both. We had our meal and peacefully smoked. Jock suddenly shook his head in doubt. 'I don't like this bloody quiet, Jack!' he said abruptly.

'No,' I answered. 'Jerry has something waiting for us. There's some machine-gunners hidden up along our route, and we shall get beans.' My despondency returned.

'Bit of a change fightin' on green fields, though.'

'Quite refreshing! There'll be no shell-holes as shelter from the bullets.'[30]

Private Frank Brooke, 1/4th Seaforth Highlanders, 154th Brigade,
51st Division

Shortly after the battalion fell in and recommenced its advance, Brooke's fears became reality:

The edge of the wood was passed and we entered another sunken road. Still that unnerving quiet, broken only by the clatter of accoutrements and the plodding of tired feet. I was in an agony of dreadful anticipation, and keyed to high tension. A detachment of cavalry was resting; its horses were in the shelter of the sunken road. All was quiet and peaceful.

Then, as our last platoon came out of the sunken road a vicious rat-tat-tat and deadly storm of bullets tore through our ranks from those chimneys and roofs. It was a withering blast, and the kilties went down in swarthes [sic]. 'Down, down, down!' screamed officers and non-coms. Some were down, for ever. Every roof seemed a hotbed of sniping and machine-gunners. The bullets whistled stingingly above our heads. Yet the order came to advance up the ridge in extended order, on our stomachs. The enemy had to be cleared from the village. We commenced the attack, crawling up the slope, seeking depressions in the ground for shelter, then away again in spasmodic rushes. I saw the company commander, Lieutenant Macintosh [sic], lent to us from the Fifth Battalion, get a bullet between his eyes. He stood bolt upright and paid the penalty for such foolishness.[31]

Private Frank Brooke, 1/4th Seaforth Highlanders, 154th Brigade,
51st Division

This may have been the 24-year-old poet, Lieutenant Ewart Mackintosh, who was certainly attached to 1/4th Seaforth Highlanders from the 1/5th battalion when he was killed in action. Mackintosh had been at Oxford University when war broke out. When he tried to join the army he had originally been rejected because of poor eyesight before getting a commission. He was wounded at High Wood on the Somme in August 1916 and spent a year in Britain before returning to the front. His poems included 'In Memoriam', 'Recruiting' and 'War, The Liberator'. Mackintosh recognized the war as, for some at least (himself included), an opportunity to experience a life of excitement otherwise denied: 'Say what life would theirs have been, that it should make you weep for them, A small grey world imprisoning the wings of their desire?'[32]

After the first shock, Brooke was quickly at work along with other bearers. Wounded men were dragged or helped into the farmhouse. An aid-post was hurriedly established in the cellars. Now Brooke's fear had left him:

It was surprising – I thought – how I never worried about the stinging, wasp-like noises denoting the passing of bullets, when working so hard. Whereas one was always conscious of shell explosions – they forced and blasted their way to your innermost consciousness – bullets swept round practically unnoticed, excepting for such mild irritation as a bluebottle would cause.[33]

Private Frank Brooke, 1/4th Seaforth Highlanders, 154th Brigade,
51st Division

These tasks completed, Brooke observed amazed as two British cavalrymen then appeared, seemingly oblivious to the danger around them.

At the brow of the hill they reined in, and coolly, one unslung his binoculars and keenly scanned the country. For quite half a minute, his glasses glued to his eyes, he sat patiently, only the two horses fidgeting nervously. He replaced the glasses, and with his companion, 'about-turned', and the horses immediately began a swift trot. Suddenly the man with the glasses fell from his horse. Instantly the other caught the riderless horse and rode off at a headlong gallop.[34]

Private Frank Brooke, 1/4th Seaforth Highlanders, 154th Brigade,
51st Division

Rushing to the wounded man's aid, he found him propped against the roadside, with one leg doubled under him. He was smoking a cigarette, and sweating profusely:

'Your leg?' I asked. 'Yes.' I cut through his thick riding-pants with my jack-knife and soon had the neat bullet wound exposed. His late companion returned, zig-zagging to avoid stray bullets. 'I had ta tak t'hosses in,' he explained. 'hoss is worth 'undreds o' men ta t'cavalry, an' it's t'first question asked – "Wot abart t'hosses?" '[35]

Private Frank Brooke, 1/4th Seaforth Highlanders, 154th Brigade,
51st Division

The two unwounded men then carried the wounded cavalryman to the recently created aid-post.

I wished him luck and left him to the ministrations of our MO. Charlie Cliffe was in the farmyard and I stopped for short rest and a chat. Then, as I stepped off to rejoin the platoon, snick! A stray bullet ploughed its way across my left knee leaving a neat furrow. Painful, but not dangerous.[36]

Private Frank Brooke, 1/4th Seaforth Highlanders, 154th Brigade,
51st Division

This seemingly innocuous incident's consequences saw Brooke first taken to a Casualty Clearing Station and then invalided home. It was his 'Blighty ticket'. Brooke was sure the reason for this surprising denouement lay in his Yorkshire roots:

I was amazed to hear, on all sides, homely Yorkshire dialect from the RAMC wallahs. It was explained in conversation with one, for the unit was from Leeds. I was made a fuss of, and the doctor who attended me had a huge splint put upon my leg. It was done deliberately, I honestly believe. No man who had walked as far as I had needed a splint. The veriest tyro in first-aid knows that much. But splint cases were usually marked for straight on board and I spoke loudly about Leeds being my home when the doctor was attending the next case to mine. He couldn't help but hear![37]

Private Frank Brooke, 1/4th Seaforth Highlanders, 154th Brigade, 51st Division

Unlike so many of his friends, Brooke had survived and would go home.

Outside Cantaing, Douglas Wimberley was trying to ascertain the tasks expected of him and his machine-gun company. He made his way forward past horrors that, for him, matched those of the Ypres Salient:

Here there was a nasty sight. A half burnt tank straddled half across the road and outside the door were two dead members of the crew, blackened and half burnt, one had an appalling wound in the body as he had tried to get out at the door, and his entrails were out of his body in the road. It nearly made me sick – though after Ypres I didn't think a corpse could affect me . . . Later on in the day the mess was cleared up, but for days afterwards it was interesting to see how every horse that passed shied violently at the place, smelling the blood and burnt flesh.[38]

Major Douglas Wimberley, 232nd Company, MGC, 51st Division

Discovering Brigadier General Buchanan's headquarters were established in Cantaing, he at once went off to report his sixteen guns ready for action, 'though in my heart of hearts I hoped we would get a respite, as the men were very tired, so were we officers. I was told that I was not then wanted, so went back to the company.'[39]

Meanwhile, in the absence of other support, 154th Brigade, whose attack had stalled in front of Fontaine, were ordered to wait on the arrival of tanks before making a fresh effort. Seven tanks of 'H' Battalion were assigned to assist them in taking Fontaine. The commander of this enlarged 'section' was Daniel Hickey:

There was a ridge to be crossed before we reached Fontaine, and since we had already seen the mess that the enemy had made of tanks as they topped a ridge, we didn't feel too comfortable about it – especially as we now knew he was prepared for tanks. At half-past one seven tanks were drawn up in a line, at about 200 yards' interval, as though for a race.[40]

Captain Daniel Hickey, H28 'Hadrian', No. 23 Company, 'H' Battalion, Tank Corps

Hickey had chosen to ride in the tank 'Hadrian', commanded by Lieutenant George Hardy. Their initial advance was relatively uneventful:

It was a clear, cold winter afternoon when we went into action for the second time in forty-eight hours. The first half hour was uneventful and we rolled on comfortably over firm, smooth ground. After passing a farmhouse at La Justice, on our left, Hardy, peering through his front port-hole shouted: 'See them running like rabbits!' The enemy had seen the tanks approaching and were beating a strategic retreat.[41]

Captain Daniel Hickey, H28 'Hadrian', No. 23 Company, 'H' Battalion, Tank Corps

Crossing a sunken road, the tanks assisted the 1/7th Argyll and Sutherland Highlanders overcome lingering opposition from Cantaing Mill before breasting the final ridge and the run over exposed terrain towards Fontaine:

We found ourselves in the thick of a bombardment. Two enemy batteries of field guns were blazing at the advancing tanks, one from the southeast edge of Bourlon Wood and the other from near Fontaine church . . . 'Hermosa' had taken a more direct route to Fontaine and was out of sight. One of the crew at the rear reported that 'Havoc' was following, but that 'Hydra' and 'Harlequin' were knocked out. All I could see through a revolver loop-hole was Viveash's tank 'Hong Kong' slightly ahead and about 200 yards to our left. She was coming in for the concentrated fury of the guns. Breathless, we watched her zig-zag as the shells dropped nearer and nearer. Clouds of earth flew up like water-spouts, some so close that a dozen times we thought she'd been hit . . . We realized that whether she got through or not, in a minute or so we should be going through the same hell. Hardy gave orders to keep on changing direction. Miraculously, 'Hong Kong' escaped and charged down the slope into the valley. It was our turn now! Shells were bursting all round us, and fragments of them were striking the sides of the tank. While the four gunners blazed away, the

222

rest of the perspiring crew kept the tank zig-zagging, to upset the enemy's aim.[42]

Captain Daniel Hickey, H28 'Hadrian', No. 23 Company, 'H' Battalion, Tank Corps

Their hope of salvation lay in keeping going and following as erratic a course as possible. Then disaster struck.

Just at this critical moment the 'auto-vac', supplying petrol to the engine, failed. The engine spluttered and stopped. We were now a stationary target, incapable of moving one way or another. In the sudden silence we could hear the thud, thud of falling shells, and metal and earth striking the sides of the tank. At any moment it would be kingdom come! Automatically, I tightened my tin-hat, and adjusted my metal mask, with the feeling of: 'Those about to die, salute thee, O Caesar!'[43]

Captain Daniel Hickey, H28 'Hadrian', No. 23 Company, 'H' Battalion, Tank Corps

Now their lives depended on the skill of one crew member. In the hot, foetid air of the stalled tank, they sweated and watched:

It was a trying moment! With tense faces the crew watched the imperturbable second driver as he coolly and methodically put the auto-vac right, ignoring all the proferred advice to give it a good hard knock. To the adjurations to hurry up or the tank would be blown to blazes, he replied with his habitual stutter: 'Why d-don't you m-mind your own b-bloody b-business?'[44]

Captain Daniel Hickey, H28 'Hadrian', No. 23 Company, 'H' Battalion, Tank Corps

It was only a matter of minutes before they got started again, but for Hickey it seemed a lifetime. The tank's final drive on Fontaine was exhilarating:

How we weren't hit during that brief period Providence alone knows! Then, down the slope we charged in 'top' speed, with guns blazing, and the enemy batteries ceased firing. The tanks advanced straight for the village and then wheeled along it, firing into it and silencing the machine-guns.[45]

Captain Daniel Hickey, H28 'Hadrian', No. 23 Company, 'H' Battalion, Tank Corps

The long advance under constant fire from all sides had sadly depleted the advancing infantry. Their casualties were estimated at nearly 70 per cent. Of 375 Seaforths who had passed La Justice in the attack, there were now about 120 remaining. The Argyll and Sutherland Highlanders had suffered almost equally heavily. With the infantry now occupying Fontaine, the three surviving tanks 'Hadrian', 'Havoc' and 'Hong Kong', started back to their rallying point 'lumbering along like circus elephants, one following the other'.[46]

On the left, 62nd Division's attack was still being driven forward by the energetic Roland Bradford. To support his infantry in the attack on the 21st, Bradford was allotted twenty tanks and the 11th Hussars. Based on the previous day's experiences, Bradford expected little resistance and, when he met the Hussars' commander, Lieutenant Colonel Rowland Anderson, he proposed the cavalry should clear Bourlon Wood with two squadrons and occupy Bourlon with the third. Anderson counselled caution and was sensibly concerned that if his cavalry were asked to operate in Bourlon Wood, their value would be greatly diminished since, dismounted, they would become the equivalent in firepower terms of an infantry company. Bradford concurred and the Hussars were instead ordered to move around the wood preceded by patrols to ascertain the exact situation. Bradford set his brigade's objectives as the capture of Anneux and a line in front of Bourlon Wood before a second blow to clear Bourlon village from the west to the south-east corner of the village. It was soon clear, however, that the expectation of an easy advance was not likely to be fulfilled.

At 10.00 a.m. the attack by infantry and tanks captured Anneux and, after considerable fighting, the edge of Bourlon Wood was reached. The chief centres of resistance were Anneux on the right, the trenches of the Hindenburg Support system on the left (where 36th Division also had considerable difficulty in making progress) and in the centre, most problematic of all, Bourlon Wood from which machine-gunners poured fire into all sectors off the division's attack. Against such opposition, 186th Brigade did well to accomplish what they did.

The tanks made an important contribution, as the terse description of one tank commander indicates:

Left rallying point at 8.30 a.m. for Graincourt. Arrived Graincourt, proceeded with difficulty through the village. On nearing the end of the village got my 6-pounder sponson jammed in narrow street. Backed out and proceeded on to Anneux round another way. Advanced on Anneux slightly behind the rest of the tanks.

Very fine sight to see tanks advancing on Anneux and surrounding the village. Got good shooting here with 6-pounder. Then proceeded to left of the village and worked down houses to the end of the village. Crossed a small road and proceeded to Anneux–Cambrai road.

Good shooting here at a sort of factory full of Huns. Did not cross road as I saw no signs of infantry behind. Turned round and found a Hun aeroplane overhead dropping green lights over me. Went on as fast as possible towards infantry near Anneux.

Shelled on the way evidently as a result of Hun aeroplane. None very near. Found infantry officer who asked me to try and keep Hun machine-guns off his men while digging in. Set off again and tried to do this but could not see any, although bullets were coming fast. Saw tanks returning from Arras–Cambrai road so followed them. Engine running very badly all the day, getting short of petrol.

Followed 'buses' back past Graincourt all along the valley to near Havrincourt. Got orders to take tank to T Wood, did so and camouflaged. Crew and I then ordered to proceed for rest to Havrincourt Wood. Arrived wood about 12.00 p.m. Turned in.[47]

Lieutenant Christopher Burton, G4 'Gloucester II', No. 21 Company, 'G' Battalion, Tank Corps

By the day's end, Bradford's brigade had almost reached Bourlon and its wood, but they had now accomplished as much as they could reasonably be expected to. The brigade, having captured more than 1,200 prisoners and 38 guns, was relieved in the evening by 185th Brigade.

CHAPTER EIGHT

Hope Dies Hard

THE LATE AFTERNOON and evening of 21 November was a crucial point in the battle. On the right flank of the attack, Pulteney's III Corps were clearly impeded by the difficulties of getting sufficient men, horses, guns and tanks across the few surviving crossings over the canal and river. A small bridgehead had been established east of Masnières and Marcoing but resistance at Crèvecoeur, Rumilly and Flot Farm prevented it from being expanded towards Cambrai. Failure to take Crèvecoeur meant that any prospect of French participation in the battle was now ended. With Noyelles all but captured and Cantaing taken, the direction of the attack was now north and north-east. Fontaine, held only by the badly mauled companies of the Seaforth and Argyll & Sutherland Highlanders, was a dangerous salient in IV Corps' front. Bourlon Wood, a dark, seemingly malign mass of still largely undamaged trees straddling higher ground and dominating the battle-field for the defenders, must be captured for real success in the battle.

The ridge, village and wood at Bourlon had been objectives for the first day. Looking back from a different century and with the considerable benefit of hindsight, it might seem that this was the moment for Haig to shut down the battle – just as he had told Byng he would do if, after 48 hours, the results gained and the general situation did not justify continuation. His diary entries for 20 and 21 November show he was well informed regarding the battlefield situation and, clearly, the prospects for using cavalry to exploit the battle's successes were now limited. He had few reserves (although the three divisions of V Corps had not yet been committed to the fight) and still faced the prospect of the loss of more divisions to the Italian front. Dawn on 22 November would see the end of the 48-hour period after which German reserves might be expected to arrive in strength. It was surely time to end the battle.

Ironically, had he done so, Haig would have provided ample demonstration of why Fuller's idea of a 'tank raid' was flawed. Firstly, the attackers could not now simply occupy the new line they had reached. There must, inevitably, be a withdrawal to the best defensive positions – probably on Flesquières Ridge on IV Corps' front and, presumably west of the canal in III Corps' sector. In this case, what would have been accomplished beyond an attritional victory, albeit with a deeper advance than those achieved during Third Ypres? (Indeed, Fuller's 'raid' would have been an attritional victory *without* the advance.) The withdrawal would not only be problematic but would certainly provide a boost to German morale. However, Haig did not call the attack off. His philosophy was that successful commanders pursue (and, of course, achieve) ambitious objectives. For Haig, possession of the Bourlon Ridge offered great strategic rewards for exactly the same reason it was already threatening the success of Third Army's attack: observation. The ability to observe German positions to the north-west meant a greatly enhanced ability to bombard these positions with artillery. This might, in turn, prompt a German withdrawal from positions east of Arras. Looking east, Cambrai's position as a supply railhead would also be threatened.

Byng and his staff at Third Army headquarters had continued to entertain the hope and belief that much could still be accomplished. Even after Byng's chief of staff, Major General Sir Louis Vaughan, had had a lengthy discussion with Sir William Pulteney, III Corps' commander, regarding the prospects of further operations by the latter's corps, Third Army staff still issued preliminary orders for more operations by III Corps on 22 November. As the Official History pointedly observed, 'Hope died hard at Army headquarters.'[1] Nevertheless, in the evening Haig showed no hesitation in closing down III Corps operations and ordering Pulteney through Byng to take defensive measures to retain possession of what had been captured. His decision concerning Bourlon Ridge was equally determined. With the gains of the opening days' fighting behind him, Haig must surely have known that he could afford not to give immediate direct aid to Lloyd George's pet project: Italy. Furthermore, continuation of the battle could be justified not only by reference to the potential strategic gains attendant on the capture of Bourlon but also as a means to occupy German forces in France and thereby indirectly relieve pressure on his Italian allies. Confirmation from the Chief of the General Staff, Sir William Robertson, that he might hold on to two of his divisions ear-marked for the Italian front made his choice certain. The attack towards Bourlon would continue. However, a fresh effort could not be made until a properly coordinated assault could be organized and fresh troops brought up. The availability of 40th Division for an attack on 23 November offered an opportunity to relieve the tired and depleted units of 51st and 62nd Divisions. It was decided that, on the day before IV Corps would maintain pressure with its left flank divisions (36th and 56th) along the western slopes of Bourlon Ridge. Meanwhile, Byng's other reserves – the Guards and 59th Divisions – were also moved a step closer to the front.

On the ground, some could see the vulnerability of the Fontaine position:

> 154 Brigade had established itself in Fontaine, along the road to Cantaing and that village itself. Hardie, the shrewd, looking at his map and seeing Fontaine like a pistol pointing into the Boche line, suggested that eight of my guns should go up and help 154 Machine-Gun Company in the consolidation, but this the General judged as unnecessary, as reports from Colonel Unthank, commanding the 4th Seaforths in Fontaine, said there was not a Boche in sight.[2]
>
> Major Douglas Wimberley, 232nd Company, MGC, 51st Division

However, it was not so obvious to the high command, who knew little of the weakness of Fontaine's garrison. Only time would prove the error of Buchanan's decision.

The issue of supplies, together with reinforcements, was predominant in the minds of many British senior officers that night. The German destruction of the bridge over the Canal du Nord on the Bapaume–Cambrai road on the first morning of the battle was now starting to present IV Corps with considerable logistical problems.

Charles Weaver Price and his tank supply column of six lorries had spent the entire day battling along the road from Albert. At 6.00 p.m. they reached Metz-en-Couture where he was solemnly warned by an Assistant Provost Marshal not to be fool enough to attempt to get through. 'As my orders were to "get through" I had to ignore his counsel, and so pushed on to Trescault.' He now braved four lines of traffic, two up and two down, with frequent traffic jams, reaching Trescault after several hours.

> The scene here, to use a Press phrase, 'beggars description'. I shall never forget the 'Jock' private who was the sole representative of the traffic control people. Try to visualise the Bank at the busiest time of day, and then imagine one policeman attempting to regulate the traffic . . . [you get] a faint idea of what the 'Kiltie' was doing – and really doing it well. Punctuated with shouted orders to drivers of all description of vehicles, he told them that all roads forward were 'done in by Jerry'. I left him swinging his lantern, the only light allowed on the patch.[3]
>
> Captain Charles Weaver Price, 'Q' Branch, Headquarters, Tank Corps

He now discovered the mine crater the Germans had blown in the road here. Furthermore, cavalry hooves had broken the road's hard surface exposing the putty-like substance underneath. Lorry traffic was, therefore, out of the question. Extricating his lorries and resolving to try an alternative route by Havrincourt, Weaver Price soon discovered this road too was blocked. It was time for a new plan.

> Just before dawn we evolved a scheme that we at once commenced carrying out. The supplies were dumped in a field off the road side; a guard was borrowed from a Divisional Ammunition Column; the lorries were sent home, while we proceeded to Ribécourt, via Metz. Here we made arrangements for tanks to make a cross-country journey to pick up the goods. This was successfully done, and thirty-nine hours after leaving it I reported to HQ at Albert.[4]
>
> Captain Charles Weaver Price, 'Q' Branch, Headquarters, Tank Corps

Dramas such as these were being enacted all over the battle front, but without such supplies any decision regarding continuation of the battle would have been rendered irrelevant.

Once again, night time brought intense activity – some of it especially unwelcome to resting troops:

That night 232 Company slept, rested and refreshed. When I say slept,
I should say rather with many interruptions. A little after dark we heard
a great clatter upstairs, and shrill laughter mingling with the loud
laughs of the Jocks. On going upstairs we found that the first refugees
from Cantaing and Fontaine had arrived, with as many of their household goods as they could either carry or bring in hand carts. All night
long they flocked in, in uproarious spirits, and most of them chose our
courtyard to break their journey for an hour or two. The men
thoroughly enjoyed themselves kissing all the girls and having huge
jokes – but to one trying to sleep underneath it was trying to say the
least of it.[5]

Major Douglas Wimberley, 232nd Company, MGC, 51st Division

During the night and early morning units were relieved and others
moved into the front line. Hunger was the repeated refrain of many
now. Supplying rations for the many front line troops was as problematic as the supply of munitions and other stores. What food did get
forward was welcome:

The Battalion by this time had reached the village of Cantaing. We
took possession of a large dugout just outside the village which had
formerly been a German Red Cross Dressing Station and here we
stayed for the night. As soon as it was dark, one of our field kitchens
managed to get up to within a few hundred yards of us and made some
porridge which was greatly enjoyed as we were having nothing but two
very hard biscuits each day.[6]

Private Stan Bradbury, 1/5th Seaforth Highlanders, 152nd Brigade, 51st Division

With the decision largely to consolidate on the fronts held by III
Corps and 51st and 62nd Divisions, many of the infantry in reserve
had their opportunity to indulge in a much-favoured (possibly favourite)
pastime: scrounging.

We had nothing to do unless the Germans attacked, so we all went into
the town looking around for souvenirs. Masnières had been occupied
by civilians when we attacked, some of these had gone back with the
Germans and some had joined the English and been taken to the rear.
We found a piano in a neighbouring house and had it taken into our
room. I went around with my servant and found some live rabbits and

some flour – nearly every house we went into had several live rabbits. The French peasants seemed to keep rabbits for food. I had heard that there were some tunnels in the town, which were supposed to go right to Cambrai . . . Nothing was found in these tunnels but the number of rumours of parties of Germans caught in them was too ridiculous.[7]

Second Lieutenant George McMurtrie, 7th Somerset Light Infantry, 61st Brigade, 20th Division

The opportunity to pillage abandoned farms and houses certainly brought variety in its spoils. For McMurtrie's battalion, perhaps the greatest delight came from the 'liberation' of two cows, which were brought to battalion headquarters and placed in adjacent stables. Some of the men who were farmers tended these cows and for the next few days the officers at least enjoyed fresh milk daily.

For others it was an opportunity to examine the scene of tank carnage on Flesquières Ridge and to speculate on how the large number of tanks here had met their fate:

After a meal I went up to the gun position at Flesquières and carefully examined the German position. As far as I could see by the piles of shell cases, only two guns were used and they were in the open behind the battery position, having been pulled out of the battery to fire at the tanks. From their position they could fire as the tanks showed, coming up the hill and before any armament of the tanks could be brought to bear. I carefully went round the broken tanks and in no case could the tanks' gunners use either the 6-pounders or machine-guns before they were hit.[8]

Major Edward Carter, No. 8 Company, 'C' Battalion, Tank Corps

Another who examined the Flesquières position was Geoffrey Dugdale:

The first thing we came to was a German field battery, every gun out of action with the exception of one. By this was lying a single German officer, quite dead. In front of him were five tanks, which he had evidently succeeded in knocking out himself, single-handed, with his gun. A brave man.[9]

Captain Geoffrey Dugdale, Headquarters, 60th Brigade, 20th Division

Neither Carter nor Dugdale suggested that one man was responsible for all the tank casualties of 'D' and 'E' Battalions on Flesquières Ridge. Undoubtedly, however, they admired the anti-tank work of the German artillerymen and, in Dugdale's case, of one man in particular whom, he speculated, had worked his 77mm gun alone.

Respect for a brave foe might soon have faded from memory had it not been for the visit of a more illustrious personage to the same spot that day. Field Marshal Sir Douglas Haig had set out from his advanced headquarters that morning to view the battlefield himself.

> The Commander-in-Chief with the Corps Commander and Divisional
> Commander passed by our Station. They went just up the road to
> Trescault and stood on the high ground where a view of the country
> towards Bourlon Wood could be had. After a survey through their field
> glasses they returned. I learnt afterwards that he [DH] had visited 62nd
> Divisional Headquarters to congratulate the Division on the splendid
> advance they had made.[10]
>
> Second Lieutenant Benjamin Parkin, 2/4th Duke of Wellington's Regiment, 186th
> Brigade, 62nd Division

Haig visited both Harper and Braithwaite's headquarters and, later, recorded some censure of the two divisional commanders for positioning their headquarters too far behind the front line, recognizing the manner in which this compounded the problems of communication with the front line. However, it was his reconnaissance of Flesquières Ridge that did much to establish one of the most entrenched Cambrai myths. He noted his impressions in his diary that evening:

> On the ridge about Flesquières were a dozen or more Tanks which
> were knocked out by artillery fire. It seems that the Tanks topped the
> ridge and began to descend the ridge into the village . . . then came
> under direct artillery fire. An eyewitness stated that on the appearance
> of the first Tank all the personnel of a German battery (which was in a
> kind of chalk pit) fled. One officer however was able to collect a few
> men and with them worked a gun and from his concealed position
> knocked out Tank after Tank to a number of 8 or 9. This officer was
> then killed. This incident shows the importance of infantry operating

with Tanks at times acting as skirmishers to clear away hostile guns and reconnoitre.[11]

Field Marshal Sir Douglas Haig, General Headquarters, BEF

Haig was to repeat the assertion of his unnamed eyewitness in his Official Despatch concerning the battle in February 1918. In doing so, he set a hare running. Who was the courageous German artillery officer? After the war, the Germans tried to identify him and concluded that the likeliest candidate was Unteroffizier Theodor Krüger of *8 Batterie Feld Artillerie Regiment 108*. The basis for this assumption was somewhat slim, however.

But Haig's diary entry makes two important points. The first was that the dead German officer *might* have accounted for *at most*, perhaps, 9 tanks. Since 'E' Battalion alone had lost 28 tanks knocked out, ditched or broken down, it was clearly not the work of a single German gunner that had led to the check at Flesquières.

Secondly, Haig rightly concluded that a key lesson was the need for skirmishing infantry to tackle artillery crews before they could bring their guns to bear using direct fire against tanks. That the infantry were not available at the right time on Flesquières Ridge on 20th November was because of a complex mix of factors and not flawed tactics. Undeniably, as evinced by the events that day, the prior anti-tank training the artillery of the German *54th Division* had received was of crucial importance. If an unknown officer had kept his head whilst others suffered 'tank panic', it was as much due to this training as his own personal courage.

All this activity in the support and reserve areas did not mean that the Germans had lapsed into peaceful acquiescence concerning the British offensive. Whilst the operational pause on the 22nd brought a welcome respite and an opportunity to bring further reserves up, nevertheless General Georg von der Marwitz (commanding *Second Army*) remained concerned that artillery reinforcements were only arriving piecemeal. Nevertheless, the front-line commander of the sector under most pressure, Generalmajor Otto Havenstein of *107th Division*, was pressed to continue counter-attacks against the British. In particular, there was uncertainty about the British thrust on Fontaine. So, as soon as reinforcements from *119th Division* arrived, several companies were urged forward towards Fontaine, which was now only defended by the battered 1/4th Seaforths. The 1/7th Argyll and Sutherland Highlanders who had helped capture it had been moved to cover the Bourlon Wood flank. Defence was not in the thoughts of Douglas Wimberley, who had ridden forward that morning to Cantaing:

> We went to the village outskirts and had some difficulty in finding our front line. There were of course no trenches. Not a Boche was to be seen, and Cambrai with its tall spires a mile and a half away seemed within a stone's throw. A cavalry subaltern informed me that the evening before some troops had wandered all through La Folie Wood without seeing a single Boche.
>
> I am convinced that had we attacked again at dawn we could have had Cambrai almost without opposition. At the same time it is easily understood that a breakthrough for such a depth on the very limited frontage on which we were attacking would have rendered us particularly prone to being attacked in the flanks – cut off and isolated.[12]
>
> Major Douglas Wimberley, 232nd Company, MGC, 51st Division

The calm was deceptive. Certainly it prompted others to be less cautious in their actions than they might otherwise have been. Captain Robert Bruce of the Royal Army Medical Corps (RAMC) was visiting various Battalion Aid Posts, accompanied by Reverend Andrew Grant who, like many Catholic priests in the war, wanted to be where the action was:

> We set off together, soon leaving Flesquières behind. An open country stretched before us, and we trudged along a good enough road, here and there gaping with nasty shell holes. It led in the direction of Fontaine . . . Passing the small Bois de L'Orival on our left, we soon came to the farm of La Justice, where was the first Aid Post. I spent some time ascertaining and noting the inevitable wants of the MO, who had a room full of wounded and no means of evacuating them.[13]
>
> Captain Robert Tennant Bruce, RAMC, 51st Division

Except for an occasional gruesome reminder that this was a battlefield, Bruce and Grant continued forward like two Scottish gentlemen out for a stroll:

So far there had been little in the way of shelling to trouble us and the walk had not been unpleasant. On the outskirts of Flesquières we had passed a derelict tank, with two headless bodies lying beside it.[14]

Captain Robert Tennant Bruce, RAMC, 51st Division

Having visited a second aid post, Grant and Bruce continued towards another close to Anneux.

Some shells were falling in the dip between Anneux and Fontaine, but none at all near us. Half way to Anneux we met a 7th Argyll, who had been sent back in guard of prisoners, resting in a sunk pit by the side of the road on his way back to his battalion, which he said (with a sweep of his hand including Bourlon Wood and Fontaine) 'We're holding that ridge!'[15]

Captain Robert Tennant Bruce, RAMC, 51st Division

A little further on, having been warned of the potential threat from a sniper, the padre and medical officer paused to consult on the battle-field situation:

It seemed to me that the large forest, the famous Bois de Bourlon, on our left front must be in our hands as it dominated both the Bapaume Road and Fontaine. Unless we held it I failed to see how our troops could be in Fontaine. Our choice of routes to the latter place was between the main road, which skirted the Bois de Bourlon less than a mile north of Anneux, and directly across the country over which the sniper was said to lie busy.

Everything being quiet, and the road not appealing to us, we decided to chance the sniper, and . . . proceeded across country in the direction of Fontaine.[16]

Captain Robert Tennant Bruce, RAMC, 51st Division

However, at Fontaine events took a dramatic turn. Captain James Kingstone of the Queen's Bays on the outskirts of Cantaing described how

the show commenced with a very heavy shellfire on Cantaing village, which luckily did us no damage. Soon after this we saw considerable activity on the high ground near Bourlon Wood, and were able to see large numbers of German troops moving apparently from Cambrai towards Fontaine-Notre-Dame. Very soon heavy rifle fire broke out, and the troops who had been in the village the previous night were driven out. The Germans then began to debouch from the village in large numbers, but their progress was eventually stopped some four or five hundred yards from Cantaing by very heavy accurate fire from a Field Artillery Brigade somewhere to our left rear. We ourselves were unable to fire, owing to the fact that the infantry were between us and the Germans, and it certainly looked at one time as if the very small numbers of our infantry that were there would be driven back to the village.[17]

Captain James Kingstone, 2nd Dragoon Guards (The Queen's Bays), 1st Cavalry Brigade, 1st Cavalry Division

The defenders of Fontaine were undoubtedly surprised:

As we began to leave the village, the Boche started a little quiet shelling – about three shells a minute, and just as we left we saw a Seaforth officer run round shouting to the men to 'stand to' as the Boche were massing at the far end of the village to attack. Hardie and I looked at each other and decided it was quite time to move as neither of us were directly responsible in the defence of the village, but we both thought it was probably a 'wind up'. Whenever one captures a position there are five alarms for attack for every one that comes off.[18]

Major Douglas Wimberley, 232nd Company, MGC, 51st Division

Wimberley's initial impressions of needless panic soon gave way to a realization that something was afoot.

About five minutes later when we were half way across country to Cantaing, the shelling got heavier and we could see Boche running out of Bourlon Wood and from La Folie on the east. Our artillery were not retaliating at all. At this moment an orderly on a horse bent double passed us going at full gallop, getting a few bullets at him. This we learnt later was Colonel Unthank's, 4th Seaforths, runner, riding hell for leather with news for the Brigade.[19]

Major Douglas Wimberley, 232nd Company, MGC, 51st Division

It was now clear that a German counter-attack was in progress and Bourlon Wood was quite definitely *not* in British hands – although at least one member of the Army Medical Corps and an Army Chaplain did not appreciate the fact until it was too late:

> We still walked through quiet but pretty scenery, and were troubled very little by shells. If there were a sniper he took no notice of us. As we were nearing the road, however, our steps were arrested by shouts coming from our left. The padre said he saw some men he took to be West Yorks on account of their short coats and woolly jackets. We halted, listened, and again heard the shouts, coming apparently from the edge of Bourlon Wood quite close to us. I could see nothing.
>
> Thinking it possible that some wounded might by lying there, I suggested to the padre we should slant in the direction of the shouts and ascertain what was the matter . . . On getting close to the main road we were hailed by unmistakably Boche voices, a number of soldiers with rifles at the present sprang into view on the edge of the wood and we were fairly caught! Escape was out of the question. The sunken road was too far behind us, neither of us particularly fleet of foot, and we would in any case have been riddled with bullets before we had gone fifty yards. 'Hands up' we were ordered, and hands up it was till we reached the wood.[20]
>
> Captain Robert Tennant Bruce, RAMC, 51st Division

In the sky above Fontaine, Arthur Lee, now promoted to Captain, had a bird's eye view of the counter-attack in progress:

> I then realised that a fierce fight was going on for possession of Fontaine. I saw khaki and field-grey figures clustering close to the walls on either side of the crossroads, firing at one another round corners, but it was all very mixed up, and there was nothing I could do there. So I switched my attention to a group of field-greys filtering off the main road southwards into a large field flanked by a wood with a canal behind it. I dived low and began to spray them, but after one long burst, my guns jammed, first one then the other.[21]
>
> Captain Arthur Gould Lee, 46 Squadron, RFC

However he soon became far more preoccupied with attempts to ensure his own survival after a shell burst immediately beneath his Sopwith Camel:

Chunks of shrapnel tore through the fabric of the plane, one piece going *clang!* somewhere in the engine, which didn't stop but vibrated horribly.

I expected the machine to fall to bits, as it began to wobble violently. The joystick felt loose, with no lateral control and fore-and-aft like lead. I closed the throttle, switched off, held her off the ground as long as I could, and flopped – I couldn't call it a landing but at least I didn't turn over – on the large grassy field that was fortunately still beneath me. Fortunately, also there was next to no wind. She trundled along for fifty yards, while I unbuckled my belt, just in case, then she stopped halfway between the wood I'd just circled and a sunken road.[22]

Captain Arthur Gould Lee, 46 Squadron, RFC

The large field he had landed in was quiet enough, but fitful rifle fire came from the direction of Fontaine:

Otherwise, all seemed peaceful enough . . . when – Crak! Crak! Crak! Crak! – and a sharp rattle of gunfire from my right. Startled, I turned, saw a machine-gun flashing in the trees. I was out of the cockpit like a jack-in-the-box. I ran as hard as my full flying kit would allow towards the sunken road, keeping the machine between me and the guns, though I could still hear the vicious crak-ak-ak-ak! as bullets passed fairly close to me. They were after me because they were the bunch I'd just been shooting up and they were only 200 yards away. I had nearly 100 yards to run and with every step was astonished they didn't hit me. Then the ground dropped away, and I slithered down the bank into the road. I was safe – for the moment. I was gasping for breath – sprinting and flying kit don't go together.[23]

Captain Arthur Gould Lee, 46 Squadron, RFC

His feelings of safety did not last long:

Suddenly I heard footsteps. I had no gun with me, and didn't know what to expect, so I dropped into a funk-hole by the ditch . . . I kept low until they passed, then looked out – it was a wounded infantry-man, arm in a sling. I caught him up and found he was a Seaforth Highlander. The bullet had gone through his shoulder. He said they were being pushed out of Fontaine, the Boche had brought up too many troops. I knew it already, I'd just been shooting some of them up.[24]

Captain Arthur Gould Lee, 46 Squadron, RFC

Back in Cantaing, Douglas Wimberley provided what information he could to the commander of 154th Brigade's reserves, 9th Royal Scots:

As soon as we got to Cantaing we went down to Colonel Green, 9th Royal Scots, in his dugout and told him the news. He instantly rang up the artillery, and messages were sent all round for the 9th Royal Scots and 1st Cavalry Brigade troops in Cantaing to stand to.

We later got the bad news that Fontaine was lost and that a lot of the Seaforths were taken prisoner, killed or wounded. The attack was a purely local affair and a line was taken up from Cantaing in front of Anneux. The attack had been well carried out, the Boche had massed in La Folie and Bourlon, close to the village, and had then rushed it, its situation being in an acute salient between woods, rendering it particularly liable for this type of attack.[25]

Major Douglas Wimberley, 232nd Company, MGC, 51st Division

This was an accurate summation of how Fontaine was lost. The hard-pressed Seaforths had given a good account of themselves but had eventually been overwhelmed. Wimberley could only speculate on how his machine-gun company might have influenced the outcome:

I often wonder what the result would have been if there had been the fire power of the additional machine guns of mine, lying idle in Flesquières, which was offered to General Buchanan and refused, as by Colonel Unthank's report he was perfectly safe and satisfied with his position.[26]

Major Douglas Wimberley, 232nd Company, MGC, 51st Division

Arthur Gould Lee, now with a company from 9th Royal Scots, had observed the Seaforths' retirement from Fontaine:

I had a good view of my immense field, with the Camel perched there looking pathetically abandoned, and also of the wood facing us, some 300–400 yards distant, which I now learned was La Folie Wood. From here too I could see how the ridge on which Bourlon Wood lies dominates the whole area . . . On the crest of the slope, I saw the Seaforths from Fontaine taking up position along the sunken road, so placing my Camel in the centre of No Man's Land.[27]

Captain Arthur Gould Lee, 46 Squadron, RFC

Here it was to remain as a landmark for the rest of the battle. Lucky to have escaped with his life, the intrepid pilot was left to mourn the loss of his watch, shoes and shaving gear still in the aircraft. He made his way to the rear via an Advanced Dressing Station on the Marcoing–Anneux road, which was crowded with wounded. He volunteered to do some stretcher-bearing – something he soon regretted:

I joined three RAMC bearers, and, accompanied by a bunch of walking wounded, we set out for the field hospital at Flesquières, nearly two miles away. We were carrying a Seaforth, and I soon began to notice that he was a heavy man. In my flying kit I found the going hard. Halfway there, some approaching troops spotted me and my unaccustomed garb, and one came up and cried to the others: 'Eh, look lads, a bleeding Jerry flier.' 'Bleeding Jerry yourself!' I retorted indignantly, at which our Seaforth laughed so much his wound gave trouble, and we had to rest him on the ground for a few minutes, much to my relief.[28]

Captain Arthur Gould Lee, 46 Squadron, RFC

Captain Robert Bruce RAMC, a prisoner in Bourlon village, where the story of the 'Artzt' and 'Pfarrer' produced good-humoured amusement among his German captors, could only rue his own misfortunes:

I don't know how the padre felt, but for my part the shock was pretty great and I felt most horribly depressed. It had come on so suddenly. At one moment we were free and having a walk which was enjoyable enough considering where we were and what was afoot; the next we were prisoners. We had suddenly dived behind that impenetrable screen before which we had moved for nearly three years. It was an unexpected plunge behind the scenes![29]

Captain Robert Tennant Bruce, RAMC, 51st Division

The fall of Fontaine was not an isolated chance. German counter-attacks were also launched against 62nd Division on the British left and against the Queen's Bays on 51st Division's right. The latter might have been better warned if Private Nobby Clarke and his mate had made a more effective reconnaissance of La Folie Wood:

An officer ordered me and another chap to recce the wood. We had a good look along the fringe and a few yards inside but couldn't see any Jerries so we came back and reported all clear. About 15 minutes later they reported 'Action Front!' The Jerries attacked with 15 rounds rapid from the left hand side of the wood. So we let them have everything we could. They had been so well hidden in the wood that the attack was a complete surprise.[30]

Private William 'Nobby' Clarke, 2nd Dragoon Guards (The Queen's Bays), 1st Cavalry Brigade, 1st Cavalry Division

Since early morning heavy machine-gun fire had been directed against the entrenched positions of 185th Brigade. It soon began to take its toll on Billy Kirkby's section:

So deadly was it in both accuracy and volume we lost man after man, killed outright as we endeavoured to locate something to shoot at. First to go was Albert Chadwick, falling lifeless into the bottom of the trench, quickly followed by Jim Smithson, both lying there forming a cross of bloody humanity below me, looking down shocked beyond description at the suddenness of it all.[31]

Private Billy Kirkby, 2/6th West Yorkshires, 185th Brigade, 62nd Division

Though still under heavy fire whilst watching and waiting for the expected counter-attack, Kirkby began to feel he and his men might escape further losses. Then it happened.

I saw someone crash down as though hurled by some gigantic force. Instinctively, I knew it was old Sam Taylor. He could not have known what had hit him . . . Jim Turnbull looked across at me with that shattered look, so common to fighting men when they see great friends and comrades killed before their eyes, then he turned to carry on like the great soldier he was . . . The Germans in their position of advantage on the higher ground above and around us maintained their devilish machine-gun fire, sweeping the top of this ghastly trench with an unending hail of bullets while we kept up our rifle fire though rapidly running out of ammunition. Lewis guns had jammed, the gunners swearing away as they fought, without success, to bring them into action again.[32]

Private Billy Kirkby, 2/6th West Yorkshires, 185th Brigade, 62nd Division

Kirkby's battalion was in the path of the main force of the German thrust. The trench was now choked with dead, with an ever increasing pool of blood around them.

In the midst of this our Company Commander, Captain Moorhouse, entered our bay, seeing the carnage around us. Looking up at me standing on the fire step, [he] ordered me down saying 'I will see what the Boche are up to,' his whole bearing one of utter disregard for his own safety . . . I watched, dreading the inevitable end. Suddenly it came – he slowly sank down and down onto my fire step, coming to rest full length, face upwards, still, so very still, so very silent in death . . . His eyes were wide open as though still looking upward to the heavens. I was shocked beyond description. He had just taken over command of the company, we all admired him so much, hoped to continue to serve under him until the end of the war, if any one of us could survive.[33]

Private Billy Kirkby, 2/6th West Yorkshires, 185th Brigade, 62nd Division

Moorhouse's death was a grievous loss and, indeed, the battalion lost nearly all its officers. Forced back to the Cambrai road, the West Yorks still managed to rally and regroup here. Their efforts were helped somewhat by an attack along both sides of the Canal du Nord by 36th Division at 11.00 a.m. The attack on the east side made little progress but on the west side, the 12th Royal Irish Rifles managed to get into and almost through the village of Moeuvres. But, without reinforcements and under pressure from heavy machine-gun fire and a strong counter-attack, they were eventually forced to withdraw to their starting positions.

With the main British attack now towards Bourlon Wood, the fighting was shifting further west. Consequently, 56th Division carried out a bombing attack supported by artillery fire in the form of an exceptionally slow barrage which moved forward at a rate of 50 yards every five minutes and by 5.30 p.m. Tadpole Copse was occupied by the 1/16th London (Queen's Westminster Rifles) Regiment supported by the 1/5th London (London Rifle Brigade). The surge in fighting was obvious to all here.

> It was obvious that the Germans had brought up reserves and were becoming more aggressive. We found it necessary to canter down the Cambrai road from one end of Boursies to the other, as the village was being severely strafed and houses were toppling down in quick succession . . . Gradually this region was developing into a battlefield of the recognised type. Big guns were coming up in fair numbers: blazing oil-drums, gas shells and other devilries landed in profusion in the German lines, the Cambrai road was completely transformed.[34]
>
> Rifleman Aubrey Smith, 1/5th (London Rifle Brigade) Battalion, London Regiment, 169th Brigade, 56th Division

By the following morning Generalleutnant Otto von Moser's *Arras Group* holding the right sector of *Second Army* facing IV Corps, would have six divisions at his disposal. He took over responsibility for the defence of Bourlon Village and Wood from von Watter's *Caudry Group*, which now held the front from Fontaine to Bantouzelle. Preventing the loss of Bourlon Wood was to be von Moser's obsession from this point forward. He was inspired by the challenge:

> There is an enormous number of things to attend to, but the support of my staff is outstanding . . . My first priority is to ensure that the defence of Bourlon Wood is placed in the hands of a reliable commander . . . Towards 10.00 a.m. a powerful attack takes place; at 1.00 p.m. *214th Infantry Division*, which is holding the line Moeuvres–Bourlon Wood, has to beat off a similar attack . . . *21st Reserve Division*, which is arriving by rail, is subordinated to me as an *Eingreif** division. I request, in addition, the subordination of *3rd Guards Infantry Division* which is still on the move. Enemy artillery fire becomes heavier, reaching down as far as Aubencheul . . . There are hundreds of other matters to organise: liaison in all directions, preparation of sketches of the positions and dugouts along a front which previously was not our responsibility, communications to the rear, supply of ammunition and

* i.e. counter-attack.

rations, setting up of field hospitals, allocation of accommodation for the reinforcing artillery and the fresh divisions, which are arriving constantly. The hours fly by . . . the entire staff is constantly working as fast as it can.[35]

Generalleutnant Otto von Moser, *XIV Reserve Corps*

For the British the same divisions that had made the original attack were still in the front-line. The men were tired and, whilst morale was still generally good, supply problems and the November weather were beginning to take their toll:

We were not relieved after the attack as we expected to be; the men had no overcoats and the weather was very cold. It was also very difficult to provide the troops with hot food, therefore their spirits became rather low as time went on, especially as prospects of relief were dim.[36]

Captain Geoffrey Dugdale, Headquarters, 60th Brigade, 20th Division

Amongst the units most affected by losses, of course, no amount of success could relieve the pain of lost pals. Billy Kirkby's battalion had suffered a terrible mauling but had clung on. Yet fate had one more cruel blow to deal Kirkby:

In the darkness I stood at the side of the Bapaume–Cambrai road, watching our casualties being brought in. I saw Dick Hardy a short distance away but was unable to get near him owing to the crowded road and the gloom of the November night. He was alright at the time, watching as I was, but was hit later and died of wounds the following day. I did not know until later. How I should have appreciated the opportunity to be with him before this great friend of mine passed out of this life . . . [37]

Private Billy Kirkby, 2/6th West Yorkshires, 185th Brigade, 62nd Division

Kirkby's only good fortune was that his division was about to be relieved by the 40th Division.

Finally, for the men of the Royal Flying Corps already under strain to assist in every way possible the ground offensive, there was a worrying, but hardly unexpected, development.

Above Field Marshal Sir Douglas
Haig. (Photograph courtesy of the
Imperial War Museum (henceforth
IWM) HU 98270)

Above right General Hon. Sir Julian
Byng (here photographed whilst a
Lieutenant General commanding
the Canadian Corps). Admired for
his integrity and humanity.
(IWM CO 1370)

Right Lieutenant General Sir
Thomas Snow, commander of
VII Corps – a 'safe pair of hands'.
(IWM HU 98271)

'He had a touch of showmanship which troops like when it is combined with efficiency.' Major General 'Uncle' Harper, commander of 51st Division, and his faithful dog. (IWM Q 5368)

Tank Corps staff at Bermicourt Chateau. The 'immensely popular' Hugh Elles (third left) with 'the brightest and most gifted of the undoubtedly talented and relatively young Tank Corps staff' John Fuller (extreme left). (Tank Museum)

A tank (F1 'Firespite II') demonstrates how to pass through barbed wire, Wailly, October 1917. (IWM Q 6425)

'The sheer logistical effort involved in moving the tanks to the railhead before they were deployed to their various starting points was immense . . .' Tanks bearing fascines at Plateau Station. (IWM Q 46932)

'Every ruined house, every hedge and hollow concealed them, perfectly hidden from view by most careful and elaborate camouflage.' A 6-inch 26 cwt howitzer in action under camouflage netting on the Cambrai front. (IWM Q 10595)

Men of 6th Division with machine-guns in a captured second line trench, Ribécourt, 20 November 1917. (IWM Q 6279)

'Whistling Percy', a German 5.9-inch (150 mm) naval gun captured in Lateau Wood by 6th Royal West Kents, 12th Division, after first being bombed by Arthur Gould Lee and Sopwith Camels from 'C' Flight, 46 Squadron, 20 November 1917. (IWM Q 6338)

Officers of 51st Division watch the progress of the attack, 20 November 1917. (IWM Q 6326)

'Much nasty messy cavalry about in the area, all over the road as usual and blocking traffic in all directions ...' Battle traffic on a road near Ribécourt, 22 November 1917. Both cavalry and the motorcycle sidecar combinations of the Motor Machine Gun Corps would be used much more effectively in an exploitation role in 1918. (IWM Q 6311)

'It was pitiful to see them.' A group of German prisoners carry a wounded British soldier on a stretcher. (IWM Q 3188)

German 77mm field gun. An effective anti-tank weapon on 20 November and subsequently, and capably employed in close support of the German counter-attacks on 30 November. (IWM Q 56490)

British tanks including 'Edinburgh II' of No.12 Section, 15 Company, 'E' Battalion, knocked out on Flesquières Ridge, 20 November 1917. Photograph probably taken in February 1918. (IWM Q 56824)

Second Lieutenant Edmund Fisher, 36th Divisional Ammunition Column. 'The more I see of mules, the more I think they will win the war – I shall never wish for a horse except for hunting.' (IWM DOCS FisherEMP)

Above Second Lieutenant Benjamin Parkin, 2/4th Duke of Wellington's Regiment. (IWM DOCS ParkinB)

An artillery observation officer on top of a ruined wall at Havrincourt, 20 November 1917. (IWM Q 3205)

Second Lieutenant Joseph Gordon
Hassell, 'H' Battalion, Tank Corps.
(IWM DOCS 250)

The 'conscientiously brave' Captain Elliot
Hotblack, Tank Corps chief intelligence officer.
(Tank Museum)

F22 'Flying Fox II' lying in the wreckage of the collapsed canal crossing at Masnières
'like the husk of a monstrous creature from a very different era.' Photographed in February
or March 1918. (IWM Q 42813)

Men of the 51st Highland Division clean up in Flesquières, 23 November 1917. (IWM Q 6324)

Lieutenant Harcus Strachan VC with a squadron of the Canadian Fort Garry Horse passing through Epéhy, while moving up to the forward area. (IWM CO 2295)

Refugees in Marcoing, 22 November 1917. 'The first refugees ... had arrived, with as many of their household goods as they could either carry or bring in hand carts.' (IWM Q 6309)

Royal Army Medical Corps men in Marcoing, 23 November 1917. (IWM Q 3198)

Captain James McCudden,
56 Squadron, RFC.
(IWM Q 46099)

Manfred von Richthofen (left)
with fellow pilots after his 62nd
victory on 23 November 1917.
(IWM Q 63148)

Kaiser Wilhelm II (centre) studying operational maps with Field Marshal Paul von Hindenburg (left) and General Erich Ludendorff (right). (IWM Q 23746)

Crown Prince Rupprecht of Bavaria. (IWM Q 45320)

General Georg von der Marwitz, commander of *Second Army*. (IWM Q 68033)

Indian cavalry. 'Imperial troops many thousands of miles from their homes fighting with lances on horseback alongside, and against, the most recent technological innovations in warfare'. These are men of 9th Hodson's Horse, Ambala Brigade, 5th Cavalry Division. (IWM Q 2061)

Captain C. Raymond Hulsart (left) with fellow officers of 11th Engineer Regiment (Railway), American Expeditionary Force. (IWM Q 6361)

German troops advancing to the assault. During the German counter-attack at Cambrai the assault units chiefly came from 'line' infantry regiments. (IWM Q 55483)

Dugouts in a quarry near Gouzeaucourt. Offering a false sense of security and undefendable against counter-attack. (IWM Q 45578)

Men of the crews of captured British tanks being transported to Germany by train, December 1917.
(IWM HU 98269)

The Kaiser examining a captured British 60-pounder in Bruges, December 1917.
(IWM Q 52816)

We hear that the bad Baron has arrived with his red devils and Fokker Triplanes, and so now I suppose things will get more hectic.[38]

Captain Arthur Gould Lee, 46 Squadron, RFC

Manfred von Richthofen's 'circus' had come to town.

CHAPTER NINE

Dogs of War

I T IS DIFFICULT not to ascribe a sense of 'make or break' to the 23 November attack. The previous evening Haig had visited Byng at his headquarters in the battered town of Albert, bordering the desolation of the Somme.

> I urged capturing Bourlon Wood *tomorrow*. If we did not get it to-morrow, it would be harder to take the next day and in view of the demands made on me for Italy I could not continue a wasting fight.[1]
>
> Field Marshal Sir Douglas Haig, General Headquarters, BEF

Haig had now heard from General Sir William Robertson to the effect that he had the government's backing in exploiting the success so far achieved, but that the demands of the wider strategic situation (and especially Italy) together with the paucity of manpower for the army after the year's fighting meant he must be cautious in deciding how far he should pursue any success.

The time for limiting the operation was surely before it commenced. The War Cabinet's response was only a mealy-mouthed attempt to prevent Haig's ambition overreaching itself as at Third Ypres (as Lloyd George would see it). In part, at least, because divisions had been sent to Italy, there never had been adequate reserves to ensure a really major exploitation – although others might argue that Haig had squandered his reserves in his earlier Flanders offensive.

The plans for 23 November envisaged a coordinated attack to retake Fontaine and capture Bourlon village and wood, with the main thrust by three infantry divisions (51st, 40th and 36th) supported by large numbers of both tanks and artillery. Another infantry division (56th) would operate to protect the attack's west flank, whilst 9th Cavalry

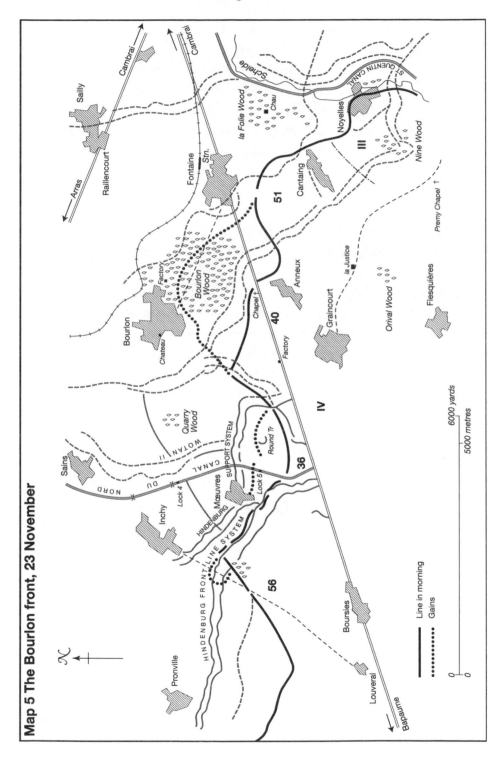

Map 5 The Bourlon front, 23 November

Brigade from 1st Cavalry Division were to exploit the recapture of Fontaine, if it was achieved. However, during the day many units from this division were being withdrawn to Metz-en-Couture where the water supply (essential for horses) was better – an order which Haig persuaded Byng to reverse when they met.

A not inconsiderable number of the heavier howitzers and guns had now been moved forward to positions where they could support the attack, including 6-inch, 8-inch, 9.2-inch and even 12-inch howitzers. In total over 400 guns were amassed in support of the attack. More might have been engaged, but the relatively narrow salient meant it was difficult to site the batteries; the problems of the Ypres Salient repeated. The three tank brigades assembled 92 tanks from six battalions. Understanding the need to screen these tanks from hostile artillery fire, the British gunners were specifically tasked with neutralizing any anti-tank batteries which might operate on the southern and eastern slopes of Bourlon Wood and a smoke barrage was to be employed as well.

Despite the talents of the Tank Corps staff, preparations for the attack were far from smooth. Firstly, there was the question of supplies. William Watson was charged with moving every available tank of his company to Graincourt. He did so, expecting to collect ammunition and stores from a large dump that was being established at a chapel on the Havrincourt–Flesquières road:

> Foolishly credulous, I moved my tanks to the appointed place and waited for the dump to appear. We had, however, entered the state of open warfare, and we soon began to realise its disadvantages. My messengers scoured the countryside without success, and at last, when it grew dusk, I despaired and sent on my tanks to Graincourt.[2]
>
> Major William Watson, No. 11 Company, 'D' Battalion, Tank Corps

Clearly, the Tank Corps were struggling with a situation they had never encountered before, something beyond the rigid conventions of trench warfare. It proved a major challenge.

Secondly, Watson's tanks were ordered to attack in the morning with 40th Division and take Bourlon Wood. Watson was concerned about the lack of opportunity for reconnaissance; nor had there been an opportunity to meet the cooperating infantry from 40th Division, since they were already making their way into the forward positions. He knew how vital such liaison was to successful cooperation.

The relief of 62nd Division by 40th Division was completed with much difficulty during the night of 22/23 November. Advancing through positions captured by 62nd Division on the first day, one experienced battalion commander was astonished by the scenes of devastation:

> There was no recognisable feature left at all in the landscape after our barrage of 20 November had done its business, and the sight of that descent towards the Canal Du Nord was one of utter desolation. It was still light enough to get some idea of the lie of the land as I crossed the canal some way ahead of my command, and though I had seen many a fair landscape changed into a desert on many occasions before this, it seemed to me that the scenery in this spot was just of the kind that Dante would have chosen as the final abode of his worst enemies.[3]
>
> Lieutenant Colonel Bernard Baker, 13th Green Howards, 121st Brigade, 40th Division

Because the Bapaume–Cambrai *pavé* road was badly congested, by the time the front-line positions had been reached, many of the men were very tired. Some elements of the divisional headquarters took fifteen hours to cover nine miles and the problems concerning supplies persisted. Operation orders for the attack contained caveats regarding the firing of barrages 'having regard to the ammunition situation', whilst the planned smoke barrage on Bourlon Ridge never materialized – because the ammunition never materialized. It remained mired in the traffic on the clogged-up road.

During this relief not every man from 62nd Division was withdrawn. Second Lieutenant Benjamin Parkin, on duty for the fourth consecutive day at his aeroplane dropping station, heard about the relief but was himself instructed to remain at his post. This was hard on a man who had been separated from his battalion for several days and who craved news of their endeavours.

The newly arrived 40th Division was an unusual formation. It had been raised in late 1914 as a New Army 'Bantam' division, consisting of volunteers who did not reach the regulation height of five foot three inches. However, there were insufficient numbers of these short and stocky men to form twelve battalions and so the standards of general physique were also relaxed to get the required numbers of volunteers from the 'Derby Scheme' and conscripts. Numbers were one thing; the ability of such men to withstand the strains of active service was another. Inevitably, it became necessary to weed out many whilst the division was still in Britain. In one case, a battalion's notional strength of 1,000 was reduced to about 200. The division was then strengthened by the 'import' of four battalions whose men were of acceptable physique. According to the division's history, by the time it went to France in June 1916 its infantry roughly comprised a mix of one-half English, one-third Welsh and one-sixth Scottish. However, a significant proportion of the men could still definitely be described as 'Bantams'.

The division's commander was a Coldstream Guardsman of some breeding, being the son and grandson of generals and a descendant of the Earls of Bessborough. Among his brigade commanders was another Guardsman: the Honourable Charles Heathcote-Drummond-Willoughby, second son of the Earl of Ancaster. His younger brother, the Honourable Claud (another Guardsman), was also present at Cambrai as commander of 'H' Battalion, Tank Corps to which he had brought the Guards' 'high ideals of discipline and military achievement'. Claud imbued every tank officer with an understanding that 'he was a member of an intricate organization which demanded of him obedience, smartness, unselfishness and, above all, teamwork'.[4] His elder brother set similar standards for his infantry brigade.

By contrast, another brigade commander, Frank Crozier, was a veteran of several campaigns in Africa who had been forced to leave the army in 1908 over a catalogue of irregular financial dealings. He had returned via the Ulster Volunteer Force and, when its units were incorporated into the British Army on the outbreak of war, he lead one of the resulting battalions of the Royal Irish Rifles. Crozier was short and rather stout himself (possibly as a result of a drink problem he had now conquered). He was also a tough and uncompromising man who had, if possible, been hardened even further by the experience of war. When taking over 119th Brigade, he was said to have made himself so unpopular with the officers that a number of them had transferred to the RFC. One who served under him recalled his style of command:

After the war our Brigadier Crozier made a name for himself by writing a book titled 'A Brass Hat in No Man's Land' . . . I must admit that I never saw the Brigadier in No Man's Land but quite frequently in the Front Line. On one occasion he caught three or four of us sitting down on the firing step and said 'You (pointing to one of us) go and fetch your Company Commander.' When the CO arrived, he got a wigging for allowing the men to be idle when there was plenty of work to be done.[5]

Lance Corporal Frank Turner, 19th Royal Welsh Fusiliers, 119th Brigade, 40th Division

Crozier urged his subordinate officers to act as 'war dogs' and aspired to hone his brigade into a killing machine. War had made strange bedfellows in 40th Division.

Crozier was convinced his brigade could take Bourlon Wood 'on their heads'. However, mindful of the lessons of fighting in South Africa where a British commander had failed to secure a complete victory when he abandoned a position gained at great cost in casualties, Crozier's final words to his battalion commanders before the battle were menacing. 'Remember Spion Kop. If I want you to come back, come back. I decide your fate. You hold on or die.'[6]

The attack of 40th Division was to be made by two brigades. Whilst Crozier's 119th was to take the wood with the assistance of 13 tanks from 'D' Battalion (which Crozier perceptively reminded his men were a luxury and not to be relied upon), Brigadier General John Campbell's 121st Brigade's objective was Bourlon Village and the western shoulder of the ridge. For this his lead battalions, 20th Middlesex and 13th Green Howards, would be supported by 16 tanks from 'G' Battalion and the machine-guns of 121st Machine-Gun Company. Amongst its officers was Lieutenant Algernon Hyde Villiers, who had enjoyed the 'great fun' of his company's training for the battle under 'Uncle' Harper's watchful eye. Now it was for real. Given the mayhem about to commence, the deeply religious Hyde Villiers appeared remarkably calm to his superior when the latter visited the machine-gunners' positions just after dawn.

I found him sitting under a bank – asleep. I woke him, and we talked over the orders which he had had some hours before. We both knew he had a dangerous task to perform. He had read his orders, decided on his plans, and gone off peacefully to sleep.[7]

Major Sydney Davey, 121st Company, MGC, 40th Division

In fact, in recent days Hyde Villiers' faith had caused him to wrestle with a particular dilemma – as he explained in a letter home two days before the battle began:

> It is extremely difficult to say that one is a Christian, and there is no other way of saying that one is seeking to follow Christ. Unfortunately, the word Christian has become so closely associated with moral perfection that one cannot call oneself the former without appearing to lay claim to the latter. It is offensive, and indeed absurd, to say, 'I did this, or feel so, because I am a good man,' isn't it? But that's what one will be understood to mean by saying one is a Christian. I want some way of saying that I believe in Christ without implying that I am like Him.[8]

Lieutenant Algernon Hyde Villiers, 121st Company, MGC, 40th Division

Perhaps Hyde Villiers' placid calm on the morning of 23 November meant that, in the midst of a major battle, he had finally resolved his quandary.

On 40th Division's left, 36th Division's attack was once again divided into two by the Canal du Nord. The 8th Royal Irish Rifles of 107th Brigade would have 11 tanks of the battered 'E' Battalion that had suffered badly on Flesquières Ridge on the east side of the canal. On the west side, however, 108th Brigade was not allotted any tanks but was tasked with taking Moeuvres.

To retake Fontaine, 51st Division would have to employ infantry battalions that had been involved in the initial attack on the Hindenburg Line three days and, seemingly, a thousand years before. Infantry from 152nd Brigade would initially have support from 36 tanks from 'B', 'C' and 'H' Battalions. The brigade commander, Henry Pelham Burn, proposed attacking with two infantry battalions and one in support. In fact, he had a total of seven battalions at his disposal. This method, possibly designed as an attempt to minimize casualties by not employing men needlessly and thereby exposing them to greater risk, was clearly favoured by the divisional commander, Harper. Its shortcomings had been demonstrated on 20 November. Nevertheless, Pelham Burn was confident he was deploying the appropriate numbers of infantry for the task.

Once more, news of the impending attack reached those it involved late on the eve of the battle.

> I was just hoping for a few hours' sleep when I was sent for by Hardie and told that 152nd Brigade were to attack Fontaine next morning and that eight of my guns were to help. All that night I was busy planning out gun teams, orders for pack animals, etc. There was a long piece of open ground in front of Fontaine and as we were to attack in broad daylight, limbers were out of the question, and we decided to use pack transport. The Brigade were to form up on the Graincourt–La Justice road before daylight – Brigade Headquarters to be at La Justice itself . . . The rest of the night was spent in loading pack animals with guns, tripods, belt boxes and condensers and petrol tins, and getting food and drink for man and beast. I went with the guns to the sunken road where we assembled, most of the troops being in good trim.[9]
>
> Major Douglas Wimberley, 232nd Company, MGC, 51st Division

The day dawned brighter than any for several days past. One cavalry officer near Flesquières recalled the early morning scene in almost rose-tinted terms:

> November 23rd remains in my mind as one of the few picturesque days in the whole war. It was fine and warm, and in the plain to the south-east of Bourlon Wood, squadrons were manoeuvring in line. Generals cavorting about with orderlies carrying pennons, and the whole scene like an eighteenth-century battle-print, with only a few strong puffs of shrapnel to mar the harmony. We were all elated by the feeling that at last something was doing in the cavalry world.[10]
>
> Captain Alan 'Tommy' Lascelles, Bedfordshire Yeomanry, 9th Cavalry Brigade, 1st Cavalry Division

A battalion commander too recalled the fine morning:

> The morning came in with a blustering north-east wind sending cloud-shadows chasing over the undulating ground. An occasional scud of sleet made way for spells of sunshine in which Bourlon Wood

to the east glowed in ragged autumn finery, while Moeuvres church tower stood out above the ruins of the village . . . By 9.30 a.m. the forms of tanks moving up from the south loomed up more plainly . . . [11]

Lieutenant Colonel Bernard Baker, 13th Green Howards, 121st Brigade, 40th Division

Unfortunately, the tanks Baker saw were not those intended for co-operation with his battalion. The traffic problems had prevented petrol supplies reaching 'G' Battalion in time and the battalion was almost an hour and a half late in getting into action.

If Baker could see the tanks, without a shadow of doubt the Germans in Bourlon Wood could.

It was an unpleasant wait in the road, I remember, for the Boche had seen the tanks lumbering up to lead the attack and was shelling the road, killing a few horses and a good few of the Jocks, particularly one shell which killed five or six Gordons of 152nd Brigade near us. [12]

Major Douglas Wimberley, 232nd Company, MGC, 51st Division

On 51st Division's front, the artillery barrage came down at 10.10 a.m. in front of Fontaine. Twenty minutes later it lifted 200 yards and continued to do so every 20 minutes. The tank advance began when the barrage first lifted:

After what seemed a long wait, the leading waves started off behind the tanks – and I presently gave the order for my mules to start off in line with the Battalion Headquarters, moving up in a little cluster of men surrounding their Regimental pennons. [13]

Major Douglas Wimberley, 232nd Company, MGC, 51st Division

Wimberley watched with fascination as the events of the battle began to unfurl before him:

It was now a beautiful morning and larks were singing above us. The tanks were forging well ahead followed by the assaulting lines towards Fontaine and dark-looking La Folie Wood. The Boche artillery fire was light, but machine-gun and rifle fire was very heavy from both flanks, both Bourlon and La Fontaine, not to mention frontal fire from the village. Through my glasses, I saw the attack held up though the tanks

254

were still going on, and my men unloaded the guns and sent the animals back as they waited for the infantry to advance. I had an animal hit, but was lucky not to lose more.[14]

Major Douglas Wimberley, 232nd Company, MGC, 51st Division

On the right of the attack, attempts by three tanks of 'C' Battalion with a company of 1/6th Gordon Highlanders to take La Folie Wood and the chateau in it failed. This was in all likelihood as much because of the folly of trying to use tanks against wooded positions as the lack of adequate numbers of infantry and tanks in the first place.

Since the woods were not taken, the remaining companies of the Gordon Highlanders were enfiladed in their attack on Fontaine. Repeated attempts to cross this fire-swept zone meant only a part of one company reached the village outskirts. Casualties, though especially heavy amongst the officers, were fewer than they might have been. Nevertheless, they were bad enough and the battalion commander described it as 'one of the worst days I have ever spent, we lost many a good lad to no purpose whatever. It's a sad and weary business, this war, to those who are in personal touch with the sacrificed.'[15] On the other hand, the tanks of 'B' and 'C' Battalions were able to advance at their top speed on the village and were heartened by the initial effect of their advance on the German defenders:

We were doing a good 4 mph when, on nearing the village, German infantry ran out of a shallow fire trench. First a few, then about two companies got up and legged it from the village. There was great excitement in the tank. Those who were handy to the Lewis guns took turns in firing at the fleeing infantry. We bowled over quite a few, and I heard an awful shriek of fear and pain as we ran over one . . . Sergeant Stewart seemed exceptionally excited as he was laughing and gesticulating wildly, trying to tell me something.[16]

Captain Cyril Grimley, 'H' Battalion, Tank Corps

Stewart's excitement was at seeing a 6-pounder shell he fired cut a German in half. 'This was a wrong use of the gun, of course,' as Grimley observed in officious censure. Barricades erected by the German defenders of the village and unmanned field guns at the village edge were swiftly overcome; some being crushed under the tracks of the tanks. But there was an abrupt change as the tanks entered the streets of Fontaine.

> So far it was all our luck – all smiles, laughter, excitement and thrills – but hell was let loose as we turned into the street. We were being fired at from the roofs – front, back and sides. A combination of splash and armour flaking made it most difficult to see anything when handling a gun. We tried the vizor-chain masks, but took them off as we couldn't see properly. The gun ports were all lit up with sparks.[17]
>
> Captain Cyril Grimley, 'H' Battalion, Tank Corps

Machine-guns firing from the upper storey of the surviving houses were a particular problem.

> In order to put sufficient elevation on the gun, we had to get the tank on the other side of the street. Bateman and Chappel on the port-side 6-pounder put three out of action in one house, the shells going below the sills and taking gun and crew I should imagine most successfully.[18]
>
> Captain Cyril Grimley, 'H' Battalion, Tank Corps

The storm of German machine-gun fire was not the only problem. The Germans had brought two lorry-mounted anti-aircraft guns from *K.Flak Batterie 7* into the village, sighted on the western entrance to the village. When these guns opened fire they, together with the determined company of infantry from *Reserve Infanterie Regiment 52*, accounted for seven tanks. The company commander described his men's part in this fight:

> We saw the tank about 100 metres ahead of us advancing and holding the entire village street under fire. However, we quickly sprang into and behind the farm buildings. We had found a hand grenade dump . . . and tried at first to throw the hand grenades under the tracks of the tank. That succeeded. The single grenades, however, were too weak. I then ordered that empty sandbags be brought and four hand grenades be placed in them, with one grenade tied near the top of the bag so that only the firing spring showed.[19]
>
> Leutnant Spremberg, *Reserve Infanterie Regiment 52, 107th Division*

Whilst the tanks were kept under fire, Spremberg's men completed their preparations and waited until the right moment. Then,

Musketeers Buttenberg and Schroeder . . . rushed upon the firing giant and, from throwing distance, tossed two bunched hand grenades under the tracks. A single explosion, the tracks on the left side flew in the air and the tank stood still. At this there was a cheer from our little group.[20]

Leutnant Spremberg, *Reserve Infanterie Regiment 52, 107th Division*

A disabled tank could still inflict heavy loss on infantry foolish enough to approach it in the open, and the Germans' attention was soon taken by the appearance of a second tank which now effected a dramatic rescue of the crew of the first:

Suddenly, a second tank appeared, armed with guns, and opened fire, penetrating the lower house wall so that we had to flee into the farmyard. We saw to our dismay that it moved to the right side of the tank which we had disabled . . . The second tank evacuated the crew of the first and, firing constantly, departed like a roaring lion.[21]

Leutnant Spremberg, *Reserve Infanterie Regiment 52, 107th Division*

Cyril Grimley's tank had survived a hard pounding by the Germans in Fontaine – although two of the crew were wounded – when its batteries caught fire:

I thought, 'death by fire or bullets – well, bullets for my choice.' They were banging away on the door like large hail stones on plate glass. I took the pyrenes to the fire, however, and managed to put it out. On we went, firing away at likely machine-gun hiding places. Then I saw two tanks of another section on fire in the centre of Fontaine, obviously hit by a field-gun firing up the street. I looked round for the infantry – but none had followed. So I turned about and led my section out to find the Gordons.[22]

Captain Cyril Grimley, 'H' Battalion, Tank Corps

He found them still held up by fire from La Folie Wood. Firing his remaining 6-pounder rounds at the wood, he then realized there was little more he could do.

I then led my three tanks away as we were useless, first putting up the tank and infantry cooperation flag 'Coming out of action for supplies.' At this juncture I met Captain Hotblack.[23]

Captain Cyril Grimley, 'H' Battalion, Tank Corps

Once more the intrepid senior Tank Corps Intelligence Officer was close to the action to gain first-hand knowledge of the tanks' performance in the fighting. Although the Germans were offering strong resistance in Fontaine, Eliot Hotblack was unhappy with the lack of 'fight' shown by some tank crews and its moral effects on the infantry:

> About an hour after reaching their objectives one section of tanks left the eastern end of the village and returned towards our lines. The Section Commander told me that he was slightly wounded and that one of his tanks had run out of ammunition. I told the commander of the third tank who had had no casualties and still possessed ammunition that I thought he was leaving his objective too soon. He returned to the end of the village and was seen to dislodge several nests of Germans and to kill a considerable number. There is no doubt that the withdrawal of tanks from a village early in the day has an extremely bad morale effect on infantry that may be hung up outside. During the day tanks returning from the village for various reasons not only caused the infantry to consider that the position was too hot for them, but also to cause them to give up a good deal of ground which they had already gained.[24]
>
> Captain Eliot Hotblack, Headquarters, Tank Corps

Nevertheless, the tanks operating without real infantry support in Fontaine could not succeed alone, and those that were not destroyed withdrew to regroup and take on more ammunition. Douglas Wimberley, witnessing the return of one, could only express professional admiration for his German counterparts:

> I listened to the subaltern's report to his Major. Apparently tanks had got into both village and wood to find them bristling with machine-guns. These did not bother the tanks, but mowed down the infantry if they tried to advance, and the Boche machine-guns were too many and well hidden for the tanks to deal with. They quietened down when the tank was near or its very limited field of vision was on them, only to fire again when it passed – very good and brave work too by the German machine-gunners.[25]
>
> Major Douglas Wimberley, 232nd Company, MGC, 51st Division

To the left of Fontaine, between it and Bourlon Wood, 'H' Battalion tanks operating with 1/6th Seaforth Highlanders encountered equally determined opposition from men of the newly arrived *3rd Guards Infantry Division* amongst whom, occupying a hastily dug trench line, was the 19-year-old Miles Reinke and his fellow cavalrymen of *2.Garde-Dragoner-Regiment.* For the Germans too, the battle had created a crisis in which dismounted cavalry were thrown into the fighting simply to increase the number of rifles available. Reinke described, in occasionally eccentric English, his encounter with tanks:

> It was something like a *cauchemar** when I saw these tremendous machines. We didn't know what they were – we never had seen them before. When they approached us, coming over a hill and on top of the hill they were just dipping a bit before they went downwards towards the trenches. I was not in the first line, but I was in the third line. So I had ample time to watch.[26]
>
> Dragoner Miles Reinke, *2.Garde-Dragoner-Regiment, 3rd Guards Infantry Division*

His fears overcome by curiosity, Reinke was able to witness the courage and ingenuity of his fellow defenders:

> When the first tanks passed the first line, we thought that we would be compelled to retreat towards Berlin . . . I remember only one by the name of 'Hyena'. This tank advanced very far and then suddenly stopped about 800 to 1000 yards from my little dugout. Some of the boys of the first line had discovered that they could stop the tanks by throwing into the manholes which was on top of the tank a hand grenade. Once this was known to the other fellows, it very fast became known and all the boys also had realised that there was a 'dead angle' [where] the machine-guns couldn't reach every part around the tank. These points were very important in the defence.[27]
>
> Dragoner Miles Reinke, *2.Garde-Dragoner-Regiment, 3rd Guards Infantry Division*

As the tanks crossed the trenches and pits dug by the Germans, they presented an opportunity for the latter to use their hand grenades. The watching Reinke was appalled by the results:

* i.e. a nightmare

I was shocked, and I felt very sorry for those fellows in the tanks because there was no escape for them. Once a man was on top of a tank, these tanks were doomed to failure and the poor fellows were not able to escape. There was not much room for them and the fuel started to burn. After about an hour and a half or two hours we only saw spots of burning tanks in front of us and some of them also behind us.[28]

Dragoner Miles Reinke, *2.Garde-Dragoner-Regiment, 3rd Guards Infantry Division*

Reinke's compassion for his British opponents was matched by that of the regiment's two chaplains:

Our Catholic and our Protestant preachers rushed up to one man who [managed] to escape by the side door. He lived for a couple of hours. The preacher . . . Mr Klinker was his name . . . he said he never had seen more horror on a face than on the face of this dying brave British tank soldier.[29]

Dragoner Miles Reinke, *2.Garde-Dragoner-Regiment, 3rd Guards Infantry Division*

Reinke then described how, without tank and artillery support, the infantry attack was beaten off:

The approaching infantry behind the tanks had still to overcome the machine-guns of our infantry which had still a great effect because the British artillery had to stop shooting at the very minute when the tanks were advancing. Naturally some of the little machine-gun nests, as we called them, were still in full action. Anyhow, the attack came to a standstill and we now expected, as I am from the cavalry, that several squadrons or regiments of cavalry would now sweep up and drive us towards Berlin.[30]

Dragoner Miles Reinke, *2.Garde-Dragoner-Regiment, 3rd Guards Infantry Division*

His fears and expectation were unrealized. His section of the line was not attacked again that day.

Prior to the advance of 40th Division, there had been confusion for Frank Turner's company of Royal Welsh Fusiliers. Shortly before dawn, on receipt of orders from battalion headquarters, they had retired from the ditch they had been occupying back across the Bapaume–Cambrai road. Then, in the hours before zero, Turner himself had been sent to battalion headquarters for further instruction:

> We were told to wait. There appeared to be some indecision some-
> where along the line but at last we were given a message for Captain
> Richards. 'Proceed back across the main road and man the ditch' –
> where we had been before. But it was now broad daylight.[31]
>
> Lance Corporal Frank Turner, 19th Royal Welsh Fusiliers, 119th Brigade, 40th Division

Runners like Turner had to get their messages as quickly as possible to the intended recipient, regardless of the dangers. It was a hairy return journey for him:

> Suddenly machine-gun bullets were flying around our ears and we
> made a dash for the last 30–40 yards, leading to the nearest point of
> the ditch which the Company were occupying. We dived headlong
> in, much to the annoyance of the lads we fell on – but we weren't hit.
> We pushed our way past them up to where Captain Richards was
> talking to the other officers. He was visibly annoyed at receiving the
> instructions I brought as it meant the whole company had to cross the
> main road again but this time in broad daylight. This was accomp-
> lished in rushes by small parties and luckily, few casualties occurred
> from the machine-gun fire. We were to await further instructions
> from HQ.[32]
>
> Lance Corporal Frank Turner, 19th Royal Welsh Fusiliers, 119th Brigade, 40th Division

These instructions revealed that Zero Hour would be at 10.30 a.m. Fretting over the last minutes, Turner was concerned about how a recently joined draft of young lads would behave when the attack began: 'I did not have much time to talk to any of them but understood that most of them had not been in action before.'[33] Then it was time.

> The barrage . . . lifted from the edge of the wood and over we went. I
> beside Captain Richards . . . There was, of course, plenty of noise and
> as we clambered out, there were a few gaps. Some of the new lads were
> hesitant to get out of the ditch. We walked along and encouraged them
> and they all made it. As we breasted the slope, machine-gun fire
> opened – it seemed to come from half-right behind us. A few chaps

dropped and as the barrage had lifted, some of us started to run for the cover of the wood.[34]

Lance Corporal Frank Turner, 19th Royal Welsh Fusiliers, 119th Brigade, 40th Division

The 19th Royal Welsh Fusiliers, despite the machine-guns and the shells plastering their advance, were the first to enter the wood, which offered some cover from the German fire. However, it was a strange and confusing environment.

Soon after gaining the cover of the wood (which was quite dense – the barrage hadn't done much damage) two of us were together and I had lost touch with Captain Richards – I never saw him again. We met up with another fellow in our Company and the three of us continued to move forward together. No sign of any Germans. We came to a road running through the wood and after ensuring there was no one about, crossed it. After a time we decided that we should go back, so crossed the road again. We (all of us were lance corporals), decided to wait for some of the others and after a short time we found ourselves being heavily shelled.[35]

Lance Corporal Frank Turner, 19th Royal Welsh Fusiliers, 119th Brigade, 40th Division

Watching the barrage and tank advance on 40th Division's front at zero, the tank company commander, William Watson, realized there was little he could now do for his men and their machines:

At 10.30 a.m. the barrage fell and we could see it climb, like a living thing, through the wood and up the hillside, a rough line of smoke and flame. To the left of the wood we could mark the course of the battle – the tanks with tiny flashes darting from their flanks – clumps of infantry following in little rushes – an officer running in front of his men, until suddenly he crumpled up and fell, as though some unseen hammer had struck him on the head – the men wavering in the face of the machine-gun fire and then spreading out to surround the gun – the wounded staggering painfully down the hill, and the stretcher-bearers moving backwards and forwards in the wake of the attack – the aeroplanes skimming low along the hillside, and side-slipping to rake the enemy trenches with their guns.[36]

Major William Watson, No. 11 Company, 'D' Battalion, Tank Corps

Watson's inability to influence events on the battlefield was only too clearly brought home by what happened next.

> We watched one tank hesitate before it crossed the skyline and our hearts went out to the driver in sympathy. He made his decision, and the tank, brown against the sky, was instantly encircled by little puffs of white smoke, shells from the guns on the reverse slope. The man was brave, for he followed the course of a trench along the crest of the hill. My companion uttered a low exclamation of horror. Flames were coming from the rear of the tank, but its guns continued to fire and the tank continued to move. Suddenly the driver must have realised what was happening. The tank swung towards home. It was too late. Flames burst from the roof and the tank stopped, but the sponson doors never opened and the crew never came out . . . When I left my post half an hour later that tank was still burning.[37]
>
> Major William Watson, No. 11 Company, 'D' Battalion, Tank Corps

In the wood, Crozier's brigade had quickly penetrated the dense undergrowth and shattered trees where they captured several prisoners and a number of machine-guns. Although the British artillery maintained a barrage on the northern edge of the wood and a few tanks using some of the rides cut through the wood also assisted, the infantry were largely on their own now. The 'soldier's battle' of Bourlon Wood had begun. The fighting fractured into many small, but deadly combats between little groups of men or individuals. German artillery shells and British 'shorts' fell indiscriminately. One victim was Frank Turner:

> I was looking back over my shoulder and saw a shell burst in a tree no more than twenty feet away. I felt as though someone had given me a heavy kick behind my knee, and fell. The others helped cut away my trouser leg and applied a tourniquet and field dressing to the front – the exit wound is always the larger. They propped me up against a tree and then one of them said he had a piece in his foot. They applied a dressing and the unwounded chap said he would help the second one, who could walk, back to the first aid post. They left their water bottles with me. I never knew what happened to them. Soon after the Captain of 'A' Company came through, on his own –

stopped and asked me if I was OK. I saw a few others and then all was quiet.[38]

Lance Corporal Frank Turner, 19th Royal Welsh Fusiliers, 119th Brigade, 40th Division

Alone, wounded and undoubtedly scared, Turner patiently waited for the stretcher-bearers. The quiet Turner noted was unquestionably a freak possibly caused by the vegetation deadening any noise. Deeper into the wood, the fighting raged on and here the chatter of German machine-guns and of the British Lewis guns combined with the continuing crash of shells. The Fusiliers and their fellow assault battalion, 12th South Wales Borderers, continued to make good progress, despite the German opposition. By 11.40 a.m. they had reached the Fontaine–Bourlon road running through the middle of the forest and less than an hour later were working to establish a line of posts around the north-eastern edge.

The attack of 121st Brigade led by the 20th Middlesex on the right and 13th Green Howards on the left, and with 'D' Battalion tanks in front, started well as one battalion commander from 119th Brigade observed:

I saw the 121st Brigade, under cover of tanks, move forward to attack Bourlon village. It was rather a nice sight seeing the men moving leisurely along as if they were having a day out.[39]

Lieutenant Colonel James Plunkett, 19th Royal Welsh Fusiliers, 119th Brigade, 40th Division

Unfortunately, the superficial calm had completely deceived Plunkett. Very soon after they began to advance the attackers came under enfilade fire from the left where 107th Brigade from 36th Division was unable to get on and were suffering great losses. Nevertheless, the attack made some progress towards Bourlon village. The attackers were supported by a section from 121st Company, Machine Gun Corps; Algernon Hyde Villiers' section being the one chosen. To facilitate cooperation with the infantry, Hyde Villiers, cigarette and walking stick in hand, advanced with the last infantry wave, while Second Lieutenant Thomas Thorpe followed about 400 yards behind with the section of four guns.

Our first objective was a ridge on the left of Bourlon Wood, and just outside it, known as '100 Spur'; and our second, Bourlon village and the high ground beyond. All went well as far as the first objective, and the brigade on our right, which attacked the wood, seemed to be going well. We were held up by machine-guns at '100 Spur' and [Hyde Villiers] came back to help me to get the guns into action, to try and help the troops in front to advance. I was hit in the thigh as we were doing this, he turned to me and shouted, 'Hard luck!' as a farewell message, for, of course, in a show like this, once a man is wounded no more notice can be taken of him by the people who are advancing. My last view was of him directing the guns' fire and encouraging his men in face of a pretty deadly fire. On my way down to the dressing-station, a man overtook me with a message from him to the CO, so I know that he was all right half an hour after I got hit. I heard a rumour of his death at the dressing-station but I kept on hoping against hope till I saw his name in the casualty list.[40]

Second Lieutenant Thomas Thorpe, 121st Company, MGC, 40th Division

Villiers' death (shot through the head whilst directing his machine-guns and maintaining a pretence of sangfroid despite the threat of snipers) might appear to capture the very essence of war's futility. And yet, almost certainly, he would not have seen it that way himself. For this was how officers of his ilk led their men, and did so in full knowledge that they might pay the ultimate price.

Although the 13th Green Howards were still held up, the infantry of 20th Middlesex (soon reinforced by their sister battalion, 21st) reached the edge of Bourlon behind tanks of 'D' Battalion at about noon but could get no further. In the village, the tanks encountered a similar situation to Fontaine and, without adequate infantry to clear the houses, they were forced to pull out. It was not until 1.00 p.m. that the Green Howards reached the western outskirts of the village – a position they could not hold for long because of heavy losses. Throughout the rest of the afternoon, 121st Brigade conducted a desperate fight to retain its gains.

The problems of 36th Division (and especially 107th Brigade) on 40th Division's left are well illustrated by the accounts of the commanders of 'E' Battalion tanks who attacked with them.

On moving off towards my first objective, I met Captain Roberts about 500 yards south of Round Trench who told me that the objective of the first wave of tanks was not yet taken by the infantry and that I should find considerable opposition there. I went forward and crossed the front line of this trench firing at the enemy and going up and down. Tanks 'Eve' and 'Esme' were with me, and we continued thus until 'Esme' became ditched. I myself was ditched for about half an hour in the German front line, the trenches being very wide, and my crew suffered one man killed and four wounded by bombs in our attempts to fix the underching gear. We used our guns freely, but were subjected the whole time to considerable rifle fire and bombing. By working the tank backwards and forwards we finally got out. Shortly afterwards my tank got two direct hits. I ordered the crew to get ready to evacuate and just then I got a third direct hit which set my tank on fire, I then evacuated and remained in shell holes until dusk when I withdrew.[41]

Second Lieutenant Bertrand Carter, E38 'Eileen II', 'E' Battalion, Tank Corps

Without fascines, the wide trenches of the Hindenburg Line presented precisely the expected problems, as another tank officer discovered:

When I arrived at Round Trench I saw a few enemy whom I fired at and they ran away. I couldn't see where. I waved my Red and Yellow Flag. I didn't see any of our infantry come on immediately, so after waiting a bit I went towards Lock 5 as I heard considerable fire coming from there. I fired at several enemy machine-gun emplacements which I think I knocked out and again waved my flag. I could see our infantry lying down about 900 yards from my tank. They appeared to be under heavy enfilade fire from the direction of Moeuvres. I heard further firing from Round Trench so turned my tank and went back and found the enemy had reoccupied portions of it. I got ditched in part of Round Trench and some Germans closed in on my tank and began bombing it. I could not do any good from my tank as she was at such an angle that the guns I wanted to use were in the mud. One gun had been shot away. I evacuated my crew on the other side and got into the traverse where I remained for about half an hour.[42]

Second Lieutenant Leonard Johnson, 'Esme', 'E' Battalion, Tank Corps

Round Trench was one of the chief centres of resistance to 107th Brigade's advance. Second Lieutenant Carlyle Fairbank in 'Eve' describes what happened after he found the crew of 'Esme' in shell holes close to the German position:

> I was at and about Round Trench until about 3.00 p.m. As no infantry were there I sought out an infantry officer and took him up in my tank to show him what was in front of him. He said he had only a very depleted company and that in his opinion it would require at least a battalion with two companies in reserve to take the trench. I asked him what he wished me to do and he said: 'Wait until I have interviewed my Colonel and I will then let you know.' I went on rolling out wire in the interval, a few minutes afterwards I got a direct hit from a field gun which set my tank on fire.[43]
>
> Second Lieutenant Carlyle Fairbank, E36 'Eve', 'E' Battalion, Tank Corps

Despite the tanks' efforts, 107th Brigade could not get forward and, indeed, by 3.30 p.m. it was back at its start line. 108th Brigade on the canal's west bank did better, pushing the Germans back almost as far as Moeuvres. On the far left, 56th Division bombed its way further along the Hindenburg front system, whilst a Royal Engineers Field Company which had finally built a light bridge across the canal on the Bapaume–Cambrai road during the previous night, repaired it under constant fire and began to construct a second.

By mid-afternoon, neither Fontaine nor Bourlon had fallen, although Crozier's 119th Brigade had taken almost all the wood and defeated counter-attacks by units of *3rd Guards Infantry Division*. However, it was obvious that the woodland would be difficult to hold if the two villages were not captured and the Germans now poured artillery fire onto the potential routes of reinforcements. As Herbert Gregory found when given a message from his 21-year-old company commander, Major Douglas Amery-Parkes, to the machine-guns in the woods:

> About 1.00 p.m. I was called to go with my first dispatch. They could give me no information as to where I should find the officer that I wanted. A barrage was lying between the two opposing forces, and only open country to go through. This was going to be very dangerous work, and great care would have to be used to get through. I made across country until I got to the end of the road in front of the wood at the left-hand side. I was safe so far, but as I looked on that road it was a blazing,

screaming, shell-bursting barrage all the way along, and if ever there was an inferno outside of Hell it was this road. It was one mass of flame the whole length. As the shells came hurtling over, they cut the trees down with a crash. This was an added danger. But I had to get on somehow. I took my courage in both hands, set my teeth, and made a start on that death-defying journey. As the shells came over, I dodged them as best I could, keeping my eyes open for a falling tree, and dodging from behind one tree to another. I at last reached my destination.[44]

Private Herbert Gregory, 119th Company, MGC, 40th Division

The news Gregory received in the wood was shocking:

Nearly half our company were gone, and the other half must carry on somehow. The infantry had fared just as badly. After delivering my dispatch, and getting one to take back telling of the plight they were in, I made my way back along that shell-swept, blazing road once more always dodging, every nerve strained listening for the shells, and trusting in Providence. I eventually arrived back at Headquarters, and on giving my message to our Commanding Officer, his face turned an ashen grey. The company in the wood had suffered terrible casualties.[45]

Private Herbert Gregory, 119th Company, MGC, 40th Division

During the fighting, 119th Company, MGC, was to lose all its guns and most of the men were to become casualties in Bourlon Wood.

Meanwhile, there was considerable activity in the air. The RFC was keen, after criticism from the infantry of its performance on the previous day, to demonstrate a commitment to cowing its opposite number. Fifty machines from four fighter squadrons were allotted to provide close support for the infantry. However, the German air force had now received considerable reinforcements – including Rittmeister Manfred von Richthofen's elite squadrons. There was, therefore, a series of clashes – especially in the vicinity of Bourlon Wood. In one, an experienced British flyer had the first of many encounters with the pilot of an instantly recognizable Albatros aircraft:

About 10.00 a.m. on the 23rd my patrol left the ground and we flew at once towards Cambrai at 3,000 feet, for [we] could not get any higher owing to the clouds. We crossed the lines south of Bourlon Wood and very soon saw four Albatroses over Cambrai. We got close enough to open fire, and I engaged an Albatros, who was painted with a red nose, a yellow fuselage, and a green tail. He also had the letter K on his top plane. This Hun was destined to be always fighting my patrol somehow, and for the next three months we were continually meeting him. After I had fired a short burst at this machine he spun down a little, but at once came up again.[46]

Captain James McCudden, 56 Squadron, RFC

Having driven off these four German aircraft, McCudden and his patrol flew westwards, and spotting a reconnaissance aircraft over Cantaing attacked. The German immediately turned east and fired a signal flare.

I had seen many Hun two-seaters do this, so I suppose that is a signal, 'Jagdstaffeln – to the rescue!' This Hun went down in a devil of a hurry, but I did not finally get him.[47]

Captain James McCudden, 56 Squadron, RFC

However, McCudden and his remaining companion were luckier in their next encounter.

By now most of my patrol had dwindled away, and I only had Fielding-Johnson with me. We sighted two Albatros scouts attacking a Bristol Fighter over Marcoing, so at once we went to the rescue. The Bristol, seeing us coming, skilfully drew one of them after him. The remaining one, who was just about my level, saw me and fairly stood on his tail endeavouring to scrape up a foot more height than my machine.

By the time I got to him and zoomed, the S.E. just went up a little higher. Then we both turned inwards and, the Hun losing height, I at once did a quicker turn and got behind him. After a short burst from my Vickers, the Hun's hat fell out of his machine, for apparently he was wearing an ordinary service cap; and after that the V-strutter went down and hit the ground, in a vertical dive with the engine on – a fearful whack. I looked where the Hun had crashed and found it was near Rumilly.[48]

Captain James McCudden, 56 Squadron, RFC

The Albatros which McCudden shot down was his 20th victim. This type of aerial combat was now increasingly prevalent over the Cambrai battle. However, the ground attack squadrons were still committed to their tasks and whilst the battle raged to wrest Bourlon Wood from the Germans, Lieutenant Frederick Huxley of No. 68 (2 Australian) Squadron saw three British tanks held up in the wood by a German battery. He dropped four bombs on the guns from a hundred feet, silenced them and enabled the tanks to advance.

One German pilot described how 'Over Bourlon Wood, whole swarms of English squadrons are cruising around, close together in massed formations; single-seaters and multi-seaters, machines of all types.'[49] Yet matters changed decidedly at around 2.00 p.m. when Richthofen's *Jagdgeschwader I* made its first appearance – 'The commander lets his machine-guns rattle, and the first Englishman goes rushing downward out of the swarm.'[50] Richthofen's 62nd victim was Lieutenant James Boddy, who was flying a DH5 of No. 64 Squadron. Richthofen's combat report provided an unemotional description of the encounter:

> Shortly after I had forced an Englishman to land at the west side of Bourlon Wood, I attacked a DH5 north of Fontaine (Notre Dame) at about 100 metres height. After the first shots, the Englishman started to glide downwards, but then fell into the south-east corner of Bourlon Wood. I could not observe the plane hitting the ground.[51]
>
> Rittmeister Manfred von Richthofen, *Jagdgeschwader I*

Like many of Richthofen's victims, Boddy had known little, if anything, about the attack in which he was shot down. A bullet fractured his skull and he broke both legs when his plane crashed into Bourlon Wood. A fellow pilot from 64 Squadron, Captain Henry Fox Russell, whose aircraft might perhaps have been the one Richthofen had forced down prior to shooting down Boddy, saw Boddy crash and rescued him with the help of a tank crew. Boddy was then taken to a dressing station on board the tank. Despite his prompt rescue, Boddy still lost a leg as a result of his savaging by Germany's 'Red Knight'.

Further attacks were planned for Bourlon and Fontaine in the afternoon. Stan Bradbury was with 1/5th Seaforths' headquarters and described how:

Battalion Headquarters established themselves in a miserable dugout in a sunken road on the outskirts of Cantaing. In the dugout were two or three wounded Germans, one of whom had some awful wounds but never gave way to his pains and sufferings, remaining perfectly stolid. During the day, many attacks on Fontaine were made with the aid of tanks; first one battalion, then another, of our brigade attempting to capture the place; each one in turn suffering heavily and meeting with fluctuating success.[52]

Private Stan Bradbury, 1/5th Seaforth Highlanders, 152nd Brigade, 51st Division

Brigadier General Pelham Burn intended to use his reserve battalion, 1/5th Seaforth Highlanders, against Fontaine but was prevented when the Germans counter-attacked 40th Division's units in Bourlon Wood, forcing him to use the Seaforths to bolster their sister battalion, 1/6th, in the front line. Instead twelve tanks of 'I' Battalion went into action without infantry support against Fontaine meeting what must surely have been, by now, predictable failure.

During this second attack, the chaos and confusion in the fight for Fontaine was appalling and the casualties amongst both the defenders and the tank crews were heavy. The ferocity of the German resistance was remarkable; on at least one occasion German infantry hung onto the guns of the tanks in an attempt to prevent them firing. The village remained untaken.

The counter-attack against 40th Division was launched at about 3.00 p.m. following a heavy bombardment. The attack threatened to overwhelm the front line troops of 119th Brigade until the 18th Welsh Regiment arrived to save the day and help drive the Germans back until only the northernmost portion of the wood was still in German hands. The 18th Welsh's commander, Lieutenant Colonel William Kennedy, according to one of the weary defenders, 'rode right up to us on horseback, jumped off when he got up to us, rushing in front, rallied us and waving his cane urged us on; he had only gone about half a dozen yards when he fell dead, shot by the Bosch [sic].'[53]

For Lance Corporal Frank Turner, still lying wounded and oblivious of all this in Bourlon Wood, the afternoon brought much-anticipated succour and aid:

It must have been in the afternoon that a stretcher-bearer, mopping up, saw me and said 'Hang on, mate – I'll go and get a stretcher.' He wasn't gone long before he came back with a stretcher, but he had lost his partner. But he made me comfortable on the stretcher before going off to find his mate. Eventually they returned together and said 'one of your pals is over there with both legs nearly off – would you mind if we take him back first?' So they helped me off the stretcher and propped me against a tree again. That was late on Friday afternoon 23rd November.[54]

Lance Corporal Frank Turner, 19th Royal Welsh Fusiliers, 119th Brigade, 40th Division

Patiently, Turner continued to wait but his hopes of rescue were to be cruelly dashed:

They never found me – possibly they were knocked out – there was still shelling going on and I was expecting to be hit again, but my guardian angel was certainly doing her best![55]

Lance Corporal Frank Turner, 19th Royal Welsh Fusiliers, 119th Brigade, 40th Division

Throughout the day Byng at Third Army headquarters had great difficulty discovering what was actually happening in the fighting in and around Bourlon Wood and could do little but offer support to IV Corps staff in their push to take the Bourlon Ridge. The urgings by Army to Corps to use cavalry if possible in mounted operations if the opportunity presented itself changed later in the day to a more practical decision to form a dismounted battalion from 9th Cavalry Brigade.

In the wood every available man was thrown in to reinforce Crozier's brigade. Two hundred men of 19th Hussars from 9th Dismounted Cavalry Battalion were followed by the brigade's attached Royal Engineers and, at 7.15 p.m., by 14th Argyll and Sutherland Highlanders from 120th Brigade. Lieutenant Colonel Robert Benzie (once of the Ceylon Planters' Rifle Corps and now commanding 12th South Wales Borderers) was given command of the troops in Bourlon Wood. Under his direction, a continuous defensive line was finally established and a German counter-attack at 11.45 p.m. was beaten off.

The intense bombardment was kept up all through the night. We knew now that we were in for the toughest proposition of our lives, and those who came through this trying ordeal must consider themselves lucky.

Our men had done that which they had set out to do: that was to get into the wood. The question now was could they hold what they had got with the depleted force?[56]

Private Herbert Gregory, 119th Company, MGC, 40th Division

Haig had already expressed concerns about the withdrawal of units of 1st Cavalry Division from the line back to Metz-en-Couture. As a consequence, Byng had reversed this decision. Now Haig sent a special order urging Byng to use dismounted cavalry 'in any numbers' to take Bourlon Ridge. This meant 1st and 2nd Cavalry Brigades were also to act in this manner.

Rumours were now flying about that we were to move up, dismounted. At dusk, orders came to be in readiness at a moment's notice. Eight, nine, ten o'clock came, but no order to 'fall in'. 'Let's get down to it,' said Nobby Clarke, and we were just dozing off when 'Fall in' sounded. We grumbled and cursed at the fates that had beguiled us. It was about 11 p.m. and inky black. Our blankets, rolled in ground-sheets, were worn bandolier-fashion over our ammunition bandoliers. (A cavalry-man working as an infantryman is an awkward-looking creature. He has to wear kit which would otherwise be worn by the horse.)[57]

Private Chris Knight, 2nd Dragoon Guards (The Queen's Bays), 1st Cavalry Brigade, 1st Cavalry Division

Moving across country in the dark, they stumbled and slithered forward to occupy reserve trenches:

It was a night of blasphemous utterances. Our thoughts dwelt too much on comfortable beds – beds at home, beds in barracks, and even beds of straw in barns behind the line.[58]

Private Chris Knight, 2nd Dragoon Guards (The Queen's Bays), 1st Cavalry Brigade, 1st Cavalry Division

Now dismounted, and as a general reserve to the infantry, the contrast with the cavalry's anticipated role on the first day of battle could not have been greater. Captain 'Tommy' Lascelles was struck by how different it all was compared with the morning's gay scene:

That night came disillusion, and off we went on our feet to that infernal sugar factory at Graincourt . . . We had no trenches, we had no

definite orders, it rained and we were shelled and sniped with increasing intensity; the men lay on their stomachs in the grass, on an
improvised line.[59]

Captain Alan 'Tommy' Lascelles, Bedfordshire Yeomanry, 9th Cavalry Brigade, 1st
Cavalry Division

These cavalry units represented only the equivalent of weak strength
infantry companies and were not in themselves sufficient to bolster the
attackers. With the majority of the rest of the cavalry having been
ordered to withdraw into reserve, Byng decided it was time to send in
the Guards.

CHAPTER TEN

'To certain hell accompanied by a snowstorm'

O N THE MORNING of 23 November, the Guards Division were close to the battle zone after moving forward from south-east of Bapaume. For Captain Charles Dudley Ward of 1st Welsh Guards the preliminaries to another major engagement were further complicated by the internal politics of his battalion and in particular the relationship between the battalion CO, Lieutenant Colonel Grenville Douglas Gordon ('DG'), and other officers in the battalion – especially the second-in-command, and Dudley Ward's personal friend, Major Humphrey 'Broncho' Dene. Furthermore, when the battle opened and the cycle of operation orders and conferences had gradually clarified the Guards' proposed role in the fighting, experienced officers became increasingly concerned. Nervous tension manifested itself in surprising, and unpleasant, ways:

> When we heard the rough outline of the scheme, Broncho and I went for a walk to discuss it: It was a glimpse of the real 'simplicity' of war. Broncho was very serious, not a smile on his face but at the same time he was suffering as he does most days from most violent indigestion and so he made strange noises from both ends of himself and once stopped to piss in an open field – but he never ceased talking. And when you consider that he had probably never been more earnest you realise on what a slender foundation good behaviour as understood in a drawing room is built on.[1]
>
> Captain Charles Dudley Ward, 1st Welsh Guards, 3rd Guards Brigade, Guards Division

Yet this was not all 'piss and wind'. Dene's earnest concerns were based on sound knowledge of war's realities and the shortcomings of the battalion in which he served.

The burden on his mind was the poor quality of officers we now have should the attack succeed and we be engaged in open warfare – for that is to be our part, to go through the hole made by others. Of course we came to no conclusion, the whole question being could they ever act quickly? The plan itself we thought might be a huge success and could not be a serious failure.[2]

Captain Charles Dudley Ward, 1st Welsh Guards, 3rd Guards Brigade, Guards Division

The Welsh Guards were the rear battalion of their brigade and had reached Beaumetz.

We were much closer to the line and the Bosche was dropping an occasional shell nearby but not so close as to worry. We had lunch in comfort and then came an order that we were to march that night and take over the line. Men were to be in battle order etc. This meant an afternoon of worry dishing out ammunition, bombs and so on, and arranging for coats, blankets and caps to be stored. Later we were told we should go first into support.[3]

Captain Charles Dudley Ward, 1st Welsh Guards, 3rd Guards Brigade, Guards Division

Observing the Guards' advance from his aeroplane dropping station, Benjamin Parkin could not conceal his admiration:

I have a very vivid recollection from this day of seeing the 'march up' of the Guards – or of portions of them . . . Now, what did the marching up of the Guards mean? . . . Their march up was different from that of any other division I had seen. The 62nd Division battalions always left their packs behind – the 40th had done the same. But here were the Guards marching as steadily as if on the Barrack Square – with full pack and equipment and all as clean and spick and span as a new pin.[4]

Second Lieutenant Benjamin Parkin, 2/4th Duke of Wellington's Regiment, 186th Brigade, 62nd Division

What Parkin could not observe was the seething undercurrent of battalion politics that still boiled in the 1st Welsh Guards. Charles Dudley Ward was stunned on the eve of battle to find himself replaced as company commander by Captain Philip Dickens and ordered to join the battalion headquarters staff. This, perhaps inevitably, provoked more angst from 'Broncho' Dene:

Broncho came to me and said he hated the whole arrangement and was getting most anxious. Everyone had been sent off on courses. Lisburne was already so fagged out he was gaga. Roderick had never been other than gaga, Hargreaves was the only one left in whom he had any confidence as Dickens had only been in the line once and got hit – all of which is true. If anything happened to DG 'these are my orders,' said Broncho, 'you are to take charge of the battalion till I arrive and pay no attention to any paper seniority.' Nice position![5]
Captain Charles Dudley Ward, 1st Welsh Guards, 3rd Guards Brigade, Guards Division

Worse was to follow as the Guards made a confused approach to their battle positions:

We marched at 9.00 p.m., the whole brigade and as a brigade. Soon the road was so bad we had to march in single file . . . The rear could not keep up and were running – they lost touch. We were no longer following the road we had been told of and had no idea of our destination. DG raced along following the leading battalion and being followed by some thirty men. At every corner we left a man to direct – it was a fearful game. At last we came to a halt and discovered the staff who told us the route had been changed at the last moment and that guides had arrived. The rest of our journey we finished, when the battalion had closed up, at 6.00 a.m. on the 24th. We were met and guided by an amiable Scotsman who had just returned from attacking the Bosche.[6]
Captain Charles Dudley Ward, 1st Welsh Guards, 3rd Guards Brigade, Guards Division

The 1st Guards Brigade actually took over the forward positions whilst the Welsh Guards and 3rd Guards Brigade were in support at Flesquières. The relief of units of 51st Division by the Welsh Guards was considerably more amicable than that by some other Guards units. For example, Stan Bradbury related how there had been a little unpleasantness between the men of the two divisions owing to the Guards making a few nasty remarks on the non-capture of the whole of Fontaine – with the result that our men commenced fighting the Guards and for a time there was quite a 'set to' with a few casualties on both sides.[7]

Private Stan Bradbury, 1/5th Seaforth Highlanders, 152nd Brigade, 51st Division

Nevertheless, for the weary 51st Division, the relief was welcome:

We marched, or shall I say 'straggled', back to Flesquières where we sat on the pavements for over an hour whilst the officers in charge endeavoured to find us billets for the night, but getting properly fed up, impatient, and being dead tired, we entered the cellar of a big ruined house and after a bit of patching up succeeded in making it comfortable; someone gathered some fuel and a fire was made then one by one we fell asleep on the floor.[8]

Private Stan Bradbury, 1/5th Seaforth Highlanders, 152nd Brigade, 51st Division

For Douglas Wimberley, the relief of his machine-guns by those of 1st Guards Brigade could not come quickly enough.

I hastily wrote relief orders for the limbers to come up, and then rode down in the dark towards Graincourt to meet my opposite number. After a long wait, the Brigade came by and stopped for ten minutes' halt by the roadside.

I was very much interested listening to the talk of the Guardsmen, of the Coldstreams, nearby where I was sitting. They had marched fifteen miles or more it seemed, and wondered if they were going into good billets. Billets indeed! They had no idea that they were going into two foot trenches already several inches deep in water, and that within eight hours they would be once more facing those same machine-guns which had accounted for so many of our Jocks that morning.[9]

Major Douglas Wimberley, 232nd Company, MGC, 51st Division

More than half of the 15 miles the Guards had marched had been over difficult terrain in the dark. But Wimberley's hopes of withdrawal were premature:

The Brigade Machine-Gun Company were last of all in the column, and the OC was riding at the head. The first words, almost, he said to me were, 'I haven't any guns to relieve you with tonight. They are with the transport which has gone round by Hermies and Havrincourt, and won't be at Flesquières for some hours.' My heart went to zero. My men were dead beat; I had lost about nine men killed and many wounded out of the sections, and teams were consequently weak, and I calculated that if my guns were there next morning it meant another attack for them.[10]

Major Douglas Wimberley, 232nd Company, MGC, 51st Division

Despatching a runner to look for the Guards' limbers and guide them up, Wimberley was not optimistic. Therefore, he rode back to pour out his woes to his brigade commander, Pelham Burn. Finding the latter with his Guards' opposite number, Brigadier General Sir Claude Champion de Crespigny, nicknamed 'Crawley', Wimberley secured his men's much needed release:

'PB', wonderful man, fixed it up with him that I should withdraw my guns without relief and that his own Brigade Company's guns should be handed over to the Guards, and the men come out . . . I, of course, was delighted, for it meant that I could get my men out at once.[11]

Major Douglas Wimberley, 232nd Company, MGC, 51st Division

Snow fell during the night and was followed by rain. Conditions were miserable. So were many of the men. But daylight on 24 November offered the first opportunity for Charles Dudley Ward and the Welsh Guards to survey their new position:

Our dugout is in a small quarry in a little copse and is part of the very strong support system of the Bosch. Our first look round in daylight was most interesting. The battlefield was all in front of us – the smashed tanks, smashed German aeroplanes, the deep German trenches with Bosch dead and kit lying about in the utmost confusion, and then the tracks of the tanks showing where they had cruised down the lines obliterating the wire and shooting down the trenches – great work and a very fair advance. The ground is all clean grassland with scarcely a shell hole.[12]

Captain Charles Dudley Ward, 1st Welsh Guards, 3rd Guards Brigade, Guards Division

The newly arrived Guards did not attack that day. Already Third Army were concerned about the losses 40th Division had sustained in the previous day's fighting and contemplated the division's relief. Meanwhile two more divisions (2nd and 47th) were now in the vicinity and might be employed as reinforcements or, at least, to replace losses. Another division, 59th, stood ready to be used. However, these reserves had not all been available when the attack commenced. Had they been, Bourlon Ridge might already have fallen.

Nevertheless, the British prepared another assault. IV Corps' chief objective for 24 November was the capture of Bourlon village. Orders issued at 12.50 a.m. allotted two Cavalry Battalions (1st and 2nd) to 40th Division, together with 12 tanks from 'I' Battalion. These tanks and dismounted cavalry would bolster 121st Brigade. Bourlon Wood, where 119th Brigade had been further reinforced during the night by two more companies of the 14th Argyll and Sutherland Highlanders, eight machine-guns and about two hundred dismounted cavalry, was to be held but no further advance was planned there at this stage.

At 8.30 a.m. German counter-attacks on the flanks of 119th Brigade near the villages of Bourlon and Fontaine pre-empted any British action, but were beaten off by rifle and artillery fire. Further attacks were, however, expected. Shortly afterwards, Lieutenant General Charles Woollcombe, IV Corps' commander, arrived at 40th Division's head-quarters in Havrincourt to meet Major General Ponsonby, the divisional commander. Perhaps news of the German counter-attack was a contributory factor in Woollcombe's decision to postpone the attack on Bourlon. In any event, Woollcombe had also succumbed to the increasingly prevalent view amongst British commanders that large quantities of tanks would ensure success in such attacks. To his mind the twelve from 'I' Battalion were clearly not enough. What such an analysis failed to recognize was that the attacks at Fontaine and Bourlon had not failed because of an insufficiency of tanks but because the cooperation between those used and the infantry was wholly inadequate.

The shelling of Bourlon Wood and its approaches continued unabated. Private Herbert Gregory observed one awful incident close to his company's headquarters when two limbers with badly wounded men from the wood on board were hit by shell fire.

The men were all bandaged up: head wounds, arm wounds, and leg wounds. They were singing as they came down the road in the limbers, which were drawn by two mules. When the limbers got to within thirty yards or so of the hospital, a tremendous shell came hurtling over and exploded, crash, right under the two limbers. The men and limbers were scattered in all directions, all being killed instantly. The mules lay dead in a pool of their own blood, while the limbs of the unfortunate men were scattered about all over the road: legs, arms, and heads being severed as with a scythe. The limbers were splintered to matchwood. These men, only a few seconds before, were happy in the thought that they would soon be in 'Blighty'.[13]

Private Herbert Gregory, 119th Company, MGC, 40th Division

On 40th Division's left front where there was, by comparison, considerably less activity at this time. 'Tommy' Lascelles recalled

the arrival of a hare, which had prudently decided to evacuate Bourlon Wood, and ran the length of our line and that of the 19th [Hussars]. All the men fired at it; the hare escaped to our left flank amid prolonged cheering.[14]

Captain Alan 'Tommy' Lascelles, Bedfordshire Yeomanry, 9th Cavalry Brigade, 1st Cavalry Division

Was this one lucky hare or an example of some very bad shooting? If the latter, it was hardly an auspicious augury.

At 11.00 a.m. the Germans launched a second counter-attack against Bourlon Wood. This too was beaten back, but the British casualties continued to mount. The defenders were also harassed from the air. One of those in the wood recalled

very marked activity by enemy aeroplanes flying at very low altitude, in some instances skimming the tops of the trees and firing their machine-guns at intervals, but very much at random.[15]

Private William Falconer, 14th Argyll and Sutherland Highlanders, 120th Brigade, 40th Division

The lack of RFC opposition on 24 November was taken by German pilots as a sign that the British had been cowed by the arrival of Richthofen's squadrons:

The word seems to have gotten around on the other side of the lines that the 'Baron's' red machines have arrived. There is hardly any other way to explain the fact that there are conspicuously few airmen visible on this day. In return, the *Staffeln* have plenty of time to get themselves settled at their new airfields in the vicinity of Avesnes-le-Sec.[16]

Hauptmann Karl Bodenschatz, *Jagdgeschwader I*

The truth was that once again the conditions over the RFC airfields prevented many squadrons from getting airborne:

An absolute gale stopped everything, except in the early morning. At 5.00 a.m. I took seven pilots to collect new Camels from Candas, but two crashed on landing because of the gusty wind. Candas are supplying fifty Camels a day to make good the losses of the squadrons engaged in this push.[17]

Lieutenant Arthur Gould Lee, 46 Squadron, RFC

Meanwhile orders postponing the attack on Bourlon had reached the supporting artillery, but 121st Brigade did not know of the cancellation until it was too late. Consequently, at 3.00 p.m., at almost the same time as a further German attack was launched against 119th Brigade in the wood, the twelve tanks and the infantry from 14th Highland Light Infantry (HLI) (attached from 120th Brigade) and 12th Suffolk Regiment attacked Bourlon village.

The tanks led the way. The attack had already been delayed on their account because of a lack of petrol. Evidently they were seen as essential to the attack's success. The lateness of the attack meant there was only a short period of daylight in which to operate. One tank commander was Second Lieutenant George Parsons, now commanding I28 'Incomparable'. His first tank had been knocked out by artillery fire on Welsh Ridge on 20 November wounding his section commander, 'Jake' Wilson.

We moved across the main Bapaume–Cambrai road and up the narrow road to Bourlon crest. There were eight tanks in Indian File – I was fifth and remember seeing Major Vandervell and Captain Keane literally staggering back down the road, white as sheets. I heard afterwards that with Captain Monaghan they were near the crest, when a shell took Monaghan's head right off.[18]

Second Lieutenant George Parsons, I28, 'Incomparable', 'I' Battalion, Tank Corps

Close to the top of the ridge the tanks stopped.

> We just sat there being mildly shelled. I don't know why but there were no orders – nobody knew anything, so I decided I wouldn't be trapped like that, and swung left – climbed out of the sunken road, went about 200 feet and faced the enemy.[19]
>
> Second Lieutenant George Parsons, 128, 'Incomparable', 'I' Battalion, Tank Corps

Driving 'Incomparable' was Private Fred Keyworth. His recollection was that:

> We were travelling along a sunken road which led into the wood and after going some distance my officer told me to take the tank up the bank of the road and go across the field and into the wood, because he thought the enemy had mined the road.[20]
>
> Private Fred Keyworth, 128, 'Incomparable', 'I' Battalion, Tank Corps

Out of the confines of the sunken road, Parsons' route to Bourlon Village seemed clear:

> I drove to the top of the rise, and there was Bourlon Village, just a little way ahead. I saw nobody and only a little smoke in the morning haze. Then I got into high gear and moved in with both front machine-guns firing continuous bursts. It was exhilarating – believe me! I don't think anything hit the tank. Well, I was about one-third of the way to the first farm building when the tank fell into an excavation and stuck at 45°. The engine stopped and we couldn't start it at any price. Then Jerry got machine-guns on us and made life very miserable. I had to abandon [the tank] – but how? The high side doors were a little bit 'away' from the enemy, and we took single turns struggling out, and sprinting to safety.
>
> I don't know what I fell into – it might have been an old farm foundation.[21]
>
> Second Lieutenant George Parsons, 128, 'Incomparable', 'I' Battalion, Tank Corps

His driver was much surer concerning what had happened:

> I did as directed and had travelled a short way across the field when we fell into a tank trap. The Germans had dug a large hole and covered the top of the hole with chicken wire and put the turf back so as to look

283

like the surrounding terrain. We fell to the bottom of the hole; the tank turned over on its side and the right hand door which was on top was the only door we could get out of.[22]

Private Fred Keyworth, 128, 'Incomparable', 'I' Battalion, Tank Corps

Of the rest of the tanks, most reached and entered the village but possibly over-cautious because of the lateness of the day, when the infantry did not appear, the tanks withdrew again. Only four rallied; the rest were destroyed or had mechanical breakdowns. Soon after the tanks' withdrawal, 14th HLI reached the houses and pushed through the village to the railway line north-east of Bourlon. However, the three leading companies became cut off from the fourth company and the battalion headquarters, whilst 12th Suffolks suffered enfilade fire and, consequently, made less progress. As soon as it was known that 121st Brigade had attacked Bourlon, the division's commander placed the remaining battalions of 120th Brigade under 121st Brigade's commander, Brigadier General John Campbell.

Although not committed to this fighting, the dismounted cavalry near the sugar refinery were still exposed to German fire, as 'Tommy' Lascelles discovered:

At some point in the proceedings I and my other officers . . . foregathered in the sunken road leading north-west from the factory to read some orders. We huddled into a little excavation in the bank in the road. A 5.9 shell pitched on the other bank; I was knocked end over end, with a sensation of being violently hit on the arm; I was only half-conscious for some time and practically lost the use of my tongue. Smee and Pentelow picked me up and walked me down to a dressing-station in the bowels of the ruined sugar factory. There I was laid down, given a dose of morphia and, after my arm had been examined, told I was to be evacuated. The next hour was one of the happiest of my life, in spite of the fact that Graincourt was being heavily shelled.[23]

Captain Alan 'Tommy' Lascelles, Bedfordshire Yeomanry, 9th Cavalry Brigade, 1st Cavalry Division

Whilst Lascelles lay in opiate-induced ecstasy, the fighting resulting from the renewed German attack on Bourlon Wood grew heavier and more chaotic. Scouting on the right flank of 14th Argyll and Sutherland

Highlanders, Private William Falconer had found himself about one hundred and fifty yards from the north edge of the wood when he encountered a cavalryman from 15th Hussars. This woodland meeting was interrupted by German rifle fire but the two managed to drive their assailants off. They then decided to try to get back to the main body, crawling through the undergrowth. Soon the Hussar grew impatient and suggested a series of tree-to-tree rushes.

> I did not approve of this suggestion but he was headstrong and intended to carry it out. So I said, 'All right. Do as you like, but I will carry on the way I have been doing.'[24]
>
> Private William Falconer, 14th Argyll and Sutherland Highlanders, 120th Brigade, 40th Division

The cavalryman reached one tree safely but before he could reach a second, he was killed by a single rifle shot 'like a rabbit in a ride' and dropped silently. Falconer, however, reached his platoon commander, Second Lieutenant John Allison, who promptly sent Falconer in command of five men to clear up the situation on the same right flank. This party soon came under heavy fire and all but Falconer and one other man were killed. The loss of his chum, Charles McKay*, prompted Falconer to wild action. Jumping up and waving his rifle in furious rage, he faced four astonished Germans: 'They looked at me in amazement, more like startled deer than men,' as Falconer shouted, 'Come on, you dirty German bastards!' Remarkably, it was two of the German party who fell to rifle fire, not Falconer. German machine-gun fire then impelled Falconer and his surviving companion to retire back to his platoon.

Allison, the platoon commander, decided this machine-gun should be captured but attempts to do so resulted in dismal failure and the loss of a valuable NCO.

> Our officer was not discouraged with this blow [but] about two hundred yards away, German Very lights were being sent up, it appeared in the form of a semi-circle; they were fired four at once. The

---

* According to the Commonwealth War Graves Commission Debt of Honour website, Private Charles McKay died on 26 November 1917. However, Falconer's account suggests he was killed outright on 24 November.

officer said, 'What are they up to now?' so I formed the conclusion that we were being surrounded, as any sane man would have thought likewise; our party was only seven men and an officer, the latter a gallant soldier and gentleman. So, after a discussion as to our procedure we decided to retire and form a line of resistance.[25]

Private William Falconer, 14th Argyll and Sutherland Highlanders, 120th Brigade, 40th Division

These events typified the confused defence the British maintained here. Their opponents knew how crucial it was for them to retake the wood. The German *3rd Guards Infantry Division*'s continued pressure, combined with the losses suffered during the course of the day, was driving back the British right until it faced eastward across the centre of the forest. However, at about 4.00 p.m. a mixed force from all the infantry and cavalry units in Bourlon Wood, commanded by Lieutenant Colonel James Plunkett of 19th Royal Welsh Fusiliers and with his battalion staff acting as section leaders, counter-attacked and drove the Germans northwards back out of the wood where they were caught by a British artillery barrage, which inflicted heavy casualties. Later, much needed reinforcements arrived in the shape of men from 11th King's Own and 2nd Scots Guards. Lieutenant Wilfrid Ewart was an officer in the latter battalion:

At nine o'clock that evening the order came to move up to Bourlon Wood, which we did as a Battalion, getting shelled a bit going across the open. Bourlon Wood was a nightmare sort of place – pitch dark and no one knew its tortuous ways or quite where the Germans were. It is a big wood divided up by rides and summer roads. After going halfway through it, very heavy rifle and machine-gun fire broke out in front on the farther edge of the wood, lights going up all round. Several men got hit, and down the ride there came a surging mob of cavalrymen, infantry, and engineers absolutely out of control, shouting and yelling that the Germans had broken in and were coming through the wood. It was a fine example of New Army discipline. Our men fixed bayonets, lined the ride, expecting every moment a terrific German onslaught. Nothing happened. We then went on through the wood, which was pitch dark, nobody knowing whether the Bosches had been driven out or not, and eventually dug in. We then found some very windy

Highlanders and dismounted cavalry, and we got orders to push on and drive the Bosches out at daybreak.[26]

Lieutenant Wilfrid Ewart, 2nd Scots Guards, 3rd Guards Brigade, Guards Division

Ewart's training as a Guards officer undoubtedly accounted for much of his rather sneering comments. Schooled to believe that the Guards were quite simply the best the British Army had, Ewart's attitude reflected this superiority complex. Soon he too would discover the particular horrors of Bourlon Wood.

That night 'Tommy' Lascelles was evacuated to a Casualty Clearing Station. In fact, he had to make his own way there:

I was roused from my state of happy coma and asked if I could walk to Havrincourt. By that time the shelling had increased to such an extent that I was only too glad of the opportunity to walk anywhere. So, in company with a sergeant of the Scots Guards, who had been wounded in the head, I started off down the Havrincourt road in bright moon-light. It was a very long walk, punctuated by a great deal of attention from the Germans, but we eventually reached a CCS and were despatched in a motor-ambulance to railhead.[27]

Captain Alan 'Tommy' Lascelles, Bedfordshire Yeomanry, 9th Cavalry Brigade, 1st Cavalry Division

Less fortunate was Frank Turner of the Royal Welsh Fusiliers whose terse description of his time in Bourlon Wood from the evening of 23 November to the morning of 25 November suggests an experience more horrifying than could be detailed in words:

At last as darkness fell [on 23 November] the shell firing ceased and quiet reigned. I expect I slept, I do not remember and next day, Saturday, I saw no one. Probably I slept that night, I had lost a lot of blood but never lost consciousness as a result. Next day I was feeling a bit desperate and tried to crawl – I didn't get far and propped myself up against another tree rather exhausted. It was, of course, late November and the ground was covered with a deep layer of leaves.[28]

Lance Corporal Frank Turner, 19th Royal Welsh Fusiliers, 119th Brigade, 40th Division

How many other men during the course of this terrible conflict felt their lives leach away into the earth whilst lying alone and uncomforted?

How many lost hope and allowed death to take them? Frank Turner must surely have been aware that his time and his chances were running out.

The last reserves of 120th Brigade (and therefore of 40th Division) had been brought forward during the afternoon. The march up of 13th East Surreys was marked by several ill omens of what awaited them:

> As we marched along a sunken road, we came to what I thought was a man resting against the bank. Within a few yards of him I saw that he was wearing a blue [signallers] band. I turned to one of our signallers marching beside me and said, 'There you are Seager, there's a "blue band" having a rest.' I looked at Seager as I spoke and noticed he went a sickly yellow. Then I saw why. We had reached the 'resting' man and we could see he was stone dead and had a hole as big as a saucer in his chest. His jacket and shirt had been pulled aside (by someone who had tried to help him I expect) and we saw the gaping hole so suddenly. It was not so much the wound that upset Seager, we had seen many before, it was the fact that the man was wearing a blue band, as we were for the first time. A few yards further on we saw what had happened. A shell, or possibly two, had landed right in the centre of an artillery gun and limber. There were bodies of men and horses and mules covering the road for about forty yards, all mixed up with bits of the gun carriage and limber. We skirted round the worst part and went on.[29]
>
> Corporal Fred Wynne, 13th East Surreys, 120th Brigade, 40th Division

After dusk the battalion spent several hours in a sunken road within sight of Bourlon Wood:

> A shell dropped now and again, very accurately, in the sunken road. One shell dropped about ten yards ahead of us among the men of 'A' Company. They bandaged up the wounded and passed them back. We moved forward a few yards and in the darkness I saw, leaning against the bank, a man I had known very well at the Shaft Barracks Dover. He was 'Jock' Harris, a Scotsman who, for some reason unknown to us, was serving in the East Surreys. As I got to him I said 'Hello Jock,' and then I saw him properly. He also had been hit in the chest and was dead.[30]
>
> Corporal Fred Wynne, 13th East Surreys, 120th Brigade, 40th Division

Wynne's fellow signaller, Seager, was a tall, well-built, handsome young man who was well liked and regarded as honest and straightforward. On previous occasions in the line he had behaved calmly and rationally under shell fire but now he began to lose his nerve.

> He started saying 'What are we waiting here for? We'll all be killed in a minute. Can't we move away? Can't we go back?' He went on and on like this for nearly half an hour. I tried to quieten him by saying: 'These shells are nowhere near us' or 'We'll soon be moving on'. But it was no use. He got worse and worse, making me even more jittery than I was. At last the platoon officer, who was sitting the other side of me, said 'Take hold of yourself, Seager. Pull yourself together, man.' A shell dropped fairly near and that finished it. Seager was a shaking wreck. Someone took him away and I never saw him again.[31]
>
> Corporal Fred Wynne, 13th East Surreys, 120th Brigade, 40th Division

Finally, the battalion occupied a line of shallow 'scrapes' across a field very close to Bourlon village.

> We lay down in a firing position awaiting further orders. It was pitch black and drizzling with rain. A cold miserable rain and from about 2.00 a.m. to 6.30 a.m. it never stopped. We were soaked through to the skin, stiff with the cold and inactivity and as spiritless as drowned cats.[32]
>
> Corporal Fred Wynne, 13th East Surreys, 120th Brigade, 40th Division

On the evening of 24 November, IV Corps issued orders for a renewed attack by 40th Division 'with tanks' on Bourlon at 7.00 a.m. the next day. Woollcombe and his chief staff officer, Major General Hugo De Pree, in pressing to complete their allotted task, committed a serious error at this point. On the morning of the same day, Third Army had, in fact, ordered all tanks (except those of 'I' Battalion already in action) to be withdrawn into reserve to refit and to permit the tank crews to recuperate. Later that evening, IV Corps headquarters staff compounded the error when asked by 40th Division to provide twelve tanks to support the 14th HLI now known to be in Bourlon village and who expected to be counter-attacked the following morning. The staff of 40th Division issued orders for an attack in the morning to relieve the

HLI in Bourlon based on IV Corps' promise to provide tank assistance. Yet there were no tanks.

Haig, Third Army and IV Corps, although having learned that Bourlon had not been taken, were still planning for the cavalry to complete the breakthrough the next day, pressing 40th Division to secure the railway cutting beyond Bourlon village for the cavalry to pass through. The 2nd Cavalry Division was moved forward on the morning of 25 November to Ribécourt. It was a windy, showery morning after a stormy night in which 'tarpaulins were torn off roofs and tents flattened'.[33] Only the day before, Captain Frank Ash and several fellow officers of the 4th (Queen's Own) Hussars had been entertained by the divisional pierrot troupe at Villers-Faucon. Now they were going back into the line.

> Saddled up at 6.00 a.m. in the pitch dark, pouring with rain. Went up to Ribécourt. The whole Brigade halted and dismounted on an open hillside, part of which was in full view of the Bosches. We had some sausage and dog biscuits. Captain Scott and I then went to the top of the hill and had a splendid view of Cambrai away to our right front.[34]
>
> Captain Frank Ash, 4th (Queen's Own) Hussars, 3rd Cavalry Brigade, 2nd Cavalry Division

And here they remained; a brigade of cavalry drawn up in the open on a hillside waiting for action – an attractive target for German artillery.

Preparations in 121st Brigade's sector for the attack on Bourlon to relieve the HLI were hampered by the chaotic mix of units there. Eventually, it became the task of one solitary battalion, Lieutenant Colonel H.L. Warden's 13th East Surreys, whose ranks included Fred Wynne.

> We had lain on the wet grass until Captain Linge looked at his watch and told us to pass the word along the line to advance quietly when he gave the signal. A few minutes later, at 6.30 a.m. he gave the signal. We got up. I couldn't walk properly for several minutes. I just staggered and the others looked much the same. About a hundred yards away, immediately in front of us, was a very high unkempt hedge beyond which appeared to be a road running parallel with the hedge. We could

see the outline of the roofs of one or two cottages above the top of the hedge. We walked forward and found gaps in the hedge and all assembled on the roadway.[35]

Corporal Fred Wynne, 13th East Surreys, 120th Brigade, 40th Division

The East Surreys' orders were for a 'mopping up' operation:

We had to 'mop up' the village and relieve the two companies of the Highland Light Infantry who were entrenched beyond the village but were surrounded and cut off. So we did not expect any firing in the village. All the same we went forward very cautiously. The centre road in the village was fairly wide and had small houses on each side. We cautiously crept along the road, hugging the house walls where they existed and cautiously entering each house to clear out any Germans who might be there.[36]

Corporal Fred Wynne, 13th East Surreys, 120th Brigade, 40th Division

They had almost reached the centre of the village when suddenly several machine-guns opened fire.

We were sitting ducks. It was impossible to be certain where the machine-guns were, but without doubt the bullets came from the upper windows of the houses somewhere near the crossroads. We fired into every window we could aim at. The machine-guns then stopped. Of course we thought, or hoped, that the hundreds of bullets we had fired into the windows had effectively destroyed the machine-gun nests. They were silent.[37]

Corporal Fred Wynne, 13th East Surreys, 120th Brigade, 40th Division

Once more the East Surreys advanced cautiously. Abruptly, a blizzard of fire opened again.

Whereas previously the German machine-guns fired in bursts, they now fired with hardly a pause. Out of the hundred or so men stealthily advancing along the street, more than half were wounded or killed in the first two minutes of the fusillade. The shouts for stretcher-bearers from the wounded who were unable to walk or limp to safe cover were unnerving. On many occasions the unhurt ran to drag the helpless to the shelter of a house wall, in several cases resulting in further casualties, but within about ten minutes all those who needed help were dragged to cover and only the dead or those who appeared to be dead were left on the roadway or in the gutters.[38]

Corporal Fred Wynne, 13th East Surreys, 120th Brigade, 40th Division

Those who still lived were pinned down.

We tested the enemy fire by occasionally raising a helmet as a target and more often than not a spattering of bullets was the result. 'Where were all those tanks?' was the general feeling. We had seen some scattered over the plain in front of Cambrai, disabled and deserted, but there must have been scores in fighting condition pulled back out of harm's way. We had the same feelings towards them as we had for some of the Guards battalions. Months of preparation for a battle, into the fight fresh and strong and out again in no time, whereas the line regiments would be just as much in the fighting but would have been holding the trenches months before the assault and would still have to hold the line after the assault had been successfully or unsuccessfully concluded, with only perhaps a week out of the line for re-equipping.[39]

Corporal Fred Wynne, 13th East Surreys, 120th Brigade, 40th Division

Wynne did not know of the blunder IV Corps had made regarding tank support, but he was sure that 'One tank could have wiped out the enemy machine-guns that held up a whole battalion and accounted for something like four hundred dead or wounded.'

The surviving East Surreys left the main street and worked their way round the back gardens of the houses, encountering more opposition as they did so:

At one point we were again held up by machine-gun fire. It seemed to come from the upstairs room of a house about twenty yards away. Every time any of us moved the machine-gun would stutter out a very short burst – about ten rounds only. The gunner was certainly a cool customer. The tendency is to fire more rounds than necessary, even at an elusive or imaginary target, but this gunner didn't waste a round.[40]

Corporal Fred Wynne, 13th East Surreys, 120th Brigade, 40th Division

Thinking he saw a movement in the window of one room Wynne took aim and fired.

Just as I pressed the trigger one of our chaps crawled up beside me with his head in line with the muzzle of my rifle, his ear no more than six or seven inches away. I fired, concentrating on my target and not realising his head was so near. I must have split his eardrum. He spun round, held his head and called me quite a lot of colourful things. He was quite right of course, particularly as my bullet was wasted. The machine-gun spat out another short vicious burst very near the four of us (including Captain Linge).[41]

Corporal Fred Wynne, 13th East Surreys, 120th Brigade, 40th Division

Orders were received after an hour or so of this cat and mouse exercise to regroup in the field where they had started from that morning. Gradually, in ones and twos, what remained of Wynne's company cautiously retreated, still frequently under fire.

Attempts to reach the HLI companies near the railway on the village's north side were, therefore, continually baulked. When their ammunition ran out, their resistance was overcome and they were forced to surrender. Unaware of this fact, Lieutenant Colonel Warden with his headquarters staff had found their counterparts of 14th HLI in a house on the Fontaine road at the entrance to Bourlon. This they set about converting into a strongpoint which soon became the linchpin of the British line on the village edge of Bourlon Wood. A battery of trench mortars arrived as reinforcements and many of the surviving East Surreys rallied here. However Captain Linge despatched Corporal Wynne and seven men through the wood to lead an attempt to outflank and overcome the German machine-guns.

Wynne recalled that, here at least, the wood remained largely undamaged by shellfire:

It was a beautiful wood. Tall upright trees, leafless then but very majestic. The trees were well spaced, seven or eight feet apart of irregular pattern . . . We advanced very slowly, dodging from the shelter of one tree to the shelter of the next. I couldn't see very many of my party as the trees obscured them. Occasionally we heard a bullet smack against a tree particularly as we got deeper into the wood and on several occasions I could hear someone shout for help.[42]

Corporal Fred Wynne, 13th East Surreys, 120th Brigade, 40th Division

Eventually Wynne and two others of his party reached a narrow sunken road leading into the village. Apart from an occasional stray bullet, all was quiet.

> I told them we would wait for the others to arrive before we moved further. We waited but no one joined us . . . We concluded that at least three were wounded or killed and the other two, making up the five, might have been helping them back. We also considered sending someone back to inform Captain Linge that we had reached a sunken road looking down on the village, and decided against it as the possibility of anyone getting back for certain was doubtful in view of the fact that only three out of eight had arrived there. A wrong decision, probably. It is hard to say.[43]
>
> Corporal Fred Wynne, 13th East Surreys, 120th Brigade, 40th Division

Here they remained for several hours observing the top floors of the houses about two hundred yards away and firing at any possible targets in the windows.

In the wood, the Scots Guards had attempted a short advance in the morning:

> As soon as it got light the three companies advanced in extended order, and it was not long before the bullets began to fly, and Howard's Company got hung up by machine-guns on the left. Consequently, we could not get on. Desultory and sometimes very sharp fighting went on for about two and a half hours. We sniped a lot of Bosches. Then Howard got badly wounded, and it was obvious the Bosches were too strong for us.[44]
>
> Lieutenant Wilfrid Ewart, 2nd Scots Guards, 3rd Guards Brigade, Guards Division

Now Ewart began to understand the unique character of wood fighting. A second attempt to advance and clear the wood was ordered for two in the afternoon:

> I had the wind up as never before, feeling certain that it was impossible to take the place owing to the machine-guns which were supposed to be rushed with the bayonet, but which nobody really knew the where-abouts and number of. We lined along a summer ride and went over just at the tail end of a sleet-storm. There was a short and quite useless

machine-gun barrage, no artillery. Just after we had gone over, Tyringham tried to stop us, as the Command realised the hopelessness of it, but it was then too late.[45]

Lieutenant Wilfrid Ewart, 2nd Scots Guards, 3rd Guards Brigade, Guards Division

Accompanied by Sergeant James Fotheringham, who was 'wonderful from first to last' and who 'kept bringing the men on in the most magnificent way', Ewart's company reached a more open part of the wood. Here Captain Archibald Menzies, the Company Commander, Sergeant Roderick Maclean and the leading men of 'F' Company were mown down trying to rush the machine-guns.

At the same moment the two machine-guns slewed round on to us, and I realised that we were only about fifteen yards from one of them. Of course we flung ourselves down, Sergeant Fotheringham, a man called Grant . . . and myself; and for the next twenty minutes there was nothing but a young oak tree between us three and eternity. The machine-gun fired absolutely point blank, but could not quite reach us on account of the tree.[46]

Lieutenant Wilfrid Ewart, 2nd Scots Guards, 3rd Guards Brigade, Guards Division

Most of the platoon got down in a depression about twenty-five yards behind, but about eight men, including two Lewis gunners, remained close by Ewart, firing for all they were worth until they were killed. Soon only Ewart, Fotheringham and Grant of the advanced group were still alive.

Then the Bosche started throwing phosphorous bombs at the dead and wounded, which set light to them and burnt them up. I thought I had seen most of the nasty things in this war, but this was the nastiest by a long way. We three were still lying behind the tree, unable to move an eyelid. However, after about twenty minutes the Germans got tired of shooting, and we decided to get away if possible one by one. Grant went first, and got across the open all right, though fired at from each side. Then Sergeant Fotheringham volunteered to try and get one of the Lewis guns away. He had his arm shattered at once, but managed to crawl back, only to die at the dressing station. He was a great friend of mine and I feel his loss very much.[47]

Lieutenant Wilfrid Ewart, 2nd Scots Guards, 3rd Guards Brigade, Guards Division

Ewart himself waited for five minutes and then made his attempt. Bullets flew around him, yet he got back safely. For Ewart,

It was an experience I shall never wish to repeat, and it is no compensation for the loss of people like Menzies, and Sergeants Fotheringham and Maclean to know that what they were asked to do was absolutely impossible.[48]

Lieutenant Wilfrid Ewart, 2nd Scots Guards, 3rd Guards Brigade, Guards Division

Thus no further significant progress had been made in Bourlon Wood.

When rescue came that day for Frank Turner, lying wounded in Bourlon Wood, it was sudden and surprisingly swift:

I think it was probably about midday when I heard what appeared to be marching – I gave a shout and sure enough a corporal came and found me. He and a couple of others were escorting a party of about a dozen Germans to the rear. They all came over and one of the Germans took off his long grey coat and put it round me. Then four of them picked me up – there was no stretcher – as best they could and the party continued to the rear.[49]

Lance Corporal Frank Turner, 19th Royal Welsh Fusiliers, 119th Brigade, 40th Division

Turner was taken out of the woods to a large field seemingly covered with stretchers and bodies. Medical officers and orderlies worked among the stretchers. Turner's leg was examined.

Sometime later, four RAMC men came to me and said, 'You're next.' They lifted me on to their shoulders and set off. After what I thought was a short period, they put me down and had a smoke, giving me one. When I really looked at them, it was obvious that they were almost worn out. They had been at it for hours and the journey to the nearest point the motor ambulances could reach was nearly four miles. So we continued in short spells until we came to the road where they again put me down and said, 'This is it. An ambulance will be here shortly.'[50]

Lance Corporal Frank Turner, 19th Royal Welsh Fusiliers, 119th Brigade, 40th Division

When the ambulances arrived, Turner was loaded into the 'upper deck' of one of them. He had had nothing to eat since Friday morning –

it was now Sunday evening. In due course they arrived at No. 33 Casualty Clearing Station. Here an RAMC orderly approached Turner:

He had a 'dorothy bag' and said 'I am putting your personal belongings in here and it will travel around with you.' Some of the RAMC personnel had been named 'Rob All My Comrades' but I always took it with a grain of salt, especially as the only previous experience of them had been the quartet which had carried me about four miles. I admired them and was sure they were doing a necessary and dangerous job.[51]

Lance Corporal Frank Turner, 19th Royal Welsh Fusiliers, 119th Brigade, 40th Division

Unfortunately, Turner's faith in the fundamental goodness of human nature proved misplaced:

My pack had, of course, been dumped in Bourlon Wood as soon as I was hit and the only possessions I had were in my pocket. These consisted of a gun-metal pocket watch and silver chain, a German razor and other odds and ends. The watch and chain had been sent to me by one of my sisters who had gone to Australia about 1903. It was for my 15th birthday, probably not of great intrinsic value, but since I received it I had always carried it with me. So the orderly started to empty my pockets; I fear I was not particularly interested but when some time later I did dive into the bag, there was no watch and chain. I think he must have decided I was not going to make it.[52]

Lance Corporal Frank Turner, 19th Royal Welsh Fusiliers, 119th Brigade, 40th Division

The odds were heavily in favour of the thief's assessment. It quickly proved necessary for Turner's gangrenous leg to be amputated and he was subsequently moved to a hospital at Le Treport where his wound continued to trouble him greatly.

I felt a sore place in the middle of my stump and told the sister when she was dressing it. She asked me to show her the location and when she pinched it there was quite a lot of pain. She asked one of the nurses to fetch the surgical trolley. Having rubbed some local anaesthetic on the spot, she got a scalpel and made an incision. Grasping a pair of tweezers, she burrowed away and came out with a piece of shrapnel. The entry wound was on the other side of the thigh and after hitting the femur, it was flattened on one side and had worked its way to the inside of the thigh. She had it washed and gave it to me in a little bag.[53]

Lance Corporal Frank Turner, 19th Royal Welsh Fusiliers, 119th Brigade, 40th Division

Subsequently, more of Turner's leg had to be amputated. Yet despite his wound and his ordeal in Bourlon Wood, Frank Turner survived. The understatement in his account cannot wholly mask the courage he displayed throughout it all.

That morning, Benjamin Parkin had rejoined his battalion, 2/4th Duke Of Wellington's (West Riding) Regiment at Bertincourt after 'WX' Aeroplane Dropping Station had finally been closed down. He was shocked by what he encountered:

We reached the Battalion at 10.00 a.m. I immediately dismissed my party and tumbled into 'A' Company shanty hoping to get a change of work and a meal and some rest, for I had had little rest for a whole week. I had not undressed. I was somewhat shattered with the nerve-strain of the week. I was ready to shiver and shake every time I heard the noise of shells. I was hungry and ready for a change for I was lousy and uncomfortable. But there was nothing like what I wanted just then. All was bustle and confusion preparing at short notice to go back to Bourlon Wood in two hours' time. I saw Zohrab and Fitch and that was all. Zohrab was Company Commander and (poor man!) he was different altogether from the Zohrab before the Stunt. He was a broken man. His welcome to me was 'You lucky devil! You were well out of it.'[54]

Second Lieutenant Benjamin Parkin, 2/4th Duke of Wellington's Regiment, 186th Brigade, 62nd Division

Parkin knew his own experiences were nothing compared to those of Reginald Zohrab and the rest of the battalion. He learned of the fate of several fellow officers and the doings of the battalion in the previous days. According to Zohrab:

The first day of battle had been a walk-over. Hardly any casualties and the boys had plenty of souvenirs. The second day – our company's day – had not been too bad until those flank attacks came from Flesquières which the 51st had not taken. The third day was terrible. The shelling of Bourlon Wood by the Germans was an indescribable affair. They couldn't get away from it and added to the noise of the bursting of the shells was the crashing and the falling of the trees. The Medical Officer's Aid Post in the Quarry was a shambles. As men waited to be dressed they were killed by further shells. Zohrab had not been hit but he simply dreaded going back. He was very downhearted and so were the men. For some reason or other they seemed rather bitter – but they gave most of their bitterness to the 40th Division who, they were convinced, had lost some of the ground they had gained – and now they had to go back again and regain it once more. There was one consolation and that was the company this time of the Guards.[55]

Second Lieutenant Benjamin Parkin, 2/4th Duke of Wellington's Regiment, 186th Brigade, 62nd Division

62nd Division was going back into the line with the intention of relieving 40th Division. However, because he had been on duty for over a week, Parkin found he was again to be left out of the battalion's return to the fighting. Zohrab asked him to censor the men's mail.

I got a peep into the soul of those men who had acted so bravely for three days of battle. There were very few exaggerations but there were many references to General Bradford's address. They were letters of thankfulness and relief. They gave good news and bad news – news of advance and capture – of the tanks and the fear of the Germans – of the enemy's machine guns and the shelling in Bourlon Wood – of pals being killed and wounded at their side. One man, writing to his mother, said he went down on his knees when he was relieved by another battalion soldier and could march out of the line.[56]

Second Lieutenant Benjamin Parkin, 2/4th Duke of Wellington's Regiment, 186th Brigade, 62nd Division

The march of the battalion's remnants away from Bertincourt was impressive and sad.

They were all down in the dumps – from the Colonel downwards – I can see him now – going doggedly forward. It seemed a very small Battalion; they had been thinned by casualties and they were going to certain thinning again . . . before evening it was snowing. It snowed hard during the night and our boys were to relieve the 40th during the

299

night. Poor fellows! What a relief! To certain Hell accompanied by a snow-storm.[57]

Second Lieutenant Benjamin Parkin, 2/4th Duke of Wellington's Regiment, 186th Brigade, 62nd Division

During the afternoon Fred Wynne and his small 'forlorn hope' in the sunken road on the edge of Bourlon Wood remained in a paralysis of inaction.

We had become, in common with all soldiers in modern war, a bit witless, dulled by primitive conditions but with a developed sense of self-preservation and, to a great extent, self-concern. The lance corporal was keeping cover eight or nine yards to our left while the signaller and I were standing talking, discussing what to do. Our heads were only just showing above the bank of the sunken road. All we could see in front was the mass of well spaced trees. I had just said to him 'We're on a bloody fine job,' and half turned away when the lance corporal shouted out: 'Look out, corporal, he's been hit.' I turned my head again and there he was, stone dead, with a bluey-red lump on his cheek just below the eye, like a plum. I didn't hear the bullet or the man fall. He was a very nice chap with whom I did my signalling training in Dover.[58]

Corporal Fred Wynne, 13th East Surreys, 120th Brigade, 40th Division

Towards the end of the afternoon, Captain Linge arrived with a party of men.

We put our helmets on top of our rifles and raised them so that we could not be mistaken for suitable targets. When they saw who we were, we waved them in. Captain Linge saw me and said 'Why didn't you send me a message that you were here?' 'There were only two of us left', I replied. 'I see,' he said. 'You did the right thing but we could have been here hours ago if we had known'. I think I missed an opportunity.[59]

Corporal Fred Wynne, 13th East Surreys, 120th Brigade, 40th Division

The lane was soon occupied by more East Surreys of Linge's company who lined the bank of the sunken road, digging out footholds and a breastwork to form firing positions. When darkness fell sentries were posted and the remainder sought shelter for the night.

It was inevitable that the waiting 2nd Cavalry Division at Ribécourt would be shelled at some point in the day:

> About 1.00 p.m. the Huns spotted us and began to shell us with HE and shrapnel. They were evidently very disorganised, as they only turned one gun onto us and that only fired ten rounds. Not much damage done. The 16th Lancers had four horses killed and the Oxford[shire] Hussars an officer killed, the Greys about ten horses and half a dozen men wounded and killed. No orders yet.[60]
>
> Captain Frank Ash, 4th (Queen's Own) Hussars, 3rd Cavalry Brigade, 2nd Cavalry Division

These losses were unnecessary and the result of negligence in exposing the men and horses in this way. When the orders did arrive at about 4.00 p.m., however, it was not for the anticipated mounted action but for the horses to be sent back and for a dismounted party to go up into the trenches

> Trew and I were on it. Captain Scott in command. We took as many men as possible, leaving one man to four horses. The horses left for Fins at 6.00 p.m. We billeted where we stood in the blinking field. Scott and I had the luck to get into a tent belonging to two artillery officers. They gave us a good dinner and plenty of whisky. The men had a good feed off the horses lying around. Did not sleep much as was very cold. Only had a flea bag and mack without the lining as everything I carry now has to be carried by myself and not on the saddle.[61]
>
> Captain Frank Ash, 4th (Queen's Own) Hussars, 3rd Cavalry Brigade, 2nd Cavalry Division

The decision to use these cavalry dismounted was tantamount to an admission that all hope of a breakthrough was gone. From now on, it was a slogging match for Bourlon Ridge.

In the evening, the first troops of 62nd Division arrived to relieve 40th Division. 186th Brigade took over the Bourlon Wood position from 119th Brigade and its attached troops. The 2nd Scots Guards were withdrawn to support and replaced by 4th Grenadier Guards. In front of Bourlon village, 187th Brigade relieved the 121st Brigade, but 1st and 2nd Cavalry Battalions remained in the line and in support positions respectively. Lieutenant Colonel Warden and his men in the 'redoubt' they had constructed on the edge of the village were not relieved, since the orders Warden received were hours old and did not reflect the local situation as it now was.

When Douglas Haig was made aware of the events of 25 November and the failure to complete the capture of Bourlon Ridge, he laid the blame squarely on the shoulders of Woollcombe and IV Corps, feeling that 'something was lacking in the conduct of the operations'.[62] He urged Byng to take control of operations personally 'because I am not sure that Woollcombe has a real grip on it'.[63] Mindful now of the need to justify his actions to Lloyd George and the War Cabinet, he telegrammed Sir William Robertson with an explanation of his instructions to Byng.

> My orders to Byng are to complete capture of Bourlon position and such tactical points on its flanks as are necessary to secure it. The positions gained are to be held and troops to be ready to exploit any local advantage and follow up any retirement of enemy. Nothing beyond above to be attempted.[64]
>
> Field Marshal Sir Douglas Haig, General Headquarters, BEF

Perhaps feeling that his actions required further elaboration, he added, 'Bourlon hill is a feature of great importance because it overlooks Cambrai and the approaches to the town as well as the country northwards to the Sensée marshes.'

Third Army sent orders to IV Corps at 11.35 p.m. for the capture 'not later than Tuesday 27 November' of the Bourlon Ridge as well as the villages of Fontaine and Bourlon. Another division (2nd) was now placed under Woollcombe's command, but IV Corps decided that its attack would be made by the Guards and 62nd Divisions.

The fight for the Bourlon Ridge had given many British soldiers a grudging admiration for their determined and indefatigable enemy. One artillery officer wrote home that evening telling his wife: 'Fritz is putting up a stout fight now and I'm afraid it is not like him to break and let us on,'[65] whilst a divisional staff officer recognized there were similar problems for the BEF in this battle as there had been in battles earlier in the year:

> Although the Boches must be still considerably disorganised and especially his administrative services dependent on Cambrai – they really have done very well to stop the rot. After the first surprise attack a sort of paralysis seems to descend on us – just the same as Arras. If we had pushed on three divisions instead of one, things might have been different. But it is easy to criticise after events than to foresee and one does not of course know all the circumstances attending the original idea.[66]
>
> Lieutenant Colonel Edwin Collen, Headquarters, 12th Division

Throughout the night the Germans continued to press and probe against the positions around Bourlon, producing a vigorous, but nervous, response:

> We were awakened by repeated 'Stand tos' from the sentries above. We scrambled up, lined the bank and opened fire. It was the biggest concentration of rifle fire I had ever heard. Eardrums vibrated with the noise and the yard or so of immediate front was continuously illuminated by the flashes from the rifles. This went on for about ten minutes until a sergeant went along the line ordering the 'cease fire'. All was quiet then and shortly afterwards 'stand down' was ordered and those of us not on sentry returned to our holes to sleep. The enemy attacked six or seven times that night and on each occasion there was the scramble to line the bank.[67]
>
> Corporal Fred Wynne, 13th East Surreys, 120th Brigade, 40th Division

26 November was a fine, bright, windy day. There were no major attacks made by either the British or the Germans on that day. Nevertheless, there was much activity by the British at least in planning and preparing the attack for the following day. One major battle that did take place was across a conference table at 62nd Division headquarters in the grounds of Havrincourt chateau. Here Woollcombe met Major-Generals Geoffrey Feilding and Walter Braithwaite, commanding Guards and 62nd Divisions respectively to discuss the proposed assault. Feilding was appalled at the prospect of this attack, which he termed 'ill-conceived'. His division was tasked with an advance partially

through the wood and partially in the open for the capture of Fontaine. In the open, it would be exposed to artillery fire from high ground near Rumilly, which he felt should also be assaulted. Although the whole operation was on too narrow a front in his opinion, his own division's attack frontage would broaden to 1,800 yards by the time it reached its objective. With 1st and 3rd Guards Brigades already occupying front-line positions, he only had six fresh battalions for the attack. Furthermore, Feilding must have known about the tenacious defence of Fontaine and the consequent failure of the tanks and 51st Division on 23 November. (In the event, the availability of 12 tanks to cooperate did nothing to assuage Feilding's fears – the Guards Division's experiences of previous operations with tanks had, in the main, been less than happy.) He wanted artillery support and had already requested the preparatory bombardment to be as heavy as possible.

Feilding had a wealth of experience commanding Guards Division on which to draw. By contrast, this was Woollcombe's first major battle as a corps commander. It cannot have been far from Feilding's thoughts that he was arguing with an elderly, but higher-ranking, officer who appeared out of his depth. Woollcombe was saved at this point by the arrival of the army commander.

Byng listened to Feilding's concerns. However, he was only too painfully aware of the burden of additional responsibility placed on his shoulders by Haig's urgings of the previous evening for him to take *personal* responsibility for the conduct of operations. He ordered the attack to proceed. Feilding's response was one of weary resignation: 'We shall do our best, sir, but you ask a lot of us.'[68]

Soon afterwards, Haig himself arrived. With the deliberate bombardment of the British artillery already pounding German positions in preparation for the assault in the background, Haig reiterated the necessity of the attack. The present positions occupied by the front line troops were under artillery observation and, admitting that a lack of resources now meant no further operations for big goals could be attempted, he wanted the attack to capture and hold a good defensive line for the winter. In this regard he and Feilding had been thinking along similar lines, although the latter had suggested a withdrawal to prepared positions on Flesquières Ridge.

There was therefore a finality about the impending attack.

Whatever its result, no further operations would be attempted after-wards. In such a Valkyrian environment, it is entirely understandable that Feilding fought so hard to get the attack plan changed or cancelled.

Elsewhere, 26 November was undoubtedly a memorable day for Arthur Lee of the RFC, but for entirely the wrong reasons. Soon after dawn, he had led his small command on a mission over Bourlon Wood to locate and attack ground targets, which meant,

> I had to find the targets and then bomb them and shoot them up. This is quite tricky in a battle like this, where ground is won and lost and won again every day, for you don't know from hour to hour where our front-line troops are positioned. Bourlon Wood, for instance, has changed hands two or three times. There's no set line, no clearly recognisable no man's land, with barbed wire. You may see trenches, but you can only find who's in them by flying low enough to distinguish khaki or field-grey. If in doing this you go down to 100 feet or lower, you're an easy target, and dozens of guns will be turned on you. If you stay higher you may not know you're over Boche troops until they open fire at you.[69]
>
> Lieutenant Arthur Gould Lee, 46 Squadron, RFC

Deciding to see whether the Germans had retaken Bourlon Village and part of the wood, Lee led his flight in echelon across the Bapaume–Cambrai road.

> All of us weaving constantly to prevent gunners getting too easy a bead on us, and all intently searching the wooded slopes on our right for signs of field grey. I had just decided that some moving figures among the trees along the top of the ridge were Boche when I saw flashes among them, from three or four guns. Followed by the two others, I went into a flat dive and opened fire. A few seconds later there was a terrific metallic clang behind, and I felt the thud of bullets.[70]
>
> Lieutenant Arthur Gould Lee, 46 Squadron, RFC

The reason for the noise was easily discernable:

> I looked over my tail, and my heart positively stopped. Trailing out thirty feet behind me was a wide plume of bluish-white vapour. It was

petrol! Pouring out of the tank and being vaporised by the hot exhaust gases from the revolving engine. Exactly as I'd seen happen to planes in air fights just before they burst into flames.[71]

Lieutenant Arthur Gould Lee, 46 Squadron, RFC

Lee did the only thing he could in such circumstances.

Instantly, I switched off and dipped my nose steeply towards the ground. I didn't care where I came down, scarcely even looked – all I craved for was the solid earth before some spark set everything alight. The ground rushed up. I flattened out, held her off for what seemed a long time until she slowed down to landing speed, touched wheels, ran into a trench, and tipped over into it. I was upside down, hanging on my straps, half concussed – and the petrol was pouring over me. In a sudden panic I unbuckled my harness, dropped head first into the trench, and crawled along it until I was clear.[72]

Lieutenant Arthur Gould Lee, 46 Squadron, RFC

Soaked in petrol, Lee was soon fortunate to find himself in the care of an RFA battery, which was using German gun-pits already occupied by two large German artillery pieces. The relative lack of offensive activity on the ground during the day gave Lee an opportunity to roam the battlefield whilst waiting for some means to return to his squadron.

We walked to Flesquières, and examined the scene at the corner of the chateau wall where the Hun artillery major and a handful of men had held up the advance early on the 20th by catching the tanks at point-blank range as, one by one, they topped the brow of the slope to his front. It was an amazing sight. In a crescent a few hundred yards long, facing his grave, lay a whole line of disabled tanks. One had advanced to within thirty yards of the battery, but this too was hit and burned out. It was named *Egbert II* and alongside were the graves of the crew.[73]

Lieutenant Arthur Gould Lee, 46 Squadron, RFC

The myth of the German artillery officer was spreading fast.

Returning to the dugouts occupied by the artillery battery, Lee discovered he would have to spend the night there. When he had set out on his mission that morning he had hoped to learn the fate of his Camel aircraft, in which he had been shot down on 22 November near

Fontaine. He had speculated on who had 'won' his watch, shoes and shaving gear after he had left them in the plane. Now he had what he assumed would be an unsolicited grandstand ticket for the Guards' attack on Fontaine.

The preparations for the attack were well under way. Second Lieutenant Carroll Carstairs, an American officer with 3rd Grenadier Guards, had feared his chance of participating in a major battle had once again been dashed. He was on his way with his company to occupy a section of the line near Anneux, when he heard the sudden announcement that an attack would take place. It was a moment to test the very core of his moral strength.

> I found 'Billy', who was much excited. He told me what was up, but I could not take it in. His announcement affected me physically before I had mentally grasped it. I felt it like a shock, like a blow, turning me sick. The Battalion was to attack the following morning. Once the words had been formulated and the brain had recorded and repeated them there occurred an emotional ebb, leaving the system drained. Gradually I rallied to the fact itself, inevitable. All this within the space of a few seconds. I had morally run away, fallen, picked myself up, while remaining steadfastly on one spot.[74]
>
> Second Lieutenant Carroll Carstairs, 3rd Grenadier Guards, 2nd Guards Brigade, Guards Division.

Units of 3rd Guards Brigade were already being moved into Bourlon Wood to support 2nd Guards Brigade who would make the attack in the morning. Others like 1st Welsh Guards were given their orders that evening:

> DG took me off to Brigade HQ where a conference was going on and we saw how war is made. The conference was in a country house at the outskirts of a village – no windows, doors or furniture, but only a few shell holes. All the floors and passages were covered in wet mud from the many people who were passing in and out. One door was covered in bits of sacking and part of a window shutter but the other rooms were open to view from the passage and seemed to be full of people apparently engaged in making tea or watching it being made. Everyone was smoking and everyone looked dirty. We pushed aside the sack

curtain and found a lot more people bending over a table on which were maps and a number of candles in bottles and on tins. These were the Brigadier and COs discussing the attack. And here it was we received orders to move up at five in the morning.[75]

Captain Charles Dudley Ward, 1st Welsh Guards, 3rd Guards Brigade, Guards Division

For Charles Britten this meant time in the company of two of the Guards Division's most highly-regarded battalion commanders: Lord Gort and Harold Alexander.

I was ordered to meet Lord Gort, our CO at the 2nd Brigade Irish Guards [sic] headquarters in the shooting box in the centre of the wood. The Battalion was commanded by Colonel Alexander, then about 25 years old. The Chalet had been used as a Dressing Station and [was] full of dead and wounded. Shells and bombing from the air was intense but Colonel Alexander stood on the steps leading up to the house giving out his orders for an attack at dawn as if in peacetime.[76]

Captain Charles Britten, 4th Grenadier Guards, 3rd Guards Brigade, Guards Division

The imperturbable Alexander was already establishing a remarkable reputation in the division as a precociously talented officer. Nevertheless, he and Gort had unquestionably never faced the prospect of an attack through such terrain as Bourlon Wood before.

The belated decision to include tanks in the attack meant a period of furious activity from mid-afternoon for Major Philip Hamond:

At about 3.00 p.m., the Brigadier came for me and we went up to see the Guards Division about an attack on Fontaine. It was one of those – side shows not half thought out and conceived in a hurry and everything to be done in a muck sweat. These shows always fail and lead to a loss of good men and gear. I had to rush back to Ribécourt and get my tanks out and ready, no time to properly choose the route or lay tapes to drive along at night. Anyway we went off, raining and sleeting like the devil. We were all worn out, and the tanks pretty rocky. I thought it was not likely that we should get more than half of them there. I started with thirteen and only one broke down on the road, so we got rid of the unlucky number early. We got by some miracle to the starting point.[77]

Major Philip Hamond, No. 18 Company, 'F' Battalion, Tank Corps

*

That evening it had turned bitterly cold again and at 10.00 p.m. snow began to fall. Still in the front line near Bourlon, Fred Wynne and his fellow East Surreys faced another night of alarms and wild firing:

> As darkness closed down the enemy got active. Several times during the night attacks were made. We lined the bank and fired a blistering curtain of bullets, but how far the bullets went it was impossible to say . . . In the early hours of the morning the enemy really tried to obliterate us. Perhaps we occupied a position dangerous to his plans. The infantry attacks having failed, he then used artillery. The shells, more frequently than not, hit the tree tops, burst into shrapnel and rained down on us like hail, bringing lumps of trees with it. We took what cover we could but some of us had to stay in the sunken road. It was sheer hell. The bursting of shells, the explosions like momentarily looking into a blazing furnace. The deafening noise that left our eardrums singing for days afterwards. It must have lasted a long time, but how long it is impossible to say.[78]
>
> Corporal Fred Wynne, 13th East Surreys, 120th Brigade, 40th Division

The snow had turned to drizzling rain during the night, but it was cold and a biting wind developed during the morning. Second Lieutenant Carroll Carstairs was awoken at 4.00 a.m. by his commanding officer, Andrew 'Bulgy' Thorne.

> The candles, stuck in bottles on the table, burned as straight as on any altar. Each step up the twenty-two of the dugout was a conscious movement. Now we were at the entrance. The night was still, breathless. It had been raining. The ground was soggy and the going difficult. The mud stuck to our boots until we were walking on huge pads.[79]
>
> Second Lieutenant Carroll Carstairs, 3rd Grenadier Guards, 2nd Guards Brigade, Guards Division

Together they made a last tour of the battalion, whilst Thorne checked his company commanders were prepared. First was No. 1 Company.

> The Commanding Officer went down a dugout to have a last word with 'Mary' Bowes-Lyon while I remained and joked with the two

309

subalterns. How is it one can jest at such a time? It's a question of tuning up. Laughter is the loophole through which joy enters the soul.[80]

Second Lieutenant Carroll Carstairs, 3rd Grenadier Guards, 2nd Guards Brigade, Guards Division

Then they were slipping along again through the mud once more to find Captain Wilfrid 'Nibs' Beaumont-Nesbitt and No. 2 Company.

An interminable walk to go a few yards. But we had missed No. 2 Company and were out in No Man's Land heading for the enemy. We made for the road which divided the Battalion. By the time we had reached Nos. 3 and 4 Companies they were forming up. Sinister shadows filling the gloom, as silent as the night itself, only the immense discipline of the Brigade of Guards kept one from remembering they were men cold and wet and dulled with fear.[81]

Second Lieutenant Carroll Carstairs, 3rd Grenadier Guards, 2nd Guards Brigade, Guards Division

Arthur Lee's hosts, the RFA battery, were to participate in the barrage so Lee himself was up early, whilst after a quiet night, the artillery officer, Philip Keightley, had started on his task of laying a telephone line to his forward observation post.

Everything was quiet in the grey, solemn light. The only moving thing I saw was a party or two of stretcher-bearers, with their pitiful burden, trudging back along a trench to a dressing station, a mile or so in the rear, and a few more, led by a padre, carrying their stretchers and going forward on their noble errand.[82]

Captain Philip Russell Keightley, 262 Siege Battery, 54th Brigade, RGA

But, a little further on, there were ugly and terrible indications of past fighting. For an artilleryman like Keightley, it was a shocking opportunity to witness the dreadful power of his own arm of service:

I had gone about two hundred yards down the track when my sense of smell warned me of what was coming. Here were a couple of horses possibly three days dead, and then I stumbled on all that remained of what was once a German – and another – and another – in awful and rapid succession. I thought of leaving the road, but found the going too heavy in the shell-holes . . . so I was forced to come back upon the track . . . At one spot the road for about a hundred and fifty yards was literally paved deep – I do not exaggerate – with German dead, ghastly, mutilated, contorted. I noticed a few khaki-clad figures here and there. I cannot tell you how glad I was to reach my destination.[83]

Captain Philip Russell Keightley, 262 Siege Battery, 54th Brigade, RGA

These were the victims of previous days' fighting but, soon afterwards, the artillery burst forth with a new outpouring of violence; the dawn of another day of death and mutilation.

Dawn was showing 'dirty white'. At 6.20 a.m. our barrage came down and while I thought of the Battalion as a unit, five hundred men had begun their perilous progress towards the enemy trenches.[84]

Second Lieutenant Carroll Carstairs, 3rd Grenadier Guards, 2nd Guards Brigade, Guards Division

Arthur Lee's grandstand ticket proved an 'obstructed view' and he could see nothing of the attack because of the fold in the ground. It was perhaps as well that he could not. But he could hear the phenomenal noise.

For the Guards Division's attack, three battalions of 2nd Guards Brigade were used. Bitter experience had shown the effect that flanking fire from Folie Wood could have on any attack on Fontaine from the south, so the Guards' attack was to be in an easterly direction. On the right astride the Bapaum–Cambrai road were 3rd Grenadier Guards, with 1st Coldstream Guards in the centre and 2nd Irish Guards on the left. The right of the division's front was held by 1st Scots Guards. The attack was supported by artillery and machine-gun fire and a total of 13 tanks from 'I' and 'F' Battalions. Notwithstanding the noise of the barrage, however, only a small proportion of the available heavy artillery had been used in the preliminary bombardment against Fontaine itself – a fatal error.

A medical officer, Captain Harold Dearden, was appalled by the maelstrom of battle when the attack commenced:

I have never known such machine-gun fire as we met going across the first hundred yards. They just sounded like a continuous scream. The Boche put down a terrific barrage, too, and our poor lads went down like grass before a reaper. They still kept steadily on though, and we reached the village on time. I got a good many walking wounded back, but the fire was hopeless for bearers, and I had half of them knocked out before the village was reached.[85]

Captain Harold Dearden, RAMC, Guards Division

Despite changes in the axis of attack, on the right the two attacking companies of 3rd Grenadier Guards were almost wiped out by machine-guns firing from La Folie Wood. Only one sergeant and six men fought their way through to Fontaine church.

In the centre, both Charles Dudley Ward and Carroll Carstairs tried to discern the progress of the Coldstream Guards from observation posts close behind the front line, but the drizzling rain made this too difficult. Soon Carstairs received orders to go into the village and relay news of progress back to battalion headquarters.

The full orchestra of battle was on. The air seemed alive with invisible wires being twanged, while the earth was thumped and beaten. The bullets zipped, whizzed, whistled, spun, sung, and sighed according to their proximity and their point of flight. They constituted in reality the spray off the wave of lead being poured into Nos. 1 and 2 Companies, although I scarcely realised this at the time.[86]

Second Lieutenant Carroll Carstairs, 3rd Grenadier Guards, 2nd Guards Brigade, Guards Division

All but one of the nine tanks allotted for the attack on Fontaine succeeded in getting forward into the village, with Philip Hamond commanding them.

It was all badly and hurriedly thought out and we had not near enough infantry, though those we had were the best infantry in the world. The machine-gun fire from the right toward La Folie was simply terrific and cut up the Guards badly. Anyway we got all the tanks into the town and then indeed pandemonium broke loose. The Boche shelling was very heavy even in the west outskirts of the town itself, and our half-baked barrage was poor. The houses were full of Boches and we went down the streets firing into the houses till the infantry could rush in and bayonet them. My people did most splendidly.[87]

Major Philip Hamond, No. 18 Company, 'F' Battalion, Tank Corps

The storm of fire so decimated the Grenadier Guards that although they managed to advance well into the village and even reach their first objective, they had insufficient numbers to clear the houses and the cellars of the Germans, who went to ground just as they had in Flesquières, Bourlon and the other villages when confronted by infantry and tanks.

> By the time we had got through the village to the station, there were practically no infantry left to follow, only little knots of four and five in the doorways. About twenty of us tried to dig in at the station on the line we had been ordered, but it was hopeless without reinforcements. It wanted a division to hold the place, not only a brigade. The Boche was like hundreds of rats in a stack running everywhere. The Boche infantry chucked it up easily, but the machine-gunners and the artillery stuck it well and the machine-gun fire in the streets and the shells was a thing to remember.[88]
>
> Major Philip Hamond, No. 18 Company, 'F' Battalion, Tank Corps

Carroll Carstairs and his small group of battalion headquarters men found their way into the village without suffering loss. Still trying to find the two companies that had lead the attack, he came across three wounded Germans in the act of surrendering. What happened next was clearly disturbing for Carstairs, and yet he felt powerless to act:

> They were holding up their hands. One had his foot in a bandage and was being helped by the others. They looked frightened and miserable. While they were chattering in German, a wounded Grenadier turned up, quite off his head. 'That's all right, sir,' he addressed me. 'I'll kill them.' 'I wouldn't do that,' I remonstrated. 'Oh, that's quite all right. You just leave them to me.' He threatened them with his rifle. The wounded German started to whimper and shuffled off. The Grenadier followed, herding his little party together. He used his rifle like a shepherd's staff. Could he have been a shepherd in civilian life? They disappeared in the direction of an out-house.[89]
>
> Second Lieutenant Carroll Carstairs, 3rd Grenadier Guards, 2nd Guards Brigade, Guards Division

Confronted by the possibility of an act of atrocity, Carstairs could only speculate lamely: 'Whatever happened to them? They were not heading strictly for the British lines.'[90]

Shortly afterwards he received messages from the two Grenadier Guards companies who had formed the second wave of the attack. They had captured their objectives, but were held up by heavy machine-gun fire and had suffered considerably. They desperately required reinforcements. There was no word from either of the two lead companies, which was a bad sign. At this point, the battalion commander, Colonel Thorne, arrived.

> I saluted as though on parade. He looked anxious. 'We must go up and see what is happening'. Together we proceeded up the main street, down which machine-gun bullets were pouring with the volume of water from a fire-hose. We hugged the houses to minimize the danger of being hit. We reached the crossroads and I marvelled that a man could get so far and remain alive.[91]
>
> Second Lieutenant Carroll Carstairs, 3rd Grenadier Guards, 2nd Guards Brigade, Guards Division

During this advance, Carstairs (a connoisseur of fine art and a lover of all things beautiful) was moved, despite the raging battle, to pass admiring comment regarding the fine form of Fontaine church, only to exclaim 'Damn! The fools have spoilt it' as a shell ripped into the structure.

Reaching No. 3 Company, he and Thorne were greeted by Lieutenant Arthur Knollys.

> His Company Commander had been wounded. He was holding his position with about forty men and one machine-gun. It was almost all that was left of the Battalion. Nos. 1 and 2 Companies had been, as a matter of fact, wiped out. All officers (including both Company Commanders killed), both Sergeant Majors, and all Sergeants casualties, and two-thirds of the men.[92]
>
> Second Lieutenant Carroll Carstairs, 3rd Grenadier Guards, 2nd Guards Brigade, Guards Division

Carstairs now tried to track down the remnants of No. 4 Company – reportedly holding out on the attack's left.

I found Carrington with about thirty men, all that was left of No. 4 Company. He looked exhausted. Our consultation was interrupted by the appearance of a tank. It stopped, and out of it an officer descended. 'Do you want me any more?' 'No.' I felt as though I were dismissing a taxi. He climbed back into the tank and down the street it waddled away.[93]

Second Lieutenant Carroll Carstairs, 3rd Grenadier Guards, 2nd Guards Brigade, Guards Division

Philip Hamond's recollection differed slightly, but essentially the end result was the same:

At last in accordance with our orders we began to draw off, a few Guards were consolidating on the objective and we were told to go, though I knew there were not nearly enough to hold it. The Boche had field-guns in the doors of yards and houses, I think five in all, but they did not tend to make the streets any more healthy. One of my tanks coming down the main street was pretty well blown in two by a gun at ten yards' range. It killed three men outright and seriously wounded another, leaving the officer, the driver and one man alive . . . Well, we started to pull out then, and I got them all back except the ruined one. We had done our best in a hopeless show.[94]

Major Philip Hamond, No. 18 Company, 'F' Battalion, Tank Corps

The British infantry in Fontaine were now pitifully small in numbers and clearly ripe for counter-attack. Urgent requests for reinforcements were sent back to Brigadier General Bertram Sergison-Brooke, 2nd Guards Brigade's commander, and a desperate race ensued to get adequate support for the beleaguered Guards in Fontaine before the Germans struck back.

Meanwhile, in Bourlon Wood, the advance of 2nd Irish Guards through 4th Grenadier Guards was witnessed by Charles Britten.

At dawn in cold and wet the attack started. The 2nd Irish Guards advanced in column of companies, but shortly after passing through my line were met by intense rifle fire.[95]

Captain Charles Britten, 4th Grenadier Guards, 3rd Guards Brigade, Guards Division

However, Britten soon found he too had much to contend with when the Germans launched an attack on his company.

> The German infantry shortly afterwards counter-attacked, and when visiting my platoons I was shot at short distance in my right arm. The pain was intense and I was unable to take further part in the battle. I was taken down by the stretcher bearers to battalion headquarters where the first aid post was situated. I reported to Lord Gort and was taken down by ambulance to the Casualty Clearing Station.[96]
>
> Captain Charles Britten, 4th Grenadier Guards, 3rd Guards Brigade, Guards Division

With few anti-tetanus injections available, it seemed likely Britten would lose his arm but he managed to persuade the doctors not to amputate and, luckily, he survived intact.

Commanding a company of 2nd Irish Guards was Lieutenant William Rea:

> Our objective was the right half of the northern edge of the wood. I was on the right flank of the second wave, 50 yards behind the first wave. We had a hard struggle through the thick undergrowth and suffered very heavily from the enemy machine-guns which were very numerous and active as our artillery support was very weak in fact almost nil. I reached the objective with about 50 men all told. I never saw any sign of the first wave except a few stragglers whom I picked up on the way. I found I was the senior officer left, and there were two others, Lieutenant Wreford and Lieutenant Dame. The former was wounded and had to be sent back almost immediately after we reached the objective.[97]
>
> Lieutenant William Rea, 2nd Irish Guards, 3rd Guards Brigade, Guards Division

Having taken their objective, the remnants of the company now had the difficult task of holding on to it. Rea's problem was the paucity of men with which to do so. Contact with 1st Coldstream Guards on the right had at least been maintained, but of troops from 186th Brigade of 62nd Division on the other flank there was no sign.

> Having so few men I could not form a continuous line in the usual way, so I arranged a series of posts about 15 yards inside the wood so that the posts would be sheltered from view as much as possible and at the same time have a good field of view. On my extreme left I placed a post in a

shell-hole 15 yards in front of the wood, from which there was a good view of the northern edge of the wood and the enemy lines 200 or 300 yards in front. I put Lieutenant Dame in command of the right flank. I myself took the left where I formed a defensive flank – with the assistance of a machine-gun.[98]

Captain William Rea, 2nd Irish Guards, 3rd Guards Brigade, Guards Division

Here too, the problem was the absence of reserves to compensate for the losses suffered in the initial attack. Having dug-in, Rea sent back several messages giving full details of his position and shortage of ammunition, and asking for assistance. In the meantime, they had to stand.

As ever, captured Germans taken in the attack were pressed into service as stretcher-bearers. Carroll Carstairs persuaded one party to use a house door to carry their putative escort, a wounded Grenadier Guardsman:

I showed them what I wanted done and they complied with alacrity. Soon they were off, carrying the wounded Grenadier. It must have been a heavy load. I could not help fearing they would drop him half way in their eagerness to get out of danger. But if they had any thought of doing so it was intercepted by a German shell which burst in their midst after they had gone two hundred yards.[99]

Second Lieutenant Carroll Carstairs, 3rd Grenadier Guards, 2nd Guards Brigade, Guards Division

But at his aid post in Cantaing Mill the medic, Harold Dearden, had problems with one recalcitrant German:

One fellow didn't want to carry and I had to clout him over the head to make him lend a hand. When we got back to the aid post he sat down on the steps of the dug-out, and every time I came near him he kept plucking me by the coat and saying something. I took no notice of him, but it struck me as curious that he hadn't gone downstairs to be gorged with 'enemy' cocoa and bread, as most of them do at once.[100]

Captain Harold Dearden, RAMC, Guards Division

A near miss by a German shell that damaged the aid post's entrance revealed the reasons for the German's reluctance:

It put the wind up me all right, but when I turned round there he was still sitting quietly as before, and I knew he must be hit or something. I went over to him, and when I saw his face I was certain. He didn't look hurt, he looked dead, and dead a long time at that. Then I saw he was holding his trousers together with one hand; and when I pulled his hand away the entire contents of his belly just spilled itself over his knees. I tucked them in again, covered him up, and gave him two grains of morphia to suck. It was the best I could do for him, poor devil. But I wish now I hadn't hit him. I wish that quite a lot.[101]

Captain Harold Dearden, RAMC, Guards Division

Although Brigadier Sergison-Brooke acted quickly to reinforce his units so drastically winnowed by the scything machine-gun fire and raging artillery, nevertheless, it was the Germans who struck first. From concealment in La Folie Wood (which had always been a thorn in the side of any British attack in this sector), as many as ten German infantry battalions spewed forth in a counter-attack that crashed through the thin lines of British infantry into the heart of Fontaine and against the Irish Guards' posts on the edge of Bourlon Wood.

The last message I sent off at 10.30 a.m. I then crawled out to the advanced post having seen all was in order in the other posts – it was while doing this I was wounded in the face.[102]

Captain William Rea, 2nd Irish Guards, 3rd Guards Brigade, Guards Division

Whilst the solitary machine-gun maintained its supporting fire, Rea's men held on to their gains. However, it was a different situation approximately fifteen minutes later when the machine-gun began to be troubled by stoppages. Immediately,

the enemy, about 150 in number, burst out of the wood behind us, driving before them sixty of our men. I, with the seven men in the post, was just swept up and carried along with the others. Personally, I don't think I would have been saved, only one of our men seeing me wounded pulled me along by the arm saying, 'You will only be bayoneted if you stay there!'[103]

Captain William Rea, 2nd Irish Guards, 3rd Guards Brigade, Guards Division

Rea was saved from a German bayonet, but not from capture. The Irish Guards desperately clung on with mounting casualties and little hope.

In Fontaine, a momentarily resting Carstairs had been roused to action by a sergeant's warning that the Germans had got behind No. 3 Company's position.

> To be suddenly shooting at grey uniformed Germans was accompanied by no thrill. How big they were! Was it because he was aiming straight at my head that this German appeared so big? The motion of his rifle coming up to his shoulder increased his stature. My revolver lost power to hurt, for after I had fired the Germans remained in the same position. And yet they were so near it would have seemed impossible to have missed them. (A week before I had hit an envelope at 20 paces.) It did not seem as though I was missing but rather as though my bullets, turning into pellets, were bouncing harmlessly off. Nor did the German's rifle seem to function. There was no smoke, no flash, and I heard no bullet whistle uncomfortably close to my head. The whole thing took on the unreality of a 'movie' until one of the Germans dropped. It seemed the signal for which his fellows had been waiting, for with one accord they spun round and ran away. I have never seen people run so fast. I can see again that man as he turned the corner, the play of his big grey legs from hip to knee.[104]
>
> Second Lieutenant Carroll Carstairs, 3rd Grenadier Guards, 2nd Guards Brigade, Guards Division

It was the signal for the Grenadiers to flee too. With their position clearly in danger of being overwhelmed and their line of retreat cut off, Carstairs recognized the need to get out of Fontaine.

> It was true enough. We could soon expect an attack in force, and from several directions. The rest of the Company had joined us. Some thirty Britishers in the village of Fontaine. The apparently deserted houses seemed haunted. The windows took on the semblance of glassy eyes. Soon we should be the victims of a dangerous game of hide and seek.[105]
>
> Second Lieutenant Carroll Carstairs, 3rd Grenadier Guards, 2nd Guards Brigade, Guards Division

The withdrawal of this small band of survivors was accomplished successfully, even as the Germans beat through the village driving out, capturing or killing any surviving British soldiers in similar groups.

The losses of 2nd Guards Brigade in this attack were quite appalling. Of perhaps 1,350 men of the three attacking battalions, only 200 Grenadiers, 180 Coldstream, and 80 Irish Guards returned to the start line. The reinforcements sent by Sergison-Brooke arrived too late to prevent this, but in time to stop every attempt by the Germans to exploit their success at Fontaine. By 1.00 p.m. it was all over.

On the Guards' left, 62nd Division, which had relieved 40th Division, also attacked. Brigadier General Roland Bradford's 186th Brigade on the right was to clear the northern part of Bourlon Wood and the eastern end of Bourlon village, whilst on the left Brigadier General Reginald Taylor's 187th Brigade was to overcome all resistance in the main part of Bourlon.

The 2/5th Duke of Wellington's (West Riding) Regiment on 186th Brigade's right made little progress, struggling to make contact with its neighbours from the Guards. Its sister battalions, 2/6th and 2/7th, did achieve more in Bourlon village with the assistance of four of the twenty tanks allotted to the division. However the attacks so weakened these battalions, which had already seen action in the first days of the battle, they were doomed to fail in their attempts to gain their objectives. Because they were in a salient, they were subsequently withdrawn from the eastern end of Bourlon to the high ground behind.

The attack of 187th Brigade into the village itself was led by tanks of 'F' Battalion. Here the BEF's inability at this stage of the war to coordinate tank and infantry in attacks on villages was again evident. The 2/5th York & Lancaster and 2/5th King's Own Yorkshire Light Infantry (KOYLI) got into the village with the tanks but the narrow streets were barricaded and the barriers well defended. After two hours of futile efforts, the infantry and tanks withdrew with heavy losses. By 9.30 a.m. Brigadier Taylor was aware of the failure and ordered no further attacks to be made, preferring to ensure he maintained possession of the crest of Bourlon Ridge.

About this time orders were finally despatched for the remnants of 13th East Surreys to withdraw from Bourlon Wood.

Parties of ten men under an officer or NCO were sent out at intervals of
fifteen minutes to make their way as best they could to the Hindenburg
Line where battalion headquarters were. Eventually it became my
turn . . . In front of us in the path of our destination the enemy had put
down a barrage. Shell barrages were not new to us and this one was not
formidable. We advanced to within thirty or forty paces of the barrage
line, lay down on the grass, and as soon as a shell burst in front of us we
sprinted (if rheumaticy [sic] old men can sprint) across the recent shell
hole and ran on until we dropped from exhaustion – which wasn't very
far. We went on like walking dummies, eventually coming within sight
of the Hindenburg Line.[106]

Corporal Fred Wynne, 13th East Surreys, 120th Brigade, 40th Division

Having survived the efforts of German artillery and low-flying
aircraft, Wynne and his fellow survivors encountered a truly welcome
sight on their arrival back at the captured Hindenburg Line trenches.
And this feeling was reciprocated.

We saw our second-in-command, a major seconded from a Scottish
regiment, excitedly waving to us. 'Come on lads,' he said and, as we
reached him, he said 'Get out your canteens and have some rum or
stew. Which do you want first, rum or stew?' I handed him the lid of my
canteen. 'Rum, sir, first'. He gave me some rum which I drank without
taking breath, hardly. 'Now,' said the major, 'throw your equipment on
the limber' which was standing with mules harnessed ready for moving
off, 'take your stew and go down in the dugout. There are bunks there.
Have a good sleep and you'll be taken to the rest area later on in
lorries.' He was so excited to see us. Relieved to see every man who
returned from Bourlon Wood. The rumour had got around that almost
the whole battalion had been wiped out and every man who came back
was a ray of hope.[107]

Corporal Fred Wynne, 13th East Surreys, 120th Brigade, 40th Division

Only later did a shocking realization take hold of some of the survivors:

I slipped off my equipment, got ready to fling it on to the limber, but
the rum on an empty stomach had acted like magic. The limber and all
the rest of the world went round in circles. I stumbled to the entrance of

the dugout with my canteen of stew, went down the steps, climbed on to the chicken wire bunk and lay down in a stupor. In the next bunk was a young man almost in tears, standing by him was Lieutenant Beaurepaire. The boy was sobbing 'We're lucky to get out of there, sir. We're lucky to get out of there.' Lieutenant Beaurepaire was very commiserating. 'Yes, lad. It's all over now. Pull yourself together.' He patted him on the head and went to see the other men.[108]

Corporal Fred Wynne, 13th East Surreys, 120th Brigade, 40th Division

In the afternoon, 1st Welsh Guards was ordered to relieve Alexander's Irish Guards in the wood. Two companies had already been sent forward as reinforcements. Charles Dudley Ward was sent by 'DG' to establish contact with the Irish Guards' commander and tell him of the relief.

> I remember in the night going in to relieve the Irish Guards. We couldn't find them. So our Captain now, Roderick, said 'Fix bayonets' and we went into this wood. I'd never seen so many dead in all my life. Finally we had to dig in with our entrenching tools – we had no shovels – and scrape a little pile of earth in front of us.[109]
>
> Lance Corporal Charles Evans, 1st Welsh Guards, 3rd Guards Brigade, Guards Division

At the hunting lodge, which had been Alexander's battalion headquarters, Dudley Ward found chaos.

> I reached the wood and found most fearful confusion. The roads, or tracks, were filled with men and pack horses – shells were bursting all over the place and had a fearful echo through the wood. The place we made for was a small chalet in the centre and round it were loads of men from every sort of unit (the rotters) and heaps of wounded. It was so filled inside and out I had to pick my way through. Alexander of the Irish was not there, having moved his HQ to his front line.[110]
>
> Captain Charles Dudley Ward, 1st Welsh Guards, 3rd Guards Brigade, Guards Division

It took Dudley Ward some time to find anyone who knew where their colonel was. Experience told him not to go plunging about a wood at dusk which had not been cleared of enemy. Eventually, however, he found Alexander

> on the high ground of the wood in a dugout just below a tall tree with observation platforms built amongst the branches. He told me all there was to tell, how there was a strong point filled with machine-guns inside a corner of the wood, and that it had defied all efforts to capture it. He traced his line on the map for me, gave me guides and departed.[111]
>
> Captain Charles Dudley Ward, 1st Welsh Guards, 3rd Guards Brigade, Guards Division

Similar reliefs were accomplished in 62nd Division's sector.

The struggle to take the Bourlon Ridge was over. The British simply did not have the resources in men and *matériel* to complete the task. Most worryingly, when the Germans had counter-attacked at Fontaine they had done so in such strength that the scales had tipped significantly in their favour. It was clearly time to close the offensive operations down. Of course, fighting still simmered and flared in Bourlon Wood and on the edge of the village; artillery shells still obliterated men and terrain. Rifle and machine-gun fire still rang out all along the front; men still lived, ate, slept and fought with the constant threat of death or mutilation. The fight for Bourlon might be over, but the killing went on.

> It was getting dark when we went in and Sergeant 'Tim' Daly said, 'We'll pitch the gun here' and he pitched the gun. We hadn't had time to separate – we were all round it – when a shell exploded in front of us. I remember being blown over a tree trunk, and when I picked myself up I grabbed my spare barrel (that was my duty; we all had something to look after – one had the tripod, the other one had the gun, another one had a box of ammunition, I had the spare barrel) and was going to look round to find where the rest had gone when I heard a call out and went over. It was Mick Scanlon. He was our No. 2. I went to him. He was badly wounded. All I can remember him saying was 'Don't leave me. Don't leave me. Don't leave me.' He kept repeating it, 'Don't leave me.' Well, I stayed with him a little while. Then I heard another voice – Sergeant Daly's voice – calling out. So I said to Mick, 'There's Tim calling. I'll just and go see what he wants.' He was only a few yards

away. He was terribly badly wounded – in fact he died in just the few minutes I was with him. So, then I went back to Mick Scanlon and he was dead. They were both dead in that short time.[112]

Private Fred Holmes, Cavalry Machine-Gun Corps; attached 12th Lancers, 5th Cavalry Brigade, 2nd Cavalry Division

CHAPTER ELEVEN

'An equal, but opposite, reaction'

NINE DAYS AFTER the opening of this remarkable offensive, Byng's Third Army found itself with its head in a sack, facing the definite possibility of a noose being slipped around its neck and pulled tight. The attack had created a salient thrusting into the German lines nine miles wide and four miles deep.* The German high command was not blind to the opportunities such a newly formed, and therefore as yet insecure, position offered for a counter-attack. Any such attack would not be merely opportunistic, however: it was *demanded* by the German Army's tactical doctrine. Therefore, as early as 23 November, whilst the British were making strenuous attempts to take Fontaine and Bourlon, preparations were set in train for a counter-offensive.

Ironically for the British, the focus of Byng and his staff on pressing to take the Bourlon Ridge offered both advantages and disadvantages when these attacks were stopped. On the one hand, although IV Corps had failed to take all the ridge and 51st, 62nd, 40th and Guards Divisions had been through the mill and suffered correspondingly, three fresh divisions were put into the line to hold the captured positions. There was also more than adequate artillery support here as well. It was on the east and south sides of the salient where the greatest problems existed. Here the same divisions that had made the initial attack still held the line and had not been reinforced. Furthermore, the problems of a salient – well known to the BEF from its experiences in and around Ypres – were only too obvious once again. It had proved extremely difficult to find suitable artillery positions in land recently occupied; the front held by 29th Division had the St Quentin Canal

* Figures quoted in the Official History, p.164.

immediately behind it and was overlooked by German observers on the higher ground north-east of it; in other places where the terrain fell away from the Bonavis Ridge the reverse was true and observation of any possible attack was severely limited. The junction of III and VII Corps was an especially vulnerable point after the combination of 12th Division's attack and 55th Division's diversionary operations paradoxically meant the British defence of the northern edge of the Banteux Ravine was seriously weakened.

> On our right was a weak division holding a long front and their left was the weak spot. We thought it so weak that we would not put any more batteries at Villers Guislain and General Vincent felt so certain of an attack that he packed up and sent away most of his papers, etc.[1]
>
> Lieutenant Colonel Edwin Collen, Assistant Adjutant and Quartermaster General, Headquarters, 12th Division

Brigadier General Berkeley Vincent, commanding 35th Brigade, was by no means alone in his conviction of the likelihood of a German attack. The commander of VII Corps, Lieutenant General Sir Thomas Snow (tall with a fine bristling moustache and a shock of white hair to rival 'Uncle' Harper's), and the commander of 55th Division, Major General Hugh Jeudwine were also aware of the threat. Jeudwine's particular concern was how to defend his exceptionally long divisional frontage of over 9,000 yards with inadequate artillery support, and no depth to his position. Many of his infantry battalions were under strength. But it was Snow in particular who grew daily more convinced that a German counter-attack would be launched at some point given the activity opposite his Corps front.

> We had instructions every morning to be prepared for eventualities. This we did not take very seriously, as we had heard our guns in the distance, pounding away at Cambrai for the last week – our already weakened companies had been further reduced by men being sent on courses.[2]
>
> Lance Corporal William Evans, 1/6th King's Liverpool Regiment, 165th Brigade, 55th Division

Each day, despite great pain from an injured pelvis suffered during the BEF's 1914 retreat from Mons, Snow viewed his forward positions

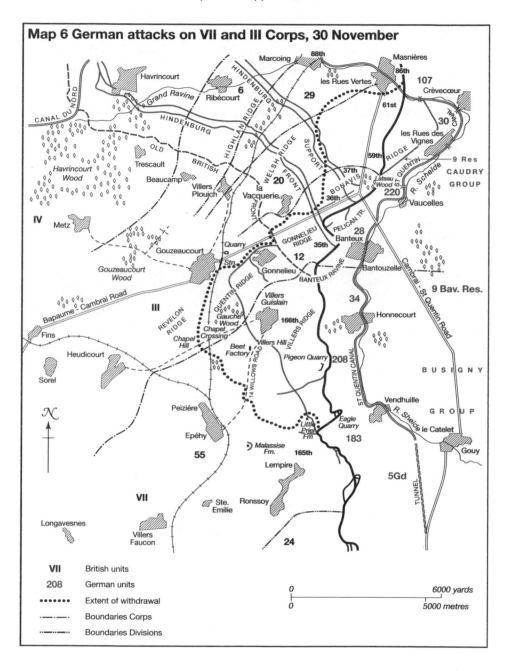

Map 6 German attacks on VII and III Corps, 30 November

from the Ronssoy–Epéhy ridge and observed clear signs of German preparations for an attack. He reported his concern to Third Army, even suggesting a probable date for the attack: 29 or 30 November.

German planning for a counter-attack was led by General Georg von der Marwitz, *Second Army*'s commander, and coordinated by Crown Prince Rupprecht of Bavaria, who commanded the Army Group which included *Second Army*. On 27 November, with preparations well under-way in those divisions not engaged in the fighting on the Bourlon front, Rupprecht met his superior, Erich Ludendorff, at *Second Army*'s head-quarters in Le Cateau and presented, in outline, his scheme for the German attack. It is worthy of note that in the German Army in late 1917, the *Generalquartiermeister* Ludendorff (a Prussian, but not strictly speaking a *Junker*), was superior to a Bavarian Crown Prince on at least two counts – and in political terms considerably more powerful.

It was the volatile but talented Ludendorff, always with his focus on the wider strategic picture, who first perceived greater possibilities for the attack. In Ludendorff's grander vision, with sufficient troops an attack on the southern flank of the British salient could be 'rolled up' towards the north. 'There has never been such an opportunity,' Ludendorff told those present. This was not hyperbole, but it was ambitious. The German Army in late 1917 was not the force it had been at Verdun and on the Somme. Its gritty defence during the previous days of the Cambrai battle was a remarkable achievement but of a piece with most of its combat experience of the previous three years. Furthermore, whilst offensive operations had been conducted against the French in the interim, this would be the first offensive launched against the British on the Western Front since the gas attack at Second Ypres in April 1915. Ludendorff was undeterred and his subordinates were more than happy to follow his lead.

However, when outlining his plan to his subordinates, Ludendorff unwittingly ensured the *Second Army*'s attack did not unfold in the in-tended manner:

> At the Le Cateau conference Ludendorff stressed the importance of the Flesquières heights and, making a bold line on the map with a charcoal pen, indicated how the heights were to be seized. At this General von

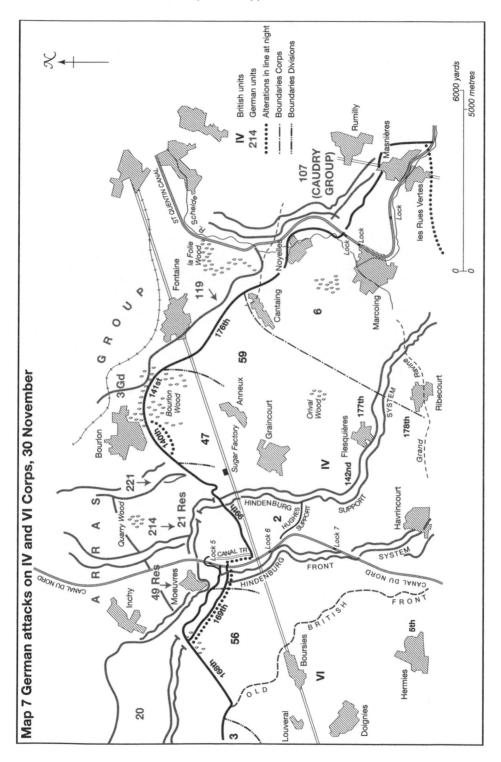

Map 7 German attacks on IV and VI Corps, 30 November

Legend:
- IV British units
- 214 German units
- •••••• Alterations in line at night
- –··–··– Boundaries Corps
- –···–···– Boundaries Divisions

6000 yards
5000 metres

der Marwitz stated, 'I shall pay particular attention to this curve.' As a result *Second Army* placed the main emphasis on the direction of Trescault instead of Metz-en-Couture.[3]

Kronprinz Rupprecht von Bayern, *OHL, Kaiserliches Heer*

That evening Rupprecht issued orders to *Second Army* and the various formations under its command in confirmation of Ludendorff's decision. The attack would be launched on 30 November, with its main blow from the south of the British salient towards Metz-en-Couture, capturing Flesquières and Havrincourt Wood and perhaps cutting the base of the new salient. An attack would also be made from west of Bourlon Wood towards the south. This too would involve significant numbers of troops but the attack from the south was definitely the chief one. Rupprecht hoped that: 'The minimum outcome of the offensive . . . has to be the recapture of Second Army's *Siegfried I* Positions.'[4] To disguise the German intentions from the British, *Generalleutnant* Otto von Moser's *Arras Group* was to shell Bourlon Wood on 28–29 November using gas and high explosive shells as though in preparation for an attack. The devastation of Bourlon Wood was now compounded by the reek of poison as Frank Ash witnessed:

November 29th: 1.00 a.m. Heavily shelled with shrapnel for 15 minutes, also a lot of tear gas shells. Put our helmets on for half an hour. 3.00 a.m. More gas shells. 5.00 a.m. More gas shells. From 6.00 to 7.00 a.m. they turned all their guns on and the wood became a mass of bursting shells, falling trees, smoke and gas. We all stood to, bayonets fixed, expecting heavy attack and the front line to be driven in on to us. Nothing happened. No heavy attack. Shelled off and on all morning. Fairly quiet in the afternoon, all the shelling was further back, but they came whizzing just over us, some hitting trees and bringing tops and big branches down, very unpleasant dodging them. Ventured out to a mud hole to fill my water bottle. Got it half full and got a whiff of tear gas; did not alarm me as it is non-poisonous. Got another whiff and an awful burning in the lungs. Spotted that the brutes had mixed some poison gas with the tear gas. Dropped everything. Held breath and did a hundred yards sprint back to where I had left my gas hat in the scrape. Blew into it for about ten minutes absolutely done to a turn, lungs felt all on fire. Quite alright after ten minutes except for slight cough. Returned and filled bottle. Had some tea. Relief came up at 7.00 p.m.[5]

Captain Frank Ash, 4th (Queen's Own) Hussars, 3rd Cavalry Brigade, 2nd Cavalry Division

The fact that they possessed no tanks was of little consequence to the German high command who saw artillery as the chief means to effect a breakthrough of the British defences. Consequently, the battle plan was for a short, intense, artillery bombardment of between thirty minutes and an hour's duration, with gas and smoke shell mixed in with it. Suspected headquarters, battery positions and observation posts were to be subjected to particular attention by the artillery. Some of the 77mm field guns of the type used so successfully as anti-tank weapons on Flesquières Ridge were to accompany the infantry in the attack, whilst light trench mortars (*Minenwerfer*), supposedly relatively static weapons of position warfare, which could be moved on wheeled carriages allowing them to be hauled forward with the infantry, were to offer close support in action.

The infantry themselves were to employ a new form of infiltration tactics. The first waves would move in their squads passing round strongpoints and villages, leaving them to be isolated and overcome by the following formations. Dissemination of these assault tactics was the responsibility of *Stosstrupp*, sometimes termed *Sturmtrupp* (assault detachments) and in 1918 the term 'stormtroop' would be used to describe these tactics. However, at Cambrai the assault units came principally from existing infantry regiments who practised the methods under the supervision of *Stosstrupp* immediately prior to the attack. Indeed heavy rain and sleet prevented some key units, such as *34th Division*, from practising the new tactics until 28 November – two days before the attack.

For the German infantry, the prospect of making a major counter-attack after long periods of hard pounding in defensive positions by British artillery offered a significant morale boost. But the orders were not received without some misgivings amongst even the most hardened and ardent:

We were delighted, certainly, to change the part of the anvil for that of the hammer at last; but we had some reservations on account of the

331

men, after their recent exhaustion in Flanders. Nevertheless, I had entire confidence in the spirit of my company and its iron backbone, in my experienced platoon commanders and excellent NCOs.[6]

Leutnant Ernst Jünger, *Füsilier Regiment 73, 111th Division*

On 28 November as gas shells rained down, the British divisional reliefs took place: 47th Division replacing 62nd Division in Bourlon Wood, whilst 59th Division completed the relief of the Guards facing Fontaine.

We got out about midnight. The wood was blocked with troops and horses and shelling continuous. To add to the enjoyment the Bosch started gas shelling and I, as guide to HQ, fairly legged it having lost my gas mask. In my anxiety to avoid that area I struck too far to the left and lost myself. However we only went a mile or so further than we need have done and reached our billets about four in the morning.[7]

Captain Charles Dudley-Ward, 1st Welsh Guards, 3rd Guards Brigade, Guards Division

Overall command of Bourlon front was now to become the responsibility of Lieutenant General Edward Fanshawe's V Corps. Woollcombe's IV Corps was to be relieved on the afternoon of 30 November. Woollcombe was clearly regarded as worn out by the staff of Third Army.

Another tired and relatively old corps commander, the 59-year-old Snow, was more than sufficiently experienced in the ways of war to perceive the great threat to men under his command from the obvious German attack preparations. At 7.00 p.m. on 28 November he made a further attempt on his own and Jeudwine's behalf to prompt Third Army into action over the menace to its southern flank. In a telephone conversation between Snow's chief staff officer, Brigadier General 'Jock' Burnett-Stuart and Major General Sir Louis Vaughan, Byng's Chief of Staff, however, Vaughan was content to offer reassurances about the availability of the Guards Division as an immediate reserve. Cavalry could also be moved up if necessary and a fresh division, 61st, was arriving in Third Army's sector on 30 November. Byng, Vaughan and many Third Army staff were already aware of much of the German activity indicating attack preparations but intelligence reports suggested that German losses in Flanders and at Cambrai were so severe that any heavy counter-attack was very unlikely.

In truth, of course, Vaughan had only outlined what in terms of manpower resources there was available. The problems of a salient were again evident. Only a certain number of divisions and their associated artillery, supply and medical units could be accommodated in the few square miles gained in the British attack. Aside from the Guards, of the divisions used in the fighting by IV Corps only 62nd Division remained close by; 40th and 51st Divisions were already 18 and 24 miles away respectively. But neither Byng nor Vaughan took any other steps to ensure a better supply of ready reserves. Brigadier General Vincent reiterated his fears to his divisional commander, Major General Arthur Scott, in a telephone call on 29 November. As a consequence, 12th Division at least made additional preparations in anticipation of the expected attack.

As if the warnings of Snow and Vincent were not enough, when 2nd Division attempted a small-scale operation to improve the situation on its front to the west of Bourlon Wood, the attackers suffered very heavy casualties amounting to 75 per cent of those engaged, mostly from machine-gun fire. Clearly, the time for offensive operations was over for the BEF. Now was the time to consolidate and defend the gains. The impending challenge was fast approaching.

It began as a barely perceptible increase in German artillery fire on the south and eastern edges of the salient. Soon after 6.00 a.m. on the dark and misty morning of 30 November, when the infantry stood to arms prior to dawn as the daily routine of trench warfare demanded, some amongst the ranks of 55th Division in particular detected a different pattern to the 'normal' shellfire that provided the constant accompaniment to trench life. The sounds of shells in flight and their explosions started to build and merge until the whole noise assumed the distinctive characteristics of what the Germans termed *trommelfeuer* ('drum fire'), punctuated only by the discordant plop of many gas shells. Trench mortar shells fell thickly on the front line trenches. Very soon the artillery fire broadened in frontage and as it grew heavier, all communication between the front trenches and the rear was cut off. At 7.05 a.m. signal rockets, the defending infantry's emergency means to call for artillery support, began to appear all along 55th Division's front. What artillery VII Corps possessed immediately opened fire but was of little use against the weight of the German attack.

No assault was launched on 55th Division's southern neighbour, 24th Division. The main strike was against the three battalions of 166th Brigade holding the left of 55th Division's front. The German infantry advanced at 7.00 a.m, initially with three divisions, with their assault waves of *Gruppe* moving in small columns and, in some cases, lead by men armed with flame-throwers. In places, the initial bombardment and *Minenwerfer* fire gave the defenders little option but to surrender almost immediately. Private John Lee offers a plain, unvarnished account of the abrupt end to his wartime role as a fighting soldier:

> Had a visit from German troops and taken prisoner about 8.00 a.m. Had been standing to since 5.00 a.m. and had missed breakfast. We were driven across No Man's Land with hands up at the point of the bayonet. Shrapnel bursting and machine-gun bullets whizzing all round. Got through danger zone safely.[8]
>
> Private John Lee, 1/10th (Liverpool Scottish) King's Liverpool Regiment, 166th Brigade, 55th Division

Although in places stands were made around various 'Posts' (strongpoints behind the front defensive line), the German infantry swiftly overwhelmed the weakened battalions. In the case of 1/5th South Lancashire defending the area around Banteux Ravine, their commanding officer was captured and scarcely a man survived death, wounds or capture. The German *34th Division* was thus able to press on towards Villers Guislain and into the flank and rear of III Corps, almost without tackling the front-line defenders of 12th Division.

The experience of the right battalion of 165th Brigade was not untypical of many in this sector. The 1/6th King's were defending the vicinity of Eagle Quarry:

> Our front line trenches were separated from the Germans by some 300 yards of grass land. Crossing No Man's Land was a country road, overgrown with grass and where the road crossed our trench we had a bombing post of which I was in charge. Thrown across the road we had a barricade of sand bags, some four feet high. For this reason my post

was named the 'Barricade'. The road in the immediate rear entered the chalk quarry, 30 feet in depth. As this afforded ample cover, a dugout had been hewn, having three entrances and capable of accommodating half a company of men, in addition to forming a store for 'flying pigs' and TMB (Trench Mortar Battery) shells.[9]

Lance Corporal William Evans, 1/6th King's Liverpool Regiment, 165th Brigade, 55th Division

The trench mortar battery's commander was Lieutenant John Lomax:

My command was well forward with no continuous front line, and behind a quarry with no visibility forwards. The infantry defenders consisted of a solitary platoon, of whom we saw nothing during the battle except a stretcher party carrying out their young officer, killed that morning.[10]

Lieutenant John Lomax, X Trench Mortar Battery, RFA, 55th Division

It was immediately obvious to the British occupants of this sector that the Germans had targeted the quarry area, recognizing it as a key point in the defences:

German shells seemed to be dropping all round my post, as it was in close proximity to the quarry and the head of the communication trench. The Germans had evidently detailed a few extra guns on these objectives. Immediately orders were flying about, almost as thick as shells, from the officers and sergeants, in obedience to one of which I doubled across the road to see how two men I had posted there were getting on. A rabbit could not have scuttled across in quicker time.[11]

Lance Corporal William Evans, 1/6th King's Liverpool Regiment, 165th Brigade, 55th Division

In fact, it was as much the German use of concentrated *Minenwerfer* fire as the artillery that shattered the resistance here, leaving only isolated groups of defenders fighting for survival. Most could not discover if this was the prelude to a major attack or an extreme example of the 'morning hate'. Evans found only one defender at the 'Barricade' post, an Irishman called Shannon:

'What shall we do, Corporal?' shouted Shannon. 'How the hell do I know? Keep your head down!' I yelled. We then attempted to go further down the trench where it was not so unhealthy and where the others had apparently gone, but a big shell exploded in the trench in the next bay – we turned back. The Irishman, however, had another try which was apparently successful, and I was left alone at the Barricade, with a pain in my stomach.[12]

Lance Corporal William Evans, 1/6th King's Liverpool Regiment, 165th Brigade, 55th Division

Alone, with the noise and dangers of the bombardment, and the growing nervous tension it engendered in his bowels, Evans could only wait for the shelling to cease.

This terrific upheaval had been proceeding for some little time when I was startled to see a figure with staring eyes in the trench on the other side of the road. I was relieved, however, to see Holman, a runner, who, like myself, had been left alone and had crawled along in the hope of finding someone to share his loneliness. We shouted and invited one another to cross the road. Eventually, I again emulated the rabbit, scuttled over and threw myself into the trench.[13]

Lance Corporal William Evans, 1/6th King's Liverpool Regiment, 165th Brigade, 55th Division

They exchanged experiences and shared a cigarette. Holman was very nervy, anxious to run the risk of retiring to the quarry dugout. Eventually Evans agreed.

In spite of our equipment and greatcoats, [we] did the few yards in the open in record time. I tumbled into the trench, took a breather, climbed out and again commenced running down the quarry towards the dugout. Holman was about 20 yards in front. I had just got into my stride when I was thrown flat upon my back, still clutching my rifle. I got up at once, rushed at the dugout, properly blown, to meet several of our fellows with open mouths and surprise written all over their faces. It seems it was a heavy shell, which had buried itself in the side of the quarry, which had blown me off my feet. Fortunately, it was a dud, otherwise I should have got it all to myself and it certainly would not have been a 'Blighty' one, but a general distribution![14]

Lance Corporal William Evans, 1/6th King's Liverpool Regiment, 165th Brigade, 55th Division

The dugout offered a false sense of security to its occupants, but the relief at being out of the bombardment was immense for Evans. His fellow defenders may have been less than delighted at his release.

> I took the opportunity, when I had recovered my breath of relieving the pain in my stomach and then found there were about a dozen men in the dugout, including the Trench Mortar Battery officer.[15]
>
> Lance Corporal William Evans, 1/6th King's Liverpool Regiment, 165th Brigade, 55th Division

Lomax, Evans and the dugout's other occupants soon came to understand the bogus safety of the quarry dugout.

> About mid-morning coloured rocket signals were fired from a line five hundred yards from our positions but in rear. Meanwhile, we came under rifle fire from the rear and both flanks. We had no defensive weapons; maybe half a dozen rifles and revolvers. The enemy had got well behind us before we knew that their assault had begun. After a spell of what resistance we could make, a second wave of the enemy lined the quarry lip and showered us with bombs.[16]
>
> Lieutenant John Lomax, X Trench Mortar Battery, RFA, 55th Division

Caught in the undefendable quarry, surrender was inevitable but still the attempt to resist was made:

> Suddenly the cry went up 'They are in the quarry!' We saw the Germans swarming down the side and flinging their bombs at us. We retired into the dugout. The TMB officer called for a machine-gun which, of course, was not there, neither did there appear to be a supply of bombs, although I saw one of the TMB crew throw one at the Germans. I raised my rifle over his head to fire at a German when a bomb exploded right in front and knocked out the TMB man. Added to this the Germans threw what appeared to be a piece of rope about 1½ feet long. This had been ignited and thick fumes that smelt like phosphorous quickly penetrated the dugout. The fumes started everyone coughing and choking and we were, for a short space, overcome.[17]
>
> Lance Corporal William Evans, 1/6th King's Liverpool Regiment, 165th Brigade, 55th Division

Apparently under the impression the defenders were dead or otherwise *hors de combat*, the attackers drew off and began to consolidate their
hold on the quarry.

> This gave us time to recover and watch their activities and to formulate
> a plan of lying 'doggo' until a counter-attack materialised and we could
> get the Germans in the rear. We thought it could only be a raid and
> when our artillery, which had been strangely quiet, again became
> active, that we should have no difficulty in dislodging them.[18]
> Lance Corporal William Evans, 1/6th King's Liverpool Regiment, 165th Brigade, 55th
> Division

The flaws in this optimistic assessment were almost immediately
revealed. Evans was also under the impression that the trench mortar
officer had voluntarily surrendered during the clash at the dugout's
entrance. But, as Lomax explains, it was not a matter of choice:

> We had been scattered and the scene was utterly unexpected and
> bewildering. Retreat never entered my head. With one of the rifles I
> was firing at anything that moved to the flanks when I spotted a
> German taking aim at me: he actually fired before I could get my gun
> up and his bullet went through my collar, drilling a neat hole in and out
> but not touching me. At the same time another German from the
> quarry lip must have dropped a bomb from above. The explosion
> knocked me over and for a spell I lay stunned in the dust. When I
> recovered my wits and tried to rise there was a German NCO standing
> over me with a massive pistol pointed at my head and, with a furious
> roar of words, he waved me back to where a soldier was standing guard
> over a few of my men.[19]
> Lieutenant John Lomax, X Trench Mortar Battery, RFA, 55th Division

Lomax's capture meant his battery sergeant was the senior man in
the quarry dugout. As Evans readily admitted, their plight was hopeless
and surrender the only option.

> The sergeant now shared an understandable coyness to lead the way as
> the leading German was some 20 yards away, bomb in hand, ap-
> parently ready for any emergency. It seemed to me that our only hope
> lay in advancing to meet the Germans, rather than that he should enter

the dark dugout and probably blow up the side of the quarry, as there was stored, by the entrance, a good quantity of trench mortar ammunition. I therefore decided to lead the way and instructed the men to shout 'Kamerad'. This at once attracted the attention of the advancing German.[20]

Lance Corporal William Evans, 1/6th King's Liverpool Regiment, 165th Brigade, 55th Division

This was the worst moment for any surrendering soldier. How would his captor react? Evans was all too aware that a man with the excitement and tension of battle coursing through his blood could kill a surrendering opponent out of hand without the least compunction.

I advanced just beyond the entrance, calling 'Kamerad' and hesitated. The German did not anticipate anyone coming from that direction, having apparently overlooked the side entrance. I expected to receive that bomb for myself, but he lowered his arm and shouted, 'Come, Tommy.' I came, and turned round to call the others to follow. They, however, held back, no doubt anxious to see what reception I received but as I did not suffer a violent death the rest followed to the evident delight of our captors, who, I think, had visions of the Iron Cross![21]

Lance Corporal William Evans, 1/6th King's Liverpool Regiment, 165th Brigade, 55th Division

The safety of the captives was not yet guaranteed. Their captors' delight attracted the attention of other German troops:

One, a hulking brute of a fellow, detached himself and advanced on me bomb in hand, in a very threatening attitude, no doubt with the kindly intention of knocking me on the head! Our captor, a much smaller man, however, flew at him and there ensued a fierce altercation. This attracted the attention of their officer, who curtly ordered the man with the 'kindly intentions' to get on with his job. This he accordingly did with some reluctance. We were then directed out of the quarry and over No Man's Land, our late post being occupied by half a dozen Germans.[22]

Lance Corporal William Evans, 1/6th King's Liverpool Regiment, 165th Brigade, 55th Division

The journey through the counter-bombardment was fraught with danger. The prisoners were led back through the British barrage with frequent halts to take cover and help the wounded, but after reaching the German lines, the captured men were generally treated with kindness.

> There the first enemy I saw was a bearded warrior with a benevolent expression who pointed to my face, which had been peppered with bomb splinters and was bleeding in streams. He insisted on binding up my face with paper wrappers and smeared the wounds with something. This must have made me seem very stricken but, in fact, the cuts were only superficial and before the end of the day I had pulled off the bandaging.[23]
>
> Lieutenant John Lomax, X Trench Mortar Battery, RFA, 55th Division

The story was similar all along the brigade front. Against the sudden German onslaught dogged resistance also came from some artillery batteries and their personnel, many of whom barely had time to get into action when the Germans were almost upon them and they could only fire at point-blank range. First were the field guns and 4.5-inch howitzers of the Royal Field Artillery. Sergeant Cyril Gourley of D/276 Battery, on the flank of the attack at Little Priel Farm, managed to keep one of his section's howitzers constantly in action despite being under heavy shellfire, aircraft attack and fire from machine-guns and rifles. The battery resisted throughout the day and that night the guns were withdrawn. Gourley received the Victoria Cross for his resolute defence. Elsewhere, however, similar positions were overrun before guns could be withdrawn or the breech-blocks and dial sights removed from the weapons.

The rapid German advance meant it was soon the turn of the heavy guns of the Royal Garrison Artillery. In and about Villers Guislain, 34th Heavy Artillery Group with its 6-inch howitzers and 60-pounder guns was dramatically overrun by men from *Infanterie Regiment 67* who suddenly appeared through the mist, advancing confidently up the slope from the north-east at about 8.00 a.m.

> My billet was an old house which was hit early on. The top was blown off and then the living room collapsed with a very heavy bump which left very little house. With several others I made my way across some

gardens towards the Officers' Mess through a perfect shower of shells. I soon discovered retreat was impossible as we were surrounded and the greatest sensation of my life was when I saw a German taking deliberate aim at me with his rifle. His first shot glancing off my steel helmet, the next flattened itself in a wall just in front of my nose. I then crawled through a hole in a house only to be captured by a German officer who levelled his revolver at me. How I did it, I never knew but I got away from him and ran into two others and was compelled to throw up my arms and surrender.[24]

Gunner Alfred Newman, 32nd Siege Battery, Royal Garrison Artillery, 34th Heavy Artillery Group, III Corps

Astonishingly, 24 6-inch howitzers, 26 18-pounders, four 60-pounders and four 6-inch howitzers were lost when Villers Guislain fell: 58 artillery pieces. This would have been nothing less than a disaster on the Somme in 1916, but for the BEF in late 1917, supported by a war economy at home now geared towards the production of huge numbers of guns, it was possible to overcome such losses. Some field guns close to the village did get into action and the captured Newman had the satisfaction of seeing the results.

We were put into a group and then later into fours, counted, and marched off under an armed guard some sorry looking objects. I shall never forget the sights through the lines. Although we lost a lot of men, the enemy's losses must have been three times more killed.[25]

Gunner Alfred Newman, 32nd Siege Battery, Royal Garrison Artillery, 34th Heavy Artillery Group, III Corps

At 55th Division's headquarters Jeudwine could get little news of events on his division's front. However, it was soon clear that the situation was critical and that everything must be done to staunch the smashing drive of the Germans. Of his reserves, 164th Brigade was so weak after its diversionary attack on 20 November that its four battalions could muster fewer than 1,400 rifles; full strength infantry battalions were supposed to have over 1,000 men. Nevertheless, this brigade was used to form the basis of a line of resistance and its numbers were bolstered by pioneers, engineers and working parties – anyone who could hold a rifle.

They were joined by survivors from the front line battalions, some of whom were perhaps not unreasonably reluctant after their earlier experiences to face more enemy fire. The army did not offer such choices, however. Unarmed artillery crews, infantrymen (some of whom had been captured and then escaped), engineers and men from a variety of other units swarmed rearwards in the face of the onslaught. Amongst them were lesser numbers of the walking wounded together with the terrified and the cowards who had thrown away their arms. Having been subject to the army's discipline since they first joined or were conscripted, men knew the risks if they committed such an act. An infantryman who could not explain the loss of his rifle was likely to be incapable of defending himself against his own army's scrutiny as well as his German pursuers. Only the truly desperate and those gripped by the worst forms of panic fled without some prepared explanation for their actions.

In the neighbouring 12th Division's sector, the first Brigadier General Vincent and his staff knew of the Germans' swift progress was when they appeared beyond Villers Guislain. His Brigade Major, Broadwood, dashed down into the headquarters dugout to burn any useful papers and was captured along with the clerks.

> The Boches were through Villers Guislain before anybody had any warning and no one here knows how they got through the division on our left without any SOS signal. One of our Field Ambulances had an Advanced Dressing Station there and Rankin (the Commanding Officer) and some men were taken prisoner. The Divisional Burial Party got away by the skin of their teeth and lost everything they possessed.[26]
>
> Lieutenant Colonel Edwin Collen, Assistant Adjutant and Quartermaster General, Headquarters, 12th Division

Despite being so badly surprised, however, Vincent hastily dressed and immediately began to organize an effective defence, calling on whatever men were on hand. His headquarters personnel, a company of Royal Engineers and a machine-gun and crew resisted all attempts to dislodge them from a rise west of Villers Guislain for some time. Finally, the few survivors fell back to the shelter of Gauche Wood. Here, bolstered by about a hundred artillerymen, engineers and infantry stragglers and cut off from his brigade, Vincent organized his new (albeit tiny) command into four platoons. This body of men, 'Vincent's Force', then conducted a fighting withdrawal from the wood, via the relative protection of a railway embankment, to a position on Revelon Ridge a further half mile to the rear. The mongrel horde of signallers, sappers, runners and gunners fired rifle volleys at their pursuers as if engaged in some colonial frontier skirmish. Yet it was effective. However, as their ammunition ran out, their fate hung in the balance and depended on the immediate arrival of reinforcements.

Vincent and his men were fortunate that help came. When it did, it was from a variety of sources. When the first reports from allied airmen of Germans massing opposite Villers Guislain arrived at 12th Division headquarters, Lieutenant Colonel Edwin Collen collected about 800 reinforcements encamped nearby and formed them into a Provisional Battalion. By 9.00 a.m., this battalion was moving to engage the Germans. Meanwhile, the divisional reserves consisting of two battalions, 6th Queen's and 11th Middlesex, the latter under the command of Lieutenant Colonel Tom Wollocombe, advanced from Heudicourt.

> At 7.30 a.m., the Brigade Major (36th Brigade) rushed into our billets and told me to get on parade as soon as possible as the line had been broken. The battalion was actually at breakfast. I had to collect the company and platoon commanders and had no time for a proper preliminary reconnaissance, though I made a personal one as soon as possible and rode forward with the vanguard most of the way into action. We were moving off in ¾ hour.[27]
>
> Lieutenant Colonel Tom Wollocombe, 11th Middlesex, 36th Brigade, 12th Division

Even Wollocombe was not aware, however, of the effort required by some of his officers to get into action that morning, until subsequently informed by one of his subordinates:

> You may remember that I and a few other officers dined with you at battalion headquarters the night before and, fortunately for me, I slept through a barrage. When ordered to report to you, I was fully dressed and booted as the result of your hospitality, and my breakfast that morning consisted of the remains of the soda siphon.[28]
>
> Captain H Stuart Cook, 11th Middlesex, 36th Brigade, 12th Division

With a raging hangover, Stuart Cook took command of the Middlesex's vanguard. Unaware as yet of Vincent's Force and its desperate fight for survival, the two reserve battalions had orders to assist in retaking Villers Guislain and Gonnelieu – now also known to have fallen to the German advance.

> We and the Queen's were ordered immediately to occupy the high ground south-west of Gonnelieu and west of Villers Guislain, respectively. The Middlesex were unable to carry out their orders as the enemy had already passed the point which we were to occupy and we were obliged to deploy before coming to the top of the hill north of Revelon Farm.[29]
>
> Captain Guy Chipperfield, 11th Middlesex, 36th Brigade, 12th Division

As Stuart Cook's company led off, his battalion commander was elated at the prospect of the type of action they were about to encounter:

> It was one of the most interesting and, in many ways, enjoyable days of my life. I was one who hated the trench warfare routine, into which we all fell of necessity, and insisted for the year I had command of that battalion on at least one open warfare scheme every time we came out of the line. So you can imagine my joy when the chance came to carry out an advance guard 'show' in open country. My instructions were that the Germans had broken through the front and we were to march on a certain objective, find them and stop them.[30]
>
> Lieutenant Colonel Tom Wollocombe, 11th Middlesex, 36th Brigade, 12th Division

In accordance with Wollocombe's open warfare 'scheme', Stuart Cook's company was on the move within a quarter of an hour, receiving an extra iron ration and ammunition as they filed along the road.

> We went to Quentin Mill Ridge where we met details coming in the opposite direction in all states of attire – gunners – sappers – pioneers – signallers. I well remember meeting General Vincent just before I reached the brow of the ridge. He was in Gum Boots and 'British Warm' over his pyjamas. He asked me where I was going. I said my orders were to hold Quentin Mill Ridge. He walked up the ridge a

short way with me and there was a target such as we had longed for, the Bosch about to ascend the further side of the ridge like rabbits.[31]

Captain H Stuart Cook, 11th Middlesex, 36th Brigade, 12th Division

Lieutenant Colonel Collen and his Provisional Battalion also arrived at this point.

When we arrived, I met General Vincent with about forty men and some gunners, pioneers and sappers. He had fought a rearguard action from Villers Guislain. Just as they had practically fired their last round, up came these three battalions and the Boches were stopped there. This mixed force really saved the situation on this side. I saw the Boches come over the rise and they were received with five rounds rapid.[32]

Lieutenant Colonel Edwin Collen, Assistant Adjutant and Quartermaster General, Headquarters, 12th Division

The battalion frontage for the 11th Middlesex's advance was over a mile – incredible for a battalion with a strength of only about 500 rifles. The vanguard company's leading platoon, and especially its Lewis gun, made the first check to the advancing German infantry on Revelon Ridge. They got to the top of the ridge just in time as the Germans were coming up the other slope. Soon afterwards, the rest of the battalion began to arrive:

We immediately fixed bayonets and occupied the crest of the hill. On our left we could see the scratch forces of RAMC, tunnellers, roadmen, railway troops, etc who had been collected together to act as a sort of screen, retiring gradually from the direction of Villers Guislain. The Queen's succeeded in getting their objective by a few minutes and were able to get their machine-guns into play. It is the one who gets to the top first who has the advantage on these occasions.[33]

Captain Guy Chipperfield, 11th Middlesex, 36th Brigade, 12th Division

Now that they held the higher ground, they could effectively blunt any further German advance.

On our front the Boches were pouring into the valley in streams, but in a very unorganised manner. We got every machine-gun, Lewis gun and rifle we possibly could into play and it was like duck-shooting; in about twenty minutes there was not a live Boche to be seen for they had all cleared back or taken cover.[34]

Captain Guy Chipperfield, 11th Middlesex, 36th Brigade, 12th Division

Having deployed in the best positions they could find, the Middlesex could do no more for the time being.

It was a similar story at Brigadier General Charles Owen's head-quarters on the outskirts of Gonnelieu where, despite more determined work by the men of several artillery batteries, a number of other guns were lost to the Germans. This time, however, it was a more calculated withdrawal and sights and breech-blocks were removed before the artillerymen retired. Nevertheless, Gonnelieu's fate was sealed. According to Edwin Collen, 'General Owen and his staff got away with what they stood up in but poured petrol all over the place, set it alight and cut for it.'[35]

Owen's brigade front was actually further east on the Gonnelieu Ridge. Here Corporal Tom Bracey was in charge of a Vickers machine-gun crew supporting 9th Royal Fusiliers in part of Pelican Trench southeast of La Vacquerie. The Fusiliers fought hard here under the example of their commander, and Bracey rendered spirited assistance from a position in the former Hindenburg Support Line:

> The Colonel put me in a position there with the machine-gun. On my right was some German barbed wire that hadn't been touched going for about 400 yards and about 10 or 15 feet wide. Suddenly the Lance Corporal said 'Here! The Germans are over there!' They'd come on our right. Nobody was on my right. But about from where we started on the bloody Germans were coming that way! I said to the Colonel 'Looks as though we're going to be taken prisoner, Sir,' because they were coming back from where we'd come in! He said 'Here's one they don't take' – he'd shoot himself before he'd be taken prisoner.[36]
>
> Corporal Tom Bracey, 36th Machine-Gun Company, 12th Division

Bracey, like many of his fellow machine-gunners, was aware of the rumours that the Germans shot captured machine-gun crews out of hand. This, he suspected, drove many of his fellows to make a particularly determined fight:

I said to Frank, our Lance Corporal, 'What are you firing at, Frank?' He said, 'The Germans over there.' He was afraid, I knew he was afraid, afraid that we were going to be surrounded, afraid that we'd be shot.[37]

Corporal Tom Bracey, 36th Machine-Gun Company, 12th Division

Bracey's position was guarding against a German bombing attack up their former trenches. His gun was sited on a bombing 'stop', or barricade, in the trench with a door in it:

The lot was coming up the trench throwing their bombs and coming towards me. Well, there's me on the gun . . . I was about 30 yards away from that door. I was confident as anything all on me own. They came up to a stop there, come up with bombing and I thought to myself 'Why the bloody hell didn't I fire at their arms?' They came to near that stop but they stopped there. That was me waiting there. And then I suppose they must have got a sniper. I see him put his rifle up. He just put his head up and I went bang bang – two shots. But I was a bit too low, but the next two wasn't. And as I did that the Colonel must have given the order to attack.[38]

Corporal Tom Bracey, 36th Machine-Gun Company, 12th Division

This counter-attack relieved the pressure on the Royal Fusiliers who then withdrew to positions closer to La Vacquerie.

Although for some time the British thought that the attack was focused solely on 55th Division's front, this was chiefly because the attack of the *Caudry Group* north of Banteux Ravine started an hour later than that of the *Busigny Group* to the south. Thus, the left brigade of 12th Division, together with 20th Division, were still surprised in much the same way as the British units further south when two further German divisions attacked.

Shortly after daybreak about 7.30 a.m. Kidd and I were awaked suddenly by the unmistakable sound of bursting shells, and the din of a hostile bombardment. As K and I hastily climbed down from our 'beds', K said 'How long has this been going on?' 'Just started' was the reply. K commenced to pull on his boots, and asked me to go and find out what was the matter. I dashed upstairs and a glance showed me that our front line was being heavily shelled, and that a box barrage was being placed on our communications. There could be only one inference, that the enemy was contemplating an attack, and I conveyed that information to K. Hardly had I returned to the dugout, when K was called to the 'phone. The order to 'Stand-to' had come from Battalion HQ.[39]

Second Lieutenant Wilfrid Taylor, 6th Buffs, 37th Brigade, 12th Division

In their support positions, Taylor's company had little clue yet as to what was going on, but they were soon harassed by artillery and low-flying aircraft as the Germans set out to take Lateau Wood.

An enormous flight of enemy planes appeared, coming up fast from the direction of Cambrai, and flying very low. The sky was black with them, and throughout the day they dominated the situation, firing on our infantry, harassing communications, and putting many batteries out of action. I never saw a friendly plane the whole day long. A few minutes later there appeared a few – very few – elements of our front line battalions dribbling out of Lateau Wood, and close behind them hordes of Boche. W and I instantly called our platoons from the dugouts, and lined them up behind a fold in the ground, where the few survivors of the Kents and Surreys speedily joined them. I recognised the West Kents' Adjutant and the second-in-command of the East Surreys. We at once opened fire with rifles and Lewis guns on the advancing foe, and partially checked their advance, though I could see them still making ground on our left and threatening to turn that flank. The enemy barrage on our sector had lulled, and I remember noting Bourlon Wood away to our left wreathed in smoke, and the lurid glare of a burning dump.[40]

Second Lieutenant Wilfrid Taylor, 6th Buffs, 37th Brigade, 12th Division

The northern attack had also begun. However, Taylor's attention was now wholly taken with events in his immediate vicinity. He was soon despatched to brigade headquarters 300 yards to the rear to ask for reinforcements.

Captain Alan Thomas was at Brigadier General Incledon-Webber's 37th Brigade headquarters when the Germans 'announced' their offensive.

I was shaving in the deep dugout that was Brigade headquarters. I had finished lathering and was just getting busy with the razor, when a great gust of air was blown down the entrance. It was caused by the bursting of a shell. Another shell followed, then another and another. The next moment an orderly came rushing down the steps with the news that the Boche was attacking. 'They're on top of us!' he shouted. I went up and found that he was right. A field-grey figure was lying at the entrance to our dugout – dead. A furious bombardment was going on but most of the shells were falling well behind us. The German who was lying at my feet was evidently one of the advance-guard. 'Get your tunic on, Thomas, and come with me!' It was the General speaking. He was standing on top of the little trench which led to our dugout, looking at Lateau Wood through his field-glasses. I was in my braces and my face was half-lathered and half-shaved. I dived down as quickly as I could, seized my tunic and my revolver and came up again just as the General was striding off towards the front.[41]

Captain Alan Thomas, Headquarters, 37th Brigade, 12th Division

The approaching Germans proved little distraction to Incledon-Webber, who still found time and opportunity to 'rip a strip off' one of his battalion commanders, Lieutenant Colonel Arthur Smeltzer of 6th East Kents ('The Buffs'). The 36-year-old Smeltzer was a career soldier with considerable fighting experience who had risen through the ranks. His focus was the threat of the oncoming Germans, not his commanding officer.

Colonel Smeltzer was an old soldier, keen as mustard and as brave as they make them, but seemingly without phlegm. We found [him] giving orders right and left and so preoccupied that he didn't appear to have time for the General. 'Listen to me, Smeltzer,' commanded the General. He began to explain what the dispositions were to be. But the colonel was only half attending. His eyes were roving over the landscape and every now and then he turned away from the General to see what was going on. Knowing the General's temper I could have given Smeltzer a word of advice. But that was not my job. Then it came – as I knew it would. 'Damn you, sir, stand to attention when your General is speaking to you!' The Germans were now only five hundred yards away and advancing in hordes. But the General's words counted for more than any Germans. They awoke in the colonel far-off memories of the barrack square when obedience to your superior officer took

349

precedence of every other loyalty – even of your obedience to God. 'Stand still, sir!' The colonel stood still – his eyes unwaveringly fixed on those of the General, his thumbs in line with the seams of his breeches. I also stood still – but, unlike the colonel, I had half an eye cocked at the advancing Germans.[42]

Captain Alan Thomas, Headquarters, 37th Brigade, 12th Division

Having witnessed this 'barrage', Thomas was charged with organizing the brigade headquarters' defence.

It soon became clear that if the headquarters was to be defended we ourselves should have to defend it. We had a few men – cooks, signallers, some bandsmen doing duty as batmen, runners and mess waiters – about twenty in all, I suppose. The General put me in charge of them and told me to counter-attack if I could, or failing that to hold my ground.[43]

Captain Alan Thomas, Headquarters, 37th Brigade, 12th Division

Thomas never veered from his seemingly hopeless task, yet the German advance appeared inexorable.

I got the men into an extended line and we advanced about twenty yards. Then a machine-gun opened fire on us and we lay down. We could see the Germans quite plainly ahead of us. They were coming on in close formation making easy targets for our Lewis gun. I told the cook, who happened to be lying next to me, to get busy. Unfortunately he hadn't the faintest idea how the gun worked.[44]

Captain Alan Thomas, Headquarters, 37th Brigade, 12th Division

Having personally got the Lewis firing, Thomas barely had time to direct the defence before he was wounded.

I lifted my head, to see what the chances were of our going forward again. Instead, I received a stunning blow in the jaw – as though a heavyweight boxer had caught me with an upper cut. Blood was falling on to my tunic and I realised that I had been wounded. I think I must have passed out for a little. When I turned over I found that I was lying in the Brigade headquarters trench with my servant, Lavender, bending over me. My jaw was now covered with a field dressing.

'D'you think you can walk, sir?' asked Lavender. 'The General says

I'm to take you down.' I got up on to my feet and felt all right. I asked how the men were doing and Lavender said they were doing fine. I asked who had the Lewis gun. He couldn't say. As we were talking the General turned up and asked me how I felt. I told him I was all right and argued with him for a time, speaking as best I could without moving my jaw. Then he ordered me to get out of it and told Lavender to see me as far as the Casualty Clearing Station. So we turned our backs on the Germans and left.[45]

Captain Alan Thomas, Headquarters, 37th Brigade, 12th Division

Meanwhile, Wilfrid Taylor had been told by General Webber to reconnoitre their right flank, on the high ground overlooking the St Quentin Canal. He took a Brigade signaller named Ferguson with him. They managed to get about sixty yards from the brigade headquarters before a block in the trench forced them to move into the open ground.

We had proceeded about 5 yards from the trench, when a warning shout from Ferguson who was behind me attracted my attention. Almost at the same moment I caught sight of a Hun kneeling about 200 yards away to fire at us. I at once flung myself down, but as I did so he fired and I was hit.[46]

Second Lieutenant Wilfrid Taylor, 6th Buffs, 37th Brigade, 12th Division

Ferguson recalled two shots:

One bullet just whizzed by my head and the other struck Mr Taylor in the right thigh. I promptly dropped flat and laid still for a few moments and then crawled across on my stomach to Mr Taylor and managed to pull him about 40 yards to the trench. It was a very tedious journey, as we had to keep flat on the earth owing to the danger of the sniper observing our movements. Mr Taylor who must have been in terrible agony bore the journey well – I got him into the trench and got him on my back – I was almost dropping from exhaustion when luckily I observed one of our men and he assisted me to get him back to the Brigade Headquarters where we dressed his wound. The Signals Section then received orders to retire at once so we had unfortunately to leave him but we made him as comfortable as possible under the circumstances.[47]

Sapper James Ferguson, RE Signals, Headquarters, 12th Division

Incledon-Webber had already withdrawn and it was clear to Taylor that Colonel Smeltzer and his staff would soon follow.

> I asked Ferrie* if he could get me away and he replied 'I'll do my best for you, Taylor. I've sent down three messages already for stretcher-bearers, but none have come yet. I'll send them for you as soon as ever they come.' He and Turk and the CO then left me. The morning began to slip away, and still the handful of men I had left in the support lines showed no signs of retreating. Every minute I hoped that some stretcher-bearers might appear, but none came.[48]
>
> Second Lieutenant Wilfrid Taylor, 6th Buffs, 37th Brigade, 12th Division

All Taylor could do was lie and wait to be captured whilst the Buffs' rearguard delayed the German advance as long as possible.

It was not only brigade commanders who were caught unawares by the Germans. The commander of 29th Division, Major General Beauvoir de Lisle, was compelled to quit his headquarters in haste too. However, de Lisle was especially keen to clarify the exact circumstances in which he did so.

> For twenty years I have ignored the published story that the general who had to run away in his pyjamas was myself. I knew who it was, and did not want to give him away. As a matter of fact, I had finished breakfast and was just about to start to visit my front line with my ADC.[49]
>
> Major General Beauvoir de Lisle, 29th Division

'So there,' he might have added. What was certain was that his departure was not a leisurely one and was considerably hastened by the large shell that pitched into the quarry in which his headquarters were located, wounding his senior artillery officer, who subsequently had to be left behind and was captured. Generals do not lightly abandon senior members of their staff in the face of the enemy. It seems likely, therefore, that de Lisle's flight was more precipitate than he would have us believe, although he also stated that:

> I ordered my Headquarters to evacuate the quarry and to *run for it*. As we got away and were running down the road to Gouzeaucourt, a

* The Battalion Medical Officer

machine-gun opened on us from the hill behind at a range of 500 to 600 yards. This was unpleasant and I lost my GSO3, who was killed, and several were wounded; but the most unpleasant of all was the fire from two low-flying aeroplanes, less than 150 feet up. It was not easy to run that mile, and my ADC, Captain Nickalls, was soon 'all in' and required all the encouragement I could render to continue the struggle.[50]

Major General Beauvoir de Lisle, 29th Division

De Lisle does not appear to have 'remembered with advantages what deeds he did' that day, since he describes an hour's work spent putting Gouzeaucourt into a state of defence. Yet there was barely time before the Germans, hot on his heels, entered the village. The 29th Division staff offered some resistance, assisted by men of the III Corps cyclist battalion, a few pioneers and sappers and a detachment of American railway engineers. The latter were at Gouzeaucourt to re-establish the railway yard.

The troops were detailed to different parts of the yard and work was well under way at about 8 o'clock when a barrage moved over the ridge and roughly halfway to the track. No warning of an advance by the Germans had been received and at that time no retreating troops had been seen. I still thought that we need fear only the shelling which was moving south, so I ordered all the troops to board the work train which had begun to move out. The barrage then moved forward to the track in the vicinity of the train and the locomotive was uncoupled and ran south. I ordered the men to leave the train, to scatter in the fields to the southwest (south of Gouzeaucourt) and to hurry over the hill in that direction.[51]

Captain C Raymond Hulsart, Company B, 11th Engineer Regiment (Railway), AEF

British troops were seen retreating over the ridge and across the track, and the Americans realized this was an attack in strength.

To the engineers, the situation as it affected them was painfully clear. They were unarmed and, therefore, unprepared for any offense [sic]. The senior officer [Major Burbank] present recognising that his men were being uselessly sacrificed, very properly ordered a withdrawal. The men consequently became somewhat scattered, though not disorganised. Some succeeded in making their way under the command of their officers through Gouzeaucourt, some sought refuge in dugouts from the downpour of high explosive and gas shells, while some were rallied into an improvised unit and offered some resistance. They seized any weapons at hand, although some fought effectively with their picks and shovels until overcome. It is related that one fellow was seen to lay low five of the enemy with only a shovel before he fell.[52]

Major William Barclay Parsons, 11th Engineer Regiment (Railway), AEF

Their action was spirited, if ultimately futile, although it delayed the German advance along the main Cambrai–Gouzeaucourt road, giving a little extra time for the reinforcements to be organized and sent forward. There were casualties however and most of the men in the dugouts were captured. The remaining American engineers managed to get away. The previous day had been Thanksgiving, now the survivors had cause to give thanks for the manner in which they had escaped.

By 9.00 a.m. Snow understood the desperate need for reinforcements for his battered corps. Third Army's response to his appeal came soon enough but the lack of preparedness of Byng's staff was demonstrated by their failure to have an adequate defensive plan in place and the ill-coordinated response to VII and III Corps' appeals for assistance. Thus the Cavalry Corps was ordered to send a division towards Villers Faucon, but when Snow asked for the Guards Division to come to his aid, he was told they had already been placed under III Corps, as was 2nd Cavalry Division. One dismounted battalion of this division had only just been relieved the evening before from the horrors of Bourlon Wood.

The cavalry from three divisions (4th Cavalry Division was soon ordered to follow 5th) was soon on the move. The Guards also responded promptly to their orders when finally received – despite having just been withdrawn from the line. The 1st Guards Brigade under Champion de Crespigny led the way. The other brigades came on separately behind. The advance by De Crespigny's brigade, witnessed by one artillery officer, was 'the most amazing sight',

> Over the ridge in front of us was streaming infantry, wagons, and so on
> – all coming hell for leather from the horizon through our lines. Even

the artillery troops were coming back pretty fast and we could see ourselves having to have our guns round 180 degrees. And then a marvellous thing happened – the Guards Brigade came up the road in column of fours as if they were on a peacetime routine march and the band! Leading them was the Brigade Commander, Champion de Crespigny, on a horse! The effect on morale was terrific. They went through our lines like that and when they got up a bit further they shook out into battle order.[53]

Captain John Murray Rymer Jones, 'A' Battery, 74th Brigade, RFA, Guards Division

The desperate nature of the situation even produced a request for the Tank Corps, already in the process of withdrawing to winter quarters, to commit whatever resources it could in terms of men and machines. In order to move tanks by train and pass under the French rail system's narrow bridges, it was necessary for crews to unbolt the tank sponsons and swing them into the tank body to reduce their width. Joseph Gordon Hassell and men from 'H' Battalion were engaged in this task in preparation for the battalion's entrainment when 2nd Tank Brigade's commander, Brigadier General Anthony Courage, arrived:

He ordered us immediately to prepare for action. Out sponsons again; load ammunition; get rations; climb aboard and set off in improvised companies. My orders were simply to go and meet the enemy, to rally upon a certain map reference. A staff officer on horse galloped up to me and asked did I want a map? Yes, I had none. I found the map plain uncoloured. Whilst Sergeant Callaghan drove, I 'layered' the map with coloured chalks. I had always been taught to carry them for just such an emergency. Thus valleys and hills stood out clearly according to their contours. This was to prove invaluable, and I believe saved the life of the tank and of my men.[54]

Second Lieutenant Joseph Gordon Hassell, No. 22 Company, 'H' Battalion, Tank Corps

The unnamed staff officer was Courage's energetic Brigade Major, Stephen Foot. He and Courage had been on the point of leaving their headquarters at Templeux La Fosse on an inspection tour when III Corps' commander, Lieutenant General Sir William Pulteney, telephoned with the news of the German breakthrough. It was Foot who secured the petrol the tanks desperately needed, before riding forward to reconnoitre the situation on Revelon Ridge. His 'fragmentary recollections' were of:

> The queer mixture of gunners, sappers, and elderly men from a Labour Battalion who were occupying a trench overlooking the valley between the ridge and Gauche Wood – their officer clad in khaki trousers, sweater and Sam Browne belt – his anxiety as to what I thought of his dispositions for defence – the way they cheered up when I told them that the tanks were coming.[55]

Major Stephen Foot, Headquarters, 2nd Tank Brigade, Tank Corps

It was as a boost to morale that the tanks did their best service that day since they were essentially offensive weapons and therefore of only limited value in the defensive. Their slow speed made them something of a liability when the salient was under threat. Whilst attempts were made to get some tanks into action, equally strenuous efforts were made to get others *away* from the Germans. This was the case with 'F' Battalion's tanks, which were mostly in a desperate state of ill-repair.

> There was very heavy firing away to our right, and our right rear by Gonnelieu, and also to our left and left rear at Bourlon and to the west of it. I did not like the sound of it much as we were right out in the salient, and it was evident that something was going on on both flanks and to the rear of us, but I didn't say anything to anyone except the Colonel as I did not want to frighten worn-out men. While I was talking to him, a staff officer arrived white as a sheet, and with the wind right up him, and said to us quietly that: 'The Boche is back in La Vacquerie and coming on, and if you don't get on now you will be surrounded.' Then he pushed off 'toot sweet'.[56]

Major Philip Hamond, No. 18 Company, 'F' Battalion, Tank Corps

Colonel Summers and Hamond agreed that the former would evacuate the men and stores, whilst the latter would stay with a few men to drive the movable tanks.

> I warned everyone to get ready quickly to go at once, and took the men I wanted up to the tanks to get them started. They all thought I had got the wind up about the shelling. Do you think I could get either officers

or men to get a move on, not a bit of it! They messed about collecting blankets and rubbish, and all the time I was cursing this adder of horrible knowledge in my bosom. At last in desperation, I said, 'Damn you, can't you get busy? If you want to hear something worth knowing, the Boche is damned near behind you at this moment, and in another hour he will get you if you don't buzz off.' You never saw such a change come over any proceedings, the whole lot had got their kit and were fallen in in the yard to march off in about two seconds. They shot about on the *pavé* until the sparks came off their boot heels. I handed them over to a section commander and they marched off.[57]

Major Philip Hamond, No. 18 Company, 'F' Battalion, Tank Corps

Hamond was successful in getting the movable tanks away, but others had to be left in the hope they could be recovered later.

Ten miles to the northwest, at Bapaume, there were chaotic scenes as 61st Division, already on its way to join Third Army, suddenly received the news that provided an additional imperative for their move:

As soon as we were clear of the station, the CO received orders from a Staff Officer of V Corps to the following effect: 'The enemy attacked this morning and have broken through. They have got as far as Gouzeaucourt already. The 61st Division has been transferred to V Corps. You will fall your battalion out on the field at the side of the road as soon as you are clear of the town. Motor omnibuses are on their way to take you up to the battle front.' A fine 'kettle of fish'. The transport have gone by road and will not get into this area till late tonight. All our Lewis Guns, Bombs, etc. are on the transport! I have not even got a Box Respirator or a Steel Helmet! Everyone is full of rumours, many of them of a very alarming nature.[58]

Captain James Wyatt, 2/4th Gloucestershire Regiment, 183rd Infantry Brigade, 61st Division

Major Geoffrey Christie Miller, 2/1st Oxfordshire & Buckingham-shire Light Infantry, was equally appalled by the poor staff work that left the division so ill-equipped for immediate action:

Infantry battalions were entrained without any Lewis Guns or stores as these came down from Arras by road on the regimental transport,

357

which also carried the SAA* reserve, bombs and rifle grenades. The Bucks who shared a train with another infantry battalion were met at Bapaume by a somewhat excited staff officer who announced that the Huns had broken through, and that motor 'buses' were waiting in the station yard to convey both battalions to the line, and that our CO as the senior officer was to take command of the half-brigade . . . The feelings of the CO can be imagined when asked to take command of two battalions with no Staff, no information, no maps beyond ½ inch-scale (and not many of these), no Lewis guns and no reserve of SAA.[59]

Major Geoffrey Christie Miller, 2/1st (Bucks) Oxfordshire & Buckinghamshire Light Infantry, 184th Brigade, 61st Division

Nevertheless, given the seeming scale of the developing crisis, there was no other choice – although the prospects of action under such circumstances looked bleak for 61st Division.

General de Lisle's escape from near-capture had been a clear enough sign of the seriousness of the situation, but of greater significance was the very real danger developing for the men of his division from the success of the German advance against 12th Division's left-hand neighbours, 20th Division. This advance soon enabled the attackers to threaten the right rear of 29th Division in and around Masnières and Marcoing.

Initially, the defenders of 20th Division had thought the German attack was only against the divisions to their south. When it became clear that this was not the case and their own front was threatened, they soon discovered just how difficult it was to defend their positions. There was something absurd in George McMurtrie's introduction to this violent day of battle:

I was eating some Devonshire cream and a cake which I had received in a parcel from home the night before when suddenly the Germans started a very heavy bombardment. Luckily for us they did not know that we had dug in the night before in new positions and so we watched in comparative safety all their shells dropping on our old posts. Andrews had not returned from Battalion HQ and so the command of

* Small Arms Ammunition, i.e. rifle ammunition.

the company fell on me. I immediately got everybody standing to. After almost 15 minutes shelling, we saw Germans advancing. We had plenty of ammunition so opened fire on them. We soon stopped them as they were being killed in huge numbers and we had all our Lewis guns firing in a most perfect manner.[60]

Second Lieutenant George McMurtrie, 7th Somerset Light Infantry, 61st Brigade, 20th Division

The division's defence scheme was clear and simple and McMurtrie understood his role within it. However, putting it into practice proved a far more difficult proposition:

The plan of defence was as follows: we were holding an outpost line but against any big attack we were to withdraw to the main line of defence where we should be reinforced and where we were to fight to the last. For a time I held on in our posts firing away at the Germans and for the time being stopped them. Soon, however, the battalion on our right withdrew and thus our right flank was threatened. Almost immediately the Germans started working round my right flank and so I gave the signal to withdraw.[61]

Second Lieutenant George McMurtrie, 7th Somerset Light Infantry, 61st Brigade, 20th Division

For the men of the division's reserve brigade, the skilful use of smoke and gas by the Germans from the outset of the attack disguised any clear indication of the attack's progress:

We could not see the front, but we could hear our artillery firing as quickly as they could load the guns. Very soon after this the Germans lengthened their range; their barrage was now concentrated just in front of the sunken road where we were. I was ordered to proceed at once to my observation post in the rear as best I could. When I got there an astonishing sight met my eyes. On our brigade front I could see our troops retreating with the Germans following them. The enemy were then amongst our batteries.[62]

Captain Geoffrey Dugdale, Headquarters, 60th Brigade, 20th Division

60th Brigade soon also became a target for the German guns and news began to filter back from the division's front:

All of a sudden the enemy opens heavy drum fire upon us; at first just in front, then their barrage lifts, and they are shelling these trenches and the shells are flying over us into the village of Gouzeaucourt behind. A runner appears with the news that the enemy are counter-attacking in force, and that our men are falling back from the forward positions. I dash up the steps of the dugout. The shells are whizzing and crashing all around now, and I have to take myself in hand before I can find the courage to leap from the top step of the dugout. Once in the trench I am alright again and running forward to join my party who are manning our old front line. On our right our men are retiring past us in small parties, carrying Lewis guns and equipment. The situation is a nasty one. I can see our own men occasionally and the enemy not at all, but there is a barrage before and behind us and the smoke is very thick.[63]

Captain Horace Raymond Smith, 12th Rifle Brigade, 60th Brigade, 20th Division.

George McMurtrie's battalion, like all those in 61st Brigade and many in 59th, had much of their strength in the vulnerable forward positions of the outpost line. The Germans attacked in such strength and advanced so swiftly that many defenders of these outpost positions were rapidly overwhelmed and what should, theoretically, have been a steady withdrawal to the main defence line became, in several places, an uncontrolled rout.

German aeroplanes began coming over, flying about 60 feet above us and firing their machine-guns into us as we withdrew. Men were falling right and left, the Company Sergeant Major fell and I thought he was shot through the head. My puttee began to come down and so I tore it off. I sent a runner to Battalion HQ to tell the CO that we had withdrawn. After an awful race, we at last got to the main line of resistance only to find that we were almost surrounded and there were no other troops to reinforce us, so I gave the order to withdraw still further back as we had no chance of doing any harm to the advancing Germans and it was simply a waste of life to remain there.[64]

Second Lieutenant George McMurtrie, 7th Somerset Light Infantry, 61st Brigade, 20th Division

McMurtrie could sense the onset of panic in those around him. Desperation prompted a desperate response:

> We went a little further back and came across some more men. I turned round and tried to stop them all. Everyone wished to clear out, everyone was out for himself and his own preservation. I remembered a lecture that we had had at Sandhurst by a Staff Sergeant and he had told us that if withdrawing and the men tried to run away, then get out your revolver and threaten them and if that was not enough, shoot some of them. This was a similar situation, all the men had panicked and just commanding them was not enough. The place we had got to was quite a good place for making a stand and so I cocked my revolver and started threatening them with it. Immediately they turned around and faced the enemy and began firing away again. I saw Jenks doing the same thing further down on the left. For a time this was alright but the enemy kept on advancing, their aeroplanes were firing down on us, they had their machine-guns playing on us unmercifully and once more they started getting round our right flank.[65]

Second Lieutenant George McMurtrie, 7th Somerset Light Infantry, 61st Brigade, 20th Division

What artillery support the infantry had was soon overwhelmed by accurate German gunfire and it was a similar case with the machine-gun companies. Once again infantry, engineers and gunners fled back towards La Vacquerie and Welsh Ridge and the gains made on 20 November were abandoned to the Germans.

> Jenks and I decided to withdraw further back, hoping that reinforcements would turn up. We gave the signal to withdraw and we went back, across the La Vacquerie valley to some half-dug German trenches and here we made another stand. Jenks was hit through the chest and so I helped him along till some stretcher-bearers took him. I saw Paul, the signals officer, firing away just by the light railway. There were some Cornwalls in the trench when we got there and soon a major turned up and took command.[66]

Second Lieutenant George McMurtrie, 7th Somerset Light Infantry, 61st Brigade, 20th Division

This was Major James Macmillan, commanding 7th Duke of Cornwall's Light Infantry, who for a time led an effective defence here. However, when Macmillan was killed, a further retirement became necessary.

> Across the other side of the valley we saw the Germans advancing in huge numbers and they soon got round our right flank once more. We therefore had to withdraw under very heavy machine-gun fire. We went back several hundred yards to a sunken road which we lined and here we brought the enemy at last to a standstill. By this time I had lost all my men and so went around looking for them. There were no signs of any near me and so I reported to the nearest company commander who happened to be in the 11th Battalion, Rifle Brigade.[67]
>
> Second Lieutenant George McMurtrie, 7th Somerset Light Infantry, 61st Brigade, 20th Division

The Rifle Brigade battalion was, in fact, part of 59th Brigade – indicating the extent to which the defenders were now a rather heterogeneous mix of units of the division. Despite the still-present dangers, McMurtrie felt relief at his survival. With this relief, inevitably, came a flood of other emotions:

> I was under someone's command and I had no responsibility; I was therefore able to think of myself. My nerves went then and for the rest of the day and all the night I was in rather a bad state. I could not help thinking of what a narrow escape I had had from either being killed, wounded or taken prisoner. During the German attack, I never thought I should get back. We had no support from the artillery, not one of our aeroplanes appeared and there we were under a hail of machine-gun bullets both from aeroplanes and the attacking troops, shells bursting everywhere.[68]
>
> Second Lieutenant George McMurtrie, 7th Somerset Light Infantry, 61st Brigade, 20th Division

20th Division's defence had been greatly weakened by the decision of its commander, Major General William Douglas Smith, to send several units of his reserve brigade, 60th, to assist 12th Division when the first German attack was launched. Yet the divisional commander's implacability in the face of the developing crisis impressed, and reassured, those around him.

The scene at divisional headquarters at Villers Plouich was sensational. There were crowds of officers from the division on our right, many of them in a state of undress, but although it was reported at the time that these officers were caught in their pyjamas I did not see any myself; the General received me in his dugout perfectly calmly. He said he was very pleased to see me; would I have a cup of tea? He also said that as far as the 61st Brigade was concerned he had no idea where they were, and he would be very glad if I would tell him something about them. I did my best to explain what had happened, and showed him our position on the map.[69]

Captain Geoffrey Dugdale, Headquarters, 60th Brigade, 20th Division

Yet amongst the ranks too there were those who could remain calm in any crisis:

Hours pass and we still hang on, with apparently no supporting troops on either flank. At length a runner appears with news that the Boches are in Gouzeaucourt, immediately in our rear. He also brings a message from Battalion Headquarters that I am to occupy a short sector of Chalk Trench to the right of our present position. We settle down in the new line and despite the fact we are being shelled more heavily now, my servant places a spirit stove on the floor of the trench and calmly proceeds to make tea![70]

Captain Horace Raymond Smith, 12th Rifle Brigade, 20th Division

20th Division's position had been difficult to hold and the defenders were quickly thrown back. Their defence on the slopes of Welsh Ridge stopped the German advance to some extent but pushed it off course in a northerly direction. It now became a very real possibility that Masnières would be lost and, with it, the men of two brigades of 29th Division on the east side of the canal would be cut off and forced to surrender. In a very real sense, the actions of one man were about to play a very important part in saving a whole division and preventing an even greater disaster for the BEF.

The initial frontal attack on 29th Division had been beaten back chiefly by rifle and machine-gun fire. None of the attackers got within 400 yards of the main position. However the division was only very weakly

supported by artillery. What guns there were were soon almost overwhelmed by the tasks they were called upon to perform, since the
breakthrough on 20th Division's front meant large numbers of German
infantry were streaming towards Marcoing and across the division's
rear. They entered Les Rues Vertes, capturing an entire Royal Engineers company and an advanced dressing station and putting the
canal crossings under direct threat.

Les Rues Vertes was in 86th Brigade's rear area and home to the
brigade's grenade and ammunition dumps – the responsibility of
Captain Robert Gee, the brigade's 43-year-old Staff Captain. Gee was
a seasoned veteran with over 21 years' service in the ranks before
receiving a wartime commission. Contrary to the image of the effete
staff officer, Gee was a hard man; his personal weaponry included a
heavy stick shod with a cavalry lance head. At 8.00 a.m., Brigadier
General 'Ronnie' Cheape had telephoned Gee, informing him of the

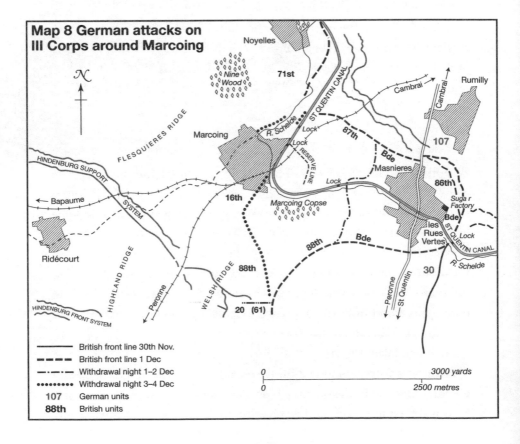

German breakthrough and ordering him to form a defensive flank immediately. Gee's available forces consisted of twelve orderlies and signallers and 200 men of 1st Guernsey Light Infantry, many of whom had no ammunition.

Nevertheless, Gee set about his task with a will. He established a secure left flank on the canal and then, accompanied by six men, concentrated on defence of the village itself. Evacuation of his position, and loss of the brigade dumps, was unthinkable. Yet, almost immediately, he saw German infantry in fours marching down the La Vacquerie road. Gee despatched one man to fetch a Lewis gun and two more to get material to form a barricade; another was killed by the Germans. However, the deadly rifle fire of Gee and his remaining companions prevented the German infantry rushing them and a barricade of chairs, tables and a feather-bed was constructed. Gee informed the others that this was bullet-proof, but when the Lewis gun arrived, it was found necessary to blow a hole through the feather-bed as it was too big to fire over, somewhat undermining his assertion. With this block established, Gee went to check the brigade ammunition store and the rest of the village. Sensing he was being followed, he turned and laid out his pursuer with a blow from his stick, breaking it in the process. It was one of his own men.

Discovering the ammunition dump guards dead, at this point Gee was set upon by two Germans. He reacted by driving the point of his stick into the stomach of one man and then struggled with the other. A sudden rifle shot at very close range killed the German. It was fired by the man whom Gee had previously rendered unconscious. Shortly afterwards, Gee's rescuer was killed by German rifle fire.

Gee then organized bombing attacks to drive the Germans out of the houses before leading a special party to clear the brewery, the Germans' last foothold in Les Rues Vertes. This was accomplished with little opposition but when Gee saw a German machine-gun entrenched near the La Vacquerie road he rushed it and, using his two revolvers to good effect, killed the crew.

Gee was later wounded in the knee and ordered by Brigadier General Cheape to get treatment in Marcoing. On the way, however, he was forced to evade capture by jumping in the canal and swimming across to safety. The subsequent award of the Victoria Cross was well merited.

Gee's inspired defence of Les Rues Vertes was a model of its type and formed a breakwater against the tide of the German attack. It allowed his brigade commander time to organize the village for all-round defence from which the 'besieged' and the surviving supporting artillery could frustrate the German onslaught.

> We were encircled. About 10.45 a.m., the 15th Brigade RHA, who were completely isolated, were obliged to abandon their guns, all of which were captured. Very shortly after this German infantry appeared on the crest above us. I turned two batteries on to them. This was not easy, as they were on our right rear, but we got our guns round in time, and were able to hold them up until some of our infantry were found to counter-attack, when the Germans were driven back on to the crest beyond. All day my batteries were hanging on by their eyelids, expecting to be cut off at any moment. But the men were as steady as rocks. The 29th Division infantry didn't yield a yard of ground, in spite of heavy attacks. If they had broken it would have meant the whole line going. I constituted myself CRA,* collected another brigade and organised a defensive barrage. Very weak it was, but it sufficed, and we were able to give the infantry a good deal of support.[71]
>
> Lieutenant Colonel Walter Murray, 17th Brigade, RFA, 29th Division

The advent of the German attack again prompted the hasty withdrawal of units (especially of non-combatants) out of its path. However, the absence of a heavy German attack on Marcoing meant that infantry there were soon able to come to the relief of the besieged 86th Brigade. Company after company of infantry from Marcoing marched out of the village and came into action on the slopes of Welsh Ridge. This counter-attack drove the Germans back until a line was established facing south from Les Rues Vertes and linking up with the defensive positions established by 20th Division.

At about 12.30 p.m. 1st Guards Brigade reached Gouzeaucourt Wood and learned that the village itself was occupied by the Germans.

---

* Commander Royal Artillery, i.e. a division's chief artillery officer.

Meanwhile, 3rd Guards Brigade followed on. Champion de Cres-pigny's immediate response on assessing the situation at Gouzeaucourt was to order an attack, despite the absence of artillery support. Three Guards battalions had been drawn up behind the crest of the high ground west of the village prior to their advance in immaculate forma-tion over the ridge.

> The ridge beyond Gouzeaucourt Wood was held by a thin line of dismounted cavalry and some tanks, and it was a stirring sight, that visibly shamed some faint-hearted stragglers, to see a battalion of the Irish Guards come up to the counter-attack as if they were in Hyde Park, marching at attention with their band playing.[72]
>
> Lieutenant Frederick John Salmon, 3rd Field Survey Company, Royal Engineers

The battalions deployed into assault waves and stormed on into the village through German artillery and machine-gun fire. The tanks had little chance to cooperate.

> My next memory was seeing the Guards Division in line, counter-attacking between Gouzeaucourt and Gonnelieu. I swung left behind them and staggered after them. I don't remember the tank firing a shot, but it may have, by this time I had become an automaton. I just drove.[73]
>
> Second Lieutenant George Parsons, No. 26 Company, 'I' Battalion, Tank Corps

Private Norman Cliff, a stretcher-bearer with 2nd Grenadier Guards, recalled the attack and the need for the Guards to conduct themselves in a manner befitting their status:

> We felt 'We are the Guards. We'll show them,' and we knew we had to keep cool, and maintain a disciplined line. Orders were passed along verbally. Over undulating down we went, and still no sign of Germans, but when we drew near Gouzeaucourt Wood and, crossing a deserted trench, reached the crest of a hill, they met us with a blizzard of fire. Mates fell on all sides, and the order came to fall back to the trench. Many wounded were left behind, and I crept out and started to drag in a heavy fellow badly wounded in the legs. It wasn't easy going and, desperately, I appealed to him: 'Make an effort, chum.' 'Effort be damned!' he exclaimed, and it struck me as so comic a situation, with

bullets spattering around, that I had to pause and chuckle before resuming the pull to the trench. Helping hands hauled him over the parapet to safety, and that was the last I saw or heard of him. He must have been swiftly carried to the rear. As I fell into the trench someone said 'You'll get the DCM for that' and, emotionally tensed as I was, I retorted angrily 'Don't talk like that!' and broke down in tears.[74]

Private Norman Cliff, 2nd Grenadier Guards, 1st Guards Brigade, Guards Division

Any check to the advance was only temporary and the village was soon taken. Those Germans occupying Gouzeaucourt that were not killed or captured retreated quickly. The recapture of Gouzeaucourt had, indeed, been so rapidly accomplished that it even took other British units by surprise – so much so that the Guards narrowly missed being shelled by their own artillery:

At about noon all the Divisional Headquarters signallers, cooks, orderlies, etc attached themselves to our line and a few tanks came up. We were ordered to do a counter-attack on Gouzeaucourt at 2.00 p.m. Very shortly before this hour we were suddenly informed that the Guards had retaken the place. We did not know they were there even, but they came in on the left flank much to our surprise. Of course I had no telephone communication with the rear or I would have called for an artillery barrage of sorts I expect, and then what would have happened to the Guards?![75]

Lieutenant Colonel Tom Wollocombe, 11th Middlesex, 36th Brigade, 12th Division

After the Guards' attack, there was a pause before cavalry and tanks made separate attempts to drive the Germans back still further.

The tanks went on ahead and, when the cavalry came up, they streamed over the hill and rode down into the valley. They did not get far. On the opposite side of the valley to where I was, the Boches had installed one of our 18-pounder batteries which they had captured (not from our Division) and they fired point blank at the advancing cavalry.[76]

Captain Guy Chipperfield, 11th Middlesex, 36th Brigade, 12th Division

Chipperfield mistakenly thought the cavalry were from the Royal Scots Greys, but they were in fact 8th Hussars and 12th Lancers from 5th Cavalry Division. Their objective was Gauche Wood:

Through my glasses I could see the Boches round the guns, see the flash and then the burst on our side. Some of the shells landed right amongst the horses, knocking out several, and the rest turned and took flight, bolting madly back again. Some of the Greys succeeded in getting inside the trajectory of the guns and rode right past where our men were deployed, several being kicked. I saw one little section, their officer twenty yards or so in front heading for the guns and then disappear in one of the numerous sunken roads.[77]

Captain Guy Chipperfield, 11th Middlesex, 36th Brigade, 12th Division

Somewhere between Gouzeaucourt and Gonnelieu, Geoffrey Dugdale watched as 20th Division's reserve brigade arrived to bolster the survivors of 12th Division before launching their own counter blow, supported by dismounted Indian cavalry.

I had a wonderful view of the counter-attack made by the 60th Brigade and the Guards. They put up a wonderful show, driving the Germans out of Gouzeaucourt and part of Gonnelieu . . . An SOS at this time was sent for the cavalry to come to the rescue. Their arrival gave us great encouragement and was a magnificent sight. They dismounted and came into the battle as infantry.[78]

Captain Geoffrey Dugdale, Headquarters, 60th Brigade, 20th Division

Further north, on 12th Division's left flank, Smelzer's Buffs battalion had finally been forced back to a position between the Hindenburg support and front trench systems. Wilfrid Taylor, still lying where Sapper Ferguson had dressed his wounds close to the Buffs HQ, watched the last of the retirement:

The situation continued until at last the men began to give ground, and about 3.00 p.m. the last of the battalion passed me; they had put up a splendid fight against hopeless odds. Now as the men passed me I received much sympathy and many cheery messages from amongst them.[79]

Second Lieutenant Wilfrid Taylor, 6th Buffs, 37th Brigade, 12th Division

The imminent possibility of capture raised a thorny problem for Taylor:

I had realised by now that I might be captured, and I therefore threw away a small automatic pistol which I had in my possession, and which had once belonged to a German officer. To my surprise, however, the enemy did not come on at once, and when darkness came soon after 4.00 p.m., I saw that I was lying in a new No Man's Land, and that the Very lights were going up on either side of me, those from friend and foe alike being fired as it seemed some hundreds of yards away.[80]

Second Lieutenant Wilfrid Taylor, 6th Buffs, 37th Brigade, 12th Division

His battalion still held on grimly to their new position, but there were not sufficient reinforcements to recapture more lost ground. Taylor was, without any effort on his part, in the worst possible situation for medical care.

I still hoped that some friendly stretcher-bearer might be on the prowl, so I shouted at intervals till about 10.00 p.m., but my efforts met with no success. Meantime it had become piercingly cold, the ground was freezing, and it became apparent that if I lay where I was, I must inevitably freeze to death. Moreover I had no food or water, and only one blanket as covering, which Ferrie had found for me before he left.[81]

Second Lieutenant Wilfrid Taylor, 6th Buffs, 37th Brigade, 12th Division

The cold ultimately prompted Taylor into action:

I began to entertain the wild thought of trying to crawl towards our lines . . . Then I remembered the dugout, the entrance of which lay a few yards behind my head as I was lying, and I determined to try and get down it for shelter. I pulled myself along backwards towards it, and commenced to descend the stairs feet foremost.[82]

Second Lieutenant Wilfrid Taylor, 6th Buffs, 37th Brigade, 12th Division

Taylor was to spend most of the rest of the night in his attempt to get shelter from the elements.

Throughout the day German attacks continued but British rein-forcements of all kinds were coming up now and, after the Germans had been driven out of Gouzeaucourt, a defensive line of sorts was re-established along most of the southern flank of the salient by mid-afternoon. Yet the Germans had made considerable gains and inflicted heavy losses on the 55th, 12th, 20th and 29th Divisions – despite suffering heavily themselves. Although the defence held, however, the danger was by no means over. In particular, the situation of 86th and

87th Brigades on the eastern side of the canal was still precarious and it was clear that the Germans would make further attacks in the morning. Third Army therefore issued orders in the evening for a counter-attack to be made by VII and III Corps, with support from the Cavalry Corps and any available tanks, early on the following day. Zero was eventually fixed for 6.30 a.m.

The attack on the northern flank of the salient was markedly different to the attack from the south. Generalleutnant Otto von Moser's *Arras Group* intended to achieve success by using massed artillery to support the four assault divisions. Since the attack began well after those of the *Caudry* and *Busigny Groups*, there was no likelihood of achieving surprise. Instead, the infantry were supported by the fire of 390 light and 118 heavy guns and accompanied by more than a hundred low-flying aircraft. Gas was also used in great quantities. The assault fell on 59th, 47th and 2nd Divisions of IV Corps (all of whom had moved into the line after the Corps' last attempts to take Fontaine and Bourlon on 27 November) and 56th Division on the left who had been in the line since the British offensive opened.

From dawn onwards, whilst events were taking their dramatic course in the south, a staggering artillery duel developed on the northern flank:

> Fritz started a very intense bombardment at about 7.30 a.m., which developed into a barrage, besides shelling all roads and tracks leading to the guns and trenches, making it very difficult to get ammunition up.[83]
>
> Driver William Grant, 173rd Brigade, RFA, 36th Division

A large proportion of Third Army's heavy guns were still able to bring fire to bear on this flank from locations around Louverval and Demicourt to the south-west of Bourlon Wood. But German heavy artillery fire continued to bombard the British positions along, and on either side of, the Bapaume–Cambrai road throughout the day. It was one such shell that claimed the day's most noted casualty. Brigadier General Roland Bradford's 186th Brigade was in reserve near Lock 6 on the Canal du Nord. The precocious 25-year-old was fatally wounded in the spine by a shell splinter at some time between 10.00

a.m. and 2.00 p.m. whilst visiting units of his command. His death was a shocking loss, as his divisional commander acknowledged:

> He was a very exceptional man, though only a boy, and would have risen to any height in his profession. His power of command was quite extraordinary. He certainly knew every officer in his Brigade, although he had only commanded it for quite a short time, and I honestly believe he knew every non-commissioned officer, and a great many of the privates. He had extraordinary personality, and that personality, linked with his undoubted military genius, made him a very extraordinary character and a very valuable commander of men.[84]
>
> Major General Walter Braithwaite, 62nd Division

The artillery duel continued, but at 8.50 a.m., the Germans' field guns and *Minenwerfer* launched a fierce hurricane bombardment of the British front line prior to the infantry assault. The first effort was made towards Cantaing on 59th Division's front on the British right at 9.00 a.m. but this was broken up by British artillery. From this point forward, the story was of a series of separate, distinct, repeated and determined attacks at different start times against the four British divisions. In many cases, the German infantry massing for these attacks were subjected to withering artillery and machine-gun fire and smashed before, or soon after, they began their attack – as was the case with a second attack on 59th Division at 11.00 a.m. However, where the assault was pressed with greater resolve, there were frantic struggles.

The front trenches occupied by 47th Division in particular, dug when the British advance had first taken this ground a week before and hardly improved since, offered little cover from the *Minenwerfer* fire and the casualties began to mount.

> An order now came along for every man with a rifle to line the trench, and immediately we surmised that Fritz was counter-attacking. The Labour Companies had to turn out into the trench and I felt sorry for them, as they were mostly elderly men, and didn't handle their rifles as if they were used to them – I don't suppose many of them had fired a shot previously on active service, as their duties were trench digging, road making, etc. Still, they were to be useful now. This was my first taste of being amongst the attacked, and it wasn't a very pleasant

sensation. Although we were in the support position, our boys were firing rapidly at masses of Germans who were advancing down a slope some distance away and this, together with the fire of the front line troops, kept Fritz at bay.[85]

Private Frank Dunham, 1/7th London Regiment, 140th Infantry Brigade, 47th Division

On the left, 56th Division's artillery acted as soon as the Germans were seen preparing to attack.

From the bank just above my battle headquarters we had an excellent view of Bourlon Wood and the surrounding country. At 9.00 a.m. we could see at least 3 battalions of Germans coming over the open at us, and with his field guns being brought into position by horse teams. Needless to say not a moment was lost in getting our own artillery on to them and their columns were severely cut up. However, their attack was by no means entirely stopped, and my men had a long and bitter bombing fight in the trenches – the Boches *nearly* turned us out, but we counter-attacked and succeeded in keeping our positions. The fight continued until about 4.00 p.m. and it was a long and anxious day for us all.[86]

Brigadier General Edward Coke, Headquarters, 169th Brigade, 56th Division

A Royal Engineers officer, Kenneth Palmer, was watching from a reserve trench as the German advance commenced.

Never have I seen so many Germans, the whole forward landscape seemed literally alive with them; thousands of them were attacking; they looked like swarms of insects covering the landscape but those insects had a very nasty sting in their tails.[87]

Lieutenant Kenneth Palmer, 513th Field Company, RE, 56th Division

In many cases the Germans came on in massed assault waves and thus presented excellent targets. Nevertheless, to one watching German officer, viewing the panorama of battle from a reserve position, events seemed to be progressing well:

At 9 o'clock* our artillery broke into heavy bursts of fire, and increased between 11.45 and 11.50 to drum-fire. Bourlon Wood, which owing to

* German time.

373

the strength of its defences had been left out of the frontal attack, disappeared under yellowish-green clouds of gas. At 11.50 we saw the attacking waves through glasses, as they emerged upon the vacant expanse of shell-holes; while further back, batteries harnessed up and raced forward to new positions. A German scout shot down an English captive balloon in flames, and the observer jumped out with a parachute.[88]

Leutnant Ernst Jünger, *Füsilier Regiment 73, 111th Division*

What Jünger did not see was the manner in which the attackers advancing from Quarry Wood towards 2nd Division were subjected to enfilade fire by 47th Division and by artillery and machine-guns in positions north of the sugar factory on the Bapaume–Cambrai road. This drove the Germans westwards and, soon after midday, they were seen retreating in disorder back over Bourlon Ridge. The artillery of the British 36th Division, operating in support of 2nd Division, worked all out to perform its job:

About 11.30 a.m. all wagon teams were ordered up with ammunition, the gun teams and limbers being ordered to go up and wait behind the guns, in case of emergency, as we got the news that the Germans had broken through on our right at Gouzeaucourt and Fins and was likely to get in on our rear. From our Observation Post we got the news that the German cavalry were coming up the crest that lay in front of our guns, so all the guns were laid on the crest, and got on them just right. One Section of our 'B' Battery was firing point blank into them, as well as one battery out of the 2nd Division who we were covering. About 1.30 p.m. things began to die down a bit as we had stopped him on our front and drove him back to where he had started, but we could still hear them hard at it on our right.[89]

Driver William Grant, 173rd Brigade, RFA, 36th Division

Whilst this attack was in progress, a major crisis for 2nd Division occurred on the left where 6th Brigade was astride the Canal du Nord. Here the 13th Essex beat back an attack at 9.30 a.m. with rifle and Lewis-gun fire but, an hour later, the German artillery fired a 'box barrage' around Lock 5, thereby isolating 'D' Company and preventing its reinforcement. Repeated attempts were made under covering fire from mortars and artillery to reach the survivors. All failed. Their Commander-in-Chief subsequently described their fate and paid tribute to these brave men in his Official Despatch describing the battle:

> After maintaining a splendid and successful resistance throughout the day, at 4.00 p.m., this company held a council of war at which the two remaining company officers, the Company Sergeant Major, and the platoon Sergeants were present, and unanimously determined to fight to the last and have 'no surrender'. Two runners who were sent to notify this decision to Battalion Headquarters succeeded in getting through to our line and delivered their message. During the remainder of the afternoon and far into the following night this gallant company were heard fighting, and there is little room for doubt that they carried out to a man their heroic resolution.[90]
>
> Field Marshal Sir Douglas Haig, General Headquarters, BEF

This 'forlorn hope' held out for 22 hours until 7.20 a.m. on the following morning when the exhausted men were overwhelmed. Their defence was a first-class example of the spirit in which the infantry conducted themselves on that day.

On the right of 2nd Division's front, 17th Royal Fusiliers responded in similar fashion when attacked whilst attempting to withdraw some of its men from advanced positions in the Hindenburg Support Line. Desperate fighting, in which a party of men under Captain Walter Stone fought to the last, eventually drove the attackers off and re-established the defensive line. Stone was posthumously awarded the Victoria Cross. The situation was deemed serious enough to warrant reserves from 5th Brigade being hurried forward to reinforce 2nd Division amidst an atmosphere of potential panic.

> I said to myself, 'Now we are for it,' and at noon the 52nd [i.e. the Ox. & Bucks. Light Infantry] moved up to support the two brigades in the front line. We stayed at Lock 7 for some time and then orders were received for the regiment to counter-attack the Sugar Factory on the Bapaume–Cambrai road. As a matter of fact this factory had never been captured by the enemy though it was being pasted to hell.[91]
>
> Captain James Neville, 2nd Oxfordshire & Buckinghamshire Light Infantry, 5th Brigade, 2nd Division

Such misleading reports were not uncommon, but many of the support troops such as artillery and engineers were well aware of events to the south and there was a general unease at the prospect of being attacked from the rear.

Throughout the day there was a grim and deadly struggle west of the Canal du Nord where a German attack from the shattered remains of Moeuvres drew into the fighting elements of four British battalions before the old German front line could be held and consolidated. Mortar shells and grenades flew thickly and both sides had many killed or grievously wounded. It is difficult to convey the combination of determination, fear, resilience and animal instinct that drove men on in such terrible circumstances. Yet their survival depended on answering such German fury with even greater ferocity.

For the British defenders, there was another serious crisis shortly after 2.00 p.m. when a renewed German attack after a heavy bombardment drove a wedge between 47th and 2nd Divisions. The situation was restored by a counter-attack by men of the reserve and headquarters companies of 1/6th London Regiment 'The Cast-Iron Sixth', and the line was restored. There were further crises for 56th Division as well but where defensive positions could not be held, several battalions successfully conducted fighting withdrawals – usually to the former German front line. In at least one case, an additional retirement to the original British front line was contemplated, but proved unnecessary with the onset of night – although fighting continued in the form of fierce bombing attacks in the darkness.

German designs for the northern offensive had definitely been foiled on this day by the courageous resistance of the British infantry. Equally, the many heavy artillery batteries used by IV Corps in the British attacks towards Bourlon Wood remained in position until the German assault opened and did much to interrupt the work of their opposite numbers; fire was truly met with fire. The manner in which, after years of offensive operations, the divisions conducted themselves in the defence was admirable and, for the high command, offered considerable reassurance regarding discipline and morale. All four British divisions faced, and repulsed, massed German infantry attacks and endured artillery fire perhaps more powerful and intense than they had ever previously encountered. For the German infantry, acceptance of failure came slowly:

> At eleven o'clock I got orders to proceed to the former front line and to report to the CO of the battalion in the line, under whose orders the 7th Company was. I gave the order to fall in and led the company forward . . . on through overcrowded trenches to battalion headquarters. I went in and found a mob of officers and orderlies in an atmosphere that could be cut with a knife. I was told that the attack on the front had not achieved much and that it was to be renewed the next morning. The feeling in the air was not very hopeful. Two commanding officers began a long discussion with their adjutants. Now and then from the height of their bunks, that were as crowded as hen-roosts, the specialist officers threw a few crumbs into the debate. The cigar fumes were suffocating. Batmen endeavoured to cut bread for their officers in the throng. A wounded officer who burst in aroused a passing alarm with the news of an enemy bombing attack. Finally, I was able to take down my orders for the attack. I and my company were to roll up Dragon Alley and as much of the Siegfried Line as possible.[92]
>
> Leutnant Ernst Jünger, *Füsilier Regiment 73, 111th Division*

The plans to 'roll up' Dragon Alley were plainly a reversion to the bloody attritional fighting method of trench-by-trench bombing attacks to secure local tactical gains – an admission that the major attack had failed. The *Arras Group*'s losses were such that there was little, if any, prospect of recommencing large-scale operations in support of the *Caudry* and *Busigny Groups* on the following morning. Clearly the hammer was still intact to inflict further harm on the southern flank, but without an anvil in the north.

Many of the preceding accounts indicate the extent to which the hard-pressed British ground troops, frequently menaced by large numbers of low-flying German aircraft which machine-gunned and bombed British positions, remained firmly convinced that they had been let down by the 'fly boys' of the RFC. Where were *our* fliers? The truth was they were everywhere they could be. Men like McCudden were hardly likely to stand by and let Richthofen's 'circus' rule the roost, whilst others like

Arthur Lee, flying a dawn patrol and already a comparative veteran in ground-attack work, did all they could to assist the defenders.

> The clouds were low, about 2,000 feet, and heavy, and there were patches of mist. As we entered the salient just below the cloud base, looking for Huns to fight, I saw that there was great activity around Bourlon, with widespread shelling and smoke, but even more on the southern flank, for the whole area was seething with smoke, shell-bursts and Very lights. I led the flight down to 800 feet and from there we could plainly see that the Boche had broken through to a depth of 3–4 miles. Pockets of our infantry, cut off in the sudden advance, were firing lights of every colour as SOS signals. At first there wasn't a lot that we could do. It was difficult to distinguish the Boche from our troops, as they were deployed and our people were scattered. We couldn't tackle this problem in formation, so I gave the signal to break up and attack independently.[93]
>
> Lieutenant Arthur Gould Lee, 46 Squadron, RFC

Lee instantly knew what his responsibilities were in such a situation – to render whatever assistance he could to those below.

> Flying at 200 feet, I found that the Boche soldiery were too busy fighting their way forward to give much attention to me, and so when I dived to attack, the job was akin to beating up rear areas. But the trouble was to find groups sufficiently large to attack, and with such fleeting targets you had to be very careful not to put your shots into fleeting targets in khaki![94]
>
> Lieutenant Arthur Gould Lee, 46 Squadron, RFC

However, the work of Lee and those like him was rendered much more difficult and dangerous by the presence of *Schlachtstaffeln* or 'battle-flights' of two-seater German Halberstadt aircraft which were used in force for the first time. These, in turn, were protected by large numbers of Albatros scout aircraft flying above them, waiting for any opportunity to pounce on their British opposite numbers. Much of the 'normal' work of artillery spotting, aerial observation and reconnaissance and contact patrols performed by the aircraft from both sides suffered as a consequence. Air fighting largely revolved around scouts supporting ground attack aircraft. McCudden was not to be diverted from his purpose though and, after an indecisive clash with Albatros scouts over Bourlon Wood, he shot down a reconnaissance two-seater:

> I now saw seven two-seater machines coming west over Cantaing, so we flew to the attack, and I settled my opponent at once, for he started gliding down emitting clouds of steam. While I had been tackling him the enemy gunner had hit my radiator with an explosive bullet which knocked a big hole in it, so, having to go down in any case, I landed alongside the Hun. Just as I had almost stopped my wheels ran into a small shell-hole and my machine stood gracefully on its nose. I got out and, after having pulled the tail down, ran over to where the Hun was and found the pilot having a tourniquet put on his arm, for he was badly shot, whilst the German gunner, a weedy-looking specimen, looked on very disconsolately. The pilot died on the way to hospital, and the gunner, a Corporal, was marched off.[95]
>
> Captain James McCudden, 56 Squadron, RFC

The damage to his aircraft effectively wrote McCudden out of further involvement in the day's air fighting but it was doubtful if he alone could have prevented *Jagdgeschwader I* enjoying considerable success on that day. Sheer weight of numbers, rather than the skill of the individual 'ace', was now ensuring a sea-change in the character of aerial warfare. Richthofen's 'circus' operated in such strength on the day that it greatly increased its chances of inflicting grievous harm on the RFC. One of the Rittmeister's charges distilled some of the essence of Richthofen's outstanding abilities when recalling how he had shot down a DH5 fighter over Bourlon Wood.

> Immediately after the landing, Richthofen congratulated me, but at the same time rebuked me because after my first attack I had not followed the crippled aircraft into the first turn. I had had to turn away because of the attack by another Englishman who, as we used to say in front-line German, 'was spitting into my crate from behind'. I mention this to show how closely Richthofen kept watch over the whole battle scene.[96]
>
> Leutnant Georg von der Osten, Jasta 11, Jagdgeschwader I

Here was utter ruthlessness, combined with an ability to observe with clinical detachment through the swirling dogfights and to pass on the lesson that might, in future, save his less-experienced fellow pilot's life and make him a more efficient killer. Richthofen himself scored his 63rd victory that day when he shot down an SE5 of No. 41 Squadron flown by Lieutenant Donald MacGregor over Moeuvres. MacGregor's aircraft went down in flames and its 22-year-old pilot was killed.

Arthur Lee had attempted to tackle one of the German ground-attack aircraft but the rear gunner was alert and Lee was forced to break off. Nevertheless, he subsequently shot down a reconnaissance plane, which crashed between Havrincourt and Flesquières. Almost immediately, however, he was attacked by three of the supporting scouts and he was forced to run for home. On his next sortie he once more pitched in with machine-gun and bomb against a variety of targets:

> I found a body of infantry moving in mass along the very road which, ten mornings ago, Charles had led 'C' Flight in the bombing of Lateau Wood. I flew along the column at 100 feet and released a bomb. The explosion jerked up my tail. With a target like this, from so low a height, I couldn't miss. It was appalling to look back as I swerved away, and see what I can only describe as a hole that the bomb had made in a crowd of human beings. Next, I saw a Camel diving. It was Robinson, who had found a big group of guns lining a hedge, and after making sure that they were Boche, I joined him, got rid of my remaining bombs as well as some long bursts with my gun. Between us we put those batteries out of business for some time.[97]
> Lieutenant Arthur Gould Lee, 46 Squadron, RFC

On his return he found the aerodrome very busy with Camels and DH5s from 3, 64 and 68 Squadrons as well as his own. All were engaged in the same work.

> Although there was an air of subdued excitement as we waited for our buses to be made ready, nobody spoke much. In fact, there was an oppressive feeling. Almost everyone had been winged in the previous jobs, and I felt that people were inwardly asking: 'How long can my luck last out?'[98]
> Lieutenant Arthur Gould Lee, 46 Squadron, RFC

By the time he was making his third sortie, Lee was doing the job mechanically – seeking out targets to bomb and firing at any groups of men in field-grey uniforms. On his fourth, he attacked a German headquarters in a house on the edge of Bourlon Wood before encountering an Albatros DV scout.

> As it slid by, I saw the pilot looking out of the further side of his cockpit at the smoke of battle below. He hadn't seen me. I swung steeply down on to his tail, and caught him up so quickly he seemed to be coming back towards me. At twenty yards' range I pressed the triggers. The tracers flashed into his back. The machine suddenly reared up vertically in front of me and I banked to the right to avoid him. He fell over sideways, and went down in a vertical dive. I swung over and followed him down for a thousand feet, but he was going too fast. He didn't pull out, and crashed west of Bourlon village.[99]
>
> Lieutenant Arthur Gould Lee, 46 Squadron, RFC

In less than ten hours, he had flown four missions, shooting down two German aircraft and attacking a variety of ground targets. He had had several near misses but was then forced down for the third time in the space of ten days.

> There was a sudden crump of 'archie'. Then crump, crump, crump. Black bursts all round me – a clang in the cowling – a thud somewhere in front. My engine stopped dead. Not even a splutter. A great blast of noise came up from below – exploding shells, guns firing, trench mortars, the rattle of machine-guns, the continuous sharp crackle of rifle fire.[100]
>
> Lieutenant Arthur Gould Lee, 46 Squadron, RFC

Without power, Lee could only glide steadily down and hope he could land on the British side of No Man's Land.

> I had to find somewhere to come down, but the ground ahead was a shamble of trees, hedges, guns firing, dumps, trenches. I spotted a short stretch of clear ground off to the right, about the size of a couple of tennis courts . . . I put her down gently, she trundled to the edge of a trench, and was pulled up by the parapet. Field guns were firing somewhere near me. I sat there tensed, waiting for it, too petrified to look around. For five long, long seconds I just didn't know whether I was a prisoner or not. Then a couple of tin helmets appeared alongside

the cockpit. I sank thankfully into my seat. They were ours, flat and
basin-like, not the Boche coal-scuttle.[101]
Lieutenant Arthur Gould Lee, 46 Squadron, RFC

The German air force's decision to strike in large formations of
ground-attack aircraft supported by concentrations of scouts meant
their interventions in the battle were significant and highly effective
(and very obvious to many of the ground troops). However, RFC losses
indicate that the British fliers were by no means passive in the face of
the offensive. But perhaps symbolic of the German air force's success on
30 November was the scene Lee witnessed with Lieutenant Mills of 'Q'
Anti-Aircraft Battery after his forced landing:

As darkness drew on, the machines gradually thinned out until only
odd ones were left. Then about twenty 'Tripes' and V-strutters appeared, in a final sweep of the salient at 3,000. Lieutenant Mills, who
had come back again, said they were the Circus. Two of them dropped
down, and one dived after a solitary DH5 that came from the Cambrai
direction, and fired successive bursts at him as they flashed across our
front twenty feet up, the DH zigzagging along the road to Bapaume,
and duly keeping to the right, I hope. The second Hun came down at
my Camel, and put a long burst into it. Mills and I dived into the trench
at the first bullet, though he did no damage that I could see. But this
little episode persuaded me that I'd had enough for one day.[102]
Lieutenant Arthur Gould Lee, 46 Squadron, RFC

Throughout the night men on both the north and south sides of
the salient worked hard in preparation for the renewal of the attacks
tomorrow. The strain and stress was appalling and the darkness full of
horrors:

The sunken roads leading from the trenches are littered with dead men
and dead mules, wrecked General Service waggons and limbers. The
night is worse than the day, as the hellish shelling continues. By the
flashes of the bursting shells one gets strange momentary pictures – the
tired, strained faces of nerve-wracked men, and the wet shining of steel
helmets, and the waterproof groundsheets which most of the men have
round their shoulders. My men work steadily on, carrying boxes of

SAA and bombs. As we leave the dump I see a man sitting beside his load – two long boxes of Mills bombs. 'I can't go on, sir; I'm done in; you see, I'm forty-eight,' he says in response to my question. I reply that it is not my fault he is out here, but I help him with his load and so we go on. There is a rending scream and a terrific crash just behind, and then a terrible half-human cry of agony. It is from a poor mule mortally wounded. Its driver appears out of the darkness and borrows my revolver to put his mule out of his agony. There is a flash and a sharp report in the darkness near at hand and there is no more screaming. The driver returns and silently hands me his revolver; there are tears in his eyes.[103]

Captain Horace Raymond Smith, 12th Rifle Brigade, 60th Brigade, 20th Division.

The slaughter of helpless animals and men did not cease. With the morning it would continue with renewed vigour in the inevitable slogging match after the first dramatic thrust of the German attack. For the Germans knew that they must test their opponent's resolve to the limits of endurance. As evening approached, it became known that the *Arras Group* had only made slight progress on either side of Bourlon Wood. But Rupprecht's particular frustration was that in the southern attack, despite repeated reminders by the Army Group, *Second Army* had failed to shift its point of main effort to the left flank of the attack. This had cost the Germans dear.

Crown Prince Rupprecht wrote in his diary: 'Although the success is nowhere near as great as we might have expected; nevertheless a painful blow has been struck against the enemy and so far 2,500 prisoners have been captured.'[104] With perhaps one more strike, who could say what all-encompassing victory might be achieved? Hadn't the British defenders been hammered into submission by the powerful combination of artillery and *Minenwerfer* fire before the survivors were driven like sheep before the infantry's assault?

Altogether nine divisions had been deployed. Yet, knowing full well that they did not have the resources to secure a major strategic victory from their initial tactical success, the German High Command, like that of the British on the evening of 21 November, now succumbed to the temptation of 'one more blow'. It remained to be seen whether 1 December would bring definite success for their plans.

CHAPTER TWELVE

'A Bad Dream'

AS NOVEMBER TURNED to December, across the battlefield the night shrouded many human stories of endurance and endeavour, tragedy and courage. For the wounded Wilfrid Taylor, the hours of darkness centred on an agony of effort to descend twenty-five steps to the relative security and warmth of a deep dugout.

> After about 4 hours' hard work, I eventually reached the bottom.
> About halfway down I found a bottle of soda water, and to me, in the
> condition in which I then was, it was the sweetest drink that I ever
> tasted. Near the bottom I also found a blanket and a petrol tin full of
> drinking water. These I took in tow, as I knew they would prove useful.
> There were two other wounded men in the dugout. Both were on
> upper wire beds and were helpless. I found a resting place on the
> ground beneath them, and to my delight there lay close to hand several
> tins of bully and some loaves of bread.[1]
>
> Second Lieutenant Wilfrid Taylor, 6th Buffs, 37th Brigade, 12th Division

Thus it was that in a dugout in what was now No Man's Land, Taylor and his two companions remained undisturbed by the fighting above throughout 1 December.

The experiences of men taken prisoner in the fighting are frequently marginalized during accounts of any battle. They are especially worthy of mention here, however, since they indicate that, to some degree at least, the Germans had been unprepared for the scale of success of their operations on the southern flank. Private John Lee had been captured in the first hour of the German attack on 55th Division:

March to 'cage' was very tiring. We reached 'cage' at 4.30 p.m. completely done up. During the evening, the number of prisoners increased to about 2,000. A tub of water was brought in, but no food. Very hungry. Slept the night in the filth and woke early next morning feeling famished.[2]

Private John Lee, 1/10th (Liverpool Scottish) King's Liverpool Regiment, 166th Brigade, 55th Division

The experiences of Lee and his fellow prisoners of war in the subsequent days are also salutary regarding what the phrase 'For you, the war is over' *really* meant.

December 1st: Left 'cage' at 10.00 a.m. Received one small loaf between 8 men. First to eat for 40 hours. Bread very coarse and sour, but could have eaten anything. Marched to station at Busigny. Received cup of hot coffee on the way from a civilian; very good. Entrained for Le Quesnoy, arriving 5.00 p.m. About 2,500 men in one room. Packed like sardines, and had to sleep on top of another. No further food.

December 2nd: Spent a bad night. Could not sleep owing to crowded conditions. Everybody astir early. Never felt so hungry in my life. Received bread and coffee at 10.00 a.m. At 11.30 a.m. we paraded four deep outside for dinner, and marched round grounds until 2.30 when the dinner gave out, and about 500 of us had none. Stayed all night in same building.

December 3rd: Took good care to be early on the scene for bread and coffee. Paraded at 11.00 a.m. for dinner. This time managed to get near the front, and after walking around for about 3 hours obtained a bowl of sour kraut [sic] and black peas. Not very palatable, but went down. We entrained at 4.30 p.m. for Münster, 48 men to a truck . . .

December 5th: Still travelling. Most uncomfortable journey. No light in van except from a small hole in roof. Wondered when we were going to get any food again. Could not [help but] keep thinking of the good things I had left behind in my 'shack'. Very thirsty. Nothing to smoke. At 5.00 p.m. we were taken out for another bowl of soup. Could have eaten a bucketful.[3]

Private John Lee, 1/10th (Liverpool Scottish) King's Liverpool Regiment, 166th Brigade, 55th Division

Lee eventually reached Münster on 6 December. Whilst others like Lieutenant John Lomax experienced better treatment, Lee's experiences were not untypical. One common problem was that described by Gunner Alfred Newman. Although the night was relatively mild, for men who had experienced the twin blows of combat and capture, and who had perhaps not eaten for many hours, it was shockingly cold; it was December:

[We were] put into a wire cage in an open field, no food being given us and nothing to eat all day. The night of 30th November–1st December was bitterly cold with a thick fog – the cold was terrible – my clothes consisting only of tunic, trousers, shirt and tin hat. My overcoat being taken from me by a German officer to whom I said a few kind words. Luckily for me he knew no English. [At] 6 o'clock in the morning they put a tub of water near the pen with only your hands to get it in. At ten o'clock we were counted again and given a loaf between eight, marched about eight kilometres and put into railway trucks and despatched to Le Quesnoy arriving here at 8.00 p.m. Put into an empty factory. No food the next day. The officer in charge of this camp was the worst type of German I ever met, and I have seen some _____ in my travels while a prisoner.[4]

Gunner Alfred Newman, 32nd Siege Battery, Royal Garrison Artillery, 34th Heavy Artillery Group, III Corps

Inevitably, there was a randomness which dictated the manner in which men were treated. Some, like William Evans, had few complaints when moved to the rear, away from the dangers of the battlefield:

We filed into a church which at one time must have been a very beautiful place. But now the floor was encumbered with sleeping and wounded soldiers lying on straw. Fresh bundles of straw, which were very wet, were brought in and we, of the new party, bedded down. Sleep, however, was a long time coming, food was our most pressing need. We were therefore agreeably surprised when we were roused and told to come for soup. We were given a generous supply of a thick vegetable soup, which also had a flavour of meat. We did full justice to this very welcome meal and did not worry over-much about the ingredients. In any case, it was very satisfying and warming and we were able to find sleep without tossing and turning, although the wet straw was not an ideal couch. In the morning we had another meal of the same soup and felt a bit more cheerful.[5]

Lance Corporal William Evans, 1/6th King's Liverpool Regiment, 165th Brigade, 55th Division

It would be wrong also to suggest that the treatment of these men was necessarily worse than that of German prisoners at British hands. But in the case of a nation struggling to sustain its fighting men in the field, let alone feed its civilian population adequately, the needs of prisoners were, perhaps inevitably, sometimes less conscientiously dealt with.

The night cloaked the reliefs of shattered units and the arrival of reinforcements on both sides of No Man's Land. At Gouzeaucourt, some of the heavy howitzers lost and then recaptured by the British were withdrawn by mechanized tractors, whilst elsewhere batteries of guns that had previously supported IV Corps were moved to compensate, to some extent, for the losses III Corps had suffered. The men of 1st Guards Brigade in Gouzeaucourt gorged themselves on the contents of a recaptured supply train. Captain Henry Dundas, 1st Scots Guards, described the 'great fun looting in Gouzeaucourt, though as the Brigadier said, it was rather melancholy looting, as it was all British stuff retaken from the Boche'.[6]

Infantry reliefs were also carried out. Captain James Neville's battalion, 2nd Oxfordshire & Buckinghamshire Light Infantry, had moved up from reserve on 2nd Division's front. During the evening they had moved into Hughes Support Trench, whose former occupants had already gone forward into action, leaving their packs stacked high in the bays of the trench. Here the infantrymen were subjected to the terrifying destructive fire of German heavy artillery:

We were packed like sardines, my platoon occupying half a traverse only. Some very heavy stuff was coming over at odd intervals. You can hear these very heavy birds coming from a considerable distance: they seem to take ages to arrive, and there is always a second during their flight when you know whether they are going to fall near or far from you. I heard this particular bird from afar, and felt relieved that he was going to plant himself away from us. Then I began to doubt my supposition; a second later, it was touch and go, and then I realised that it was probably going to blot me out. I lived through one agonising second of uncertainty. There was no way of escape; we could not dodge the brute, as we were far too cramped for space. With a tearing, rushing, mighty roar as of an express train screaming at top speed through an enclosed station, it crashed in the next bay from me.[7]

Captain James Neville, 2nd Oxfordshire & Buckinghamshire Light Infantry, 5th Brigade, 2nd Division

The shell had fallen in the middle of Neville's platoon, killing twenty men. Rushing around the corner of the traverse, Neville found a bloody shambles:

It had fallen plumb in the centre of the trench – a magnificent shot from the enemy's point of view. Among the killed was Sergeant Archer, Platoon Sergeant of No.7, and a damned good chap. The only man who escaped untouched of all the men in that bay, was sitting on the top of a pile of packs, at the foot of which the shell had landed. The packs were utterly destroyed and he was lifted off his perch but unhurt![8]

Captain James Neville, 2nd Oxfordshire & Buckinghamshire Light Infantry, 5th Brigade, 2nd Division

In a scene that was by no means unique in the dismal reality of this appalling conflict, the grim task of disposing of the shattered remnants of humanity took place under cover of darkness. There was little dignity in their death and scant respect in their burial ceremony:

As soon as it got dark, we collected some bits of men, put them in a sandbag, carried out the recognisable bodies over the top and dumped them in a shell hole, and Billy Barnard said the Lord's Prayer over their remains. I think it was probably the only prayer he knew for certain![9]

Captain James Neville, 2nd Oxfordshire & Buckinghamshire Light Infantry, 5th Brigade, 2nd Division

Yet amidst the squalor and terrors of the battlefield at night, some could still find a terrible beauty in the violence of mankind. Whilst 'D' Company, 13th Essex fought its desperate struggle for survival through the night, at a distance James Neville observed the ill-starred attempts to extricate them:

> We watched these attacks from our front line. It was very thrilling. We could see the shrapnel bursting over the enemy trenches, and the smaller flashes of flame from Mills bombs. The darkness, meanwhile, was continually lit up by Very Lights which burst high in the frosty night and fell into the rolling clouds of smoke. They were rather grim firework displays.[10]
>
> Captain James Neville, 2nd Oxfordshire & Buckinghamshire Light Infantry, 5th Brigade, 2nd Division

The night was kinder to another unit of reinforcements – a troop from 'A' Squadron, Lord Strathcona's Horse of the Canadian Cavalry Brigade which occupied a sunken road to the right of Gauche Wood.

> One of my men returning from a patrol on our front asked me if I would like a Bass ale, and much to my surprise produced it. The patrol had found a deserted artillery canteen, which still had some supplies in it. This information, which was soon public property, proved unfortunate to those so foolhardy as to try to forage in the light of day. Our position was quite exposed. Amongst the prizes brought to our lines was a small keg of SRD* rum. This I had buried, as I knew we were to advance, and contrary to many others we never, to my knowledge, had rum before a fight.[11]
>
> Sergeant Henry Rebitt, Lord Strathcona's Horse, Canadian Cavalry Brigade, 5th Cavalry Division

It is remarkable that men like Rebitt possessed an utterly unshakeable conviction that they would be able to return to recover such a prize, for it was by no means certain that, with the morning, the ground his unit held would remain in their hands.

Third Army's order issued the evening before had constituted something more by way of a rallying call than simply a directive for counter-attacks. *'Tout le monde à la bataille!'* it seemed to cry. All three corps were to do all

---

* Supply Reserve Depot (other, more ironic, interpretations of the initials have included: 'Seldom Reaches Destination', 'Service Rum Diluted' and 'Soon Runs Dry'. Thanks to my colleague, Alan Jeffreys).

they could to drive the Germans back, or at least stop their advance. There is surely a place for this kind of thing in warfare, but what was needed from Third Army staff after its failings of the previous day was coordination of the various attacks by the different units. This it signally failed to offer. So it was that a variety of units on the southern flank made ineffectual and damaging piecemeal attacks when the morning came.

Two divisions, therefore, of the Cavalry Corps were tasked with attacking in cooperation with the Guards Division south and east of Gouzeaucourt. Courage's 2nd Tank Brigade had produced almost forty serviceable tanks for the attack, whilst almost as many again had come from 1st Tank Brigade. Dismounted troops from 5th Cavalry Division and the Lucknow Brigade from 4th Cavalry Division were assigned Villers Guislain and Gauche Wood as their objectives. Nineteen tanks from 'H,' 'A' and 'B' Battalions were to cooperate, whilst the Mhow Brigade from 4th Cavalry Division had orders to take advantage of this attack's use of tanks and seize Villers Ridge in a mounted operation. The Guards Division, further north, was also to assault Gauche Wood whilst seizing Quentin Ridge and Gonnelieu. Twenty more tanks from 'H' Battalion had been assembled, with twenty more from 'D' and seventeen from 'E' also allotted.

The preparation and planning of the attack was a hurried affair, and matters relating to both cavalry and tanks soon began to unravel. The Indian cavalry of the Mhow Brigade had been used dismounted on the previous day to reinforce 166th Brigade near Lempire. As a consequence, their traditional arms (lances and swords) had been left on wagons. Now, called upon to assemble near Epéhy for mounted action, they met a problem:

> During the whole of that day [30 November] no clear information as to what it was all about reached the troops. We surmised and correctly so, that the long-promised 'G in gap' had come at last – only that the gap was in our line. The trench parties rejoined at about midnight in the pitch dark. Villers Guislain was to be attacked by the Division at dawn. Our role was to make a mounted advance, seize Pigeon and Quail Ravines, and form a defensive flank to the south . . . [but] the lance and sword wagons were lost in the night.[12]
>
> Captain Dysart Whitworth, 2nd Lancers (Gardner's Horse), Mhow Brigade, 4th Cavalry Division

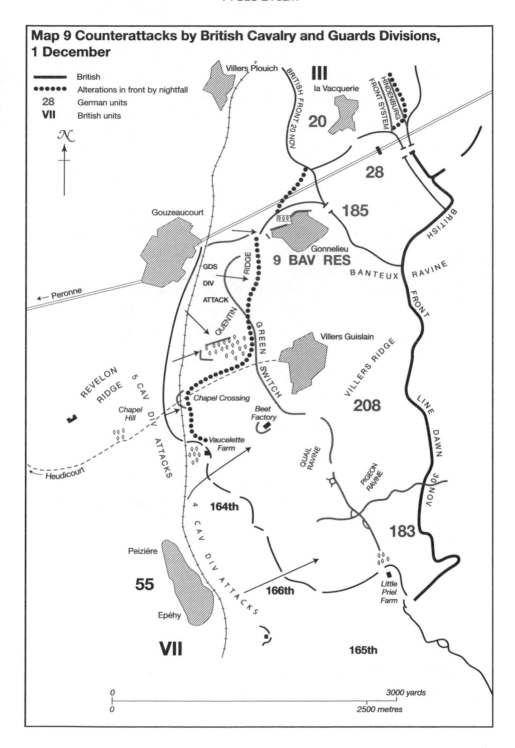

Map 9 Counterattacks by British Cavalry and Guards Divisions, 1 December

—————— British
●●●●●● Alterations in front by nightfall
28 German units
VII British units

Villers Plouich

III

la Vacquerie

BRITISH FRONT 20 NOV

HINDENBURG FRONT SYSTEM

20

28

Gouzeaucourt

185

← Peronne

GDS
DIV
ATTACK

RIDGE

Gonnelieu

9 BAV RES

BANTEUX RAVINE

BRITISH FRONT

QUENTIN

GREEN SWITCH

Villers Guislain

VILLERS RIDGE

208

REVELON RIDGE

5 CAV DIV ATTACKS

Chapel Crossing

Beet Factory

LINE DAWN 30 NOV

Chapel Hill

Vaucelette Farm

QUAIL RAVINE

PIGEON RAVINE

← Heudicourt

4 CAV DIV ATTACKS

164th

183

Peiziére

Little Priel Farm

55

166th

Epéhy

VII

165th

0   3000 yards
0   2500 metres

There were problems too regarding tank support for the Guards' attack. Firstly, 'E' Battalion tanks became lost in the darkness. Forced to rely solely on those of his own battalion, Major William Watson, who was 'Johnny-on-the-spot' and, therefore, de facto tank commander for the divisional attack, set off to finalize plans with 3rd Guards Brigade near Gouzeaucourt Wood. The brigade commander, 'Copper' Seymour, directed him to 'find the Colonel of a certain battalion of Grenadier Guards, warn him that we would make a counter-attack on Gonnelieu at dawn, and arrange, as far as was possible, pending orders from the division, the lines on which my tanks would assist.'[13]

Thus it was that Watson met another of the bright stars in the firmament of Guards battalion commanders, Viscount Gort, commanding 4th Grenadier Guards who, like Alexander of the Irish Guards, was already viewed with something approaching awe. Watson's arrival at Gort's headquarters coincided with that of Lieutenant Colonel Grenville Douglas Gordon of 1st Welsh Guards, Charles Dudley-Ward's battalion commander.

> Between twelve and one in the morning orders came to move. 'DG' and I set off to the Brigade and there 'Copper' told us we should have to attack a village and hold a hill crest. Very briefly he gave us objectives and by the time he had finished the battalion had arrived. We streamed off in the moonlight till we reached a sunken road where Douglas left us while he consulted Gort who was to be next to us.[14]
>
> Captain Charles Dudley-Ward, 1st Welsh Guards, 3rd Guards Brigade, Guards Division

On Douglas Gordon's return, Dudley-Ward and the four company commanders of the Welsh Guards went to Gort's headquarters and were briefed concerning the forthcoming attack. Neither Dudley-Ward nor Watson mention the other's presence at this meeting.

> In a small dugout we heard for the first time exactly what we had to do, and that information was meagre enough. Gort had been dodging about with his battalion all day just round there and knew the country. We were to attack with a few tanks and no barrage but he said he had watched another abortive attack and that the machine-gun fire was tremendous. However we went through the limits and boundaries of

everyone's part and just had time to go down to the jumping off ground without being able to see anything of what was in front of it, and back to the battalion when it was time to start in concert. Heavens, what a scrambled affair![15]

Captain Charles Dudley-Ward, 1st Welsh Guards, 3rd Guards Brigade, Guards Division

Watson's description of Gort's briefing so closely resembles Dudley-Ward's in key aspects that it is difficult to know why, given its importance, the latter did not record the chief matter arising from the conference's end.

I was about to go back to my tanks when two of my officers suddenly appeared, bringing the worst possible news. The tanks had run short of petrol! Their commanders in the hurry and excitement of the day naturally had not realised how much they had used . . . The attack would take place in five hours – the Guards were relying on our tanks – Gonnelieu was crammed full of machine-guns. The Colonel had just said so. I felt sick and frightened. The Guards were relying on our tanks, and Gonnelieu was crammed full of machine-guns![16]

Major William Watson, No. 11 Company, 'D' Battalion, Tank Corps

Although Watson's men frantically siphoned petrol from tank to tank in an attempt to get some moving, it was clear that, from an initial expectation of the assistance of almost forty tanks, the Guards Division could now only hope for half that number at best. Like Fontaine, it was an inauspicious set of circumstances in which to make an attack. But the die was cast. Thankfully, some tank assistance would be available for the Guards' attack in the form of 'H' Battalion's tanks.

Without the presence of the Guards, the forces assembled for 1 December might have been regarded as a ramshackle assortment scraped together for an over-ambitious battle plan at the wrong end of the hardest year of the war so far, and now to be further embroiled in a desperate fight to haul Third Army's (and perhaps even Douglas Haig's) coals from the fire. However, their efforts in the attack were to demonstrate this as a massive under-appreciation of the qualities of the individual soldiers of the BEF.

*

Without doubt, the Cambrai battle is chiefly remembered as a portend of the future. Many essential elements of warfare in the first half of the twentieth century manifested themselves (sometimes for the first time) during the course of the battle: the surprise offered by unregistered artillery shooting 'off the map', the extensive use of hefty quantities of tanks, large numbers of aircraft operating in a ground-attack role and more flying 'deep battle' missions in attempts to deny supplies and reinforcements to the front-line troops. For the more immediate future, it also presaged the offensive tactics of the German Spring Offensives of 1918 and at the same time, it must be admitted, the concomitant failings of British defensive tactics. And yet 1 December 1917 undeniably muddies the waters of the whole picture, bucking the trend in no uncertain fashion. A quite remarkable day in which imperial troops many thousands of miles from their homes fought with lances on horseback alongside, and against, the most recent technological innovations in warfare. A day which, if it did not precisely mark the cusp between nineteenth century warfare and the 'century of total war', certainly epitomized it.

For the German infantry of *183rd Division* who had successfully taken their objectives on the previous day, there was no expectation of further action and no hint of impending events:

> Everything is peaceful. There is nothing to indicate that Tommy wants to claim back the position he lost yesterday. I make myself a coffee on the spirit stove, enjoying the warming brew with a piece of dry bread, and begin to prolong my unbroken peace. I find my own little space in the open trench and, since I am covered with a 'newly bought', thick English coat, the siesta in the open is not unpleasant.[17]
>
> Leutnant Karl Christian, *Infanterie Regiment 418, 183rd Division*

The British attack was scheduled to begin at 6.30 a.m. in the darkness before the first suggestion of dawn. However, it was 6.50 a.m., by which time the morning was considerably lighter, before the Lucknow Brigade on the right went forward. It was doomed before it began. There was a late change in the route of the cooperating tanks which effectively meant they were no longer cooperating. There was no artillery support either. Two dismounted cavalry regiments had been assigned to attack but only one eventually did, largely because their brigade commander exercised caution after the stunning news concerning the tanks. Approximately 230 *sowars* accompanied by about 70 other men of a machine-gun squadron passed through the eclectic collection of men of 12th Division holding the line here but were soon pinned down by machine-gun fire after advancing less than a hundred yards.

The original Cavalry Corps operation orders had required 4th Cavalry Division, in the form of the Mhow Brigade, to be ready to take advantage of any success gained in the dismounted cavalry and tank attack with a view to advancing and occupying the high ground east of Villers Guislain. With the failure of the dismounted attack, the Mhow Brigade's commander, Neil Haig, recognized that any attack by his men would be futile. He was especially concerned about machine-guns operating from a sugar beet factory south-west of Villers Guislain. Furthermore, his cavalry were still without swords and lances. At his divisional commander's headquarters he explained his fears to Major General Alfred Kennedy and invited him to see for himself:

> Kennedy came down at once and accompanied me to the point whence I had seen the enemy's position. He had to crawl on his belly a good way, but I was able to show him the Beet Factory walls and what I took to be the wire in front of the enemy's machine-guns. Kennedy quite agreed with me that an attack on this position was impracticable, and said he would go and talk to the Corps Commander on the telephone at once and explain the situation.[18]
>
> Brigadier General Neil Haig, Headquarters, Mhow Brigade, 4th Cavalry Division

The Cavalry Corps commander, Lieutenant General Charles Kavanagh, was an altogether different proposition and of an altogether different point of view. Stung by criticism of his Corps' conduct and lack of 'push' in the British attack, Kavanagh was out to make absolutely sure that no further such accusations could be made, as Kennedy's record of their conversation makes clear:

> General Kavanagh: How is your attack getting on?
>
> Self [Kennedy]: My attack! Why, it has not started, as the dismounted attack has not made any progress. The tanks failed to turn up and there is nothing doing.

General Kavanagh: Rot! You have to carry out your attack as ordered.

Self: But my orders were to take advantage of any success gained in the dismounted attack, and, as I say, there has not been any success.

General Kavanagh: You have to carry out your attack at once.

Self: If you order me to do so I will try it.

The Corps Commander was evidently very annoyed and, from the first, spoke very rudely. I put down the phone and went across to Haig. He told me what his plan was, and I said that we had to put it into execution forthwith. I have always regretted that I did not, there and then, refuse to carry out Kavanagh's orders. I thought at the time that there might be a very slight chance of the mounted attack gaining a little ground, and that, if it did, it would certainly help the dismounted attack to get forward, so I did not refuse.[19]

Major General Alfred Kennedy, 4th Cavalry Division

Haig's brigade had stood ready since 6.30 a.m. hidden behind a low ridge – but evidently not well hidden since they were shelled by artillery and several men and horses were hit. At about 8.00 a.m. the 2nd Lancers received orders to lead the attack. It was with some relief, therefore, that as they were about to move off, Captain Whitworth witnessed the arrival of the sword and lance wagons.

A hurried issue began. This was not over when the order to move off was given. Weapons were being thrown to the men of the rear half squadron as they passed the wagons we moved off.

We passed through Epéhy and turning to the left debouched from the village at the level crossing. A hundred yards on we crossed the trenches of our very astonished – and relieved – infantry, who were expecting a German attack at any minute. We then deployed into open column of squadrons at extended distances, each column in line of troop squadrons.[20]

Captain Dysart Whitworth, 2nd Lancers (Gardner's Horse), Mhow Brigade, 4th Cavalry Division

At 9.35 a.m., the Mhow Brigade attack began. Led by 2nd Lancers, commanded by Lieutenant Colonel H.H.F. Turner, with a squadron from 6th Inniskilling Dragoons and a mounted machine-gun section, they entered what must inevitably be regarded as a shallow valley of death. At no point was the skyline to the left or right more than seven hundred yards distant, limiting somewhat German observation of the charge. Consequently, German fire was almost entirely from machine-guns and rifles, not from artillery.

> Our own infantry were astounded when we galloped through them. They cheered us like blazes. As soon as the leading squadron – Sikhs, Major Knowles – began to gallop, Boche machine-guns opened from both sides of the valley. It was Colonel Turner's intention to follow the valley for some way and then turn left-handed over the ridge. The pace soon became an all-out gallop and the cracking of machine-guns was deafening. Our pace down the valley was a good sixteen annas, and until we halted our casualties were negligible. The going was excellent – good spring turf, and only a few shell holes. There was nothing to stop the advance until within about two hundred yards of the sunken road; here we came on a single apron of wire with two gaps.[21]
>
> Captain Dysart Whitworth, 2nd Lancers (Gardner's Horse), Mhow Brigade, 4th Cavalry Division

Whitworth estimated that from the point where his unit crossed the British lines to the wire and sunken road was one and a half miles and was covered in about five minutes.

> This was the first time we have been called upon to fight as cavalry in our three years' field service. Our regiment was in the forefront of the attack, and [so was] my squadron. Thanks be to God, the attack was made with the utmost bravery and it achieved splendid results. The fury of our charge and the ardour of our war cries so alarmed the enemy that he left his trenches and fled. At first we were assailed by machine-gun fire like a rain storm from left and right, and afterwards from the front, but how could the cowardly Germans stand before the onslaught of the braves of the Khalsa?! This credit is not due to us, but to the Guru, through whose favour we speared many of the routed enemy on our lances.[22]
>
> Jemadar Jiwan Singh, 2nd Lancers (Gardner's Horse), Mhow Brigade, 4th Cavalry Division

From the German lines, the oncoming cavalry appeared by turns bizarre and then horrifying:

> What on earth is that? A lone nag runs around in front of me. I position myself up on the embankment so that I can keep within sight the hollow ground in front of me. If I haven't taken leave of my senses, I can see the heads of a mass of people creating a rather strange impression. The heads are popping up and down hilariously, like peas being shaken. Now I can see more, now bodies are appearing – and the heads of horses. Now I get it. 'Alarm! Get out! Tommy is coming!'[23]
>
> Leutnant Karl Christian, *Infanterie Regiment 418, 183rd Division*

The sight of charging lance-armed cavalry was enough to cause many occupants of the sunken lane to flee. However, some machine-gunners stuck to their task.

> 'Shoot!' I yell, 'Get the MG onto them!' The light machine-gun, damaged by damp and cold while being hauled up, goes on strike. It jams! The riders come quickly closer, under heavy fire from trench positions to left and right. But they are absolutely fearless and are put off by nothing. Now they are coming right out of the depression. And now I also know who I have before me. Indians, real Indians, savages, the brown devils from the newspaper reports.[24]
>
> Leutnant Karl Christian, *Infanterie Regiment 418, 183rd Division*

Inevitably, the barbed wire checked the charge as the cavalry were forced to squeeze through the gaps and now these machine-gunners took their opportunity. The regimental headquarters troop caught it first. Colonel Turner and all his staff were killed or wounded except Whitworth and some signallers. Turner's loss was genuinely and sincerely mourned by the men of his command:

> My friend, the black cloud came over the Regiment. We had escaped for three years; but unfortunately the 1st of December was an ill-omened day for us. Our hero, the lion-hearted one whom we all loved, and to whom the Regiment had given the title of 'The Lion' – that is to say our brave Colonel Turner – was killed. He

was a great and good and clever man. Such men are rare in this world.[25]

Sowar Khalil Ullah, 9th Cavalry (attached 2nd Lancers (Gardner's Horse)), Mhow Brigade, 4th Cavalry Division

Some of the cavalry jumped the wire, whilst others poured through the gaps. As they did so, Karl Christian grabbed two hand grenades:

I run to the point where the horde has to reach the defile and wait until it is right upon me, then pull the pin and throw my greeting into the surging mass. Horses buckle or are torn apart. But the confusion is too short. The cavalry split, one half streaking right, the other left, along the lane, looking for a more favourable crossing point. I have a second grenade and chase recklessly after the force heading right. It is a good opportunity and the grenade explodes between horses' legs. Again the troop of riders presses on. 'Get grenades over here!' I shout loudly, but there is not a soul around me. Nicely cut off – the left troop has already ridden over the position at a favourable point and overrun the thin line of men behind. Those who could not reach the rear trench in time are no doubt defending, but there are too many attackers for the men in field grey . . . I am not quite ready to turn back. An old soldier does not know how to run. Is there a rifle lying on the ground? Nothing. I am without weapons against two troops of Indians. There's nothing for it but to give up the position I took yesterday.[26]

Leutnant Karl Christian, *Infanterie Regiment 418, 183rd Division*

The majority of Germans had already fled and were pursued by a small group of cavalry led by Lieutenant Norton Broadway, who died soon after at the hands of a duplicitous German officer.

Lieutenant Broadway had, when the Regiment reached Kildare Lane, just spared a German officer who held up one hand in token of surrender. When Broadway turned away, this German drew a pistol, held behind his back in his other hand, and shot the unfortunate officer. He was promptly speared by Major Knowles' orderly.[27]

Captain Dysart Whitworth, 2nd Lancers (Gardner's Horse), Mhow Brigade, 4th Cavalry Division

Meanwhile, Leutnant Karl Christian fought for his life:

Some of the brown fellows are threateningly close. Then I remembered my pistol. There were still all nine shots in it, quite enough. One of the riders is a little ahead of the others. I let him get to a distance of twenty paces and then fire. The shot misses. The second cartridge is stuck. I squeeze the trigger. The weapon has failed and creaks softly. I fiddle about with the pistol. Something has jammed. No point in bothering with it any more. Right then, I am struck by a lance and tumble to the ground. To my amazement, I feel no pain and there is no blood. The horse jumps over me. I'm up on my feet quickly and try frantically again to get the pistol to fire. The Indian turns his horse and stabs at me again. I manage to protect myself from the blow with my arm, but in doing so drop my faithless pistol.[28]

Leutnant Karl Christian, *Infanterie Regiment 418, 183rd Division*

Although then attacked by an officer with a sabre and a number of lancers, Christian continued to defend himself with his right arm. Wounded several times and covered in blood, he feigned death until he could get away.

Meanwhile, the cavalrymen occupied the sunken lane, dismounted and began to defend the position they had seized. The lane was now a mass of men and horses. In order to ease overcrowding, most of the horses were led to the rear but this resulted in heavy casualties to both the horses and the men leading them.

Whilst the Lancers defended themselves, attempts to get word back to brigade headquarters were decided upon and volunteers called for.

Two men immediately came forward – Sowar Jot Ram and Lance Dafedar Gobind Singh. They started together, but took different routes. Jot Ram was shot down almost at once. Immediately after Gobind Singh's horse came down, and we thought that he had been killed too. An hour later, however, he appeared with an answer from the Brigade. He had managed to make his way on foot through the German posts, falling down whenever they fired at him and lying doggo until their attention was attracted elsewhere.

He had started back from Brigade on another horse, but this too was killed, and he made his way back to us in a similar manner. An hour later another message had to go back, and he again volunteered. This time he galloped straight through the barrage to our right.

Halfway through we saw his horse cut clean in two by a direct hit. Again he finished his journey on foot, and then volunteered to return again. The Brigadier, however, thought he had done enough. This earned Gobind Singh the Victoria Cross.[29]

Captain Dysart Whitworth, 2nd Lancers (Gardner's Horse), Mhow Brigade, 4th Cavalry Division

It was richly deserved for quite remarkable courage. Elsewhere, the cavalry attacks met equally heavy machine-gun fire from the German defenders and where their advance was more exposed they suffered the effects of German artillery fire too. The Inniskilling Dragoons, who attacked very soon after Gardner's Horse began their charge, encountered machine-guns firing from the Beet Factory regarding which Neil Haig had been so concerned. Two squadrons of 38th Central India Horse suffered in similar fashion when they were sent forward as dismounted reinforcements.

Despite the bravery with which these attacks were pursued, they had enjoyed little real success. Furthermore, the overall goal of foiling further German attacks in this area by a pre-emptive cavalry strike proved an exercise in futility since the Germans had never intended any further advance here.

Further north the Guards Division, supported on its right by more Indian cavalry – this time 18th Lancers from the Ambala Brigade of 5th Cavalry Division – was tasked with taking Gauche Wood and Gonnelieu. The attack by De Crespigny's 1st Guards Brigade started at 6.30 a.m. and was a complete success. The brigade had expected twelve tanks to lead them, but these were late in arriving. Consequently, 2nd Grenadier Guards, who had over 1,000 yards of bare hillside to advance over, did so as fast as their legs could carry them, so fast indeed that the German machine-guns could not get their range and the Grenadiers soon reached Gauche Wood.

The late appearance of the tanks also affected the attack by the dismounted cavalry of the Ambala Brigade. On the previous day other regiments from the brigade had suffered heavy casualties making a mounted counterattack against the Germans. Now it was the 18th Lancers' turn to make an attack on foot, as one *sowar*, writing to a former comrade, described:

At eleven o'clock at night we were warned that we would have to counter-attack in the morning and to take the small wood in front. At 6.30 a.m. we attacked on foot. The enemy saw us coming. Great God, what am I to say? You have been here, you know. The enemy met us with so intense and rapid a fire that we were unable to advance. Consequently, we were ordered to retire to our trenches.[30]

Sowar Dalawar Chand, 18th (King George's Own) Lancers, Ambala Brigade, 5th Cavalry Division

In fact, what this soldier took to be a failed initial attack was a move away from machine-gun fire in an attempt to reduce the casualties his unit was suffering. The attack proper was delayed in anticipation of tank support – which did not arrive until 7.15 a.m. Almost immediately they had lost direction and headed towards Gouzeaucourt but came back in time to assist 2nd Grenadier Guards and the Lancers in the fight for Gauche Wood. Dalawar Chand recalled this attack too:

Later we were ordered to advance again. The enemy this time left his trenches and fled; but about fifty Germans came running towards [us] shouting 'India! Kamerad! Kamerad!' The regiment continued to advance in a dashing manner, although heavily shelled by the enemy's artillery; but by the grace of God there were no casualties, except Dafadar Sher Mahomed Khan. The enemy's aeroplanes, flying low, fired on us, and Dafadar Falk Sher Khan was slightly wounded. A German prisoner lifted Dafadar Falk Sher Khan in his arms and carried him to hospital, which was a fine deed.[31]

Sowar Dalawar Chand, 18th (King George's Own) Lancers, Ambala Brigade, 5th Cavalry Division

The timely arrival of the tanks ensured the wood was taken. Several had been knocked out by German artillery fire but Joseph Gordon Hassell's was not one of them:

I began to pick up my bearings as it got lighter; identified the wood and Gouzeaucourt village. Saw hills on left, with tanks crossing right over them being blown up. I benefited by my experience of ten days previously, and kept in the folds of the ground, thus safely getting to near edge of the wood. I crept round the edge of the wood, following its convolutions and found the advanced trench which was the Guards' objective. Here my Section Commander, Captain Batten, who had been travelling with me, left the tank and entered the trench and saw the Guards into it.[32]

Second Lieutenant Joseph Gordon Hassell, H7 'Harrier', No. 22 Company, 'H' Battalion, Tank Corps

Together the Guards and Lancers, with some tank assistance, held the wood, despite heavy losses to the former in particular, and the death of the Lancers' commanding officer, Lieutenant Colonel Edwin Corbyn in the afternoon. Meanwhile, to their left, 3rd Coldstream Guards took Quentin Ridge with valuable tank assistance.

After his success at Gauche Wood, Gordon Hassell pressed on with his tank towards Villers Guislain, coming upon a German battery, who were limbering up to take their guns away:

We peppered the horses by Lewis guns. We passed a disabled tank which had been hit (Lieutenant Cecil Scott's), and signalled to him to bring all his crew across to us. They were sheltering behind the disabled machine. They ran across and we took officer and crew in. Then still going towards enemy, my engine failed – stalled – crossing a small trench; so that my nose was elevated, forming a grand target.[33]

Second Lieutenant Joseph Gordon Hassell, H7 'Harrier', No. 22 Company, 'H' Battalion, Tank Corps

The same experience that had so far served Gordon Hassell and his crew so well now reminded them of the incredible danger they were in:

Enemy guns ranged on us, and soil and splinters were coming through into tank. Sergeant Callaghan worked like one possessed to get engine running. We were seven minutes in this perilous stationary position [but] escaped being hit. Getting her on the move, I decided to return, and then the gear-changing lever jammed, so that there was no selection, and we had to crawl home in lowest gear. Moreover, we could not steer, and came back right through the wood in a dead straight line, but managed not to be bellied. Lieutenant Scott was in a state of partial shell-shock, and I had to get him out and walk with him in front of the

403

tank, getting him to smoke a 'fag'. We rallied in sunken road and found Major Pratt with three other tanks.[34]

Second Lieutenant Joseph Gordon Hassell, H7 'Harrier', No. 22 Company, 'H' Battalion, Tank Corps

Gordon Hassell and his crew were fortunate for many of the tanks were lost in the fighting around Gauche Wood. However, despite their late arrival, their contribution was proving more than small justification for their use.

In the case of 3rd Guards Brigade's attack towards Gonnelieu over the Quentin Ridge, the tanks once more failed to appear in the dark. The attack of 1st Welsh Guards still went in, however. Charles Dudley-Ward watched the advance begin:

The men lined up on a railway line, facing a hill and though it was moonlight you could see nothing to help you. But no one had very definite instructions. It seemed to me . . . that suddenly men began to call out 'advance' and a very long line marched slowly up the hill and disappeared in the night. It was the most terrific rifle and machine-gun fire I have ever heard. I said to Broncho 'they will never get through that' and he agreed.[35]

Captain Charles Dudley-Ward, 1st Welsh Guards, 3rd Guards Brigade, Guards Division

Both Dudley-Ward and Dene had enough combat experience to know what they were talking about. The former's none-too-sanguine assessment proved correct, as one of the men who made the advance later testified:

[Under Lord Gort, Grenadier Guards] and our Colonel, Douglas Gordon, we were picked to attack the Germans. 'We haven't any artillery for you . . . but you'll find eight tanks to lead you.' Eight! Well, the tanks never turned up! Our Colonel stuck to his orders that he had to attack, which he shouldn't have done. No, we went with fixed bayonets on this morning. We walked up a slope at Gouzeaucourt, and then we got on a flat plateau and that's when the machine-guns opened out. We had 250 casualties in the first three minutes! The three companies that suffered were Nos. 2, 3 and 4; the Prince of Wales Company was in reserve down by the station.[36]

Lance Corporal Charles Evans, 1st Welsh Guards, 3rd Guards Brigade, Guards Division

Two-thirds of the attackers had been killed or wounded. In the darkness before dawn, this bloody reverse astounded the watching Charles Dudley-Ward and 'Broncho' Dene:

> In a light which must have been from star shells I suddenly saw a crowd of men on the sky line and they seemed to be coming straight for us. It was staggering in its effect. I at once thought we had struck a strong Bosch attack and yelled to the men in reserve to line the bank and prepare to fire. Broncho dashed off to one side yelling too, and then they were on us and we saw it was our own men. Never have I seen such a thing. They were sobbing and cursing.[37]

Captain Charles Dudley-Ward, 1st Welsh Guards, 3rd Guards Brigade, Guards Division

Even for an officer with Dudley-Ward's experience, to see his fellow officers and friends, and the men of the three companies, was a dreadful and shocking nightmare:

> In the pale light . . . I saw Dickens supported between two men and covered with blood and Kearton very pale between two others. Then I saw the whole attack crumbling to nothing. As they came in Broncho and I pushed them up against the bank and ordered them to face the enemy. I nearly fell over someone on a stretcher and saw it was Bowyer. I stopped for a moment and he told me they could never get through and that he was hit in three places. By this time we could see, more or less, and we then made out that about a hundred men had come back and the rest were out of sight over the hill.[38]

Captain Charles Dudley-Ward, 1st Welsh Guards, 3rd Guards Brigade, Guards Division

Unscathed, Charles Evans was amongst those still on the hillside. Cowering in what cover he could find, Evans could do little except watch as a solitary tank then appeared and advanced on the Germans. Dudley-Ward and Dene could not even do that. Their fellow officer,

Captain Arthur Gibbs, had already been sent forward to occupy a line halfway up the ridge. However, when it was daylight at about 8.30 a.m., Dene and Dudley-Ward decided to ascend the ridge to survey the battlefield. The scene that greeted them was more cause for astonishment:

> After passing Gibbs, we crawled on our tummies and looked over the top. There we saw a tank had engaged the Bosch and was firing while squatting over their trench and, what was good, the Bosch was running. So I called back to Gibbs to come on slowly, told him to watch what was happening and follow the tank as the Bosch cleared out.[39]
>
> Captain Charles Dudley-Ward, 1st Welsh Guards, 3rd Guards Brigade, Guards Division

For Charles Evans and his fellow Guardsmen pinned down on the Quentin Ridge, the appearance of the tank, followed soon after by Gibbs and the Prince of Wales Company, meant it was a case of 'Up Guards and at 'em.'

> This Captain of the Prince of Wales Company saw a lone tank coming along the trench they'd captured from us; I don't think these Germans had ever seen a tank before. He [advanced] . . . and what was left of us went with him. 200 prisoners and 28 machine-guns – the ones that had mown us down some hours earlier![40]
>
> Lance Corporal Charles Evans, 1st Welsh Guards, 3rd Guards Brigade, Guards Division

Charles Dudley-Ward arrived soon afterwards to survey the remarkable change in fortunes occasioned by the tank's appearance.

> What a sight! Such a jumble of kit and rifles and machine-guns! In the bit of trench Gibbs occupied there were 26* machine-guns. He had taken and sent down about two hundred prisoners. On the way back I found Roderick and Borough killed. Nothing of No. 4 Company was known but Wreford-Brown, shot through the wrist, and still going strong with a few men by the side of Arthur Gibbs' lot told me he

---

* Although Charles Evans says 28, Charles Dudley-Ward's figure of 26 is quoted by the Official History, p. 241.

thought they had gone right ahead. I sent this gallant boy back and attached his men to the P of W. The situation slowly cleared during the day.[41]

Captain Charles Dudley-Ward, 1st Welsh Guards, 3rd Guards Brigade, Guards Division

Yet, as it cleared, it revealed the extent of the Welsh Guards' losses and gave an opportunity for Dudley-Ward to learn the fate of his fellow officers. Writing later in his diary, he ended his roll call of the dead and wounded with three simple words summarising the battalion's (and his own) experience of the battle: 'A Bad Dream.'

To the left of the Welsh Guards, Lord Gort's 4th Grenadier Guards, aware they would almost certainly have no tank assistance, attacked Gonnelieu. Without tanks, they also enjoyed little, if any, artillery support. Amidst wildly inaccurate rumour, William Watson waited desperately for word of whether his own tanks had been of help:

The news was disquieting. The Grenadier Guards had not been able to force an entry into the village, while the Welsh Guards on their right had made little progress. Both battalions had lost practically all their officers. They had been withdrawn and replaced by fresh battalions. The dismounted cavalry had managed to establish themselves on the ridge with the help of tanks, but they could make no further advance until Gonnelieu was cleared. Tanks could be seen on the slopes of the hill. Two, silhouetted against the skyline, were burning fiercely. Of my own tanks nothing could be heard. The Colonel was doing valiant deeds in Gonnelieu.

Then came the grave rumour: 'The Colonel is badly wounded!' but a moment later he walked into the dugout, his arm in a rough sling and his face drawn with pain. They persuaded him against his will to go to the main dressing station . . . [sic] The wounded were streaming past, walking wounded and stretcher after stretcher.[42]

Major William Watson, No. 11 Company, 'D' Battalion, Tank Corps

It was the Grenadiers' further misfortune to find the village filling up with German troops from two divisions prior to the renewal of their attack. Watson's tanks did not appear and the attackers were driven back with heavy losses, including Gort himself. However, the Germans were themselves prevented from advancing when they attacked soon afterwards.

This German attack was principally directed against the British troops occupying a line between Gonnelieu and La Vacquerie and those around Masnières and Les Rues Vertes. It was impeded in some measure by the same problems that had affected British attacks in earlier days. There was a shortage of artillery ammunition and chaotic traffic congestion meant what supplies there were could not be got forward quickly. This was particularly bad near Gonnelieu which was one of the key points from which the Germans proposed to attack.

To the north-west of Gonnelieu, Captain Horace Raymond Smith's battalion, 12th Rifle Brigade, although greatly weakened in numbers after its defence the day before, was once again assailed by the Germans. The morning began quietly. In a support trench, Raymond Smith's servant was, once again, making tea.

> In half an hour the shelling starts again. They are pounding our trench now, and the chalk is flying in all directions, and hitting us from all sides. Several of my men are wounded. Suddenly there is a rising shriek and a deafening bang, and I am thrown on the ground. On rising I see a man sitting on the fire step close by me. He is coughing, and as he coughs blood spurts like a fountain from his chest, which is smashed in. I pass the word for stretcher-bearers, but a glance shows that it is hopeless. A piece of shell, which must have missed me by inches, has killed him.[43]
>
> Captain Horace Raymond Smith, 12th Rifle Brigade, 60th Brigade, 20th Division

The battered remnants of two battalions of 60th Brigade offered determined resistance for some time, but it was only when three companies of 1st Grenadier Guards counter-attacked the Germans that the position was restored.

The real crisis occasioned by the German attacks was for Brigadier General Ronnie Cheape's 86th Brigade of 29th Division. Pounded by heavy artillery and assailed from two sides, the brigade's survivors steadfastly defended Masnières and Les Rues Vertes. However, it was becoming critical that they receive reinforcements in their small salient at the head of a larger salient, otherwise Masnières might have to be abandoned. The divisional commander, De Lisle, knew there were no such reinforcements to be had. Nevertheless, through the afternoon, the defenders – many of whom were inexperienced men from new drafts thrust straight into the fighting and therefore very shaken by their first encounter with the terrible power of artillery and machine-gun fire – held out. A withdrawal, however, was inevitable and preparations were begun for this to be accomplished in the evening. Military terminology makes subtle differentiation between 'withdrawals', 'retirements' and 'retreats'. All are, essentially, undesirable but what distinguishes a withdrawal from a retreat is who provides the momentum for the motion – one's own side or the enemy. The evacuation of positions in the conjoined villages definitely constituted a withdrawal; a planned and organized process in which measures were taken in regard to ensuring the wounded, supplies and ammunition were brought out or, in the latter case, disposed of.

As 87th Brigade withdrew its last posts during the night, where the iron bridge had crossed the canal between the two villages, the tank 'Flying Fox II' remained wallowing in the wreckage of the collapsed crossing, like the husk of a monstrous creature from a very different era.

Throughout the afternoon, the fighting on the southern flank of the main British salient continued. Many were futile attempts by both sides to achieve unrealistic goals with inadequate numbers of troops. Some arose because of confusion over orders and the breakdown of battlefield communications as in the case of a dismounted attack by Indian cavalry from Jacob's Horse against the exceedingly troublesome beet factory that had caused great loss to the Mhow Brigade. After this failure, the surviving Inniskilling Dragoons and 2nd Lancers were withdrawn from their deadly outposts. After all, what more could a few hundred men at most do in such circumstances?

Another exercise in futility was the dismounted attack by Lord Strathcona's Horse in the late afternoon described by Sergeant Henry Rebitt:

At 3.00 p.m., 'A' and 'B' Squadrons made a circular approach to Gauche Wood. We had fair cover part of the way, but finally had to come out in the open on the down slope to the wood. This part we covered in rushes. We suffered several casualties from artillery fire and from machine-gun fire. Many of my men were quite exhausted on reaching the shell holes in the wood, which finally formed our line. I remember assisting some of the most exhausted ones in digging in the sides of the shell holes to afford them better shelter.[44]

Sergeant Henry Rebitt, Lord Strathcona's Horse, Canadian Cavalry Brigade, 5th Cavalry Division

During this attack, of the fifty or so casualties suffered by the regiment, two were especially remembered. The first was Lieutenant Rex Young, whom Rebitt recalled as an 'excellent officer and a brave man'. The other was Private Edward Seymour, who was seriously wounded and died of his wounds some days later. As Lord Edward Seymour, he belonged to an old and distinguished family – third son of the Marquis of Hertford and brother of 'Copper', the Guards' brigadier. According to Lieutenant Sam Williams, 'He was what would be termed today a confirmed alcoholic, which no doubt accounts for his being a private in a Canadian unit.'[45] If true, it would appear that this particular 'black sheep' from a noble house had made the ultimate sacrifice, surely wiping the slate clean in doing so. We can only speculate what his brother thought and felt when he heard the news.

In their new positions, Sergeant Henry Rebitt made contact with their neighbours, 2nd Grenadier Guards, whom 'I found to be most curious about our methods, country, etc. Most of them were quite ready and willing to share some of their (at that time) meagre food supplies.' However, with night approaching and temperatures falling, it was with some relief that Rebitt and his troop were given permission to withdraw. He had unfinished business: 'By the aid of the stars I was able to lead my troop back to our jumping-off spot and retrieved our buried treasure.'[46] It was certain that one small rum jar at least was not going to fall into German hands.

The loss of Rex Young was especially hard on his fellow lieutenant, Andy Morgan. Sam Williams recalled Morgan's desolation:

Andy went out as soon as it grew dark to search for Rex Young's body. When he had found the body, he gathered it up, and weeping

like a child carried it back to our lines. Andy and Rex were friends
and neighbours of long years standing back home before the war.[47]

Lieutenant Samuel Williams, Lord Strathcona's Horse, Canadian Cavalry Brigade, 5th
Cavalry Division

The deaths of men like Young and Seymour, although occurring in
such futile attacks, did not make their own sacrifice futile. The robust
and vigorous actions of the cavalry, tanks and infantry on the southern
flank, supported by improving and growing artillery fire, effectively
ensured that there would be no further collapse on this flank, prompt-
ing General Georg von der Marwitz, *Second Army*'s commander, in his
acceptance that the attack had 'run itself out'. Now it was Crown Prince
Rupprecht who fell victim to urging that 'one more push' might achieve
a significant victory. However, even he accepted the need to pause for
consolidation before any further effort. So, 3 December was set as the
date for another German 'push' on the southern flank.

On the salient's northern flank, the massed infantry attacks of the
previous day were reduced to the slog of trench-by-trench bombing
attacks. No matter how much the likes of Ernst Jünger might wrap this
up as an exemplar of 'the technique of the storm-troop', the fighting
here was not the incisive infiltration tactics with which stormtroops
would subsequently become identified. Yet Jünger's descriptions of the
fighting on that day gives a very real indication of the horrors of trench
fighting – beginning with the gut-gripping tension before action:

> I got up at six and made the final arrangements, in a mood peculiar to
> the last hour before an attack. There's a lonely, sinking feeling in the
> stomach as one speaks to the section leaders, tries to make jokes, and
> keeps running to and fro as if before an inspection by the divisional
> commander. In short, one tries to be as occupied as possible in order to
> escape the thoughts that drill into the brain. One of the men offered me
> a cup of coffee heated in a trench cooker. Its warmth cheered me to the
> marrow.[48]

Leutnant Ernst Jünger, *Füsilier Regiment 73, 111th Division*

Jünger's unit was involved in the strong attacks made along the old
Hindenburg front system against units of 6th Brigade including the

survivors of 13th Essex who were soon overwhelmed. Men of 1st Kings were also engaged in the fighting in which the Germans managed to get behind the headquarters of the Kings' battalion. The Germans enjoyed considerable success in these small-unit fights and took many prisoners. Jünger's company, approximately 80 strong, knew the extent of their achievement and took to looting the British positions in the captured trench:

> It was bristling with arms and equipment. On the firesteps were machine-guns, mortars, bombs, and rifle-grenades, water-bottles, sheepskin waistcoats, mackintosh capes, groundsheets, cases of bully beef, jam, tea, coffee, cocoa, and tobacco, bottles of rum, tools, revolvers, Very light pistols, clothing, gloves; in short, everything imaginable. Like an old soldier of fortune I allowed an interval for plunder, nor could I resist the temptation myself of having a small breakfast prepared for me by my batman in a dugout entrance and lighting a pipe of the 'Navy Cut' I had so long been without, while I scribbled a report to the commanding officer of the troops in the line.[49]
>
> Leutnant Ernst Jünger, *Füsilier Regiment 73, 111th Division*

For the German infantry, too long deprived of any comforts and especially the relative richness of the bounty enjoyed by their British counterparts, it was too good an opportunity to resist but must surely have been a difficult reminder of the resources of Britain and her allies.

The bloody and intimate killing of trench fighting continued into the afternoon with casualties mounting on both sides and gains measured in yards or metres. British reinforcements in the form of 17th Middlesex and, later, two companies of 2nd Highland Light Infantry, launched successive counter-attacks, which were repulsed by the Germans:

> Suddenly, there was a commotion at the barricade. Bombs flew, rifles pinged, and machine-guns rattled. 'They're coming. They're coming.' We jumped to our sandbags and fired away. One of my men, the volunteer Kimpenhaus jumped on to the top of the block in the heat of the battle and fired into the trench till he fell severely wounded in both arms . . . There followed one of those extraordinary episodes in which, great and small, the history of the war is so rich. A subaltern of the

regiment on our left who had come to get into touch with us became inspired by a boundless pugnacity. It seemed that drink had inflamed his inborn courage to madness. 'Where's the Tommy? At the dogs! Who's coming?' In his rage he pulled down our fine block and plunged on, clearing a road for himself with a roar of bombs. In front of him, through the trench, flitted his orderly, and finished off with his rifle those whom the bombs had spared . . . We were all wrought up and, snatching up bombs, ran to take part in the improvised assault.[50]

Leutnant Ernst Jünger, *Füsilier Regiment 73, 111th Division*

Jünger himself was subsequently wounded in these bombing attacks in which, as he admitted, all the non-commissioned officers and a third of the men of his company fell casualty. These, he must have known, were casualties that the Germans could ill afford. And for what purpose? In truth, after their initial success, their gains had been tiny compared with what von Moser had hoped to achieve on the previous day. Although the bombing attacks raged on, the Bourlon front was stagnating back into the attritional grind of trench fighting. Of course, this did not mean that the fighting was over but the divisions of the *Arras Group* were too tired to attempt any major operations on this front and no stormtrooper myth was going to disguise that fact.

From a British point of view, there was an element of desperation in the air as well. The arrival of Richthofen's *Jagdgeschwader I* had definitely swung the battle in the air in Germany's favour – although not necessarily in numerical terms. Richthofen now had general command of all the German air units. It must, therefore, have been disappointing for the men under his command that 1 December was a day of mist and low cloud that prevented them from any great active participation in the battle. If their tails were up, they were perhaps a little less so by the end of the day – particularly since the RFC flew a great many more low-level sorties on the day. There were only a small number of actual combats and the British had the upper hand in these.

However, the following days saw continued use of massed German formations endeavouring to out-muscle the RFC fliers from over the battlefield. Captain Howard Brokensha, commanding a flight of No. 3 Squadron, was caught in one such swirling combat:

Several thousand feet above us and right in the sun, I saw a formation of twelve or sixteen enemy aircraft. In a few seconds they were diving on our formation from all directions and the air was full of tracer and twisting and turning machines engaged in a general dog-fight. One of ours was soon in difficulties and was seen to go down out of control at the same time as two of the Huns also broke off, apparently badly damaged. We closed formation again with 'B' Flight still intact followed by two of 'A' Flight and waited for the next assault, as the Germans had mostly dived past us after their first attack and were now gaining height again. They were a squadron of Richthofen's circus and were painted in all sorts of colours and patterns, and one, I noticed, had a wavy red snake painted along the fuselage. But there was not much time to wonder at them as part of their squadron had been kept in reserve a few thousand feet above.[51]

Captain Howard Brokensha, 3 Squadron, Royal Flying Corps

Well aware that the German Albatros aircraft could out-climb and out-dive their outnumbered Sopwith Camels, Brokensha and his fellow RFC pilots' hopes of survival depended on mutual support against the second attack by these beautifully streamlined aircraft with plywood fuselages and powerful engines.

One of 'A' Flight was soon in difficulties, being surrounded by at least three of the enemy and fighting hard against such odds. To go to his assistance was of course the only thing to do, and by waggling my wings from side to side I gave the one signal we could use in those days in an emergency, for the rest of the flight to follow. But in all the excitement and tension my turn to the right was not noticed and I realised that I was alone in the rescue attempt and would have to deal with four Huns, as by the time I reached the scene our machine was already going down practically out of control, and I was quickly in a dog-fight with three highly coloured Albatroses.[52]

Captain Howard Brokensha, 3 Squadron, Royal Flying Corps

With his role changed from rescuer to hunted, Brokensha managed to loose off a long burst into one aircraft, putting the German machine out of control. Brokensha himself went into a fast full-power spin. This was the moment of greatest danger:

414

I realised my danger when I should come out of my spin and present a good target on straightening out and in a vertical dive. After falling about a thousand feet I stopped the spin, and immediately did a fast turn and climb to face two of the diving enemies as they came at me, their tracers crackling past and my guns replying, but all without apparent effect. The two Huns had dived past as I turned to meet the third machine which was following the first two and noticed his painted red nose and blue fuselage and realised, too late, that he had a bead on me. A frantic pull over on the joystick was also too late, and the next thing I knew was a stunning sledgehammer-like blow as the result of a bullet in my right thigh.[53]

Captain Howard Brokensha, 3 Squadron, Royal Flying Corps

Recovering from the shock of his wound and finding the Camel in a vertical climb through his instinctive pulling back of the stick after being hit, Brokensha's troubles were far from over.

I pulled over hard into a quick roll just in time to miss a burst from a diving Hun who was waiting above. It must have been about this time that my petrol feed pipe was partly shot through, and the escaping petrol started spraying over my right leg making it numb and cold, but my worry now was how to get out of the fight alive and reach our lines again. Three Huns were now following me down in a steep dive firing as they came, but when any of them approached too near I pulled the Camel into a vertical climb and fired bursts at the nearest, then turned and dived again towards our lines, still some miles away. These manoeuvres continued in a running fight for a long time and I began to feel a little sick through loss of blood, especially when my leg felt hot and warm instead of cold, through blood running down from my wound overcoming the previous numbness.[54]

Captain Howard Brokensha, 3 Squadron, Royal Flying Corps

In this fashion, Brokensha was hounded back to the British lines with the chill realization that the odds were against him and there were three Germans whose sole intention was to kill him.

Down to about a thousand feet and feeling pretty weak, I managed to find a stick of chewing-gum in my flying-coat breast pocket and ate that, paper and all. The Huns followed down to five hundred feet just above their trenches, then turned away as I crossed our lines at two hundred feet, making for one of our emergency landing fields.[55]

Captain Howard Brokensha, 3 Squadron, Royal Flying Corps

A difficult landing came next, but this was safely negotiated. Struggling out of his mauled aircraft, however, Brokensha saw clear evidence of how closely he had courted the same death so many of his comrades had suffered.

In getting out I could not help noticing a neat group of four bullet holes in the cowling behind my seat and about two inches behind where my head had been; an inch or two further to the rear and this burst would have hit my petrol tank and what we all feared most – to be set on fire in the air – would have happened. Why those bullets should have missed is one of the unsolved mysteries of our lives; some lasted a few weeks, others some months, but one never knew. So often had I packed up my room-mate's belongings, always left ready in case, and forwarded them to his relatives, wondering when my own turn would come – and now it had – and more fortunately for me than for most of these young pilots.[56]

Captain Howard Brokensha, 3 Squadron, Royal Flying Corps

This was the stark reality for these brave men. The strain they flew under was undoubtedly immense. Arthur Gould Lee had survived a brush with ground fire on 2 December and now hated the work of ground-strafing. His nerve was clearly going:

To fly along a winding trench, bristling with successive nests of machine-guns and mortars, and rifles by the score, all blasting up at you every time you lift up to dive, and fired by people largely hidden and protected by traverses, really makes my hair stand on end. The strain of waiting for that one bullet with your name on it, knowing that you can't dodge it like you can 'archie',* is quite petrifying. Trench-strafing can be a suicidal job, especially if you're rash, and the staff types who so casually order it can have no conception of what it demands from a pilot. They ought to try it occasionally.[57]

Lieutenant Arthur Gould Lee, 46 Squadron, RFC

* 'Archie' – anti-aircraft fire.

Yet, despite frequently being outgunned and outnumbered, the scout pilots of the RFC knew they must keep to their task of protecting their fellow fliers doing the vital work of spotting for artillery, photo-reconnaissance or contact patrols, whilst preventing the Germans doing the same. Thus, the dedicated James McCudden continued about his work day on day until the battle was over:

> On December 5th the visibility being good I went up looking for
> photographic Rumplers, and had been up about an hour and was at
> 19,000 feet when I saw a Hun over Bourlon Wood coming west at
> about my height. I at once sneaked into the sun, and waited until the
> Hun was west of me, and then I flew north and cut him off from his
> lines. I very quickly secured a good firing position, and after firing a
> good burst from both guns the Rumpler went down in a vertical dive
> and all its wings fell off at 16,000 feet and the wreckage fell in our lines
> near Hermies. I went back to my aerodrome, landed, and after having
> had lunch took my patrol out for the afternoon sports.[58]
>
> Captain James McCudden, 56 Squadron, RFC

'Business as usual' was the essence of McCudden's approach and many followed his example even if killing and being killed was the business.

Although Crown Prince Rupprecht's plan was for another large-scale assault on 3 December to try to take Trescault, or at least La Vacquerie, the fighting here did not die down – as men of the newly arrived 61st Division were about to discover. Captain James Wyatt had been sent up in the afternoon of 1 December to arrange the relief of the hard-pressed defenders of Guards, 12th and 20th Divisions. At Villers Plouich, he found the headquarters of 29th Division and three infantry brigades:

> There were two Brigadier Generals of the 12th Division, Vincent and
> Owen by name, and a Colonel acting as Brigade Commander of a
> Brigade of the 20th Division. These 3 brigades were, I gathered, pretty
> well mixed up in the Welsh Ridge–La Vacquerie area and had been
> having a pretty tough time for the past 2 days keeping their end up
> against the Bosche. Vincent seemed to be the directing spirit and when

I enquired what the situation was, led off by saying 'Well, the "situ-agger" is that everybody's got the wind up'![59]

Captain James Wyatt, 2/4th Gloucestershire Regiment, 183rd Infantry Brigade, 61st Division

Vincent's remarkable sangfroid had carried him and 'Vincent's Force' through the previous days of hellish action and chaos. It remained to be seen how 61st Division would perform when pressed. As the reliefs were carried out, the newcomers witnessed all the signs of the epic struggles that had already occurred:

That night, Saturday 1 December, we moved up into the line at La Vacquerie, or an area which had once been the village of La Vacquerie. The trenches were piled high with dead men. It was difficult to move about in places. The whole place was a scene of complete and utter disaster. Nobody knew just what part of the trenches we were supposed to take over or exactly where the Germans were . . . We did finally 'take over' from a small party of Grenadier Guards headed by a Corporal. When our Commanding Officer asked him where his officers were he replied very quietly, 'They are all dead, sir, we are all that is left' . . . He looked very young and very weary, I think his little band of survivors numbered less than a dozen men.[60]

Company Sergeant Major Walter Lockwood, 2/6th Gloucestershire Regiment, 183rd Brigade, 61st Division

The night was relatively quiet with nobody knowing where they were or what to expect when morning came. Before it did come, things soon started to happen. At 5.30 a.m., the Germans launched a bombing attack against Lockwood's battalion of Gloucesters. Lockwood, with his friend 'Mac' alongside him, was soon faced with a battle for survival:

We were in rather a stupid position really, for we had no grenades to tackle the Germans with. I got hold of a corporal and sent him off to find some. Meanwhile the Germans tried to rush us but that was a bit stupid on their part because we could just shoot them as they came round the corner. That held them up for a bit. Then the corporal returned with a box of Mills hand grenades and I just picked the pin out of one when a German grenade landed at my feet between me and Mac. It blew the sole of my right boot off and a big splinter hit me just above my right eye which then bled like fury. Some more splinters busted a finger on my right hand, broke the bone and generally made a mess of it. Fortunately I must have thrown my grenade into the Germans by instinct for I don't remember doing so, but with the pin out it wasn't a good thing to have about anyhow. Had it dropped on the floor it would have finished us both off . . . Poor old Mac was in a terrible state. He got the full blast of the German grenade in his stomach and was also half-blinded. I helped him and together we staggered to the end of the trench. Then the stretcher bearers took him away.[61]

Company Sergeant Major Walter Lockwood, 2/6th Gloucestershire Regiment, 183rd Brigade, 61st Division

Lockwood and his fellow Gloucesters repulsed this first attack, but it was only a short respite and soon a very heavy general attack began.

Finally, we were forced to get out. We didn't go back but moved sideways along the trench past a sunken road and on the other side of it we made a block in the trench and got a couple of Lewis guns at the end and held on there.[62]

Company Sergeant Major Walter Lockwood, 2/6th Gloucestershire Regiment, 183rd Brigade, 61st Division

The British were pushed back to the outskirts of La Vacquerie, but Lockwood and a party of about 90 men still held out as a pocket of resistance and a thorn in the Germans' side. With Lieutenant Claud Hughes-Games, Lockwood tried to establish the party's situation:

Hughes-Games and myself were standing together in the trench. He at the back of the trench facing me and I leaning against the parapet with a number of others standing around. Suddenly there was a burst of fire from somewhere and the soldier standing next to me got a bullet straight between the eyes and folded up against my feet, very dead of course. I felt a bullet sing past my ear and saw it bury itself in the back of the trench near Hughes-Games. Then another hit him in the upper part of his arm and cut the artery. So he started bleeding like a pig. Fortunately, two stretcher-bearers were also in the little group and they started to get a tourniquet on his arm. Poor old 'Hugo' didn't like the idea at all, declaring that he was quite all right and trying to brush them off, but he soon folded up from the loss of blood. So the stretcher-bearers completed their job and carried him away.[63]

Company Sergeant Major Walter Lockwood, 2/6th Gloucestershire Regiment, 183rd Brigade, 61st Division

For the rest of the day, the following night and into 3 December, the Gloucesters' defence was made even more hellish for Lockwood by the bitter conflict that developed between himself and Captain John Allen, the senior officer. The latter clearly demonstrated his belief that the isolated defenders' only hope was by iron self-discipline and supreme effort by one and all. Lockwood, as Company Sergeant Major, felt the pressure more than most:

> Then I had my first brush with Captain Allen. Although he must have known and seen that I was in a pretty poor state he instructed me to take out a patrol and investigate the German position. I told him that I could take any sort of old patrol that he liked to order but I thought it was complete nonsense for we knew very well what the Germans' strength was, only too well in fact. In those conditions (it was snowing heavily and difficult to see a dozen yards ahead) I was much more likely to lose my own men than to find out anything fresh. He became exceedingly unpleasant and 'pulled rank' and so I went over the top and out into the darkness into a minor blizzard. It was absolutely utterly hopeless – I knew it would be. Then a shell burst a little behind me and I felt a terrible bang in my back and passed out. I must have lain there for several hours because when I recovered my senses I found that my right foot was in a shell hole which was partly full of water which had frozen over. Then I remembered my back and soon realised that there was nothing wrong there. There was probably a good old bruise but nothing appeared to be broken and no bleeding.[64]

Company Sergeant Major Walter Lockwood, 2/6th Gloucestershire Regiment, 183rd Brigade, 61st Division

Two of his men came along and took him back to trench but, much to Lockwood's chagrin, 'Captain Allen never came near me to ask for my report or anything.'

As the siege went on, Lockwood struggled increasingly to perform any useful service. His various wounds drained his strength and the fatigue and constant tension ground him down. But Captain Allen did not let up either:

I lay on the fire step half unconscious. One of my men piled an old coat on top of me. Then of course our old friend Captain Allen came along, demanded to know who that man was under there. When he was told, he pulled the old coat away and told me to get up, my place was to lead my men and not sulk there. That really did sting. He was told that I was wounded in several places and not at all well. To which he retorted 'So are a lot of other men.' I thought one of my blokes was going to knock him down, it was touch and go and I think he realised it just in time and had the sense to go. I did manage to get up but sat down very heavily and passed out immediately afterwards, but I never got over that remark, never.[65]

Company Sergeant Major Walter Lockwood, 2/6th Gloucestershire Regiment, 183rd Brigade, 61st Division

Lockwood's party did not extricate themselves from their position until 4 December, by which time the Germans had completed the capture of La Vacquerie in a heavy attack on 3 December. It was as a result of this attack that the wounded Wilfrid Taylor and his two fellow dugout occupants were finally rescued from their lonely ordeal. Their rescuers were German infantry. Nevertheless, their appearance was a tremendous relief for the three British soldiers but there had been one final, cruel, twist:

A terrible fear began to enter our minds lest the lines should have settled down permanently, and we should be left eternally in No Man's Land. At last on Sunday night I heard a movement above, and at once called out 'Stretcher-bearers!' and then 'Wounded!' and 'Blessées!' Two Huns promptly came down, bombs in hand. They showed no signs of hostility, but on the other hand, appeared to take little interest in us, and busied themselves at once in 'scrounging' for food and souvenirs . . . Later two more Huns came down, and one of them, who was quite a boy appeared more sympathetic and in response to my appeals of 'blessées' replied 'Ja! Ja! Sanitator,' and made sundry gestures from which I gathered he would send some stretcher-bearers to our aid. All that night, after he and his comrade had gone we waited anxiously, but by daybreak on Monday no one had appeared.[66]

Second Lieutenant Wilfrid Taylor, 6th Buffs, 37th Brigade, 12th Division

When the German artillery bombardment suddenly re-opened on the morning of 3 December, Taylor and his companions briefly entertained the hope that it was a British counter-attack. It was not to be.

The shoe was on the other foot, however, and subsequently a German officer came down with a number of men. He had a stick grenade in his hand, but as soon as he saw me he said in English 'Are you wounded?' 'Yes,' I replied. 'There are three of us.' He thereupon came up to me and put his hand on my shoulder and said 'I also am a man!' I thought at once of the famous 'Homo sum nihil humani a ne alienum puto.' I asked him if he could get us away. 'Not now,' he replied, 'the English artillery is not good; it is better for you to lie blessed where you are, than to be died in the trenches.' He at once set to work, however, and made us some hot cocoa and told one of his men to re-arrange my bandage and splint – a task which the man accomplished gently and skilfully. At last in the afternoon he got us on to stretchers and we were carried away. Needless to say I shook hands with him and thanked him very much for his kindness. He is the only German I should ever care to meet again.[67]

Second Lieutenant Wilfrid Taylor, 6th Buffs, 37th Brigade, 12th Division

Whilst indecisive fighting continued on both the Bourlon and La Vacquerie sides of the salient, a serious threat had developed against the positions still occupied by British troops on the far side of the St Quentin Canal east of Marcoing. Already, on 2 December, Haig had discussed with Lieutenant General Sir Launcelot Kiggell, his Chief of the General Staff, the likelihood of a withdrawal from most of the areas captured in the British offensive. Now, such a withdrawal became a necessity. The salient was proving too costly a liability. On the following day, Byng was ordered to 'select a good winter line' and make arrangements for a withdrawal to it. Later, having met with Byng and officially sanctioned the moves the latter had decided upon, Haig acquainted his superior, General Sir William Robertson, with his reasons:

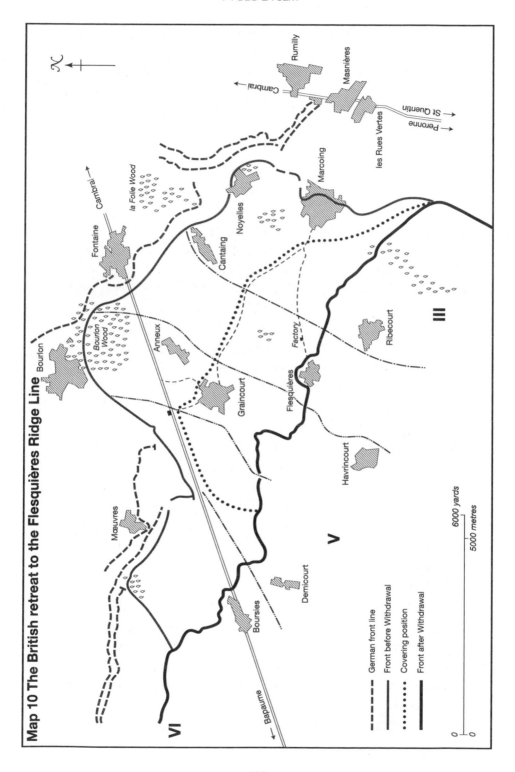

Map 10 The British retreat to the Flesquières Ridge Line

Bourlon

Bourlon Wood

Mœuvres

Fontaine

la Folie Wood

Cambrai →

Anneux

Graincourt

Cantaing

Noyelles

Rumilly

Masnières

Cambrai →

les Rues Vertes

← Peronne

St Quentin →

Marcoing

Factory

Flesquières

Ribecourt

Havrincourt

Demicourt

Boursies

← Bapaume

III

V

VI

German front line

Front before Withdrawal

Covering position

Front after Withdrawal

6000 yards

5000 metres

The present line could be held, but in view of the enemy's present activity it would use up troops which, in view of your instructions and the manpower situation, I do not feel justified in devoting to it. My available reserves to meet serious attack are very limited; and the troops need as much rest as possible after their strenuous exertions since April.[68]

Field Marshal Sir Douglas Haig, General Headquarters, BEF

With scant attempt at cunning, Haig also took the opportunity to lay down markers indicating the inadvisability of sending more precious men from his command to Italy and his inability, given his present manpower resources, to take over more of the front line from the French. These were stalling tactics. Already his mind was turning to the need to plan for what now seemed inevitable: a large-scale German offensive in the west in the New Year.

The withdrawal was skilfully accomplished during the course of the next few days despite continued pressure from the Germans. It established the British in defences that offered good observation of the ground in front and was an important reason why, when the Germans did attack what was still, essentially, a salient at Flesquières in March 1918 as part of their attempt at a war-winning offensive, these attacks suffered heavy casualties and were bloodily frustrated. This was, perhaps, poor compensation for the expenditure of lives, *matériel* and effort that the British offensive had required but, in the end, it was an important landmark on the road to British victory.

The battlefield was peppered with the wrecks of British tanks that had not been recovered after they had been broken down or knocked out by shell fire. Many remained behind German lines after their counter-attacks had recaptured lost ground. Most were cannibalized in some way by the Germans, who produced approximately 30 serviceable tanks for their own use as a result. Although these did subsequently see combat alongside Germany's own first attempt at a tank, the A7V, they did not form the spearhead of the Spring Offensives launched on 21 March 1918. That honour went to the artillery and *minenwerfers* that had served this purpose so well on 30 November 1917. For the Germans, perhaps because they had seen the effects of their own artillery fire against tanks, the tank was never regarded as a war-winning weapon, although its moral effects were recognized and acknowledged by many and, indeed, exaggerated by some. However, the moral effects of offensive action were perhaps more keenly noted as 1917 closed and plans for 1918 were laid.

The British spent much greater effort on recovering the valuable artillery pieces that had been abandoned in what had become No Man's Land or that lay in ground recaptured by British units after initial loss on 30 November. Lieutenant Sam Williams watched one attempt:

> We got a thrill from seeing the artillery rescue a big gun out in 'No Man's Land'. Shortly after we had arrived at the trench line, the artillery men went in, taking with them three teams of heavy draft horses. The horses all had sacking wrapped around their feet to insure them making no unnecessary noise, such as by striking their shod feet against stones. About an hour after they had gone in, they came back again with the teams pulling an eight-inch howitzer.[69]
>
> Lieutenant Samuel Williams, Lord Strathcona's Horse, Canadian Cavalry Brigade, 5th Cavalry Division

Len Ounsworth of 144th Heavy Battery was one who actually risked his life in another daring, and well-planned, enterprise:

> We had two guns in No Man's Land. We'd moved them forward a couple of days before and they'd been captured in front of Villers Guislain. Well, the Major determined to get these two out so we spent the preceding day or two preparing for it. The limbers wheels were all bound round with car tyres cut round the wheel rim and then wired on. The drag washers, they put leather washers in place for the time being. The horses' feet were all muffled in sandbags. Every link of the harness, all the adjusting links, they were all bound round with string. We pulled sandbags to pieces and bound it like that. The drivers' feet were in a sandbag so his boots wouldn't rattle on the stirrups. We got down into No Man's Land towards the guns which were in a hollow at the bottom and the Lovat's Scouts bloke came back and told us to stand fast, there was a Jerry patrol out. Well, we stood there for about 20 minutes and, believe it or not, not a blooming horse sneezed or anything! They seemed to realise there was something wrong and everybody stood

dead quiet. Then they came back and told us we could carry on. We got everything ready and the drag ropes hooked on and the hand spikes into the gun sockets ready for men to lift it. There were sockets and these big long ash-reinforced hand spikes. You stuck them into the trail and then four men lifted them on the limber. We got hooked in and we started off cautiously up this slope . . . We'd sixteen horses to each gun, normally there's eight . . . our horses now were still four deep but also four abreast. Then we had a drag rope as well with 30 men on either side. That was just to get the gun out of the pit. We got so far and then a gun we hadn't time to silence banked into a hole or something and made a big clatter. Well, the next thing was Jerry started shooting but he didn't seem to have any Very lights or anything, fortunately for us. The moment they started, the Major yelled out to 'Let 'em go' and with 32 horses onto the two guns, they soon were almost at a gallop up that slope. They didn't find the spot where the trenches were filled in, but the horses jumped over the infantry who were swearing like hell at us for crashing over them! We got up the way we'd come and when we got behind Vaucelette Farm, the old man halted us. I thought 'Christ, let's get out of this.' But, he knew what he was doing. Less than a minute later, the road from Vaucelette Farm down to Heudicourt was just one mass of shell bursts! He kept that up for about ten or fifteen minutes and we stood there watching it all. After he'd finished, we waited about another ten or 15 minutes and then the Major just said to the Sergeant Major 'I think we may go home now, Sergeant Major.' We never had a casualty taking those two guns out like that![70]

Corporal Len Ounsworth, 144th Heavy Battery, RGA

Similar scenes took place all over the battlefield. With a likely German attack in the New Year, the value of every artillery piece was that much more inflated than that of, for example, a tank. In a very real sense this was, and always remained, an artillery war.

Amongst those who had survived the fighting, many experienced the sheer *joie de vivre* of being alive after surviving the terrors of the battle. George McMurtrie had been in the first attack and experienced the unreality of the splendid initial success. Then he had remained in Masnières under increasing German artillery fire and the growing pressure of a potential counter-attack before becoming embroiled in the frantic scenes and the fight for survival against the German counter-attack. He had survived what he knew was 'some of the fiercest, bloodiest and heaviest fighting that had taken place throughout the war'. After the final withdrawal, safely ensconced behind British lines, he took the opportunity of an exceptionally mild December day to ride out:

> It was a lovely sunny, warm autumn day and it was a pleasant change to be riding back just as it was getting dark – with a warm hut, good tea and blazing fire to return to; instead of a wet, muddy trench and rumours of stand-tos, alarms and counter-attacks. It was great and I don't think I have ever experienced a stronger feeling of life and happiness than on that day, after having gone through two weeks of nerve-wracking strain and danger.[71]
>
> Second Lieutenant George McMurtrie, 7th Somerset Light Infantry, 61st Brigade, 20th Division

Benjamin Parkin's experiences had almost shattered his nerves but he also survived. His descriptions in writing to his wife of the pastoral delights of 'rest' were almost lyrical:

> Ah! Luxury! Happiness! Rest! Glorious! I woke from a beautiful night's rest this morning to the sound of cocks crowing, children playing, clock striking, dogs barking. What joy! What peace! It's more than I can say. A cat sits by me while I scribble this. I have just been buying eggs, vegetables, bread. Ah! Luxury! I won't tell how we've existed for the last fortnight – that is – what remains of us. I am so thankful we are here. The guns can still be heard – but a long way off. Oh! Joy! I am so glad, you don't know. I wanted to give you a taste of my joy and peace. The cock's crowing delights me after the time we've had.[72]
>
> Second Lieutenant Benjamin Parkin, 2/4th Duke of Wellington's Regiment, 186th Brigade, 62nd Division

Both must surely have known such delights were temporary. The war was not over. It had not yet been won. The Germans were not defeated. That would come almost a year later towards the end of 1918, though these men were not to know that. So, for now, they enjoyed life in a way that only men who have known such horrors of death and destruction as we would never wish to see could. This war was not to be won by a single strike as attempted at Cambrai, but by a bloody, battering, slogging fight. In a war fought with weapons that could blot out one's being in an instant and leave no trace, what could young men such as these do but enjoy every last drop they could eke out of life. Who knew what tomorrow might bring?

'Scattered memories remain'

It would be invidious not to detail the casualties suffered by both sides during the battle. Between 20 November and 8 December 1917, Sir Julian Byng's Third Army lost 44,207 men killed, wounded or missing. During approximately the same period, German losses totalled between 41,000 and 53,300 (the latter figure resulting from attempts to make the method of calculating these casualties comparable with that used for the BEF's losses). After the withdrawal to the Flesquières Ridge, the British front line here was approximately two miles further forward than on 20 November. However, elsewhere on the battlefield, it was the Germans who had accomplished a similar depth of advance.

'The results of the battle, measured in terms of ground gained and lost, showed little profit.'[1] So concluded the Cambrai volume of the British Official History – the last of the series to be produced. Published in 1948, after another global conflict in which, once more, Britain had emerged exhausted on the side of the victors, its account and conclusions excited little interest amongst a general public tired of war and facing the austerity of post-war Britain. Perhaps also because of its 'modern' nature, with many of the features of war that characterized the fighting from North Africa to the Elbe and Dunkirk to the Reichswald, the significance of this landmark in warfare was diminished. Cambrai no longer indicated 'the shape of things to come'.

However, this was not all. The events of the battle and their significance in the wider context of warfare had already been appropriated and reinterpreted by certain individuals in the inter-war years. Principally they did so to draw focus to one aspect of the battle and that alone: the massed employment of tanks. Despite the corrective the Official History attempted to provide to this monocular view, it was too late. Through the writings of John Frederick Charles Fuller, Basil Liddell Hart, Christopher Baker-Carr, and Winston Churchill, together with the popular histories of the war written by Arthur Conan Doyle and John Buchan, the public's imagination was already captured with a simple equation: Cambrai equalled tanks. There was essentially, therefore, nothing new to learn about the battle.

Aside from Buchan and Conan Doyle, each of these men had particular reasons for promoting the image of Cambrai as 'the first great tank battle'. In Fuller's case, they were twofold. Firstly, as the Tank Corps' chief staff officer at the time, it was in his interests to promote the role of the tank and the extent to which his tactical methods had been employed and contributed to the initial success. Secondly, as an inter-war British Army officer, writer and military theorist, he was a leading champion of a mechanized British army. Consequently, he did all he could to perpetuate the myth of 'invincible armour' in pursuit of this goal.

In this, his views were largely supported and shared by Basil Liddell Hart. It is difficult to indicate the position these two men (and especially Liddell Hart) held in the public's regard in the 1920s and 1930s. In Liddell Hart's case, his position as Military Correspondent of the *Daily Telegraph* from 1925 to 1935 and *The Times* between 1935 and 1939 gave him unparalleled status in pressing his views on war strategy and tactics. A prolific writer, he did much to promote a negative view of British military conduct of the war. It was inevitable, then, that he should see Cambrai as Haig's lost opportunity. However, in the case of both men, many of their writings were as much about the internal strife of the inter-war army as about the realities of the Great War. Of perhaps greater relevance concerning his analysis of the tank aspects of the Cambrai battle, however, was Liddell Hart's authorship of the regimental history of the British tank arm – hardly suggesting a critical analyst of the tanks' performance.

In 1930, Christopher Baker-Carr's *From Chauffeur to Brigadier*, his autobiographical account of his war service, was published. In it, Baker-Carr repeatedly asserted that he had spent much of his war fighting those within the British army establishment who had neither the wit nor the wisdom to share his views on the development and use of machine-guns and, later, tanks as the means to win the war. This was not all.

Regarding Cambrai, he asserted that the principle reason for the British offensive's failure had been 51st Division's inability to take the ridge and village of Flesquières and that this failure was due to the divisional commander, Major General Montague Harper, who had employed his own tactical drills in the battle contrary to the advice and guidance of Fuller and the Tank Corps. This was plainly rot. Like so much else in this most unreliable of books, Baker-Carr's description of events and apportionment of blame bore little relation to reality. In this case, it is sufficient to point out that it was Baker-Carr's own tank brigade that, together with 51st Division, failed to take Flesquières and that he made no criticism of the division's tactics at the time. It is impossible, therefore, to discount bias from his highly partial account. The narratives of tank officers like Horace Birks, Wilfrid Bion and William Watson soon prove the lie to Baker-Carr's words. Unfortunately, subsequent historians have repeatedly accepted Baker-Carr's account without qualification, thereby embedding it more deeply in the collective consciousness.

Winston Churchill, a man who can rightly claim to have been one of the key individuals responsible for the development of the first tank, expounded his view on Cambrai in his book *The World Crisis*:

> Accusing as I do without exception all the great Allied offensives of 1915, 1916, and 1917 as needless and wrongly conceived operations of infinite cost, I am bound to reply to the question, 'What else could be done?' And I answer it, pointing to the Battle of Cambrai: 'This could have been done.'[2]
>
> Winston Churchill

This suggests that had greater time and resources been devoted to developing and employing the tank earlier, the war might have been won considerably sooner and with a great deal less loss. Furthermore, it implies that the opening of the Cambrai offensive had been an unqualified success – the epitome of the perfect all-arms battle. It is worthwhile mentioning here, therefore, the response of a seasoned and knowledgeable tank officer whose battlefield experience meant his views cannot be ignored – the five times wounded, many times decorated Eliot Hotblack: 'I suggest that the short and perhaps impertinent answer is "Not with THOSE Tanks, it couldn't".'[3] Reading the descriptions of the battle preparations and of the first day's fighting presented here the reader will, I hope, see the many flaws that manifested themselves in Fuller's 'Clockwork Battle'.

The myth of Cambrai as primarily a tank battle and (by virtue of the number of tanks deployed en masse) the *first great* tank battle, was in no way diminished by a desire amongst tankophiles to focus on the first day of the battle. This was not, however, the attitude of the British High Command, and especially Douglas Haig. Overall, a stunning success had been achieved on that day – but a success that fell comprehensively short of complete victory. In order to account for that failure, Haig was obliged to detail what he felt were the reasons. His analysis was principally completed through the medium of his Official Despatch on the battle published on 20 February 1918 which (rightly given the prevailing strategic circumstances at the time it was written) gave as much attention to the German counter-attack as the British offensive. However, Haig's Despatch also helped create another myth within the larger myth. In seeking to explain the failure of tanks and infantry to capture Flesquières on the first day he wrote:

> Many of the hits upon our tanks at Flesquières were obtained by a German artillery officer who, remaining alone at his battery, served a field gun single-handed until killed at his gun. The great bravery of this officer aroused the admiration of all ranks![4]
>
> Field Marshal Sir Douglas Haig, General Headquarters, BEF

Haig was merely repeating the assertion of the unnamed eyewitness he had heard during his tour of the Flesquières Ridge on the third day of the battle. Nevertheless, in doing so, he developed and sustained an uncorroborated story that was doing the rounds in the BEF within days of the battle's opening. After the war, the cynical (such as Basil Liddell Hart) suggested that he did so as a critic of tanks hoping to show that well-trained and well-handled artillery could nullify any tank attack in a future war. Yet it is clear Haig was rather attempting to indicate how hard the fighting had been in and around Flesquières and how desperate the German defence there had been. It should be noted that when he wrote his Despatch, the German Spring Offensives of 1918 had not yet begun and he knew nothing of the prior training in an anti-tank role that the defending German *54th Division*'s artillery had received.

Furthermore, Haig's Despatch clearly acknowledged the valuable contribution the tanks had made:

> Throughout these operations the value of the services rendered by the tanks was very great, and the utmost gallantry, enterprise and resolution were displayed by both officers and crews. In combination with the other arms they helped to make possible a remarkable success.[5]
>
> Field Marshal Sir Douglas Haig, General Headquarters, BEF

In this last sentence Haig also indicated that he now had a clear understanding of how to employ tanks to maximum effect in the fighting on the Western Front. Although the BEF's combined all-arms attacks that brought victory in the second half of 1918 were still some months away, for the BEF's senior commander a crucial element of the tactical conundrum of trench warfare had fallen into place.

Amongst those who had taken part, the reality behind the 'great tank battle' myth provoked frustration. Jim Davies, the officer who had taken Sonnet Farm without tank assistance, spoke for many of the infantry on this matter:

> I've told this to tank officers who celebrate it as the great birthday of the tanks! . . . Personally, I had a very poor opinion of the tanks at the Battle of Cambrai![6]
>
> Second Lieutenant Jim Davies, 8th Royal Fusiliers, 36th Brigade, 12th Division

This was not merely a post-war 'problem'. Corporal Fred Wynne, who had survived the fight for Bourlon Village, captured the dichotomy that remained within the BEF concerning the value of the tank in battle, even as the Germans counter-attacked:

> We heard the news [of the German counter-attack] while queuing up for a rum issue in an 'elephant iron' hut. The semi-darkness in the hut adding to the depression of losing so many of our friends and now the news of the damning of our hopes for an early end to the war . . .
>
> We had, or some of us had, lost faith in the tanks. Those abandoned hulks scattered in front of Cambrai proved to some that their usefulness was limited. Those big bundles of tree loppings carried on top ready for dropping into an otherwise impassable widened trench demonstrated their limitations. And, some said, what was wrong with some of the

hulks we had seen (and closely examined) lying around abandoned? Some with not a visible scratch or a sign of serious damage, but left there as sitting targets for enemy field guns. But we who had been in Bourlon village knew that one tank at the right time at the right place could have avoided the slaughter of two or three hundred men on that damp chilly morning of November 26th 1917.[7]

Corporal Fred Wynne, 13th East Surreys, 120th Brigade, 40th Division

By returning to the accounts of those who participated, produced during the ninety years following the battle, I have endeavoured to provide a balanced assessment of the battle. Selection of such accounts must inevitably be partial but their value is in taking us away from the myths. Some accounts quite literally speak the truth for themselves. To take one example, there are those that show the clear understanding amongst those who fought of the strategic context in which the attack was launched – if not of the fine detail of the war situation. Thus, on 11 November, Lieutenant Algernon Hyde Villiers wrote:

The news is as bad, isn't it? One really requires all one's fortitude to contemplate the conquest of Venetia and the final *pourriture* of Russia under Lenin. How long shall we and the French be able to keep loyal in the midst of so much collapse? I don't really doubt that we both shall be able to hold on, but this winter will evidently be a time of supreme strain and testing.[8]

Lieutenant Algernon Hyde Villiers, 121st Company, MGC, 40th Division

Similarly, there are accounts illustrating how, within the BEF, many knew that the Western Front was where Germany could, and must, be defeated for the war to be won:

The war is becoming pretty serious now, from all appearances. The enemy seems to have plenty of men, due to the splendid support to our side given by Russia! We do seem to back the wrong horse. I do wish that the capture of Jerusalem and the advance in Mesopotamia could make some difference; these side-shows use a great many men and make no material difference to the ultimate issue.[9]

Captain James Neville, 2nd Oxfordshire & Buckinghamshire Light Infantry, 5th Brigade, 2nd Division

However, other aspects of the battle cannot be illustrated by a single quote but only by drawing together many accounts to reach a balanced conclusion. From the many accounts presented here it is possible to construct the following narrative.

In 1917, prior to the battle of Cambrai, there was a convergence of strategic, political, scientific, technological and tactical factors that, together with chance, produced a marked change in how the BEF fought its battles from this point. The changes produced by these factors were first seen in combination on 20 November 1917, a day that can legitimately be seen as marking the commencement of a 'Modern Style of Warfare'. However, despite the major change wrought overall in the conduct of fighting on the Western Front, Cambrai was only a milestone on the road to ultimate victory. It did not provide all the answers.

Generally, the attack enjoyed remarkable success. However, there were three key points at which success evaded the attackers. The failure of tanks and 51st Division's infantry to take Flesquières has been mentioned and provides one example of how preparations for the attack were defective. The divisional commander's decision not to commit his reserve brigade to secure the capture of Flesquières on the first day was a serious error. This arose from a combination of Major General Harper's excessive caution in trying to husband his resources for the second and subsequent days of fighting, the division's over-extended command and communication infrastructure and the German Army's understanding that this village was the lynchpin of their defence in this sector and must be held at all costs.

The collapse of the bridge at Masnières under the weight of the tank 'Flying Fox' demonstrated a crucial flaw in the plan frequently ignored or only vaguely referred to in many accounts – the limitations that the St Quentin Canal imposed on options for actions with tanks and, to a lesser extent, cavalry. Once this crossing had gone and any other option on the right flank had been denied to tanks and other arms, the main focus of both British and German attention shifted to the left flank and Bourlon. Here the failure to capture the crucial first day objective of Bourlon Ridge, despite the considerable advance achieved by Roland Bradford's 186th Brigade, might have been compensated for by its capture early on the second day.

When this did not happen, Byng and Haig were faced with a decision concerning whether to go on attacking or close down the offensive. *Based on the evidence before him at the time*, it seems entirely understandable that Haig chose to continue. That he did so, however, without adequate infantry reserves for the task meant both tanks and cavalry were repeatedly committed to attacks in a manner in which the operational plan had never intended. In the case of the tanks, the inevitable consequences were exhausted crews, poor communication and liaison with the other arms and a series of penny-packet attacks for which the Tank Corps' command and supply infrastructure was not prepared.

The attacks on Fontaine and Bourlon on 23 November provided a clear illustration of the shortcomings of the British use of tanks at this stage of the war. Once more their use against woods and villages resulted in major problems. At La Folie and in Bourlon the shell-damaged woodland meant any tank operations were limited and largely doomed to fail from the start, whilst in the attacks on Bourlon and especially Fontaine the problems encountered by 51st Division at Flesquières on the first day re-emerged. The BEF did not have its tactics for village fighting right at this stage. Having fought for several months against defences that consisted mainly of isolated strongpoints built on or under the site of Flanders farms, this aspect of tank co-operation with infantry had been refined and integrated into the minor tactics of the infantry platoons. There had been no such opportunity since Arras to develop tactics for the capture of villages – especially one in which many of the houses survived largely undamaged. However, after Cambrai, the lessons of the fighting were applied in tactical and technological changes. Thus, for example, the need for tank crews to be able to fire at targets in the upper storeys of buildings resulted in the new Mark V tanks introduced in mid-1918 being equipped with a machine-gun mount on its roof precisely for this purpose.

From 23 November onwards, the resilient defence offered by the German infantry facing the continued attacks between the Canal du Nord and Fontaine ensured that, as reserves and reinforcements arrived on the battle front, the German high command could not only gain in confidence regarding its ability to resist the British attacks but also begin preparations for a counter-strike. Yet, at this point, both sides were obliged to continue the fight for Bourlon Ridge. Its capture by the British would ensure artillery observation over a considerable section of the German back areas to the north-west and east (including Cambrai), whilst its retention by the Germans offered similar observation over the ground newly-won by the British between Havrincourt and Marcoing.

The final British attacks on 27 November produced wholly unnecessary casualties and were doomed to failure from the first. The spirited opposition of the Guards Division's commander, Major General Geoffrey Feilding, was admirable but, ultimately, the desire to remove the twin thorns of Fontaine and Bourlon from Third Army's side overwhelmed the Corps and Army commanders and even the British commander-in-chief. It was undoubtedly Haig's urgings that ensured the attack went ahead. That his concerns regarding German observation over the front-line positions were ultimately addressed in the manner Feilding had initially argued (that is, by a withdrawal to the Flesquières Ridge) must have been no consolation to the Guards' commander.

All too often the German counter-attacks commencing on 30 November have been marginalized in the picture of Cambrai as a 'tank battle'. Yet they deserve more detailed attention to provide much-needed balance to this picture. That Ludendorff's grandiose vision of an attack to roll up the British defences from the south came close to realization is a remarkable indication of the quality of the German Army facing the BEF in late 1917. That a successful deep advance was achieved on the southern flank without the assistance of tanks is equally worthy of note. This success was principally achieved through a skilful combination of artillery, trench mortars and infantry. However, whilst the German plan when implemented included many of the tactical elements employed in their 1918 Spring Offensives, the stormtroop tactics employed in November 1917 were, at best, only an embryonic version of those that enjoyed considerable success in March 1918.

Furthermore, the 'classic' elements of the 1918 attacks were almost wholly absent in the attack on the northern flank where no surprise was attempted and infantry were largely employed in massed formations, hoping to overwhelm the defenders in and around Bourlon Wood by sheer weight of numbers. It was on this flank that the continued presence of large numbers of British guns following the failed attempts to take Bourlon Ridge ensured that these massed attacks were defeated and heavy casualties inflicted on the Germans.

Some important aspects of the German success should also be stressed. The Germans faced nothing comparable in terms of barbed wire defences to those the British had encountered and, where they did, for example where the positions the British occupied incorporated the wire of the Hindenburg Line, the defence was generally more success-ful. The German infantry's training for their task was, in several cases, inadequate – a fact masked by the manner in which the violent artillery and *minenwerfer* bombardment shattered the British defences. Neverthe-less, important and useful lessons were learned about the offensive tactics employed. These were inculcated during the winter into the tactical training of the infantry and artillery that would make the assault on 21 March 1918 when Germany began what proved to be her final series of attempts to win the war by a decision on the battlefield.

The German counter-attack was a major shock for the British. Amongst politicians and the general public the chief focus was on the dramatic German drive to seize Gouzeaucourt. There was considerable disquiet concerning stories of mobs of men fleeing in the face of the German attacks and, in the process, throwing away their arms. Al-though GHQ attempted to focus attention within the army on the successful defence of 47th, 2nd and 56th Divisions by publishing a pamphlet entitled '*The Story of a Great Fight*', the need to address the failings on the opposite flank was accepted. Haig had no intention of minimizing the seriousness of what had occurred. However, in pre-paring a report for the War Cabinet, he relied almost exclusively on Sir Julian Byng's version of events.

Byng concluded that there had been no surprise, that his reserves were disposed appropriately to meet the attack and that the principle causes of failure were inadequate training of the junior officers, NCOs and men and the lack of determination shown by machine-gunners in the defence. He subsequently defended all his senior commanders and essentially argued that, although the forces of VII Corps and III Corps were weaker than was desirable, there had been adequate troops and, as Haig repeated 'the enemy should not have succeeded in penetrating any part'[10] of the British defence. Byng, despite his renowned empathy with his men, placed the blame solidly on their shoulders.

Remarkably, this undoubtedly flawed version of events was subsequently supported by the findings of both military and civilian investigators. Indeed, only Haig modified the version of events generally shared by suggesting that the defenders had probably been overwhelmed by weight of numbers and that the machine-gunners had been unable to open fire because of retreating British troops who got in the way. Still, Haig was not content to let matters lie with this version. On 21 January 1918, he convened a Court of Enquiry which took evidence from 25 witnesses. That these witnesses did not include Byng, his chief staff officers or any of the Corps commanders, makes the value of the exercise questionable. Besides, this enquiry reached much the same conclusions as previous investigations.

It was, therefore, not until a period of thirty years had elapsed that a detailed examination of the events between 30 November and 4 December produced rather different conclusions regarding the factors contributing to German success in the vicinity of Gouzeaucourt and Gonnelieu. This was the chief value of the Official History Cambrai volume. Finally, a more just and balanced account of the British defence in this sector was produced – an account with which my own closely concurs.

Both Third Army and III Corps were surprised by the German counter-attack and did not make adequate preparations in anticipation of such an attack. On the other hand, VII Corps' commander, Snow, and 55th Division's commander, Jeudwine, did fear and expect an attack and made what limited provision they could. Because Third Army's focus was still on the Bourlon flank, there was little they could do. Jeudwine's division was exhausted and considerably weakened in numbers and ought to have been relieved. This was true of 29th Division and, to some extent, 12th and 20th Divisions on III Corps' front too. Yet the initial German bombardment was so violent that many front-line defenders had little or no opportunity to defend themselves before they were overwhelmed. Those who could, fought hard, but as at Gouzeaucourt the German advance was often so rapid that there was little time before the Germans were upon the defenders.

Undoubtedly men threw away their arms and ran. However, there was some exaggeration in the numbers of men who did so, in the speed with which they retreated and in the arms of service to which they belonged. Many were transport men, gunners or engineers who were often falling back in steady fashion after abandoning their guns or positions only when it was deemed sensible for them to do so. It is worthwhile noting the words of Wilfrid Taylor concerning the defence of men from the Buffs and other units he witnessed whilst lying wounded on 30 November 1917:

> Amongst them I noticed our company cook and one of our sanitary men, non-combatants under ordinary circumstances, at this juncture full of spirits and blazing away with their rifles, as though they had been used to it all their lives. One had perhaps throughout 1917 felt rather despondent and been inclined to listen too much to the grousings and grumblings of the ordinary Tommy, and consider that perhaps his heart was not in the business , but in an action like this when the men had their backs to the wall, one could see how completely groundless was such despondency.[11]
>
> Second Lieutenant Wilfrid Taylor, 6th Buffs, 37th Brigade, 12th Division

Loyalty to mates was one bond that did much to underpin the dogged defence offered to the attack but the many occasions on which retreating men were rallied to provide spirited opposition further proves their mettle. Many only needed leadership and direction as a focus. It was this which had most frequently been lost by them, not their courage. The way in which units rallied and fought on and the spirit with which counter-attacks were launched to stop the German advance demonstrated that the BEF's morale, on the whole, remained high. Even the events of this near-disaster soon came to provide a source of amusement for the tommies' dark humour, so that on 9 December an artillery officer, Edmund Fisher, wrote: 'Most exciting and amusing things have happened lately. A Major General flying miles in pyjamas carrying his dispatch box, another captured in his bath, etc, etc. Episodes to relieve depression.'[12] This morale would be more sorely tried in 1918 but, once again, it would not break.

Ninety years after the battle, the stories of the courage and endurance of the men who fought at Cambrai should still excite our admiration and wonder. Regardless of its status as a landmark in military history, it was for many who fought in it an episode that shaped, or even defined, their lives. Many thousands of combatants from Britain, Germany, India, Canada, the United States, Australia, China and a host of other nations died during its brief course. Of those who survived, some went on to greater things – the Guards battalion commanders Harold Alexander and Viscount Gort both rose to hold very high rank in the Second World War. Prior to doing so, in September 1918, Gort won a VC on the same battlefield. Of the senior commanders, Haig remained as commander-in-chief of the BEF and led it to victory over the German Army, whilst Byng continued to lead Third Army. It conducted a successful defence in 1918 against the German offensives before becoming one of the two chief armies leading the BEF's final advance on victory in the fighting of late 1918. All the corps commanders except, perhaps surprisingly, Kavanagh, were replaced in early 1918 – chiefly on the grounds of their age. On the other hand, both Harper and Braithwaite were promoted to corps command. Both remained highly regarded by their commander-in-chief.

Amongst the junior officers, NCOs and men, more died in the battles of 1918. Edmund Fisher of 36th Divisional Ammunition Column died in hospital on 31 March 1918; he was 46. The 21-year-old Major Douglas Amery-Parkes, who had commanded a machine-gun company in Bourlon Wood, died of wounds received in the fighting of April 1918 as part of the German Spring Offensive; his fellow machine-gun company commander, Major Sydney Davey, died aged 25 on 25 March 1918 in the Third Army's defence against the German March offensive. James McCudden and Manfred von Richthofen had only a few months to live at the end of 1917. The Australian flyer, Harry Taylor, who had been awarded the Military Cross for his courageous fight after being shot down on 20 November 1917, died in a training accident in August 1918.

Some survived and thrived. Lieutenant Colonel Algernon Lawson of 2nd Dragoon Guards (Queen's Bays), whose resolve in his intention of 'doing something' on the evening of 20 November was rewarded by the capture of Cantaing on the following day, was promoted to command 2nd Cavalry Brigade in April 1918. Captain Robert Gee VC became an MP in 1921 after he defeated Ramsay Macdonald in a by-election at

Woolwich East. Others like Fred Wynne, Charles Dudley Ward, Douglas Wimberley, Billy Kirkby, John Lomax, Miles Reinke, Arthur Gould Lee, Benjamin Parkin, Eric Potten and Wilfrid Bion would survive the war where, in some cases, their achievements considerably exceeded their wartime exploits. Yet they all felt moved to provide an account of their war service and, specifically, their involvement in the Cambrai battle. Clearly, they understood and accepted its crucial influence on their lives.

Of those who became prisoners of war, almost all endured a year or more of captivity before repatriation. Of the wounded, some were adjudged fit enough to return to the front in time for more service before the war's end but for others, such as Frank Turner, who had lain undiscovered in Bourlon Wood for several days, the loss of a leg ended his war. With no organized national system of health and welfare provision, the post-war years were very hard for the thousands upon thousands of maimed war veterans. It is impossible to calculate the war's ongoing cost in terms of premature deaths, suicides and broken lives that occurred in all the combatant nations after November 1918 or what influence these 'forgotten casualties' had on the lives of their loved ones and those who held them dear.

George Parsons assuredly spoke for many participants in the battle when, reflecting on his involvement, he wrote: 'I suppose I can claim to have been in the battle of Cambrai from start to finish, although I don't really think my overall contribution amounted to very much. Scattered memories remain.'[13] With the passing years, the memories, and those who possessed them, became fewer and more scattered. When former Private Fred Holmes was interviewed by the Imperial War Museum Sound Archive in 1985 he was suddenly struck whilst describing his unit's fighting and losses in Bourlon Wood by the thought that 'I'm probably the only one who knows what happened to them . . . I *am* the only one!'[14] However, the stories these men told and the accounts they wrote still have the capacity to move us today. We must hope never to experience what they experienced and we must acknowledge that we can never truly feel the depth of emotion they felt. Yet the power of their words is truly remarkable, even in recounting a simple incident – a moment – in the course of a momentous battle:

One of our young fellas, he was an officer's runner. He'd been up with his officer and his officer got his legs blew off . . . He came running down to me and said 'I'm going to go over there. Will you watch him?' I said 'Yes'. I went over and I looked at him. This officer lay there and he'd got his cover drawn over, but it was his eyes looked at me. I shall never forget his look. I knew he wouldn't get better. He seemed like he looked right through you somehow . . . You get so used to them, but you never forget these things. I used to lie there and think about them. They're there and they'll always be there.[15]

Private Fred Collins, 'B' Battalion, Tank Corps

This story might have been dominated by the steel and fire of tanks and guns but such human tales and emotions, forming as they do a vital other dimension to the battle, could not and should not be forgotten.

Glossary of Terms and Abbreviations

AAR	After-Action Report
ADC	Aide de Camp
AEF	American Expeditionary Force
Archie	Anti-aircraft fire
ASC	Army Service Corps
AW FK8	Armstrong-Whitworth F.K.8 (a two-seater aircraft used for aerial reconnaissance, tank contact patrols and anti-tank ground attack roles)
BEF	British Expeditionary Force. The title given to the forces of the British army sent to fight in France and Belgium in the opening months of the First World War. This remained the official title for British forces serving on the Western Front until the end of the war.
CGS	Chief of the General Staff
CIGS	Chief of the Imperial General Staff
CO	Commanding Officer
CRA	Commander, Royal Artillery (the usual term for a divisional artillery commander)
CSM	Company Sergeant Major
DH5	De Havilland Airco fighter/scout biplane aircraft
DLI	Durham Light Infantry
DMO	Director of Military Operations
DSO	Distinguished Service Order
Fascine	A brushwood bundle intended to facilitate crossing wide trenches
FSR	Field Service Regulations
GHQ	General Headquarters. The main British Expeditionary Force staff
GOC	General Officer Commanding
GS waggon	General Service waggon – a horse-drawn supply cart
GSO1, 2, 3	General Staff Officer, Grade 1, 2 or 3, belonging to the
(I)/(O)	(Intelligence) or (Operations) branch of the Staff
HBMGC	Heavy Branch, Machine Gun Corps

HE	High Explosive
HLI	Highland Light Infantry
HQ	Headquarters
IWM	Imperial War Museum
IWM DOCS	Imperial War Museum Department of Documents
Junker	One of the landed nobility of Prussia and Eastern Germany who dominated the German Army's officer corps
KOSB	King's Own Scottish Borderers
KOYLI	King's Own Yorkshire Light Infantry
KRRC	King's Royal Rifle Corps
KSLI	King's Shropshire Light Infantry
LCLU	Liddle Collection, Leeds University Library
LHCMA	Liddell Hart Centre for Military Archives
MC	Military Cross
Mebus	German 'pillbox' or strongpoint. From MEBUs *Mannschafts Eisen-beton Ünterstande* ('reinforced concrete personnel dugouts')
MG	Machine-gun
MGC	Machine-Gun Corps
MO	Medical Officer
NCO	Non-Commissioned Officer
[n.d.]	No date. Used for undated documents in footnote references
OC	Officer Commanding (like 'CO')
O.H.	British *Official History*
OHL	*Oberste Heeresleitung* – German Army's General Staff
OP	Observation Post
psc	Passed Staff College (and hence a trained staff officer)
QF	'Quick Firing' (artillery)
RA	Royal Artillery
RAMC	Royal Army Medical Corps
RE	Royal Engineers
RFC	Royal Flying Corps
RFA	Royal Field Artillery
RGA	Royal Garrison Artillery (heavy artillery)
RHA	Royal Horse Artillery
SAA	Small Arms Ammunition
SE5a	Royal Aircraft Factory 'Scout Experimental' fighter/scout biplane aircraft
Sowar	Indian Army cavalry trooper
Sponson	Wedge-shaped gun housings mounted on each side of the tank's hull in Marks I to V*
TM	Tank Museum
TMB	Trench Mortar Battery
TNA	The National Archives

Orders of Battle

IV Corps: Lieutenant General Sir Charles Woollcombe

36th (Ulster) Division: Major General Oliver Nugent

107th Brigade

8/9th Battalion, Royal Irish Rifles	15th Battalion, Royal Irish Rifles
10th Battalion, Royal Irish Rifles	1st Battalion, Royal Irish Fusiliers

108th Brigade

2nd Battalion, Royal Irish Rifles	12th Battalion, Royal Irish Rifles
11/13th Battalion, Royal Irish Rifles	9th Battalion, Royal Irish Fusiliers

109th Brigade

9th Battalion, Royal Inniskilling Fusiliers	11th Battalion, Royal Inniskilling Fusiliers
10th Battalion, Royal Inniskilling Fusiliers	14th Battalion, Royal Irish Rifles

62nd (West Riding) Division: Major General Walter Braithwaite

185th Brigade

2/5th Battalion, West Yorkshire	2/7th Battalion, West Yorkshire
2/6th Battalion, West Yorkshire	2/8th Battalion, West Yorkshire

186th Brigade

2/4th Battalion, Duke of Wellington's	2/6th Battalion, Duke of Wellington's
2/5th Battalion, Duke of Wellington's	2/7th Battalion, Duke of Wellington's

187th Brigade

2/4th Battalion, KOYLI	2/4th Battalion, York and Lancaster
2/5th Battalion, KOYLI	2/5th Battalion, York and Lancaster

51st (Highland) Division: Major General Montague Harper

152nd Brigade

1/8th Battalion, Argyll & Sutherland
   Highlanders
1/5th Battalion, Seaforth Highlanders

1/6th Battalion, Seaforth Highlanders
1/6th Battalion, Gordon Highlanders

153rd Brigade

1/6th Battalion, Black Watch
1/7th Battalion, Black Watch

1/5th Battalion, Gordon Highlanders
1/7th Battalion, Gordon Highlanders

154th Brigade

1/9th Battalion, Royal Scots
1/4th Battalion, Seaforth Highlanders
1/4th Battalion, Gordon Highlanders

1/7th Battalion, Argyll & Sutherland
   Highlanders

56th (London) Division: Major General Frederick Dudgeon

167th Brigade

1/7th Battalion, Middlesex
1/8th Battalion, Middlesex

1/1st Battalion, London Regiment
1/3rd Battalion, London Regiment

168th Brigade

1/4th Battalion, London Regiment
1/12th Battalion, London Regiment

13th Battalion, London Regiment
1/14th Battalion, London Regiment

169th Brigade

1/2nd Battalion, London Regiment
1/5th Battalion, London Regiment

1/9th Battalion, London Regiment
1/16th Battalion, London Regiment

III Corps: Lieutenant General Sir William Pulteney

6th Division: Major General Thomas Marden

16th Brigade

1st Battalion, Buffs
8th Battalion, Bedfordshire

1st Battalion, KSLI
2nd Battalion, York and Lancaster

18th Brigade

1st Battalion, West Yorkshire
11th Battalion, Essex

2nd Battalion, DLI
14th Battalion, DLI

71st Brigade

9th Battalion, Norfolk
9th Battalion, Suffolk

1st Battalion, Leicestershire
2nd Battalion, Sherwood Foresters

12th (Eastern) Division: Major General Arthur Scott

35th Brigade

7th Battalion, Norfolk
7th Battalion, Suffolk

9th Battalion, Essex
5th Battalion, Royal Berkshire

36th Brigade

8th Battalion, Royal Fusiliers
9th Battalion, Royal Fusiliers

7th Battalion, Royal Sussex
11th Battalion, Middlesex

37th Brigade

6th Battalion, Queen's
6th Battalion, Buffs

7th Battalion, East Surreys
6th Battalion, Royal West Kents

20th (Light) Division: Major General William Douglas-Smith

59th Brigade

10th Battalion, King's Royal Rifle
   Corps
11th Battalion, King's Royal Rifle
   Corps

10th Battalion, Rifle Brigade
11th Battalion, Rifle Brigade

60th Brigade

6th Battalion, Ox & Bucks
6th Battalion, KSLI

12th Battalion, King's Royal Rifle
   Corps
12th Battalion, Rifle Brigade

61st Brigade

7th Battalion, Somerset Light Infantry
7th Battalion, DCLI

7th Battalion, KOYLI
12th Battalion, King's (Liverpool)

29th Division: Major General Sir Beauvoir de Lisle

86th Brigade

2nd Battalion, Royal Fusiliers
1st Battalion, Lancashire Fusiliers

16th Battalion, Middlesex
1st Battalion, Royal Guernsey

87th Brigade

2nd Battalion, South Wales Borderers
1st Battalion, KOSB

1st Battalion, Royal Inniskilling
   Fusiliers
1st Battalion, Border

88th Brigade

4th Battalion, Worcestershire
2nd Battalion, Hampshire

1st Battalion, Essex
1st Battalion, Royal Newfoundland

Cavalry Corps: Lieutenant General Sir Charles Kavanagh

1st Cavalry Division: Major General Richard Mullens

1st Cavalry Brigade

2nd Dragoon Guards (the Queen's Bays)

5th (Princess Charlotte of Wales's) Dragoon Guards
11th (Prince Albert's Own) Hussars

2nd Cavalry Brigade

4th (Royal Irish) Dragoon Guards
9th (Queen's Royal) Lancers

18th (Queen Mary's Own) Hussars

9th Cavalry Brigade

15th (King's) Hussars
19th (Queen Alexandra's Own Royal) Hussars

1/1st Bedfordshire Yeomanry

2nd Cavalry Division: Major General Walter Greenly

3rd Cavalry Brigade

4th (Queen's Own) Hussars
5th (Royal Irish) Lancers

16th (The Queen's) Lancers

4th Cavalry Brigade

6th Dragoon Guards (Carabiniers)
3rd (King's Own) Hussars

1/1st Oxfordshire Yeomanry

5th Cavalry Brigade

2nd Dragoons (Royal Scots Greys)
20th Hussars

12th (Prince of Wales's) Lancers

3rd Cavalry Division: Major General John Vaughan

6th Cavalry Brigade

1st (Royal) Dragoons
3rd (Prince of Wales's) Dragoon Guards

1/1st North Somerset Yeomanry

7th Cavalry Brigade

1st Life Guards
2nd Life Guards

Royal Horse Guards

8th Cavalry Brigade

10th (Prince of Wales' Own Royal) Hussars

1/1st Essex Yeomanry
1/1st Leicestershire Yeomanry

4th Cavalry Division: Major General Alfred Kennedy

Sialkot Brigade

17th (Duke of Cambridge's Own) Lancers

19th Lancers (Fane's Horse)
6th King Edward's Own Cavalry

Mhow Brigade

6th (Inniskilling) Dragoons
2nd Lancers (Gardner's Horse)

38th King George's Own Central India Horse

Lucknow Brigade

29th Lancers (Deccan Horse)
36th Jacob's Horse

Jodhpur Lancers

5th Cavalry Division: Major General Henry Macandrew

Secunderabad Brigade

7th (Princess Royal's) Dragoon Guards
20th Deccan Horse

34th Prince Albert Victor's Own Poona Horse

Ambala Brigade

8th (King's Royal Irish) Hussars
9th Hodson's Horse

18th (King George's Own) Lancers

Canadian Cavalry Brigade

Royal Canadian Dragoons
Lord Strathcona's Horse

Fort Garry Horse

Other divisions involved in the battle:

55th (West Lancashire) Division: Major General Hugh Jeudwine

164th Brigade

1/4th Battalion, King's Own
1/4th Battalion, Loyal North Lancs

2/5th Battalion, Lancashire Fusiliers
1/8th Battalion, King's (Liverpool)

165th Brigade

1/5th Battalion, King's (Liverpool)
1/6th Battalion, King's (Liverpool)

1/7th Battalion, King's (Liverpool)
1/9th Battalion, King's (Liverpool)

166th Brigade

1/10th Battalion, King's (Liverpool)
1/5th Battalion, South Lancashire

1/5th Battalion, King's Own
1/5th Battalion, Loyal North Lancs

Guards Division: Major General Geoffrey Feilding

1st Guards Brigade

2nd Battalion, Grenadier Guards

2nd Battalion, Coldstream Guards

3rd Battalion, Coldstream Guards

1st Battalion, Irish Guards

2nd Guards Brigade

3rd Battalion, Grenadier Guards

1st Battalion, Coldstream Guards

1st Battalion, Scots Guards

2nd Battalion, Irish Guards

3rd Guards Brigade

1st Battalion, Grenadier Guards

4th Battalion, Grenadier Guards

2nd Battalion, Scots Guards

1st Battalion, Welsh Guards

40th Division: Major General John Ponsonby

119th Brigade

19th Battalion, Royal Welsh Fusiliers

12th Battalion, South Wales Borderers

17th Battalion, Welsh

18th Battalion, Welsh

120th Brigade

11th Battalion, King's Own

13th Battalion, East Surrey

14th Battalion, Highland Light Infantry

14th Battalion, Argyll & Sutherland
  Highlanders

121st Brigade

12th Battalion, Suffolk

13th Battalion, Yorkshire

20th Battalion, Middlesex

21st Battalion, Middlesex

61st (2nd South Midland) Division: Major General Colin Mackenzie

182nd Brigade

2/5th Battalion, Royal Warwickshire

2/6th Battalion, Royal Warwickshire

2/7th Battalion, Royal Warwickshire

2/8th Battalion, Royal Warwickshire

183rd Brigade

2/4th Battalion, Gloucestershire

2/6th Battalion, Gloucestershire

2/7th Battalion, Worcestershire

2/8th Battalion, Worcestershire

184th Brigade

2/5th Battalion, Gloucestershire

2/4th Battalion, Ox & Bucks

2/1st Buckinghamshire Bn, Ox &
  Bucks

2/4th Bn, Royal Berkshire

47th (2nd London) Division: Major General Sir George Gorringe

140th Brigade
1/6th (City of London) Battalion, London Regiment

1/7th (City of London) Battalion, London Regiment

1/8th (City of London) Battalion, London Regiment

1/15th (County of London) Battalion, London Regiment

141st Brigade
1/17th (County of London) Battalion, London Regiment

1/18th (County of London) Battalion, London Regiment

·1/19th (County of London) Battalion, London Regiment

1/20th (County of London) Battalion, London Regiment

142nd Brigade
1/21st (County of London) Battalion, London Regiment

1/22nd (County of London) Battalion, London Regiment

1/23rd (County of London) Battalion, London Regiment

1/24th (County of London) Battalion, London Regiment

2nd Division: Major General Cecil Pereira

5th Brigade
17th Battalion, Royal Fusiliers

24th Battalion, Royal Fusiliers

2nd Battalion, Ox & Bucks

2nd Battalion, Highland Light Infantry

6th Brigade
1st Battalion, King's (Liverpool)

2nd Battalion, South Staffordshire

13th Essex

17th Middlesex

99th Brigade
22nd Battalion, Royal Fusiliers

23rd Battalion, Royal Fusiliers

1st Battalion, Royal Berkshire

1st Battalion, King's Royal Rifle Corps

Although 59th and 3rd Divisions also played important roles in the operations, for reasons of space they have not been included here.

GERMAN INFANTRY DIVISIONS OF GENERAL GEORG VON DER MARWITZ'S *SECOND ARMY*

3rd Guards Division
Guard Fusilier; Lehr Regiment; Grenadier Regiment Nr. 9.

20th Division
Infanterie Regiment Nrs. 77, 79, 92.

28th Division
Fusilier Regiment Nr. 40; Leib Grenadier Regiment Nr. 109; Grenadier Regiment Nr. 110.

30th Division
Infanterie Regiment Nrs. 99, 105, 143.

34th Division
Infanterie Regiments Nrs. 30, 67, 145.

54th Division
Infanterie Regiment Nr. 84; Reserve Infanterie Regiment Nrs. 27, 90.

107th Division
Reserve Infanterie Regiment Nrs. 52, 227, 232.

119th Division
Infanterie Regiment Nrs. 46, 58; Reserve Infanterie Regiment Nr. 46.

183rd Division
Infanterie Regiment Nrs. 184, 418; Reserve Infanterie Regiment Nr. 440.

185th Division
Infanterie Regiment Nrs. 65, 161; Reserve Infanterie Regiment Nr. 28.

208th Division
Infanterie Regiment Nrs. 25, 185; Reserve Infanterie Regiment Nr. 65.

214th Division
Infanterie Regiment Nrs. 50, 358, 363.

220th Division
Infanterie Regiment Nr. 190; Reserve Infanterie Regiment Nrs. 55, 99.

221st Division
Infanterie Regiment Nr. 41; Reserve Infanterie Regiment Nr. 60; Reserve Ersatz Regiment Nr. 1.

9th Reserve Division
Infanterie Regiment Nr. 395; Reserve Infanterie Regiment Nrs. 6, 19.

21st Reserve Division

Reserve Infanterie Regiment Nrs. 80, 87, 88.

24th Reserve Division

Reserve Infanterie Regiment Nrs. 104, 107, 133.

49th Reserve Division

Reserve Infanterie Regiment Nrs. 225, 226, 228.

20th Landwehr Division

Landwehr Regiment Nrs. 384, 386, 387.

9th Bavarian Reserve Division

Bavarian Reserve Regiment Nrs. 11, 14; Bavarian Ersatz Regiment Nr. 3.

Acknowledgements

This book has been written in difficult and trying circumstances. These difficulties and trials were of a very different nature to those faced by the men whose stories I have described. Nevertheless, in the same way in which many of those men were sustained and supported through the travails of their war service by enduring friendships and the very best qualities displayed by their fellow human beings, I have been the fortunate beneficiary of the same 'loyalty of mates' and spontaneous acts of kindness. As a consequence, I have been able to complete what I had always intended to be a tribute to the endurance and courage of those who fought in the Great War.

It is, therefore, with these friends that I should begin when acknowledging the contributions to the research and writing of this book. Peerless amongst these chums stands the colossus that is Peter Hart, who bullied and cajoled me into preparing a proposal for this book, offered advice, identified sources and commented (in his inimitable fashion) on the early drafts. Constantly cheerful, despite the many disadvantages of his life (such as his choice of football and cricket teams), his advice that 'fun is more important than history' was frequently taken by myself in entirely the wrong spirit to which it was intended. I will be forever in his debt – as he will, no doubt, constantly remind me.

A similarly glowing tribute should go to my great friend, Chris McCarthy, whose enthusiasm for the study of the BEF in the Great War has remained undiminished and whose knowledge of the minutiae of this vast subject is immense. His frequent acts of generosity have been really appreciated and his willingness to share his thoughts and ideas have greatly expanded both my interest in, and knowledge of, the Great War. It was Chris who first encouraged me to begin researching my postgraduate interests through primary sources and who was always interested in the development of my own ideas and knowledge. His current work on the location and movement of the units of the BEF will, I am sure, provide a major step forward in our knowledge and understanding of the incredible organization that Haig's command became.

Philip Dutton, a talented and knowledgeable historian and writer and a perfect gentleman (probably the nicest man I know) offered gentle, but valuable critical comment on my drafts. Another great friend whose kindness deserves greater

456

appreciation on my part. Dr Andy Simpson's comments and suggestions were of immense value in demonstrating the shortcomings in my knowledge of the English language and of the finer points of the genesis of the Western Front. Having previously benefited from his dissection of my doctoral thesis, I was more than happy to benefit from his assistance again. A fine mind and a fine man. Another great chum, and my fellow convenor of the museum's History Group, Alan Jeffreys also deserves thanks for his enthusiasm and support and for positive comments on my work. John Paylor's occasionally eccentric comments on the final text and his assiduous efforts to make the whole thing more readable were greatly appreciated.

In 1983, as part of my undergraduate degree course at the University of Birmingham, I studied Britain and the Great War under Dr John Bourne. Almost twenty-five years later my interest in the events of that war and in British military involvement in the conflict that John's course first prompted in me has remained undiminished. I cannot miss this opportunity to express my admiration for John's superb work on aspects of the war and his fine scholarship in his various writings and lectures on the subject. However, most of all I am grateful to him for setting me on the course I have continued to follow since my days as one of the original self-styled 'Bourne Boys'. His creation of a Centre for First World War Studies is a hugely important achievement and I am proud to be an Honorary Research Fellow there.

At the Imperial War Museum I would especially like to thank the following for their help with my research: Penny Bonning, Simon Offord, Tony Richards, Simon Robbins, Rod Suddaby, Wendy Lutterloch, Ellen Parton and Mandy Mason in the Department of Documents; Jane Rosen, Belinda Haley, Mary Wilkinson, Richard Golland, Katherine Moody, Christopher Hunt and Angela Wootton in the Department of Printed Books; Margaret Brooks and John Stopford-Pickering in the Sound Archive; Rose Gerrard, David Parry, and Alan Wakefield in the Photograph Archive. A host of friends and colleagues (past and present) also helped me through. I could not have achieved anything without the huge support I have had from my great friend, Jan Bourne – 'the Gunner's Wife'. However, Tom McVeagh, Abigail Campbell, Steve Grace, Gael Dundas, Elizabeth Bray, Simon Bourne, Polly Napper and Gavin Birch all deserve honourable mentions. The assistance of James Taylor and Dr Claudia Condry with German sources was enormously appreciated. Jack Sheldon kindly provided material at indecently short notice and gave generously of his knowledge. I look forward to his book on the German Army at Cambrai.

Elsewhere, Katie and Dave remained supportive and interested in my work during my 'Streatham days' whilst Alice, David, Kerry, Robert and Rebecca in the Lincolnshire Fens all helped. Tim Roberts and Phil Johnson kept me going when times were perhaps hardest.

All this gratitude for my friends is wholeheartedly endorsed and understood by my family, who never ceased to remind me of how lucky I am to have such good friends as these. However, they also deserve a special thank you. My mum and dad have been a constant source of practical and emotional support throughout my life.

They are truly wonderful people. My brother and best friend, Dave, backed me every inch of the way and shouldered a greater burden than anyone ought. He and I have shared for most of our lives a common understanding that needs no explanation: nothing but the best is good enough. He is possibly the only man who could rival Phil Dutton as the world's 'nicest man'. My sister, Sarah, has been a rock of advice and support, backed by Kevin, Tom, Simon and Emily. Abby, Holly and Bryn remain the most important people in my life. Their unqualified love is a huge boost to flagging morale. This book was written despite the enormous pain I felt each time they and I were apart. Amongst 'family' I also number Guy Callaby, a lifelong friend and as close to being another brother as I could wish. Both he and Dave demonstrated their faith in me by placing advance orders for this book as soon as the opportunity arose. Greater love hath no man than this!

During my research I received great help from the staff of a number of archives and other organizations. Particular mention must be made of David Fletcher, the Historian at the Tank Museum and his colleague, Janice Tait, both of whom helped me in every way they could in researching the experiences of the tank men. The staff at the National Archives, Liddell Hart Centre for Military Archives and the Liddle Special Collection at Leeds University were always polite, professional and helpful. I am grateful to all these organizations for permission to quote from the sources I have used here. Thanks to all those individuals who gave me permission to quote from the sources for which they hold copyright. Similar thanks must go to the publishers of the various books from which I have quoted for allowing me to do so. I hope all those I have been unable to contact or trace, despite my best endeavours, will grant me their forebearance.

I am especially grateful to all those at Weidenfeld and Nicolson who showed faith and confidence in my abilities and who backed me from the first with this book. I hope I have delivered on their investment in time and support. Words fail me when expressing my thanks to my editor, Keith Lowe, whose patience and tact meant more to me during the process of writing this book than perhaps he will have realized. Undoubtedly, his guidance in helping me turn my manuscript into the final version made this book. I wish him nothing but constant good fortune in all his future endeavours.

My ideas and thoughts on the Great War in general and Cambrai in particular have benefited greatly from reading the works of the many excellent historians working on this subject. However, the additional opportunity of discussing aspects of both with many of these individuals and to have their help in shaping my knowledge has been particularly helpful. I must, therefore, thank the following who all gave me their valuable time and thoughts. The late John Terraine, whose contribution to the scholarship of the BEF and its commander-in-chief was so profoundly important. The writings of, and discussions with, Professor Peter Simkins, Dr Paul Harris, Professor Gary Sheffield, Dr William Philpott, Dr Stephen Badsey, Major Gordon Corrigan, John Lee, Michael Orr, Philippe Gorczynski and Jean-Luc Gibot all directly influenced my views of Cambrai. I must also thank the many contributors to the Great War Forum on the web where

Acknowledgements

I received generous assistance with a variety of aspects of the battle. I should particularly like to mention: Ralph J. Whitehead, Bob Coulsdon, Paul O'Rorke, Adrian Wright, Steve Beeby and Phil McCarty. Colin Campbell, co-author of *Can't Shoot a Man with a Cold*, provided valuable material on E. Alan Mackintosh.

The quotations from letters, diaries, personal accounts and oral history interviews used in this book have occasionally, where necessary, been lightly edited for overall readability. Punctuation and spellings have been largely standardized, material has occasionally been re-ordered and irrelevant material has been omitted, usually without any indication in the text. Occasionally, minor additions such as individuals' ranks or forenames have been inserted in the text for clarification and elaboration. Such additional information is enclosed in square brackets. Nevertheless, changes in the actual words used in the original sources have been avoided wherever possible.

Notes

Chapter 1 – Waiting for the great leap forwards

1 'Mark Severn' [pseudonym of Frank Lushington], *The Gambardier: Giving Some Account of the Heavy and Siege Artillery in France 1914–1918* (London: Ernest Benn, 1930), p. 13.

2 Hans von Hentig, *Psychologische Strategie des großen Krieges* (Heidelberg: [unknown], 1927), quoted in Peter Simkins' preface to Chris McCarthy, *The Somme: The Day by Day Account* (London: Arms & Armour Press, 1993).

3 Timothy T. Lupfer, *The Dynamics of Doctrine: The Changes in German Tactical Doctrine During the First World War* (Leavenworth Papers No. 4) (Fort Leavenworth, Kansas: Combat Studies Institute, 1981), p. 15 quoting from *The Principles of Command in the Defensive Battle in Position Warfare.*

4 Captain D.G. Browne MC, *The Tank in Action* (Edinburgh and London: William Blackwood, 1920), pp. 233–234.

5 Captain Wilfrid Miles, *History of the Great War Based on Official Documents by Direction of the Historical Section of the Committee of Imperial Defence: Military Operations France and Belgium, 1917. The Battle of Cambrai.* (Nashville, Tennessee: Imperial War Museum and Battery Press, 1991 (repr. of 1948 edition)) (henceforth *O.H., 1917*, Vol. 3), Preface, p. iii.

Chapter 2 – Armies and Weapons

1 IWM DOCS: S Bradbury typescript (1923), 81/35/1.

2 Ibid.

3 IWM DOCS: W R Kirkby typescript (c1978), 78/51/1.

4 IWM DOCS: F W Paish typescript (1977), 96/29/1.

5 Thomas Suthren Hope [pseudonym], *The Winding Road Unfolds* (London: Putnam, 1937), p. 252.

6 Ibid, pp. 253–254.

7 IWM DOCS: R C Foot typescript (1964), 86/57/1.

8 Ibid.

9 Ibid.

10 IWM DOCS: F W Paish typescript (1977), 96/29/1.

11 John R Innes, *Flash Spotters and Sound Rangers: How They Lived, Worked and Fought in the Great War* (London:

George Allen & Unwin, 1935), p. 19.

12 IWM DOCS: F W Paish typescript (1977), 96/29/1.

13 IWM Sound Archive: Kenneth Page interview, 717.

14 'Mark Severn' [pseudonym of Frank Lushington], *The Gambardier: Giving Some Account of the Heavy and Siege Artillery in France 1914–1918* (London: Ernest Benn, 1930), pp. 167–168.

15 Ibid, p. 169.

16 F.J. Salmon, 'With the Field Survey Units in France, 1915–19' in *Empire Survey Review*, Vol. II, No. II, January 1934, quoted in Peter Chasseaud, *Artillery's Astrologers: A History of British Survey and Mapping on the Western Front 1914–1918* (Lewes: Mapbooks, 1999), p. 359.

17 IWM DOCS: F W Paish typescript (1977), 96/29/1.

18 IWM DOCS: H C Edwards typescript (undated), 02/29/1.

19 The invention of Corporal William Sansome Tucker, formerly a lecturer at Imperial College London. He was later Director of Acoustical Research, Air Defence Experimental Establishment, Biggin Hill.

20 IWM Sound Archive: Kenneth Page interview, 717.

21 Major General Ernest Swinton, *Eyewitness* (London: Hodder & Stoughton, 1932), p. 64.

22 All material regarding Hugh Elles is taken from Evan Charteris, *H.Q. Tanks* (Privately Published, 1920), p. 15.

23 IWM Sound Archive: Horace Birks interview, 870.

24 Major General J.F.C. Fuller, *Memoirs of an Unconventional Soldier* (London: Nicholson & Watson, 1936), pp. 89–90.

25 This meant that, strictly speaking, the first working prototype 'Mother' was a 'male' tank since it was armed with 6-pounder Hotchkiss guns rather than a 'female' carrying only machine-guns.

26 IWM Sound Archive: Horace Birks interview, 870.

27 IWM Sound Archive: Reginald Johnson interview, 9172.

28 IWM Sound Archive: Robert George Parker interview, 492.

29 IWM Sound Archive: Edward Leigh-Jones interview, 4161.

30 IWM Sound Archive: Norman Dillon interview, 9752.

31 IWM Sound Archive: Horace Birks interview, 870.

32 IWM Sound Archive: Eric Potten interview, 11042.

33 IWM DOCS: R.E. Beall typescript (c.1939), 82/22/1.

34 IWM Sound Archive: Norman Dillon interview, 9752.

35 IWM Sound Archive: Horace Birks interview, 870.

36 Quoted in Peter Kilduff, *Richthofen: Beyond the Legend of the Red Baron* (London: Arms & Armour Press, 1995), p. 169.

Chapter 3 –
The Clockwork Battle

1 [Anon], 'More Light on Cambrai, 1917' in *The Army Quarterly*, Vol. XXXV, No. 1, October 1937, p.143.

2 IWM Sound Archive: Kenneth Page interview, 717.

3 IWM Sound Archive: Charles Austin interview, 11116.

4 Captain Geoffrey Dugdale, *'Langemarck' and 'Cambrai': A War Narrative, 1914–1918* (Shrewsbury: Wilding and Son Ltd: 1932), p. 96

5 Ibid, p. 95.

6 Ibid, p. 96.

7 Quoted in J.P. Harris, *Men, Ideas and Tanks: British Military Thought and Armoured Forces, 1903–1939* (Manchester, Manchester University Press, 1995), p. 108.

8 Gary Sheffield & John Bourne (ed.), *Douglas Haig: War Diaries and Letters 1914–1918* (London: Weidenfeld & Nicolson, 2005), pp. 325–326.

9 Edward L. Spears, *Prelude to Victory*, (London: Jonathan Cape, 1939), p. 316.

10 Colonel W.N. Nicholson, *Behind the Lines*, (London: Jonathan Cape, 1939), p. 143.

11 Ibid, p. 149.

12 Ibid, p. 141.

13 Spears, *Prelude to Victory*, p. 316.

14 Cyril Falls, *The Gordon Highlanders in the First World War, 1914–1919*, (Aberdeen: University Press, 1958) p. 104.

15 IWM DOCS: General Sir Ivor Maxse Papers, PP/MCR/C42 & Con Shelf & 69/53/18A-B, File 41, XVIII Corps No.G.S.82., Maxse to Fifth Army, 27 September 1917.

16 IWM DOCS: Major R C Foot typescript (1964), 86/57/1.

17 Ibid.

18 Quoted in Harry Moses, *The Fighting Bradfords: Northern Heroes of World War One* (Durham: County Durham Books, 2003), p. 97.

19 IWM DOCS: R Ross typescript (c1930), 99/22/1.

20 Ibid.

21 Ibid.

22 F.J. Salmon, 'With the Field Survey Units in France, 1915–19' in *Empire Survey Review*, Vol. II, No. II, January 1934, quoted in Peter Chasseaud, *Artillery's Astrologers: A History of British Survey and Mapping on the Western Front 1914–1918* (Lewes: Mapbooks, 1999), p. 357.

23 IWM DOCS: F W Paish typescript (1977), 96/29/1.

24 IWM DOCS: Major F W Webster typescript (1970s), PP/MCR/C53.

25 The National Archives [TNA PRO]: CAB 45/118 Fuller to Edmonds, 19 March 1945.

26 Major General J.F.C. Fuller, *Memoirs of an Unconventional Soldier* (London: Nicholson & Watson, 1936), p. 194.

27 IWM Sound Archive: Norman Dillon interview, 9752.

28 IWM Sound Archive: Horace Birks interview, 870.

29 IWM Sound Archive: Frederick Collins interview, 8229.

30 IWM Sound Archive: Stuart Hastie interview, 4126.

31 General Erich Ludendorff, *My War Memories 1914–1918*, Vol. II. (London: Hutchinson, 1919), pp. 494–495.

Chapter 4 – 'Simple tactical exercises . . . colossal binges'

1 Wilfrid R. Bion, *The Long Week-End, 1897–1919: Part of a Life* (Abingdon, Oxfordshire: Fleetwood Press, 1982), p. 150.

2 Ibid, pp. 151–152.

3 Major W.H.L. Watson, *A Company of*

Tanks (Edinburgh: William Blackwood, 1920), p. 163.

4 IWM DOCS: The Papers of Major General H.L. Birks. CAMBRAI and the attack on FLESQUIERES RIDGE, 72/7/1.

5 TNA PRO: WO 95/2846 '51st (HIGHLAND) DIVISION. INSTRUCTIONS No: 1 Training Note. Tank And Infantry Operations Without Methodical Artillery Preparations', 7 November 1917.

6 The National Archive: CAB 45/118 Standish Craufurd to Edmonds, 3 August 1944.

7 IWM DOCS: W R Kirkby typescript (c1978), 78/51/1.

8 Ibid.

9 IWM DOCS: G D J McMurtrie typescript (1918), 78/23/1.

10 Quoted in *Letters and Papers of Algernon Hyde Villiers* (London: Society for Promoting Christian Knowledge, 1919), p. 149.

11 IWM DOCS: E Marchant transcript, DS MISC 26, letter to 'Dad', 4 November 1917.

12 General Sir Beauvoir de Lisle, *Reminiscences of Sport and War*, (London: Eyre and Spottiswoode, 1939), p. 158.

13 Charles Weaver Price, "Q' Reminiscences' in *The Royal Tank Corps Journal*, Vol. 13, No. 31, 1921, p. 159.

14 Arthur Gould Lee, *No Parachute: A Fighter Pilot in World War 1* (The Adventurers Club, London: 1969), pp. 152–154.

15 Ibid, p. 157.

16 Ibid, p. 158.

17 IWM DOCS: Captain H Brokensha transcript (1973), 73/185/1.

18 Ibid.

19 Arthur Gould Lee, *No Parachute: A Fighter Pilot in World War 1* (The Adventurers Club, London: 1969), p. 158.

20 Ibid, p. 160.

21 IWM DOCS: E Marchant transcript, DS MISC 26, letter to 'Dad', 15 November 1917.

22 Ibid.

23 Gary Sheffield & John Bourne (ed.), *Douglas Haig: War Diaries and Letters 1914–1918* (London: Weidenfeld & Nicolson, 2005), p. 341.

24 IWM DOCS: B D Parkin manuscript (c1929), 86/57/1.

25 Ibid.

26 Ibid.

27 IWM DOCS: W.R. Taylor, 'Diary and Reminiscences of the War' (typescript, undated), 01/60/1.

28 Tank Museum [TM]: 'Diary of F W Apthorpe, Tank Corps,' E1986.64.4.

29 Frank C. Brooke, *'Wait for It'* (Bingley, West Yorks., typescript, n.d.)

30 H.C.C. Uniacke, *The Royal Artillery war commemoration book: a regimental record written and illustrated for the most part by artillery men while serving in the line during the Great War* (London: G. Bell and Sons, 1920), p. 223.

31 Ibid, pp. 222–223.

32 Ibid, p. 223.

33 Ibid.

34 IWM DOCS: F W Paish typescript (1977), 96/29/1.

35 Ibid.

36 F.J. Salmon, 'With the Field Survey Units in France, 1915–19' in *Empire Survey Review*, Vol. II, No. II,

January 1934, quoted in Peter Chasseaud, *Artillery's Astrologers: A History of British Survey and Mapping on the Western Front 1914–1918* (Lewes: Mapbooks, 1999), p. 357.

37 Brevet-Col. J.F.C. Fuller, *Tanks in the Great War, 1914–1918* (London: John Murray, 1920), p. xv.

38 (Hon) Evan Charteris, *H.Q., Tanks 1917–1918* (Privately Printed, 1920), p. 88.

39 IWM Sound Archive: Norman Dillon interview, 9752.

40 Ibid.

41 Ibid.

42 Ibid.

43 Ibid.

44 IWM DOCS: R Beall typescript (c1939), 82/22/1.

45 IWM DOCS: J K Wilson Papers, Wilson transcript (c1970), PP/MCR/100.

46 IWM DOCS: A E Hodgkin diary, 14 November 1917, P399.

47 IWM DOCS: G Dent, PP/MCR/226, transcript of letter to Mother, 19 November 1917.

48 Ibid.

49 Ibid.

50 Captain S.H. Williams, MC, *'Stand to your Horses': Through the First Great War with the Lord Strathcona's Horse (R.C.)* (Altona: D. W. Friesen & Sons, 1961), p. 156.

51 Major General The Rt. Hon. J.E.B. Seely, *Adventure* (London: William Heinemann, 1930), pp. 273–274.

52 IWM DOCS: Edmund Fisher, 'Letters from France, 1917,' 97/4/1, transcript of letter to 'My Dear Roddles' from 'PAPA', 10 November 1917.

53 IWM DOCS: S Bradbury typescript (1923), 81/35/1.

54 IWM DOCS: R Ross typescript (c1930), 99/22/1.

55 IWM DOCS: G D J McMurtrie typescript (1918), 78/23/1.

56 Ibid.

57 Ibid.

58 IWM DOCS: B D Parkin manuscript (c1929), 86/57/1.

59 Captain Wilfrid Miles, *O.H., 1917*, Vol. 3, p. 48.

60 IWM DOCS: R Ross typescript (c1930), 99/22/1.

61 Captain Geoffrey Dugdale, *'Langemarck' and 'Cambrai': A War Narrative, 1914–1918* (Shrewsbury: Wilding and Son Ltd, 1932), p. 104.

62 IWM DOCS: H L Adams typescript (undated), 83/50/1.

63 IWM Sound Archive: Charles Austin interview, 11116.

64 IWM DOCS: G D J McMurtrie typescript (1918), 78/23/1.

65 IWM DOCS: W R Kirkby typescript (c1978), 78/51/1.

66 IWM DOCS: Captain H Brokensha transcript (1973), 73/185/1.

67 Ibid.

68 IWM DOCS: Air Vice Marshal Sir Ranald Macfarlane Reid, 'Fly Past' (1972), 88/30/1.

69 IWM DOCS: G D J McMurtrie typescript (1918), 78/23/1.

70 IWM DOCS: Douglas Wimberley typescript (1958–63), PP/MCR/182.

71 Quoted in Everard Wyrall, *The History of the 62nd (West Riding) Division, 1914–1919*, Vol. 1 (London: John Lane, 1925), p. 79.

72 IWM DOCS: W R Kirkby typescript (c1978), 78/51/1.

Chapter 5 – Shock and Awe

1 IWM DOCS: W R Kirkby typescript (c1978), 78/51/1.
2 IWM Sound Archive: Horace Birks interview, 870.
3 IWM DOCS: R Ross typescript (c1930), 99/22/1.
4 Tank Museum, Bovington (TM): EXTRACT from a letter from BASIL HENRIQUES, 27.11.17, WW1 Diaries/ 7/G Bn. TC/ Henriques Papers.doc.
5 IWM DOCS: Douglas Wimberley typescript (1958–63), PP/MCR/ 182.
6 IWM DOCS: B D Parkin manuscript (c1929), 86/57/1.
7 Ibid.
8 Ibid.
9 IWM DOCS: F W Paish typescript (1977), 96/29/1.
10 Ibid.
11 Ibid.
12 IWM DOCS: K Palmer typescript (1960s), 76/80/1.
13 TM: Letter from Colonel E J Carter to Major General N W Duncan containing observations on RTR history draft, 15 October 1959, WW1/Personal Accounts/Carter/ 17AC.doc.
14 TM: Unsigned account of action of A29 'Apollyon' in N.M. Dillon papers [no. ref.]. Lieutenant Kenneth Wootton was the commander of A29 'Apollyon' on 20 November 1917.
15 TM: 'Some Reminiscences of Cambrai and the German March Offensive by 97218 Private George Brown', E2007.591.
16 IWM Sound Archive: Reginald Beall interview, 4013.
17 TM: Unsigned account of action of A29 'Apollyon' in N.M. Dillon papers [no. ref.].
18 Ibid.
19 IWM Sound Archive: Edward Leigh-Jones interview, 4161.
20 IWM Sound Archive: Norman Dillon interview, 9752.
21 Ibid.
22 IWM Sound Archive: Eric Potten interview, 11042.
23 IWM DOCS: G D J McMurtrie typescript (1918), 78/23/1.
24 TM: Letter from Carter to Major General Duncan re: RTR history draft, 15 October 1959, WW1/ Personal Accounts/Carter/ 17AC.doc.
25 IWM DOCS: G D J McMurtrie typescript (1918), 78/23/1.
26 IWM DPB: Artur Pries, *Das R.I.R. 90, 1914–1918* (Erinnerungsblätter deutscher Regimenter, Truppenteile des ehemaligen preussischen Kontingents; der Schriftenfolge 153. Band), (Gerhard Stalling, 1925), pp. 236–247.
27 IWM DPB: Alexander Schwenke, *Geschichte des Reserve-Infanterie-Regiment Nr. 19 im Weltkriege 1914–1918* (Oldenburg: Stalling, 1926), p. 285.
28 Ibid.
29 Ibid, p. 286.
30 IWM DOCS: Captain H Brokensha transcript (1973), 73/ 185/1.
31 Ibid.
32 Ibid.
33 Major James Thomas Byford McCudden, *Five Years in the Royal Flying Corps* (London: The 'Aeroplane' & General Publishing Company Ltd, 1918), pp.270–271.
34 Arthur Gould Lee, *No Parachute: A Fighter Pilot in World War 1* (The

Adventurers Club, London: 1969), pp. 161–162.

35 Ibid, p. 162.

36 Ibid, p. 163.

37 Ibid.

38 Ibid, pp. 163–164.

39 He was born in Birmingham.

40 Quoted in F M Cutlack, *Australian Official History, Vol. VIII, The Australian Flying Corps in the Western and Eastern Theatres of War, 1914–1918* (11th Edition, 1941), p. 186.

41 Ibid, p. 186.

42 Ibid, pp. 186–187.

43 Ibid, p. 187.

44 Ibid, p. 187.

45 Major James Thomas Byford McCudden, *Five Years in the Royal Flying Corps* (London: The 'Aeroplane' & General Publishing Company Ltd, 1918), pp.270–271.

46 IWM Sound Archive: Jim Davies interview, 9750.

47 IWM DOCS: G D J McMurtrie typescript (1918), 78/23/1.

48 IWM DOCS: J K Wilson Papers, Wilson transcript (c1970), PP/MCR/100.

49 IWM DOCS: J K Wilson Papers, PP/MCR/100, letter from George Parsons to 'Jake' Wilson, January 1969.

50 IWM DOCS: J K Wilson Papers, Wilson transcript (c1970), PP/MCR/100.

51 IWM DOCS: G D J McMurtrie typescript (1918), 78/23/1.

52 TM: Unsigned account of action of A29 'Apollyon' in N.M. Dillon papers [no. ref.].

53 Ibid.

54 IWM Sound Archive: Charles Austin interview, 11116.

55 Ibid.

56 Ibid.

57 Ibid.

58 Ibid.

59 Ibid.

60 Ibid.

61 Ibid.

62 Captain Geoffrey Dugdale, *'Langemarck' and 'Cambrai': A War Narrative, 1914–1918* (Shrewsbury, Wilding and Son Ltd: 1932), pp. 105–106.

63 IWM Sound Archive: Norman Dillon (*sic*) interview, 9752.

64 Quoted in Captain B H Liddell Hart, *The Tanks: The History of the Royal Tank Regiment and its predecessors Heavy Branch Machine Gun Corps, Tank Corps and Royal Tank Corps 1914–1945: Volume One: 1914–1939* (London: Cassell, 1959), pp. 138–140.

65 Quoted in Liddell Hart, *The Tanks*, pp. 138–140.

66 TM: 'Some Reminiscences of Cambrai and the German March Offensive by 97218 Private George Brown', E2007.591.

67 Quoted in Loraine Petrie, *The History of the Norfolk Regiment, 1685–1918*, Vol. 2, (Norwich: Jarrold & Sons, 1924), pp. 274–275.

68 Quoted in Loraine Petrie, *History of the Norfolk Regiment, 1685–1918*. There is a mystery here. Captain Samuel Frederick Blackwell DSO is listed by the CWGC as a Tank Corps casualty and yet he is clearly described here as a Norfolk's officer. He won the DSO in 1916 on the Somme.

69 Quoted in Loraine Petrie, *History of the Norfolk Regiment, 1685–1918*, p. 276.

70 Ibid.

71 Ibid, p. 277.

72 Ibid.

73 IWM DOCS: R Ross typescript (c1930), 99/22/1.

74 Ernest M Thwaites, 'The Chronicles of an Amateur Soldier' in *The Tank Corps Journal*, Vol. 2, No. 19, 1920, p. 162.

75 IWM DOCS: W R Kirkby typescript (c1978), 78/51/1.

76 Ibid.

77 Ibid.

78 Ernest M Thwaites, 'The Chronicles of an Amateur Soldier' in *The Tank Corps Journal*, Vol. 2, No. 19, 1920, p. 170. For his actions on this occasion, Ernest Sykes was subsequently awarded the Military Medal.

79 Major W.H.L. Watson, *A Company of Tanks* (Edinburgh: William Blackwood, 1920), pp. 173–174.

80 Ibid, p. 175.

81 IWM DOCS: Douglas Wimberley typescript (1958–63), PP/MCR/182.

82 Ibid.

83 IWM DOCS: S Bradbury typescript (1923), 81/35/1.

84 IWM Sound Archive: Douglas Wimberley interview, 4266.

85 IWM DOCS: S Bradbury typescript (1923), 81/35/1.

86 Wilfrid R. Bion, *The Long Week-End, 1897–1919: Part of a Life* (Abingdon, Oxfordshire: Fleetwood Press, 1982), p. 161.

87 Ibid.

88 IWM Sound Archive: Horace Birks interview, 870.

89 IWM DOCS: R Ross typescript (c1930), 99/22/1.

90 Ibid.

91 Ibid.

92 Major William John Alderman had begun the war as a Quartermaster Sergeant.

93 IWM DOCS: J K Wilson Papers, Wilson transcript (c1970), PP/MCR/100.

94 Ibid.

95 IWM DOCS: Parsons to 'Jake' Wilson, January 1969 in J K Wilson Papers, PP/MCR/100.

96 IWM DOCS: J K Wilson Papers, Wilson transcript (c1970), PP/MCR/100.

97 IWM DOCS: Parsons to 'Jake' Wilson, January 1969 in J K Wilson Papers, PP/MCR/100.

98 TM: Unsigned account of action of A29 'Apollyon' in N.M. Dillon papers [no. ref.].

99 Ibid.

100 Ibid.

101 Ibid.

102 Ibid.

103 Ibid.

104 Ibid.

105 TM: Letter from J E Mossman, (Pte 76631) to Bryan Cooper, 19 December 1967, E2006.2470.

106 TM: Letter from W Wilkinson to Bryan Cooper, 21 November 1968, E2006.2470.

107 Ibid.

108 TM: Letter from J E Mossman to Bryan Cooper, 19 December 1967, E2006.2470.

109 IWM Sound Archive: Edward Leigh-Jones interview, 4161.

110 IWM DOCS: W R Kirkby typescript (c1978), 78/51/1.

111 Ibid.

112 Ibid.

113 Ibid.

114 Lieutenant Colonel William Barclay Parsons, *The American*

Engineers in France (Appleton & Company, London & New York, 1920), p.120.

115 Major General H.L. Birks, 'Cambrai' in *The Royal Armoured Corps Journal*, Vol. 3, No. 4, October 1949, p. 212.

116 IWM DOCS: Douglas Wimberley typescript (1958–63), PP/MCR/182.

117 IWM DOCS: S Bradbury typescript (1923), 81/35/1.

118 Quoted in Jean-Luc Gibot & Phillippe Gorczynski, *Following The Tanks: Cambrai 20th November–7th December 1917* (Arras: Privately Published, 1999)

119 Wilfrid R. Bion, *The Long Week-End, 1897–1919: Part of a Life* (Abingdon, Oxfordshire: Fleetwood Press, 1982), p. 162.

120 Ibid, p. 164.

121 Ibid, p. 165.

122 Ibid.

123 IWM Sound Archive: Horace Birks interview, 870.

124 Ibid.

125 Ibid.

126 Ibid.

127 Watson, *A Company of Tanks*, pp. 176–177.

128 Second Lieutenant Heap, who survived the attack, was awarded the MC for his conduct in this battle. His tank, 'Deborah' remained in the village until the Germans retook the village in March 1918. It was then moved to the western edge of the village and buried in a large hole as part of a plan to use it as the basis of a defensive strongpoint. Here it remained until November 1998 when, principally through the efforts of Philippe Gorczynski and Jean-Luc Gibot, an excavation revealed the tank. Its identity was confirmed by David Fletcher, Librarian at the Tank Museum. It was subsequently moved to become part of a museum about the battle at Flesquières.

Chapter 6 – 'Unravelling'

1 IWM DOCS: G D J McMurtrie typescript (1918), 78/23/1.

2 Captain Geoffrey Dugdale, *'Langemarck' and 'Cambrai': A War Narrative, 1914–1918* (Shrewsbury: Wilding and Son Ltd, 1932), p. 107.

3 Captain S.H. Williams, MC, *'Stand to your Horses': Through the First Great War with the Lord Strathcona's Horse (R.C.)* (Altona: D. W. Friesen & Sons, 1961), p156. Williams states his regiment's order to advance arrived just *after* 12 noon.

4 Correspondence between Major Lorenzen and Major Tom Crouch, published in *The Royal Tank Corps Journal*, Vol. XIII, No. 156, 1932, pp. 340–341.

5 Quoted in Jean-Luc Gibot & Phillippe Gorczynski, *Following The Tanks: Cambrai 20th November – 7th December 1917* (Arras: Privately Published, 1999), p. 78.

6 IWM Sound Archive: Edward Leigh-Jones interview, 4161.

7 IWM Sound Archive: Norman Dillon interview, 9752.

8 TM: Letter from Major Philip Hamond to Rita Hamond, 26 November 1917, Hammond [sic] Papers, E2005.41.3.

9 Ibid.

10 Letter from Lieutenant Colonel [sic]

D.M. Feuerheerd to the Editor of the *Daily Telegraph*, 3 April 1932, reprinted as 'Lost Chance at Cambrai' in *The Royal Tank Corps Journal*, Vol. XVI, No. 181, 1934, p. 2.

11 TM: Philip Hamond to Rita Hamond, 26 November 1917, Hammond (*sic*) Papers, E2005.41.3.

12 TM: Alfred Ballard, 'Submarining in a Tank', E2007.256.

13 TM: Philip Hamond to Rita Hamond, 26 November 1917, Hammond Papers, E2005.41.3.

14 Ibid.

15 TM: Alfred Ballard, 'Submarining in a Tank', E2007.256

16 Ibid.

17 IWM Sound Archive: Eric Potten interview, 11042.

18 TM: 'Some Reminiscences of Cambrai and the German March Offensive by 97218 Private George Brown', E2007.591.

19 TM: 'THE BATTLE OF CAMBRIA 21st [sic] November 1917: A Short Account of the Battle of Cambrai by Alfred BRISCO, H Battalion Tank Corps,' E2007.635.

20 TM: 'Some Reminiscences of Cambrai and the German March Offensive by 97218 Private George Brown', E2007.591.

21 TM: Copy of '8th TANK BATTALION HISTORY 1916–1919' with annotations by J Gordon Hassell, E2007.643.

22 Captain D E Hickey, *Rolling into Action – Memoirs of a Tank Corps Section Commander* (London: Hutchinson, 1936), p. 108.

23 TM: Copy of '8th TANK BATTALION HISTORY 1916–1919' with annotations by J Gordon Hassell, E2007.643.

24 Major S.H. Foot, 'Some Cambrai Reminiscences' in *Tank Corps Journal*, Vol. 5, No. 55, 1923, p. 192.

25 Ibid.

26 Ibid.

27 IWM DOCS: Major H C Boxer papers, 96/12/1, letter from 'Boy' to 'Dearest Mater', 7 December 1917.

28 IWM DOCS: B D Parkin manuscript (c1929), 86/57/1.

29 Ibid.

30 Major W.H.L. Watson, *A Company of Tanks* (Edinburgh: William Blackwood, 1920), p. 177.

31 Ibid, pp. 177–178.

32 Wilfrid R. Bion, *The Long Week-End, 1897–1919: Part of a Life* (Abingdon, Oxfordshire: Fleetwood Press, 1982), p. 166.

33 IWM DOCS: Douglas Wimberley typescript (1958–63), PP/MCR/182.

34 Ibid.

35 TM: EXTRACT from a letter from BASIL HENRIQUES, 27.11.17, WW1 Diaries/ 7/G Bn. TC/ Henriques Papers.doc.

36 Quoted in Everard Wyrall, *The History of the 62nd (West Riding) Division, 1914–1919*, Vol. 1, (London: John Lane, 1925), p. 72.

37 IWM DOCS: Major R C Foot typescript (1964), 86/57/1.

38 Captain Geoffrey Dugdale, *'Langemarck' and 'Cambrai': A War Narrative, 1914–1918* (Shrewsbury: Wilding and Son Ltd, 1932), p. 109.

39 Ibid, p. 110.

40 IWM DOCS: W R Kirkby typescript (c1978), 78/51/1.

41 Captain Geoffrey Dugdale, *'Langemarck' and 'Cambrai': A War Narrative, 1914–1918* (Shrewsbury: Wilding and Son Ltd, 1932), p. 109.

42 After-action report by Captain D.T. Raikes, quoted in Jean-Luc Gibot & Phillippe Gorczynski, *Following The Tanks: Cambrai 20th November–7th December 1917* (Arras: Privately Published, 1999), p. 80.

43 Franz Giese, *Geschichte des Reserve-Infanterie-Regiment 227 im Weltkriege 1914/18* (Halle a. d. S: Selbstverlag des Vereins ehemal Angehoriger des R.I.R. 227, 1931), p. 416.

44 IWM DOCS: G E V Thompson transcript *'Summer Holiday'* (undated), 75/36/1.

45 IWM DOCS: Captain Geoffrey Dent typescript, letter to Father, 28 November 1917, PP/MCR/226.

46 Captain S.H. Williams, MC, *'Stand to your Horses': Through the First Great War with the Lord Strathcona's Horse (R.C.)* (Altona: D. W. Friesen & Sons, 1961), p. 156.

47 Ibid.

48 Report of Lieutenant Colonel R W Paterson in War Diary of Fort Garry Horse, November 1917, National Archives of Canada website [www.archives.ca], RG9, Militia and Defence, Series III-D-3, jpeg images: http://data2.collectionscanada.ca/e/e046/ e001130779-e001130780.jpg

49 Ibid.

50 Captain S.H. Williams, MC, *'Stand to your Horses': Through the First Great War with the Lord Strathcona's Horse (R.C.)* (Altona: D. W. Friesen & Sons, 1961), p. 157.

51 Report of Lieutenant Colonel R W Paterson in War Diary of Fort Garry Horse, November 191, National Archives of Canada website [www.archives.ca], RG9, Militia and Defence, Series III-D-3, jpeg images: http://data2.collectionscanada.ca/e/e046/ e001130779-e001130780.jpg

52 IWM DOCS: E Marchant transcript, DS/MISC/26, letter from Second Lieutenant F E M Barford to Mr Marchant, 8 December 1917.

53 IWM DOCS: E Marchant transcript, DS/MISC/26, letter from Lieutenant Colonel Sir George Stirling to Mr Marchant, 9 December 1917.

54 Captain S.H. Williams, MC, *'Stand to your Horses': Through the First Great War with the Lord Strathcona's Horse (R.C.)* (Altona: D. W. Friesen & Sons, 1961), p. 157.

55 Ibid, pp. 157–158.

56 Report of Lieutenant Harcus Strachan in War Diary of Fort Garry Horse, November 191, National Archives of Canada website [www.archives.ca], RG9, Militia and Defence, Series III-D-3, jpeg images: http://data2.collectionscanada.ca/e/e046/ e001130780-e001130781.jpg

57 Ibid.

58 Ibid.

59 IWM DOCS: Lieutenant Colonel EHE Collen manuscript diary (1917), 79/21/1 & Con Shelf.

60 IWM DOCS: G D J McMurtrie typescript (1918), 78/23/1.

61 Ibid.

62 Ibid.

63 Ibid.

64 IWM Sound Archive: Edward Leigh-Jones interview, 4161.

65 IWM Sound Archive: Frederick Collins interview, 8229.
66 Ibid.
67 Ernest M Thwaites, 'The Chronicles of an Amateur Soldier' in *The Tank Corps Journal*, Vol. 2, No. 19, 1920, p. 162.
68 IWM DOCS: W R Kirkby typescript (c1978), 78/51/1.
69 Quoted in C E W Bean, *Australian Official History, Vol. VIII, The Australian Flying Corps in the Western and Eastern Theatres of War, 1914–1918* (11th Edition, 1941), p. 187.
70 Captain S.H. Williams, MC, '*Stand to your Horses': Through the First Great War with the Lord Strathcona's Horse (R.C.)* (Altona: D. W. Friesen & Sons, 1961), pp. 160–161.
71 Ibid, p. 161.
72 IWM DOCS: Captain F.H. Ash diary (1917), 77/36/1.
73 Frederic Whyte and A Hilliard Atteridge, *A History of the Queen's Bays (The 2nd Dragoon Guards), 1685–1929* (Jonathan Cape, London, 1930), p. 394.
74 IWM DOCS: G.H.L.M. Samuel correspondence (1917), 86/77/1.

Chapter 7 – Going on

1 H Raymond Smith, *A Soldier's Diary: Sidelights in the Great War, 1914–1918*, (Evesham: The 'Journal' Press (printers), 1940), p. 109.
2 Charles Weaver Price, "Q' Reminiscences' in *The Royal Tank Corps Journal*, Vol. 13, No. 31, 1921, p. 159.
3 Ibid.
4 Ibid.
5 IWM DOCS: W R Kirkby typescript (c1978), 78/51/1.
6 Wilfrid R. Bion, *The Long Week-End, 1897–1919: Part of a Life* (Abingdon, Oxfordshire: Fleetwood Press, 1982), p. 166.
7 Captain Geoffrey Dugdale, '*Langemarck' and 'Cambrai': A War Narrative, 1914–1918* (Shrewsbury: Wilding and Son Ltd, 1932), p. 113.
8 IWM DOCS: G D J McMurtrie typescript (1918), 78/23/1.
9 Ibid.
10 Ibid.
11 H Raymond Smith, *A Soldier's Diary: Sidelights in the Great War, 1914–1918*, (Evesham: The 'Journal' Press (printers), 1940), p. 110.
12 Frank C. Brooke, '*Wait for It'* (Bingley, West Yorks.: typescript, n.d.), p. 274.
13 Ibid, pp. 274–275.
14 Ibid, p. 275.
15 IWM DOCS: B D Parkin manuscript (c1929), 86/57/1.
16 Quoted in Frederic Whyte and A Hilliard Atteridge, *A History of the Queen's Bays (The 2nd Dragoon Guards), 1685–1929* (Jonathan Cape: London, 1930), p. 395.
17 Ibid.
18 Quoted in C.B. Purdom (ed.), *Everyman at war: sixty personal narratives of the war* (London: Dent, 1930), pp. 161–162.
19 IWM DOCS: W Clarke typescript (1986), 87/18/1, p. 14.
20 IWM DOCS: S Bradbury typescript (1923), 81/35/1.
21 Quoted in C.B. Purdom (ed.), *Everyman at war: sixty personal narratives of the war* (London: Dent, 1930), pp. 162.
22 Quoted in Frederic Whyte and A Hilliard Atteridge, *A History of the Queen's Bays (The 2nd Dragoon Guards),*

1685–1929 (London: Jonathan Cape, 1930), p. 395.

23 Ibid.

24 Herbert Ulrich, *RIR 52 im Weltkriege. Erinnerungsblätter deutscher Regimenter* (Oldenburg: Stalling, 1925), p. 405.

25 Ibid.

26 Captain F.H. Hotblack, 'Recollections of Cambrai, 1917' in *Tank Corps Journal*, Vol. 5, No. 55, 1923, pp. 188–189.

27 IWM DOCS: Douglas Wimberley typescript (1958–63), PP/MCR/ 182.

28 Frank C. Brooke, *'Wait for It'* (Bingley, West Yorks.: typescript, n.d.), p. 276.

29 IWM DOCS: Douglas Wimberley typescript (1958–63), PP/MCR/ 182.

30 Frank C. Brooke, *'Wait for It'* (Bingley, West Yorks.: typescript, n.d.), p. 277.

31 Ibid, pp. 278–279.

32 Taken from 'War, The Liberator' in E A Mackintosh MC, *War, The Liberator and Other Pieces* (London: The Bodley Head, 1918)

33 Frank C. Brooke, *'Wait for It'* (Bingley, West Yorks.: typescript, n.d.), p. 279.

34 Ibid, p. 280.

35 Ibid, pp. 280–281.

36 Ibid, p. 281.

37 Ibid, pp. 282–283.

38 IWM DOCS: Douglas Wimberley typescript (1958–63), PP/MCR/ 182.

39 Ibid.

40 Captain D E Hickey, *Rolling into Action – Memoirs of a Tank Corps Section Commander* (London: Hutchinson, 1936), p. 110.

41 Ibid.

42 Ibid, p. 112–113.

43 Ibid, p. 114.

44 Ibid.

45 Ibid, p. 115.

46 Ibid, p. 116.

47 TM: Papers of Captain Burton, "G" / 7 Battalion

Chapter 8 – Hope Dies Hard

1 Captain Wilfrid Miles (compiler), *History of the Great War Based on Official Documents by Direction of the Historical Section of the Committee of Imperial Defence: Military Operations France and Belgium, 1917. The Battle of Cambrai.* (Nashville, Tennessee: Imperial War Museum and Battery Press, 1991 (repr. of 1948 edition)), p.107.

2 IWM DOCS: Douglas Wimberley typescript (1958–63), PP/MCR/ 182.

3 Charles Weaver Price, "Q' Reminiscences' in *The Royal Tank Corps Journal*, Vol. 13, No. 31, 1921, p. 159.

4 Ibid.

5 IWM DOCS: Douglas Wimberley typescript (1958–63), PP/MCR/ 182.

6 IWM DOCS: S Bradbury typescript (1923), 81/35/1.

7 IWM DOCS: G D J McMurtrie typescript (1918), 78/23/1.

8 TM: Letter from Colonel E J Carter to Major General N W Duncan containing observations on RTR history draft, 15 October 1959, WW1/Personal Accounts/Carter/ 17AC.doc.

9 Captain Geoffrey Dugdale, *'Langemarck' and 'Cambrai': A War*

Narrative, 1914–1918 (Shrewsbury, Wilding and Son Ltd: 1932), p. 109.

10 IWM DOCS: B D Parkin manuscript (c1929), 86/57/1.

11 Gary Sheffield & John Bourne (ed.), *Douglas Haig: War Diaries and Letters 1914–1918* (London: Weidenfeld & Nicolson, 2005), p. 348.

12 IWM DOCS: Douglas Wimberley typescript (1958–63), PP/MCR/ 182.

13 Quoted in David Rorie, *A Medico's Luck in the Great War: Reminiscences of RAMC Work with the Highland Division* (Aberdeen: Milne & Hutchison, 1929), p. 170.

14 Ibid.

15 Ibid, p. 171.

16 Ibid.

17 Quoted in Frederic Whyte and A Hilliard Atteridge, *A History of the Queen's Bays (The 2nd Dragoon Guards), 1685–1929* (London: Jonathan Cape, 1930), p.398.

18 IWM DOCS: Douglas Wimberley typescript (1958–63), PP/MCR/ 182.

19 Ibid.

20 Quoted in David Rorie, *A Medico's Luck in the Great War: Reminiscences of RAMC Work with the Highland Division* (Aberdeen: Milne & Hutchison, 1929), p. 172.

21 Arthur Gould Lee, *No Parachute: A Fighter Pilot in World War 1* (The Adventurers Club, London: 1969), p. 171.

22 Ibid.

23 Ibid, p. 172.

24 Ibid.

25 IWM DOCS: Douglas Wimberley typescript (1958–63), PP/MCR/ 182.

26 Ibid.

27 Arthur Gould Lee, *No Parachute: A Fighter Pilot in World War 1* (The Adventurers Club, London: 1969), p. 173.

28 Ibid, p. 174.

29 Quoted in David Rorie, *A Medico's Luck in the Great War: Reminiscences of RAMC Work with the Highland Division* (Aberdeen: Milne & Hutchison, 1929), p. 173.

30 IWM DOCS: W Clarke typescript (1986), 87/18/1, p.14.

31 IWM DOCS: W R Kirkby typescript (c1978), 78/51/1.

32 Ibid.

33 Ibid.

34 Rifleman Aubrey Smith, *Four Years on the Western Front: Being the Experiences of a Ranker in the London Rifle Brigade, 4th, 3rd and 56th Divisions* (London: Odhams Press, 1922), p. 288.

35 General Otto von Moser, *Feldzugsaufzeichnungen als Brigade-Divisionskommandeur und als kommandierender General 1914–1918* (Stuttgart: Chr. Belserche Verlagsbuchhandlung, 1923), pp. 311–312.

36 Captain Geoffrey Dugdale, *'Langemarck' and 'Cambrai': A War Narrative, 1914–1918* (Shrewsbury: Wilding and Son Ltd: 1932), p. 113.

37 IWM DOCS: W R Kirkby typescript (c1978), 78/51/1.

38 Arthur Gould Lee, *No Parachute: A Fighter Pilot in World War 1* (London: The Adventurers Club, 1969), p. 175.

Chapter 9 – Dogs of War

1 Gary Sheffield & John Bourne (ed.), *Douglas Haig: War Diaries and Letters*

1914–1918 (London: Weidenfeld & Nicolson, 2005), p. 349.

2 Major W.H.L. Watson, *A Company of Tanks* (Edinburgh: William Blackwood, 1920), p. 184.

3 Colonel H.C. Wylly, *The Green Howards in the Great War, 1914–1919* (Richmond, Yorks : [Privately printed], 1926), p. 370.

4 TM: Copy of '8th TANK BATTALION HISTORY 1916–1919' with annotations by J Gordon Hassell, E2007.643. The Guards colours (red and blue) were also adopted for 'H' Tank Battalion's insignia.

5 IWM DOCS: F Turner typescript (1982), 83/23/1.

6 Brigadier General F.P. Crozier, *A Brass Hat in No Man's Land* (London: Jonathan Cape, 1930), p. 179.

7 Quoted in *Letters and Papers of Algernon Hyde Villiers* (London: Society for Promoting Christian Knowledge, 1919), p. 12.

8 Ibid, pp. 156–7.

9 IWM DOCS: Douglas Wimberley typescript (1958–63), PP/MCR/182.

10 Quoted in LJC Southern, *The Bedfordshire Yeomanry in the Great War* (Bedford: Rush and Warwick, 1935), p. 71.

11 Colonel H.C. Wylly, *The Green Howards in the Great War, 1914–1919* (Richmond, Yorks: [Privately printed], 1926), p. 371.

12 IWM DOCS: Douglas Wimberley typescript (1958–63), PP/MCR/182.

13 Ibid.

14 Ibid.

15 David Fraser [ed.], *In Good Company: The First World War Letters and Diaries of The Hon. William Fraser, Gordon Highlanders* (Salisbury: Michael Russell, 1990), p. 179.

16 Quoted in Bryan Cooper, *The Ironclads of Cambrai* (London: Pan Books, 1970), p. 144.

17 Ibid, p. 145.

18 Ibid.

19 Herbert Ulrich, *RIR 52 im Weltkriege. Erinnerungsblätter deutscher Regimenter* (Oldenburg: Stalling, 1925), p. 427.

20 Ibid.

21 Ibid, pp. 427–428.

22 Quoted in Bryan Cooper, *The Ironclads of Cambrai* (London: Pan Books, 1970), p. 145.

23 Ibid.

24 LHCMA: Captain Eliot Hotblack, 'Confidential Report', 23 November 1917 in Fuller Papers, I/BCI/I/2/80/a.

25 IWM DOCS: Douglas Wimberley typescript (1958–63), PP/MCR/182.

26 IWM Sound Archive: Miles Reinke interview, 4207.

27 Ibid.

28 Ibid.

29 Ibid.

30 Ibid.

31 IWM DOCS: F Turner typescript (1982), 83/23/1.

32 Ibid.

33 Ibid.

34 Ibid.

35 Ibid.

36 Major W.H.L. Watson, *A Company of Tanks* (Edinburgh: William Blackwood, 1920), p. 189.

37 Ibid, p. 190.

38 IWM DOCS: F Turner typescript (1982), 83/23/1.

39 Quoted in Lieutenant Colonel F E Whitton, *History of the 40th Division*

(Aldershot: Gale & Polden, 1926), pp. 104–5.

40 Quoted in *Letters and Papers of Algernon Hyde Villiers* (London: Society for Promoting Christian Knowledge, 1919), pp. 159–160.

41 LHCMA: Lt Col. E J Burnett, SUMMARY OF OPERATIONS 20th NOVEMBER TO 23rd NOVEMBER 1917: REPORT BY O.C., 'E' BATTALION TANK CORPS ON THE ACTION of 23rd NOVEMBER 1917 with 36th DIVISION, Fuller Papers I/TCOI I/4/2ll-I/4/2ss.

42 Ibid.

43 Ibid.

44 H. Gregory, *Never Again: A Diary of the Great War* (London: Arthur H. Stockwell, 1934), pp. 72–73.

45 Ibid, pp. 73.

46 Major James Thomas Byford McCudden, *Five Years in the Royal Flying Corps* (London: The 'Aeroplane' & General Publishing Company Ltd, 1918), pp. 272–273.

47 Ibid.

48 Ibid.

49 Karl Bodenschatz, *Hunting with Richthofen: the Bodenschatz Diaries: sixteen months of battle with JG Freiherr von Richthofen No.1* (London: Grub Street, 1996), p. 50.

50 Ibid.

51 Peter Kilduff, *Richthofen: Beyond the Legend of the Red Baron* (London: Arms & Armour Press, 1993), p. 160.

52 IWM DOCS: S Bradbury typescript (1923), 81/35/1.

53 Quoted in Lieutenant Colonel F E Whitton, *History of the 40th Division* (Aldershot: Gale & Polden, 1926), p. 101.

54 IWM DOCS: F Turner typescript (1982), 83/23/1.

55 Ibid.

56 H. Gregory, *Never Again: A Diary of the Great War* (London: Arthur H. Stockwell, 1934), pp. 73–74.

57 Quoted in C.B. Purdom (ed.), *Everyman at war: sixty personal narratives of the war* (London: Dent, 1930), pp. 163–164.

58 Ibid, p. 164.

59 Quoted in LJC Southern, *The Bedfordshire Yeomanry in the Great War* (Bedford: Rush and Warwick, 1935), pp. 71–72.

Chapter 10 – 'To certain hell . . .'

1 IWM DOCS: Major C H Dudley-Ward diary (1917), 94/30/1.

2 Ibid.

3 Ibid.

4 IWM DOCS: B D Parkin manuscript (c1929), 86/57/1.

5 IWM DOCS: Major C H Dudley-Ward diary (1917), 94/30/1.

6 Ibid.

7 IWM DOCS: S Bradbury typescript (1923), 81/35/1.

8 Ibid.

9 IWM DOCS: Douglas Wimberley typescript (1958–63), PP/MCR/182.

10 Ibid.

11 Ibid.

12 IWM DOCS: Major C H Dudley-Ward diary (1917), 94/30/1.

13 H. Gregory, *Never Again: A Diary of the Great War* (London: Arthur H. Stockwell, 1934), pp. 79–80.

14 Quoted in LJC Southern, *The Bedfordshire Yeomanry in the Great War* (Bedford: Rush and Warwick, 1935), p. 72.

15 Quoted in Lieutenant Colonel F E Whitton, *History of the 40th Division* (Aldershot: Gale & Polden, 1926), pp. 126–127.

16 Karl Bodenschatz, *Hunting with Richthofen: the Bodenschatz Diaries: sixteen months of battle with JG Freiherr von Richthofen No.1* (London: Grub Street, 1996), p. 50.

17 Arthur Gould Lee, *No Parachute: A Fighter Pilot in World War 1* (London: The Adventurers Club, 1969), pp. 176–177.

18 IWM DOCS: J K Wilson Papers, PP/MCR/100, letter from George Parsons to 'Jake' Wilson, January 1969.

19 Ibid.

20 TM: Frederick L Keyworth account, E2007.952.

21 IWM DOCS: J K Wilson Papers, PP/MCR/100, letter from George Parsons to 'Jake' Wilson, January 1969.

22 TM: Frederick L Keyworth account, E2007.952.

23 Quoted in LJC Southern, *The Bedfordshire Yeomanry in the Great War* (Bedford: Rush and Warwick, 1935), p. 72.

24 Quoted in Lieutenant Colonel F E Whitton, *History of the 40th Division* (Aldershot: Gale & Polden, 1926), p. 128.

25 Ibid, p. 129.

26 Wilfrid Ewart, *Scots Guard* (London: Rich & Cowan, 1934), pp. 146–147.

27 Quoted in LJC Southern, *The Bedfordshire Yeomanry in the Great War* (Bedford: Rush and Warwick, 1935), pp. 72–73.

28 IWM DOCS: F Turner typescript (1982), 83/23/1.

29 IWM DOCS: F Wynne typescript (undated), P148.

30 Ibid.

31 Ibid.

32 Ibid.

33 IWM DOCS: EHE Collen diary (25 November 1917), 79/21/1 & Con Shelf.

34 IWM DOCS: F H Ash diary (1917), 77/36/1.

35 IWM DOCS: F Wynne typescript (undated), P148.

36 Ibid.

37 Ibid.

38 Ibid.

39 Ibid.

40 Ibid.

41 Ibid.

42 Ibid.

43 Ibid.

44 Wilfrid Ewart, *Scots Guard* (London: Rich & Cowan, 1934), p. 147.

45 Ibid, pp. 147–148.

46 Ibid, p. 148.

47 Ibid, pp. 148–149.

48 Ibid.

49 IWM DOCS: F Turner typescript (1982), 83/23/1.

50 Ibid.

51 Ibid.

52 Ibid.

53 Ibid.

54 IWM DOCS: B D Parkin manuscript (c1929), 86/57/1.

55 Ibid.

56 Ibid.

57 Ibid.

58 IWM DOCS: F Wynne typescript (undated), P148.

59 Ibid.

60 IWM DOCS: F H Ash diary (1917), 77/36/1.

61 Ibid.

62 Captain Wilfrid Miles, *History of the*

*Great War Based on Official Documents
by Direction of the Historical Section of the
Committee of Imperial Defence: Military
Operations France and Belgium, 1917.
The Battle of Cambrai.* (Nashville,
Tennessee: Imperial War Museum
and Battery Press, 1991 (repr. of
1948 edition)), (henceforth *O.H.,
1917*, Vol. 3), p. 148.

63 Gary Sheffield & John Bourne (ed.),
*Douglas Haig: War Diaries and Letters
1914–1918* (London: Weidenfeld &
Nicolson, 2005), p. 351.

64 Quoted in *O.H., 1917*, Vol. 3,
p. 148.

65 IWM DOCS: Edmund Fisher,
'Letters from France, 1917,' 97/4/
1, transcript of letter, 24 November
1917.

66 IWM DOCS: E.H.E. Collen diary
(25 November 1917), 79/21/1 &
Con Shelf.

67 IWM DOCS: F Wynne typescript
(undated), P148.

68 Feilding quoted in Robert
Woollcombe, *The First Tank Battle:
Cambrai 1917* (London: Arthur
Barker, 1967), p. 169.

69 Arthur Gould Lee, *No Parachute: A
Fighter Pilot in World War 1* (London:
The Adventurers Club, 1969),
p. 177.

70 Ibid, p. 178.

71 Ibid.

72 Ibid.

73 Ibid, p. 179.

74 Carroll Carstairs, *A Generation
Missing* (Stevenage: Strong Oak
Press, 1989 [reprint of 1930
edition]), p. 122.

75 IWM DOCS: Major C H Dudley-
Ward diary (1917), 94/30/1.

76 IWM DOCS: C R Britten
typescript (1974), 74/11/1

77 TM: Philip Hamond to Anthony
(his son) and Rita Hamond (his
wife), 9 December 1917,
E2005.41.3.

78 IWM DOCS: F Wynne typescript
(undated), P148.

79 Carroll Carstairs, *A Generation
Missing* (Stevenage: Strong Oak
Press, 1989 [reprint of 1930
edition]), pp. 123–124.

80 Ibid, p. 124.

81 Ibid.

82 Captain Philip Russell Keightley,
RGA, *Among the Guns: Intimate Letters
From Ypres and the Somme* (Belfast:
privately printed, n.d..), p. 50.

83 Ibid.

84 Carroll Carstairs, *A Generation
Missing* (Stevenage: Strong Oak
Press, 1989 [reprint of 1930
edition]), p. 125.

85 Harold Dearden, *Medicine and Duty:
A War Diary* (London: William
Heinemann Ltd, 1928), p. 223.

86 Carroll Carstairs, *A Generation
Missing* (Stevenage: Strong Oak
Press, 1989 [reprint of 1930
edition]), p. 125.

87 TM: Philip Hamond to Anthony
(his son) and Rita Hamond (his
wife), 9 December 1917,
E2005.41.3.

88 Ibid.

89 Carroll Carstairs, *A Generation
Missing* (Stevenage: Strong Oak
Press, 1989 [reprint of 1930
edition]), pp. 127–128.

90 Ibid, p. 128.

91 Ibid, p. 130.

92 Ibid, pp. 130–131.

93 Ibid, pp. 131–132.

94 TM: Philip Hamond to Anthony
(his son) and Rita Hamond (his

wife), 9 December 1917,
E2005.41.3.

95 IWM DOCS: C R Britten
typescript (1974), 74/11/1.

96 Ibid.

97 The National Archive: WO 339/
69390.

98 Ibid.

99 Carroll Carstairs, *A Generation
Missing* (Stevenage: Strong Oak
Press, 1989 [reprint of 1930
edition]), pp. 131–132.

100 Harold Dearden, *Medicine and Duty:
A War Diary* (London: William
Heinemann Ltd, 1928), pp. 223–
224.

101 Ibid, pp. 224–225.

102 The National Archive: WO 339/
69390.

103 Ibid.

104 Carroll Carstairs, *A Generation
Missing* (Stevenage: Strong Oak
Press, 1989 [reprint of 1930
edition]), pp. 134–135.

105 Ibid.

106 IWM DOCS: F Wynne typescript
(undated), P148.

107 Ibid.

108 Ibid.

109 IWM Sound Archive: Charles
Evans interview, 10487.

110 IWM DOCS: Major C H Dudley-
Ward diary (1917), 94/30/1.

111 Ibid.

112 IWM Sound Archive: Fred
Holmes interview, 9147.

**Chapter 11 – 'An equal, but
opposite, reaction'**

1 IWM DOCS: E H E Collen
manuscript diary (1917), 79/21/1.

2 IWM DOCS: W Evans typescript
(c1920s), Con Shelf.

3 Kronprinz Rupprecht von Bayern,
In Treue Fest. Mein Kriegstagebuch,
(Zweiter Band) (München: 1929),
pp. 299–300. I am especially
grateful to Jack Sheldon for material
from Crown Prince Rupprecht's
memoirs.

4 Ibid, p. 298.

5 IWM DOCS: Captain F H Ash
diary (1917), 77/36/1.

6 Ernst Jünger, *The Storm of Steel*
(London: Constable, 1994 (repr. of
1929 edition)), p. 222.

7 IWM DOCS: Major C H Dudley-
Ward diary (1917), 94/30/1.

8 IWM DOCS: J Lee manuscript
(1918), 98/31/1.

9 IWM DOCS: W Evans typescript
(c1920s), Con Shelf.

10 IWM DOCS: J Lomax typescript
(1960s), 88/27/1.

11 IWM DOCS: W Evans typescript
(c1920s), Con Shelf.

12 Ibid.

13 Ibid.

14 Ibid.

15 Ibid.

16 IWM DOCS: J Lomax typescript
(1960s), 88/27/1.

17 IWM DOCS: W Evans typescript
(c1920s), Con Shelf.

18 Ibid.

19 IWM DOCS: J Lomax typescript
(1960s), 88/27/1.

20 IWM DOCS: W Evans typescript
(c1920s), Con Shelf.

21 Ibid.

22 Ibid.

23 IWM DOCS: J Lomax typescript
(1960s), 88/27/1.

24 IWM DOCS: A J Newman
manuscript (1917–18), 01/8/1.

25 Ibid.

26 IWM DOCS: E.H.E. Collen manuscript diary (1917), 79/21/1.
27 IWM DOCS: T Wollocombe typescript correspondence (1944), 89/7/1.
28 Ibid.
29 Ibid.
30 Ibid.
31 Ibid.
32 IWM DOCS: E.H.E Collen manuscript diary (1917), 79/21/1.
33 IWM DOCS: T Wollocombe typescript correspondence (1944), 89/7/1.
34 Ibid.
35 IWM DOCS: E.H.E Collen manuscript diary (1917), 79/21/1.
36 IWM Sound Archive: Tom Bracey interview, 9419.
37 Ibid.
38 Ibid.
39 IWM DOCS: WR Taylor, 'Diary and Reminiscences of the War' (typescript, undated), 01/60/1.
40 Ibid.
41 Captain Alan Thomas, *A Life Apart* (London: Victor Gollancz, 1968), p. 139.
42 Ibid, pp. 139–140.
43 Ibid, p. 140.
44 Ibid.
45 Ibid, p. 141.
46 IWM DOCS: WR Taylor, 'Diary and Reminiscences of the War' (typescript, undated), 01/60/1.
47 IWM DOCS: WR Taylor, 'Diary and Reminiscences of the War,' 01/60/1, letter from Private J Ferguson to Mrs Taylor, 13 December 1917.
48 IWM DOCS: WR Taylor, 'Diary and Reminiscences of the War' (typescript, undated), 01/60/1.
49 General Sir Beauvoir de Lisle, *Reminiscences of Sport and War*, (London: Eyre and Spottiswoode, 1939), p. 158.
50 Ibid. My italics.
51 Quoted in *United States Army in the World War, 1917–1919: Military Operations of the American Expeditionary Forces* (Washington: Historical Division US Dept of the Army, 1948).
52 Lieutenant Colonel William Barclay Parsons, *The American Engineers in France* (London and New york: Appleton & Company, 1920), pp. 128–129.
53 IWM Sound Archive: Murray Rymer-Jones interview, 10699.
54 TM: Copy of '8th TANK BATTALION HISTORY 1916–1919' with annotations by J Gordon Hassell, E2007.643.
55 Stephen Foot, *Three Lives, an autobiography* (London: William Heinemann, 1934), pp. 202–203.
56 TM: Philip Hamond to Anthony (his son) and Rita Hamond (his wife), 9 December 1917, E2005.41.3.
57 Ibid.
58 IWM DOCS: J.D. Wyatt typescript (1924), 83/12/1.
59 IWM DOCS: Colonel Sir Geoffrey Christie-Miller typescript (1919–20), 80/32/2.
60 IWM DOCS: G.D.J McMurtrie typescript (1918), 78/23/1.
61 Ibid.
62 Captain Geoffrey Dugdale, *'Langemarck' and 'Cambrai': A War Narrative, 1914–1918* (Shrewsbury: Wilding and Son Ltd, 1932), p. 116.
63 H Raymond Smith, *A Soldier's Diary: Sidelights in the Great War, 1914–1918*, (Evesham: The 'Journal' Press (printers), 1940), p. 111.

64 IWM DOCS: G D J McMurtrie typescript (1918), 78/23/1.

65 Ibid.

66 Ibid.

67 Ibid.

68 Ibid.

69 Captain Geoffrey Dugdale, 'Langemarck' and 'Cambrai': A War Narrative, 1914–1918 (Shrewsbury: Wilding and Son Ltd, 1932), p. 117.

70 H Raymond Smith, A Soldier's Diary: Sidelights in the Great War, 1914–1918, (Evesham: The 'Journal' Press (printers), 1940), p. 112.

71 H.C.C. Uniacke, The Royal Artillery war commemoration book: a regimental record written and illustrated for the most part by artillery men while serving in the line during the Great War (London: G. Bell and Sons, 1920), pp. 224–225.

72 F.J. Salmon, 'With the Field Survey Units in France, 1915–19' in Empire Survey Review, Vol. II, No. II, January 1934, quoted in Peter Chasseaud, Artillery's Astrologers: A History of British Survey and Mapping on the Western Front 1914–1918 (Lewes: Mapbooks, 1999), p. 361.

73 IWM DOCS: J K Wilson Papers, PP/MCR/100, letter from George Parsons to 'Jake' Wilson, January 1969.

74 Norman D. Cliff, To Hell and Back With the Guards (Braunton, Devon: Merlin Books, 1988), pp. 85–86.

75 IWM DOCS: T Wollocombe typescript correspondence (1944), 89/7/1.

76 Ibid.

77 Ibid.

78 Captain Geoffrey Dugdale, 'Langemarck' and 'Cambrai': A War Narrative, 1914–1918 (Shrewsbury: Wilding and Son Ltd, 1932), p. 118.

79 IWM DOCS: WR Taylor, 'Diary and Reminiscences of the War' (typescript, undated), 01/60/1.

80 Ibid.

81 Ibid.

82 Ibid.

83 IWM DOCS: W J Grant diary (1917), 97/16/1.

84 Quoted in Harry Moses, The Fighting Bradfords: Northern Heroes of World War One (Durham: County Durham Books, 2003), p. 102.

85 R.H. Haigh & P.W. Turner (eds.), The Long Carry: The War Diary of Stretcher Bearer Frank Dunham 1916–1918 (Oxford: Pergamon Press, 1970), pp. 96–97.

86 IWM DOCS: Lieutenant General Sir Thomas D'Oyly Snow Papers, 76/79/1, letter to Lieutenant General Thomas Snow from Brigadier General Edward D'Ewes Coke, 6 December 1917.

87 IWM DOCS: K Palmer typescript (1960s), 76/80/1.

88 Ernst Jünger, The Storm of Steel (London: Constable, 1994 (repr. of 1929 edition)), p. 223.

89 IWM DOCS: W J Grant diary (1917), 97/16/1.

90 Lieut. Col. J.H. Boraston [ed.] Sir Douglas Haig's Despatches (December 1915–April 1919) (London: J.M. Dent & Sons, 1979 (reprint of 1919 edition)), 5th Despatch (Cambrai Operations), 20 February 1918, pp. 166–167.

91 Captain J.E.H. Neville, The War Letters of a Light Infantryman (London: Sifton Praed, 1930), p. 74.

92 Ernst Jünger, The Storm of Steel (London: Constable, 1994 (repr. of 1929 edition)), pp. 223–224.

93 Arthur Gould Lee, *No Parachute: A Fighter Pilot in World War 1* (London: The Adventurers Club, 1969), p. 184.

94 Ibid.

95 Major James Thomas Byford McCudden, *Five Years in the Royal Flying Corps* (London: The 'Aeroplane' & General Publishing Company Ltd, 1918), pp. 279–280.

96 Peter Kilduff, *Richthofen: Beyond the Legend of the Red Baron* (London: Arms & Armour Press, 1993), p. 167.

97 Arthur Gould Lee, *No Parachute: A Fighter Pilot in World War 1* (London: The Adventurers Club, 1969), pp. 185–186.

98 Ibid, p. 186.

99 Ibid, pp. 188–189.

100 Ibid, p. 189.

101 Ibid, pp. 189–190.

102 Ibid, p. 190.

103 H Raymond Smith, *A Soldier's Diary: Sidelights in the Great War, 1914–1918*, (Evesham: The 'Journal' Press (printers), 1940), p. 113.

104 Kronprinz Rupprecht von Bayern, *In Treue Fest. Mein Kriegstagebuch*, (Zweiter Band) (München: 1929), pp. 298–299.

Chapter 12 – 'A Bad Dream'

1 IWM DOCS: W R Taylor, 'Diary and Reminiscences of the War' (typescript, undated), 01/60/1.

2 IWM DOCS: J Lee manuscript (1918), 98/31/1.

3 Ibid.

4 IWM DOCS: A J Newman manuscript (1917–18), 01/8/1.

5 IWM DOCS: W Evans typescript (c1920s), Con Shelf.

6 Quoted in *Henry Dundas (Scots Guards): A Memoir* (Edinburgh: William Blackwood, 1921), p. 199.

7 Captain J.E.H. Neville, *The War Letters of a Light Infantryman* (London: Sifton Praed, 1930), p. 74.

8 Ibid.

9 Ibid, p. 75.

10 Ibid.

11 Quoted in Captain S.H. Williams, MC, *'Stand to your Horses': Through the First Great War with the Lord Strathcona's Horse (R.C.)* (Altona: D. W. Friesen & Sons, 1961), p. 169.

12 Quoted in Colonel E.B. Maunsell, *Prince of Wales's Own The Scinde Horse, 1839–1922* (Regimental Committee, 1926), p. 167.

13 Major W.H.L. Watson, *A Company of Tanks* (Edinburgh: William Blackwood, 1920), p. 204.

14 IWM DOCS: Major C H Dudley-Ward diary (1917), 94/30/1.

15 Ibid.

16 Major W.H.L. Watson, *A Company of Tanks* (Edinburgh: William Blackwood, 1920), p. 204.

17 Leutnant d. R. Karl Christian, *Das Heldenbuch vom Infanterie-Regiment 418* (Frankfurt a. M.: Vereinigung ehemaliger Angehöriger I.R.418, 1937), p. 125.

18 Letter from Brigadier General Neil Haig to Colonel E.B. Maunsell, 30 June 1925, quoted in Colonel E.B. Maunsell, *Prince of Wales's Own The Scinde Horse, 1839–1922* (Regimental Committee, 1926), p. 155.

19 Ibid.

20 Captain Dysart Whitworth in Colonel E.B. Maunsell, *Prince of*

Wales's Own The Scinde Horse, 1839–1922 (Regimental Committee, 1926), p. 167 and Captain D. E. Whitworth, *History of the 2nd Lancers (Gardner's Horse)* (London: Sifton Praed, 1924), p. 165.

21 Ibid, p. 105.

22 Letter from Jiwan Singh to Pensioned Subedar-Major Bhagat Singh, 10 December 1917, quoted in David Omissi [ed.], *Indian Voices of the Great War: Soldiers' Letters, 1914–18* (Basingstoke: Macmillan Press, 1999), p. 339.

23 Leutnant d. R. Karl Christian, *Das Heldenbuch vom Infanterie-Regiment 418* (Frankfurt a. M.: Vereinigung ehemaliger Angehoriger I.R.418, 1937), p. 125.

24 Ibid.

25 Letter from Jiwan Singh to Pensioned Subedar-Major Bhagat Singh, 10 December 1917, quoted in David Omissi [ed.], *Indian Voices of the Great War: Soldiers' Letters, 1914–18* (Basingstoke: Macmillan Press, 1999), p. 339.

26 Leutnant d. R. Karl Christian, *Das Heldenbuch vom Infanterie-Regiment 418* (Frankfurt a. M.: Vereinigung ehemaliger Angehoriger I.R.418, 1937), p. 126.

27 Captain D. E. Whitworth, *History of the 2nd Lancers (Gardner's Horse)* (London: Sifton Praed, 1924), p. 107.

28 Leutnant d. R. Karl Christian, *Das Heldenbuch vom Infanterie-Regiment 418* (Frankfurt a. M.: Vereinigung ehemaliger Angehoriger I.R.418, 1937), pp. 126–127.

29 Captain Dysart Whitworth in Colonel E.B. Maunsell, *Prince of Wales's Own The Scinde Horse, 1839–1922* (Regimental Committee, 1926), p. 169.

30 Letter from Dalawar Chand to Ressaidar Wali Muhammad Khan, 28 December 1917, quoted in David Omissi [ed.], *Indian Voices of the Great War: Soldiers' Letters, 1914–18* (Basingstoke: Macmillan Press, 1999), p. 343.

31 Ibid.

32 TM: Copy of '8th TANK BATTALION HISTORY 1916–1919' with annotations by J Gordon Hassell, E2007.643.

33 Ibid.

34 Ibid.

35 IWM DOCS: Major C H Dudley-Ward diary (1917), 94/30/1.

36 IWM Sound Archive: Charles Evans interview, 10487.

37 IWM DOCS: Major C H Dudley-Ward diary (1917), 94/30/1.

38 Ibid.

39 Ibid.

40 IWM Sound Archive: Charles Evans interview, 10487.

41 IWM DOCS: Major C H Dudley-Ward diary (1917), 94/30/1.

42 Major W.H.L. Watson, *A Company of Tanks* (Edinburgh: William Blackwood, 1920), pp. 207–208.

43 H Raymond Smith, *A Soldier's Diary: Sidelights in the Great War, 1914–1918*, (Evesham: The 'Journal' Press (printers), 1940), p. 113.

44 Quoted in Captain S.H. Williams, MC, *'Stand to your Horses': Through the First Great War with the Lord Strathcona's Horse (R.C.)* (Altona: D. W. Friesen & Sons, 1961), p. 169.

45 Ibid, p. 168.

46 Ibid, p.169.

47 Ibid, p. 170.

48 Ernst Jünger, *The Storm of Steel*

(London: Constable, 1994 (repr. of 1929 edition)), p.227.

49 Ibid, p.229.

50 Ibid, pp. 231–232.

51 IWM DOCS: Captain H Brokensha transcript (1973), 73/185/1.

52 Ibid.

53 Ibid.

54 Ibid.

55 Ibid.

56 Ibid.

57 Arthur Gould Lee, *No Parachute: A Fighter Pilot in World War 1* (London: The Adventurers Club, 1969), pp. 193–194.

58 Major James Thomas Byford McCudden, *Five Years in the Royal Flying Corps* (London: The 'Aeroplane' & General Publishing Company Ltd, 1918), pp. 279–280.

59 IWM DOCS: J D Wyatt typescript (1924), 83/12/1.

60 IWM DOCS: S W D Lockwood typescript (1970s), 90/21/1.

61 Ibid.

62 Ibid.

63 Ibid.

64 Ibid.

65 Ibid.

66 IWM DOCS: W R Taylor, 'Diary and Reminiscences of the War' (typescript, undated), 01/60/1.

67 Ibid.

68 Quoted in Captain Wilfrid Miles, *History of the Great War Based on Official Documents by Direction of the Historical Section of the Committee of Imperial Defence: Military Operations France and Belgium, 1917. The Battle of Cambrai.* (Nashville, Tennessee: Imperial War Museum and Battery Press, 1991 (repr. of 1948 edition)) (henceforth *O.H., 1917*, Vol. 3), p. 258.

69 Captain S.H. Williams, MC, *'Stand to your Horses': Through the First Great War with the Lord Strathcona's Horse (R.C.)* (Altona: D. W. Friesen & Sons, 1961), p. 163.

70 IWM Sound Archive: Len Ounsworth interview, 332.

71 IWM DOCS: G D J McMurtrie typescript (1918), 78/23/1.

72 IWM DOCS: B D Parkin manuscript (c1929), 86/57/1.

Conclusion – 'Scattered memories remain'

1 Captain Wilfrid Miles, *History of the Great War Based on Official Documents by Direction of the Historical Section of the Committee of Imperial Defence: Military Operations France and Belgium, 1917. The Battle of Cambrai.* (Nashville, Tennessee: Imperial War Museum and Battery Press, 1991 (repr. of 1948 edition)) (henceforth *O.H., 1917*, Vol. 3), p. 273.

2 The Rt. Hon. Winston S. Churchill, *The World Crisis, 1911–1918* (Vol. II) (London: Odhams Press, 1938), p. 1220.

3 Liddle Collection, Brotherton Library, Leeds University, F E Hotblack miscellaneous recollections; GS0804.

4 Lieut. Col. J.H. Boraston [ed.] *Sir Douglas Haig's Despatches (December 1915–April 1919)* (London: J.M. Dent & Sons, 1979 (reprint of 1919 edition)), 5th Despatch (Cambrai Operations), 20 February 1918, p. 155.

5 Ibid, p. 157.

6 IWM Sound Archive: Jim Davies interview, 9750.

7 IWM DOCS: F Wynne typescript
(undated), P148.

8 *Letters and Papers of Algernon Hyde
Villiers* (London: Society for
Promoting Christian Knowledge,
1919), p. 149.

9 Captain J.E.H. Neville, *The War
Letters of a Light Infantryman* (London:
Sifton Praed, 1930), p. 74.

10 Quoted in *O.H., 1917*, Vol. 3,
p. 295.

11 IWM DOCS: W R Taylor, 'Diary
and Reminiscences of the War'
(typescript, undated), 01/60/1.

12 IWM DOCS: Edmund Fisher,
'Letters from France, 1917,' 97/4/
1, transcript of letter, 9 December
1917.

13 IWM DOCS: J K Wilson Papers,
PP/MCR/100, letter from George
Parsons to 'Jake' Wilson, January
1969.

14 IWM Sound Archive: Fred Holmes
interview, 9147.

15 IWM Sound Archive: Frederick
Collins interview, 8229.

Index

Page references in **bold** refer to maps.